*Oracle Press*™

Oracle Designer Handbook

Second Edition

Peter Koletzke
Dr. Paul Dorsey

Osborne/**McGraw-Hill**

Berkeley New York St. Louis San Francisco
Auckland Bogotá Hamburg London Madrid
Mexico City Milan Montreal New Delhi Panama City
Paris São Paulo Singapore Sydney
Tokyo Toronto

Osborne/**McGraw-Hill**
2600 Tenth Street
Berkeley, California 94710
U.S.A.

For information on translations or book distributors outside the U.S.A., or to
arrange bulk purchase discounts for sales promotions, premiums, or
fund-raisers, please contact Osborne/**McGraw-Hill** at the above address.

Oracle Designer Handbook, Second Edition

1234567890 AGM AGM 90198765432109

ISBN 0-07-882417-6

Publisher	**Copy Editors**
Brandon A. Nordin	Kathy Hashimoto,
	Claire Splan
Editor-in-Chief	
Scott Rogers	**Proofreader**
	Stefany Otis
Acquisitions Editor	
Jeremy Judson	**Indexer**
	Caryl Lee Fisher
Project Editor	
Mark Karmendy	**Computer Designer**
	Jani Beckwith
Editorial Assistant	Ann Sellers
Monika Faltiss	
	Illustrator
Technical Editor	Lance Ravella
Leslie Tierstein	Beth Young
Contributing Editor	**Series Design**
Douglas Scherer	Jani Beckwith

Peter Koletzke is a consulting manager who specializes in Designer and Developer work for Millennia Vision Corporation (www.mvsn.com), a strategy-through-implementation Oracle solutions provider that concentrates on custom development, Oracle Applications, data warehousing, Oracle training, supply chain command, electronic commerce, finance strategy, and Web applications in the Silicon Valley region of California. He is also a principal instructor for the company, a member of the Board of Directors of the International Oracle Users Group — Americas, and a frequent contributor to national and international Oracle newsletters and users group conferences.

Millennia Vision Corporation (MVC) is a strategic consulting partner, implementer, and reseller of various technologies (database, tools, data warehousing, e-commerce, financial applications/ERP, and others) in the enterprise space. It is unique in terms of experience, breadth, methodology, and referenceability. MVC's charter is to provide integrated business solutions to enable competitive advantage. A key differentiator for MVC is that it combines business depth and technical expertise to deliver "end-to-end" solutions. With core competencies in high technology manufacturing, banking, finance, retail, and telecommunications, its business specialists understand the key market drivers, business processes, and opportunities for competitive advantage.

Dr. Paul Dorsey is the founder and President of Dulcian, Inc. (http://www.dulcian.com) He specializes in project management, system design, and application development. He is co-author with Joseph Hudicka of *Oracle8 Design Using UML Object Modeling* from Oracle Press. He is also co-author with Peter Koletzke of an upcoming book from O'Reilly Press, on Very Rapid Application Development (VRAD) in Oracle Developer. Paul is an Associate Editor of *SELECT* Magazine. He is the Vice President of the New York Oracle Users' Group. Paul is very active in the Oracle user community and an award-winning speaker.

Dulcian, Inc. provides a wide variety of consulting services, customized training, and products for the Oracle development environment. They provide products and services to large government and private sector companies worldwide. Services include new project development, auditing existing efforts and rescuing failed projects. Training is available on all Oracle products, relational or object/relational data modeling, and DBA mentoring. Available products support virtually all development activities from analysis to data migration. Dulcian's vision is to deliver top quality systems in record time. To this end, they have automated or streamlined every possible portion of the development lifecycle to create a flexible strategy that is adapted for each project.

Files containing code from examples in this book are available from the authors' web sites.

Contents

PART I
Getting Started

PART II
Life Cycle Phases

PART IV
Additional Oracle Designer Activities

Oracle Designer Contents at a Glance

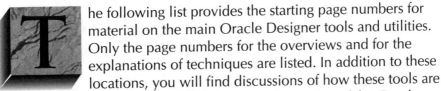

The following list provides the starting page numbers for material on the main Oracle Designer tools and utilities. Only the page numbers for the overviews and for the explanations of techniques are listed. In addition to these locations, you will find discussions of how these tools are used in system development in the introductory section of the Oracle Designer chapters.

Tool or Utility	Description	Location
Application Design Transformer	Overview	50
	Introduction	458
Application Programmatic Interface	Overview	72
	Introduction	971

Acknowledgements, Second Edition

he objective of this second edition was clear: "Update the technical material to reflect the new features of Oracle Designer 2.1." However, what seemed on the surface to be just an update quickly turned into a nearly total rewrite of this technical material because the product had increased so much in features and scope. The size of the book you have in your hands is more than three-quarters larger than the last edition largely because of this and because of our increased coverage of alternative development methods.

In the last edition, I likened the production of a book to the mounting of a stage production. This time, the metaphor is a railroad engine. Paul and I were only part of the team on that train and the credit for finishing this work on time goes to numerous others who stoked the engine and kept it on track.

Leslie Tierstein of W R Systems, Ltd., our Technical Editor, who sat on top of the engine, surveyed the track ahead and behind, and made sure the cars (our chapters) behind us were in line and solidly connected. I appreciate her contributions in the form of constant challenges, encouragement, ideas, painstaking attention to detail, and numerous pieces of supplemental text. I recognize the enormous amount of time she poured into the review process and am thankful for the depth and breadth of skill she brought to both method and methodology sides of this book. If anything remains unclear or technically inaccurate, it is likely due to my misinterpretation of her comments.

Douglas Scherer of Core Paradigm, Inc., our Contributing Editor, jumped on the engine at the last moment to flip the secret switch and avert a wreck when two weeks somehow vanished from our schedule. He took control and co-authorship of updates to the first edition that were needed for Part IV and wrote supplemental text for Chapter 18. Douglas' knowledge of the Oracle Designer product and expert sleuthing abilities added much technical value and depth to those chapters. We really appreciate his dedication and willingness to take on such a large task on such short notice. He spent many a sleepless night at the keyboard to make the book a reality.

Kudos to my co-author Paul Dorsey, and to Caryl Lee Fisher of Dulcian, Inc. for committing to and sticking to the nearly-impossible deadline schedule this train was on despite their other pressing deadlines for the *Oracle8 Design Using UML Object Modeling* book. Caryl Lee spent many long hours providing the daily coordination of schedules and files and somehow mastered the version control necessary to keep straight the various copies of all the chapters from both books.

There are many others who stoked the boiler in the engine so it would arrive on time and intact.

Most importantly, my work on this book would not have been accomplished without the support of my employer, Millennia Vision Corporation, who sponsored key portions of my time and materials, both of which are valuable commodities to a consulting company. Thanks too, to my boss, Guy Wilnai, Director of Custom Solutions and cofounder, for encouragement and co-dedication to the demanding schedule the writing team set for itself.

My appreciation goes also to Tony Ziemba, editor of Pinnacle Publishing's *Oracle Developer* technical journal who first published the articles Douglas and I wrote on information flow which made their way into Chapter 29. Tony got me started, for better or worse, in presenting and writing about Oracle development, and this has proved to be a rewarding part of my life.

I'd also like to acknowledge the efforts of the Oracle Press/ Osborne/McGraw-Hill staff, especially Jeremy Judson, our acquisitions editor, and Mark Karmendy, our project editor, who pulled some stops on their own to facilitate the book's release, as well as Ron Hull, and our copy editors, Kathy Hashimoto and Claire Splan. My gratitude also goes to Dai Clegg, of Oracle Corporation, for clarifications on the object support in the product; Monica Tucker, of Oracle Support, for asking questions and sharing information on the module component API; and Joe Strano, of Dulcian, Inc. for assistance tracking down an unpublished API feature.

Thanks goes too, to all those who contributed in an indirect way by writing articles, papers, or e-mail tips on the IOUG-A forum, ODTUG list servers, and various Oracle user conferences. This book includes ideas posted to these valuable sources. Now, with nearly universal acceptance of web technology, this kind knowledge flow is easier than ever. Hopefully this book will contribute something back to that flow.

Finally, I would like to thank my wife, Anne, for bearing with the large drains on my time that this book schedule demanded, and my parents and brother for their apparent interest in what must seem to them to be a boring topic. When writing this book I relied upon two principles my folks taught me: "You are cared for" and "Cut a strip sapling."

Peter Koletzke
Menlo Park, CA
September 1998

Even as we release this book into its second edition, I am struck with how much more I would like to do with the topic. Maybe we should have just focused on the many features of Oracle Designer rather than try to write about how best to use the product. But finally, Peter, Leslie (the Second Edition technical editor) and I believe that combining methodology and tool usage is the right approach for the book.

First, I would like to acknowledge Peter Koletzke, my co-author. To attempt to cover all of the new Designer features adequately in such a short space of time was truly a Herculean effort, which Peter accomplished with his usual grace and meticulousness (a rare combination of qualities). While I was finishing the *Oracle8 Design Using UML Object Modeling* book, Peter carried the effort on his own for many months. Most of the credit for this second edition rightly belongs to him.

Leslie Tierstein, our technical editor, gave this book the kind of careful attention that an author can only dream of. Her competence, expertise, and dedication helped us to avoid numerous misstatements, errors, and inconsistencies. Any errors that remain are probably due to us ignoring her advice. We have invited Leslie to join us as a co-author on the next edition. Our only reservation is how we can ever replace her as technical editor.

Of course, the book could not have been written without the amazing Caryl Lee Fisher. Caryl Lee edited and re-edited the manuscript. She was the main source of communication between the authors and Osborne/McGraw-Hill, ensuring that everything ran smoothly in the writing and editing processes. If she was any more of a contributor, we would have to add her as a third author.

Thanks to our editors at Osborne/McGraw-Hill. Jeremy Judson, Mark Karmendy, and Ron Hull were instrumental in getting this project completed on time.

Many thanks to my co-workers at Dulcian, Inc. They are, without exception, the finest set of IT professionals that I have ever worked with. Much of what I have learned about excellence in project design, I have learned from them. Thanks, gang.

Special mention must go to Joe Hudicka, my business partner, who contributed the material for the data migration chapter.

My love and gratitude go to my wife, Kathie Duliba. She not only put up with me working on two books simultaneously, but also contributed the material for the BPR chapter. I promise to spend more weekends at home.

Finally, my apologies to my dog, Popper, for not spending enough time with him. Fortunately, he is getting old enough that he is content to sleep most of the day.

Paul Dorsey
Lawrenceville, NJ
September 1998

Acknowledgments, First Edition

eciding to write a book is the easy part. Actually starting and, more importantly, finishing the process is another story. Although there are only two authors' names on the cover of this book, it would have been impossible to accomplish this work without the help and support of many other people throughout the months of deadlines, schedule juggling, missed sleep, and a complete lack of a social life. The fact that you are reading this is a tribute to their patience and perseverance.

Many thanks to Christine Hall of Detroit Edison, who became much more than a technical editor. She was a major contributor to the book. Without her astute insights sprinkled with humorous comments, which cheered us on as we worked, this book would be something far less than it is.

A special mention must go to Caryl Lee Fisher who helped write, edit, and re-edit the manuscript, and re-edit the manuscript, and re-edit the manuscript…

Love and gratitude to Katherine Duliba, my wife, for contributing the section on business process re-engineering that we include in the Analysis chapter, and for putting up with me throughout this arduous process.

Also, thanks to many other people who have, by design or inadvertently, contributed ideas to this book, including Ian Fisher and Dai Clegg of Oracle Corporation, for their support; Eyal Aronoff, who contributed the ideas surrounding the political environment of a project; Bonnie O'Neil, for her ideas concerning business rules; Michael Hillanbrand II, for his information on database security and thoughtful comments; Mike Martin, for his thoughts on process-centric versus data-centric analysis; Tony Ziemba, for innumerable ongoing conversations and support; Erik Enger, for his contributions to the sections on the Designer/2000 generators; and Jim Phipps of Oracle Corporation, for his valuable insights on the Analysis phase.

Many thanks to Wendy Rinaldi, Daniela Dell'Orco, Judy Ziajka, and especially Emily Rader, of Osborne/McGraw-Hill for all their efforts and support on this project.

And finally, heartfelt apologies to my dog, Popper, for having neglected him for the last six months.

Paul Dorsey
Lawrenceville, NJ
September, 1996

In a theatrical show, the actors provide their talent to the production and enjoy, as well as suffer, the spotlight. The show could not exist as a vehicle for the actors, however, without the backstage personnel in charge of lighting, scenery, costumes, and stage management. These people contribute to the show their hard work, expertise, and creativity, but receive little or no public recognition.

Writing a book is much like mounting a theatrical show. (I speak from experience, because my previous career was as a stage manager and lighting technician.) The authors of this book are like actors who are in the spotlight, and the book itself is like the production. There were also numerous "backstage" people who assisted in "raising the curtain" and "lighting the lights" of this book. Since we cannot list all of these as co-authors, it is appropriate to at least mention their contributions and offer gratitude and thanks for their efforts.

I greatly appreciate the efforts of all involved at Osborne/McGraw-Hill: Wendy Rinaldi, acquisitions editor; Daniela Dell'Orco, editorial assistant; Emily Rader, project editor; and our unknown (but all important) friends in production. Thanks also to Judy Ziajka, our copy editor on the book. At the start of this project, we set quite an ambitious schedule, and all at OMH dedicated themselves to work many hours to finish it. Particular thanks to Emily, who went out of her way to speed us needed copies of review material. How could we not meet our deadlines when all these people were giving up so much personal time to meet theirs?

Ian Fisher, Vice President of Designer/2000 Product Marketing for Oracle UK, assisted us by supplying us with an early copy of Designer/2000 1.3. Without that jump-start, we would have lagged behind our early deadlines by a few weeks. Thanks Ian.

Our technical reviewer, Chris Hall, provided astute, uncompromising, and accurate opinions and judgments of the work-in-progress. She put much time into carefully reviewing the drafts and caught some potentially embarrassing typos and unclear sentences.

Many thanks go to Titus Bocseri and Dr. Zhongsu Chen, for base material on the Forms and Reports generators. Their hard work, timeliness, enthusiasm, and expertise was of key importance to the Build chapter.

Caryl Lee Fisher cheerfully endured the daily phone calls and more frequent e-mail. Her phone was rarely silent and most of the traffic was related to this book. Caryl Lee was really the authors' stage manager, as she organized our work and focused us on the proper tasks at the proper times with gentle reminders. All that hard work and commitment is greatly appreciated.

My wife, Anne, as well as my parents and brother, bore with the difficult schedule that I imposed on myself. They also provided momentary diversions when the work started to be too intense, and listened empathetically to me while I explained each step of the book production process. I now understand the reasons why everyone who writes a book must recognize their family's assistance.

Finally, thanks to all my major teachers of the last 30 years from whom I learned much: Gilbert, Todd, Art, and Sai. Hopefully the torch is passed without diminishing its flame.

Peter Koletzke
New York City, NY
September, 1996

Introduction

12-Step Program for Traditional System Development

1. Come up with a cool acronym and figure out a mission-critical system that fits the acronym.

2. Get a bunch of money to build the system and divert the money to other over-budget projects.

3. Use junior developers because everyone else is too busy.

4. Hire inexperienced consultants because they give you the best rate.

5. Don't bother with system requirements because you already know what the users want.

6. Fire the consultants. They were too slow. Hire a new team from a big expensive consulting firm.

7. Have each developer design their own portion of the database because they know exactly what tables they need.

8. Do your prototypes in MS Access even though you will be deploying with Developer Web Forms.

9. Just start coding, because the project is way behind schedule.

10. Don't bother with system or user documentation, since no one reads that stuff anyway.

11. Have the developers do user acceptance testing because they are the only ones who really understand how the system should work.

12. Write vague and misleading status reports to give the illusion of progress. Then write a system work request to propose what you actually accomplished. Backdate it and declare victory.

The process of designing and building automated information systems is greatly influenced by the software tools used to assist in the process. Systems analysts, designers, and developers turn to Computer-Aided Software Engineering (CASE) programs to capture information about business requirements, create a design for the data structures to fulfill these requirements, and generate front-end and server program code. Since CASE tools automate much of the manual, repetitive, and error-prone work needed for system development, they can, when properly used, greatly increase the productivity of those who produce the systems. They can also greatly increase the accuracy of the design and robustness of the implementation. These tools become such an important part of the mechanics of creating systems that it is impossible to separate the process from the tools.

Oracle Designer, Oracle Corporation's CASE product now at Version 2.1 (formerly called Designer/2000), represents an unparalleled achievement in Oracle's ability to support all phases of traditional, as well as alternative, System Development Life Cycle methods. One such method is presented in Richard Barker's Oracle CASE books, which serve as excellent overviews. Unfortunately, these books are often misused by developers who follow them dogmatically, or mistakenly believe that the books, together with the Oracle Designer product, form a complete development methodology. These books were never intended to serve as complete methodology guides, as each step in the development life cycle really deserves its own book.

The Approach of This Book

This book represents a revision of the first development method fully integrated with Oracle's Oracle Designer product. Its purpose is to show the practical steps and methodological phases of producing software, in addition to specific ways in which the Oracle Designer tool can support them. Our work here has two objectives. The first is to revise and expand on the CASE method. We have gone into more detail than have the original CASE books, added more deliverables, and restructured the whole process in addition to discussing the features of Oracle Designer v. 2.1. The second objective is to describe how Oracle Designer can best be used to support our revised CASE method.

We call this revised method the CASE Application Development Method (CADM). This book represents a serious departure from traditional books about the System Development Life Cycle and traditional books about software products. It is an integration of these two distinct types of books. Rather than saying, "this is a book on how to build systems" or "this is a book about how to use Oracle Designer," we say "this is a book about how to build systems using Oracle Designer." We have combined the best industry practices for system development with the best integrated CASE tool on the market—Oracle Designer.

One of the main goals of this book is to present a development process that tracks the path of a business requirement from its original source, typically gathered during Analysis, to its eventual implementation in the system. We wanted to formulate a process that would guard against encountering the scenario in which a user shows up at the end of a project with interview notes gathered six months earlier, points to a paragraph, and says, "We wanted this in our system and it's not here. You signed off on this. Where is it?" In order to avoid this frightening scenario, our entire development process is driven by business requirements. This book discusses the methodology itself—what you need to think about, talk about, and do as you progress through the System Development Life Cycle.

Another goal of this book is to include a very strong quality assurance component with virtually every aspect of every phase of the development process. It doesn't matter that you have a great application development method if the developers don't follow it carefully. The key to the success of CADM is making sure that each phase is correctly completed prior to moving on to the next.

While this book presents an expanded variation of the traditional "waterfall" life cycle, we recognize that there are many other valid methodologies used successfully. We find, however, that these alternative methods have many of the same features, and even in some cases, even the same phases as this waterfall approach, although these phases may be expanded or collapsed. Therefore, the techniques presented in this somewhat traditional, but arguably, complete approach should be portable to other methods.

The exciting part of this is that Oracle Designer supports these alternative methods as well as the CADM described in this book. The way it is both compartmentalized and integrated hides many of the complexities involved with how it can support these different methods. The foundation for all system development work you do is in intelligent use of a well-structured, central repository of information about the system you are creating or maintaining. This is where Oracle Designer excels and this is what makes it a perfect tool for every design and development environment.

The book also contains information on what processes Oracle Designer can support in each of the CADM phases and how it supports them. It supplies details, not found in other sources, for effective use of the tools, and explains what information is important to gather at each stage. The book also mentions where to find this information for each step of the development process. Interspersed in these discussions, as well as discussions of the methodology itself, are tips and techniques for productive work in the tool.

Comments on the Second Edition

Since writing the first edition of this book, there have been two important changes in our development environment. The first is that Oracle Designer has matured as a product. The quality of the user interface has greatly improved, as has Designer's ability to generate code. Second, over the last few years, we have changed some of our thinking about systems development.

We now recognize that the development phases are not as discrete as we initially believed. Instead, many activities and deliverables refuse to fall neatly into one phase or another, but span the whole systems development life cycle. At some points, we may even break out a portion of a project and carry it through to production in order to validate the development effort. As opposed to "top-down" development (the traditional SDLC model) or "bottom-up" development (a more RAD-oriented approach), this is "middle-out" development and it deserves serious attention as a formal methodology.

Like systems development, this book is also a work in progress. In this edition, because our thinking has changed, we have added some chapters on topics we felt were missing in the first, such as data migration and adapting CADM to a rapid development environment, and reorganized some aspects of the development phases. There are still many things to learn. As we discovered while working on the first book, the tools greatly influence the methodology. This became one of the core principles behind CADM and will doubtless influence our direction again in the next edition.

Despite the substantially increased length of this book, it is still a cursory overview of the topic of how to use Oracle Designer for effective systems development. Many sections deserve to be books in their own right. In fact, this has already been done with Database Design in Oracle Press' *Oracle8 Design Using UML Object Modeling* (Dr. Paul Dorsey & Joseph Hudicka, 1999) and another Oracle Press book specifically about the Oracle Designer generators. Additional books could easily be written on the topics of Analysis, Testing, Application Design Standards (including GUI and coding standards), Data Migration, and WebServer Generation.

Organization of This Book

This book is divided into four parts. Part I contains an overview of the CADM methodology and of Oracle Designer in Chapters 1 and 2, respectively. Part II (Chapters 3-21) provides details on each phase of the methodology, as well as on the Oracle Designer tools and utilities that support each phase. Each phase is discussed in one or two chapters, although discussions of the Test, Implementation, and Maintenance phases are combined in one chapter. The material on Oracle Designer is woven into this methodology discussion and picks up where the installation process leaves off. Following the chapter on each phase is another chapter that discusses the Oracle Designer support for activities in that phase.

The CADM life cycle we present in this book progresses in a linear way from one phase to another. We recognize, however, that system development is not a simple, linear process. The scope of a project can change at any time. New user requirements can be discovered anywhere in the process, even in the Test phase. In addition, quality-control checks can fail. In general, reality always creeps into our theoretically clean process. Therefore, Chapter 21 discusses how to respond to the unexpected.

Part III, new in this edition, addresses topics that fall beyond the traditional SDLC. Chapter 22 covers a Rapid Application Development (RAD) modification to CADM for small to medium-sized projects. Chapter 23 discusses how to modify the CADM process when you need to "start in the middle" of a previously attempted project. Chapter 24 covers Business Process Reengineering, and Chapter 25 discusses the often overlooked, but critical to the success of a project, topic of Data Migration.

Part IV contains information on several Oracle Designer features and facilities that you use throughout the methodology phases. In particular, Chapter 26 outlines application system and repository maintenance, Chapter 27 discusses Oracle Designer's User Extensibility options, and Chapter 28 introduces the Application Programmatic Interface. Chapter 29 covers the all-important topic of how information flows within the repository and how element definitions in one phase are copied to definitions in another phase.

Since many Oracle Designer tools and utilities are used in more than one phase, discussion of a particular tool may be spread across more than one chapter. You can refer to the "Oracle Designer Contents at a Glance" following the Table of Contents, if you are interested to know where in the book to find the major discussions of a particular tool or utility.

The Sample Data Model

You will find examples throughout the Oracle Designer chapters of this book based on a student registration tracking system called CTA (Computer Training Associates), which is also the name of a fictitious company. These examples do not use a case study approach so the business rules and implementation details are not critical to the discussions. Nevertheless, it is useful to go through a quick explanation of what the CTA system can do.

The CTA system tracks the registration of students in the program, enrollment of students in classes, and grading of students for course work. It manages the assignment of instructors to sections (instantiations of a course). It also stores profile information of the students and instructors and provides the ability to issue invoices based on the enrollment information, and grade reports based on work that the students complete.

Each of the main entities in the system is represented by a table that stores its information: STUDENTS, INSTRUCTORS, COURSES, SECTIONS, ENROLLMENTS, WORK_GRADES. Since the volume of students is quite high, the postal code information is stored in a separate structure ZIPCODES, which can be joined to the STUDENTS and INSTRUCTORS tables to look up the city and state portion of the address. These principles should help in understanding the examples in this book.

Why Use Oracle Designer?

Oracle Designer is still the best integrated CASE product on the market. Its capabilities greatly influence the CADM process. Oracle Designer's ability to track data and process information in a single repository makes it an invaluable aid. In addition to its built-in breadth and depth, Oracle Designer offers User Extensibility and the Application Programmatic Interface (API). These features allow you to extend the capabilities of Oracle Designer to support aspects that the Oracle product designers chose not to implement in the core product, or that are specific to your working environment.

In general, Oracle Designer promises to make application system development more accurate and flexible, as shown in the following table. This is because Oracle Designer provides a way to capture and manage the often voluminous data associated with a new or current system. The data can be so unmanageable that systems designers end up ignoring or overlooking key business needs, or spending too much time developing the system and, along the way, lose sight of the requirements.

Development Aspect	With Oracle Designer	Without Oracle Designer
System development	Structured	Usually ad hoc
Maintenance costs	Low	High
Generation of database	Automated (low cost)	Manual (high cost)
Code generation	Partially automated	Manual
System documentation	Mostly stored in the repository	Ad hoc

NOTE
Oracle Designer 2.1 was originally called Designer/2000 and you may find references to that name in the help system and other documents from Oracle and third-party sources.

Why CASE Projects Fail

CASE tools have historically been viewed as a waste of time and resources because project leaders who bought into the concept could not support the huge learning curve required for their staff. If time was not devoted solely to learning the tools and how they were supposed to work, the project was delayed significantly or failed totally. Due to these early negative experiences, a stigma was attached to the word "CASE," and many companies would not touch it. Oracle (as well as other CASE vendors) has therefore reworked the idea and expunged the word "CASE" from documentation and discussions of the current product. Oracle Designer is, nonetheless, a CASE tool, and while the product is much deeper and easier to use than previous versions, the learning curve is still significant. Ignoring this fact may still cause projects to fail.

Another major reason for the failure of CASE projects was that CASE users who did not understand the software development process relied on the product to lead them through the life cycle, one step at a time. While this is somewhat possible in the current version of Oracle Designer, it was not, and still is not, possible to expect the CASE tool to do the driving. After all, CASE is "Computer-Aided" not "Computer-Driven" Software Engineering. A CASE tool should not be confused with a methodology. The methodology, rather than the tool, defines our procedures.

Determining the Methodology

When developing a system, care and attention must be given to the development methodology. One of the important influences of a methodology is the tool selected for the task. In particular, CASE tools have the strongest impact on the development method because of their direct influence on all phases of the project. As we just mentioned, the danger is that the CASE tools become the methodology. If the tools perform many of the development tasks, it is easy to assume that they support and drive all development tasks. This tool-driven methodology encourages developers to miss essential steps in the development process because those steps are not explicitly handled by the tool.

We all would like an easy, no-thought-required design process. We would like checklists, detailed deliverables, and precise standards. We would like to give up our responsibility of having to think about what we are doing. In reality, though, this will never work, because every system is different, and developing systems is an intellectual exercise. Developers must ask the following questions:

- Is there a theoretically sound plan that will take the project where it should go?

- How will we know when a task or phase has been accomplished?

- How will we measure success?

These are the kinds of questions that must be asked at each phase. Unfortunately, it is far too easy to be blinded by the work plan, the delivery deadline, and the demands for immediate results.

Where Does CADM Fit?

After writing this book, we recognized that, after all, CADM is a traditional System Development Life Cycle (SDLC) approach. Our experience has been that developers and users are more satisfied with the finished product when the analysis and design are carefully done. Most of us have worked on systems where failures have been of biblical proportions. These failures usually happen because shortcuts are taken and the proper methodology is not followed or performed with enough care. Oracle Designer helps us to do better analysis and design by providing a unified repository to store most of the analysis and design information.

While CADM does not emphasize prototyping, we do believe that prototypes can be developed in order to show proof of concept. In this second edition, a RAD-CADM approach is described in Chapter 22. Prototyping can occur throughout any system's life cycle in order to better communicate the overall vision of the system to users. This gives users useful feedback about how the completed system eventually will look before a significant amount of money is spent building it. In the Pre-Design phase, we suggest that developers produce a prototype so that users can experience the look and feel of the system. By the time the system is ready to be built, the users have helped the system evolve through its life cycle.

At the risk of looking like traditionalists (i.e., non-forward-thinking radicals) who are bucking the trend toward the rapid prototyping environment, we strongly advocate a traditional SDLC, but one that is done better, faster, more efficiently, and with better organization. We believe that Analysis should be done carefully and correctly. When it is, valuable time and money can be saved by not having to redo what should have been done right the first time.

When we first started writing this book, we envisioned a much smaller work. Nevertheless, now that we've finished it, we have to acknowledge that even though it is larger than we originally thought it would be, it is merely an overview of the application development process. Time and time again, we found ourselves wanting to write more about a topic, but the practical limitations of the project prohibited this. Even in this revised and expanded second edition, we do not claim that this book is a complete treatment of how to use Oracle Designer to build systems, as that would take many volumes. However, we do feel that it is a complete overview of our vision of the best way to build systems using Oracle Designer.

PART
I

Getting Started

CHAPTER
1

Introduction to System Design Methodology

A poorly planned project will take five times as long as anticipated. A well-planned project will take only three times as long as anticipated.

he key to a successful system design project lies in the coordination of several critical success factors—namely the right people, the right technology/tools, and the right method. An effective combination of these three factors is necessary for system success. This is not just a how-to book about the Oracle Designer tool set, nor is it a college textbook on systems analysis and design. Rather, this book serves as a guide for systems developers on how to successfully build systems using the Oracle Designer tools based on actual project experiences of the authors.

You will be exploring each step in the system development process in detail in the following chapters. This chapter presents short summaries of all of the steps to give you an idea of the individual phases. The detailed steps will be easier to follow if you first have a broad understanding of the entire process. Chapter 2 gives an overview of the Oracle Designer tools and explains their role in system development.

Overview of CASE Application Development Method (CADM)

There is no magic about the System Development Life Cycle (SDLC). It has been documented in every book on analysis and design for the last 20 years. With the exception of a few radical shifts, such as prototyping methodology in the mid-1980s, there hasn't been a fundamental shift in the SDLC since it was described decades ago. Essentially, it boils down to the fact that all methodologies, regardless of whether they are developed in-house or purchased from a software project management or consulting firm, address a structure to plan, analyze, design, build, and implement business applications. What differentiates them is their level of detail, techniques, and their integration with people, processes, and technology.

Since Oracle Designer is an Oracle product, many readers of this book may be familiar with the SDLC steps known as the CASE method and outlined by Richard Barker in *CASE Method: Tasks and Deliverables* (Addison-Wesley, 1990). Richard Barker was one of the driving influences behind Oracle's CASE products and the CASE methodology. He spearheaded the development of Oracle's CASE tool set, which eventually evolved in Oracle Designer.

We will use the same major phases and terms utilized by Barker as a starting point. However, to achieve the objectives of this book, we found it necessary to modify and enhance the CASE method. No explicit assumption is made that the reader is familiar with Barker's method, but for those readers already familiar with it, we hope that our remaining consistent with Barker's terminology will help avoid confusion.

The basic phases in Barker's method are Strategy, Analysis, Design, Build, Documentation, Transition, and Production. We found the basic steps of the CASE method too broad so we added several additional phases. What this book attempts to do is lay out the goals, deliverables, and methods for evaluating the success and completion of each phase. Not all tasks in the various phases of the CASE method are supported by the Oracle Designer tool. A list of the basic phases of our revised development method and what tasks each supports is presented in Table 1-1.

Revised CASE Design Phases	Supported by Designer	Not Supported by Current Version of Designer	Can Be Supported by Designer with User Extensibility
Strategy	Strategy ERD Process flows	Strategy document Cost-benefit analysis Workplan	
Analysis	Analysis ERD Function hierarchy Dataflow diagrams	User interviews Prototypes Storyboards	System requirements Report audit
Design	Most modules	Very complex modules	Design specifications

TABLE I-I. *Simplified CADM Development Phases and What Designer Supports in Each Step*

Revised CASE Design Phases	Supported by Designer	Not Supported by Current Version of Designer	Can Be Supported by Designer with User Extensibility
Build	Most modules	Very complex modules	
Test		Automated testing	Test plan and execution
Implementation	Rollout plan		
Maintenance	Versioning		

TABLE 1-1.   *Simplified CADM Development Phases and What Designer Supports in Each Step* (continued)

We have added the transition phases of Pre-Analysis and Pre-Design to the basic methodology and have included Test, Implementation, and Maintenance in the overall process. We have named this revised method CASE Application Development Method (CADM).

We have also added some topics that have become critical components of applications development methodology and technology in the years since the publication of Barker's book. Since many current development projects must replace preexisting legacy systems, data migration has become an increasingly important part of these efforts. Also, because of its importance in today's development environment, a section on business process reengineering (BPR) has been included. Prototyping and rapid application development (RAD) concepts have been employed throughout the process, although the book does not present a strict prototyping methodology.

Beyond the Waterfall

The "waterfall" method of development starting from Strategy and moving through various phases to Implementation is the traditional foundation that drives the way systems are built. The real-world process of system development is not nearly as clear cut. Some level of analysis is taking place in every phase of the project. Major portions of the project can be developed and, in some cases, put into production before Analysis is complete. Phases overlap, and development is never a linear process from one phase to the next. Portions of the system may be completed ahead of schedule, while others may completely fail and need to be redesigned.

Few design efforts are undertaken from the ground up. More often, the successful design and development of a system does not occur the first time the effort is attempted. A project may begin on the ruins of a previously failed attempt. Major portions of the Analysis phase may remain incomplete, but for political or other reasons further contact with users may be greatly restricted until some success is achieved.

There may be political deliverables that must be completed, which have little or no relevance to the actual development process. In government contracting, there are sometimes large milestone deliverables that may even interfere with a logical development process.

For the reasons just stated, actual implementation of every step in the approach described in this book should not be slavishly followed. What should be followed are the engineering principles and theories behind CADM. Events may occur in a different order. CADM deliverables may need to be partitioned and delivered in stages, but the theory remains sound. In no place should any of the deliverables be shortcut or eliminated, although the same objectives can sometimes be met using different tasks or deliverables than those detailed in this book.

CADM Critical Success Factors

CADM has all of the necessary audit and control points designed to ensure that the project undertaken is designed to the best of the development team's abilities. However, three additional critical managerial elements are required in any project:

- Top management support to commit adequate resources to the project

- A Project Administrator role to ensure that the principles behind the development method are rigorously followed

- Competent technical lead person to guide the strategic technical decisions on the project, managing the architecture of the database and applications, development method, and coding environment

Without these factors, the method alone is not adequate to ensure project success.

Rapid Application Development-CADM (RAD-CADM)

For small projects, where requirements are reasonably well defined at the start of the project or easily and quickly determined, it is possible to use a RAD project development approach. CADM is already a RAD approach to some extent, incorporating many of the aspects of RAD such as prototyping in the Analysis phase. This concept can be taken one step further by doing a very limited Analysis phase and moving right into iterative development. While such an approach can decrease project costs, it often increases the risks and exposure of the development team. We will discuss the RAD-CADM approach in more detail in Chapter 22.

For RAD-CADM to succeed, a skilled development team with a good relationship with the user community is required. In addition, the project should have a clearly defined and limited scope.

"Start in the Middle"

It is very common to enter a project at some middle point. Usually, all that is recoverable from a failed attempt is some of the Analysis phase work. Most design work, including database design, is often so badly flawed as to be unsalvageable.

Critical challenges to entering a project in the middle are often political. Bad feelings may exist between developers and users. Users are tired of answering the same questions over and over again. Existing developers may resist throwing out any prior work.

When entering a project in the middle, the important thing to accomplish is to determine what can be salvaged and to find some way of proving that what is salvageable is of use in the new effort. Even accepting that Analysis was done properly, work from this phase will still need to be audited. Without an audit, you must accept the risks of building a system based upon a questionable foundation.

Entering a project that is proceeding well but lacking in sound project administration presents similar challenges. If appropriate audits have not been done or control points have not been included in the development process and work has proceeded, a decision must be made to either accept the work done up to that point or perform the audits. In either case, the political risks and challenges are usually greater than the technical ones.

Business Process Reengineering (BPR)

BPR is a very different type of system design requiring a much higher level of involvement from the user community than is usual in a systems development project. No matter how hard large consulting firms try to convince us otherwise, systems cannot be reengineered from the outside. The users, perhaps with guidance from a development team, must be the drivers of a BPR effort.

BPR can greatly lengthen the Analysis phase of any project. Paradoxically, if the BPR effort is successful, the overall cost of the project may not change or even decrease, because it may be easier to develop and implement a reengineered process than it is to "pave the cowpath."

BPR efforts involve radical redesign of the underlying business process. This often involves a complete rethinking of the way that an organization does business. Prior to designing a major information system is an ideal time to undertake a BPR effort. Never asking the question "Is there a better way to do things?" guarantees that you won't find the answer. Unfortunately, cost-conscious and shortsighted organizations often fail to recognize that their business processes can be improved upon and the question is rarely asked.

Data Migration

Data migration involves moving data from the legacy system into the new system structure. This is a task that is usually greatly underestimated, if not completely ignored. Usually, the scope and difficulty of a data migration is impossible to assess until the migration itself is almost complete.

In virtually every system we have worked on, users insisted that the data in the database was "clean" and that we would not have significant difficulties in migrating the data. In our experience, every data migration performed has been more difficult and time consuming than anticipated. There are five main causes for these difficulties:

■ The first problem is the difference in structures between the legacy and new systems. Even legacy systems built on relational platforms are often heavily denormalized. Migrating this data into a modern, normalized database, often created using generic modeling techniques, requires very complex mapping routines not supported by most data migration products.

■ Whenever data integrity rules are not enforced by the database, violations of these rules creep into the data. Each unenforced database constraint in the legacy system may be violated in 10 percent or more of the rows in a given table. The cleansing of this dirty data prior to its migration to the new system is a very difficult task.

■ Data-related business rules in an organization change over time. Multiple maps are needed for any given table to map rows from different points in the history of the organization. Changes in business rules can increase the complexity of a migration by as much as 50 percent.

■ In many cases, migration must occur from more than one source. In addition to the main legacy systems, other departmental databases and spreadsheets built to supply functionality that the legacy system could not must also be incorporated into the new system. Migrating and harmonizing data from a variety of sources can greatly increase the cost of a migration effort.

■ You can almost always find expert functional users of the current systems. However, if the legacy systems are old enough or were not developed in-house, it may be difficult to find systems professionals who can help you decipher the data that is actually stored in the legacy database.

For all of these reasons, we have seen data migrations consume up to 80 percent of the budget for a project. In Chapter 25, we will discuss how a successful data migration should be accomplished.

Strategy

In the Strategy phase, the entire focus is on the business. The goal of the Strategy phase is to gain a clear understanding of the business area's goals, objectives, processes, direction, and needs in order to structure and document the vision of a project. This "vision document" has been referred to as a project charter, project definition document, and scope document, depending upon your organization's preference. For our purposes, we will call it the Strategy Document. The *Strategy Document* outlines the scope of a project and defines an agreement about what the project is committed to deliver. It also includes the estimated budget, time frame, resources, controls, and standards within which the project must be completed. It is the foundation for moving forward and preparing detailed plans.

Strategy is the most often neglected phase of a systems project. The Strategy Document is usually quite brief and not well thought out. Barker states very clearly that "the objective of the strategy phase is to produce, with user management, a set of business models, a set of recommendations and an agreed plan for information systems development."

Many analysts view Strategy as a protective step. It is used to limit later finger pointing and enable analysts to justify cases in which they went over budget.

Preparing the Strategy Document is a complex step that must be completed before going forward. Development of business models requires understanding of the organization. A few meetings with top management are not usually sufficient. In the Strategy phase, one of the goals is to intimately understand the business. The system requirements are going to change over the course of the project. (Has there ever been a project during which user needs did not evolve?) By thoroughly understanding the business, the analyst will be prepared to evolve with the project.

At the completion of the Strategy phase, it is important to deliver a high-quality strategy document that includes the following parts: a Strategy ERD, a top-level requirements document, an analysis of the political environment, a work flow plan, strategy-level process flows, and a strategy evaluation. For this overview, we have described only some of the sections. A complete list and discussion of all parts of the Strategy Document can be found in Chapter 3.

Strategy ERD

The purpose of the Strategy ERD is to identify the primary data or main entities of a business area. The Strategy ERD serves to demonstrate a preliminary understanding of the business area. There should be little thought at this point in the process as to how the system will eventually be implemented. The only goal is to capture the users' needs at the highest level.

Strategy ERDs should focus on readability rather than on relational theory. Good drawing and naming techniques, such as those proposed by David Hay, should be used. All you are trying to do is draw a picture. It is not necessary to completely fill in all Oracle Designer element entities with descriptions; nicely named relationships and a few key columns are sufficient.

Keep Strategy ERDs small enough to be useful. Several small models of 10 to 20 entities each are better than one complicated (and often intimidating) model.

Strategy Document

A comprehensive Strategy Document is essential to the success of a project. Although most of the system requirements are gathered during the Analysis phase, the key system requirements should be included in the Strategy Document. The keys to a good Strategy Document are planning and organization. The main goal of this document is to scope the project—to identify and describe high-level requirements. The "real" Requirements Document comes later. Another goal is to sell the system. A cost-benefit analysis of the system should be included.

Business and Formal Sponsorship

Systems analysts need to be aware of the political environment within the organization in which they are working. The existing political environment can have a major impact on how the project phases proceed. This environment, including its players and methods for resolving potential conflicts, should be documented.

High-Level Workplan

A high-level workplan identifies the major phases, activities, milestones, key deliverables, resources, and duration of the project. The workplan outlines the steps to be followed as the system goes forward and can largely be boilerplate text. It should be clear to the reader not only how long things will take but also that the plan will produce the desired results. Personnel requirements and deliverables should be included in the workplan.

Strategy-Level Process Flows

Business process flows are typically defined as part of the Analysis phase. However, the key business processes should be identified and modeled at this point as process flows.

Strategy Evaluation

The evaluation of strategy requires input from both users and developers. Unfortunately, users may not understand the process of development well enough to evaluate whether the Strategy phase has been properly completed. Therefore, it is important to educate users as necessary so they can effectively evaluate the project strategy. The challenge on the side of the developers is to not delude themselves that the strategy is complete when it isn't. Developers must understand the basics of the system they are developing.

At its core, the Strategy Document is a contract. There must be a meeting of the minds if the contract is to make sense and be honored. Developers must understand the needs and direction of the business; users must have confidence that the developers have grasped a level of understanding sufficient to move forward. The Strategy Document is the vehicle for making this mutual understanding possible.

Pre-Analysis

The goals of Pre-Analysis are to plan the analysis process and to begin to set standards. Users and developers together must develop a strategy that ensures that the analysis will be performed correctly. Therefore, the first step is to decide on the goals of the Analysis phase.

Barker describes Analysis as expanding Strategy to "ensure business accuracy, feasibility and a sound foundation for Design." However, Analysis is more than this. The goal of Analysis is to capture all user specifications for the project and to completely detail all business processes that will be involved in the system design.

Analysis therefore focuses on the user rather than on the system. It attempts to figure out what the users want and how their business works. Later, items can be declared out of scope or budget. At this point, there is no reason to argue with users about their requirements. The only goal is to understand these requirements.

The Pre-Analysis Document should include the following: Analysis Plan, plan for implementing CASE analysis standards, and pre-analysis evaluation.

Analysis Plan

Before Analysis can begin, there must be an Analysis Plan. Steps and deliverables must be included. "Analysis" is not a well-defined word. Different analysts explain this step very differently. The developer must include a statement of the scope of the analysis.

Plan for Implementing CASE Analysis Standards

The developer must specify how CASE analysis standards will be implemented. How will the CASE tool be used? What properties will be filled in and with what information? How will entities and attributes be named? How detailed will the descriptions be? Will functions be numbered or named? What will be ignored? These are some of the many questions that must be answered before the project can go forward into Design.

Pre-Analysis Evaluation

Pre-Analysis is finished when everyone agrees that there is an appropriate plan for gathering all system requirements. As with other phases, both users and developers have to agree that the Pre-Analysis phase is complete.

Assessment of the Analysis Plan is similar to that of an ERD. To "break" an ERD, you try to come up with a data example that the model can't handle. In Pre-Analysis evaluation, it is helpful to have users try to come up with requirements that the process will not gather. For example, in one system a veteran on-site developer asked: "We have requirements hard-coded in our old C routines that must make it into the new system; how will we find out about those?" Because of that one question, the Analysis Plan was expanded.

Analysis

The goal of the Analysis phase is to capture all of the user specifications for the project and to completely detail all business processes that will be involved. This is the most important step in systems design.

The ERD and function hierarchy are built with the user directly and indirectly through the Requirements Document; good analysts do not just work with the user for an hour and then come back three months later with a product that they developed on their own.

The existing business processes, the legacy system, and the users themselves are all sources of the requirements information. The amount of information gathered will be so large that its management is a task in itself. A thorough Requirements Document can easily fill several thousand pages.

The main focus of the Analysis phase is the generation of the Requirements Document. However, there are other deliverables. These should be included in the overall Analysis Document, which is the deliverable for this phase. The Analysis Document consists of the following parts: Analysis ERD, process flows (logical), Requirements Document, and analysis evaluation.

Analysis ERD

The goal of the Analysis ERD is to completely represent as many business rules as possible. Any rules that cannot be represented in the model must be written down. In Analysis, the focus is still on the user, so there is no need to worry about how the system will be implemented.

Process Flows (Logical)

The developer needs to document logical process flows. What are the tasks? Who performs them? What tasks precede other tasks? Process flows modeling major business transactions attempt to answer these questions, with one flowchart used for each business transaction. The Oracle Process Flow Diagrammer is the ideal tool for this task.

Requirements Document

The Requirements Document is a critical aspect of the Analysis phase. A missing or inadequate Requirements Document can lead to client dissatisfaction and, ultimately, system failure. A Requirements Document must include the following:

- **Detailed business objectives and critical success factors for each business area that the system will support** It is not sufficient to simply try to understand what the new system has to do. A thorough understanding of the underlying business is critical to the success of the system. Therefore, the business objectives and critical success factors should be carefully gathered as a key portion of the Requirements Document.

- **Legacy system documentation** Any existing legacy systems to be replaced should be modeled. A small Oracle database that tracks existing files, fields, applications, and menu screens is easy to build and is a great help in making sure that the new system does not lose any legacy system functionality. The legacy documentation database should be mapped to the new system database and function hierarchy to ensure functional and data completeness of the new system. This mapping can also be used to validate the completeness of the data migration plan.

- **Requirements list** A list of all requirements should be elicited directly from users and other sources. User interviews should be structured so that user requirements are easily identified and assigned to functional areas. Each interview should generate a document that is returned to the user for sign-off.

- **A report audit** Developers need to know which reports in the current system will be brought forward into the new system.

- **Process flows for all major business functions** Process flows document the way business is done in the organization. These flows help guide the workflow of the new system. If any business process reengineering is planned, both the legacy flow and the reengineered flows must be included.

- **Function hierarchy** An analysis function hierarchy should capture all basic business functions. This hierarchy can include manual functions, which will never be mapped to modules, so the main goals here are completeness and readability.

- **Business rules** The developer needs to take all system requirements and distill them down to business rules. Business rules are represented in two places. One is in the Analysis ERD. Not even all data-level business rules can be reflected in the ERD, however. Therefore, these requirements need to be tracked in text and, in the Build phase, translated into database triggers.

- **Requirements mapped to the function hierarchy** To prove the completeness of the function hierarchy, all requirements from the detailed requirements list should be mapped to the function hierarchy. Any functions not representing a user need should be reexamined and, in most cases, dropped. Requirements that cannot be mapped to existing functions require the creation of new functions.

The completed requirements document can then be used as a cross-check to ensure that the proposed data and function models are complete. A Requirements Document of this type greatly increases the likelihood of system design success.

The importance of the Requirements Document is evident in the following example of a situation in which no Requirements Document was originally planned. The client wanted a Requirements Document and also pushed for documentation of system requirements. Unfortunately, the senior consulting staff was not responsive to the client's requests. They fought the construction of a full list of all the project's requirements. They felt that creation of such a document would be a duplication of effort because the CASE tool already allows for descriptions for each function. However, this was not enough for the client. The client wanted a list of everything, from detailed requirements to process flows. This client tired of the consultants coming onto the site and taking information directly from users and putting it into the functional models and ERDs. This tactic made it impossible for the information to be cross-checked. The project manager could not track who authorized what functions, especially when information, such as the source and topic, that could have been noted in the CASE tool was left out.

Development effort was spent on complex ERD modeling when some of the data being modeled was not even required for the system. Furthermore, duplicate functions were hard to find, while exactly who needed a certain function could only be inferred from the description of the function.

With a Requirements Document, it is possible to cross-reference requirements by entity model, function model, and source. Then a tool can be constructed that enables both user and analyst to validate the information transfer. By mapping system requirements to the Oracle Designer deliverables, the ERDs and functional hierarchies can be cross-checked. Analysts can receive the users' and management's approval on the requirements and model them in a way that achieves the appropriate goal. Without the Requirements Document, it can only be hoped that developers and users can keep all of the requirements in their heads while they validate the ERDs and functional hierarchies.

Analysis Evaluation

The first question in analysis evaluation is whether the set of requirements is complete—and the answer is always no; there is always something overlooked. If requirements are sorted by detailed function and shown to users, users frequently will find something new at this point. In-house systems people should also spend time evaluating the requirements. They frequently know more about what really goes on at the detail level than many users. Finally, it is up to the developers to make sure that requirements related to system performance are specified. Response time, accuracy, and volatility are all factors that users frequently take for granted but which have profound impacts on the design.

The next question is whether the ERD is correct. A correct, logical ERD is a third normal-form representation of as many data-related business rules as possible. Any data-related business rules that cannot be represented in the ERD can be represented in a non-ERD supportable business rules document. The developer must ensure that the ERD can support all of the organization's business transactions. The way to accomplish this is to take the most complex examples of everything stored and make sure this data can be represented. People often think that their model is correct until someone tries to put data into it. Every data business rule must be captured in the ERD. Any rule that can't be modeled should be written as trigger specs that accompany the ERD.

The final question in analysis evaluation is whether the function hierarchy is correct. The purpose of the function hierarchy is to show the business process and make sure all system requirements are on schedule for implementation. The function hierarchy is used mainly for organizational purposes. If all major business functions are represented, all requirements are mapped to at least one function, and each function has at least one system requirement associated with it, the analysis evaluation is finished.

Pre-Design

In the phase between Analysis and Design, the rest of the project is planned. Only after Analysis does the developer know exactly what the system is required to do. As the process moves from Analysis into Design, several steps need to be taken. Some people firmly believe that these steps belong in Analysis; others vigorously assert that they should be in Design. To avoid controversy, this book includes them as steps in the transitional, Pre-Design phase.

The Pre-Design phase includes the following: design plan, process flows (physical), design standards, screen concept prototype, and pre-design evaluation.

Design Plan

The plan for the Design phase must move comfortably from logical design to physical design. The plan should then specify the results of consultation with the users regarding what will be part of the new system and what will remain as a manual process. The next step in the plan should be to iteratively develop prototypes of the system with screen designs that are supported by physical level process flows; when the developers are satisfied that they have a strong design, they should go back to the functional hierarchy and redo it at the physical level. Next, the designers should identify elemental functions in preparation for the generation of modules.

Process Flows (Physical)

Physical process flows differ from logical process flows in that logical flows model the business whereas physical flows model the proposed system. The development of physical process flows is the first attempt at a functional system design. These process flows describe the way the new system will work functionally. They are modified throughout the Design phase as the system design matures.

Design Standards

Design standards describe the layout of the proposed system. Decisions must be made concerning the following:

- Screen layout, including colors, fonts, and buttons

- Navigation methods, including menus and buttons

- Help

- Documentation

- Functionality

- Coding standards

- Naming conventions

One of the best strategies for developing design standards is to create several archetypal applications and then to reverse-engineer the standards into Oracle Designer templates and libraries using the design capture utilities. Archetypal applications should include the following types:

- Simple, single table

- Master-detail

- Complex

This task must be performed knowing how Oracle Designer will generate applications. The goal is to produce standards that are easily generated by Oracle Designer.

Screen Concept Prototype

The developers should create a screen prototype, sometimes called a storyboard. This prototype is a major deliverable that will validate the design standards and the analysis. Screen design prototypes implement the physical process flows and design standards. Through prototypes, users can evaluate the ability of the system to meet their needs. The storyboard does not need to access data, although some functionality is helpful when trying to get users to understand the design strategy.

Pre-Design Evaluation

In pre-design evaluation, the focus shifts from the user to the system. Systems professionals should have a greater say in this phase than should the users. Users should feel comfortable with the design plan, but systems people are the ones who will have to implement it, so their influence should be as great as that of the users.

The Pre-Design phase is complete when users are happy with the screen prototypes and process flows. Both users and developers must approve the design standards and design plan.

Design

The Design phase is where the blueprints are drawn for building the system. Every detail should be laid out before generation. The vision of iterative development using CASE is still a fantasy for large projects. So much time is spent preparing modules for generation and cleaning up after generation that it is important to have a clear picture of the system before the first generation.

The Design phase is divided into two parts: database design, which is discussed in Chapters 13 and 14, and application design, covered in Chapters 15 and 16.

Database Design

Database design involves the designing of the tables and columns along with the detailed specification of domains and check constraints on the columns. Database design also includes the denormalization of the database to improve performance along with the associated triggers to support that denormalization. You do not have to worry about more physical-level issues such as disk striping and tablespace layout. Those final parts of the design work occur in the Build phase.

Design Data Model

The design data model is the final physical design of the database. Here is where any necessary denormalization takes place. Low-level details should be considered; table designs should be rigorously tested with sample data before implementation.

The data model must be built with the assistance of the database administrator (DBA). The time is over for any shoulder-shrugging comments that "we will worry about this later." It is later *now.* Not only must the system encapsulate the user needs, but it must work in the real world. Here is where the best and most experienced DBA talent should be used. If good in-house talent is not available, this is a cost-effective place to hire a consultant. The main downside to using an outside consultant is that a consultant will not have to live with the design day in and day out. Therefore, if possible, an in-house DBA should be the main driver of this effort.

Naming Standards

Naming standards for the database must be finalized and strictly adhered to at this point in the development process. Not applying naming standards can greatly increase the cost of development because of the lack of consistency.

Performance Tuning

Basic performance tuning should begin at this point and continue as an ongoing process through the end of the project.

Application Design

In addition to the design of specific applications and reports, application design involves decision making about what product (for example, Visual Basic, Forms, HTML, or C++) will be used for those designs.

Screen Design

Screen designs should be built according to what will realistically be generated using Oracle Designer. Efficient system design is predicated upon staying as close as possible to what Oracle Designer will generate.

There is no point in showing users a prototype that will be inferior to the final system.

Module Specification

After the screens are designed, we can specify the modules and map them back to the functions from the Analysis phase. Requirements are then brought forward from the functions to the modules.

Design Book

Each module to be generated should have a set of information associated with it. Beyond the information associated with the tool, each module has functions that should be documented. The goal here is to generate a folder for each application that fully describes that application. This folder acts as the primary unit-testing document. The tester need only ensure that the application meets the specifications listed in the folder. In addition, the physical process flows should be a part of the design book to assist in system testing.

Design Evaluation

Design is complete when the design documents could be handed over to another team to build, with each application having its own screen (or report) design, list of detailed functionality, and create-retrieve-update-delete (CRUD) report.

Generation and Post-Generation Development

During the Design phase, modules are generated using the Oracle Designer generators and post-generation development work is identified.

Build

The Build phase involves two areas: the database and applications. If all of the preceding steps have been performed carefully and thoroughly, this phase should proceed smoothly.

Database Build

Database building involves direct generation using Oracle Designer. All triggers and data structures can be kept within the physical model in Oracle Designer, so the building of the database is a straightforward operation.

About the only specific work to be done at this point is making a final decision regarding tablespace sizes and physical disk locations. Also, a final decision needs to be made as to how many Oracle instances will be used. An *instance* is a self-contained Oracle environment. It is common practice to use three (develop, test, and production). However, this book advocates five instances, which are described in more detail in the Pre-Design phase discussion in Chapter 11.

Before building applications, you need a sample database to test whether the applications are working properly. It is possible and common to build systems without this sample database. However, in those cases, you may spend a great deal of time figuring out where errors are coming from and how fast the system will run with real data. This book thus strongly advocates the use of sample data. If the migration effort has been proceeding in parallel with the development effort, you could even use migrated data in your sample database.

Application Build

Full application specification should be stored in the repository and, whenever possible, should be used to automatically generate the modules. With the improved functionality of the application generators, cleanly generating the layout and code for all but the most complex applications is now possible.

Before you finish the Build phase, you must subject the system to a first-pass unit-level test. You should be sure to perform this testing while building the application because the application will at that point still be fresh in your mind. Then immediately pass the system to a tester to check that the system meets the design book specifications and that functionality from the user standpoint is working properly.

Documentation

Documentation should be an ongoing process occurring throughout the system development process. It should accompany the first prototype that the user sees and every other software deliverable. Documentation should not simply be a separate step at the end of the process.

There are two main types of documentation: system documentation and user documentation.

We all know the nightmare stories of developers who come in to modify an existing system for which there is no documentation. In the worst cases, the system not only has no system documentation but also has no source code for the applications. Let us resolve not to inflict this situation on future developers. By preparing careful system and user documentation throughout the life cycle of the project, developers are not left with a major task at the end. In addition, frequently little or no client money is left at this point to pay to extend the development process further.

Just as the applications of a system are tested, the documentation must also go through a testing process. Testing the system itself is impossible before the system documentation is written because there will be nothing to test against. The point is that no system is finished until both system and user documentation are completed satisfactorily.

System Documentation

The development of system documentation has been going on throughout the Design phase. During the Build phase, we collect and finalize the system documentation.

User Documentation and Help

One of the most unbelievable but common occurrences in a systems project is that user documentation is written before the applications are built. You cannot write user documentation on a system that hasn't been built yet. The system will change significantly during the Design phase. Developers need to be involved in the user documentation but are usually too busy during the Design phase. Therefore, user documentation should be developed during the Build phase.

The help system is an integral part of the user documentation and should not be considered separately. The trend in software is to have more and more of the user documentation available as help rather than in manuals. Whether or not you agree with this strategy, user documentation and help should be considered as one unified effort.

Test

Test is one of the most important but usually most poorly conducted phases in the system design process. The key to proper testing is to use multiple tests. No single test, no matter how carefully conducted, will find all of the errors in a system. It is better to perform several different tests less carefully; these usually catch more errors at less cost to the organization.

Test Plan

By the time you reach the Test phase of the development process, you should not need to audit the logical or physical design of the database. This should already have been done at the end of the Analysis and Design phases. The first goal at this stage is to audit the correctness of the applications: do they meet the requirements?

Unit Testing

To achieve this goal, you must perform unit-level tests application by application. The testing process should be meticulous, using test data, automated testing scripts, code walkthroughs, and interviews with the system developer.

Integration Testing

You also must perform overall database-level checks, including the following processes:

- Run a test deck (large amount of sample data) through the applications.

- Perform a consistency check on the database by running many procedures.

- Compare report output from the new system with that from the old system.

- Build small simple forms applications to help visually inspect the data.

- Run SELECT DISTINCT on all columns in all tables to check for valid data values.

User Acceptance Testing

The second goal of the Test phase is to perform user acceptance testing. Give users the applications to work with and perform real (not sample) transactions using the new system. Perform a final validation check on the user interface.

Load Testing

Systems often work well in a development database with a few hundred rows but are inadequate to support the millions or tens of millions of rows that can exist in production tables. Similarly, locking problems are often only discovered when a large number of users work with the system simultaneously. Prior to putting the system in production, you need to simulate production quantities of records, peak number of transactions per unit time, and number of simultaneous users performing typical tasks.

Implementation

At some point, the finished system needs to be turned over to the users and brought into production (after user training on the new system, of course, has taken place). There are various schools of thought on Implementation. The first is the "big bang" approach. The second is phased implementation.

Big Bang Approach

The big bang approach entails pulling the plug on the old system and bringing up the new system and insisting that everyone use it. In this approach, there is no turning back. If you use this approach, it is critical that the system is well tested.

The advantage of this approach is that it is cheaper to do everything at once and not have parallel systems running simultaneously. In theory, this approach involves much less work because it forces 100 percent commitment from the entire organization. Some large consulting firms advocate the big bang approach. However, this book does not, in general, advocate its use.

The major disadvantage of the big bang approach is that there is no way to test a system so extensively that a developer can guarantee that it will work. However, if you really have confidence in your system, this approach can save time and money—so long as you are willing to assume the risks.

Phased Implementation

The second, more common, approach is phased implementation. Various portions of the new system are brought up one at a time, either by subject or by class of users. In most cases, running the new system in parallel with the legacy system requires double entry into both systems while the bugs are being worked out. It may also entail writing temporary interfaces between new system components and functions still implemented in the old system. Such an approach is clearly more costly than the big bang approach, but if something goes wrong, there is always the legacy system to fall back on.

Training

Another important part of the Implementation phase is devising a user-training strategy. How will users be trained? Options include training manuals, classes, and the creation of a computer-based training (CBT) system. However, for all but the largest organizations, the creation of a CBT is too slow and much too costly to be effective. As the system evolves and changes, modification of the CBT is expensive and time consuming.

Help Desk

Another consideration at the Implementation phase is the help desk strategy. How will support be provided for users of the new system? The help desk strategy may include the following:

- One centralized person who is trained to provide support
- Several designated experts on portions of the new system who receive extra training
- User manuals
- E-mail or telephone support

The help desk strategy should be thoroughly considered before the new system is up and running.

Maintenance

Even when a system is "finished" and brought into production, it is still in a state of flux. There will, of course, be some problems with any new system along with the need for user enhancements, requests for changes in the way the system functions, the need for new reports, missing fields, and so on. The major goal of the Maintenance phase is to provide a process for screening, ranking, and then handling these problems and changes in the system. It is necessary to recognize that changes not only affect the database and applications, but also must be reflected in the system and user documentation and training. The people involved in the help desk functions must also be kept apprised of any changes.

Versioning

Versioning is the key to efficient system maintenance. You can't just make changes to the system one by one and implement them throughout the system. These uncontrolled changes are potentially dangerous for the integrity of the production system. Changes must also proceed through a process that includes testing and quality assurance (QA).

Prioritization of Enhancement Requests

Finally, changes are not cheap to make. To minimize costs, desired changes should be bundled along with all associated documentation and help desk updates. Because projects often are large and can take months or even years to complete, it is likely that by the time the Implementation phase is reached, the system requirements will have changed from those determined in the Analysis phase.

Emergency Fixes

Periodically, "showstopper" bugs are encountered that cannot wait for the next system release. Designers should recognize that just because fixing a bug is mission-critical does not mean that testing of the change isn't equally critical. Implementing an emergency bug fix with inadequate testing can cause far more problems than the original bug.

Conclusion

This chapter has provided an overview of the basic CASE methodology phases along with other phases that this book proposes should be added to the system development process. If all of the phases are completed carefully and thoroughly, the likelihood of system success is greatly increased. Part II provides more details and specific information on the methodology.

As you proceed through this book, you will learn how you can integrate Oracle Designer with the extended CASE methodology presented here, which we call CADM. This information should make the development process for a system using Oracle Designer faster, easier, more efficient, and more effective. The ultimate result will be satisfied developers and users.

CHAPTER
2

Introduction to
Oracle Designer

Here is the answer which I will give.... Give us the tools, and we will finish the job.
—Winston Churchill (1874-1965) Radio broadcast, 9 February, 1941

s you may have gathered from the preceding chapter, you need to capture an enormous amount of information for successful system development. Missing information can cause a project to fail or, at least, not fulfill some of the intentions of the system. In addition, ignored information on requirements or lost business rules has the potential to cause inaccuracies that seriously affect the business. It is therefore critical to the success of a system that you store the information about the system in a place where it can easily be retrieved and modified. Traditionally, before the advent of CASE tools, this place was paper documents and human memory (people's heads). This method was probably successful in some cases, and companies were able to deal with the flood of paper that emanated from the analysis and design processes. However, modifications to the system after implementation meant relying on documentation inside existing programs or in system documentation (if that was ever created).

The original intention of CASE tools was to assist in managing system information so information technologists could effect system implementations and upgrades by referring to the documentation stored in a central place online. Therefore, one major component of a CASE tool is the *repository*, or central storage place. The other is the front-end products that allow users to enter and query data in this repository.

Oracle Designer follows this traditional component setup. It contains a repository, implemented using Oracle's relational database management system—currently Oracle8 (although later versions of Oracle7 are also supported). The repository consists of database objects that store information on the system you are analyzing, designing, and building. Since the repository is contained in a standard Oracle database, it has all the benefits and considerations of a multiuser system: security, connectivity, concurrency, and availability. The biggest benefit, of course, is that an entire team of developers can access the definitions and work on a common model. The Oracle Designer front-end component contains many screens and utilities to manipulate the repository data. In addition, Oracle provides a method for you to develop front-end products to access the repository outside the Oracle Designer tools.

This chapter discusses the major aspects of the repository and the front-end tools to give you an idea of the scope of the product as well as an overview of the different areas in which you will work while using Oracle Designer. Subsequent chapters describe the methodology for system development and the use of Oracle Designer to support each of the phases in this methodology.

Oracle Designer supports a broad range of tasks and is considered an *integrated CASE (I-CASE)* tool because it supports work in the Strategy, Analysis, and Design phases as well as finished code generation for the Build phase. Not very many CASE products accomplish all of these tasks. Many stop with the Analysis (and sometimes Design) phases; such products are known as *upper CASE* products because they cover activities only in the top part of the CASE Application Development Method (or whichever method you use). Oracle Designer will take you through the full life cycle and generate fully working and bug-free forms, Web applications, reports, and menus in addition to the SQL code needed to create the database objects. If you use development methods other than CADM or other variations on the traditional waterfall, Oracle Designer is flexible enough to support your work as well.

No matter what your experience with previous versions of Oracle CASE tools, you should work through the book-based tutorial that Oracle provides with the product before you proceed further in this book. This tutorial, also available in the online HTML files, which you can reach by selecting Start Here from the Oracle Designer 2.1 program group in the Start menu, will give you good hands-on practice with the tools. It will also give you an idea of the kinds of activities you will be doing in the tool set. The discussions in this book assume that you have either completed the tutorial or have had some hands-on experience with the Oracle Designer interface.

The Repository

The repository consists of the tables and views you use to interact with the data and the procedural code to manage them. It essentially stores the details of the system you are developing. Later in this chapter you will see how the Oracle Designer front-end tools allow you to access these details. First, though, it is useful to review the basic concepts behind the repository.

Makeup of the Repository

The repository is contained in the schema or domain area of a single user (the *repository owner*) in the Oracle database. Therefore, before installing Oracle Designer, you either create a new user account or choose an existing user account that will own all the tables and code for the repository. The repository owner then grants access on its tables to existing Oracle users who also need to be Oracle Designer users and creates synonyms in their accounts. This procedure sets up the *repository users*, essentially Oracle users with special access privileges to the repository, who will be able to manipulate the repository objects, such as entity and table definitions.

What the Repository Stores

The repository holds *meta-data*—or data about data—as definitions of objects or elements you are using to create the system design. These may include entities and their attributes or tables and their columns, all of which have individual aspects, called *properties*, that define them. For example, a table definition includes properties for *Name*, *Alias*, *Display Title*, and various text descriptions. Each of these items is a property of the table, and all of these properties together make up its definition. There is a hierarchy of elements, with the top level being the application system that contains all objects for a certain system development project or part of a project. Figure 2-1 shows an example of this hierarchy from the Entities node.

Application System

Repository users create one or more application systems (if they have rights to do so) and grant other repository users access to the application system. The application system *owner* (creator) can *share* objects from another application system into their application system. The shared objects appear as part of that application system although they may not be changed. Therefore, the elements you work on in an application system are those that are directly owned by the system and also those that other application systems share with that system.

Elements

The application system owns two types of elements: primary access controlled (PAC) elements, which exist on the highest level of the element

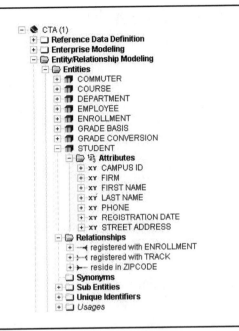

FIGURE 2-1. *Sample of the Oracle Designer hierarchy of objects*

hierarchy under the application system, and secondary access controlled (SAC) elements, which depend on and are owned by the PAC elements. Figure 2-1 shows an example of this relationship. In this example, an entity definition is a PAC, and attribute definitions for that entity are SACs, as are the relationships and synonyms.

Associations

An *association* is a special type of repository element that links one element to another. An association, for example, may specify a link between ENTITY1 and FUNCTION8. The repository stores this association—in this case, a Function Entity Usage—as a separate definition and links it to the two elements.

Properties

Each element definition has a set of properties that describe it. The set of properties for a type of element (such as Entities) is always the same, but the values for the properties differ for each instance of a definition. Figure 2-2 shows two tables that have the same set of properties, but different values for each.

NOTE
Keep in mind that meta-data is not the actual data structure. For example, table definitions in the repository are not actual tables in the database. Rather, they only contain the information needed to create actual tables that may or may not exist in the database. The repository stores the table definition and its property values, but no table exists in the database until you run a CREATE TABLE statement to create it. This is an important, but not necessarily obvious, concept.

What the Repository Looks Like

At the lowest level, the repository consists of a handful of tables and a large number of procedure packages stored in the database in PL/SQL (Oracle's procedural language extension of SQL). These tables have many views (most are named with a CI_ prefix) defined for them that correspond roughly to the elements and associations in the application system. For example, a view called CI_TABLE_DEFINITIONS shows the properties of a table definition, and you can perform a SQL query on this view to get information on a particular table definition.

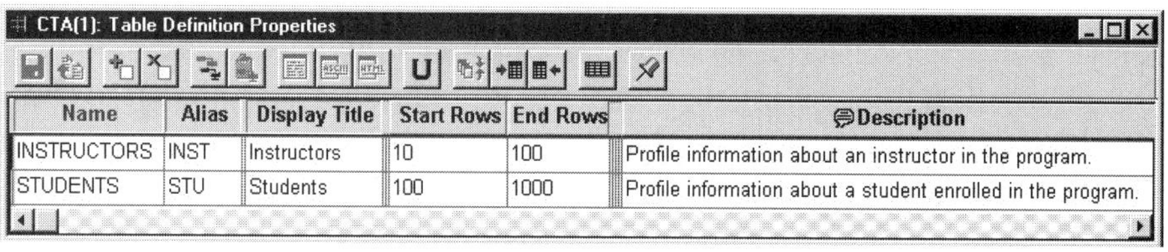

Name	Alias	Display Title	Start Rows	End Rows	Description
INSTRUCTORS	INST	Instructors	10	100	Profile information about an instructor in the program.
STUDENTS	STU	Students	100	1000	Profile information about a student enrolled in the program.

CTA(1): Table Definition Properties

FIGURE 2-2. *Table Definition Properties showing two different table definitions*

The Oracle Designer online help system contains full explanations for all these views under the item "Application Programmatic Interface" (in the Oracle Designer 2.1 Start menu program group). In addition, the hard-copy documentation shipped with Oracle Designer contains diagrams representing these views and their relationships. If you refer to both of these sources, you can usually determine what view to use for a particular element. This topic is discussed further in Chapter 28, which describes the Oracle Designer Application Programmatic Interface (API).

The API PL/SQL code packages that access the repository tables correspond roughly to the views themselves. You can write code to access a particular definition for Insert, Update, Delete, or Select by calling the package that corresponds to the view where the repository displays that definition. For example, the CI_TABLE_DEFINITIONS view has a corresponding PL/SQL package called CIOTABLE_DEFINITION. This package allows you to safely manipulate the table definition repository data through your own code. The online help system just mentioned also has documentation on these PL/SQL packages, and Chapter 28 discusses these packages further.

The Front-End Tools

The best feature about Oracle Designer is that while you could use a number of methods, such as the API, to access the repository, you do not need those methods for most tasks, because the front-end tools that Oracle provides will do the job. This section describes the major tools and utilities in Oracle Designer to give you a sense of the scope of the product. This chapter assumes that you are familiar with the tasks and deliverables needed for a software development project and the development life cycle phases in which they are completed. These phases and their tasks and deliverables are discussed in detail in subsequent chapters.

A Word About Installation and System Requirements

While this book is intended to pick up where the installation process leaves off, a few extra words of advice may be helpful. The Start Here documentation also contains a link to the *Oracle Designer Installation Guide*. This guide, also supplied in hard copy form with the product, gives the details of installing the Oracle Designer repository and front-end tools. Be sure to pay close attention to the System Requirements section of this document when planning the installation. You will be happiest, when working in Oracle Designer, if your client machine has as much RAM and processor speed as possible. (RAM is more important if you have a choice between the two and 64MB of RAM on an NT machine is a good place to start).

TIP
A large monitor running a high resolution (at least 1280x1024 pixels) is also an essential tool for productive use of the front-end programs. This advice is especially critical for tools that have multiple windows with multiple parts, like the Design Editor.

A procedure that you may miss in the installation process is one that you should do whenever installing a new Oracle product. The Start In directory on the shortcut for Oracle Designer is set to a directory in the ORACLE_HOME tree. The problem is that this tree is reserved for Oracle software and is not where you would normally want to place your files. All files you create in the Oracle Designer session will go into that directory unless you give an explicit path (which you cannot do in some cases). The procedure you should follow is to change the Start In directory for the shortcut to some directory specific to Oracle Designer work. Consult the Windows help system if you need a refresher on how to do this, but the secret is in opening the Start menu and navigating down to the icon (shortcut) that runs Oracle Designer, then opening the properties and changing the value for the *Start In* property.

Front-End Programs

You work with Oracle Designer's front-end tools under a Microsoft Windows 95 or Windows NT platform. You can generate code for other platforms, but the front end itself has a standard Windows interface (written in C++) with toolbars, menus, and dialog boxes. Oracle Designer provides many different front-end programs, but they all fall into two categories of interface styles: diagrammers and repository utilities.

Diagrammers

The diagrammer is one of the major interface paradigms that Oracle Designer uses to store system analysis and design information in the repository. Diagramming tools are available to enter many element definitions, so you, as the repository user, can interact with the repository in a visual way. The diagrammers work directly with the repository objects, so when you draw an entity, for example, in an entity relationship diagram, Oracle Designer inserts that entity definition directly in the repository. This procedure works the same way for all objects. You can also define the object in one diagram and use the same object in another diagram of that type or of a different but compatible type. For example, you can diagram the same function elements on the Function Hierarchy Diagrammer, Process Modeller, and Dataflow Diagrammer.

The repository stores the diagram itself as an object with associations to the objects on the diagram. You can view these diagram definitions by using the Repository Object Navigator, or, for some diagrams, the Design Editor, but you need to run the diagrammers themselves to make changes to the layout. The Repository Object Navigator and Design Editor also provide ways to edit the properties of an element. In addition, you can access these properties of the diagrammed objects directly in the diagrammer itself. This feature allows you to easily change or refine the definition of an object without leaving the diagrammer.

Repository Utilities

The other major interface type that Oracle Designer supplies for entering or manipulating data is that of the Repository utilities. These are all nondiagrammatic interfaces that use GUI dialog boxes, object navigators, and property palettes to assist you in entering repository data. Some utilities actually insert the data for you. For example, Oracle Designer provides a utility to convert your existing entity definitions into table definitions—the Database Design Transformer. It inserts repository information for tables based on the entities you have already defined. You can modify the rough table definitions that this utility produces and refine them manually, but the utility does a large amount of work for you.

Some repository utilities only cross-check data rather than insert new data. Others manage application systems, generate database or client code, or allow you to run reports listing the properties of various element definitions. Oracle Designer also provides utilities to manage the repository and its users;

assist in installing, upgrading and checking the repository; back up and restore the repository objects; and extend the set of repository elements.

Oracle Designer Functional Categories

Oracle Designer has four major functional categories, each consisting of front-end diagrammer and utility programs:

- **Modelling System Requirements** for Strategy and Analysis work

- **Generating Preliminary Designs** for transition to Design or Pre-Design work

- **Designing and Generating** for Design and Build work

- **Utilities** for work throughout the life cycle

These functional categories correspond to the areas on the Oracle Designer window launchpad application—the starting point for all Oracle Designer work—shown in Figure 2-3.

The first three functional categories support the major System Development Lifecycle phases. The last category involves Oracle

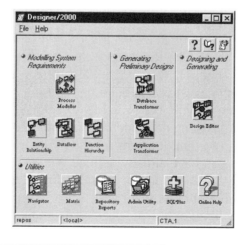

FIGURE 2-3. *Oracle Designer window*

Designer-specific activities. The following sections describe these categories and the tools they provide.

Modelling System Requirements

You use the tools in this area to model business processes and data in the Strategy and Analysis phases. The models are designed to be implementation independent. That is, the actual data structures and programs that access them are not part of the model. What you are interested in is the business area itself and being complete in representing its most important components. There are four main tools used to represent the data and processes or functions that make up a system:

■ Process Modeller

■ Function Hierarchy Diagrammer

■ Entity Relationship Diagrammer

■ Dataflow Diagrammer

Process Modeller

The Process Modeller, sometimes abbreviated as BPM (for Business Process Modeller), displays processes and flows as well as the organization units that perform them. You can use this tool to assist you in business process reengineering, which can be a full phase or part of a phase in some system development life cycles. It also supports work in representing processes during the Strategy and Analysis phases. You use the Process Modeller to conceptually show and possibly redefine what happens in the current system or what will happen in a new system.

One unique aspect of this diagrammer is that you can use it to create a diagram that represents the departments or groups in a company and show which processes, dataflows, and datastores each owns. In addition, you can drill-down from a high-level process to a lower level process and diagram the subprocesses that compose it. This tool also lets you diagram the data flowing between processes and datastores. There is no facility for detailing the data (for example, entities and attributes that make up a flow or store), because the purpose of this tool is to create a visual representation of existing or new business activities, the flows of data, and the organizational units that own them.

Another unique aspect of this diagrammer is that you can use it to show external triggering events from and outcomes to processes in your business area. Using this concept of triggers and outcomes, you can show that some external process or source is providing the stimulus for one of your processes (*triggers*), and conversely, which processes in your business area provide data (*outcomes*) to targets outside it.

The diagrams you produce in the Process Modeller are capable of multimedia enhancement, so you can show, for example, an animated flow from one process to another. In addition, you can embed video and sound clips to emphasize or clarify a point or process. You can also link to external programs, so you could, for example, run a slide show from a presentation program to help clarify a particular process, or show a spreadsheet or graph of sales representing activities in another process. You can also simulate the time sequence of a series of business processes by assigning time parameters to the processes and flows and then "running" the diagram to give you an idea of the events that occur simultaneously and the processes that may be bottlenecks in the system. All these assist in communicating your understanding and intention to the customer, client, or user.

Figure 2-4 shows a sample session in the Process Modeller.

Function Hierarchy Diagrammer

The Function Hierarchy Diagrammer (sometimes abbreviated as FHD) lets you show the different levels of system processes or functions (terms that Oracle Designer treats as synonymous) in your system in one diagram. You can tell at a glance from this type of diagram the decomposition of functions and, consequently, the lowest level and the highest level in a series of processes. This tool frees you from the need to define flows as you would do in the Process Modeller and Dataflow Diagrammer.

Once you have represented the data by creating entity and attribute definitions in the Entity Relationship Diagrammer or elsewhere, you can use this tool to declare which data elements you wish to associate with each process. Oracle Designer calls this association of data and functions the *data usage,* which includes not only the data elements but also the actions that will be performed on them (Insert, Update, Delete, Select). This concept is used later in the Design and Build phase tools as well. You can create, reposition, and *level* (decompose) functions in this diagrammer or just redisplay the same functions you created and diagrammed in the Dataflow Diagrammer or Process Modeller diagram.

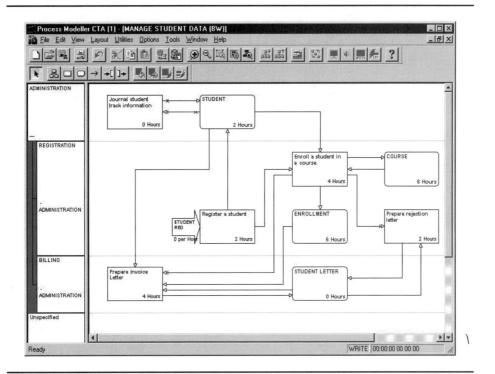

FIGURE 2-4. *Process Modeller session*

Figure 2-5 shows a sample session with the Function Hierarchy Diagrammer.

Entity Relationship Diagrammer

The Entity Relationship Diagrammer (or ER Diagrammer) shows entities with their attributes and relationships that represent the logical model of the data. As with the other diagrammers, once the definition for an element—in this case, an entity—is in the repository, you can produce different diagrams to show all or some of them in different layouts. The entities you create here are the source for the function data usage associations in the Function Hierarchy Diagrammer (FHD), so you typically use the ER Diagrammer at the same time as the FHD or before you associate the functions on the FHD with entities.

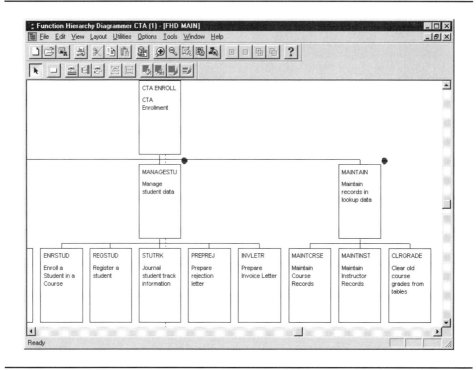

FIGURE 2-5. *Function Hierarchy Diagrammer session*

The ER Diagrammer has a rich set of symbols and provides support for subtype/supertype entities and arc (mutually exclusive) relationships. The entity and attribute definitions that this tool diagrams are separate from the definitions of the physical (design-level) elements or tables. Therefore, you can have two different data models in your system—a logical one and a physical one. This fulfills a need to keep these two models separate because typically they have different objectives and contents.

Figure 2-6 shows a sample Entity Relationship Diagrammer session.

Dataflow Diagrammer
The Dataflow Diagrammer (DFD) allows you to display functions, dataflows, and stores as does the Process Modeller. It displays the same information as

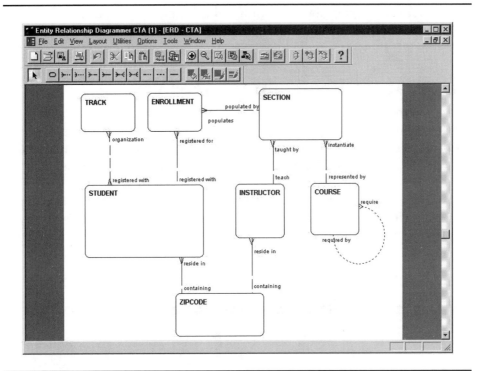

FIGURE 2-6. *Entity Relationship Diagrammer session*

the Process Modeller but in a different type of diagram that may be more familiar to analysts and users.

One of the features of the Dataflow Diagrammer that is missing from the Process Modeller is the association of the data elements—entities and attributes—with functions, flows, and stores. You can also represent entities that are external to your system in this diagram and show data flowing in and out of these entities. This representation is similar in concept to the triggers and outcomes in the Process Modeller, but this diagrammer lets you define the actual data elements (entities and attributes) that are flowing to and from your system to those externals.

Since this diagrammer is so similar to the Process Modeller, the decision about which one to use is really a matter of personal choice. You can use either diagrammer to define and display processes in the Strategy and Analysis phases, but if you choose the Process Modeller, you will need to seriously consider using another tool like the Function Hierarchy Diagrammer or Matrix Diagrammer to fill in data usages.

Figure 2-7 shows a sample Dataflow Diagrammer session.

Generating Preliminary Designs

When you move from Analysis to Design in Oracle Designer, you have to transfer definitions from the logical to the physical: entities to tables, attributes to columns, relationships to foreign key columns and constraints, functions to modules, and function data usages to module component table usages. The Database Design Transformer and Application Design Transformer assist with this move and give you a rough-cut application and database definitions that you can refine. The Transformers also save you much of the time-consuming, repetitive, and error-prone work that needs to

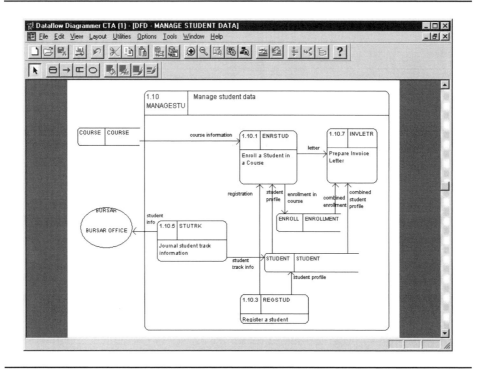

FIGURE 2-7. *Dataflow Diagrammer session*

be done in this transition and, although they may not be able to guess exactly what you have in mind, there are ways to make the results of the utilities closely match your needs.

Database Design Transformer

The Database Design Transformer (DDT) copies the entity and attribute definitions to tables and columns in the design area. It can resolve many-to-many, subtype/supertype, and arc relationships, so you can implement them as relational database tables. It can create columns based on the attributes in the entities and foreign key constraints based on the relationships between entities. You can run this utility more than once and modify or create particular elements that were not defined properly or completely the first time you ran it. The logical elements will remain in the application, so you will have many more definitions in your application system after the utility runs. Figure 2-8 shows the DDT opening dialog.

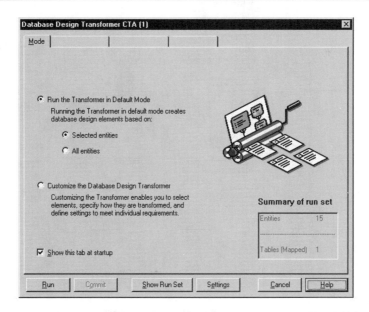

FIGURE 2-8. *Database Design Transformer session*

Application Design Transformer

The Application Design Transformer (ADT) transforms functions to modules and links modules together based on common business units. It uses a well-documented set of rules to perform the combination and produces both the modules and the menus (module structures). The *candidate modules* you create as output from this utility are subject to your approval and modification before they become working modules. Figure 2-9 shows the ADT opening dialog.

Designing and Generating

After you create the design-side elements using the transformers, you can model and refine them using the Design and Generation tools. These tools are typically used in the Design and Build phases and are applied to the wide range of activities performed to define the physical database and application. You can also create the design elements directly in these tools whether or not you have created logical elements. This latter approach is

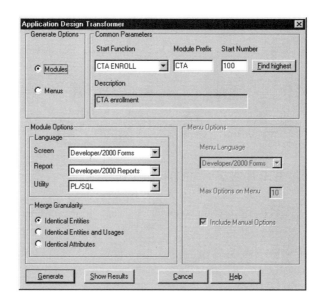

FIGURE 2-9. *Application Design Transformer session*

useful for rapid prototyping because you can skip the Analysis phase elements and jump right in, entering the definitions for design elements or capturing the design of existing elements from the database or file system.

Whatever the source of the objects you use in the design and generation tools, this source provides the basis for work in these tools. Therefore, you first spend time ensuring that the repository definitions are complete and accurate and that they truly represent the analysis work. These tools provide what you need to denormalize the data structures, modify the names of elements such as tables and columns, fill out any necessary PL/SQL code definitions, design the modules that make up the application, and perform other design activities.

The code generators in Oracle Designer are utilities that are highly functional and feature-full and can give you complete, bug-free code if you have supplied the proper definitions. While it is true that you can realize many of the benefits of Oracle Designer without even using the code generators, the ability to produce working applications is one of the main strengths of the product. The strategy is to complete the module definitions and their table usages; specify the language in which you wish to generate the application; set up preferences for the target language; and run the generators. Oracle Designer includes two types of generators: those that generate database objects and those that generate front-end code.

Oracle Designer includes the following tools or categories of tools for designing and generating the physical database and application model:

- Object Database Designer

- Design Editor

- Generate Database Utilities

- Front-End Code Generators

- Design Capture Utilities

The following briefly describes and shows a sample screen for many of the parts of these tools and categories so you can have a taste of what they do.

Object Database Designer

The Object Database Designer (ODD) is the tool you use to create definitions of object-relational database structures (such as Object Types,

Collection Types, Object Tables, and Object Views). It also offers a Unified Modelling Language (UML) diagrammer that allows you to create a Type Diagram to support the Oracle8 Object Database extensions. Figure 2-10 shows an Object Database Designer session with typical work areas open.

Several tools within the ODD support deliverables in the Design and Build phases as follows:

- Type Diagram
- Server Model Diagram
- Transformation utilities

ODD also allows you to call the Generate Database utilities and the C++ Generator described later in this chapter.

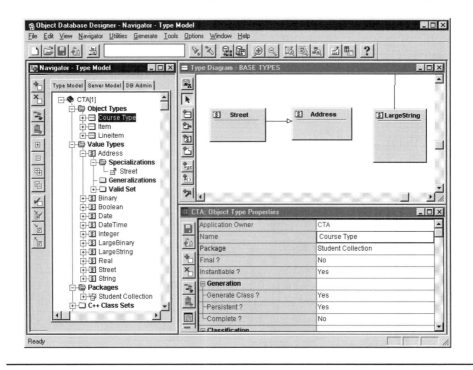

FIGURE 2-10. *Object Database Designer session*

TYPE DIAGRAM   The Type Model is the area where you use UML to define the Object Types, Value Types, and their associations, and to enter details for these elements. In addition, you can use the Type Diagram to represent the types visually. This UML modeller lets you create informative associations between object types to depict generalizations and specializations. Figure 2-11 shows a sample Type Diagram.

SERVER MODEL DIAGRAM   The other diagram you work on in the ODD is the Server Model Diagram. This diagram is based on definitions in the Server Model area. It shows the relational and object-relational database objects that you will create in the database, including relational database tables, views, snapshots, and relationships, as well as Oracle8 types. As with all other diagrammers, you can create diagrams of different subsets of these elements to represent a particular business area.

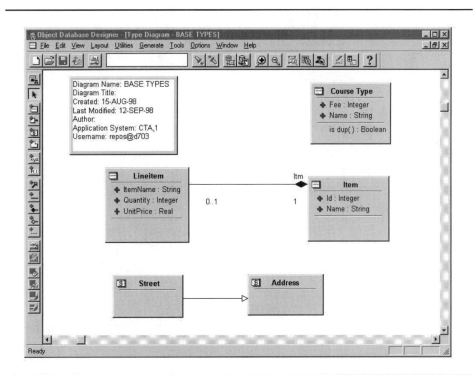

FIGURE 2-11.   *ODD Type Diagram*

The Server Model Diagram can also be used to define columns and constraints including primary and foreign keys. At first glance, this diagram seems to include the same elements that the Entity Relationship Diagrammer shows. There is a difference in symbols, but the biggest difference is in what these symbols represent. In the Server Model Diagram these symbols represent physical design objects that you will eventually implement in the finished system; in the Entity Relationship Diagrammer, the symbols represent only the logical data structures, which may or may not be the same as the physical ones. Figure 2-12 shows this diagram.

TRANSFORMATION UTILITIES   The ODD also includes a number of utilities to transform element definitions to and from the Type Model and Server Model. It also contains a utility, shown in Figure 2-13, that allows you to transform Server Model realtional definitions to Server Model object-relational definitions.

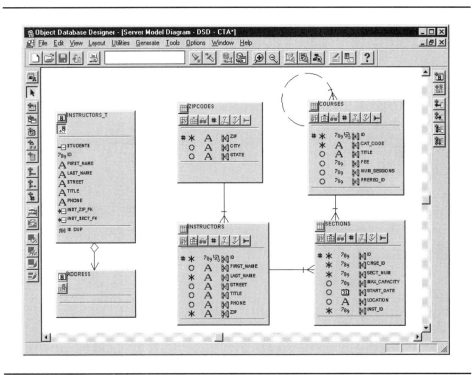

FIGURE 2-12.   *ODD Server Model Diagram*

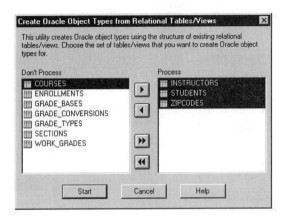

FIGURE 2-13.   *Create Oracle Object Types from Relational Tables/Views dialog*

You can also perform the transformation in another direction (from Type Model to Server Model) using an option in the Generate Database from Type Model utility.

Design Editor

The Design Editor (sometimes abbreviated as DE in this book) encompasses all diagrammers and utilities you need for the design and generation of relational and object relational database objects and application modules. The interface looks and acts like the ODD interface. Figure 2-14 shows a typical Design Editor session.

The Design Editor incorporates a number of tools that you would use to support the production of the deliverables for the Design and Build phases. These tools are:

- Server Model Diagram
- Logic Editor
- Generator Preferences
- Module Network Viewer
- Module Diagram

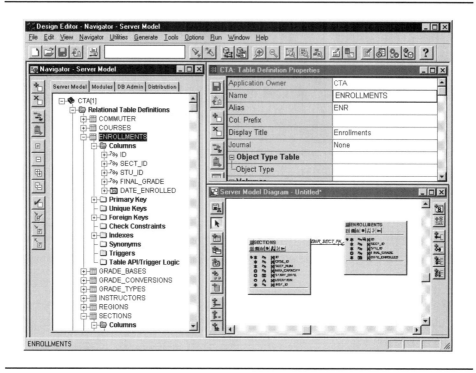

FIGURE 2-14. *Design Editor session*

The Design Editor also contains generators for database objects and front-end code as well as the design capture utilities, as discussed following this section.

SERVER MODEL DIAGRAM   The Server Model Diagram shows and allows you to enter definitions for tables, views, snapshots, and object types. It is the same tool as in Object Database Designer, described previously and shown in Figure 2-12.

LOGIC EDITOR   When you move to the Design and Build phases, you enter definitions for PL/SQL code that you will store in the database. These PL/SQL definitions—packages, procedures, functions, and cursors—will eventually become code on the database side or client side. The Logic

Editor helps you create the PL/SQL definitions and fill out the code. It contains a versatile interface with drag and drop of PL/SQL constructs, navigation through the code by means of an outliner, and a customizable look and feel. The code you enter in this tool is stored automatically in the repository. Figure 2-15 shows a sample Logic Editor session.

GENERATOR PREFERENCES   When Oracle Designer generates modules, it relies on a large number (more than 400) of user-defined settings when making decisions as to how to produce the finished code. You can change these settings, or *preferences*, using the Generator Preferences window in the Design Editor. The Oracle Designer generators rely on these preference values when forming the user interface and internal code for a particular module. For example, one preference might specify the type of decoration or box the generator puts around a radio group, and another

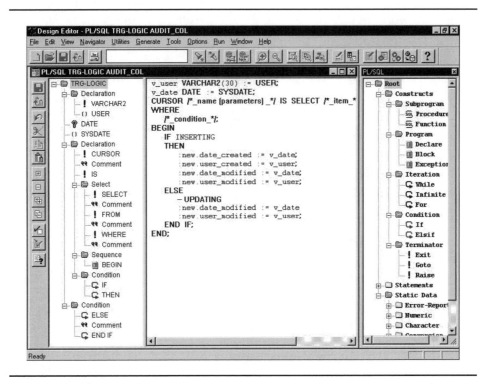

FIGURE 2-15.   *Logic Editor session*

might specify where the label for that radio group appears. Preferences are also used in ODD for C++ and type model generation.

You can set preferences on different levels, from the application down to the individual item. These preference values become part of the application system in Oracle Designer, and all modules in the system can use them or override them on an individual basis. Figure 2-16 shows the Generator Preferences window for a table definition.

MODULE NETWORK VIEWER The Module Network Viewer shows how a module is linked to other modules in the application. This diagrammer represents the system of navigation the user will employ to get from one module to another. The application menu system or navigation command buttons in the forms or reports will be the actual mechanism for this navigation; and this diagrammer shows the links between modules that provide this mechanism. In addition, PL/SQL code modules can call other modules as well as be called by other modules. All of those calls show as module networks in this tool. Figure 2-17 shows the Module Network Viewer.

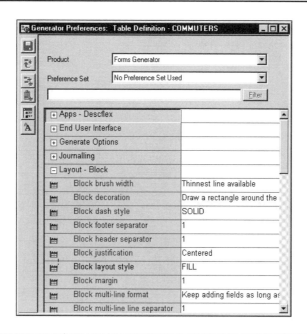

FIGURE 2-16. *Generator Preferences window*

FIGURE 2-17. *Module Network Viewer*

MODULE DIAGRAM   The Module Diagram shows the data usages for a module and its links to parent and child modules. Each module actually consists of one or more *module components*, each of which reflects a grouping of the data elements used in the module. For example, an order entry application would have two module components—one for data from the master or header section (order date, customer), and the second for the details on each order item (product, number ordered). The order details (or any other module component) can include information from multiple tables—in this case, an ORDER_ITEMS table where data is inserted, and a PRODUCTS table which is used to look up the product being ordered. The module diagram shows the two module components and their relationship within the module. Figure 2-18 shows a sample Module Diagram.

Generate Database Utilities
The Generate Database utilities create Data Definition Language (DDL) scripts from repository definitions. You can also choose to have the generator run those scripts after it creates them. These generators are contained in the Design Editor, and some also are available in the ODD.

GENERATE DATABASE FROM SERVER MODEL UTILITY   The Generate Database from Server Model utility, is available in both the Designer Editor and ODD. Like the Generate Database from Type Model utility, the Generate Database from Server Model utility generates SQL scripts that contain the DDL that will create database objects in an online database. The generated DDL is based on the definitions in the repository for database objects such as tables, columns, views, snapshots, sequences, and tablespaces. When you run this utility, you specify the objects which

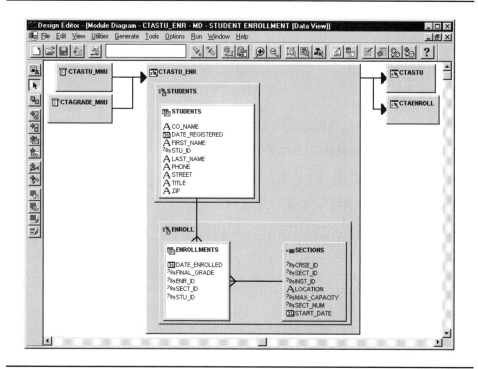

FIGURE 2-18. *Module Diagram*

you want to create, and the generator generates the scripts to create the objects. Figure 2-19 shows the opening tab of this utility.

A related utility is the Generate Database Administration Objects utility, also available in both the Design Editor and ODD, which is responsible for creating scripts for database objects such as tablespaces, users, roles, rollback segments, profiles, directories, and even the database itself. This utility is similar in scope, appearance, and operation to the Generate Database from Server Model utility.

OTHER GENERATE DATABASE UTILITIES   Other utilities in the Design Editor create scripts to create the Table API, which is server PL/SQL code that supports access to tables, and the Module Component API, which is PL/SQL code used by generated forms to access the Table API.

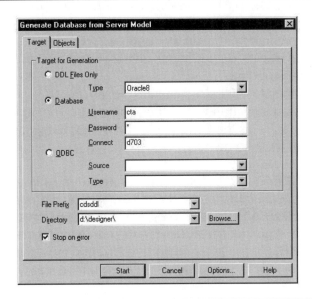

FIGURE 2-19. *Generate Database from Server Model utility*

Front-End Code Generators

The front-end generators have different outputs according to the language you are generating. Each produces a working program using the preferences you set in the Generator Preferences, the module definition you enter in the Design Editor Module Diagram, and for some, a product-specific template, starting file, or object library. You can customize the templates and object libraries supplied with Oracle Designer to control the output of the generators. All of the generators are started via dialog boxes which vary from generator to generator but may include detailed options which affect the generator's operation.

The Forms, Reports, Library, and WebServer generators generate code which can be compiled and run by an Oracle product: Oracle Developer or SQL*Plus and the Oracle Application Server. The other generators require you to go to another vendor and buy the development tool specific to the language to compile the finished product.

The following sections briefly explore the specifics for each front-end code generator. All front-end code generators are available in the Design Editor except the C++ Generator which is run from the Object Database Designer.

FORM GENERATOR   The Form Generator creates .FMB (form binary) source files. Its main inputs are the object library, template, module definitions, preferences, and generator options. You can see some of the control you have over its output by looking at Figure 2-20, which shows the main Form Generator dialog.

The Form Generator will also generate menus (.MMB files) that you can attach to forms for navigation within the application. The dialog for menu generation is the same as the Form Generator dialog with many disabled items that do not apply to menus.

LIBRARY GENERATOR   The Library Generator creates .PLL (PL/SQL library) files from definitions in the repository. You record information in the repository including code for each program unit, and run the generator to create the library. You can attach this file to Form and Report modules in the repository and those links (attached libraries) will be included in the generated form or report binary file. This gives you the ability to share code

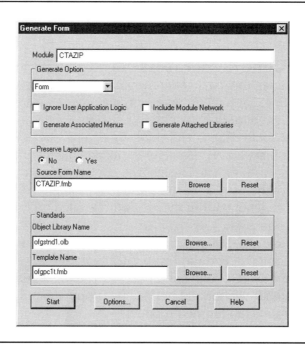

FIGURE 2-20.   *Generate Form dialog*

among multiple programs and maintain that code separately from the form or report. The Library Generator Options dialog is shown in Figure 2-21.

REPORT GENERATOR   The Report Generator creates .RDF (report definition) files that you can use to produce screen previews of reports or create .PDF or .HTML format files for publishing on the Web. The input to this generator is the same as the others and the generator dialog specifies similar options to the Form Generator, as Figure 2-22 shows.

WEBSERVER GENERATOR   The WebServer Generator creates PL/SQL packages from modules that you define in the repository, preferences, and optional templates. You run these PL/SQL scripts in a database that is accessible by the Oracle Application Server (a separate product) to create the Web application. When the user connects to a special Uniform Resource Locator (URL) the server routes the request to the database, which then calls the PL/SQL procedure to dynamically construct an HTML page. This page is sent back to the client and displayed in the client's browser. The options in the WebServer Generator dialog just specify a password and option to include the module's network. The complexity of this generator is

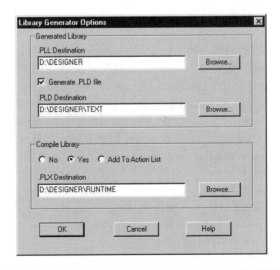

FIGURE 2-21.   *Library Generator Options dialog*

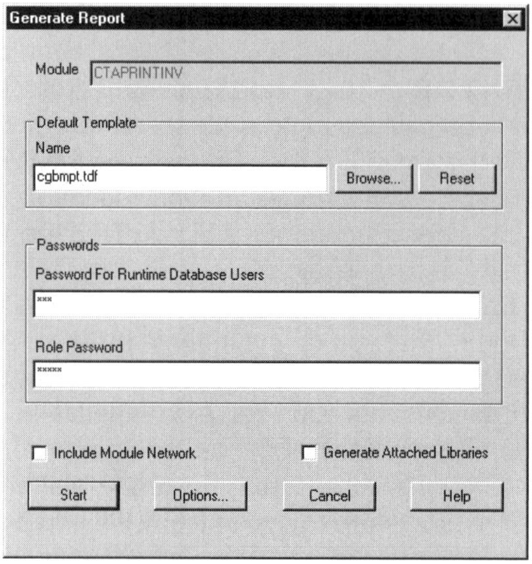

FIGURE 2-22. *Generate Report dialog*

in the setup of the application server and in writing customized server- and client-side code, which can include Javascript and HTML as well as PL/SQL.

VISUAL BASIC GENERATOR   The generator for Visual Basic (VB), like the Form Generator, takes a particular module and set of language-specific preferences as input to create Visual Basic code. You can take the code from this generator and load it into the Microsoft Visual Basic 4.0 or 5.0 development environment (a separate product) to create the finished application and executable. The options in the Visual Basic Generator dialog simply allow you to create the project, merge it into an existing one, and include the module network.

MS HELP GENERATOR   The MS Help Generator creates .HLP files that attach to your Forms and Visual Basic applications. You enter the help text as you create the modules and table definitions. The generator extracts this text, loads it into a file, and creates the hypertext links you expect from a Windows help system. This system is an alternative to the traditional Oracle

Designer help tables that query text from the database and present it in a called form. These help files can save on database activity because they are solely file-based and compiled as part of the runtime application. This utility produces files that need the Microsoft Help compiler (a separate product) to generate the WinHelp-format finished files. Figure 2-23 shows the dialog for the MS Help Generator.

C++ GENERATOR   The application design and generation work you do in this tool consists of defining and generating C++ class libraries to support access from C++ applications to Oracle object and relational definitions. The C++ Generator creates code that you link to your C++ application for easy access to Oracle object and object-relational database structures. These generated classes remove the complexity of defining data access from your hand-written application code.

You need to do some work outside of Oracle Designer, including compiling the generated classes with the rest of the C++ code you write elsewhere and linking it with the C++ libraries to create the finished application. The benefit of this utility is that you can concentrate on the C++ code for the rest of the application and rely on Oracle Designer to create the data-specific code.

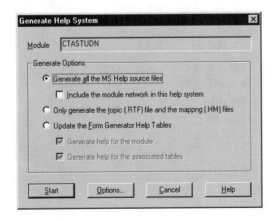

FIGURE 2-23.   *Generate Help System dialog*

Design Capture

Oracle Designer can load the repository with information from external sources. The process of creating or changing repository definitions from information outside the repository is called *design capture*. You can capture the design of both database objects and client code. All design capture utilities are available in the Generate menu of the Design Editor.

CAPTURE DESIGN OF SERVER MODEL   The Design Editor includes a utility called Capture Design of Server Model From Database. This utility reads the online data dictionary and creates repository element definitions to match. This is particularly useful in maintaining or upgrading legacy systems where you need to start working with details on a current system. This utility saves you the work of entering the element definitions manually. You can design capture from a DDL file or an ODBC database as well as from an Oracle database. Figure 2-24 shows the dialog for the Capture Design of Server Model From Database utility.

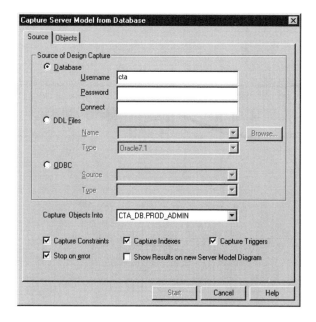

FIGURE 2-24.   *Capture Server Model from Database dialog*

CAPTURE DESIGN OF FORM, REPORT, LIBRARY, VISUAL BASIC
The process of capturing the design of client application source files into the
repository consists of first capturing the design of the tables used by the
applications, then running the specific Capture Design of... utility to read the
source file and create a definition in the repository. This allows you to
supplement or rework the modules in preparation for generating them with
new table definitions or other information from the repository. You can
capture the design of Form Builder .FMB and .PLL (form and library) files,
Report .RDF files, and Visual Basic .VBP files. You can also capture the
design of the application logic only from Forms, Reports, and Visual Basic
projects. Figure 2-25 shows the dialog for the Capture Design of Form
utility. Other languages have similar dialogs with fields and properties
specific to that language.

Utilities
Throughout the work you do in Oracle Designer, you will find a need for
various utilities to check, change, or supplement the repository work you do

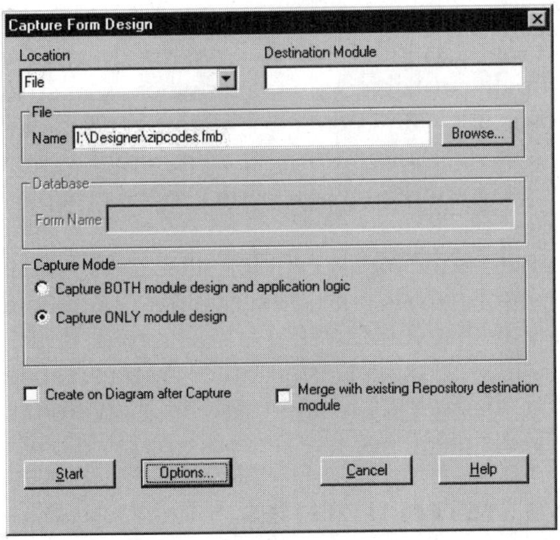

FIGURE 2-25. *Capture Form Design dialog*

in the Oracle Designer diagrammers, generators, and other utilities. The following sections explore the major repository utilities that fulfill this need:

- Repository Object Navigator
- Matrix Diagrammer
- Repository Reports
- Repository Administration Utility
- Application Programmatic Interface
- User Extensibility

Most of these utilities are called from the Oracle Designer window. This list does not include two other icons on the Oracle Designer window, that is, SQL*Plus and Online Help. SQL*Plus is the Oracle command line interface to the database. You can execute SQL statements to do anything to the database that you have privileges for. Online Help lets you access the main Oracle Designer help file that has links to all other help files.

Repository Object Navigator

The most universal repository utility is the Repository Object Navigator, frequently abbreviated as RON. RON allows you to view and change properties of virtually any object no matter where you created it. As Figure 2-26 shows, it has an interface similar to the Oracle Developer products, with a Navigator window and a Property Palette window. You can group objects together and apply properties to the group as you can do in Oracle Developer.

RON also serves as the focal point for other tools and utilities as you can start any Strategy or Analysis phase diagrammer or utility from its menu, in much the same way that you can start any Design or Build phase diagrammer or utility from the Design Editor. You can access some utilities, such as those that manage application systems, only from RON. Similarly, you can define some elements, like Business Terminology, only from RON.

APPLICATION SYSTEM UTILITIES   There are other repository utility activities specific to application systems that you can perform through the Repository Object Navigator. These utilities govern how to partition objects

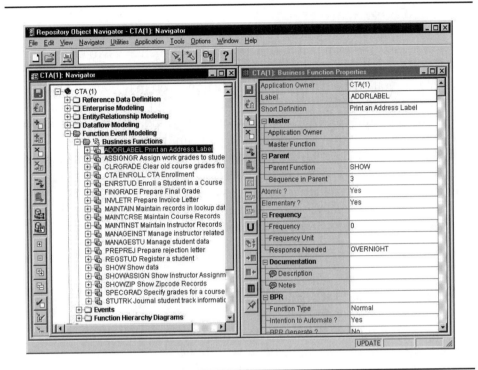

FIGURE 2-26.   *Repository Object Navigator session*

among multiple application systems; how to grant users access
to application systems; how to coordinate work by many users on many
applications and potentially in many repositories; and other activities
necessary for administering and maintaining the repository and the
applications it contains.

OTHER RON UTILITIES   RON can perform other functions on element
definitions as well. For example, it can create attribute usages for functions,
update attributes or columns in a domain for which the definition has
changed, and create module data usages. It can also create entity definitions
from table element definitions which might be needed for an existing
database that you want to rework using analysis elements (Entities and
Relationships). This is accomplished with the Table to Entity Retrofit utility.

Matrix Diagrammer

The Matrix Diagrammer is a very powerful and sometimes overlooked tool. It lets you view and maintain the relationships between any two elements in the repository that can be logically linked via a repository association. For example, as you create data usages for functions, you may want to ensure that all data can be entered or queried from some place in your function model. The Matrix Diagrammer can, among other things, report on the entity and attribute data usages in your functions so you can determine at a glance if all data is being handled. The Matrix Diagrammer presents the information in a table format with rows, columns, and intersection values. You can examine and change the values at the intersections and save the values in the repository. The diagrammer is like a create-retrieve-update-delete (CRUD) report that is connected directly to the repository.

TIP

An easy way to tell which elements have associations is to look at the Usages node under any element definition. You can also start a new matrix diagram and select one element in the row area. The associated elements will appear in the column area on the right. This means that these two elements have an association.

The Matrix Diagrammer is highly customizable so you can look at the data in almost any way; it also has navigation aids to allow you to diagram a large system and quickly go to any section you desire. Figure 2-27 shows a sample Matrix Diagrammer session.

Repository Reports

You can view all element definitions in the Repository Object Navigator and the associations with the Matrix Diagrammer; however, you might need to print out a report on a particular set of elements, such as all tables in your system. You can write your own report using your preferred reporting tool or use one of the nearly 100 predefined reports that Oracle Designer offers for displaying objects in the database. Repository Reports organizes and presents these predefined reports with variable parameters you can enter to define the output. It can display the output on screen or output the report to

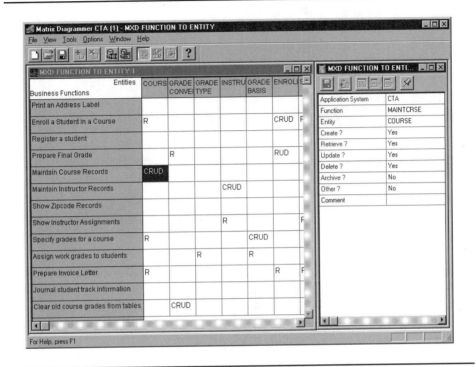

FIGURE 2-27.   *Matrix Diagrammer session*

a .PDF or .HTML file. This utility uses a navigator and a parameters window, as Figure 2-28 shows.

Repository Administration Utility

You use the Repository Administration Utility (RAU) to manage the repository itself, with all its application systems. You can use this utility to install, upgrade, and back up an instance of the repository and to grant and revoke repository user access. The first step you take after installing the front-end tools, in fact, is to use this utility to create the repository owner and install the repository data structures and code. RAU also has many utilities to check the state of the repository objects and to "pin" the base packages in memory to increase performance. Figure 2-29 shows this utility's opening screen.

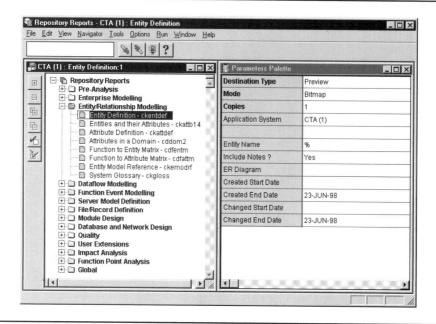

FIGURE 2-28. *Repository Reports session*

Application Programmatic Interface

The Application Programmatic Interface, or API, is not so much a utility as a documented method you can use to insert data into and modify data within the repository. As already mentioned, only a few tables store the repository data, but many views of these tables represent the actual objects, such as entities and attributes. The API includes these views so you can examine the definitions you create in your application systems. It also includes the PL/SQL packages that allow you to change the contents of the tables safely outside of the Oracle Designer front end. Thus, you can supplement the Oracle Designer diagrammers and utilities with your own front-end programs or code.

User Extensibility

You can add properties to existing elements or even add new types of elements to the repository through a facility called *User Extensibility*. This facility allows you to place site-specific objects in your application systems

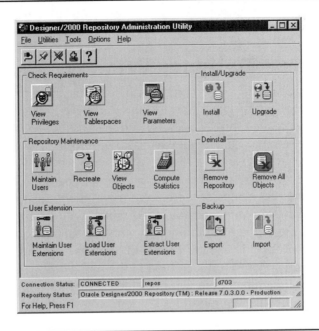

FIGURE 2-29. *Repository Administration Utility session*

that are not normally included in Oracle Designer. The RAU manages the user extensibility features and extended elements are available in the RON, Design Editor, and Matrix Diagrammer.

The Oracle Designer Interface

As already mentioned, you are strongly urged to complete the book-based tutorial (also online in HTML files) shipped with Oracle Designer to at least become familiar with the product's organization and how you accomplish tasks. Nevertheless, this section discusses briefly how to work with the Oracle Designer tools on an operator level. You can be more productive if you know how the tools are organized and if you master a few simple techniques. All diagrammers and utilities have certain functions in common (like **File→Save**), and you use common techniques to interface with them. When you learn about each tool in later chapters, these techniques will allow you to focus on the specifics for that tool instead of on basic features and techniques that are common to all Oracle Designer tools.

The Oracle Designer Window

The Oracle Designer 2.1 Start menu group contains an item for "Oracle Designer." You select this item to start the Oracle Designer window application, also called the *Front Panel* and the *launchpad*. When this utility starts, you log in to the Oracle database as the repository user and choose an application system using the dialog in Figure 2-30.

If no application systems appear in the dialog, you do not have access to existing application systems or there are none in the repository. If you have privilege to do so (the Manager privilege granted with RAU), you can create an application system in this dialog by typing the name in the Application System field and clicking Create. This field doubles as a find area and, if you have application systems, you can type in the name of the application system and the matching name will be selected. This dialog also shows the version numbers, which is important if you have more than one version of an application system.

If you click Cancel in this dialog, you will not have selected a default application system. Therefore, each tool you run from the Oracle Designer window will ask for an application system name. This might be a good effect to exploit if you are bouncing around in the repository between different application systems. Otherwise, it is merely annoying and you will want to select an application system.

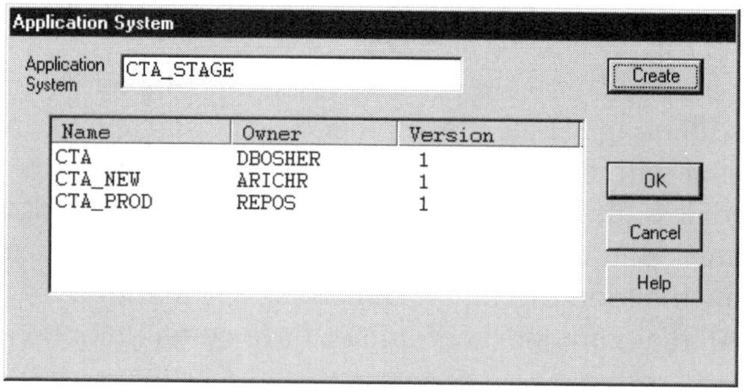

FIGURE 2-30. *Application System dialog*

Starting the Oracle Designer Window

To start the Oracle Designer window, the launchpad application, log in to Oracle, and load a particular application system automatically, provide the *Target* string (in the shortcut properties):

```
des2kxx user/password@database /a:appsys,version /s
```

where *xx* is the version number of Oracle Designer; *user/password@database* is the login string; *appsys* is the application system name; and *version* is the version number. /s indicates "no splash page."

If you omit the version number, the Application System dialog will appear. If you omit the /s (suppress splash screen) you will see the Oracle Designer logo screen.

For example, Scott, who has a password of Tiger, will log in to the Design database and EMPDEPT application system. He uses the following as a command line or Target string:

```
des2k20 scott/tiger@design /A:EMPDEPT,1 /S
```

You will need to confirm the version number part of the filename by looking in the ORACLE_HOME\bin directory. Chapter 26 provides command line syntax for some other Oracle Designer tools.

NOTE
*You can also create a new application system in RON. Select **File→New Application** from the menu, and fill in the application system name. After you click the Save (commit changes) button, Oracle Designer will create the new application system. You then work in this context until you choose Change Application System from the File menu.*

The Oracle Designer window has buttons for all major tools and repository utilities as well as links to the help system. There is also a button for Help in the Utilities area that loads the contents page of the Oracle Designer main help system. There is bubble help (also called micro-help or tooltips) on the buttons as shown shortly.

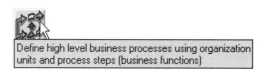

Other Menu and Toolbar Functions

The File menu contains items that are standard to most Oracle Designer tools for Change Connection (to log in as a different user) and Change Application System (to switch focus to another application system). There is also a selection for Minimize on Use, which will minimize the Oracle Designer window when one of the tool buttons is clicked.

The Help menu has selections that let you read about the changes in the new version and the table of contents for the help system, as well as a choice called About Oracle Designer, which provides a set of screens on version numbers and a license agreement.

The toolbar in the top-right corner of the window contains two help buttons. You can choose the Context-Sensitive Help (question mark) button and drop the mouse question mark icon on any other button to see the Contents help topic for that tool. The help icon with the book in the top right of that screen shows you help about getting started in the tools. The Oracle Designer icon in this toolbar minimizes the window to a toolbar as shown in the following illustration:

This reduces the size of all buttons and, since there is no bubble help for the buttons, you need to know what each icon means. Also, you lose the menu, if that is important to you. You are able to reshape the toolbar window, if, for example, you want it to be a vertical toolbar instead of a horizontal one. Fortunately, you can click the same Oracle Designer icon in the right side of the toolbar to return to the "panel" view of the window. The toolbar is handy if you are accustomed to the icons and want to save screen space.

NOTE
The status line of the major diagrammers and utilities contains information worth noticing. For example, the Oracle Designer window status line contains the application system name and version number as well as the name of the user who is logged in at that moment and the database connect string.

Help System

Two words of advice apply to the Oracle Designer help system: Use it! The help system contains conceptual overviews of each tool, instructions on how to use each tool generally, and detailed step-by-step procedures for completing tasks. Oracle Designer's scope is so extensive and its features increase so quickly that, in earlier versions, Oracle's printed manuals quickly became obsolete. In addition, well-designed help files are much easier to search for topics and find the correct information in than any printed manual—and these are well-designed help files. This section (and Chapter 26) provides details about how the help system works.

No matter what your opinion of help files may be, you should give the Oracle Designer help system a chance. For example, suppose you have not touched the tools in several months and have forgotten how to create a dog-leg (angle) relationship line for an ERD, since the procedure is a bit different than that for other Windows drawing tools. Choose **Help→Help Topics** from the ER Diagrammer and do a search on the Index tab for "dog-leg"—problem solved.

The good part of the help system is that it has a familiar interface for those who have used Windows software. The problem with the help system is that it has a familiar interface and you can be lulled into thinking you know how to use it just because you have done so in other software. The Oracle Designer help system has a certain structure and methods of obtaining information quickly. If you are aware of these, your work in the entire Oracle Designer product will be easier because you will be able to get help about a particular operation quickly.

As a quick review, Windows' 32-bit help systems are usually presented in the form of a window with three tabs: Contents, Index, and Find. The Contents tab is just that: a table of contents of all general topics in the help file. It is divided into books and topics in a hierarchical structure. The Index tab holds a searchable list of all keywords that are defined for the help file, and the Find tab lets you perform a word search on the entire file. Once you find a topic on any of these tabs, you can view it by double-clicking it; you can navigate back to the tab area by clicking the Help Topics button in the topic page toolbar.

Help System Structure

The Oracle Designer help system is divided into three sections that correspond roughly to the main functional categories of Systems Modeling, Design and Generation, and Repository Maintenance. The high-level topics listed in the help system and their responsibilities are as follows:

Modeling business system requirements	Systems Modeling
Designing and generating databases and client applications	Design and Generation
Managing the Repository	Repository Maintenance

This closely parallels the Oracle Designer opening window, which has the same categories of tools (the Utilities area of that window is represented by the "Managing the Repository" help system). The Generating Preliminary Designs opening window area (which contains the Application and Database Design Transformers) has no separate help topic but is included under the Systems Modeling category. Figure 2-31 shows a sample contents tab from the Systems Modeling category.

There are links from each category to the other two categories, as this figure shows under the node "Access to other Designer/2000 help systems." If you run the help system from the Oracle Designer window, another introductory help system will open. This system allows you to navigate to the other three help systems. There is also a separate help system for the API which you run with a menu choice in the Oracle Designer group of the Windows Start menu.

Within each help system, there are topics that describe the tools by function, not by name. This puts the emphasis on the task, not the tool. For example, in the Managing the Repository help system, there are topics for

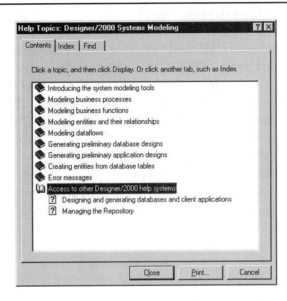

FIGURE 2-31. *Help Topics for Systems Modeling*

Administering the Repository (with the Repository Object Navigator tool), Managing application systems (the Repository Object Navigator tool), Reporting on the Repository (the Repository Reports tool), and Cross-referencing Repository objects (the Matrix Diagrammer tool).

Normally, you do not need to interact with this structure of topics because appropriate help will appear based on the task you are performing. Knowing the structure is useful, though, if you need help on a particular tool and are not working with that tool.

NOTE
Oracle Designer 2.1 received that name a month after it was released. Previously, the product was called Designer/2000, and you may still see some references to this in the help system, Start menu, and online documentation. Be aware that Oracle Designer and Designer/2000 are the same product.

Help System Common Methods

You probably already know many ways to get help. One useful way is to use the "?" button (called "Context-Sensitive Help") that appears in the toolbar for each major tool. This button changes the cursor to the "What's This" arrow and question mark. When you click this special cursor on an object on the screen or make a selection from the menu, the help system will load and jump to a topic appropriate to the object. This is great when you don't know what something is called and therefore cannot look it up in the help system index.

The other standard help system activators are the F1 keypress and the **Help→Help Topics** menu choice. Also, some dialog boxes contain a help icon in the top-right corner that shows context-sensitive help.

TIP
If you need to know what's different in a new release, you can look under the "What's new" topics in each help system.

The Online Documentation

Another source of information on some selected topics is the online documentation. This is a series of .HTML files that you view by selecting Start Here in the Oracle Designer group from the Windows Start menu. This selection will open your browser and load the links to the main Designer Documentation page (the start.htm file located in ORACLE_HOME/cdoc70). This file contains the following topics:

- *Designer/2000 Installation Guide,* which contains essential information on the steps and requirements needed for the install process.

- *Designer/2000 Product Overview,* which provides a short description of each of the Oracle Designer functional areas with information on the tools that comprise it.

- *Designer/2000 Tutorial,* which is a set of exercises that give you hands-on practice with the major tools in Oracle Designer.

- *Designer/2000 API Specifications,* which provides information on the Application Programmatic Interface packages.

■ *Designer/2000 Model*, which explains the element views in detail.

■ *Object Database Designer Installation Guide*, which you use to assist in installing the ODD.

■ *Oracle Electronic Support Services (ESS) Handbook*, which gives information on the options you have for online support for Oracle Designer.

While some of the information in this online documentation is also available elsewhere, like the API help system, this is another source of help that you can refer to whenever you need it.

TIP
Be sure to take advantage of the help system word search facility (the Find tab of the help window) offered by 32-bit Windows operating systems if you cannot find a keyword for a particular topic.

Navigator Interface

A standard Oracle Designer interface is that of the navigator. There are Navigator windows in the RON, Design Editor, ODD, and Repository Reports tools. All have similar operations and functions. The navigator presentation style is common to many Windows applications, and anyone who has used Windows Explorer will be at home in an Oracle Designer navigator.

Navigator Window

The main objective of a navigator is to provide a method for quickly finding a particular element definition (or report). Figure 2-32 shows a Navigator window from RON.

The Navigator window allows you to get to a node quickly: You find the object type, open the type by clicking the + button, and then find the object in the list under the type. You can collapse and expand nodes by clicking the – and + symbols, respectively. If no + symbol appears, there are no subordinate elements, so you do not need to expand the node. The Navigator window toolbar provides buttons for Expand and Collapse as well as Expand All (++) and Collapse All (– –) which perform those

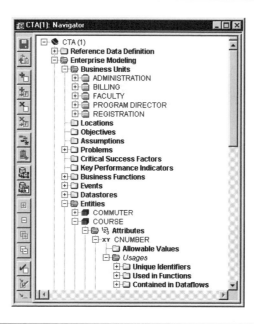

FIGURE 2-32. *Navigator window*

operations on the node that you select. There are also Expand, Collapse, Expand All, and Collapse All buttons and Navigator menu options that affect a node that you select.

TIP
Be careful of what you click on in the Navigator. Clicking the + and – symbols will expand and collapse the node. Clicking on the element icon to the left of the name selects the node; this is the proper method to use when selecting a node. Clicking the name of the node selects, but clicking again may open an edit field for that name.

You may have to open up more subnodes before finding the object you need, but the hierarchy should assist you in the search. The tool with the

Navigator window has a Find field under its toolbar that lets you search for a particular word or phrase. Enter the word and click the Find Next or Find Previous buttons to start the search.

TIP
If you press the HOME key while the Navigator window is active, the selection will jump to the top of the hierarchy. The END key will move the selection to the bottom of the hierarchy.

Property Palette

The companion to the Navigator window is the Property Palette. Once you find an object in the hierarchy and select it, the Property Palette displays the properties for that object, as shown in Figure 2-33.

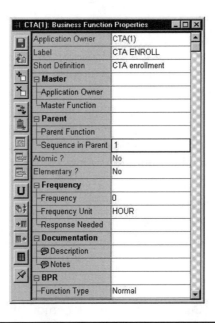

FIGURE 2-33.   *Property Palette*

You may have to explicitly display the Properties window by selecting it from the Tools menu. If the Property Palette is the active window, the Find field finds properties when you type the value and click the Find Next button.

The Property Palette contains its own editing capabilities. Property names appear on the left of the window, and values appear next to them on the right. You can navigate between properties by pressing the TAB key. This technique is useful if, for example, you want to quickly enter a definition and use the keyboard to type in values and TAB between properties without having to reach for the mouse to change properties. However, if the properties you are filling in are not adjacent, it may take more time to TAB than to click the mouse.

You can use one of three main methods for filling out property values. The first is to select from a drop-down list (if available) that appears in the field when you click the mouse in it; properties that use a drop-down list also allow you to type the value in without selecting it from the list. Another method is to type the value directly into the field. The last is to click on the bubble icon (if available) to the left of the property name and edit the text in the Text Pad editor, the internal Oracle Designer text editor.

Property Dialog

Another common interface, available in ODD and the Design Editor, is the property dialog which provides an easy to understand interface to entering properties. This interface is similar to the wizards found in most Windows products. It is intended to be self-explanatory and ensures that the user fills out at least the required properties of the definition. This is helpful to those who are not accustomed to repository work as it presents a tab interface with fields that the user answers to complete a particular definition. Figure 2-34 shows the property dialog for a table definition.

Navigator Techniques

Chapter 6 explores the Navigator and properties windows and explains them in more depth while discussing the Repository Object Navigator. There are a few techniques and features worth mentioning here that can help you work in these windows.

MULTIPLE SELECTIONS   You can select more than one element definition in the Navigator by clicking on the icon to the left of the name

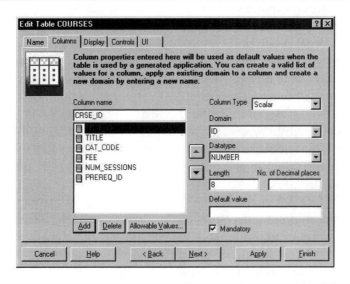

FIGURE 2-34.   *Edit Table property dialog*

while holding the CTRL key. Selecting multiple elements in the Navigator allows you to change their properties as a group in the Property Palette. If you hold the SHIFT key instead of CTRL and click on an element, you will select all elements between the previously selected node and that element.

CREATING AND DELETING DEFINITIONS   In addition to the collapse and expand buttons in the Navigator window, there are buttons for Create and Delete. If you select an element node and click the Create button, you will create a new definition for which you can define properties. The Delete button deletes a selected element (or a number of elements that you select).

COPYING AND PASTING PROPERTIES   The Navigator buttons for Copy Properties and Paste Properties allow you to transfer a complete set of properties from one definition to another. Select an element definition and click the Copy Properties button to copy the properties to the clipboard. Then select the target element definition and click on the Paste Properties button. You can view the properties in the clipboard using the **Edit→View**

Copied Properties menu item. This menu choice opens a dialog that allows you to delete properties in the clipboard in case you do not want to paste them into the target definition.

IN-PLACE EDITING   This means that you can edit the text where it is displayed. For example, you can change the name of a table definition in the navigator by clicking once on the node and again on its name. This will open an edit area where you can change the name. Clicking outside the edit area closes it. This feature is also available in the diagrammers where you can edit the name of an object in the diagram with in-place editing.

USING THE TEXT EDITORS   There are actually three text editors you can use to enter multiline text (such as the *Notes* and *Description* properties): the Text Pad, the default text editor; the ASCII text editor, which is a text editor of your choosing; and the HTML Editor, which creates HTML text versions of your text. There are buttons in the Property Palette for ASCII Editor and HTML Editor. You click on the property and click on one of those buttons to use those editors. You click on the bubble icon next to the property to use the Text Pad editor.

TEXT PAD TECHNIQUES   The Text Pad is available by clicking on an object and choosing the **Edit→Text** menu option (or by clicking on the bubble symbol to the left of the property name). This displays the Text Editor window where you add, edit, and delete the text associated with properties like *User/Help Text.* This has most common edit features in it and you use it to write the text needed to define an element. If you click the Save button in this window, you will save the whole element definition. Therefore, it is more efficient to click out of the window when you are done and complete the rest of the definition before clicking Save in the Property Palette toolbar.

AUTOMATIC UPDATES   The navigator tools that contain diagrammers (Object Database Designer and Design Editor) provide an automatic synchronization so if you update the diagram, the navigator node will automatically update. This goes the other way too, from navigator to diagram. While you do not get automatic updates like this between tools like the Entity Relationship Diagrammer and RON, you will see the broadcast indicator (red dot) if an element has been updated in another tool.

SELECT IN OTHER TOOLS   There is a menu option for Select in Other Tools (on the Utilities menu in the Design Editor and right-click menu in RON). If you check this menu item, the object you select in one tool will be selected automatically in the other tool.

PRINTING   If you select **File→Print** when the Navigator window is showing, you will print whatever the Navigator window shows at the time. The Print dialog allows you to select extra items to print (such as the page number) and to specify how many pages the printout will take up. It is useful to select **File→Print Preview** before actually printing to see if you need to change anything before printing.

Diagrammer Interface

The diagrammer tools in the Systems Modeling area all have a look and feel that is essentially the same. The standard features of diagrammers work essentially the same way in all cases and can be divided into four categories:

- Application window
- Mouse actions
- Menu system
- Toolbars

Application Window

The main application Multiple Document Interface (MDI) window for each diagrammer may contain multiple windows for different diagrams. Since you can have many diagrams of the same repository objects, each showing the objects in a different way, you might want to display these diagrams side by side in different windows. In addition, you can display different views of the same diagram in different windows.

TIP
Do not ignore the title bar. It always provides information about what you are working on. The same advice also applies to the status bar at the bottom of the window.

These diagrammers present a standard Windows interface with a diagram window, scrollbars to move the working view, page breaks, and a drawing area; the dialog and object properties window; the MDI window title that shows the name of the diagrammer, application, and diagram; a status bar for messages from Oracle Designer; a menu bar for the pull-down menu system; and Windows icons for minimizing, maximizing, and closing the diagrammer window.

There are some common techniques you can use in the diagram window to create the diagram. The first is creating *dog-legs* or angled lines. When you draw a line, such as an entity relationship line, initially from one object to another, you can click on intermediate points along the way to create angled lines. After you draw the relationship, however, you need to create the dog-leg (or angle) by holding the SHIFT key and clicking the middle of the line to create a drawing point. You can then place this drawing point anywhere that makes sense or remove it by pressing SHIFT and clicking on the point again.

Another technique you can employ in the diagrammer is copying an element between one diagram and another. If you select the element (like a table in the Server Model Diagram) and press CTRL-C (to copy), click on the other diagram window and press CTRL-V (to paste), the element will copy to that diagram (unless it is already on the diagram).

Changing the font and color on diagrammed elements is relatively easy. You select the element (and hold the SHIFT button and click other elements if you need to affect a group of elements). Click on the visual attribute toolbar button (Fill Color, Font, Line Color, or Line Width) and select the font, color, or width from the dialog that appears.

TIP
You can often apply in-place editing techniques to the objects in a diagram. For example, you can click once on the entity name in an Entity Relationship Diagram. When you click again, a field will open where you can edit the value without having to open the Property Palette or property dialog. Click outside the field to close it when you are done.

Mouse Actions

Oracle Designer is a graphical user interface (GUI) product and relies heavily on the mouse or pointer to respond to dialog boxes, change cursor focus, draw symbols in the diagrammers, and navigate the screen. In fact, you can respond to some dialogs and perform some navigation only with the mouse; the keyboard will not work. In other dialogs, the cursor navigation keys (TAB and SHIFT-TAB) will be operational. If you are not comfortable with the mouse as an input device, you might want to practice on other programs or games so you will not falter when you need to use the mouse in Oracle Designer.

You use the mouse in the diagrammers to move objects around on the screen and place new objects in the desired position. In addition, if you double-click the mouse on an object in the diagrammer, Oracle Designer displays the Property Palette or dialog for that object to allow you to make changes to its properties directly in the diagrammer. Single-clicking on a diagram object selects it so you can resize it by dragging the borders or move it by dragging the object itself. Holding the CTRL key while clicking selects multiple items, and holding the mouse button while dragging a selection box around items selects all those items when you release the mouse button. These are all standard Windows drawing actions.

In addition, there are right-click mouse menus available on most objects. The menus differ based on what object you are clicking and the location of that object. When first learning a tool, it is useful to explore these menus.

Menu System

All diagrammers have similar functions that you need to perform to manipulate the diagram as a whole, and most of these are available from the menu system and toolbar. The following sections examine the pull-down menus and the functions that are common to most diagrammers.

FILE MENU   The file concept does not really apply directly to the diagrams in Oracle Designer because they are saved in the repository, but the File menu is a standard GUI feature, and the definition of the File items can be stretched to fit repository objects. New creates a new diagram; Open presents a list of existing diagrams of that type in the repository so you can load one into the drawing area; Close unloads a displayed diagram; Save and Save As save the diagram to the repository; and Delete removes a diagram from the repository after you choose it from a list in the dialog box. There is no Rename option in these menus, but you can expand the Diagrams node in RON (in the Sets group), click on the diagram and rename it in place or change the property for *Name*.

TIP
You can change a diagram using the navigators in RON and the Design Editor to a certain degree. The navigator hierarchy contains a node for diagrams that you can expand to see all diagrams in that area. You can delete a diagram, change its summary information (in the Property Palette), or rename it using these tools. You can also open the diagram by selecting from its right-click menu.

The File menu also includes Summary Information, where you can enter information regarding the diagram as in Figure 2-35. This item creates a title block on the diagram that contains the information you indicate in the dialog. Once you click OK on this dialog box, the title block will appear in the upper-left corner of the drawing.

Change Connection and Change Application System in the File menu allow you to change the user account or application system you are connected to. Although you can also do this in the Oracle Designer window (launchpad screen), you would need to exit and restart the diagrammer before the change took effect.

The File menu also has Print, Print Preview, and Print Setup options, which open standard dialog boxes for printing. Print Setup also lets you change the page orientation so you can use a landscape (horizontal) layout instead of portrait (vertical) layout.

The last items in this menu are a list of recently opened diagrams from all application systems so you can open a diagram that was recently opened. This is faster than going through the open diagram dialog. There is also an Exit option, to close the diagrammer. You can also exit the diagrammer from the window title bar (upper-left corner) or Close icon (upper-right corner).

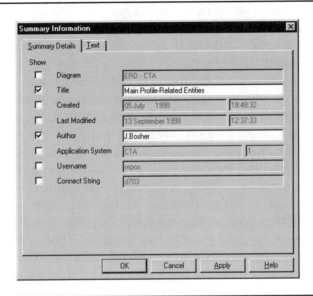

FIGURE 2-35.   *Summary Information dialog*

EDIT MENU   Redo undoes the last main change in the diagram but will not reverse a database commit (if you had created an object for example). Cut, Copy, and Paste work on selected objects the same as they do in all Windows programs; Cut removes the object from the diagram, not from the repository, and Delete From Repository deletes it from the diagram and the repository. Paste Link inserts an object that you have pasted onto the clipboard from another application. The object then appears in your diagram, but its source is the application that produced it in the first place. You can use this option to insert graphics or logos or a legend of symbols into your diagram using symbols that the diagrammer otherwise does not support. This is the concept of "Annotations" whose display you can turn on and off in the Options menu's Customize dialog.

Select All and Select Same Type let you select objects on the screen; the latter selects only the types of objects you have previously selected. The Select Same Type choice is useful if you want to change the color of all objects of the same type—for example, tables. In that case, you would click on an object, choose **Edit→Select Same Type** and click on the Fill Color button. Navigate To lets you select one object from a list of objects of a certain type. This option is useful if your diagram is large and you cannot quickly locate a particular object.

Include is the menu choice you use to put an object that already exists in the repository onto your diagram. Include displays a list of object types, and you choose one of these to display a list of objects of that type that you can include. You can choose Requery when you make changes to an object on a diagram from another tool. For example, suppose you draw an entity relationship diagram and include ENTITY1 on it. Then you go into the RON and change the name to ENTITY_1. The next time you open the diagram, the diagrammed object will be out of synch with the current definition. If you try to view the element details on the object, the diagrammer will tell you that the diagram's copy is out of date, and ask if you want to requery. This same situation can also occur if you have both the ER Diagrammer and RON open at the same time and are working in both on the same object. In this case, if you have the Network Broadcast options (as described later in this chapter) turned on, a red dot will appear next to the entity name, signalling it is out of date. The Requery menu choice lets you refresh the diagram with the current object definition.

Normally, just double-clicking an object will display its Property Palette or Properties dialog. You can also select an object and choose Properties from the Edit menu. This approach is useful if you think selecting the object could move it around on the diagram. In this case, you can select the object through the Navigate To menu item and then display the properties with the Properties menu item.

The Domains menu item (which allows you to define named datatype and values objects) appears on some menus (sometimes in the Elements menu item) to allow you to add and modify domain objects.

Insert New Object, Links, and Object handle the Object Linking and Embedding (OLE) of objects from other applications into the current one. These options are related to the Paste Link option mentioned before; Paste Link, mentioned above, handles a link from the clipboard, whereas these options handle links directly from other applications.

VIEW MENU   One powerful feature of the diagrammers is that you can look at a diagram in many different ways. Zoom In and Zoom Out move the view closer to or farther from the diagram in a preset percentage. Normal Size restores the view before you zoomed. Fit to Area prompts you to draw out an area and then fills the window with that area.

TIP
Use Fit to Area to get a particular set of objects to fill the screen. You may not be able to do this as easily with the granularity of Zoom In and Zoom Out.

Fit to Area and Fit to Diagram also let you change how much of the diagram you view. If you use Fit to Area after selecting an object or set of objects, the window will be filled with those items. If you choose Fit to Diagram, the window will fill, if possible, with the entire diagram. Fit to Selection works in the same way, but fills the window with the selected object or objects.

Grid displays a set of lines on the screen with the grid size you specify in the Options dialog. This grid helps you line up objects and can also be printed.

Toolbar, Tool Palette, and Status Bar turn those window items on or off. If you check them, they will be displayed; otherwise, they are hidden.

LAYOUT MENU The Layout menu contains selections that you use to modify the placement of the objects in the diagram. Most diagrammers have an Autolayout selection that redraws the diagram in a new configuration (Oracle Designer's best guess). If you keep pressing this button, you may (or may not) achieve the diagram layout you want without making manual modifications. Previous Layout restores the last Autolayout layout, but it will not return to a layout that Autolayout did not produce. You can customize some options that affect the Autolayout feature. Some diagrammers also have an Autolayout to New Area (or Same Area) option that lets you select an area for the Autolayout layout.

Most diagrammers also have a Minimize Number of Pages option that reduces the spread across multiple pages if the diagram will fit on fewer pages. This option fixes the situation that occurs when you move objects around and they get too close to the edge of a page and create a new page.

Rescale Diagram resizes the objects on the diagram so they fit on a specified number of pages.

UTILITIES MENU   The Utilities menu varies depending on the diagrammer you are using and includes the actions that the particular diagrammer performs on its objects. There are specific discussions on these menu items in subsequent chapters.

OPTIONS MENU   Customize displays a screen that allows you to modify the display characteristics of the diagram. Each diagrammer is slightly different, but you can specify the colors, fonts, included objects, and grid size characteristics.

Text Editor Options allows you to set up your own editor to be the ASCII Editor used to edit multiline text property values. Defining your own text editor gives you flexibility in how the text is formatted and entered. For example, after you display the Property Palette for a particular PL/SQL definition, you can select the *PL/SQL Block* (or *Package Specification*) and click the ASCII Editor button on the toolbar. The editor you set up in the Options dialog will be invoked and loaded with the text in the selected property. There is a similar field for the HTML Editor. If you fill in the name and location of your HTML Editor, you can click the HTML Editor button and the text will load into that editor. This provides you with a means to insert formatting characters, colors, graphic files, and hypertext links into the multiline text property of an item.

Broadcast Options let you specify how you want to be notified if a definition on a diagram you are working on has changed. This could occur because another user is working on the same definition. This notification appears as a *broadcast indicator*, a red dot next to the element that changed. This indicator appears in the navigator tools as well as the diagrammers and signals you use to do a requery.

Diagnostics is a way to set up a trace of the session. If you turn this on, you will see the *** *Diagnostics ON* *** message appear in the title bar of all Oracle Designer screens you start after that. There is extra processing involved with this option and you should be careful to use it only when working with Oracle Support on an issue. Having Diagnostics on will degrade the performance of your repository work.

TIP
Click the Save button in the Preferences dialog to hold these preferences between sessions of the diagrammer or utility. If you set preferences and do not save them, those preferences will not be there when you reopen that tool. Also, the preferences are saved for each tool individually, so you may have to make the same choice in several tools.

TOOLS MENU   The Tools menu is different for each diagrammer, but the menus all have the same purpose—to allow navigation to related tools. For example, in the Entity Relationship Diagrammer, the Tools menu includes the other Systems Modeller tools: Function Hierarchy Diagrammer and Dataflow Diagrammer. It also includes the Design Editor, which works on definitions of the tables that may be related to the entities in the diagram. In addition, you can access utilities such as Repository Object Navigator, Repository Reports, and Matrix Diagrammer, all of which are applicable to objects used in this diagrammer.

WINDOW MENU   The Window menu includes the standard list of open windows as well as choices for tiling, cascading, and arranging the icons of the open windows. In addition, a New Window choice enables you to create another window with the same diagram as the active diagram, so you can look at two different parts of the same diagram at once.

HELP MENU   Help→Topics displays the applicable contents page. How to Use Help displays help on the help system, and About shows a window with information on the version number of this tool. Customer Support runs SQL*Plus and creates a file containing information about your environment that you can mail or tell to the Oracle Support team when you call with problems. Show Keys, also accessible by pressing CTRL-K, shows a list of keypresses that you can use to speed up your work. Figure 2-36 shows this help topic. This help topic is available in other tools as well, such as RON.

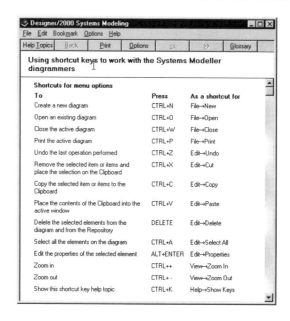

FIGURE 2-36. *Help topic—Using shortcut keys*

TIP
If a menu item or toolbar button you need to use is not enabled, check that you have selected the proper element. You can use the "What's This" button to get help on a menu item or button as described earlier. This should tell you what needs to be selected before that menu item or button is enabled. Similarly, if there is a menu, or menu item disabled or missing, the cursor may not be focused on the correct window. For example, in Design Editor, if you click on the Navigator window, a Navigator menu will appear, but if you click the Property Palette window, the Navigator menu becomes a Properties menu.

Toolbars

The button toolbars are an extension of the menu system and show the major features you need to access most frequently. To show the purpose of a button, all buttons include icons and display bubble help (tooltips) when you hold the mouse over a button. There are two main toolbars: the Toolbar and the Tool Palette.

The following illustration shows the toolbar from the Entity Relationship Diagrammer. Other diagrammers provide similar toolbars.

These represent the following menu items (from left to right):

- File buttons for New Diagram, Open Diagram, Save Diagram, and Print.

- Edit buttons for Undo, Cut, Copy, Paste, Requery Selection, and Requery All.

- View buttons for Zoom In, Zoom Out, Fit to Selection, Zoom to area, and Fit to Diagram.

- Layout buttons for Autolayout and Previous Layout.

- Diagrammer-specific buttons (the next three buttons in this illustration are to set up and manipulate arcs in the Entity Relationship Diagrammer); you'll learn more about these in subsequent chapters.

- Context-Sensitive Help—a "What's This" help button that you click to display the question mark cursor, which you can click on an item to display context-sensitive help for that item.

There is also a toolbar below the standard toolbar for drawing functions. The next illustration shows the ER Diagrammer drawing toolbar.

This toolbar provides sets of buttons for functions not on the menu:

- Select, so the mouse cursor can select an item by drawing around it.

- Object buttons where you select and then draw the object on the drawing surface. If you *pin* a button by clicking it while pressing the SHIFT key, you can lay out many objects of that type without having to reselect the button. To unpin the button, click on the Select button.

- Visual palette buttons for Fill Color, Font, Line Color, and Line Width. The visual palette buttons are not available until you select an item by clicking the mouse on it. You can select one or more objects at the same time using CTRL-click. If you apply the visual palette color at that point, you will affect all selected objects.

TIP
Although the default location of these toolbars is one on top of the other, you can actually drag and drop them anywhere. If you click and hold the mouse button on a nonbutton region within the outline of the toolbar, you can reposition the toolbar anywhere on the screen. If you drop the toolbar in the toolbar area at the top or side of the window, it will attach to the MDI window itself. If you drop it outside the toolbar, it will become a floating toolbar that you can move around inside or outside the window. This sort of toolbar is handy for maximizing the space in the drawing area because moving the toolbar out of its normal location leaves that much more area for the drawing.

Utilities Interface

The standard utilities interface is a simple one consisting of one or more tab pages. Figure 2-37 shows such a dialog for the Unload utility.

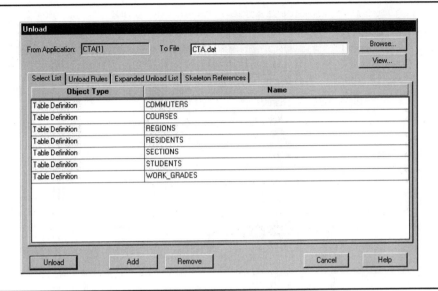

FIGURE 2-37. *Unload utility dialog*

The common features that these type of utilities share is that they start from another diagrammer or utility such as Repository Object Navigator or Design Editor. They appear in a separate dialog that is *modal*—that is, you must close that window before you can return to the calling window. They contain various Windows controls: text boxes, list items, check boxes, and radio groups. There is usually one button that starts an action, one to cancel or dismiss the dialog, and one to display help on the fields in the dialog.

A common interface item that appears, not only in the utilities, but also the property dialogs, is the customizable spreadtable. An example is the Attributes tab of the Entity properties dialog in the Entity Relationship Diagrammer. This dialog is shown in Figure 2-38.

The columns in this table-like interface are resizable. If you grab the side of one of the headings with the mouse cursor, you can drag it left or right to resize the column. You can also pin the column by right-clicking the

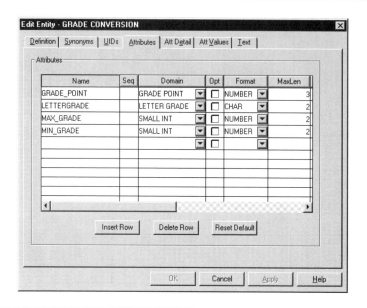

FIGURE 2-38. *Attributes tab of Edit Entity dialog*

heading and choosing Pin Column. This will ensure that, no matter how you scroll left and right, the pinned column will always remain visible.

How the Oracle Designer Tools Fit into CADM

You have now seen all the major tools and utilities in Oracle Designer. Although the main intention of most of this book is to explain how Oracle Designer supports the development life cycle, it is appropriate in this section to summarize where each tool fits into the process. Table 2-1 shows the phases, some of the main activities and deliverables, and the tools that support them.

Phase	Major Activity/Deliverable	Oracle Designer Tools
Strategy	Initial process flow model	Process Modeller or Dataflow Diagrammer
	Strategy ERD	Entity Relationship Diagrammer
Pre-Analysis	List of entities and processes	Repository Reports
	Preparation for building on strategy models	Repository Object Navigator (to version the application system)
	User Requirements to Function mapping strategy	Repository Administration Utility
Analysis (all steps)	Refinement of the strategy ERD	Entity Relationship Diagrammer
	Refinement of the strategy process flows	Process Modeller or Dataflow Diagrammer
	Attachment of the entity usages to functions	Matrix Diagrammer
	Additional functional decomposition	Function Hierarchy
	Analysis document with all repository objects	Repository Reports
Pre-Design	Designation of functions as manual or automated	Function Hierarchy
	Physical process flows	Process Modeller or Dataflow Diagrammer

TABLE 2-1.   *Methodology Phases, Major Activities/Deliverables, and Oracle Designer Tools*

Phase	Major Activity/Deliverable	Oracle Designer Tools
	Preparation to build on analysis model	Repository Object Navigator (to version the application system)
	Screen and report prototypes	Client code generators
	GUI standards	Preferences Navigator
	Refinement of templates	Oracle Developer Forms and Reports, Visual Basic; WebServer
	Physical database design: rough-cut of tables, views, and indexes	Database Design Transformer
	Application design: rough-cut of modules	Application Design Transformer
Design: Database Design	Refinement of rough-cut design	Design Editor: Server Model Diagram, Logic Editor; Object Database Designer
Design: Application Design	Refinement of rough-cut design	Design Editor: Module Diagram, Module Network Viewer, Generator Preferences; Matrix Diagrammer
Build	Completed application modules	Form, Report, Library, VB, WebServer, MS Help, C++ generators
	Completed database objects creation scripts	Design Editor: Generate Database from Server Model; Repository Object Navigator

TABLE 2-1. *Methodology Phases, Major Activities/Deliverables, and Oracle Designer Tools (continued)*

Phase	Major Activity/Deliverable	Oracle Designer Tools
Test	Cross-check for design completeness	Matrix Diagrammer
Implementation	Lists of completed modules	Repository Reports
	System documentation	Repository Reports
Maintenance	Addition to system functionality or bug fixes	Appropriate utility or tool depending on the fix
All Phases	Management of repository, repository data, and users	Repository Object Navigator and Repository Administration Utility
	Display of repository contents	Repository Reports, Repository Object Navigator, Matrix Diagrammer, Design Editor

TABLE 2-1.   *Methodology Phases, Major Activities/Deliverables, and Oracle Designer Tools* (continued)

Conclusion

This chapter has introduced you to the important concepts behind the data in the repository and to the major diagrammers and utilities that you use to access this data. The repository holds the definitions of all objects you create in the various phases of CADM. This data helps you build systems that meet the business needs of the users. It serves as the basis for the database and application code that creates a reality from the virtual elements in the repository. The Oracle Designer front-end tools provide easy entry points into the repository, as well as give structure to the development process. Now it is time to delve into the details of the methodology phases and, for each phase, to see how to harness the power of Oracle Designer.

PART
II

Life Cycle Phases

CHAPTER
3

Strategy

Why do we have to do a Strategy Document?
Can't we just start coding?

he first step in CADM is strategy. The goal of the Strategy phase is to gain an overall idea of what the system you are about to design should do and to define the scope of the project. This chapter presents an in-depth view of the Strategy phase. It provides an overview of this phase and describes its key deliverable, the Strategy Document, in detail.

Overview of the Strategy Phase

The purpose of the Strategy phase is to formulate a basic description of the overall scope of the project and how the project will proceed. It is a contract between the ultimate users of the system and the people who will analyze, design, and build the system.

Spending an adequate amount of time on the strategy portion of the project is critical. Ideally, you should spend as much time as management will allow. A better understanding of what the project is committed to deliver will reduce confusion and help keep the project on course. The more that is known about the underlying business goals and requirements early on, the less likely it is that there will be surprises during the Analysis phase or that the scope of the project will change dramatically. It is not necessary that every specific system requirement be reported at this phase, but all necessary information should be gathered. The more analysis that can be incorporated into the Strategy phase, the better. If the analyst has done a careful and thorough job in the Strategy phase, the Analysis phase will proceed more smoothly.

On some projects, problems arise when different individuals on the project team and within the organization think about the project in different ways. For example, in a data warehouse project, the systems people may focus on the migration of the legacy system information, but top management may not see this as a goal or interest, and it may not fit in with the company's overall vision for the system.

Without a clear and common vision, a project can be sidetracked and months of work can be lost or a system may be built that does not meet the core requirements. Development team after development team may come and go if they do not obtain a consensus of understanding among individuals involved at all levels as to the vision and goals of the project. There are many talented technical consultants who can write code and programs galore, but without a solid overall plan and goal, these efforts are wasted.

Rarely does anyone in a systems environment advocate cutting corners on data structures or applications without considering the impact on the system. However, there is a tendency to look upon strategic planning and methodology as an easy place to reduce costs. In the long run, this is a huge mistake and usually greatly increases the length of time for project completion.

The first task of the Strategy phase is to develop a strategy plan. This plan will help answer questions such as the following:

- What will the Strategy Document contain?

- Who will be interviewed?

- What committees will be involved in the project?

- What will the deliverables be?

- How long will the entire systems project take?

Several weeks may be necessary to produce an effective strategy plan. The development team needs the users to buy into the entire project and procedure. The plan for the Strategy Document should include criteria for determining when the Strategy phase is finished, what the expected deliverables are, and who ultimately signs off on the strategy part of the project before it proceeds to the next phase.

One useful aspect of the Strategy phase from both user and development team perspectives is that the users can contract with the development team to complete the work in this phase without committing to the full implementation of the project. Because it is impossible to accurately estimate the costs and resources necessary for completion of a project until the end of the Strategy phase (or, in most cases, the end of Analysis phase), completing the Strategy phase gives both the development team and the users a much better idea of what the proposed project will entail. The Strategy phase must be completed in order for both client and development team to have a good enough grasp of what needs to be done in order to make a decision to proceed.

Deliverables

There are three deliverables for the Strategy phase:

1. **Preliminary Project Plan**   This plan lays out the main tasks, deliverables, and schedule for the remainder of the project. This project plan will undoubtedly evolve over the life of the project.

2. **Project Contract**   In a consulting environment, the project contract is frequently developed as part of the Strategy phase. For this reason, we include a discussion of it here. In some cases, the contract is finalized before the Strategy phase begins.

3. **Strategy Document**   The main deliverable for the Strategy phase is the Strategy Document. The Strategy Document is a high-level, focused description of the proposed system. It acts as a contract between the development team and the user organization. The Strategy Document should precisely describe the scope of the proposed system and, in broad strokes, lay out the plan of how to accomplish the project.

The intended audience for this document includes the user-side project leader, everyone on the development team, and any area managers who need to be involved in system development. It should not be written for one specific person. Frequently, the Strategy Document is presented to a management committee for sign-off. In small- and medium-sized companies, this committee often is the board of directors. Therefore, there may need to be several versions of the document for different audiences. A broader version might be suitable for the development team. For other audiences, one or more sections may need to be removed, altered, or expanded.

Preliminary Project Plan

Although it is difficult to estimate costs, we can still develop an initial project plan with the understanding that it may change, even drastically. Ranges rather than precise numbers should be used in the project plan. We prefer to create three versions: best-case, worst-case, and most likely scenarios. To the extent that you can foresee them, you should try to state what types of events would contribute to a worst-case scenario; for example, a key user resource leaves the project (or company), or hardware, software or telecommunications equipment is not delivered on schedule. As the project proceeds through the various phases, the variation between best and worst cases should dramatically decrease. By the end of Pre-Design, the project plan for the remainder of the project should be very accurate.

Resources

Within the project plan, you should list the resource requirements from both the user community as well as the developer side. Incidental costs for travel, hardware, computer networking and administrative support, project administration (including status reports and presentations), and JAD sessions should all be included, since all of this nontechnical effort can add significantly to the cost of the project.

It is also important to recognize what the required user involvement will be. Access to key individuals should be carefully planned to take their availability into account. Participation by key users is essential to the success of any project. This must be understood at the outset. On one of the most successful development projects we have worked on, the users actually did most of the analysis, only using developers for mentoring and technical support. Having users on the development team not only increases the chances of project success but can also greatly decrease the cost of the project.

Roles and Responsibilities

Requisite roles for the project team must be identified for both user and developer organizations. Where possible, these roles should be associated with named individuals or very clear descriptions of what experience and skills the individual filling a particular role should have. Roles should be assigned to tasks in the project plan so that accurate estimates can be made about the number of Full Time Equivalents (FTEs) needed for each phase of the project.

Project Contract

Early in the Strategy phase, if not before, you need to draw up a contract. This is relevant for development to be performed both by internal Information System departments and by external consultants. In the case of the consultants, the contract is explicit and obvious. But even for internal development, a contract is required. Many organizations handle this through transfer pricing. Transfer pricing involves the setting of prices for goods and services when both the buyer and seller are within the same organization. It needs to be clear even for internal development teams where resources will be drawn from (the IS department? the whole organization? one particular department that stands to benefit the most?) Who is responsible for what parts of the system? Trying to determine these answers before the Strategy phase begins is difficult, since there is no formal specification of the system to be built. It is ludicrous for a Request for Proposal (RFP) to insist on a fixed-price contract based on a vaguely specified set of requirements. The Strategy phase serves to nail down specific requirements and project scope. From a contracting standpoint, it is difficult to do anything other than determine an estimate of possible costs and make a plan for completing the project.

Types of Contracts
There are several types of possible contracts for a systems project. We will describe each type separately.

FIXED-PRICE   Fixed-price contracts indicate a specified amount of money for which a system will be delivered. Users like these types of contracts, since their risks are limited. Fixed-price contracts have a very low probability of success. The development team is motivated to devote as few resources as possible to the project, performing the minimum amount of work necessary to get users to sign off on the system. Users are not motivated to make the job easier for the developers, because no matter how difficult, the price is fixed. Therefore, no one is motivated to do a careful job. Unless the fixed-price amount is extremely generous and the users extremely motivated, the probability of success is very low.

TIME AND MATERIALS   Development resources are acquired based on the cost of the hours worked and materials used. Users are motivated to help as much as possible and drive or manage the project, since every resource costs users money. Developers are motivated to keep users happy so that the project will continue but are not motivated to complete it. This type of contract can work if users take a very active (approaching managerial) role on the project. All of the risk is assumed by the users.

HYBRID   Hybrid contracts combine elements of fixed-price and time and materials contracts. One example of a hybrid contract is a time and materials contract with some percentage of billings withheld until project completion. This provides the incentive for the developers to complete the project and diverts a small amount of the risk from the users to the developers.

Another hybrid contract is created by reducing time and materials rates but adding a project phase or milestone completion bonus. This allows the risk of project overruns to be shared between the development team and users as well as providing incentive on both sides to complete the project in order to minimize costs to users and maximize developer profit.

We advocate contracting some form of the hybrid model, preferring to only contract for the next phase of the project whenever possible to minimize the probability of cost overruns. Not having a full project contract at the outset of the project is often not desirable to either users or developers, since it is impossible to accurately estimate a project before Analysis is complete. Development teams can provide estimates, but these estimates are, at best, reasonable guesstimates and, at worst, total shots in the dark.

COST PLUS CONTRACTS   Cost plus contracts, popular in government projects, involve contracting to pay the marginal costs of the contractor plus a percentage of those costs as a profit, a fixed amount, or both. If the profit is based on a percentage, this is essentially a time and materials contract. If the "plus" or some portion of the additional money is fixed, then the contract is a hybrid type. Traditionally, in cost plus contracts, some portion of the funds to be paid is withheld until project milestones are met.

Conflict Resolution Mechanism

At the outset of a project, you need to identify what the conflict resolution mechanism will be when disputes arise. These disputes often pertain to changes in scope and quality of deliverables. The rules for how such disputes will be resolved should be spelled out in advance of any significant work being undertaken. The disputes can be between developers and users or, sometimes, between different groups of users.

Strategy Document

The Strategy Document should be as complete and detailed as possible to ensure that both users and the development team have a clear understanding of what is expected. It not only should list conclusions but also should draw a reader of the document through a logically coherent argument that demonstrates how the conclusions were derived.

Gathering information for the Strategy phase is done mostly through interviewing. Interviews are usually conducted with individuals reasonably high up in the organization, since these individuals have the authority to allocate the money and resources to the project. Interview notes should be given unique document name/number identifiers, such as the person's name and the date of the interview. These notes should be kept in a binder and can be referred to by footnote in the Strategy Document. Using one's own interview document as a reference helps to make the writing tighter and less cumbersome. Instead of repeatedly writing "according to so and so" or "so and so said," footnotes can be used to reference statements in the original interview notes. All paragraphs in the Strategy Document should include footnotes citing the original interview notes. Since all interview notes will have been approved by the people being interviewed, the analyst has a defensible Strategy Document.

Goals of the Strategy Document

The Strategy Document has the following goals:

- To communicate to management and all people involved in the project just what the project entails.

- To act as a sales tool for the development team. The Strategy Document proves the need for and importance of the project, clearly explaining why the project is cost-benefit efficient and demonstrating that the proposed plan makes sense, is feasible, and is the best plan to get the job done.

- To serve as a contract between the development team and users.

■ To assess the scope of the project, list the promised deliverables, lay out the assumptions and limitations of the project, and limit the liability of the development team to what is agreed upon.

■ To provide a baseline for the proposed system, specifying the rights and obligations of both analysts and users, including the right of the analysts to rethink the project when changes in the scope of the project occur or the stable allocation of resources is altered. The document should make it clear that any major changes will affect the deliverable dates.

■ To provide a reference point and mechanism for handling conflicts that may arise.

Structure of the Strategy Document

The Strategy Document should include the following sections, each of which this chapter discusses in detail:

I. Executive summary: The *executive summary* is a short overview of the entire Strategy Document and includes an executive summary abstract. Each section is then expanded in the complete Strategy Document.

II. Legacy system description: history, current system

III. Related projects

IV. Business and financial sponsorship

V. Motivation

VI. Project scope

VII. Solution: system, ERD, process flow

VIII. Cost-benefit analysis

IX. Project organization and staffing

X. Workplan

XI. Business Impact

XII. Conclusion

I. Executive Summary

The executive summary is not just an introduction to the Strategy Document. It is a self-contained document and should be written to be read on its own. It should completely describe all of the salient features of the Strategy Document. The executive summary represents the project team's current understanding of the total project.

Consider the following anecdote, perhaps apocryphal, about a study of National Science Foundation research grant proposal applications. These proposals reflect important research projects and are typically hundreds of pages long. Millions of dollars in grant money are distributed based on decisions made regarding the worthiness of the proposals these documents describe. The study found that the average amount of time spent making a decision on an application was 15 minutes.

The point of this story for a systems environment is that much of what is written is not read carefully, if at all. How much time is a busy executive realistically going to spend reading a document? The executive summary should convince the user that they want to support the project as outlined, whether the costs are a few thousand dollars or several million. The executive summary defines the scope, solution, development method, costs, and benefits.

How long should this document be? This decision often depends on the preference of the manager being addressed. Some want two pages; others want only one. Still others may want a more detailed five- to ten-page document. The executive summary should *never* be more than ten pages. If, for some reason, the system being designed is so large that the summary exceeds ten pages, this document should have its own summary. Also, depending on the audience for this document, certain sections that appear in the larger Strategy Document (such as a description of the legacy system) can be added or removed as necessary.

A good deal of time and thought should go into the executive summary. Just because it is a short document does not mean that it should be tossed off quickly. As the analyst's understanding of the project matures, the executive summary should be refined and revised. Since some of the information in the executive summary must be extracted from the whole Strategy Document, it may be necessary to complete some work on the project before a useful executive summary can be written. Revisions may need to be made as often as every few days.

After you draft the executive summary document, you can expand it and add parts of it to other sections of the Strategy Document as you write it. It is perfectly acceptable to reuse paragraphs from the executive summary document elsewhere in the overall Strategy Document.

Executive Summary Abstract

The executive summary abstract is a quick-and-dirty summary of 100 to 200 words that forms the first paragraph of the executive summary. It should begin with a sentence of 25 words or less stating what the project intends to accomplish. This step serves as an internal validity check. If the project goal can't be stated clearly in 25 words or less, the analyst doesn't clearly understand the project and is not ready to write the Strategy Document. This statement serves as the core requirement for the system being designed.

Here is an example first sentence of an executive summary for a data warehouse project: "The proposed data warehouse will provide data structures adequate for replacing all existing production reporting and any ad hoc report requested in the last six months." If the project is very large or diverse, it may be necessary to break the 25-words-or-less rule; however, with a laundry list of several goals, it is very easy to lose sight of the core goal.

The remainder of the abstract condenses the executive summary into a few key sentences.

Business and Financial Sponsorship

Every project of any magnitude needs to have the appropriate commitment from the organization to accomplish its goals. The existing political environment within an organization strongly influences how the project phases (especially the Analysis phase) take place. The project team needs to carefully document the following:

- Who the players are
- The relative stakes in the project of each player and department
- The individual needs and requirements of each player and department
- The mechanism for conflict resolution, including who has ultimate authority

Motivation

The motivation section should consist of one or two paragraphs describing the underlying business need for the proposed project. Like the executive summary abstract, this section should also begin with a brief—25 words or less—explanation of why the project was undertaken. The motivation section must present a clear, concise, direct, and compelling statement of the user's reasons for wanting a system developed.

Here is an example of a motivation section directed to the management team of a large financial company in the Northeast that was building a new trading system: "The existing system is an antiquated COBOL system held together by patches. It is only a matter of time until there is a catastrophic program failure causing an interruption in business. New products cannot be added to the system, which is preventing us from entering new markets. The existing system is incapable of expanding into new geographic regions. Management is considering trying to support 24-hour trading. The old system cannot support this at all. The longer we wait, the more this will cost our company." This statement justified a multimillion-dollar expenditure.

Solution

The solution section should be no more than one or two paragraphs long. It should briefly describe what the analysts intend to build, the basic vision of the overall system architecture, and how the system will work. It should summarize the solution section of the overall Strategy Document, described later in this chapter.

Cost-Benefit Analysis

The benefits versus costs section is devoted to estimating the cost of the project and the resources required to complete the project. It is important for the development team to have a clear and accurate picture of the resources (hardware, software, personnel) that the user will have to provide and to present this in the document.

An ethical question arises in estimating costs. Users may be so used to being misled regarding the amount of time and money required for system development projects that they may automatically double or triple low estimates. This is a tricky issue. If the development team is honest about the time and money required, the user, who may assume that the numbers are low, may feel that the costs are unreasonable. On the other hand, if the cost estimate is low and the project ends up way over budget and late, the development team will have some very unhappy users. We believe that the best advice is to be as realistic as possible. Let your conscience be your guide. It is rare that a project does not go over budget; but if the development team has been honest with the user, budget overruns can be handled amicably.

This section of the document should also spell out exactly what deliverables the user will get. This can be a list of the hard and soft benefits that the finished project will provide, as discussed in more detail later in this chapter.

Conclusion

End the executive summary with a few concluding sentences, not with numbers. Expectations for a formal business document include a conclusion. Part of the goal of the executive summary document is to communicate to the user that the development team is well organized and can be trusted to do the job completely.

II. Legacy System Description

This section describes the legacy system, including both the history of the legacy system and its current status.

History of the Current System

It is important to understand how the existing system was created. Without a thorough understanding of the legacy system, it is not possible to redesign the system. Find out about previous attempts at system redesign. If possible, talk to people who were involved in the original system design; you will gain important information regarding the legacy system.

Include a walkthrough of the existing system and its development history in this section. The likelihood is high that this is not the first attempt to fix a system problem or design a new system. To avoid repeating past mistakes, examine the remains of earlier projects and any existing half-built structures. Documentation and analyses of these previous failures may help pinpoint the reasons for failures and help you avoid the same pitfalls. This information is well worth the time needed to gather it and incorporate it into the Strategy Document.

Some individuals in the business reengineering community might argue that a thorough review of the legacy system is unnecessary and would hamper the completion of a quality reengineering effort. The fallacy of this point of view stems from the fact that, particularly with older systems, system requirements will be embedded in the legacy system that cannot be discovered any other way except by thoroughly reviewing the system. Treat the legacy system as merely another source of requirements. To ignore this potentially valuable resource is a mistake.

Description of the Current System

A new system can't be intelligently designed without a thorough description of the system it is destined to replace. Obtaining this information will require talking to more than one person. The analyst needs to understand more than just the functional aspects of the system. He or she needs to observe the system in use to get a sense of the supporting data structures (for a computer system), inputs, outputs, how the system is used, who uses it, what they use it for, the business reason for the system, and so on. Without a baseline measure, you will not be able to discuss benefits of the new system.

This section should include an overview of the existing hardware, software, and network.

Frequently neglected aspects of the legacy system are the reports it generates. Often, even after reengineering, reports may be similar to those provided by the legacy system. The Strategy Document should list the numbers and types of reports and give examples. These reports will be completely explored in the Analysis phase.

III. Related Projects

With rare exceptions, projects do not exist in isolation. The following questions must be considered in the Strategy phase of any project:

- How is the system being developed going to interface with existing systems?

- How and when will this integration be accomplished?

It is critical to consider how the integration with existing systems will affect the amount of time needed for the new system development.

NOTE
Interfacing with existing systems can take longer than the design of the system being developed. This is true even when interfacing with an existing Oracle system. Non-Oracle database integration can take even longer because of the difficulties of dealing with different platforms. Also, in general, interfacing with packaged software takes longer than interfacing with in-house systems.

Sometimes, particularly in large systems projects, multiple teams will be working on different portions of development. In these cases, clear delineation of scope, interfacing, and deliverables is critical to project success. Trying to coordinate multiple teams on a project is exceedingly difficult and usually results in finger pointing and infighting when something goes wrong. This usually causes the project to fail. Having multiple teams, particularly from different areas, should be avoided whenever possible. However, having one team subcontract another team to fill in expertise where it is needed is acceptable.

IV. Business and Financial Sponsorship

It is not politically correct to have a section in the Strategy Document called "political environment." However, from the developer's perspective, the political environment of the organization needs to be taken into account and documented. A complete description of the existing political environment is a critical piece of the Strategy Document.

Political Environment

The political situation within an organization will influence the way any system is built. The political environment is just as important as the fundamental strategy requirements for the system. Just like changes in the scope of an ongoing project, a change in the political environment can cause the entire project to be rethought from the ground up.

Examples of changes in the political environment that can affect a project include personnel changes, department head changes, and the addition or elimination of a department involved in the project. A new person in a position of authority may have an entirely different agenda than his or her predecessor. A substantive upset in the balance of power among the players or departments can also cause a fundamental shift in project goals. Unless a way to handle these changes from the project perspective is carefully spelled out, the whole project may be in jeopardy should a change in the political environment occur. For example, if a main department head changes mid-project, the entire project may be pulled off track, and it may not be until another major organizational change occurs that the project gets back on track.

The best way to collect the necessary information on the political environment is to ask questions. Find out who the players are whose needs should be met. Define the organizational areas that the system affects. Create an organizational chart that includes all the people involved and goes high enough in the organization for its various branches to meet at a central person with ultimate decision-making power.

The deliverables in this section include the following:

- Organizational chart

- List of the names, titles, and relationships of players

- Strategy-level requirements for each of the players or a description of how the needs of various players differ (each section may need to be developed with each player using a problem/definition format)

- Conflict resolution structure

Conflict Resolution
The approval process needs to be carefully spelled out and the following questions answered:

- How will it be determined when a particular deliverable is finished?

- How will changes in scope or deliverables be handled?

- What will be the sign-off process for each phase of the project?

When there are differences of opinion in spite of these questions, there must be a process for resolving the conflict. Usually, the best way to resolve conflicts on a project is to hold a joint application development (JAD) session. At this meeting, all of the parties are brought together to lay out all of the pertinent issues and forge a consensus. If a consensus cannot be reached, there should be a clear mechanism for a higher authority to arbitrate the final decision. All those involved should have agreed to this process before proceeding. This is another example of the importance of regarding the Strategy Document as a contract between the user and the analyst. These issues are often not stated explicitly but are truly salient and material portions of the contract. Everyone involved needs to understand and buy into the process as a whole in order for the project to be successfully completed.

V. Motivation

The motivation section justifies the need for the project. The information you gathered in your interviews should include all the evidence you need. However, like a good journalist, a good systems analyst does not depend upon one source. The ultimate authority is the person with the overall responsibility for the project and the person or persons to whom the development team reports. The line of authority should be clear. If others present differing opinions regarding the project, it is the responsibility of the analyst to dig further and report these in the Strategy Document. It is important to keep the user informed at all stages of the project.

VI. Project Scope

Even though scope issues will enter into other parts of the Strategy Document, scope is such an important topic that it should be dealt with specifically. Scope can be limited by any number of factors:

- **Access to users** In one project, the scope was limited by who the development team was allowed to interview. That limitation of access restricted the quality of the analysis and therefore also restricted what the development team could deliver.

- **Subject area** One portion of a system may need to be replaced without making modifications to other portions of an existing system.

- **Interface with existing systems** This interface can restrict scope. For example, building an inventory management system is one project. Hooking that system into an existing purchase order (PO) system is a separate project.

- **Technical limitations** Developers may supply database design and application resources but not technical hardware, networking, or custom-written Windows DLLs.

- **Role of the developers** This can be restricted to analysis and development and may not include training or user documentation.

Negotiation of scope depends upon the needs of the users as well as the capabilities of the development team. It is important that the scope of a project is specifically laid out, including what is within the scope and, often more importantly, a declaration of what is out of scope and will not be delivered.

VII. Solution

The solution section should summarize all aspects of the system to be built and include a Strategy ERD and process flow diagrams.

Proposed System

The discussion of the proposed system should lay out, specifically and in depth, what the development team will do for the user. This is not the place to discuss costs. This section should discuss the following:

- **Hardware requirements** What equipment will be required to complete the project? Is a client/server environment to be assumed? Can existing hardware be reused or must new equipment be procured?

- **Software requirements** What software will be needed? What licenses will be needed? Does existing software need to be upgraded?

- **Deliverables** List the deliverables that are planned: for example, applications, reports, documentation, training, maintenance agreements.

- **Knowledge transfer** This is relevant when an outside consulting team does the development. An important deliverable is that the consulting team provide a knowledge transfer to the in-house developers that will enable them to perform maintenance and enhancements throughout the lifetime of the new system.

Strategy ERD

Depending upon the complexity of the business area and the level of knowledge of the project team and users, it may or may not be appropriate to include a Strategy ERD as part of the Strategy Document. However, this diagram should be created anyway, if only for the purpose of helping to focus the analysts' thinking.

At the Strategy level, the ERD should identify the key entities and their relationships to provide an overall perspective of the business area data. For example, for a purchase order, the key entities might be vendors, approved items, purchase order, customer, and so on. This is not the place to be overly concerned about whether an entity is a lookup table or to define the cardinality of relationships.

In addition to the diagram itself, the Strategy ERD must include narrative definitions of each entity. These definitions should be clear and concise. Errors in ERDs frequently occur because the analyst does not have a clear understanding of the entities being modeled. These definitions should come from the business users.

Entities in an ERD are not merely descriptions. They represent items of particular significance and interest to an organization about which they need to keep information. Demographic information, for example, is not an entity. The naming of an entity is a key factor in the success of an ERD. Good entity names facilitate communicating the business area information requirements. Critical to the success of an ERD are precise and accurate entity definitions. This is an iterative process, which may take some time. Good definitions of the relationships between entities are important because they reflect business rules.

The basic process for creating an ERD is as follows:

1. Identify and name the major entities. At this point, the name is only relevant from a communications perspective. It is pointless to disagree over names before clear, concise definitions are written.

2. Define relationships among entities.

3. Write the best possible entity definitions.

4. Write the best possible relationship definitions.

5. Finalize the entity names.

From these steps, often the best entity names will emerge.

The entity definition always represents something in the real world. These definitions are crucial to the accuracy of the diagram. Entity descriptions should never start with "information on . . ." nor should they describe the attributes of the entity. The entity must be a noun. For example, the entity description of an employee could be "a warm, breathing body that works here." Each instance of that entity (row in the table) therefore represents "a warm, breathing body that works here." When entities are dependent, the description should include a reference to the parent entity. For example, a description of a purchase order detail might be "the quantity of a specific item purchased using a specific purchase order." Entities should always be discussed as things that exist in the real world.

A problematic aspect of many ERDs is the naming of intersection entities. For example, the entities "student" and "class" have a many-to-many relationship. To handle this relationship, create an artificial intersection entity called "enrollment." The definition of enrollment is "the act of a specific student taking a specific class." Therefore, each row in the table represents one specific student taking one specific class.

To help others understand the ERD, generate tables and include sample data to clarify the way information is reflected in the diagram structure. The Strategy ERD should not have many entities; Strategy ERDs should be limited to 10–20 entities.

The diagram should fit on one 8-by-11-inch page. If the project consists of multiple modules, each should have its own ERD broken down by subject area. It is acceptable to have the same entity reflected on multiple diagrams.

Process Flow Diagram

A process flow is a diagram that shows business processes and their interactions. In the Strategy phase, process flows are used to demonstrate to the user that the development team fully understands the business processes within the scope of the project. At this stage, process flows do not need to be overly detailed unless more detail is needed to satisfy the user. Most of the work of creating a process flow is figuring out how the business processes interact and fit together, which usually takes place in the Analysis phase.

A strategy-level process flow can still be used to communicate the scope of the project. For example, for a purchase order (PO) system, the strategy-level process flow will show what is being included and what is not. Will the system track the distribution of goods by matching the distribution against the PO when the goods arrive? Is this tracking part of another system? Does the system include the PO authorization process? These questions can be answered by looking at the process flow diagram for the proposed PO system. If an existing system will be changed significantly, it is usually appropriate to deliver before-and-after process flow diagrams.

VIII. Cost-Benefit Analysis

The Strategy Document needs to show that the benefits of the proposed system will outweigh its costs.

Benefits

How can benefits be quantified? For a reengineering project, the cost-benefit analysis is fairly straightforward. For example, before reengineering, a report may take 14 person days to produce, and after reengineering, the same report may take only one minute to produce. Such a benefit is easy to document, and the advantages of time saved are obvious.

How can a value be placed on new flexibility within a system? One can look at the number of new reports generated by the legacy system in the last six months. If the legacy system took 10 to 12 person days to do what the new system can do in one or two days, then improvements in productivity can be realistically estimated and reflected as benefits of the new system.

Three types of benefits can be examined:

- **Process improvements** Time saved in completing tasks

- **System modification efficiencies** Changes to the system, improving performance, new reports, and so on

- **Ethereal improvements** Executive information systems, ability to expand product line or market segment, ad hoc query tools, data warehouse, and so on

How can a value be placed on these types of benefits? One way is to ask managers and users of the system what they perceive the value to be. For example, a manager can be asked, "If we could give you a new benefit—namely, bringing in a service bureau to perform ad hoc querying—what would you be willing to pay per month for that benefit?" or "In your functional area, how much would you pay to outsource a specific task?" By asking people in all functional areas related to the proposed project questions like these, it is possible to estimate the perceived value of possible benefits delivered by the proposed system.

Costs

The cost section should provide the user with a detailed account of the estimated monetary costs of developing the proposed system as well as the internal resources needed to complete and support the project. Costs can be estimated by phase. For example, the estimate for the Analysis phase should be pretty solid; however, estimates for the Design and Build phases will be less precise since there are many more unknowns in those phases at this stage of development. The true costs are never fully known until the system has been in production for one or two years.

The following should be included in the costs:

- Number of person hours required of internal systems and business people by level

- Cost of external consultants by level, based on hourly or daily rates

- Expected number of hours per day or week for each phase of the project

- Expected hardware costs

- Cost of software licenses

- Networking costs

- Cabling costs

- Number of person hours of internal user resources required

This last item is crucial to the successful completion of any project. The user needs to have a clear understanding of the need for a person or persons from his or her organization on the development team. These resources should be identified by name: for example, "We need 25 hours with Joe, 10 hours with Susan . . ." and so on. The individuals must be chosen carefully since they will function as the liaison between the analysts and the users. They may be required to devote their full time to the project until it is completed. The liaison person or persons should attend all team meetings and work side by side with the analysts building the requirements documents, designing screen shots, and so on. Their participation in all aspects of system development also helps overcome the us-them attitude of user and analyst and promote a more collaborative effort.

The input from the liaison person will play a major role in setting the direction of the project. When the project is completed, this person will be a more valuable employee to the company since the person will gain an understanding of systems development in general as well as being an expert on the new system. A rule of thumb in selecting this person is that if the users won't miss the person, he or she is probably the wrong person for the job.

Once again, it is important to keep in mind that the analysts and the users are building a contract. There must be a meeting of minds. The users are not just agreeing to pay the analyst but also must be willing to allocate the necessary internal resources to the project. The analysts must be firm about this commitment of resources from the users. For example, if the analysts need 10 to 15 hours of time from several top executives, this time must be set aside. If the resources are not made available or the user attempts to substitute lower-level employees, the analysts must indicate that this places the entire project at risk. These cheaper internal resources then become "pseudo-users," and all the analyst can guarantee is that these pseudo-users will be happy with the results. If the users are not willing to spare the appropriate employees, then the whole system development process is in jeopardy. If the analysts cannot get the right resources, then the analysts need to report that the proposed system may not be deliverable.

IX. Project Organization and Staffing

Identification of the different roles of people working on a project is a frequently overlooked step. There are numerous roles associated with a CADM project:

- ■ **Project Leader** This person coordinates all of the other roles and acts as a liaison with the business management in the organization where the project is being done. One of the main responsibilities of the project leader is to make sure that the project plan is being followed. He/she needs to communicate to the project team what steps should be followed and how these steps fit into the overall design plan.

- **Systems Architect**   This is the technical leader of the project who makes sure that the applications and underlying data are coordinated.

- **Business Analyst**   a) *Process Analyst*: This person extracts and analyzes the system requirements with the focus on analysis and representation of business processes.
b) *Data Analyst*: This individual keeps track of and analyzes entity relationships used by the business.

- **Logical Data Modeler**   This person is responsible for the complete analysis ERD representing all of the business requirements.

- **Physical Data Modeler**   This individual understands the performance considerations associated with determining the formal data structures.

- **Oracle Designer expert**   This person is responsible for helping implement the project in the software tool.

- **Repository Manager**   This person takes care of data security and working with different areas of the Oracle Designer repository.

- **GUI Design Standards Developer**   This person determines the project's GUI design standards by understanding what Oracle Designer can easily generate.

- **Application Designer**   This individual supervises the overall user interface design of the application.

- **Application Tuner**   This individual ensures that applications are correctly tuned.

- **Reports Analyst**   This person gathers and documents production and ad hoc reporting requirements.

- **Data Tester**   This individual ensures that the database meets system requirements.

- **Application Tester**   This individual ensures that the applications meet system requirements.

- **QA person**   This person is responsible for overall quality assurance for the project and ensures that things are done according to the specifications that were laid out.

- **PL/SQL Programmer**   This person takes care of complex database and application-level triggers.

- **Application Developer**   This individual is familiar with Forms and Reports or whatever application tool is being used.

- **Network Administrator**   If necessary, this person takes care of network considerations and the underlying physical network of the project.

- **Systems Administrator**   This person supports the operating systems and other systems software.

- **DBA**   This person handles backups and recovery and manages database instances.

- **Data Migration Expert**   This person manages the process of migrating data from the legacy system to the new database structures.

- **Users**   It is important to have users on the development team from each functional area, preferably full time. These individuals should sit in on all meetings throughout the life cycle of the project.

Clearly, many of these roles can and will be performed by the same person. The question arises: How big of a team is desirable? As F. Brooks describes in *The Mythical Man-Month: Essays on Software Engineering* (Reading, MA; Addison-Wesley, 1975), a surgical team model is the best approach. This means that there is one key person supported by as many others as necessary to keep that person productive. On a system development team, a few people do all of the "real" work. Others on the team do support work. We consider it irresponsible and unethical to use high-level development talent for tasks such as typing in entity descriptions or taping together ERDs. The underlying staffing principles here include the following:

- There should be various levels of talent on any team.
- Always use the cheapest, lowest-level talent qualified for any task.
- Never use low-level talent on complex tasks, except for training purposes.
- Use key people to perform key tasks.

On normal, straightforward, low-level development tasks, an expert analyst may be able to complete these tasks in half the time needed by a lower-level analyst. For complex tasks, an expert developer/analyst can often accomplish a task in one tenth of the time needed by a novice developer, assuming that the novice developer could do the task at all. Using the surgical metaphor again, a first-year medical student can suture up a minor cut but no matter how much time the student is given, he or she cannot perform brain surgery. That can only be done by a brain surgeon. Likewise, complex systems tasks require top-level talent.

For the following tasks, it is particularly important to use top-level talent:

- **Design of the logical ERD**   Lower-level talent can do requirements analysis and the first cut of the logical ERD, but the final version requires much expertise.

- **Audit of the logical ERD**   This requires a separate highly skilled data modeler other than the ERD designer. It can be a consultant brought in specifically for this purpose.

- **Design of the physical database**   Physical database design is its own specialty.

- **Audit of the physical database**   The same level talent applies to this audit as to design of the logical ERD.

- **Application design**   This person is responsible for the overall user interface for all applications.

- **GUI standards development**   GUI applications are very different from older, character-based applications.

- **DBA**   Once the database is set up, this job can be passed to a production/maintenance DBA.

- **Internal control system design**   This is crucial to the success of the project, particularly on financial systems that need to stand up to rigorous financial audits.

- **Change control system**   Once the system is in place, an experienced person needs to handle how changes are made and managed.

X. Workplan

The Strategy Document should include a high-level workplan. Other, more detailed workplans will be developed during each phase of the project. At this point, the workplan should be painted in broad strokes from a top-management perspective. Top management wants to know about the deliverables. The workplan should lay out the tasks to be performed for each major phase of the project. Management will not know when analysis is finished unless a requirements document is generated. The analyst should make sure to generate deliverables at each project point for management to review.

The Strategy Document should not simply list promises but should tell management what specifically will be delivered, and when, for the entire project. The user should have a clear picture of what the analyst intends to do and how the user will be kept informed of the project's progress. The analyst needs to instill confidence in the user that the proposed process will enable the project to be completed successfully. The user must buy into the process as well as the end result. For example, during the Strategy phase, one deliverable should be the written project plans as they are done. The user should approve each workplan.

The workplan should be an iterative, negotiated document. The first cut should be an appropriate plan based on the strategy already laid out. This plan is a refinement of the contract between the analyst and user. Each should have a clear idea of this agreement.

What should the workplan look like? It should not simply be a Microsoft Project document. A one-page chart should be included as part of the workplan, but this alone is not enough. The full workplan should describe each major process step and the accompanying deliverables in narrative form. This plan will let management know how the analyst intends to accomplish the various phases of the whole project. Management must agree to each part of the workplan.

How should the number of hours be calculated? To do this, the analyst must internally generate another level of detail. Time tends to be notoriously underestimated. Each portion and subportion of the project must be thought through carefully. Although this level of detail is not overly relevant for the Strategy Document, it is useful to have if the user wants to know how the numbers were derived. Common errors to avoid are a tendency to leave out some time-consuming steps and to underestimate how long tasks will take. This more detailed document can be shown to the key user to back up information in the Strategy Document.

Writing the workplan requires the analysts to make many assumptions. At this stage of the project, they may not know enough to go into great detail. There is still much to find out about the user-site terrain, politics, pitfalls, and so on. It is important to lay out assumptions of the size of the problem and anticipated access to resources. These factors have a direct impact on the workplan portion of the Strategy phase. It is also important to include, as a line item, unexpected disasters. These might include key resource people becoming unavailable for whatever reason and interviews that produce radically differing versions of what needs to be done. Don't underestimate the cost of unexpected disasters. If the development team has already completed a project for this user in the same area, he or she can allocate 20 percent of the overall project cost for unexpected disasters. The project team can perform a risk analysis to estimate the disaster percentage potential. If this is not possible or if this is the first project for a particular user, the development team should plan for 100 percent of the overall project cost for unexpected disasters.

At this stage, the workplan should outline the major phases and deliverables of the project. This can be done with Microsoft Project to produce a one-page document, the goal of which is to educate the user regarding the methods for building the system. The primary goal at this stage continues to be to build the user's confidence in the project team's ability to convert a vision into reality. The workplan should be as detailed as the user wants. The analyst can gauge the level of detail wanted from the user feedback.

XI. Business Impact

How can business impact be determined at the Strategy phase? The analyst will need to hypothesize, "If we had the proposed system in place, what would it do for us?" Obviously, the answer will vary greatly from project to project.

When redesigning a legacy system, whether or not business process reengineering occurs as well, the business impact will be clear: the user will get a more flexible system that can more easily respond to changes in business. Traditional systems are much less user and analyst friendly, though management is often unaware of this. A new report in Oracle Designer takes a day or two to design and build, whereas the same report may take days or even weeks to generate using the legacy system development tools.

The following common outcomes of implementing an Oracle Designer system affect business:

■ Oracle Designer provides a centralized storage place for many of the system requirements.

■ A coherent strategy exists in that all information stored in the Oracle Designer repository is linked to the applications.

■ When data is changed, it can be automatically updated in many of the applications depending on how well the applications are generated and what percent of the applications can be generated through Oracle Designer. This outcome influences the flexibility of the system with respect to regeneration.

A new Oracle Designer system is more user friendly than a legacy system. Having a centralized storage place ready in case the underlying technology changes is very useful. For example, as the work environment changes from a client/server environment to a Web server environment, by using Oracle Designer the user is better positioned to take advantage of an entirely different architecture.

On the database side, the environment is shifting to the object-oriented environment used by Oracle, and database designs are becoming increasingly object oriented. Oracle Designer will be staying on top of the latest developments in Oracle's DBMS, and a shorter time will be needed to implement changes in an Oracle Designer environment. If the legacy system is not even relational, there will be one level of improvement in moving to a relational environment and yet another level of improvement in moving to Oracle Designer. If business process reengineering is performed, even greater efficiencies can be realized, as discussed in Chapter 24.

The bottom line is that the business impact should meet the needs outlined in the motivation section. The new system should provide a solution to the stated business problems. The analyst should go back to the motivation section and make sure each need is addressed one by one and discuss how the new system will support each need.

XII. Strategy Document Conclusion

The Strategy Document should have a structured conclusion summarizing all of the sections outlined in the preceding paragraphs.

In principle, the Strategy Document should be as detailed as possible. The more analysis that can be included, the better. In reality, however, until the analysis is completed and confirmed with the users, the development team will have an incomplete vision of the scope of the project. In the final analysis, we never know the exact size of a project until it is almost finished. The full scope really can't be understood until the Design phase is complete.

Application Partitioning

It's no secret that smaller applications are much easier to build than larger ones. The number of things to consider increases exponentially as the size of the application increases. A small application with a suite of modules that operates on perhaps ten different database tables can be easily built by a couple of developers in a few weeks. A suite of modules running on 30 to 50 tables will require the efforts of a five- to ten-person development team for several months. A large effort involving several hundred modules operating on a few hundred tables can consume whatever resources are applied to it and may take a year or more, if it is ever completed.

The idea is to break the system into several independent development efforts. There is some cost to partitioning, though. For every portion of a large system that is built, you need to consider how that partition will interface with the other partitions. The system should be partitioned in such a way that the interfaces between partitions are as simple as possible. It is necessary to find a happy medium between many small systems with horrendous interfacing problems and a few large partitions with minor interface problems but that have all the other problems associated with larger systems. In the past, the tendency has been to create very large systems. Our experience has been that projects are usually not sufficiently partitioned.

How should the partitioning be done? Optimally, partitioning should be done by subject area. The main criteria to use in selecting application partitions is that it should be possible for the partition to be put into production, independent of the other partitions. In most businesses, systems can be partitioned by accounting cycles, such as purchase and acquisition, sales and distribution, or payroll.

Partitioning doesn't have to take place only during the Strategy phase. It is possible to partition your system at any point in the CADM process. In fact, the appropriate way of partitioning may not be evident until the end of the Analysis phase. At the end of every phase, the development team should audit the correctness of any system partitioning.

Scope

What we are describing in this book is the process for a complete system design involving a complete replacement of a legacy system or a new system development effort. Frequently, the scope of a project is inconsistent with the full CADM process. For example, in one project that the authors worked on, the mandate was to replace the front end of an existing character-based application. Going back to the users and starting over with a complete Analysis phase was not an option. To further complicate matters, there were other applications outside the scope of this project concurrently using the same data structures. Finally, a cursory review of the database revealed serious design flaws.

Developing the workplan for this project was quite challenging. The Analysis phase was abbreviated and only involved interfacing with existing systems personnel. An audit of the logical ERD and database was performed without a Requirements Document. We had to rely on the in-house developers to act as "human surrogates" for a Requirements Document. The rest of the workplan followed the model proposed in this book.

The main point is that in many cases the scope of the project may not include full Analysis and Design phases. At the beginning of any project, the analyst needs to evaluate what changes are appropriate to CADM in order to take into account the starting point of the project.

Strategy Document Example

The following example of a Strategy Document uses a small project as an example, because the documentation for a large project can be very long. Nevertheless, this small project illustrates the concepts being discussed.

The example project calls for redesign of a legacy human resources system. This example was chosen because every organization needs to keep track of its employees on some level. The organization in this example is XYZ Company.

The following paragraphs present the Strategy Document for the proposed project.

I. Executive Summary

Using Oracle Designer and Oracle Developer, we propose to reengineer the data structure and applications for the XYZ Staff ID database.

The XYZ Staff ID database is in need of redesign. The current system is based on a Forms 3.0 application interface; the database design has some conceptual flaws that require either applications or users to add the same information multiple times into the database. This flawed database structure will increase the overall cost and maintenance of the project because the applications will be harder to write.

We propose to not only convert Forms 3.0 to 5.0 but use this opportunity to reengineer the database and clean up its structure.

II. Legacy System Description

The existing system is an Oracle version 6.0 database with a Forms 3.0 front end. The data structure has some conceptual flaws, and the Forms 3.0 front end will require serious reworking to bring it up to modern standards.

III. Related Projects

This is a stand-alone system that has no need to interface with any other project.

IV. Business and Financial Sponsorship

This is an important project, but unfortunately, its value is not obvious. Funding will come from general department resources. Therefore, the Staff

ID database project will have to be piggybacked onto other projects that have greater political priority.

In this case, we can use this project to set up and design our GUI and Oracle Designer standards. Also, we can use the project as a watershed for the application development process using Oracle Designer.

V. Motivation

The existing system has numerous conceptual flaws. For example, people are assigned to organizations in three different places in the data structure. Three different intersection tables connect individuals and organizations, so if one individual's relationship spans more than one of these tables, that information must be stored redundantly.

The current character-based application needs to be converted to a GUI environment. Since we are now moving to a GUI Oracle Designer environment, we need to set up standards, methodology, CASE templates, and common libraries, and we need to document how applications will be designed in the future.

VI. Project Scope

In this project, we will only make essential modifications to the underlying database structure to minimize the cost of data conversion. We will develop the structure of an Oracle Designer-based methodology and GUI design standards. Then we will build an Oracle Developer-based front end to support required functionality. We will not support any ad hoc reporting or query capability or interfacing with any other XYZ systems.

VII. Solution

We propose to complete this project in two phases. Phase I will determine XYZ's GUI design and application development standards, lay out the application and development methodology, and perform some prototyping on the Staff ID database. In phase II, we will apply these standards to the problem of reengineering the Staff ID database.

We will deliver a reengineered Staff ID database and a set of applications that will act as the front end of that database. Of course, if we change the data structure, we will have to make some modifications to the Reports 2.5 application that generates the XYZ phone book.

ERD

Figure 3-1 shows the basic data model for the XYZ Staff ID system based on preliminary discussions with management. The diagram indicates that individuals can have multiple relationships of different types within an organization and that individuals can have multiple phones. The diagram also indicates that we will be tracking changes over time (history) for both people and organizations.

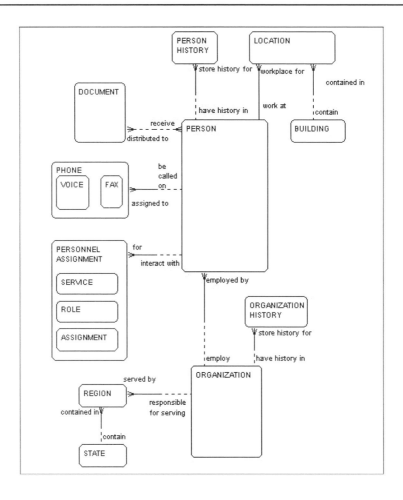

FIGURE 3-1. *Strategy ERD*

NOTE
In the diagram in Figure 3-1, the many-to-many relationship between persons and documents is not resolved, but the many-to-many relationship between persons and organizations is resolved. If this relationship had not been resolved, the diagram would be less clear. Also note that this diagram is limited because a phone cannot be shared by people and any particular phone must be of only one type. However, for a Strategy ERD, this is okay since it is just trying to capture the high-level business requirements: that is, that individuals can have only one phone.

Process Flow Diagram

One of the principal process flows associated with the system is the hiring of employees. This process is represented in Figure 3-2.

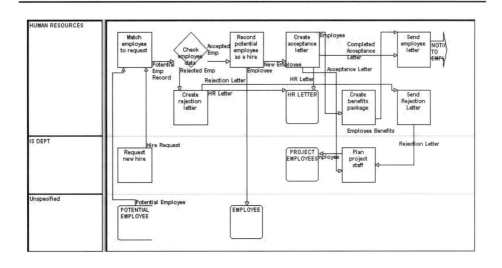

FIGURE 3-2. *Strategy process flow*

NOTE
This system would have many such process flows. This one simple example is shown to demonstrate the concept. Process flows are discussed in more detail in Chapters 4 and 5.

VIII. Cost-Benefit Analysis

The benefits of the new system for XYZ are listed next, along with the associated costs for the development of the proposed system.

Benefits

- Almost all applications will be generated using Oracle Designer so changes to the model can be propagated to the applications through a straightforward regeneration process.

- When phase I is complete, a validated Oracle Designer-based development methodology will be in place, which can be used for other application development projects.

- A solid set of GUI standards enforcing a consistent look and feel throughout all GUI applications will also be in place.

- The new system will be much more user friendly, requiring significantly less time in data entry and user training.

- At the end of phase II, the underlying data structure will be much more logically organized. This logical organization will decrease future development time because applications will be simpler to develop and the data structure will be easier for developers to use.

Costs

Both phases I and II are heavily dependent upon whether we use off-the-shelf GUI development standards already built or standards custom designed for XYZ. Assuming the first option, using GUI standards similar to those built for other users with minimal rework required, we estimate the cost of phases I and II to be approximately $50,000 per phase. This assumes a time and materials contract and represents our best estimate of cost based on currently available information.

IX. Project Organization and Staffing

The proposed system will require two developers and one project manager for the duration of the project. One person from the Human Resources department will be required half-time on the project development team.

In addition, time will be required from middle and upper management in the Human Resources area to periodically review the project status.

X. Workplan

We will complete the project in two phases. Time estimates are best guesses based on past experience and current information.

Phase I

1. Prototype application suite to validate GUI standards (1 to 10 days). Building the prototype is a simple, one-day task. If our GUI standards are not satisfactory, we will need to spend additional time modifying these standards to suit your needs.

2. Set Oracle Designer preferences (5 to 10 days). There are over 450 preferences to set.

3. Create Oracle Designer templates and PL/SQL libraries (5 to 10 days). As we dig this far into the generation process, there will be a clear need to reengineer the templates and libraries released with the product.

Phase II

1. Redesign database (5 days).

2. Create storyboard application (3 to 10 days). We will build the whole application as screen shots so you will have an idea how it will look. If you are not satisfied with our first try, extra time will be required to redo the storyboard.

3. Build detailed design book (2 to 5 days). For each application, we will need to describe how it functions. The level of complexity of the applications will determine how long this phase will take.

4. Module design within Oracle Designer (10 days). We are guessing that we will have 50 modules to build. This will take some time.

5. Generate and modify modules (10 days).

6. Engineer changes into templates, libraries, or module definitions (5 to 10 days). The time needed for this step will depend on the number of modifications required for each module. Only complex modules will need significant modification.

7. Build system documentation (5 days). Most system documentation will already be included in the design book or can be generated using Oracle Designer. We are allocating a week for cleanup and quality assurance (QA).

8. Build user documentation (5 to 10 days). With user feedback, this step always takes longer than originally planned.

9. Testing and QA (5 to 10 days). We will audit the applications to ensure that they meet the design specifications of the design book.

XI. Business Impact

Because the scope of this project is so small, the business impact was discussed under Benefits (see Section VIII).

XII. Strategy Document Conclusion

By setting up GUI and design standards that can be used for future system development and restructuring the existing database, we will make the XYZ Staff ID system more efficient and user friendly.

Modifications for Smaller Systems

A full-blown Strategy Document is appropriate only in very large projects costing a million dollars or more. However, the Strategy phase can certainly be pared down to suit smaller projects. You can stratify the size of the projects being discussed, as follows:

- **Type 1**   Multimillion-dollar projects requiring person years of effort taking place over months or years

- **Type 2**   Medium-size projects, including stand-alone systems such as payroll and purchasing systems, and systems requiring integration with existing systems

- **Type 3**   Small projects that are short term and require limited budget and resources

(Note that any project requiring integration with an existing system can be viewed as one size larger. In other words, a small project requiring integration with a functioning system should be considered a medium-sized project, and so on.)

For very small projects, the Strategy and Analysis phases are combined. For example, when building a help desk system, all that is necessary is a few-page write-up indicating the project scope and cost estimate, a Strategy ERD, and perhaps a process flow diagram. The result will be a Strategy Document with some analysis and design specifications all rolled into one. From this, the project can move to a rapid prototyping environment. With the sophistication of existing tools such as Oracle Designer, the application can be built so quickly that if it is not satisfactory, it can be rebuilt and quickly moved through the refinement process. Descriptions of the legacy system and political environment also are not necessary for small projects.

For medium-sized systems, a Strategy Document still is necessary. However, not as much time needs to be spent on this since there will be fewer users to interview. Also, since the project is smaller in scope with less money involved, you will not need to justify the plans as carefully at this stage as would be necessary in a large project. For small and medium projects, an executive summary is needed only if the Strategy Document is more than ten pages long. Legacy system and political environment descriptions may or may not be needed, depending on the specific situation.

Within this book, most of the information pertains to projects of type 1 in the preceding list. However, modifications of the proposed methodology for small- and medium-sized projects will be mentioned at the end of each phase, as in this section.

When Is the Strategy Phase Complete?

How do you determine when the Strategy phase is finished? A rule of thumb is that it is finished when all major players believe it is finished. This consensus is formalized when everyone involved signs the Strategy Document. There are no objective criteria for determining completion. However, it is important to gather and verify as much information from both users and in-house systems staff as possible. If the analyst does not get an approval from the primary user, then the definition of whether or not the system is complete is ambiguous. The analyst must put in writing that if access to the proper individuals is denied, he or she cannot be held responsible for the outcome of the total project.

It is up to the analysts to write a complete Strategy Document that covers all sections of the project. This should be a joint effort with the user community. This contract is executed when all parties sign, thus binding both analysts and users to the stated scope and deliverables.

CHAPTER
4

Oracle Designer in Strategy

O! When degree is shaked,
Which is the ladder, to all high designs,
The enterprise is sick.

—William Shakespeare, *Troilus & Cressida I*, iii, 101

 he main deliverable of the Strategy phase is the Strategy Document. This consists of written material as well as diagrammatic models of the business area. Oracle Designer provides some support for tracking documents you create as part of the Strategy Document. It also supports the diagramming work you perform in the Strategy phase, as the following table shows:

Activity or Deliverable	Oracle Designer Tool
Process flow diagram	Process Modeller
Strategy ERD	Entity Relationship Diagrammer

The Process Modeller and Dataflow Diagrammer help to represent the functions and data in the system. The diagrams you create with them are excellent tools for communicating with users or the development team, and for checking whether your understanding of what the system should do is complete and accurate.

This chapter explains in some detail how the Process Modeller works. It also introduces the Entity Relationship Diagrammer in enough detail to get you started with creating your Strategy ERDs. Chapter 10 fills out the discussion of the ER Diagrammer while covering how to use it in the Analysis phase. In addition, this chapter mentions the methods Oracle Designer provides for tracking documents. The discussion here of the methods you use to work with these diagrammers assumes that you have read the section "The Oracle Designer Interface" in Chapter 2. These diagrammers use the standard interface described in that section, and you start both from the Oracle Designer window, also discussed in that section.

Process Modeller

The objective of the Process Modeller (BPM) in the Strategy phase is to produce a complete, high-level picture of the system for communication to management or users. The Process Modeller gives you a way to diagram the processes and flows of data to and from other processes and data stores. Additionally, the BPM shows the organization units (also called org units or Business Units) that perform the processes and own the stores. This is a valuable piece of information and one to which nontechnologists can instantly relate. The idea of organization unit assignments is an essential part of the way businesses are modeled, but this type of depiction is not provided by many other CASE tools.

The Process Modeller is useful for creating a business process reengineering (BPR) diagram, where you show the current system and propose new methods for completing business tasks. In the Strategy phase, however, you are not so much concerned with BPR as with accurately identifying the current system or proposed new system, and this tool works quite well for both purposes. While the Process Modeller stores quite a few details about the data stores or flows, it does not show data usage (the entities and attributes they consist of) in detail. The strength of this tool is in the process flow information it represents and its display of the organization units.

Business Processes vs. Functions

The BPM shows business processes that may or may not be automated currently. The point of the process flow diagram is to show the steps that the business users or systems must perform to complete a certain task. The business processes represented in this flow may be quite different from the functions that a system needs to complete a task. When you get further along in the system strategy and analysis, you will need to model these functions as well. In some cases, the business processes and functions have a 1-to-1 relationship, but in many cases there is no direct correspondence between the two. For example, a business process might be "Hand final registration to bursar," but this process might be irrelevant in the final system.

In Oracle Designer, however, business processes modeled in BPM represent the same repository element as functions modeled in the Dataflow Diagrammer or Function Hierarchy Diagrammer. This gives you the flexibility to define business processes that become system functions. It also allows you to represent the same functions (processes) in this diagrammer as well as the Dataflow and Function Hierarchy Diagrammers. Although this strategy can save you time, it can also lead to confusion about whether a certain definition is inherently a process or a function. If you keep these concepts distinct in your mind, you can create a new version of the application system after performing the business process modeling. The first version would show the business processes that you modeled before moving into the analysis phase. The second version would show the functions you want the new system to fulfill. After creating the new version, you will not be able to modify the diagrams and processes in the original version, as creating a new version puts a freeze on the old version. You will, however, be able to change the process model in the new version to work the way you want to model the system functions.

Basic Techniques

Working with the Process Modeller is similar to working with the other diagrammers, since the menu, toolbars, and mouse actions follow the standard Oracle Designer interface. This discussion, therefore, concentrates on what is different about this diagrammer. Be sure to use the help system "Modeling business processes" section for detailed information on how to perform an action when you need more information.

Opening a Diagram

You open a diagram the same way as in the other diagrammers (using **File→Open** or the Open button). The diagram will appear in the Process Modeller window, as in Figure 4-1. If you need to create a new diagram, you select the New button (or choose New from the File menu) and identify the *root* (or *base*) process, which is the process that the diagram represents. The root process contains all the processes you will diagram and is not actually visible in the diagram itself. It is similar to the outer process in a dataflow diagram—all processes are within it—although the dataflow diagram (DFD) actually shows the process box in the diagram. The root process can be any process that you have already defined or, if the process does not yet exist, one that you create by clicking the Create New Root Process button.

The process definition box will pop up and give you a chance to enter the short definition and label for this new process (the "Naming Objects" section later in this chapter provides some conventions on how to name these objects). Then the drawing area will appear with one organization unit: Unspecified.

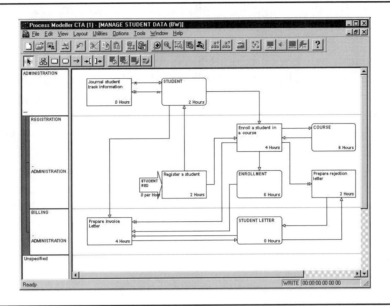

FIGURE 4-1. *Process Modeller diagram*

Drawing Objects

You place an object on the diagram in one of two ways: you create it by
selecting the button in the drawing toolbar that corresponds to the type of
object you want and drawing it on the screen, or you retrieve an existing
object from the repository with the menu sequence **Edit→Include→Process
Step**. To include an object other than a process step, you would select that
type from the **Edit→Include** menu instead of **Process Step**. A list of elements
will appear, and you can choose one or more from that list. (Hold down the
CTRL key and click to make multiple selections.) If the element is a function,
you can include the flows as well by checking the Include Flows check box.
When you draw an object such as a process, store, trigger, or outcome in
the Process Modeller, you choose an org unit to drop it into; the org unit
represents the owner or source of that element. In addition, flows require an
object on either end, so you click one process or store and hold the mouse
button while dragging the mouse to another before releasing the button.

You can create org units the same way you create other objects. When
you select the appropriate button and click in the org unit area, a new *swim*

lane representing the organization unit appears. You can create subunits of a unit by selecting the button and clicking within an existing org unit. This will make the new org unit a child of the one you dropped it into. If you just want to create a new org unit on the top level, drop it on the Unspecified unit. There are menu choices and toolbar buttons to hide or display the child org units of a parent: **View→Drill Up Organization** when you have the parent selected to hide the child units and **View→Drill Down Organization** when you have the parent selected to also show the child units. If the parent has children, it will have an expand symbol (+) in the lower-left corner to signal that children exist. Double-clicking on the expand symbol will perform the same action as the Drill Down menu choice. The Unspecified org unit is where you drop objects that have no single owner or an unknown owner.

NOTE
You can associate more than one org unit with a process using the Repository Object Navigator (Business Function node, Usages: Performed by Business Units subnode). The BPM allows only one org unit per process, and this assignment is stored in a property called Single BPR Business Unit, which is a read-only property. The value of this property will be Yes if you assigned the process to an org unit on the Process Modeller. If you perform the assignment in the Repository Object Navigator, the value will be No.

When you drop an object onto the diagram or move an existing object, it will snap to a certain location determined by an invisible grid. You cannot change the size of that grid, but you can resize all stores and processes by dragging the corner of one of them in or out. The exact dimensions of this box are also available for you to change in the **Options→Customize→ Graphics** dialog, as Figure 4-2 shows. The height of the org unit will always resize to be large enough to hold the objects you put in it. The width expands as soon as you move objects past the right boundary. You can decrease the width of the diagram if no objects occupy the space by

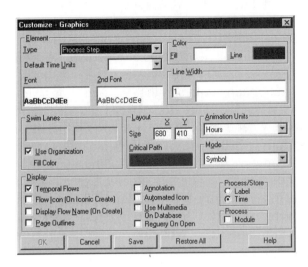

FIGURE 4-2. *Customize-Graphics dialog*

choosing **Layout→Minimize Number of Pages** from the menu. In addition,
you can select a landscape page orientation from the **File→Print Setup**
dialog box. This will change the number of pages used when the diagram
prints. In addition, checking the Fit to Page check box or specifying the
number of pages (X and Y) on the **File→Print** dialog will squeeze the entire
diagram onto one printed page.

TIP
*Pressing CTRL-F is a shortcut to move quickly to
the Customize-Graphics dialog. In fact, many
functions have shortcut keys, and you can
usually see which key to press by looking at the
label hint for the menu item. This particular
shortcut, however, is a carryover from Oracle
Designer version 1 and has no menu label hint.*

You can also modify the height of the org units. If you select an org unit on the left and hold down SHIFT while pressing the DOWN ARROW key, the org unit will increase in height. To decrease it, assuming there are no objects in the space you wish to eliminate, hold down SHIFT and press the UP ARROW key. You can move org units around by holding down CTRL and pressing the UP ARROW or DOWN ARROW key.

If you assign alternating colors to the org units, you will find that the diagram is easier to read, because the eye can more easily follow each color horizontally to see what the org unit owns. You do this in the Swim Lanes area on the **Options→Customize→Graphics** dialog by clicking on the swim lane color. Alternatively, you can specify that the swim lanes take the color of the corresponding org unit title box. Remember that you can select multiple objects in a diagrammer by holding CTRL and clicking each one.

You might want to practice this and other basic techniques so these activities do not slow you down when you are creating a diagram.

NOTE
Remember that you can create many different diagrams from the definitions in the repository. It may be necessary to eliminate a set of objects from a particular diagram when communicating with a certain group in the business area. The objects may be either confusing or misleading, or the explanation of those objects would distract from a particular purpose. You can cut objects from the diagram and save the diagram as a different name for this different purpose. This does not affect the base objects in the repository.

Naming Objects

You normally follow some naming convention when creating the objects in the Process Modeller. One common standard is the use of phrases in mixed case starting with verbs (since they represent an action) as the process names: for example, "Request new employee hire." The names of the flows themselves are usually nouns, because they represent "things," in lowercase format: for example, "employee profile." The names of data stores are uppercase nouns that are the same as or similar to the names of the flows that go into them, for example, "EMPLOYEE". Triggers and outcomes are named, in uppercase, like processes as they are events that imply action. If you change your mind and need to change the name of an object (or even its type) after you create it, you can display the properties dialog (by double-clicking the object) and making the changes in the Specific tab, as in Figure 4-3.

Using the Symbol Set

The set of symbols used in the Process Modeller, as shown in Figure 4-4, is relatively small. A *process step* represents a process or function; a *flow* is a connection between two elements that shows the data flowing from one process to another or to a store; a *store* symbolizes a collection of data that is not moving in a flow but is stored somewhere; a *trigger* is an event that starts a process from a source external to the system; and an *outcome* is an event that sends data outside the system or triggers a process outside the system.

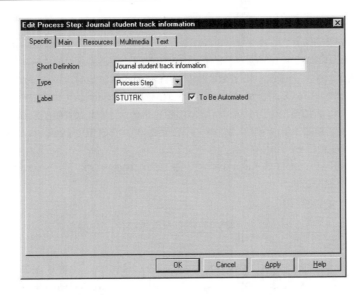

FIGURE 4-3. *Specific tab of the Edit Process Step properties dialog*

Store

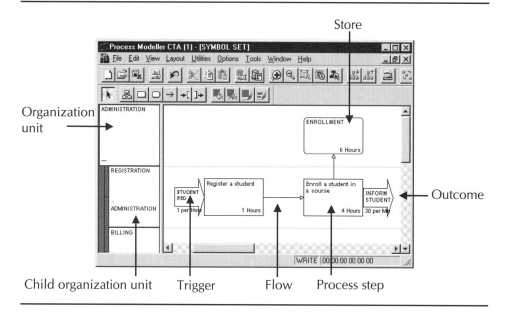

Organization unit

Child organization unit

Trigger

Flow

Process step

Outcome

FIGURE 4-4. *Process Modeller symbol set*

These symbols have different types to represent details that you might want to specify for an object. For example, a process could be a type of process step, decision point, data entry, report, external, or internal. Since the type of the object is one of its properties, you can obtain a report later on the objects and their types. In addition, the type determines how the symbol appears in Enhanced Symbol mode. You set the type in the Specific tab of the properties dialog.

Additional symbols designate how a flow line works, as shown in the following illustration:

A bar that intersects the flow line indicates OR logic. This is most useful when the process is a decision point type and you want to represent that after the decision occurs the flow will go to one output flow or another. An "x" symbol indicates that this flow or other object will not participate in the diagram animation (described in "Creating Multimedia Presentations" later).

You can view the diagram in three modes, as Figure 4-5 shows: *Symbol,* which shows boxes and flows but no distinction between types of objects; *Enhanced Symbol,* which shows the objects with distinctive symbols for different types; and *Iconic,* which shows the objects as icons or small pictures. You can choose the mode from View menu.

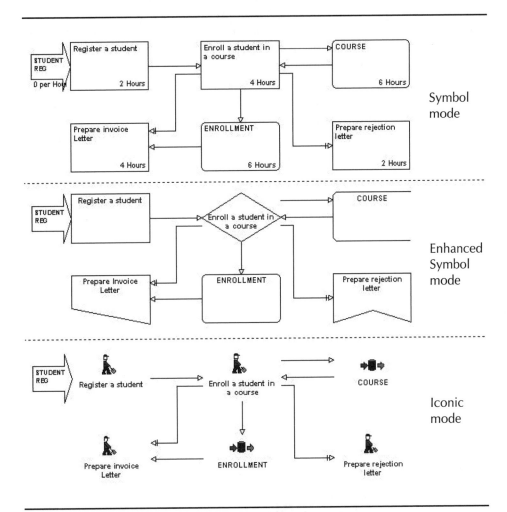

FIGURE 4-5. *Three view modes for the Process Modeller*

Performing Functional Decomposition

The Process Modeller allows you to perform *functional decomposition,* which breaks down a process (function) into its component processes. Each diagram represents one base process and the detail processes that comprise it. For each process displayed, you can create a separate diagram that represents the processes that make it up. For example, you may have a process called "Hire new employee" that has a dataflow to another process on the same diagram. You may want to break the process into the steps that compose it, so you create another diagram that has the process you want to decompose as its root process. In effect, you drill down into the details of a process. Each diagram you create in this way is a separate diagram, but it is linked to the upper-level one. Thus, if you select the process and choose **File→Open Down** from the menu, the next level of diagram opens in the Process Modeller window. If you are in a lower-level diagram, you can select **File→Open Up**, and the upper-level diagram will be displayed regardless of whether it was previously opened.

TIP
Once you Open Up or Open Down on a process, the diagrammer keeps a window open for each base process. You can switch back and forth between them faster using the Window menu window list instead of the Open Up and Open Down menu items.

Properties Text Tab

The Text tab for the process, flow, and store elements gives you a place to enter the *Notes* and *Description* properties to document the object. You can choose among several categories of text and you can cut, copy, and paste between them with the CTRL-X, CTRL-C, and CTRL-V keys, respectively. These text items serve as documentation only, and they are available for reports on the objects in the diagram.

Advanced Techniques

The techniques discussed in the preceding paragraphs will enable you to use the basic functionality of the Process Modeller and will probably suffice for the Strategy phase. If you want to enhance your diagram or add pizzazz to it for a presentation, however, you need to apply some advanced techniques.

Allocating Time and Cost

One feature that distinguishes the Process Modeller from the Dataflow Diagrammer and Function Hierarchy Diagrammer is that it allows you to assign estimated resource usage time and cost, in various units, to each process, flow, and store. This feature is useful if you are analyzing the duration of the processes and flows, particularly in a business process reengineering effort. This information is available on reports such as the *Activity Based Costing* report in the Repository Reports tool. It is also the basis for determining the time for which each element is active when you animate the diagram.

You assign time and cost amounts on the Main tab of the Edit Process Step dialog for each element, as in Figure 4-6.

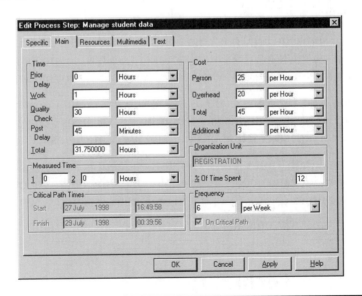

FIGURE 4-6. *Main tab for specifying time and cost*

TIME   You can track the times associated with various types for processes, flows, and stores, as measured in a unit of time (minute, hour, day, week) that you can select. You can track the following times:

■ **Prior Delay** identifies the time that elapses between the time that control passes to this element and when the actual work starts.

■ **Work** indicates how long a process or flow (or even a store) takes to act.

■ **Quality Check** designates how long a cross-check of the completed work takes, if one is performed.

■ **Post Delay** is the amount of time that elapses after the completion of the work and quality checks before control passes to the next element. If you use both a post delay on Function1 and a prior delay on Function2 that is triggered by Function1, you have to be aware that the total delay time between when Function1 stops action and Function2 begins action is the sum of the post delay on Function1 and the prior delay on Function2. You may or may not find a practical use for these delay fields.

■ **Total** sums the previous time fields automatically, and you cannot override this sum. This number and its units will appear on the drawing for processes when the view is in Symbol mode.

■ **Measured Time** gives you a way to show a minimum and maximum amount of time for this element or to assign times that you define. In other words, the definitions of these two time fields are up to you.

■ **Critical Path Times** indicates if this element is in the critical path. If so, a delay here affects the completion of the entire set of processes. These times cannot be updated and are calculated when you choose **Utilities→Calculate Critical Path** from the menu.

NOTE
The breakdown of times is really only a suggestion. If you have other needs for the fields, you can assign times for actions other than prior delay, work, quality check, post delay, and so on. Also, you do not need to fill out all times as there may be some, like Prior Delay *and* Post Delay *that do not make sense for your needs. These properties have no effect on generated code.*

The other time fields on the Main tab are *% Of Time Spent,* for designating the percentage of the total time that the organization unit this element belongs to spends on this activity, and *Frequency,* for designating the number of times this process or flow occurs in the base process you are diagramming.

COST   You can assign costs for *Person* (personnel) and *Overhead* (costs such as rent and utilities). These are actual monetary designations, and Oracle Designer adds them together into the *Total* field. As with time, you designate the unit of time to which the cost applies. You can also specify *Additional* for costs not covered by the other two categories. This cost has a per unit designation for costs of raw materials using a unit measurement.

Resources

The Resources tab in the Edit Process Step dialog, shown in Figure 4-7, has two main areas:

- **Resources** is where you indicate the amounts and types of materials you need for this process (or flow): for example, 1 typewriter.

- **Yield (Quality Percentage)** is a percentage ratio of units successfully completed to units attempted. For example, if you create 100 complete computer workstations, but only 95 of these are good enough for use, then the yield would be 95.

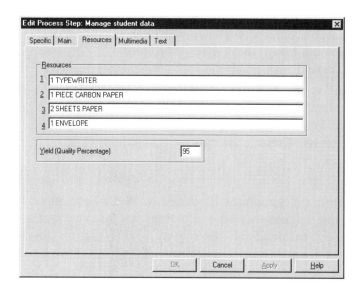

FIGURE 4-7. *Resources tab*

Global Processes

Global processes steps are those that are outside the base diagram process. Although these processes are contained within another process hierarchy, you may want to represent them on this diagram to clarify some dataflow. When you include a global process step, the hierarchy in the repository is not changed, but a reference copy is made in the diagram. This copy changes whenever the base process definition changes. For example, a diagram that represents instructors calculating grades might want to show that there is a certain grade weighting given to particular assignments and tests. The process of assigning the weightings is outside the scope of the grade calculation and so is a global process. When you include this on the grade calculation diagram, by choosing **Include→Global Process Step** from the Edit menu, the repository makes a reference copy. The location of the assigned weightings process in the process hierarchy does not move, so it is not considered a subprocess of the grade calculation.

TIP
*As mentioned in the help system, if you hold
the SHIFT key while selecting **Edit→Include→
Process Step** (or any other object) from the
menu, you will get a "global" list of all elements
of that type.*

Saving Graphical Preference Sets in the Process Modeller

You can save the graphical preferences you set for a particular diagram
in a file so you can use them in other diagrams or change them
temporarily and then restore them. These configuration files are
available to any Process Modeller diagram in any application system.
Choosing **Options→Customize→Graphics** from the menu displays the
Customize-Graphics dialog. If you press Save in this dialog, the
BPMOD10.CFG file will be created in the root directory of the drive on
which you have Windows installed. For example, if Windows is
installed on the C: drive, the BPMOD10.CFG file will be located in the
C:\ directory.

Remember that if you want to take advantage of the multiple
configuration files feature, the file must be located in the Windows
directory (examples would be C:\WINDOWS or D:\WINNT). There is a
solution, however. Here are the steps to follow so that you can use the
configuration files feature.

1. Click Save in the Customize-Graphics dialog.

2. Move or copy the BPMOD10.CFG file from the root directory to
   your Windows directory.

3. Choose **Options→Customize→Advanced** from the menu and
   choose the BPMOD10.CFG file from the Use Element Preference
   Set list. This step registers this file with the tool. Click OK.

4. Go back to the Customize-Graphics dialog and click Save again. This will display the Named Preference Set file dialog. Type in the new name of a preference set file if you want to save to a different file. The file must start with BP and use a .CFG extension (for example, BPMOD10A.CFG). Click OK.

5. Move the new file from the root directory to the Windows directory.

6. Go back to the Customize-Advanced dialog and be sure that the file is in the file list. If you missed step 5, it will not be there.

In summary, the Customize-Graphics dialog saves the configuration file in the root directory, but both it and the Customize-Advanced dialog look for it in the Windows directory.

Creating Multimedia Presentations

One powerful feature of the Process Modeller is its multimedia capabilities, which you define for each item using the Multimedia tab (Figure 4-8). You can start other programs by adding an *Execution String* property to specify the name of the program to run. This enables the Execute Program button whenever you select the object in the diagrammer, so when you click that button in the toolbar, the program assigned to the object runs.

You can also select a starting icon for animation by filling in the *Icon* name in the Animation area. This icon must have the suffix "1" and must be part of a group of files with the same name and the suffixes "2" and "3" for the animation to work (for example, BIKE1.BMP, BIKE2.BMP, BIKE3.BMP). When you press the Animate button (or use **Utilities→Animation→Start**), the Process Modeller cycles through icon files 1, 2, and 3 and repeats for a time period proportional to the amount defined on the Main properties tab.

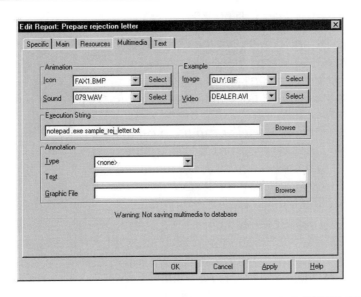

FIGURE 4-8. *Multimedia tab*

You can manipulate how long the animation will last by specifying a Time Step in the animation options dialog (**Utilities→Animation→Options**). The *Time Step* is the amount of real business time that will be represented by a half second of animation. For example, you have a process that takes two hours to run (as defined in the Work time on the Main properties tab), and you set the *Time Step* to one hour. When you animate the diagram, the process will be active for one second. By assigning times and icons to all your processes and flows, and watching the animated diagram, you will get an idea of the time (even though it may be compressed in duration) that the business process takes to complete each of its steps. This can help you identify bottlenecks in the process flows that need to be improved.

TIP
*You can set the default icons used by Process Steps, Stores, and Flows from the **Options→ Customize→Advanced** menu item. You can also set up default icons based on various words in the name of the object. For example, if you include the word "fax" in the process step name, the Process Modeller can use a certain icon. If you include the word "create" in the process step name it can use a different icon. You do this by creating a file that contains the key words and file names. For example:*

```
create    factory1.bmp
fax       fax1.bmp
```

You specify the name of this file in the same Customize-Advanced dialog. If you do not include the path, the tool looks for the file in the Windows directory or the root directory where Windows is located. This is a fast way to attach various icons without having to visit the Multimedia tab for each one.

If you check the Activate During Animation check box on the Specific tab of the flow, the flow will participate in the animation sequence. The default setting for this property is checked, so all flows will participate unless you uncheck this property. If the property is checked, you will see the "x" indicator on the flow line.

Other multimedia capabilities on this tab define image, sound, and video files that are associated with this object. If you have specified an image viewer, sound player, and video player program in the **Options→ Customize→Basic** menu item, you can attach an image, sound, or video clip (or all three) to this object. Then when you select the object in the Process Modeller, the corresponding button on the toolbar will be enabled, and you can "play" the object. This feature allows you to use a video clip or picture file to represent a process to help explain it to an audience. These image, sound, and video clips can be stored in the database if you have the resources and if you have checked the appropriate check box in the **Options→Customize→Advanced** or the **Options→Customize→Graphics** dialog boxes.

The Multimedia tab also provides a set of annotations you can attach to an object. An annotation is some text or a graphic (.BMP or .DIB) file or both that appears on the diagram next to the object, in all view modes, to explain it. To display any annotations, you must turn on the *Annotation* option (**Options→Customize→Graphics**). Annotations are useful tools for including text and images that describe your objects on a diagram.

TIP
You can run another program by clicking an object and clicking on the Execute button. The Multimedia tab lets you specify the program that the Process Modeller executes. For example, you can open a presentation software package with a slide show when you select a particular process icon. Another idea would be to run a spreadsheet with a graphic display of sales or inventory. Since this is saved with the definition, you can run this program whenever you see this process on a diagram.

Clearly, the multimedia extensions of this tool are solely for presentation purposes, but they allow you to use the data from the repository along with multimedia files to help present your view of the system, which may assist in the communication process and will surely gain attention.

Other Menu and Toolbar Functions

In addition to the standard diagrammer functions discussed in Chapter 2 and the Drill Up/Down Organization and Open Up/Down functions mentioned earlier in this chapter, the Process Modeller menu contains some other items. The toolbar buttons (other than those on the drawing toolbar) that are not part of the standard set handle some of the menu features, providing multimedia execution buttons and Drill Up/Down buttons. The Layout, Tools, Window, and Help menus all have the expected functionality and need no further explanation.

Right-Click Mouse Menus

Using the right-click mouse menus on the diagrammer itself can speed up your work because you do not need to search through the menu bar or look for a toolbar button to perform some operations. They contain, as in most Windows programs, context-sensitive items. For example, when you right-click on a store, the following menu appears:

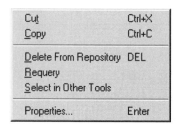

This menu offers items that you might need in order to manipulate the store itself. There are similar, but slightly different menus for process steps, flows, and org units.

File Menu

As mentioned in Chapter 2, you can include summary information in the diagram definition and also place it on the diagram as a title block. Choose the Summary Information item from the File menu and check the items you want to see on the title block.

Edit Menu

The only nonstandard item in the Edit menu is the Element item, which allows you to go to an element's properties dialog without selecting **Edit→Properties** on the menu or double-clicking on the element's symbol. This option provides a quick way to view or edit a particular element's properties and is useful on large diagrams where you may not be able to find elements easily.

View Menu

The View menu contains several nonstandard items in addition to Drill Up/Down Organization and the Symbol, Enhanced Symbol, and Iconic view modes already described. Show Annotation, if checked, displays any object annotations you defined on the Multimedia tab, and Image does the same for images defined for elements.

Utilities Menu

The Utilities menu has some unique and useful items, including options for the following:

- **Restore Graphical Preferences** restores the default set of customizations saved for a diagram after you have made changes to the preferences.

- **Update Selected** allows you to change properties of all elements in a group that you select by dragging a selection box around them or holding down CTRL and clicking to select multiple items. Changing the properties of a group of selected objects is a standard operation you can perform in the Repository Object Navigator as well.

- **Calculate Critical Path** and **Reset Critical Path** manage the critical paths of elements that affect the amount of time the whole process will take. Any changes made to a component of the critical path affect the duration of the process.

- The **Animation** submenu manages animation setup and execution.

- The **Multimedia** submenu starts a multimedia event (Image, Sound, Video, or Program) for an element that has an event defined. The multimedia toolbar buttons also activate these options.

- **Export Data** exports data to another format and creates a file with element information you can import into a spreadsheet or another program so you can print or manipulate the data.

Options Menu

The Options menu includes menu items for **Customize→Basic** and **Customize→Advanced** for specifying features of the BPM. The Customize-Basic dialog (see Figure 4-9) lets you specify up to five programs that will attach to the **Tools→User Defined Command** menu. This gives you a way to run a program directly from the Process Modeller without having to go back to the operating environment to call it. The other areas in this dialog allow you to

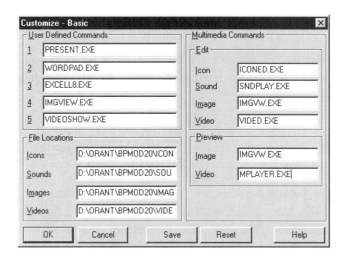

FIGURE 4-9. *Customize-Basic*

indicate which directories contain the files the Process Modeller needs for Iconic mode and multimedia capabilities and what commands or programs you use to edit and, if applicable, preview these icon, sound, image, and video files.

The Customize-Advanced dialog, shown in Figure 4-10, contains the default icon files, icon data file, and the preference set file that contains your Graphics customizations. It also allows you to specify global preferences for how the Process Modeller operates. These customizations apply globally for all diagrams in the application system, but you may need to exit the tool and restart it before some of them take effect.

Where Does This Information Go?

The objects you enter in the Process Modeller show up again when you create other diagrams using the Dataflow Diagrammer and Function Hierarchy Diagrammer. They also flow through the SDLC into the Analysis and Design phases and appear in the Repository Object Navigator's Enterprise Modeling group with the names shown in Table 4-1.

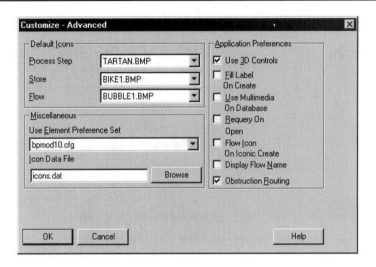

FIGURE 4-10.   *Customize-Advanced*

You can use the processes created here as functions in the Function Hierarchy Diagrammer or Dataflow Diagrammer. The flows and stores can be worked into your dataflow diagram as well. The resource allocation information and business unit assignments are relevant only in the context of

Process Modeller Element	Repository Element and Use in SDLC
Stores	Datastores; cross-checks for data usage on functions
Organization units	Business Units; used to group modules for the module network structure in the Design phase
Process steps	Business Functions; used by the Application Design Transformer to create modules

TABLE 4-1.   *Process Modeller Elements and Repository Elements*

Process Modeller Element	Repository Element and Use in SDLC
Triggers and Outcomes	Events—also called "Triggered By" and "Triggering" as subnodes of Business Functions; used to document which functions cause which others to begin
Flows	Dataflows (Source for Dataflows and Destination for Dataflows) subnodes under a particular Business Function or Datastore; used to cross-check data usage in functions and generate parameters to the modules derived from these functions

TABLE 4-1. *Process Modeller Elements and Repository Elements* (continued)

the Process Modeller, but you can report on them using the Repository Reports tool definition reports for Business Unit, Datastore, Dataflow, and Function. The business unit assignments will actually help the Application Design Transformer figure out how to group functions into modules later in the life cycle.

Entity Relationship Diagrammer

While the Process Modeller concerns itself with the process or functional side of the business area, the Entity Relationship Diagrammer (ER Diagrammer) concentrates on the data side of the business and its details. The data represented here is essentially logical; that is, there may not be actual *physical* tables or data structures that handle the entities on a 1-to-1 basis. An entity represents one instance or occurrence of an object, so an EMPLOYEE entity would appear on the diagram as a box representing one employee. In addition, the entity relationship diagram normally contains the attributes or details for each entity. Relationships appear on the entity relationship diagram (ERD) as lines with "crow's feet" (forks) to represent the "many" side of a relationship and as a single line for the "one" side of a relationship. The diagrammer shows the optionality of a relationship by using dotted lines for an optional relationship and solid lines for a mandatory (required) relationship.

In the Strategy phase, it is important to be complete in identifying entities, but it may not be necessary to identify all attributes of those entities. In fact, you could show the entity relationship diagram with no attributes at all to get a sense from the user as to whether or not the entity side is complete. The diagram at this stage need not be complex or normalized, but you should represent on the diagram all business entities you know about at this point. You will, most probably, add to this set of entities as you find out more about the business.

Relationships are as important as the entities. Oracle Designer considers that a relationship is another type of attribute that describes the entity on the many side or, in the case of a 1-to-1 relationship, on one of the "one" sides. Therefore, you do not create a separate attribute for the many side (foreign key) entity to represent the link to the unique identifier of the other entity. The relationship itself serves as an attribute, and when you create tables from those entities, the relationship creates a column in the table on the many foreign key side. Figure 4-11 shows an Entity Relationship Diagrammer session.

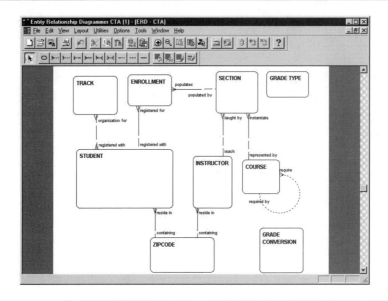

FIGURE 4-11. *Entity Relationship Diagrammer session*

Basic Techniques

The ER Diagrammer, like the Process Modeller, follows many of the common Oracle Designer interface standards mentioned in Chapter 2. However, there are particular considerations for entity relationship diagrams, and this section discusses the specific way Oracle Designer handles the objects or elements in the diagram. As before, this discussion provides the information you need to grasp the tool quickly, but you should consult the online help system for assistance with actions that you find obscure.

Opening a Diagram

You open a diagram in the ER Diagrammer in the same way as in any other Oracle Designer diagrammer: by using the **File→Open** menu choice or the Open button. If you want to create a new diagram, you just click the New button or choose **File→New** from the menu. Either method opens a new window with a drawing surface that you can fill with new objects. You can change the diagram orientation (landscape or portrait) in the **File→Print Setup** dialog box, and you can create extra pages by dragging any item off the existing page. If you have blank pages, you can choose **Layout→Minimize Number of Pages**, and the diagrammer will reduce the number of pages as best it can.

Drawing Objects

You place objects on the diagram either by creating them with the drawing toolbar buttons or by retrieving existing objects with the **Edit→Include** menu item. If you use the latter method to include existing entities, you can include the relationships between those entities at the same time. As with all diagrammers, once the objects exist in the repository, you can arrange them on any number of diagrams with different sets of other elements.

Creating objects with the ER Diagrammer is as simple as clicking the button for the type of element you want to create and drawing it on the surface. If you are creating a relationship, you have to select the correct relationship button and click once on an existing entity to start the relationship, and once more on an existing entity to end it. When placing a new entity, you can click the entity button once and then click in the drawing area once (or drag out a box and release the mouse button) to place the entity. You can resize the entity directly on the drawing surface by selecting it and dragging its corner or side in or out.

If you need to create a subtype, draw the new entity within its supertype entity. An alert dialog will notify you that the subtype is now part of the supertype. If you want to create an arc (mutually exclusive) relationship, select all end labels (using CTRL-click) on the side of the relationships where you want the arc to appear and select **Utilities→Create Arc**. If you want to delete a relationship from an arc, select the arc, select the relationship, and choose **Utilities→Remove From Arc** on the menu.

You create recursive ("pig's ear") relationships by clicking the appropriate relationship button, clicking one side of the entity, and then clicking another side of the same entity. The "from" and "to" ends will go to the same entity.

TIP

When you create a relationship, you need to draw the relationship in the order it appears on the button. Therefore, if you choose the >------ (many-to-1) relationship from the toolbar, the first entity you drop it on will be the "many" side, and the second will be the "one" side.

You can use the Autolayout feature described in the section "Diagrammer Interface" in Chapter 2 to cycle through a random set of layouts. You might consider some system other than the random one: for instance, the traditional "crows fly south and east" system, that is, all of the crows' feet (marking the "many" end of the relationships) are facing either to the top or left of the paper. This places the entities with the most frequency in the upper-left corner and those with the lowest frequency in the lower-right corner. You might choose another format, like the "dead crows" method where crows' feet face down and to the right, but some conscious system for arranging the entities will make your diagram easier to read.

TIP

*If you decide to use a layout system, here's a trick that will help your productivity. Move the entities around on the diagram to the proper position without worrying about how the relationship lines wrap. When the entities are in the right place, select one relationship line, choose **Edit→Select Same Type** from the menu, and click the Autolayout button. This will perform an autolayout on the relationship lines alone. Be sure to **Select Same Type** not **Select All** or you could undo the careful layout you just completed.*

Relationship names never seem to end up in the right place and sometimes need manual moving and resizing. You can resize the invisible box that contains a relationship name by clicking the name so you see the four corners and reshaping this box. This technique is useful if you want the relationship name to run over to more than one line. If it consists of more than one word and space is tight, you can make the box narrower but high enough for as many lines as you need. The clearest position for relationship names is close to the entity they describe. Use a standard position for the relationship lines (for example, the lower left and upper right corners of the line). Double-check your diagram to be sure each relationship name is clearly next to only one relationship and entity. If you can't tell which entity and relationship a name belongs to, select the name and the relationship will also be selected.

You can use the in-place editing technique for modifying an entity or a relationship name by clicking on the name to select it, clicking again to open an edit area, changing the text, and clicking outside the edit area. You can also create perfectly horizontal or vertical lines using the arrow keys. Click on a vertical line and press the UP ARROW and DOWN ARROW keys to straighten it. A similar technique works for horizontal lines using the RIGHT ARROW and LEFT ARROW.

TIP
*One technique that is useful with all elements
is to modify the grid size and turn Snap on
using **Options→Customize**. Then the objects
you place and lines you draw will "snap" to the
grid lines (invisible or not), and you will find
creating straight lines much easier. The
Customize option also lets you display the grid,
which will help you line up entities and
relationships. The grid will print if it is
displayed when you start printing the diagram.*

Naming Objects

Whenever you create a new element anywhere in Oracle Designer, you
have to assign it a name and certain other characteristics. Entities require a
name, short name, and plural name. If you do not fill in the latter two,
Oracle Designer will fill them in with its best guess. Usually, this is fine, but
keep in mind whenever you create an entity the Database Design
Transformer uses the entity's plural name as the name for the table it creates.
Therefore, if you do not like plural table names, you will not like Oracle
Designer's best guess in filling in this property, and you will want to specify
the plural name explicitly using whatever you want as the table name. One
common standard is to name entities with a word or short phrase that is a
singular noun (because an entity is "a thing of significance"). While you are
modeling the business in Strategy and Analysis, entity names may contain
multiple words with spaces between each word.

TIP
*When filling in the new entity dialog, if you
want the plural entity name to be the same as
the normal entity name, you can select the text,
press CTRL-C to copy, navigate to the plural
name field, and press CTRL-V to paste. These
edit keys (along with CTRL-X for cut) are
available in most text-editing boxes.*

Creating relationship names requires a bit of thought. When you draw relationships in the ER Diagrammer, you fill in the "from" name (the side of the relationship that starts it) and the "to" name (the side of the relationship that ends it). In addition to the name, you have to know the cardinality (1-to-many or many-to-many) and optionality (required or not) of the relationship. Also, you should understand how to read the entity relationship diagram.

Reading the Entity Relationship Diagram

The entity relationship diagram is a communication tool as well as an analysis tool. The diagrams you produce say much about the business you are modeling, so if you will be cross-checking the model with users or clients, it is essential that you explain everything that the diagram represents. Since people can readily understand the concept of an entity, most of your explanation should concern the relationships, which can represent sometimes complex business rules. You can use any system you want to name your relationships, but the traditional Oracle CASE Method system uses this syntax:

> **Each** *A* **[may | must] be** *relationship_name* **[one and only one | one or more]** *B*

A is the name of the entity on the "from" end of the relationship, *relationship_name* is the name of the relationship on the diagram, and *B* is the entity on the "to" end of the relationship. You choose one of the may/must and one-and-only-one/one-or-more pairs to represent the optionality of the "from" end and cardinality of the "to" end, respectively. For example, you might construct a relationship between the two entities as in the following illustration:

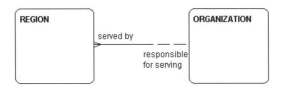

You read this diagram in the following way:

> **"Each organization may be responsible for serving one or more regions; each region must be served by one and only one organization."**

Notice that you need two independent clauses to be complete, because just as with relationships between people, relationships between entities are a two-way street. Also, both of the clauses start with "each" to clarify that the entity you are describing is a singular thing. The syntax makes both cardinality and optionality completely explicit and provides a standard and unconfusing way to read and understand the relationships. You may be tempted to say something like "There is a 1-to-many relationship between organizations and regions" or "Each organization has many regions." The problem with these statements is that they do not clarify the exact relationship; they do not indicate that there are two sides to the relationship; and they do not explain which is the many side or if it is mandatory.

Although using this syntax is not required, you should consider adopting it, because when Oracle Designer lists relationships on reports, it constructs the sentences using this template.

Using the Symbol Set

There are only two main symbols in the ERD, as Figure 4-12 shows: entities and relationships. Entities can have subtypes (entities within them) that use the same entity symbols as the supertype. Relationships can have different cardinality and optionality values, but they are all essentially just lines between entities. Arc, or mutually exclusive, relationships appear as two or more relationships joined by a rounded line symbol.

Using Attributes and Domains

A normal entity relationship diagram contains all attributes for all entities as well as designations of the datatypes and optionality. In addition, you can use domains to assist in creating attributes. A *domain* is a named collection of properties for attributes and columns, including datatype, size, decimal places, derivation (calculation expression), and the set of allowable values. When you attach a domain to an attribute, the attribute takes on all characteristics of that domain. This makes defining the attribute easier and

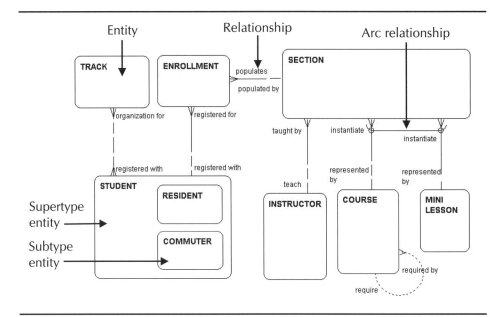

FIGURE 4-12. *Entity Relationship Diagrammer symbols*

allows you to change all attributes in a domain by changing the domain definition and running a utility to propagate the changes.

You create the attribute definitions for an entity in the Entity property dialog. In the Strategy phase, you do not necessarily need to go into attribute details.

Domains and attributes are explained more fully in Chapter 10, in the section on the Entity Relationship Diagrammer.

Other Menu and Toolbar Functions

The ER Diagrammer menus and toolbars contain a few other items not discussed in Chapter 2 nor yet mentioned in this chapter. The File, Edit, View, Tools, Window, and Help menus contain the common items discussed before. The extra toolbar buttons handle some of the commonly used functions in the menu system.

CAUTION
*It bears repeating that **Edit→Cut** removes the
element from the diagram but not from the
repository and **Edit→Delete** (or pressing the DEL
key) removes the element both from the
diagram and from the repository. When you
delete an entity, Oracle Designer also deletes
all attributes and attached relationships.*

Layout Menu

The Utilities menu provides a number of Autolayout functions. Before you
use any of these, you should save your diagram, because although you can
return to the last Autolayout, you cannot return to the original layout if you
do not like any of the random layouts you use. If you have saved the
diagram, you can always close the diagram without saving and reopen it in
its original form.

In addition to the standard Minimize Number of Pages operation, the
Layout menu also offers the Rescale Diagram item. This option resizes
elements and fonts to fit on the number of pages you specify. It is especially
useful in an automatic layout situation.

TIP
*The first time you click the Autolayout button,
you will not be able to press Previous Layout to
return to the previous layout but you can select
Edit→Undo to go back to the last layout. After
you press Autolayout the second time, the
Previous Layout button will be available, so
you can return to the previous layouts.*

Options Menu

The Options menu contains the normal Text Editor, Broadcast, and
Diagnostics items. In addition, it has the Customize item, which displays the
dialog shown in Figure 4-13. This provides the usual properties for fonts,
lines, and colors. It also allows you to modify to some degree how
Autolayout will create a new arrangement of objects. This dialog also lets

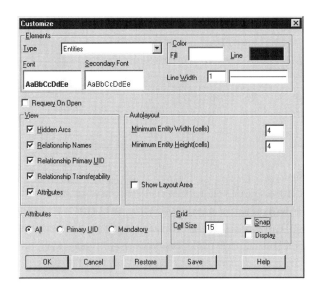

FIGURE 4-13. *ER Diagrammer Customize dialog*

you set the grid options as well as whether or not the attributes and relationships will display with the entities.

Utilities Menu

Other than the operations to create, add to, and remove from arcs already discussed, the Utilities menu contains the following options:

- **Table to Entity Retrofit** creates entity definitions from table definitions. This option is useful when you capture the design of an existing database in the Analysis phase, as discussed in Chapter 8.

- **Update Attributes in Domains** propagates changes in domains to attributes associated with those domains. Chapter 10 discusses this utility further.

- **Database Design Transformer** creates design objects (for example, tables and columns) from the analysis objects (for example, entities and attributes). Chapter 12 gives more details on this utility.

- **Function/Attribute Matrix** assigns attributes to functions if there are already entity usages for those functions. Chapter 8 discusses this utility in the context of the Dataflow Diagrammer.

- **Convert ERD 1.1 Diagrams** is helpful if you migrate the repository from Oracle CASE version 5.0 or 5.1 to Oracle Designer. It converts the entity relationship diagrams to the new format.

Where Does This Information Go?

The entity, attribute, and relationship information in the strategy ERD carries over into the Analysis phase, where you modify and add to the definitions. No other diagrammers share these elements, although the Dataflow Diagrammer and Function Hierarchy Diagrammer allow you to attach entity and attribute *usages*—which define the data sources for the process (function), flow, or store—to their elements. In the Pre-Design phase, the elements transform from logical Analysis phase elements into the physical design data elements, as Table 4-2 shows.

In addition, the table definition can reference the entity or entities it was created from. This is called a *table entity usage* and defines a link from the table to the entity for documentation and design capture purposes.

Strategy and Analysis Data Element	Design Data Element
Entity	Table
Attribute	Column
Primary unique identifier	Primary key constraint
Non-Primary unique identifier	Unique constraint
1-to-many relationship	Foreign key constraint and foreign key column
Many-to-many relationship	Intersection table and foreign key constraints
Arc and subtype/supertype relationships	Single tables or multiple tables with special columns to link them

TABLE 4-2. *Strategy Data Elements and Their Design Counterparts*

Tracking Documents in RON

While these diagrammers create the models needed for the Strategy Document, there will still be some documentation that you prepare outside Oracle Designer. The repository allows you to create references to the source documents in the repository node Documents. This is an activity that you perform in the Repository Object Navigator, as shown in Figure 4-14.

The Documents repository element definition holds information about the document such as its name, location, and status. It also includes properties for descriptions and notes. Adding this tracking information to the repository allows you to keep an online list of the documents that are important to the system. You can run a Repository Report, called *Document Definition*, to show the document definitions you created in the repository. Chapter 6 discusses the Repository Object Navigator and the methods you will use to perform the maintenance of these document definitions.

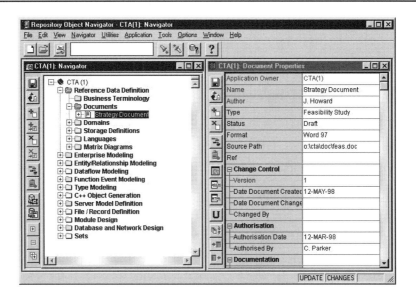

FIGURE 4-14. *Defining a Document in the Repository Object Navigator*

CHAPTER
5

Pre-Analysis

You're traveling through yet another project. A project of sight and sound but no mind. A journey into a wondrous land whose boundary is the budget. You are now entering the Analysis Zone. (Apologies to Rod Serling.)

 n the Pre-Analysis phase, the goals are to plan the analysis process and to begin establishing analysis standards for Oracle Designer. Since the goal of Analysis is to gather and organize all of the substantive user requirements, the Analysis Plan, when executed, should result in an understanding of what the business does and what kind of automated support it can use.

Overview of the Pre-Analysis Phase

The Analysis phase breaks logically into two parts: information gathering and requirements analysis. Within the information-gathering portion of Analysis, techniques for getting at user requirements include interviews, questionnaires, electronic bulletin boards and list management systems, joint application development (JAD) sessions, along with reviews of the legacy system, the report audit, and user and system documentation.

In requirements analysis, we extract the system requirements from the information gathered and place them in an organized structure. After each interview, an ERD sketch, small function hierarchy, and/or mini-process flow can be generated specific to that interview. Once some quantity of information has been gathered, some system-level requirements analysis can begin. In requirements analysis, the information from the various sources is synthesized in an effort to create the Analysis ERD, analysis process flows, and overall function hierarchy.

As this synthesis takes place, gaps in the information are discovered along with conflicting information and inconsistent requirements. Therefore, the analyst must go back to the users and ask more questions and do more information gathering, which must then be integrated into what was collected previously. Thus the two aspects of the whole analysis process are not completely discrete or linear. There is a need to move back and forth between gathering the information and analyzing it.

Because of this need to alternate between gathering and analyzing business requirements, an essential aspect of the Analysis Plan is flexibility.

As the project progresses through the Analysis phase, new sources of requirements become evident. The Analysis Plan needs to have a built-in mechanism for ongoing review to ensure that any opportunities for other areas of analysis are found and incorporated into the plan and provisions are made for resolving conflicts and inconsistencies, usually through JAD sessions. Of course, it is impossible to predict all possible new sources or areas of information that might be discovered; however, when creating the analysis budget, count on the likelihood that some unforeseen information sources will arise.

The developers are the primary users of the Analysis Plan. The plan will serve as a guide through the Analysis phase. Other users of the Analysis Plan include the project leaders and the person in charge of quality assurance.

Within CADM, the Pre-Analysis phase is a transitional period between Strategy and Analysis in which the project team initiates and performs the preparation work and obtains approval to proceed with Analysis.

It is difficult to discuss the Analysis Plan without also thoroughly discussing all of the analysis topics. This chapter lays out the structure of the Analysis Plan without going into depth regarding how each part of the plan will be executed. Details of how to execute the Analysis Plan are deferred until the appropriate sections on information gathering and requirements analysis in Chapters 7 and 9, respectively.

Deliverables

The deliverable for Pre-Analysis is the Analysis Plan. The Analysis Plan is more than just a Microsoft Project Plan. The following sections should be included in the Analysis Plan:

- **Detailed workplan and schedule for the Analysis phase** This schedule must be flexible and will be tentative at this point in the SDLC since it is difficult to estimate how long each step will take. Analysis is the vaguest part of most projects because we do not yet have a clear idea of the size and scope of the entire project.

- **Rearticulation of the project environment** In the Strategy Document, we described the political environment, motivation, project organization and staffing, business impact, and other environmental factors. The Strategy Document can be very long and much of this information can get buried. It should be modified if necessary and redelivered to make sure that all members of the project team sign off on the document.

- **Sources of Analysis information and data collection strategies for each source** You should identify all of the possible sources of information to be gathered, including complete code walkthroughs, report audits, interviews, JAD sessions, system and user documentation reviews, and any other sources of information.

- **Format, structure and content of the requirements document (which is the deliverable of the Analysis phase)** This includes specifying what deliverables are included in the Analysis phase.

- **Description of the actual Analysis phase processes** As you move through the information gathering and analysis, you must have a plan for quality controls to ensure the accuracy and completeness of the analysis process.

Goals of Pre-Analysis

From the Pre-Analysis deliverables, it should be clear what the goal of this phase is, namely to develop a detailed plan to guarantee that when Analysis is finished the requirements will have been completely and competently gathered.

All parts of the Analysis Plan should be periodically reviewed throughout the project. These reviews should be included in the Analysis Plan itself. Time required to review and modify the plan should be built into the project plan. There is little chance that you will correctly and accurately develop a complete Analysis Plan until Analysis is well under way. The Analysis Plan should and will be continually refined.

Information Gathering

No single source of information for user requirements is sufficient. The Analysis Plan should identify multiple sources and information gathering methods. Interviews should be conducted with both high-level management and low-level system users. The analysts should walk through the existing business processes with employees at different levels and, if relevant, observe how the work is done.

A thorough audit of the legacy system should also be planned. Code walkthroughs of the legacy system will be required to find the business rules implemented in the code.

The Analysis Plan should estimate the number of individuals that need to be interviewed and how much time should be spent with each one. It may be useful to conduct some of the actual interviews at this point. Doing some actual analysis as part of the Pre-Analysis phase will allow the analyst to better estimate the time required for the Analysis phase.

User-Supplied Requirements

Consider the following means of gathering information from people for inclusion in the Analysis Plan:

- Interviews

- Questionnaires

- E-mail list servers or Web-based groupware

- Joint application development (JAD) sessions

The question, of course, that arises is "Who should be interviewed or surveyed?" Never count on a single source of information. Whether this single source is an individual, a committee, or a group, all of the necessary information will not be elicited from one place. Interviews conducted with groups can be effective, but the group itself has a dynamic of its own. Each individual in the group should be interviewed individually as well.

You should interview users who have experience with the legacy system or will need to use the new system. These users can supply details regarding processes, data requirements, system functionality, and constraints.

To be successful, the analyst should talk to a variety of users. Some very important sources of information are the architects or maintainers of the legacy system. They often know more about how the system actually functions in their specific business environment than the users. Systems people, managers, and rank-and-file users may also have valuable input.

Interviews

Interviewing is a complex and important step. Open-ended interviews with users are the traditional requirements analysis method most commonly employed. In these interviews, one or more analysts sit down with one or more users. Such interviews are probably the most important source of user requirements in the design of a new system.

Interviewing managers is just as important as interviewing actual system users. Managers sometimes have a broader vision and better understanding of the overall process. They are often more open to reengineering, although they may have less understanding of the day-to-day operations and decisions faced by the end users.

Legacy system developers can often make important contributions to the gathering of user requirements. Since they are very familiar with the existing system, they can provide information about requirements that are hard-coded in the legacy system.

Analysis cannot be performed without talking to representatives from all of the groups mentioned here. Talking to only one group results in an incomplete analysis. The workplan should allocate time for interview planning (including identifying candidates, setting the date, and developing questions), conducting the interview, and post-interview documentation and confirmation.

Questionnaires

Open-ended interviews require skilled interviewers and generate a considerable amount of information that is difficult to collate and analyze. This can be a very labor-intensive process. Using questionnaires is less labor intensive and less expensive. If carefully designed, questionnaires don't even need to be administered in person; they can be administered by mail or e-mail.

Analysis and collation of information from questionnaires is inexpensive. However, the creation of high-quality interviewing instruments is difficult. Inexpertly created interview questionnaires will generate misleading results.

E-Mail List Servers or Web-Based Groupware

Two surprisingly underutilized methods of exchanging ideas and building user consensus are e-mail list servers or Web-based groupware products. These "electronic bulletin board" type equivalents can provide a relatively free flow of user input without requiring any explicit time scheduled with users.

JAD Sessions

A joint application development (JAD) session is a specific type of analysis and development interview. In a JAD session, you bring together several interested parties and attempt to move the project forward. JAD sessions are usually run with someone acting as a facilitator and can be very effective for solving specific analysis and design problems.

JAD sessions bring together many people at once, so they are very expensive and require extensive planning. A JAD session should always have a very specific agenda. If not run well, JAD sessions can degenerate into forums for venting opinions and for political posturing; run correctly, they can help forge a consensus among parties with differing needs.

Legacy System Review

In formulating the Analysis Plan, you must thoroughly review the legacy system. Unless the new system will be so radically different that the current system is irrelevant, a legacy system review is necessary. This review should include the elements discussed here.

Code Walkthrough

Business requirements are embedded within the legacy code. The analyst either needs to personally walk through the legacy system code or work with the legacy system developers to determine user requirements embedded in the code.

Report Audit

A report audit is a review and analysis of all the reports produced by the legacy system. The analysts should plan to perform a report audit to determine what reports will be retained, discarded, or changed from those in the original system.

User Walkthrough

The analysts must sit down with users and have them walk through actual business transactions in the legacy system. This will allow the analysts to see what parts of the system are being used and how they are used.

User and System Documentation Review

A review of the user documentation can frequently bring to light user requirements not found in any other source. The user documentation may discuss user requirements that, if the system is mature, may have been assumed for so long that no one mentions them. Similarly, a review of the system documentation, if it exists, can help uncover system requirements.

Requirements Analysis

All of the information-gathering mechanisms generate pages of notes that must be analyzed. Each document must be read, and the relevant user requirements must be extracted for further processing. The number of requirements varies and serves as the backbone of the Analysis phase.

Oracle Designer has an element called Objectives, which, at first glance, seems like it would suffice for storing requirements. However, there is really a difference between requirements and objectives. Nevertheless, Oracle Designer has no separate element type specifically for requirements. In addition to storing the requirements, you need to store the associations from requirements to other repository elements such as functions. One method you can use outside the repository is to build the tables for the requirements and associations to existing repository elements, as the ERD in Figure 5-1 shows.

Alternatively, you can create a new Oracle Designer repository element, called Requirements, by employing the User Extensibility feature. If you also add extensions for the association elements needed to link these to the existing elements, such as functions, the system can be implemented entirely in Oracle Designer. The implementation of these extensions in Oracle Designer is discussed in Chapter 27 on User Extensibility.

Analysis ERD

The Analysis ERD attempts to capture as many of the data-related business rules as possible in a diagram. No consideration is given to performance or to the feasibility or implementation of a rule. The only goal is to fairly represent the business requirements. Data-related business rules that cannot be implemented in the ERD are stated as text.

There is some disagreement among analysts as to the correct scope of an Analysis ERD. Many analysts advocate a higher-level approach that ignores many details. Others take performance and other aspects of physical implementation into consideration when designing their ERD. Whatever

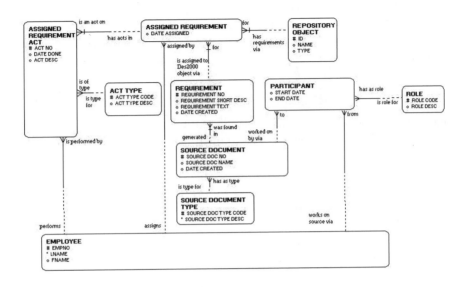

FIGURE 5-1. *Entity relationship diagram for tracking requirements*

approach you decide to take, it is essential that the approach is well documented and adhered to by all members of the design team.

Function Hierarchy

In Pre-Analysis, the function hierarchy serves to organize user requirements into functional areas. Little attempt should be made at this point to identify functions that will actually map to application modules.

Map of Requirements to Repository Elements

Each requirement must be mapped to one or more functions or entities. It is impractical and unnecessary to map functions down to the attribute level at this point, although it may sometimes make logical sense to do so.

Process Flows

Detailed process flows that show both existing business processes and proposed changes under the new system need to be shown. These process flows must be very specific, showing detailed aspects of the business.

Conflict Resolution and Change Control

Rules and procedures for handling conflicts must be specifically spelled out in the Analysis Plan—including a mechanism for dealing with conflicting user requirements.

The Analysis Plan should specify the procedures for making changes when new sources of requirements are found or when other changes need to be made to the Analysis Plan.

The Analysis Plan

The Analysis Plan describes the Analysis Document including the structure and format of the Analysis Document and how information will be gathered, tracked, and analyzed. It should describe each step in the analysis process in detail. Everything from who will be interviewed to the final format of the ERD and what the process flows will look like must be decided. For example, how will feedback to interview notes be given? Will notes be compiled at every meeting or weekly? At what point will user sign-off be required? The Analysis Plan should include answers to these questions in order to give the client a clear picture of what the analysis process will entail.

The Analysis Plan should provide estimates for a legacy system review, listing the resources needed, time estimates, and a description of interim deliverables. In addition, a process flow diagram should show how information will be gathered during the Analysis interviews and how other information-gathering activities will be organized and recorded.

Naming Conventions

As items are added to the function hierarchy, Analysis ERD, and process flows, decisions must be made about naming them. It is necessary to figure out what will be the standard for naming various objects. In general, the principle is to facilitate communication back to the users. There is nothing wrong with extremely verbose names for repository objects and extensive descriptions. Terse, obscure abbreviations have no place in Analysis. However, you may want to use some to minimize the amount of typing for the Design phase. It is appropriate to periodically print out a list of all repository objects to ensure that abbreviations are applied consistently.

A standard that is frequently employed is to use no abbreviations at all for any words within Analysis. For example, the attribute representing "Employee Last Name" would be called EMPLOYEE LAST NAME. However, it is better to employ a limited set of abbreviations where they will not obscure the meaning of the objects. For example, you might want, as an organization, to create a table such as the one shown in Table 5-1.

If such a limited set of abbreviations is going to be used, the list should be relatively small—no more than 100 abbreviations. These should be limited to only the most commonly used terms. It must be strictly enforced that these are the only abbreviations used and that they are applied consistently throughout the design process. Any word not on the approved abbreviation list must be spelled out completely. As with any standard, a precise definition of the standard is not as important as the meticulous application of the standard. The person with the role of repository manager should enforce this.

Analysis Plan Example

This section presents an example of an Analysis Plan for the redesign of a small legacy system. This small project will make relatively minor

Word	Abbreviation
company	COMPY
contract	CONTC
department	DEPT
division	DIVSN
employee	EMP

TABLE 5-1. *Sample Abbreviations*

modifications to the legacy system. The primary Analysis phase focus in this project is a thorough analysis of the legacy system.

Since this is a very small application with relatively few requirements, the requirements document will be a simple narrative with appropriate sections for each module within the system. A real Analysis Plan, however, may be dozens of pages long. Because the example system is so small, the information-gathering process can be relatively informal. A rule of thumb is that the bigger the system, the more formal the requirements gathering process should be.

Sample Analysis Plan

To complete the Analysis Plan, we will do the following:

- By looking at the data structures, we will determine the data-related business requirements.

- By looking at the applications, we will determine the required functionality that the applications must support.

- We will interview users of the system to find out what changes they want in the current system.

 NOTE
Keep in mind that even with a small system it is necessary to interview more than one user at more than one level within the organization.

- We will write up the user requirements and give them to the users for sign-off.

- As part of our analysis, we will prepare a preliminary storyboard and prototype of the revised application. Because we have a working legacy system database, we can prototype the new system against the working database using live production data.

- We will pass the storyboard and prototype to users for feedback.

- We will redesign the storyboard and prototype to reflect user feedback.

We will declare the Analysis phase complete when the users approve the revised storyboard and prototype.

Workplan

Here are our time estimates for completing the Analysis Plan:

- Legacy system analysis (2 days)
- User interviews (1 day)

NOTE
Depending upon user availability, user interviews may take more than one calendar day.

- Analysis and write-up of information (2 days)
- Presentation of analysis to users for feedback (1 day)
- Preparation of storyboard and prototype (3 days)
- Presentation of storyboard and prototype to users for sign-off (1 day)

Modifications for Smaller Systems

For a small project, the entire Pre-Analysis phase may not be required, assuming the Strategy Document provided sufficient detail to move right into Analysis. However, for medium-sized projects, a Pre-Analysis transition phase is recommended. The main reason for performing a careful analysis is to have an audit trail of points leading up to the building of the system. It is just as important to know that the user requirements have been met in a medium-sized system as it is in a large one.

As mentioned earlier, most analysts skip Pre-Analysis, even for large projects. An important statistic from many business studies going back to the 1960s and 1970s should be kept in mind: *Approximately 80 percent of all projects fail.*

One common reason for these failures is the taking of shortcuts in the methodology. Consider several real-life examples of projects that started out without a lot of structure:

- On one project, at the beginning of Analysis, the project leader had failed to set any standards for how Analysis would be done. No entity/attribute naming standards were created, nor were format for descriptions, or guidance on how to gather and record information during Analysis provided. Instead, each analyst went off on his/her own and did what was perceived to be best. This resulted in inconsistent and frequently substandard work. Much of the analysis had to be redone and many weeks were lost in trying to finalize the data model.

- In another case, rather than performing an audit of the Analysis data model, the project moved directly into development. It was later discovered that there were hundreds of errors, inconsistencies, missing attributes, and other mistakes in the data model. Correcting these mistakes, all of the associated applications had to be modified, placing the project months behind schedule.

- The third example occurred in a large state tax collection organization. Instead of putting the system through rigorous testing, because of time constraints the system was moved directly into production. This resulted in documents that were supposed to be auto scanned turning out to be "unscannable" and requiring manual entry of the information.

The lesson to be learned here is that it is critical to the success of any project to stay methodologically sound throughout CADM. There is always a danger in believing that a project is not as big as it really is and skipping crucial steps. This is especially true when the system being designed must be integrated with an existing system.

When Is the Pre-Analysis Phase Complete?

The Pre-Analysis phase can be considered complete when the lead developer, lead client, and any other primary clients are satisfied with the proposed analysis process. The project team members should feel confident that they have the right level of detail to proceed with the Analysis phase.

Pre-Analysis is one of the most difficult phases in which to assess completion, mainly, as mentioned at the beginning of this chapter, because the Analysis Plan must be flexible and may be changed throughout the analysis process. Practically, though, you should begin Analysis as soon as the project leader and management approve the Analysis Plan.

The Analysis Plan written in the Pre-Analysis phase should lay out the entire Analysis phase, from information gathering to the completion of the Analysis Document.

CHAPTER
6

Oracle Designer in Pre-Analysis

Where is the wisdom we have lost in knowledge?
Where is the knowledge we have lost in information?
                              —T.S. Eliot (1888-1965) *The Rock,* 1934

And where is the information we have lost in the repository?

 he main deliverable in the Pre-Analysis phase is the Analysis Plan. Oracle Designer provides some of the material for this plan and helps you prepare other Pre-Analysis deliverables, as Table 6-1 outlines.

This chapter describes how to use two Oracle Designer utilities, the Repository Object Navigator and Repository Reports, in the Pre-Analysis phase to complete these deliverables. You will find these tools handy for the Oracle Designer work you do throughout the CADM phases. Chapter 27 fully describes the Repository Administration Utility procedure that you might use to track system requirements in Oracle Designer, but this chapter will mention how the user extensions created in that tool can assist in this phase.

This discussion assumes that you have read Chapter 2 and know the basics of how to use the common features of the diagrammers and utilities. You should also familiarize yourself with the extensive online help system and tutorial if you need step-by-step help in performing common operations.

Activity or Deliverable	Oracle Designer Tool
Spot-check the strategy definitions	Repository Object Navigator
Create a new version of the application system	Repository Object Navigator
Produce reports on the strategy repository definitions for the Analysis Plan	Repository Reports
Map system requirements to repository elements	Repository Administration Utility

TABLE 6-1. *Pre-Analysis Activities and Designer Tools*

Repository Object Navigator

One major function you perform in the Repository Object Navigator (RON) is to access and manipulate the properties of any element in the repository. (The other, to perform administrative tasks on application systems, is discussed in Chapter 26.) You use the Repository Object Navigator in the Pre-Analysis phase to view the element definitions you created in the Strategy phase and add any missing information easily and quickly. You can also use it to create a new version of the application system created in the Strategy phase that will be the basis for the Analysis phase. Its main interface consists of a Navigator window (the same style as those in the Oracle Developer design tools) and a Property Palette. Together, these give you quick access to the properties you defined for elements in the diagrammers or other utilities. Figure 6-1 shows these two windows.

The RON menu system also gives you access to all other utilities and tools. RON serves as a common launch point outside the Oracle Designer

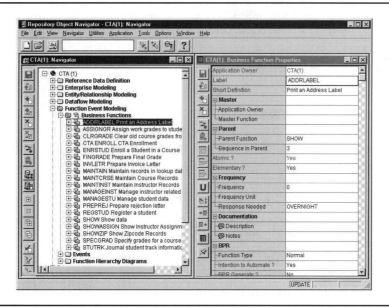

FIGURE 6-1. *RON Navigator and Property Palette*

window and has many user-friendly aspects, such as allowing you to drag and drop elements between application systems and change the properties of multiple elements in a single update operation.

You will find RON useful throughout your work in the CADM life cycle, from the birth of the application system to its versioning and completion. The more familiar you become with the methods and buttons in the Navigator and Property Palette, the easier your work will be later.

NOTE
Although diagrams appear in the Navigator window's Set group, you cannot actually create, delete, or manipulate them, but you can inspect the elements that they include by right-clicking on the diagram's icon and selecting Open Diagram from the menu.

Basic Techniques

The Repository Object Navigator is a repository utility and you interact with it in a different way than with the diagrammers. The main operations you perform here involve viewing and editing information displayed in the Navigator and Property Palette.

Arranging the Screen

You start a typical session in RON by clicking on its icon in the Designer opening window, maximizing the window and opening the application system (using **File→Open**), if it is not already on the screen. You then select **Window→Tile Vertically** (being sure the Navigator window is active, so that window appears on the left). This procedure arranges the screen as in Figure 6-1 and gives you the largest view of each window. This action reduces the likelihood that you will need to move the windows around later in the session, an activity that may be fun to some, but one that really just reduces productivity. All other actions in RON at this point consist of finding and changing properties using the two windows.

If you are used to the workings of the Oracle Developer Navigator and Property Palette, you will find many similarities in the workings of RON's

Navigator and Property Palette. There are some differences, however, such as the following:

- When you copy properties in the Property Palette in Oracle Designer, all properties will not be copied automatically; you have to explicitly select the property names by highlighting them before you copy them.

- Collapsing property categories in the Property Palette is effective only for a single session. RON forgets the setup of the collapsed categories, so when you start it again you must redo the collapsing if you want it to be in effect. This is different from Oracle Developer, which saves the collapsed property category characteristics.

Working in the Navigator Window

The Navigator and Property Palette in RON follow the same operating paradigm as the other Oracle Designer navigator utilities. The methods for collapsing and expanding nodes in the Navigator and for viewing and working with properties are the same as the standard interface outlined in Chapter 2. RON has some techniques you will use that are specific to the way it works.

NOTE
The icon next to each element in the hierarchy denotes the element type of that definition. You can also determine the element type from the node name above the definition. If you are viewing a reference and don't recognize the element type of the icon, click on the help toolbar button and click the mouse help cursor on the name of the object. The help system topic on that element type will appear.

FINDING OBJECTS IN THE NAVIGATOR RON offers you several ways of viewing and finding the elements that comprise your application. The standard hierarchy view in RON is the Group view, as Figure 6-2 shows.

This view organizes the elements into functional areas based on how you design and develop a system. The RON help system documents these

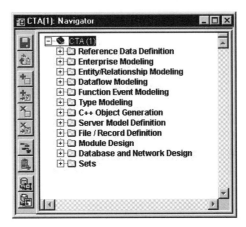

FIGURE 6-2. *RON Group view*

groups in a topic called Group View. As you browse the groups, you will see logically placed element nodes, such as the following elements in the Enterprise Modeling group:

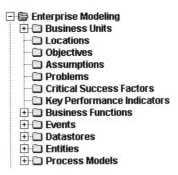

The first step to modifying or adding element definitions in RON is to find the element type in this group listing. If you know the element type you want, you can choose **View→UnGroup View** from the menu to display the Element Type view. This view shows all primary element nodes in the "traditional," Designer version 1 order, as in Figure 6-3. This order, called

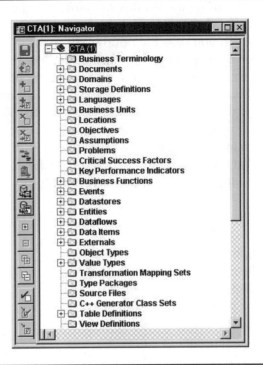

FIGURE 6-3. *RON Element Type view*

Element Type Sequence, reflects the sequence in which elements might be defined during system development, as follows:

1. Universal types used throughout the life cycle

2. Strategy and Analysis objects

3. Design and Build objects

4. Diagrams from all phases

5. User-defined sets created to help move objects between repositories

Another ordering, called *Element Type Name,* just alphabetizes the nodes without regard to the development sequence. You can choose which sort order you prefer by using the **Navigator→Sort** menu choice. This choice is available only when you select the application system node or an element node, not when you select a group node. RON remembers the view but not the sort order when you exit and reenter the tool.

The next step to modifying element definitions is to find the exact element definition to work on. Keep expanding subnodes until you find the element. If you know the name of the element you want to find, you can select the application system name at the top of the hierarchy and type the name or part of the name in the Find field next to the Print button. Then click the Find Next button directly to the right of this field. The cursor will jump to an element with that name if there is a match.

CAUTION
Be sure to expand the node you think the object will be in, or Find will not locate the object, unless the node in which the object exists has been expanded at some time in your session. Once the parent node has been expanded, even if it is collapsed when you run the search, the Find command will work properly. When you run subsequent searches, RON will start a prefix search, trying to match the item as you are still typing it.

Another, more flexible way to search for element definitions is by using the dialog you display with the **Navigator→Search Repository** menu item. If you have selected an element type or element definition, the dialog will display the properties of that element, as Figure 6-4 shows.

You enter the search criteria in this dialog and press the Search button. If there are matches, another dialog will appear, where you can select one of the matches and press the Locate in Navigator button to move the cursor selection in the Navigator to that definition. You can also press the Show Where Used button to display a list of all objects that reference the selected one. You can then navigate to one of those with the Locate in Navigator button, if needed.

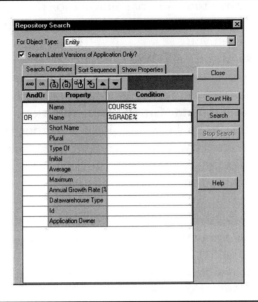

FIGURE 6-4. *Repository Search dialog*

NOTE
You can quickly load a particular diagram from the RON hierarchy by clicking the diagram name in the Diagrams node (in the Sets group) and choosing Open Diagram from the right-click mouse menu. If the appropriate diagrammer is not open at the time, it will load and open the diagram you clicked. If the diagrammer is open, focus will shift to the diagrammer, where you can perform **File→Open** *to open the diagram.*

CUSTOMIZE YOUR RON!   If the group, element type, sequence, and name sort views are not enough for you and you want more control over how the Navigator displays the elements, you can set up your own order and groupings. There are three sets of configuration dialogs you can use to do this: Navigator Groups, Navigator Views, and Filter Query.

NAVIGATOR GROUPS DIALOGS   When you display the Group view in RON, you are looking at a full set of predefined elements under each group. You can switch off the display of one or more groups using the **Options→Customize Navigator Groups** menu selection. This opens the dialog shown in Figure 6-5, where you specify the groups you want enabled and displayed the next time you open the application system. In addition, you can add your own groups to this list. Use the Customize tab of the same dialog to add groups and specify which element types will be part of each group.

   To cause the group to be displayed in the Navigator window, you must change the Navigator view. When you invoke the **View→Include Navigator Groups** menu item, the list of groups will include the new group, but it will be unselected. You need to select it, by checking its check box, so it will appear in the Navigator window. RON may not remember these settings

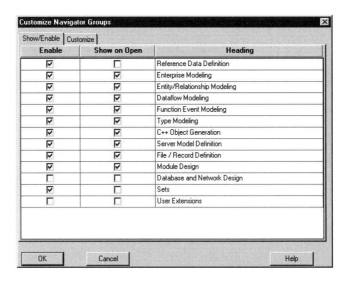

FIGURE 6-5.   *Customize Navigator Groups dialog*

when you close it, so when you reopen the application system, it will show all groups that you set as displayed in the **Options→Customize Navigator Groups** dialog. If the group was not enabled in that dialog, you will not see it in the **View→Include Navigator Groups** dialog.

The **View→Include Navigator Groups** item determines which groups of elements you see even if you are using Element Type view, where you do not see the group names themselves. For example, you display the Element Type view and want to hide all Enterprise Modeling elements like Business Units, Entities, and Business Functions. After you select **View→Include Navigator Groups** and deselect the Enterprise Modeling group, all element types that belong only to the Enterprise Modeling group will be hidden. If any element in that group also appears in another group, you need to deselect that group as well. In this example, the Entity/Relationship Modeling group also contains the Entities element so you must uncheck that group in the Include Navigator Groups dialog if you want to hide the Entities element completely.

NAVIGATOR VIEWS DIALOGS   Another way you can add nodes to the Navigator is by adding views in the **Options→Customize Navigator Views** dialog. This dialog, as Figure 6-6 shows, lets you add specific element types to a node of your naming. In addition, you can specify query conditions on various properties to filter the list. You can also

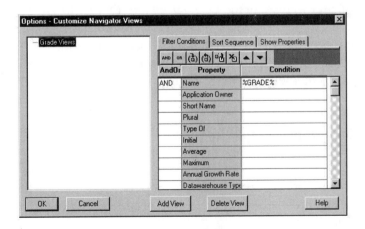

FIGURE 6-6. *Customize Navigator Views dialog*

specify a customized sort condition and designate which properties the Navigator shows.

Once you define custom views, you need to display them using the **View→Include Navigator Views** dialog. This is a list like the Include Navigator Groups list, where you put a check mark on the views you want to show in the Navigator. Once you do that, the new views will appear at the bottom of the Group View list under the Navigator Views node, as the following illustration shows:

If you are displaying the Element Type view in Sequence order, the new views will appear at the bottom of the list. In Name order, the new views will appear in alphabetical order with the other element types.

FILTER QUERY DIALOG FOR FILTERS, PROPERTIES, AND SORTS

RON allows you to set a filter so you can display only a subset of elements. This is useful if you have a large system with hundreds of functions or entities. Select the node for the element type you want to filter and choose **Navigator→Filter** to display the Navigator Filter Query dialog, shown in Figure 6-7. This dialog lets you specify query conditions by typing values in the properties lines and adding AND or OR operators at the beginning of those lines. You can group and ungroup properties to create Boolean logic, as in a SELECT statement's WHERE clause. You can also add and reorder the properties lines. All of these operations occur as a result of pressing toolbar buttons in this dialog.

Navigator→Display Properties shows the third tab of the Filter Query dialog. In this dialog, you check the properties that you want to show in the Navigator. Normally you want to show the name of the element, but there may be other properties that would help identify it more easily for a specific purpose. For example, the *Short Definition* is particularly useful in identifying functions.

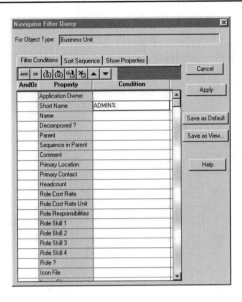

FIGURE 6-7. *Navigator Filter Query dialog*

As mentioned before, you can click on an application system or element type node and select **Navigator→Sort** to display the second tab of the Filter Query dialog. Here you specify the properties used for the sort and whether the sort is ascending or descending.

The menu choices Clear All Filters and Clear Selected Filters in the Navigator menu remove the filter settings for all nodes or selected nodes, respectively.

JUMPING TO OTHER OBJECTS   Oracle Designer provides a handy technique for jumping to an object defined somewhere else. For example, suppose you have a STUDENTS table that is based on the STUDENT entity and this table is associated with the entity under the table definition node Usages – Mapped to Entities. The blue arrow next to the entity name indicates that this is a referenced element that has a definition elsewhere. If you click the blue arrow or press the Locate Object Definition button, the selection will jump to the source element that contains the definition. Figure 6-8 shows how this looks.

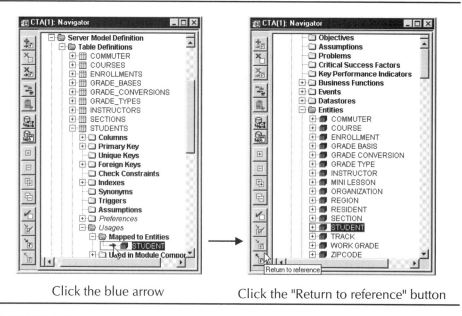

Click the blue arrow   Click the "Return to reference" button

FIGURE 6-8. *Navigating to a referenced element and returning*

This same effect occurs when you have a shared object, denoted by an open-hand icon, and you click this icon. This operation opens the application system that the object is shared from and highlights the object in that system.

You can also set a mark (like a bookmark) so you can return to a particular object. Just select the object and click the Mark button (the check mark symbol). You can then move to any other object definition and click the Goto Mark button, and the selection will jump back to the marked object.

CAUTION
Some navigator buttons may be partially hidden if your Navigator window is too small. This might even be true if your window is maximized but your monitor is set to a low resolution (under 1024×768). You can move the Navigator window up and gradually manipulate it to reveal the buttons or turn off the display of the top toolbar buttons and status line (in the View menu). The long-term solution is a higher resolution.

The mark and reference button actions also appear in the Navigator menu.

OTHER NAVIGATOR TECHNIQUES   There are a few other techniques for the Navigator window worth mentioning. One is the *in-place editing*. Once you navigate to a particular element definition in the hierarchy, you can click on the name that appears and make changes to the property value in the Navigator window itself, rather than having to switch to the Property Palette. While you can show properties other than the name, with **Navigator→Display Properties**, you cannot edit anything other than the name in the Navigator.

A technique you can use to help you view the Navigator items is to split the screen. You do this by dragging the bar at the top-right corner of the Navigator window (just above the scrollbar button) down. This splits the window vertically. You can split the window vertically by dragging the bar in the lower-left corner of the Navigator window inward. Figure 6-9 shows a horizontal drag bar splitting the screen.

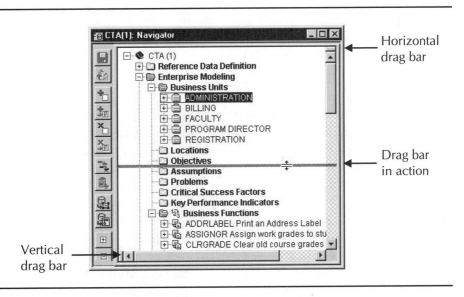

FIGURE 6-9.   *Drag bars for splitting the Navigator window*

You can also create a split view in a tab by selecting an element definition, element type node, or group node and selecting **View→Split View** from the menu. This will create a tab folder with the name of the object that was selected. This tab folder will have all object definitions under it, as the following illustration shows. **View→Remove Split View** eliminates the current split view tab folder.

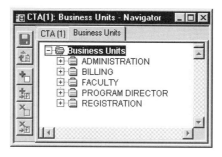

TIP

If you create split views on tab folders in the Navigator, you may have to widen the window to show them all. Otherwise, it may look as though some are not accessible.

Another useful viewing mechanism is the Association or Hierarchy view. When you click on the element type or element definition node, you can select **View→Association View** or **View→Hierarchy** (these are in a radio group, so only one is active at a time). The normal way to view an element in the Navigator is with the Association view, where an element shows its usage associations as subnodes under it, as in Figure 6-10. In this view, you have to drill down into each child element to determine the structure, and other usage nodes are shown in the same list. A Hierarchy view (selected from the View menu) appears as an element with the full hierarchy below it, as Figure 6-10 shows. An icon to the right of the function definition indicates whether you are showing the Hierarchy view. This icon does not appear if elements are shown in the Association view.

One of the best parts of the Hierarchy view is that you can drag and drop definitions from one place to another as you do in a hierarchy diagrammer. This works as intuitively as you would like it to. All you need to do is grab

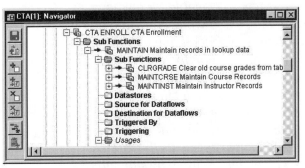

Association view

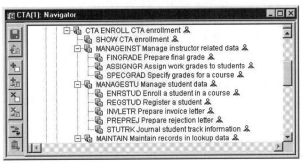

Hierarchy view

FIGURE 6-10. *Association and Hierarchy views*

an object definition in the hierarchy node and drop it in another node or in another place in the same node.

The toolbar buttons in the Navigator window perform tasks appropriate to the window. There are separate buttons for creating and deleting elements and creating and deleting associations. In addition, there are buttons for copying and pasting properties. After you select an element name, you can click the Copy properties button to save all properties to the clipboard. It is not necessary to select properties in the Property Palette. This is a different action than the Copy properties button in the Property Palette, which only copies selected properties.

TIP
The Hierarchy view is available for elements other than Functions and works the same way for those elements. In general, the hierarchy represents a self-association that has specific meaning to the particular element. For example, you can display the Hierarchy view for Entities and this represents a supertype (the parent) with its subtypes (the children). The hierarchy for Modules represents the module network (or calling hierarchy). The strength of this view is its visual representation of the associations between definitions of the same element type. It also provides a quick way to rearrange these associations.

Working in the Property Palette

Once you have found the element you want to work on, the next step to modifying element definitions is to change the properties (or delete or create a new definition in the Navigator). When you select the element in the Navigator, its properties appear in the Property Palette. The Property Palette uses colors to signify the status of each property. Although you can change these colors through **Options→Color/Font**, the default property colors are as follows:

- Normal: Black—for standard text.

- Error; Mandatory: Red—for property values that are set incorrectly and, therefore, cannot be saved or for properties that cannot be left blank.

- Modified: Blue—for property values that you have modified but not saved.

- Shared; Read Only: Green—for property values from element definitions that are shared from another application system or for property values that cannot be updated.

■ Inherited: Purple—for elements or properties that are referenced from a parent element. For example, subtype entities contain all attributes from their supertype entity. Those attributes are displayed in purple to show that they are inherited. The property values are displayed in green since you can only change them in the parent.

■ "Universal Values": Red—for properties of a module that are not valid for the language specified for that module. For example, a value of "Library" is not appropriate for the *Module Type* property of a WebServer module, so this value will appear in red.

If the Save button is enabled (not grayed out), the changes in the Property Palette have not been committed to the repository. Press the Save button or navigate to another element in the Navigator to commit the previous element's changes. Instead of pressing Save, you can press the Revert button to restore the previously saved values.

The buttons in the Property Palette allow you to save, revert, create, and delete as usual. The Copy properties button, as mentioned before, copies properties that you select. When you select properties, be sure the name is highlighted. You can use the CTRL and SHIFT keys to select more than one property. Select **Edit→View Copied Properties** to see which properties were copied. This is useful if you want to copy a certain subset of properties to another element definition. If you want all properties, use the Copy properties button in the Navigator window.

The Pin button freezes the display of the element's properties to allow you to navigate to another element, open another Property Palette (by choosing **Tools→Property Palette** from the menu or by pressing F4), and compare the two Property Palettes side by side. You need to pin one Property Palette before opening another.

The Union/Intersect button displays all properties from the selected objects or only properties in common, respectively, if you select more than one type of element in the Navigator.

To set properties for many elements at the same time, you can select elements in the Navigator window by holding down the CTRL key and clicking the elements you need or holding down SHIFT and clicking to select a range of elements from the list. The Property Palette will contain a list of all common properties, and it will display a series of hash marks (######) if the selected objects have different values for that property. You can then set a property in this grouped window, and all selected objects will have that

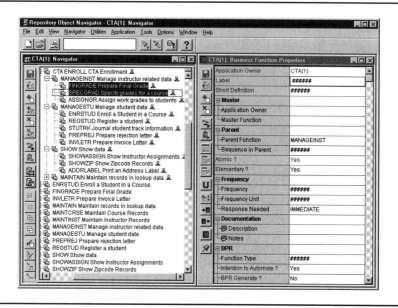

FIGURE 6-11. *Grouped element Property Palette*

value. Figure 6-11 shows a grouped list of elements and the Property Palette that applies to it.

An alternative way to work with a group of definitions is to select multiple definitions and press the SpreadTable view button. This will, effectively, turn the Property Palette sideways so you will see the selected elements as rows and the properties as columns. Figure 6-12 shows this

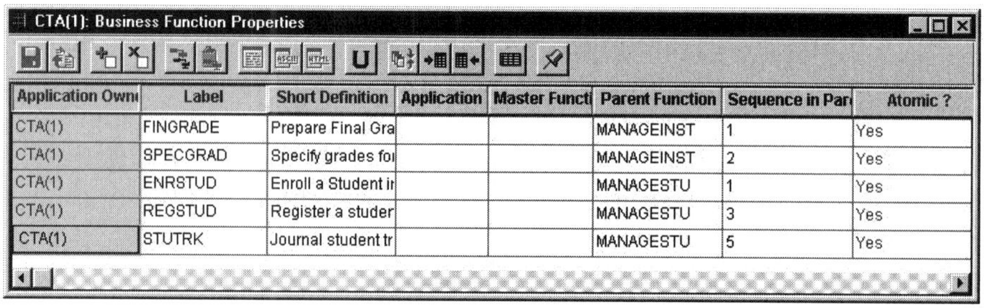

Application Owne	Label	Short Definition	Application	Master Functi	Parent Function	Sequence in Par	Atomic ?
CTA(1)	FINGRADE	Prepare Final Gra			MANAGEINST	1	Yes
CTA(1)	SPECGRAD	Specify grades fo			MANAGEINST	2	Yes
CTA(1)	ENRSTUD	Enroll a Student ir			MANAGESTU	1	Yes
CTA(1)	REGSTUD	Register a studer			MANAGESTU	3	Yes
CTA(1)	STUTRK	Journal student tr			MANAGESTU	5	Yes

FIGURE 6-12. *Property Palette spreadtable view*

view. Unfortunately, this spreadtable can get very wide very fast and may not be the way you want to look at your default properties view. It is useful, however, for the special times you want to compare or set properties from one definition to another. You can group unlike element types and show the spreadtable view of those definitions, if you want.

To switch back to the properties list, press the Default view button. When you are in the default view with grouped definitions, you can press the Next Object or Previous Object buttons to change the Property Palette temporarily so it displays only one element definition. The group will remain grouped in the Navigator and you can return to the grouped view by pressing the Set button in the Property Palette. This is useful if you want to examine one element definition after you have grouped a number of elements together but do not want to lose the group. The Set button is disabled in the spreadtable view, as it is not necessary. In that view, you can see all element definitions as individuals while still viewing the group.

TIP
If you close the Property Palette by mistake, press F4 to open it again. This keypress also works to shift focus to the Property Palette if it is displayed. To shift back to the Navigator window, press F3.

The Property Palette follows the Oracle Designer standards for this type of interface in the standard buttons and methods for editing the properties. It handles the three types of data input areas: freeform text, pick list values, and multiline text. The bubble icon identifies the multiline text:

The editor that you use with this kind of text depends on which button you press in the Property Palette to edit the value. If you click the TextPad button or bubble icon, the internal Oracle Designer text editor appears. If you press the Ascii Editor button, the editor you designate as Text Editor in **Options→Text Editor** will appear. If you press the HTML Editor button, you will use the editor you designate as HTML Editor in **Options→Text Editor**. The ability to edit HTML text means that you can embed fonts, colors, and pictures or graphics within your multiline text values.

TIP
All elements in the repository have properties called Notes *and* Description. *These are flexibly defined properties where you can enter as much text as you want using the text editors. You need to decide early in the development process on a standard for information in each of these properties. That way, you can be consistent in the type of information you store. For example, you might set a standard that* Description *will hold information not included in other properties that further defines the element whereas* Notes *will hold brief comments by the various designers who work on that definition.*

Other Menu and Toolbar Functions

The RON menu changes depending on whether you have the Navigator window or the Property Palette active. The Edit and View menus contain different items appropriate to the active window. The Navigator menu switches to become a Properties menu when you make the Property Palette active. These menus contain most actions you can accomplish using the toolbar in the appropriate window.

Oracle Designer offers a few more features in its pull-down menus. In addition to the options discussed in this section, the Edit, View, Navigator, Window, and Help menus all contain the usual items for this type of tool or the items that are discussed above.

File Menu

You can create a new application system through the **File→New Application** menu item (or by clicking the New application button). You can open more than one application system at the same time to share, copy, or transfer ownership of element definitions among them. You can also open the same application system in more than one Navigator window using **File→Open Application**. Save Uncommitted Data on this menu refers to committing changes you made to properties or objects in the application system.

When you open an application system, the Open Application dialog appears as in Figure 6-13. This dialog box lets you select one or more application systems to view in RON.

TIP
*Don't forget about the "most recently used file" list in the File menu. In the case of RON, this list contains the most recently opened application systems. It is generally easier to choose from the list than to choose **File→Open** and then select the application system.*

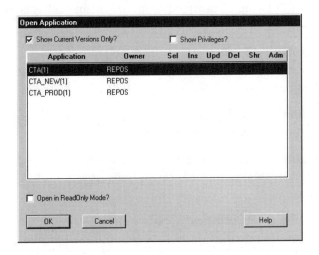

FIGURE 6-13. *Open Application dialog*

CAUTION
Remember that Oracle Designer commits work in RON implicitly when you move the cursor selection from a changed object to another in the Navigator. Therefore, if you create a new object and select another object before filling in all the required properties, the implicit commit will take place and fail because the required properties are missing. At that point you can fill in the missing properties or delete the object before moving on.

Utilities Menu

Using the Utilities menu, along with the Application and Tools menus, you can access virtually every utility and tool in Oracle Designer. The Utilities menu lets you run the repository utilities, some of which can't be launched from anywhere else. These are all discussed in future chapters, but we can get a taste for the kinds of operations they perform at this point. There are five types of utilities:

- **Design Transformers**   The Database Design Transformer and Application Design Transformer create design objects from analysis objects.

- **Table to Entity Retrofit**   This utility examines table definitions and creates entity definitions for those tables that are not associated with entities.

- **Mass change utilities**   These create or change definitions based on information already in the repository.

- **Application system utilities**   These manipulate elements in the repository between application systems or within one application system.

- **User-defined sets utilities**   These manage copying and loading data from other repositories or locking definitions within an application system.

The Force Delete option in the Utilities menu is worth singling out here. This will delete an element definition even if it has associated elements. For example, if you try a standard delete operation on a domain that has been used by columns, that delete will fail because the associated columns need that domain definition. **Utilities→Force Delete** will remove the domain and set the domain reference in the columns that use it to null. This is a powerful option, you should use it with care. When you decide to use Force Delete, be sure to examine the affected objects in the Force Delete dialog before confirming the operation. You will then be able to decide if you really want to force delete that object.

Application Menu

The Application menu contains options to maintain the application system. It includes items for freezing or unfreezing the application system to prevent or allow updates, renaming an application system, copying an application system, transferring ownership to another repository user, granting access to repository users to this application system, creating a new version, and deleting an application system. Chapter 26 will explain these in more detail.

The last items on this menu handle archiving. You can export an application system to a .DMP (Oracle Export) file that you can import into another repository. You can also import a .DMP file from this menu using the Restore option.

Tools Menu

The Tools menu gives you access to all tools and major utilities. It serves as an alternative to the Oracle Designer window, where you can also start all tools. You can also run SQL*Plus, and RON will log you in automatically.

Options Menu

As discussed before, the Options menu option lets you set up the RON environment. Other than the standard Oracle Designer items for Text Editor Options, Broadcast Options, and Diagnostics, and the Navigator Groups and Views options discussed earlier, the Options menu contains the following:

- **Color/Font** This allows you to set the colors for the Property Palette properties as well as fonts for the Property Palette, Navigator, and TextPad windows.

- **General Settings** This sets up some startup characteristics, as shown in Figure 6-14, such as what application system will load

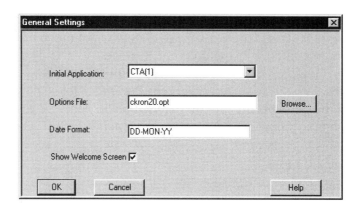

FIGURE 6-14. *General Settings dialog*

automatically into RON when you start it; the name of the options
file that stores some of the preferences for the RON working
environment; the default date format mask; and whether or not to
show the welcome screen when RON starts. If you uncheck this and
specify no opening application system in this dialog, RON will open
with the Navigator and Property Palette loaded with the application
system you chose for the Oracle Designer window.

■ **Customize Properties Palette**   This displays the Customize Property
Palette dialog, which lets you set whether you want to see the
Application system owner, audit properties, and BPR properties (for
Process Modeller elements). It also lets you specify whether you
want to be able to copy multiline text items when copying
properties. You can designate here whether you automatically want
the spreadtable mode to display when you are inserting multiple
definitions at the same time, although that option has questionable
use because it causes the spreadtable to appear by default. The
problem is that you will not see all the properties and may not
be able to easily reach the button to change back to the default
(non-spreadtable) view.

TIP
If you have used a previous release of Oracle Designer, you can consult the System Release Bulletin (SRB) on RON, found in the Start menu Designer Bulletins group, for information on the new features. In addition, there is a help topic called "What's new in the Repository Object Navigator for this release?" that you can reach from the main contents page of the help system (under "Introducing Repository Object Navigator").

Using RON to Spot-Check Your Strategy Work

You use RON in the Pre-Analysis phase to spot-check the entities and processes in your strategy ERD and process model. You may ask, "Why use RON when the diagrammers also show the element definitions as well as the diagrams themselves?" The answer is that the Repository Object Navigator is essential when you are comparing a number of element definitions because you can group elements together and view the same or different properties, either with the spreadtable view or by using multiple property palettes. This operation is not possible for Analysis elements anywhere else in the tools except in the Process Modeller for a limited number of properties. Also, in RON, you can quickly move from one definition to another without the screen redraw overhead that the diagrammers impose.

   For example, in RON you might perform a cross-check of the entities that you are diagramming in the ER Diagrammer. You can view their definitions in RON and be sure you are happy with the name, short name, and plural name for each entity. You can also fill in text information in the Description and Notes properties easier in RON than in the ER Diagrammer.

TIP
One approach you might consider is to ignore the entity properties when you are creating the entities in the ER Diagrammer during Strategy, because otherwise you have to perform another operation to open the properties window for each entity. Use RON in the Pre-Analysis phase to fill in the details in preparation for the reports and versioning tasks. This approach can speed your work in the ER Diagrammer and still provide complete entity definitions. You can use a similar strategy in other diagrammers for other elements throughout the System Development Life Cycle.

Using RON to Create a New Version

The other essential activity that RON helps with during Pre-Analysis is creating a new version of the application system. Versioning an application system in Oracle Designer creates a complete copy of the application system, increments the version number, and freezes the old copy so you cannot make changes, although you can view it. Oracle Designer cannot version individual elements or groups of elements, so application system versioning is the only way to create an online copy of the strategy elements. You must have ADMIN privilege on the application system to run the new version utility.

The reason you perform versioning at this stage is that you will (probably) radically change the element definitions in Analysis, and you need the copy that supports the strategy discussions and documents. Although you could explicitly freeze the application system so no one could make changes, you will have to start a completely new application system for the Analysis phase, and you will possibly need to reenter all your initial strategy definitions if you do that.

CAUTION
When you delete an application system, there is no way to restore it unless you have a backup.

Suppose you have versioned an application system called PRODAPP by selecting **Application→New Version** to create a copy called PRODAPP version 2 and to freeze version 1. The version number appears after the application system name in most dialog boxes and window titles; for example, PRODAPP(1) indicates application system version 1. When you open an application system, you can set an option (in the Open Application dialog) to display all the versions or only current versions. At this point, you can't change or add to version 1, but you can view it and can do anything to version 2.

NOTE
Deleting an application system or creating a new version could take some time if the application system has many elements. These operations use database resources more heavily than usual, which could affect system performance while the utility runs. Therefore, you will probably want to schedule these operations so as not to interfere with normal working hours and/or carefully plan in the initial development stages to reduce the need to delete or version application systems.

An alternative to versioning is to make a backup copy of the application system and export it. You can do this in RON by choosing Archive from the Application menu. This procedure loads the element definitions and all other details on the application system, including the diagrams, into temporary extract tables (which have names with an XT_ prefix). Once the utility has copied the element definitions into these tables, you can select **Application→Export** and create an export (.DMP) file. This file is in standard Oracle export format, so you can import it (through RON's **Application→Restore** menu item) into another repository or just use it to back up the application system. This file is a complete snapshot of all data, including diagrams, and so you could use it to hold all the strategy information in a form that cannot be changed.

The benefits of this alternative over creating a new version is that you do not take up space in the repository for a new application system and you still have data to support your Strategy phase. The drawback is that the application system is, in effect, offline so you cannot easily query it or reprint its definitions or diagrams. Since you are building on, and probably changing, the strategy elements in the one online application system, some strategy details may be "lost." You will have to restore the original application system to view the strategy details. Yet another alternative is to create another repository for the new version so there are no ties at all to the original.

Repository Reports

Repository Reports is a repository utility that lets you view the element definitions in particular formats. This utility can run nearly 100 prebuilt reports using the Oracle Developer Reports Runtime. Since you have diagrammed the Entity Model and Process Model at this point, reports to start with might be the *Entity Definition* (in the Entity/Relationship Modelling group) and *Dataflow Definition* (in the Dataflow Modelling group). You will see how to find these and other reports and groups and how to get around the Repository Reports interface. As mentioned, Chapter 2 contains the basics of the Oracle Designer interface and on how the Navigator and Property Palette work.

NOTE
A number of reports included with Designer version 1 are either obsolete or have been replaced. See the help system topic "What's new in Repository Reports for this release?" which you can reach from the Repository Reports main help contents tab (Reporting on the Repository – Introducing Repository Reports).

Basic Techniques

The Repository Reports interface is similar to that of the Repository Object Navigator. It uses the paradigm of the Navigator for its Reports window and also displays a Parameters Palette window (like the Property Palette in RON), as Figure 6-15 shows. Therefore, you follow the same procedure after opening the tool as for RON: you maximize the window and tile the windows vertically (using **Window→Tile Vertically**) while the Reports window is active (so it appears on the left). You also expand and contract

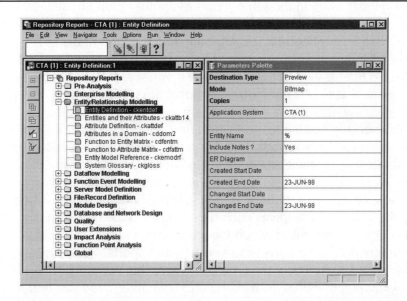

FIGURE 6-15. *Repository Reports session*

nodes and use the Find box and menu choice in the same way as in RON. The Mark and Go To Mark buttons and Navigator menu items also work exactly the same as in RON.

Running a report is a three-step process:

1. Find the report.

2. Fill in the parameters.

3. Run the report.

The following sections explain these steps.

I. Find the Report

The list of reports is so extensive that you need some help in finding the correct one. Oracle Designer gives you three ways to look at the list of reports: Group, Hierarchy, and Report Name. You can switch between these views by selecting the appropriate choice from the View menu. A given group node may contain the same report as another group node. For example, if you are viewing by hierarchy, the *Function to Attribute Matrix* report will appear under both the Attribute and Function nodes.

Group displays reports by project life cycle phase or functional area, as in Figure 6-16. This view is a good choice if you want to see what other reports are available in a particular functional area. For example, if you knew that you wanted to list Attributes you would look under the Entity/Relationship Modelling node. You find the *Attribute Definition* report there but also see other reports, like *Attributes in a Domain*, which might be useful at this stage of the CADM life cycle and might supplement the attribute report. The order of the groups is roughly the order in which you create these objects in a traditional life cycle methodology like CADM. This view is the default that appears each time you open the tool. Repository Reports does not remember which view you used in your last session.

Hierarchy displays reports by element type. Reports in this category are easy to find if you know the type of element that you need to report on. For example, if you are looking for a list of entities, you can find a number of reports under the Entities node to choose from. Figure 6-17 shows some of the Object Type nodes. This list appears in alphabetical order by element type.

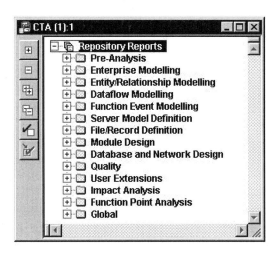

FIGURE 6-16. *Group view*

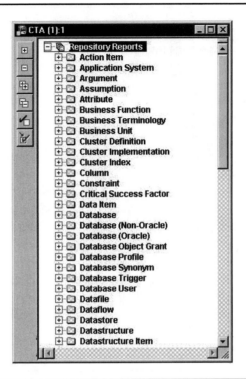

FIGURE 6-17.   *Hierarchy view*

The Report Name view of the reports is merely an alphabetical listing of all reports in Oracle Designer. This is the best method for finding the report you want if you have a copy in front of you with the name of the report or can remember the exact name (or at least the first word or two in the name). Figure 6-18 shows a list of reports by report name. The name of the file that contains the report definition appears after the report name. This is useful if you need to change the report in some way.

As mentioned previously, when you are in the Pre-Analysis phase, you might want a listing of the entities and processes you diagrammed in the Strategy phase. Use the reports *Entity Definition* (and other reports in the Entity/Relationship Modelling group) and *Dataflow Definition* (and other reports in the Dataflow Modelling and Enterprise Modelling groups) as a starting point for the Pre-Analysis work.

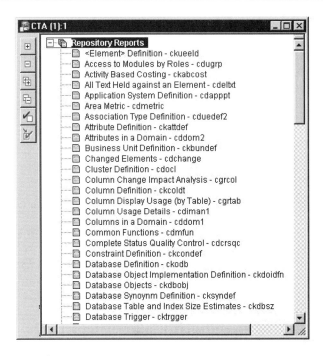

FIGURE 6-18. *Report Name view*

While the set of reports Oracle Designer provides is extensive, it is possible that the report you want is just not available. You will find some suggestions for handling this situation later in this chapter in the section "What to Do If the Report You Want Is Not Prebuilt."

TIP
Remember to use the help system to help you decide which report to choose. If you click on the Context-Sensitive Help button and then on the report name in the Navigator, the help system will show descriptions of the report, its parameters, and its output.

2. Fill In the Parameters
Each report has a set of parameters you enter to specify the elements that will be in the output. Most of these are specific to the report and are well

documented in the online help system. Just press F1 after selecting a report or search for the parameter name in the help system. This procedure opens the help system report index, where you can select the particular report you are running to see a description of the report and its parameters. Required parameters appear in red (by default); these must be entered before you run the report.

You can use the wildcard, %, if you need to specify a range of elements in any parameter. For example, to specify a Table Name parameter to indicate that you want a report of all tables, you could enter % as that parameter value. Similarly, to report on all tables with PERS somewhere in the name, you can specify a parameter value of %PERS%. This syntax is similar to that for SQL query conditions, but you cannot enter a complex condition—only a single exact value or a single value with a wildcard. Some parameters require input from a list of values (as in RON), some require typed input, and some accept both types of input (for example, the Entity parameter of the Entity Definition report).

TIP

You can include a certain subset of elements on a particular report even if the elements do not have a similar name. Some reports include a parameter for the name of a diagram on which the elements appear. For example, the Entity Definition report includes an ER Diagram parameter, which lists the existing diagrams. If you select one, Oracle Designer uses it as the source for the entities it reports on. Thus, suppose a diagram called ERD PERSON contains the entities PERSON, ORGANIZATION, and PURCHASE ORDER. You can fill in the name of the diagram in the ER Diagram parameter, and the report will include only the PERSON, ORGANIZATION, and PURCHASE ORDER. The wildcard % works here too, so if you have similarly named diagrams and specify the wildcarded name in this parameter, Oracle Designer will report on all entities on all diagrams with names that match the parameter.

PRINT TO FILE, HTML, AND .PDF FORMAT You can print a report to a file using the following parameters.

Parameter	Value
Destination Type	File
Destination Name	FILENAME.LIS
Destination Format	Dflt
Mode	Character

If you make the Destination Format HTML (Hypertext Markup Language), the file produced will be accessible with a Web browser. A file with a format of .PDF (Portable Document Format) is readable by using the Adobe Acrobat Reader. Be sure to set Mode to Bitmap for the HTML and .PDF types. If you have a browser or Acrobat Reader installed on your system, you can run them from the Run menu and view a report file you created previously.

3. Run the Report

The last step after finding the proper report and filling in its parameters is to run the report and examine its output. Running a report is as simple as clicking the Run Report button, choosing **File→Run Report**, or double-clicking the report name in the Navigator window. If you kept the default Preview value in the Destination Type parameter, the report will appear on the screen in the Oracle Developer Reports Previewer window. This window has buttons for navigating the report and printing it. If you specified a different destination, the report will go there directly.

Customize Your Repository Reports Navigator

You can add or delete the standard groups using the **Edit→Create New Group** and **Edit→Delete Group** menu choices, respectively. This allows you to modify the way the Group and Hierarchy views look to better serve your needs. The dialogs for these activities are relatively intuitive and are well documented in the help system.

In addition to tailoring the groups, you can also tailor the reports that appear within those groups. The **Edit→Add Report to Group** and **Edit→Remove Report from Group** menu items provide these functions after you select a group or hierarchy node. Again, the dialogs are straightforward and well documented. The following shows a new Group added to the navigator for Pre-Analysis reports.

You can also hide certain reports for the Repository Reports session. **Choose View→Hide Reports** from the menu to view a list of reports and choose which ones to hide. Once you hide a report, the Show Reports menu item in the View menu will be accessible so you can unhide it. The Repository Reports tool remembers which reports are hidden so when you exit and start a new session, the hidden reports will not be available. This can be a good way to reduce the list of reports if you never use a particular set of reports. It can also be a path to frustration if you forget you have hidden reports and cannot find a particular report. Use this feature wisely.

TIP
Use reports in the Quality group. These help you determine if the definitions you entered are complete. For example, there are reports called Functions without Input or Output Dataflows and Quality Checking of Relationships. These are useful at any point in the system development cycle, but particularly when you are done with a phase and trying to answer the question "When is the Strategy phase complete?"

The Output Window

The Output window, as shown next, appears when you select **Window→Output Window** from the menu.

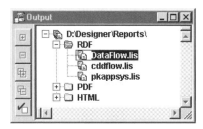

This window shows the files you have created in a certain directory (set in the **Options→General Settings** dialog) with certain extensions (.LIS for the .RDF node, .PDF for the .PDF node, and HTML for the HTML node). You can double-click on the file name to run the viewer as specified in **Options→Report Viewer Options** for ASCII and HTML formats.

If you choose File as the Destination Type and select a Destination Format, such as HTML, a name will appear in the Destination Name parameter. This name consists of the report file name and an extension based on the Destination Type. For example, it uses .HTML for HTML files. Although you can change the file name without impact, it is best to leave the directory path and extension alone, so the name will appear in the Output window and you will be sure of where to find generated output.

What to Do If the Report You Want Is Not Prebuilt

If you can't find a repository report that fulfills your needs, you can purchase a reporting tool from a third-party vendor or you can write your own report and use the following two techniques to modify the set of reports supplied as a standard:

- Add user-defined reports

- Add a parameter

Writing Your Own Reports

If you, or someone on your team, are proficient with a reporting tool, you can use it to create reports on the views in the repository. The repository views are discussed fully in Chapter 28, but it is important to know that you will have to decipher the relationships between views and the meaning of their columns. This is not an insurmountable task, but it may require some time in the beginning. One thing that can help is an application system with the repository schema (or metamodel) that is included with Oracle Designer. The schema is contained in both an application export file (.DMP) and a Load file (.DAT). You can use either file to load the application system into your repository. The Designer Release Notes explain where the files are located and how to load them. This model gives you all necessary information on the repository views and their "foreign key" links.

Once you know what to query, you can build the report using SQL*Plus, another vendor's query tool, or Oracle Developer's Report Builder. If you use one of the first two, you will not be able to link the report into the Repository Reports utility. If you use Report Builder, you can either copy an existing report module from Oracle Designer and make changes, or start from scratch and build your own. Alternatively, if you have the Designer schema loaded as an application system, you can create Oracle Reports modules in the repository and generate reports directly out of Oracle Designer.

The Report Builder requires a moderate-to-expert skill level to be able to output a report of the same class as the predefined reports. In addition, Oracle Developer is an extra cost, separately licensed package not included with Oracle Designer. However, if you use Report Builder to build reports from scratch or to modify copies of existing Repository Reports, you will create an .RDF file that you can link into the Repository Reports tool.

Adding User-Defined Reports

You can add reports you create in Report Builder to the list of reports in the Repository Reports utility. Follow these four steps to do this:

1. Create the report .RDF file from scratch or modify an existing report (as mentioned in "Writing Your Own Reports") using Report Builder.

2. Place the .RDF file into the directory specified in the **Options→ General Settings** dialog.

3. Add the report to the Repository Reports list using the **Edit→Create New Report** dialog, as shown in Figure 6-19. Be sure to click on a group or hierarchy node before trying to select this menu item.

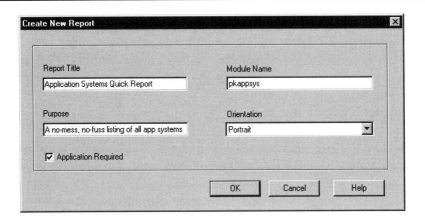

FIGURE 6-19. *Create New Report dialog*

4. Place the report in the appropriate group (as just described). The report will be in the alphabetical list of reports with a UD- prefix (user-defined).

These steps are described fully in the help system. If you need to remove a report from the available list of reports, use the **Edit→Delete Report** menu choice. Be careful of this option, because although it only "obsoletes" standard reports and preserves the .RDF file, it will delete the .RDF file for user-defined reports. If you remove a user-defined report by mistake or just want to restore one of the deleted standard reports, use the **Options→Reinstate Standard Reports** menu item.

TIP
You can edit the name of a user-defined report by clicking on its name in the Navigator and editing the existing text.

Adding a Parameter

You can add one or more parameters to any standard report. This parameter can be one used in another report or one that you define. The following are the steps you would use to create your own parameter and attach it to a report. You would use steps 2 and 3 to accomplish the same result with a parameter that already exists.

I. Choose **Edit→Create New Parameter** and define a parameter, as Figure 6-20 shows.

2. Add this parameter to the report using **Edit→Add Parameter to Report**.

3. Check that the report uses the new parameter correctly by running a report session with a value assigned to the parameter.

Use **Edit→Delete Parameter** to remove a parameter from the reports list. Use **Edit→Remove Parameter from Report** to reverse the steps just described.

CAUTION
Deleting a parameter removes it from all reports in all application systems in the repository. Be very careful when you use this feature as there is no "undelete" operation to restore a deleted parameter.

Any parameter you add must be set up for use in the report already. For standard reports, you can open the report in Report Builder and look at the User Parameters node. The names of the parameters will be there in some form (for example, the Repository Reports parameter COL_DET appears as RRI_COL_DET in the Entity to Table Implementation report – cdtents). The parameter names are available in the Add Parameter to Report dialog. For your own reports, you have to ensure that you have a parameter with an RRI_ prefix that you use in the formatting triggers or queries to restrict or manipulate the queries.

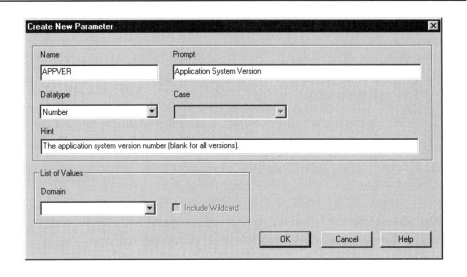

FIGURE 6-20. *Create New Parameter dialog*

CAUTION
If you are modifying existing reports, be sure to keep a backup copy. Some reports are complex, and changing one small object in them can cause major complications. Also, you should not attempt to modify an existing report unless you are very, very familiar with the way Report Builder works.

NOTE
Adding report definitions or changing the groups takes effect for all application systems in the repository regardless of which application system is active when you change the definitions.

Other Menu and Toolbar Functions

There are a few menu choices not already mentioned apart from the ones common to all Oracle Designer tools:

- The **Run menu** contains Adobe Acrobat Reader and Browse Web if you have Acrobat and a browser installed. Use these to view the .PDF and HTML files you created with the report run session. The Run menu also contains an entry for Report Builder, which loads the report .RDF file that is selected in the Navigator (provided you have Report Builder installed).

- The **Tools menu** includes options to switch back and forth between the Reports Navigator and Parameters Palette windows; you can also do this by using the F3 and F4 keys, respectively. You can also run SQL*Plus from this menu in case you want to check a particular query by typing it in at the command line.

- The **Options menu** contains items for the Export and Import of user-defined report definitions. Use these if you have created reports and defined them in this tool but need to share them with another repository. This menu also contains Color/Font for modifying how the Navigator and Parameters windows look.

Mapping System Requirements to Repository Elements

Pre-Analysis involves planning and making decisions about what will happen in the Analysis phase. One of the decisions you have to make is how to map system requirements to elements so you can cross-check later in the CADM life cycle that your design fulfills these requirements. This mapping traditionally is a manual process, if it occurs at all: someone compares the requirements list with the list of system features to ensure completeness. You can also use the table structure proposed in Chapter 5 to store the requirements and tie them to the repository definitions. Alternatively, you can use Oracle Designer to map the requirements.

Using Oracle Designer Elements for System Requirements

Oracle Designer does not provide a Requirements element type, but it does provide a Documents element where you can store the details of documents pertinent to the life cycle, such as the system Requirements Document. You can also store the document text itself in this definition using plain text or HTML format as well as associations to any other repository element. This procedure will not fulfill the need to map requirements to functions and other elements, but it can provide a list of project documents and a central storage location for certain documents.

Oracle Designer also includes an Objectives element where you can store information on objectives, which you can interpret as requirements. Objectives is actually an element that Oracle created as an extension to the normal set of objects and that has associations to elements for Critical Success Factors, Business Units, Business Functions, Documents, Key Performance Indicators, and Modules. You can use this element to store the text of your requirements and use the associations provided to map to these elements.

Using User Extensibility for Requirements

Another method for implementing a system to store requirements is to use Oracle Designer's User Extensibility feature to create your own element. *User extensions* are additional elements, associations, or properties you define as parts of the repository. You create these in the Repository Administration Utility (RAU) and then enter data into them through RON or the Matrix Diagrammer or your own front-end tool or a utility such as SQL*Plus. Since the extended objects become part of the repository, you can create reports on them in the same way as you create reports on predefined objects. Although user extensions are not available in Oracle Designer utilities or diagrammers other than RON, and to a limited extent, the Design Editor and the Matrix Diagrammer, they allow you to customize your application with items that Oracle Designer does not provide by default. Chapter 27 describes the process of creating user extensions.

Choosing Between User Extensibility and a Table-Based System

In some cases, the features that Oracle Designer provides may not meet the needs of your particular situation. For example, you may want to customize the way Oracle Designer handles project- or company-specific elements, and you will find yourself asking, "How do I accomplish this with Oracle Designer?" The answer is that you need to add something, but you have to decide whether to use a system of database tables or to use User Extensibility. Although no one can say categorically which is the better approach in every situation, if you know the benefits and drawbacks of each, you will be better prepared to decide what will work best. Table 6-2 lists the major characteristics you should consider.

The other factor that will affect your choice of method is your knowledge of what is involved in implementing the solution in each case. There is an assumption that you already know how to implement a relational database table solution. Chapter 27 discusses how to implement this solution with Oracle Designer user extensions, so you have that choice, too.

Feature	Table-Based Solution	Oracle Designer User Extensibility Solution
Ease of creating data structures	Familiar process to relational database developers	Developers need to learn the extension process.
Data structure creation process	Can generate table scripts in Oracle Designer or manually write them	Does not use scripts, only definitions in the Oracle Designer Repository Administration Utility.
Limitations on size and number of extensions	Unlimited	500 extra association types, 500 extra elements, unlimited text types, and 20 extra properties per element.

TABLE 6-2.   *Differences in Implementing User Extensions Inside and Outside Oracle Designer*

Feature	Table-Based Solution	Oracle Designer User Extensibility Solution
Front-end for loading data	Needs to be developed, but applications can be generated from Oracle Designer since they use standard SQL and table concepts	Can use RON and Matrix Diagrammer as is; if something more is needed, it must be developed outside the Oracle Designer generators and the Oracle Designer API must be accessed, a process that requires more programming than standard SQL.
Data maintenance	No ties to Oracle Designer data in the repository; if Oracle Designer data changes, changes will not automatically cascade to tables	Provided by Oracle Designer's repository.
Reporting capabilities	Reports must be created manually or through Oracle Designer	Reports must be created manually or through Oracle Designer.
Data sharing with other application systems	Nearly impossible	Built-in feature because the data is in the repository.
Support of application system import/export	None	Built in.
Support of check-in/ checkout and load/unload	None	Built in.

TABLE 6-2. *Differences in Implementing User Extensions Inside and Outside Oracle Designer* (continued)

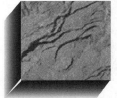

CHAPTER
7

Analysis—Information Gathering

Gather ye requirements while ye may. The old system is still a flying. And the same project that's on time today, tomorrow will be dying. (Apologies to Robert Herrick.)

nalysis is the process of gathering and analyzing system requirements. At this point in the system development process, the analyst should have the following idea uppermost in mind: "It is not possible to meet a user's need that was never discovered."

Consider this real-world example of lost requirements. The Analysis phase was almost finished when the analysts were approached by one of the client's legacy system programmers and told the following: "There are elements written into the programs that allow us to do some types of business in New Jersey and not in Pennsylvania. Most of the users are unaware of this. Where are these requirements being written down?" In this case, the confusion occurred because the project leader had not thought through the Analysis phase completely prior to its execution.

It is very easy to just begin talking to people and gathering data. However, the analyst must constantly keep in mind the following questions:

- How will the system designers find out everything that they need to know to complete the project?

- Are the resources adequate?

- Will the analysis process truly capture all system requirements?

The goal at this point is straightforward: namely, to execute the analysis plan. However, throughout the Analysis phase, the analysts need to think very carefully about the process that was outlined in Pre-Analysis.

Analysis consists of two parts: information gathering and requirements analysis. Information-gathering activities, such as conducting interviews, implementing questionnaires, holding JAD sessions, and reviewing the legacy system, are performed first. Analysis begins as soon as some information is gathered; you do not wait until all of the information is collected to begin analysis. As you are gathering information, it is constantly being analyzed. Once all of the information has been gathered, a final assembly of the information analysis must be done. Towards the end of the Analysis phase, inconsistencies among requirements are identified and resolved and a coherent statement of the new system requirements is formulated.

Deliverables

The ultimate deliverables for the Analysis phase will be discussed in Chapter 9. Independent of this final Analysis Document, specific interim deliverables are produced during the Analysis phase. These interim deliverables act as supporting documentation for the Analysis Document but may not appear in its final version. The deliverables for the information-gathering process are the following:

- Interview notes

- Narrative text

- Lists of documents reviewed

- Worksheets documenting information-gathering activities so that, at a future point in time, a review of what work was accomplished can be compiled

It is important to carefully document information-gathering activities. Of particular importance is keeping track of interview notes and documents reviewed during system analysis. The goals of information-gathering activities are not just to gather all of the relevant information but also to adequately organize and store this information for later review and retrieval.

Overview of Information Gathering

Analysts traditionally follow a two-step process:

1. They talk to users in order to understand what they want and need.

2. They build ERDs, function hierarchies, and prototypes.

Steps 1 and 2 must be linked together, however. Creating a transition step—the delivery of the Requirements Document—provides a means to cross-check the functional models and ERDs, and not just directly with the users but with a document the users approved weeks ago, about which they said, "Yes, that is the way we want it done."

This extra step also gives the users something to compare with the system function hierarchy and ERD. They first compare what they want done with their requirements list. Then they compare this requirements list (which they have already approved) to what is in the ERD, function hierarchy, and any prototypes that have been made.

During information gathering, the analysis team should be focused on determining the system requirements. If the information gathered is incomplete or inaccurate or does not reflect the users' needs, the system to be implemented will be a failure. It is important to spend an adequate amount of time to gather this information completely and effectively. In general, information-gathering tasks require both a strict information-gathering process and a separate process to analyze and document the information collected at each information-gathering activity.

Devices such as prototypes, screen shots, preliminary database models, and storyboarded applications are appropriate only insofar as they serve as vehicles to communicate back to the users what the analysts understand their needs to be.

This feedback to the users should be done at the "unit" level, interview by interview and user by user. For example, in an individual user interview, the analyst tries to collect as much information as possible. Then the analyst examines the information gathered and generates informal ERDs, process flows, or other appropriate representations to effectively feed back to the user, in an organized way, what was learned in the interview. Ideally, this unit analysis activity takes place with the help and hands-on support of the user. Unfortunately, sometimes users have neither the time nor the inclination to be this involved in the system development process.

After the unit analysis is performed, the information is passed back to the user for approval of both the interview notes and whatever analysis of the interview was performed. Until the user signs off, the interview is not complete.

The analysis process can then proceed. The analysis plan prescribes various information-gathering activities that need to be performed in a particular sequence and the degree of parallelism of these activities. Each information-gathering task follows the same process. Information gathering and unit analysis are described in the remainder of this chapter.

Eliciting Requirements from the Users

This section discusses the various methods of gathering the information necessary to understand the business area and identify requirements. These methods include:

- Interviews
- Questionnaires
- Electronic communications
- Joint application development (JAD) sessions

Interviews

Interviews that are conducted carefully can go a long way toward eliciting the necessary system requirements. The standard procedure for gathering user requirements is to interview the business users. This may sound like a straightforward and simple task, but the methods used to obtain and organize the information can greatly affect the results.

Open-Ended Interviews

Open-ended interviews consist of one or more analysts and interviewers sitting down with a user and asking questions. One of the authors of this book did a doctoral dissertation on the topic of user interviews that sought to measure how much information was discussed. Hundreds of hours of videotape of actual interviews between analysts and users were analyzed to determine the answer to this question: how is it that good analysts are able to elicit up to ten times as much information as inexperienced ones?

Some of what was discovered was consistent with the advice typically given to analysts. However, much of what was found contradicted conventional wisdom. It is critical to constantly keep in mind the nature of the analyst-user interaction and the purpose of the interview: namely, to understand the business and identify requirements. This can be supported in several ways: through good questions and comments, productive feedback, and a preexisting structure for the information to be gathered.

When conducting interviews, it is very useful to bring a person other than the interviewer to act as a scribe for the interview. In this way, the interviewer can concentrate on the questions being asked and on providing appropriate feedback, as discussed later in this section. A logical choice for this role is a junior analyst. He or she will gain experience in how to conduct an interview. The senior analyst can then review the write-up of the interview shown to the user for final sign-off.

QUESTION SYNTAX IS IRRELEVANT   Much has been written in various fields about the syntax of the questions asked in an interview and how this affects the information gathered. These studies typically stipulate that questions must be open-ended so as not to bias the feedback, and they conclude that careful attention must be paid to the exact words and syntax of the questions in order to get the most accurate answers. These conclusions were reached by looking at standardized exams, police interviews, psychiatric interviews, and teacher-student interactions.

However, there is a substantive difference between the interactions in the standard research settings and those in a systems development environment. The goal in system development is to give and receive information. The relationship between interviewer and user is *cooperative,* not adversarial, and there is no attempt to coerce or trick the person being interviewed. Both the analyst and the person being interviewed are working toward a common goal. Therefore, the syntax of the questions asked is completely irrelevant in this setting.

In the author's doctoral dissertation research, the amount of information and users' perceptions of the information transferred were precisely measured, along with the user satisfaction when the syntax of the questions was altered. In contrast to the results of the other research, this study found no appreciable differences in the responses to questions regardless of the syntax. For example, it didn't matter which of the following two questions the interviewer asked:

- "Do you want a printer?" (yes/no question)

- "How would you like to handle your printing needs?" (open-ended question)

Not only were open-ended questions no better at eliciting the desired information, but there was a statistically significant greater probability that the user would not understand these more syntactically complex questions.

The issue then remained: if the syntax didn't make a difference, what did matter in conducting a successful interview? The conclusion reached was that certain interviewer behaviors and strategies were the key factors.

LISTEN, THEN TALK   The most important factor observed from the hours of interview tapes was that the interviewers who were most successful placed themselves in a mode to receive information and stayed locked into this mode. Their primary goal was to listen, not give information. To do this, they displayed several key behaviors, some of which are covered in the literature on active listening:

- They asked good questions.

- They gave encouraging nonverbal feedback (such as note taking, head nodding, and "uh-huhs").

- They let the user say what he or she wanted to say without interruption until finished.

Interview questions should be designed to open up topics for the user to talk about. The comment "Let's talk about printing" could elicit the same feedback as yes/no or complex questions about printing. The important point is for the interviewer to always keep in mind the specific setting and situation of the interview in the business environment. The nature of this interaction is that information can go only one way at a time. Someone must be giving information, and someone must be receiving information. If both the analyst and user are trying to give information at the same time, then no one is listening.

USE FEEDBACK   Good listening behavior, however, is not enough. Attentive listening and "uh-huhs" do not communicate to unhappy users that they have been heard and understood. The most successful interviewers repeated back what they had heard, using statements like "Let me see if I understand what you are saying" or "From what I've heard, this is what you are looking for." These interviewers were able to get much more information from the users. There was a direct correlation between using these feedback strategies and getting more information. Finally, a key question that must always be asked is "Is there anything you would like to add?" This makes the person being interviewed feel that the interviewer has heard and thought about what has been said and forces acknowledgment that the user has no more to say.

USE POWER CAREFULLY   Another important issue in conducting successful interviews is that of power. In a typical interview situation, there is a clear delineation of who is in the position of power. This is not the case in an analyst-user relationship. The optimal arrangement is a relative parity in power positions between the interviewer and the user. In general, the user needs to feel comfortable enough to talk about what needs to be discussed. If a user is insecure, it is the job of the interviewer to put the user at ease. Ways that this can be accomplished include conducting the interview on the user's turf (for instance, in the user's office) and using nonverbal cues. Nonverbal cues may include note taking, head nodding, body position, and voice volume. These cues can be used to manipulate the power structure of the situation to suit the needs of the interviewer.

For example, if the user isn't letting the interviewer get a word in edgewise, the interviewer can take control by standing and walking to the white board or using paper and drawing or reviewing what has been discussed. This puts the interviewer in the place of highest power, since all attention will be focused on the person at the board. At that point, the interviewer owns the situation and is in control. Less severe power-gaining measures include controlling the actual volume (voice level) of talk. Also, the interviewer can remain in an information-receiving mode but encourage an alternation of discussion between himself or herself and the user. If done correctly, this can make for a very effective interview. Body position can also influence the power balance. If the interviewer is sitting in a relaxed pose, this is a higher power stance and tends to put the user in a weaker position.

In the opposite situation, where the user is reluctant to talk, the interviewer needs to give the user more power. This can be done with body language: for example, the interviewer can sit up in an attentive pose, waiting to receive information. Gentle cues ("Tell me about. . .") and questions can draw out the reticent user and extract the necessary information.

A related issue to that of power in analyst-user interviews is that of gender. Because of deeply rooted social norms and perceptions within society, the gender of the interviewer and user may play a role in the success of the interaction. The interviewer simply needs to be aware of this and make slight adjustments in the power structure of the interaction. If a male interviewer is dealing with a female user accustomed to a male boss, he may want to speak quietly and take lots of notes to facilitate better transfer of information. Conversely, a female interviewer with a male user accustomed to being in control may want to use more power-increasing strategies in her interviewing.

PROTECT AGAINST BIAS   One factor to be very careful about in interviewing but which can be quite difficult to detect is interviewer bias. Consider the results of a study done in the 1930s concerning the reasons for homelessness among people. Some of the interviewers sent out were temperance workers; they reported that the main cause of homelessness among the subjects they interviewed was alcohol. Other interviewers were socialists; they reported that the cause of homelessness among their subjects was economic conditions in society. These interviewers were not conducting open-ended interviews. Even though they were using precisely written questionnaires, their own biases influenced the way they asked the questions, thus influencing the responses.

The potential for bias on the part of the interviewer in an open-ended interview is even greater. The only effective way to guard against bias is to use several different analysts who will hopefully have different biases. By analyzing all of their information, a balanced picture of user requirements can be obtained.

Another way to help prevent interviewer bias is to send two analysts to conduct an interview with one user. In this way, their individual biases will have less effect. An added benefit of this strategy is that one analyst can be assigned to interview the user from a data-centric perspective and the other from a more process-centered perspective.

STRUCTURE YOUR INFORMATION RETRIEVAL   So that as many requirements as possible are uncovered and the validity of the information is explored as thoroughly as possible, three topics must be addressed during user interviews:

- What each user does

- How each user does what he or she does

- What each user needs to do his or her job

It is also important to discuss these topics, which don't relate directly to the user's current system:

- Improvements that the new system could supply

- Topics outside the range of the user's immediate job function

When asking what users do, the analyst should have them list their tasks. For each task noted, the analyst then should determine the process flow. The process flow for a task is simply how people do their jobs. Each task is further refined into subtasks. These subtasks will probably turn into functions when the information is entered into Oracle Designer. In most cases, a function becomes a screen module if the user needs to create, update, or delete information. A function becomes a report module if the user needs to retrieve the information on the screen or on paper. If the user performs quality checks on the data, the function might become an integrity constraint.

The third topic, what users need to do their jobs, includes determining what functions and data users need. The decisions a user makes during the day are often critical issues when determining the requirements of the system.

After the first three topics have been covered with the user, what the user needs in the new system can be addressed. Now that *how* the existing system works has been detailed, areas for improvement can be discussed.

Finally, the analyst should ask the user for comments that do not relate directly to the user's tasks and job. These not only shed light on processes that might affect the user indirectly, but also may open up ideas for future work. For example, a person might explain that checks are never issued on time. This may be out of scope for the current project, but an attempt to work on this related project could be made in the future.

Following this interview procedure will allow you to question users in a way that stimulates discussion. Users discuss what they do every day with coworkers and friends. In most cases, you will not get a constructive response if you ask a person, "What are the requirements of the new system from your point of view?" It is much better to put the system in perspective and have the users tell you what they do, how they do it, and what they need to do their jobs.

GROUP QUESTIONS INTO CATEGORIES   A skilled interviewer may be able to elicit a great deal of information, but without some type of format or structure, the value of the information is greatly diminished. A skilled analyst organizes his or her questions into related topics.

These structurally related questions typically start with a structural identifier. The interviewer introduces topic A and then provides contextual structural cues relating to the question to reduce the probability that the question will be misunderstood. In this fashion, subtopics A1, A2, and so on can be covered in depth. The interviewer builds a tree of information with three types of questions:

- **Validation questions**   For instance, "Is this what you are saying? Have I got this right?"

- **Horizontal questions**   For instance, "You've told me about A1 and A2. Is there an A3? Are there other areas about A that we need to discuss?"

- **Vertical questions**   For instance, "Tell me about A1. Is A1 important? How should we handle things associated with A1?"

The skilled analyst is able to organize information as it is being gathered into a structural hierarchy. The analyst begins with a list of questions and moves both horizontally and vertically through the topics. The responses can be organized into a tree structure where one topic (such as A) is the parent, and each parent topic has children (A1, A2, A3). These children are siblings and follow a horizontal format. Each child can then be further broken down into more layers of subtopics in a vertical format (A1.1, A1.2, and so on). Each horizontal and vertical topic is explored until a termination point is reached on every set of siblings in the tree. This point is reached when the answer to the question "Is there anything you would like to add?" is "no." In writing up this information, horizontal and vertical lines can be drawn at the appropriate termination points to indicate that the topic has been exhausted.

WORK FROM AN INFORMATION TEMPLATE   Having an internal information template has been found to be one of the key factors in distinguishing an experienced systems person from an inexperienced one. A large body of research on schema theory suggests that learning and comprehension of new information is strongly affected by whatever preexisting related information the learner brings to the task. This can work both ways in an analyst-user interview. The experienced analyst brings a whole range of information on system development and business applications to the interview. At his or her disposal will be many detailed questions about various types of systems that will help shape the interview and get at the desired information. Users, for their part, bring knowledge of their business and what they want the new system to be able to do. Also, they may have some expectations regarding the questions the interviewer will ask. If there is a conflict between the existing schemas of the analyst and the user, the appropriate information may be difficult to obtain.

At the highest subject level, the analyst's internal template, or schema, may be the following question: "If I'm going to build a system, what are the hardware and software requirements?" For an inexperienced analyst, this might be the whole template. A more experienced analyst would have a much more extensive, complete, and detailed set of questions to ask.

For example, to get at the system requirements for performance, a good analyst would know to ask the following questions:

- What is the acceptable time lag for each transaction?

- How up to date must information be in each context? For example, for trend analysis, work on a data warehouse that is updated monthly might be adequate. For a customer billing inquiry, information may have to be up to the second.

- What is the cost of the system going down for 1 minute, 10 minutes, 1 hour, 4 hours, 1 day, etc.?

- How many transactions per hour will the system need to support?

- How many users will be on the system at one time?

The more complex the structural template the analyst brings to the interview, the more likely he or she is to get all the necessary information to eventually create a system that successfully meets the users' needs. The ultimate goal is to get the maximum amount of information on the user's business, existing system, desired changes, and hoped-for aspects and features of the new system.

In reviewing the research videotapes in the author's doctoral study, three levels of analysts emerged based upon their interviewing procedures:

- **Inexperienced**   These interviewers took notes and did a lot of head nodding and saying "uh-huh" but elicited only a fraction of the potential information from the client.

- **Intermediate**   These interviewers followed up on particular threads of information by asking some questions but let the conversation wander. If the interviewer was lucky, the appropriate information was elicited, but it was disorganized, which made it easy to miss important points.

- **Experienced**   These analysts walked into interviews with an information template in their heads that allowed them to work through a systematic hierarchical structure of information retrieval. The user can provide a great deal of information, but the information given will not be generated in a structured format unless the interviewer provides this structure.

For example, the skilled interviewer will already have identified three important areas (A, B, and C) that need to be discussed and will begin by saying, "Tell me about A." From that prompt, topics A1, A2, and A3 will emerge. For each area, the experienced interviewer will lead the user through the information in a structured fashion, and at some appropriate point, the interviewer will review each point with the user to ensure that all the relevant information is elicited.

The interview procedure allows the analyst to develop a list of requirements and show each user what he or she said. It gives the analyst a document that can be given back to each user. The analyst can say, "This is what you told me," and ask, "Do I have it right?" Recording the details is important in big projects, where many ideas that may seem little at the time may fall through the cracks. The Requirements Document is used to explain to the user, "You want the existing system with these changes. We understand the existing system does these things." It does not get any simpler; the analyst has just outlined the scope of the project with the user's own words.

TECHNIQUES OF THE GOOD INTERVIEWER   To summarize, in order to be a successful interviewer, you should use these four important techniques:

- Go into the interview with an internal template of topics and questions relevant to the specific business situation.

- Ask the kinds of questions designed to elicit the maximum amount of information in a structured format.

- Listen actively and effectively, providing useful verbal and nonverbal feedback.

- Provide a hierarchical structure within which the information can be elicited and organized.

When all these elements are in place, the information you gather from the interviews will provide a solid base from which to start system development and will go a long way toward ensuring that users are entirely satisfied with the finished product. In addition, carefully documented and reported user interviews can be invaluable in determining the source of potential problems with the finished product and ways to solve them.

Questionnaires

Unlike open-ended interviews, the question syntax in questionnaires greatly influences their effectiveness. In questionnaires, significantly different results can be obtained depending upon the wording of the questions. The order of both questions and response selections can also affect responses. Items listed first tend to be selected more often. For instance, if asked "Which online service would you rather have access to: CompuServe, Prodigy, or America Online?" more users would choose CompuServe simply because it is listed first.

If questionnaires are administered face-to-face, the issues of bias mentioned for interviews should be taken into consideration.

A potential problem with questionnaires is not asking the right questions. Ask any teacher or professor how difficult it is to write tests and exams.

Think back to the last few times you received a questionnaire in the mail where the questions did not make sense. When composing questions, you must consider the complete range of people who will be answering them. Questions appropriate for managers may not be appropriate for end users. You may need to develop different questionnaires for different classes of system users.

In developing questionnaires, you should subject the questions to extensive testing. Present sample questions to a few users face-to-face to ensure that users interpret the questions the way you intended.

Once questionnaires have been designed and distributed, the results need to be analyzed. The analysis of the answers is a complex task that requires a skilled statistician.

Electronic Communications

Computers have changed the way we communicate within organizations. They have made communication with management much easier across the organization and have, in general, increased the amount of communication within a given organization.

Unfortunately, this communications channel is underused to support requirements analysis. There are several ways that it can be used in this capacity. Electronic information can facilitate various portions of the analysis process as well as other phases within CADM. Two are presented here.

E-mail list servers and groupware products can be used for discussion among users about the system being designed. For example, a web-based application can be set up to debate the features that the new system toolbar should include and whether the organization should go to the expense of including a user-customizable toolbar. Such an application, where any user could post or query messages, would be simple to set up. All messages would be visible to everyone using the application. The second way electronic information can be used to assist in the gathering of user requirements is by giving users direct access to the list of requirements being compiled. Users can review and respond to specific items on the list. A web-enabled application can be set up to access the Oracle Designer Repository. This would allow users to see the listed functions and their associated requirements and enable them to suggest new requirements or comment on existing requirements.

Joint Application Development (JAD) Sessions

A JAD session utilizes a workshop setting where business and technology professionals participate in the planning, analysis, and design of a system development effort. JAD sessions produce the best results when the number of participants does not exceed 20. JAD sessions should be attended by representatives from all interested groups. The organizers should ensure that the group is reasonably balanced in terms of user level.

In order to be effective, JAD sessions must have some specific purposes and goals. They should not be used for general application development work. They are very expensive and frequently not efficient.

A JAD session is an inherently political event that may often involve more political posturing than problem solving. Avoid holding a JAD session to discuss a topic when there is no decision to be made. In such a case, the main function of the session will simply be to allow users to feel as though they have been heard. Often, the outcome of these unfocused JAD sessions is the appointment of a steering committee to perform the work that the JAD session was supposed to accomplish.

If you are going to hold a JAD session, it must have a precise agenda and goal. The more precise the focus, the more successful the JAD session is likely to be. To keep JAD sessions from wasting time, a useful strategy is to schedule them before lunch. Participants are sharper and more focused in the morning, and after one or one and a half hours, they will be ready to leave. In the authors' experience, rarely has anything useful ever happened in a JAD session after the first one and a half hours.

A successful JAD session must have a trained and experienced facilitator whose job it is to work with the project team in developing the purpose, scope, and deliverable in advance of the session. The facilitator must manage the group dynamics, enforce the ground rules, and adhere to the agenda. The purpose, scope, anticipated deliverables, and the agenda should be documented and distributed to all participants well before the scheduled meeting time. The approximate amount of time allocated to each agenda topic should be indicated.

JAD sessions are useful when conflicting user requirements are encountered. A JAD session is the best place to resolve such conflicts. If there are very strong concerns, the proposed session can be used to communicate these concerns to all groups.

An additional function of a JAD session can be to convince obstinate individual users who believe they speak for a large number of other users that they may be mistaken. The JAD session can be a vehicle for overcoming the objections of one or more individuals by demonstrating a general consensus on a particular issue.

Legacy System Review

Most development projects are not brand-new stand-alone systems. They are often upgrades or replacements of existing systems. Therefore, an understanding of those systems being modified or replaced is key to the success of the new system. Just as you should learn what user requirements are from multiple sources, you need to examine the legacy system from several viewpoints to ferret out the necessary requirements. The analyst should perform a legacy system review that includes the following activities to adequately document the existing system:

- Code walkthrough

- Report audit

- User walkthrough

- Review of user and system documentation

With user interviews, you have the luxury of some redundancy— what one user forgets to mention or doesn't know, another one might bring up. However, no such redundancy is available in doing some aspects of the legacy system review. For example, there is (hopefully) only one set of source code for each program, and, if you're really lucky, one set of system documentation for the same program. Consequently, it is imperative to assign highly skilled and responsible people to perform the legacy system review.

Code Walkthrough

The legacy system frequently will contain data and application requirements that are embedded in the underlying legacy code. Particular attention should be paid to the following areas of code in trying to discover these requirements:

- Data validation

- Code that generates redundant or summary fields

- Code that supports data and application security

- Complex application logic

Code walkthroughs are difficult to accomplish if you are not intimately acquainted with the application, even if you do know the language in which it is written. Thus, they are best done with a legacy system developer or maintenance programmer. If the code has not been maintained or well documented or no legacy system developers are available, a code walkthrough may not be worth doing at all.

Report Audit

A report audit is where you ask the users to verify that they actually use each report they receive. A report audit is a cheap and easy way to determine reporting needs. During the first part of the Analysis phase, you should look at the existing reports produced by the current system. The following information should be gathered as a part of this process:

- Determine the user requirements associated with the reports: what kind of information do the system users need and use?

- Determine the reporting requirements for the new system.

- Determine how the existing reports will need to be modified.

Just because a report has been in production for ten years, analysts should not assume that it is still being read. When users are asked what information they are concerned about, they invariably will leave out important information. The systems analyst needs to look carefully at the reports in the system and how they are used by individuals in the organization.

The users should be given copies of all the existing reports relevant to their job functions and asked to rank them using a scale such as this:

- **Level 1: Mission Critical** This report must be converted and in production on day 1.

- **Level 2: Very Useful**   If possible, this report should be available on day 1; it has high priority for implementation.

- **Level 3: Useful**   Users would like to have this report in the new system.

- **Level 4: Marginally Useful**   This report may be used.

- **Level 5: Not Useful**

For all reports marked levels 1 through 3, users should use a marking pen to indicate the information that is specifically useful to them. Frequently, reports have multiple parts. Some users may look only at the summary or for a trend or sample of detail information. It may be possible to decrease the amount of information in reports to make them more concise. Some reports may have been designed for one particular user or class of users that is no longer relevant, but the system keeps churning out the reports anyway. The cost of doing this in the existing system is small, but writing a useless report for the new system is irrational.

The report audit needs to be completed by a large number of users. Unless the total number of users is very small, the audit should be completed by 10 to 20 users per reporting area (such as payroll, accounting, human resources, top management). There should be representatives from each reporting area in the audit group. The developer also needs to be aware of the different constituencies for which each report is relevant.

The results of the audit can be written in a spreadsheet with the report names listed on the left and the users and user group names across the top with user extensions in Oracle Designer. For each report, the priority number (1 to 5) assigned to the report by each user or group should be shown. The users should be asked to look at reports ranked 1 through 3 in more detail and identify the information from those reports that they want in the new system and anything that may be unnecessary.

After all this information is collected, the analyst must decide which reports to incorporate into the new system. The implications of this decision used to be huge, because putting a report into production used to take two to three person weeks. With modern reporting tools or report generation using Oracle Designer, this process now takes one to two days or less. The authors, for example, once developed nine production reports in one day.

At the end of this process, the analyst should have three binders of reports:

1. Top-priority reports that must go into the new system

2. Reports that the developer will attempt to implement in phase 1 of the new system

3. Reports without broad enough appeal to be included in the new system

Keep in mind that the first two binders may include new reports not yet in production. These binders should also include facsimiles of the actual reports or prototypes.

The cost-benefit trade-off for straightforward reports has also changed over time. Costs have been greatly reduced because of products such as Oracle Reports, with its Lexical Parameter Facility. Reports with similar layouts can be combined into a single report. Using the lexical parameters, the system can support the passing of flexible parameters to the report. With this facility, what originally looked like 200 different reports, each requiring a day or two of effort, becomes 10 reports requiring two or three days effort, with the added advantage that changes to the underlying data structure can be implemented very quickly across the entire reporting environment.

The analyst therefore needs to sort and group the designated reports to support the users' reporting needs. It is not necessary to worry about the total number of reports. As mentioned in the preceding paragraph, there may be permutations of other existing reports. It is easier to start with more reports and not be restricted to just the essential ones. Using a combination of Oracle Designer and Oracle Reports, the analyst should have the ability to support the major reporting requirements of a substantial reports system with about one month of effort.

User Walkthroughs

How a user actually uses a system may differ markedly from the way the system was designed to be used. Users are notorious for figuring out workarounds to support functionality that the system was never designed to deliver. Similarly, functionality that was designed into the system may not be as important as was originally thought and may be rarely or never used.

There is no reason to reproduce all of the functionality of the legacy system if it is not all used. For example, a reporting system may include a flexible ad hoc reporting engine that allows users to filter and break for subtotals on many fields in the database. In practice, however, the users may consider only a handful of fields, thus making a large part of the functionality of the system irrelevant.

Sometimes, the only way for analysts to find out what users actually do is to sit down with them and watch them do it. These user walkthroughs should be conducted with different users at different levels. Often, the users themselves can help the analysts select individuals who are doing interesting things with the system or who are often sought out for help with the existing system.

Here are some specific areas that analysts should target during system walkthroughs:

- Ask users to identify any workarounds and how they are performed.

- Ask questions designed to find out whether existing system features are being used as they were intended. For instance, if the system includes an employee or customer name field, ask whether this field is used for any purpose other than the stated one.

- Ask what all of the uses are for a particular screen.

User and System Documentation Review

Of course, a thorough reading of the legacy system documentation and any user documentation, where it exists, is a given. These sources will frequently point to other user requirements not mentioned elsewhere. The analyst will not get accurate or complete information on the legacy system by simply talking to users. Users often don't know how the system is designed or even how all of its functions work.

When legacy system documentation is missing or inadequate, the analysts must reconstruct it as best they can. The legacy system documentation should be organized into three sections:

- **Data structure**   The data structure section should include documentation of files and of the file structure, if the database is relational. Also, a physical ERD should be included as well as a logical ERD if these exist. Finding an ERD for a legacy system is a rare occurrence. However, even when the system is not relational, the analyst should try to design capture a physical ERD.

■ **Fields**   The analyst needs to know the purpose of all the fields in tables and files. Ideally, descriptions of all existing fields should exist for the legacy system. If these descriptions do not exist, the analyst should build them before proceeding. If fields are redundant and used only for processing, it is sufficient to identify and describe only the significant data fields.

■ **Where each field comes from**   For simple systems, a matrix can be constructed to show how a specific data element from a specific screen is populated. A simple spreadsheet or application that becomes a master-detail report can be used for this purpose.

It is also important to find out the following information on the legacy system:

■ How do data elements on the screen (the user interface) map to data elements in the database?

■ How are business transactions performed?

■ What business rules are embedded in the data structure?

It is not always possible to count on the logical, consistent mapping and file structures that developers now expect in relational databases. Fields aren't necessarily just one thing; they may serve multiple purposes. For example, a system may include a salesperson ID field, but during data migration, you may discover that although this field usually contains a salesperson ID, sometimes transactions not credited to a specific salesperson are credited to a department, and a null employee entry is made in the salesperson ID field. Consequently, the field may contain either a real employee or an unassigned employee.

The point is that the analyst needs to go into some depth in a legacy system to find out all the different kinds of information that are placed in a particular field.

The analyst should also track performance characteristics of the legacy system. How long do reports take to run? How fast is the user response in performing various tasks? The new system should at least outperform the old one. It is important to find out from the users what their performance concerns are and where performance matters less. Rank the performance issues and determine the most frequent user actions so that the new system can be more efficient.

Determining the processes embedded in the legacy system code is as important as finding out the business rules. Process-oriented people will often forget about business rules, but both aspects are important to overall project success. By observing how users actually use the existing system, analysts can get a better idea of how users will interact with the new system. A new system that is replacing a legacy system must duplicate only the business functionality of the legacy system that the users deem necessary to support their business.

The documentation of the legacy system can be handled with a small ad hoc database. The ad hoc system must track the legacy system's fields, files, modules, and data structures. The appropriate structure for this system will change from system to system. Sometimes, an Oracle Designer application can be created to store this information. For example, relational database designs can be captured directly from the database or from SQL DDL files. Designer even has properties to represent COBOL datatypes and data structures, which can be entered manually or, if volume justifies the time and cost, automatically via an API program.

Note that the legacy data structure need not be documented at the field level. The cost to achieve that level of detail outweighs the added benefits. This data model is used to map the main functionality of the old system to the new system. It is used to make sure that no legacy-supported business function is missed in the design of the new system. The data model is also used to map legacy fields to the new system attributes.

Security

It is necessary to determine the sensitivity of the information that will comprise the system. For most information, we want to have some security to prevent unauthorized manipulation of the information. In other places, we must also worry about unauthorized retrieval of information.

At this point in the information-gathering process, the goal is to determine not only the security requirements but also the costs of a security breach. The likelihood of such a breach must also be assessed. This involves the possible motivations of individuals for breaching security. For example, in a banking wire transfer system, a breach of security would allow someone the ability to initiate fraudulent wire transfers. Preventing unauthorized access to systems is particularly important where financial data is concerned. A list of a company's clients might be of great interest to a competitor. However, information concerning how much a company has paid for office supplies is of little interest.

As with other areas of system requirements, it is necessary to ask the opinions of numerous individuals at different levels within the organization to determine security requirements. In contrast to other areas of information gathering, typically the best information concerning security can be obtained from middle and upper management rather than end users because of their broader perspective on the role of information in the organization.

It is easy for users to blithely say that they want all data to be completely secure from unauthorized access or manipulation. However, there is always a cost associated with the implementation of security. No system is completely secure. It is necessary to determine the desired level of security for a specific system and the possible costs to the organization of a security failure.

Unit-Level Analysis

Chapter 9 discusses in detail the analysis of the requirements you collect. Within information gathering, you must extract the relevant system requirements from all of the interview and legacy system data that you have collected. The goal at this stage is only to understand—not to comment on, filter, dispute, or synthesize the information. As discussed in the "Interviews" section earlier, the analysts should be locked into information receipt mode.

The information collected must, however, be placed into a useful format for the Analysis phase to proceed further. To that end, you must perform unit-level analysis. User interviews will generate many interview notes. These interview notes may suggest process flows, data models, and elements that may eventually be included in a function hierarchy.

The interview notes from each user must be associated with the tasks the user must accomplish. The process flows, the tasks per user, and what information the user needs should be recorded. To allow easy cross-checking of the data, the source should also be noted with each requirement. Listing each requirement, its business function, and its source will make the project flow more smoothly. Again, it is vital that all system requirements be uncovered. Knowing who said that the system must have certain features or functions enables the team to resolve conflicting needs. It also helps the analyst weigh the information provided by each user, since some users know more about certain areas than others. In an insurance company, the user who is an expert in policy management, for example, may only be able to guess at what an underwriter would require to make a decision.

For each interview, create the appropriate business models (ERD, process model, function hierarchy) as well as any narrative descriptions to support the models. What is needed is both a graphical and narrative method to communicate to the user that the analyst has understood what was said and at the same time educate the user about some of the diagrams used by systems people—specifically, data models and process flows. This process can give novice analysts conducting interviews some experience in performing data and process analysis.

Possible feedback to the user may be as simple as a review of the notes taken during the interviews, in narrative form. For a more complex response, the analyst can map the interview to a function hierarchy. The best solution may be a combination of the two. The notes can be written, and a structured document can be generated using Word for Windows to put the information into a hierarchy. If desired, this Word document can be loaded into the Oracle Designer function hierarchy using a C program to read the file and load the data into the repository.

A copy of the user-feedback report should go for sign-off to each user interviewed. This sign-off is the ultimate feedback, since this will be the information that goes into the Requirements Document.

As you go through this book, you'll find that we advocate that nonfunctioning storyboard prototypes be delivered as part of the Pre-Design phase. However, preliminary prototypes based on unit analysis should be created even as information gathering is going on. One of the best ways to communicate understanding of particular system requirements is to show users how they might be implemented. Some level of prototyping should be ongoing throughout Analysis. Much of the thinking about how the system should look and feel should be done before the Pre-Design phase.

Modifications for Smaller Systems

You don't need to make any modifications whatsoever for smaller systems for this part of the analysis process. Information gathering is essential to any project. All that is different for a smaller project is the amount of information gathered. Procedures, interview notes, user feedback, sign-off, and so on should all be conducted in the same manner no matter how small the system.

When Is Information Gathering Complete?

Information gathering is an ongoing process throughout the System Development Life Cycle. However, it is easy to fall into the trap of "analysis paralysis," which can stall a project indefinitely. Often, what harms a project at this point is not the information that has been gathered but information that has not been kept track of properly after it has been gathered. Nothing is more infuriating to users than having a second or even a third group of analysts ask them the same questions. If a user ever asks, "Don't you people ever talk to each other?" you can conclude that the information-gathering process is flawed.

Being meticulous in all aspects of the information-gathering process is an important attribute. Obtaining requirements from so many different sources will, of course, result in some duplication of effort. However, the cost of missing an essential requirement is much higher than the cost of collecting a few requirements more than once.

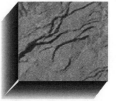

CHAPTER
8

Oracle Designer in
Analysis—Information
Gathering

*Knowledge is of two kinds. We know a subset ourselves, or we know
where we can find information upon it.*
—Samuel Johnson (1709-1784), Letter dated 4/18/1775

racle Designer offers you considerable support in the
Analysis phase, and you can produce many of the main
deliverables directly from the tools and diagrammers.
Table 8-1 lists the diagrammers and utilities that are
most useful for the information-gathering part of the
Analysis phase.

This chapter discusses how you can use each of these tools to complete
the work for these activities. As usual, you are strongly encouraged to
review the introduction to the Oracle Designer interface in Chapter 2 if you
have not had hands-on experience with this interface and to consult the
Oracle Designer help system for information on the diagrammers and
utilities if you need additional instruction.

Activity or Deliverable	Oracle Designer Tool
Interview documents: process flows	Process Modeller or Dataflow Diagrammer
Interview documents: ERD	Entity Relationship Diagrammer
Legacy System ERD	Design Editor: Capture Design of Server Model from Database utility, RON: Table to Entity Retrofit utility, Entity Relationship Diagrammer
Legacy system report audit	Repository Administration Utility (with a user extended property on the Modules element)

TABLE 8-1. *Information-Gathering Activities and Oracle Designer*

NOTE
The repository contains flexibly-defined elements you can use in the Analysis phase to categorize information not stored elsewhere in the repository. These elements, Assumptions, Critical Success Factors, Key Performance Indicators, Locations, Objectives, and Problems are available in RON. There are also some repository reports and matrix diagrams you can use to view and manipulate these elements.

Process Modeller and Entity Relationship Diagrammer in Information Gathering

During the interviewing process, you gather information about requirements, data, and process flows in the organization. You may find it useful to immediately diagram some of these processes or data entities as a visualization of the information you have gathered. Such diagrams can help you to solidify your understanding and communicate this understanding to your interviewees. The idea is to quickly translate your notes from the interviewing process into diagrams right after the interviews. You can also do this outside Oracle Designer initially and then, after checking your diagrams with users or business experts, spend more time carefully entering the information into the repository during the Requirements Analysis part of the Analysis phase.

Alternatively, you can use Oracle Designer's diagrammers to create the first-cut diagrams that you use to communicate with the users in the unit-level analysis work. The Oracle Designer Process Modeller and Entity Relationship Diagrammer can fulfill this need for a set of rough diagrams as you can quickly enter and move elements around on the screen. While these may not be the ultimate in drawing tools, the graphical features are rich enough for you to create these first-cut diagrams easily and efficiently. The benefit of using the Oracle Designer tools is that when you are done, even if the diagrams are not perfectly accurate, you will have some information in the repository that can serve as a basis for the next part of the Analysis phase: Requirements Analysis.

Completeness and correct decomposition of the process flow models and exact representation of entities are not your main concerns in this part of the Analysis phase. Rather, you should concentrate on the ideas and concepts of the functions and data. You do not want the process of drawing the interview flows and ERDs to take you away from the work of gathering information and checking it with the people you are interviewing.

Chapter 4 discusses the Process Modeller in some depth, and you should be able to use that information to complete the process flows to represent the knowledge you gained from interviews. You should also find the discussion of the Entity Relationship Diagrammer in Chapter 4 sufficiently detailed to enable you to show the entities and relationships themselves on the diagram.

Dataflow Diagrammer

The purpose of the Dataflow Diagrammer is similar to that of the Process Modeller: you use it to diagram the functions, flows, and stores in the system you are analyzing. Although the symbols and methods are a bit different, you work with the same repository objects in both. This diagrammer is really just an alternative to the Process Modeller in this part of Analysis and helps you diagram the process flows you harvest from the interviewing sessions.

You do not need to go into great depth in the dataflow diagram in the Information Gathering step of the Analysis phase. The purpose of the process flow diagrams in the initial stages of the life cycle, whether you create them in the Process Modeller or the Dataflow Diagrammer, is to document your initial understanding of the system requirements and to communicate this understanding to the clients and users. You use the Dataflow Diagrammer more heavily in the next step of the Analysis phase, when you analyze the requirements in depth. Chapter 10 describes some more features of the Dataflow Diagrammer that you might use at that stage.

Differences between the Dataflow Diagrammer and Process Modeller

Because the Dataflow Diagrammer and Process Modeller seem to accomplish the same task, it is useful to examine the differences between them. Table 8-2 lists the major differences (other than symbol sets) between these two diagrammers.

As you can see from Table 8-2, one major benefit of the Dataflow Diagrammer is that you can attach entity and attribute usages to processes,

Task	Process Modeller	Dataflow Diagrammer
Represent organization units on the diagram	Yes	No
Distinguish different types for processes, flows, and stores	Yes	Processes only
Define triggering events and outcomes	Yes	No
Run other programs from the diagram	Yes	No
Attach multimedia and text annotations to diagram elements	Yes	No
Animate the diagram and show process timing	Yes	No
Represent entities external to the system	No	Yes
Attach data usages to processes, flows, and stores	No	Yes
Use a numbering system to indicate function hierarchy levels	No	Yes

TABLE 8-2.   *Differences between the Process Modeller and the Dataflow Diagrammer*

flows, and stores in the Properties dialog box, whereas in the Process Modeller you cannot. This may or may not be a deciding factor; you will need to weigh the differences between these two diagrammers to decide which one to use. You may also need to base your decision on standards in your corporate environment or the company for which this project is being done. Your own background is a consideration as well; if you are accustomed to dataflow diagrams, you may decide to use the Dataflow Diagrammer, although learning the new features of the Process Modeller is not an insurmountable task. If you have no experience in either tool, you might seriously consider the Process Modeller for the extended set of features and presentation capabilities it offers; all you lose by making that decision is the data usage mapping—which you can perform in the Function Hierarchy Diagrammer—and the representation of external entities.

Another consideration is that you will probably not use the Process Modeller in the next stage of the Analysis phase: Requirements Analysis. In that stage, you fully define the data usages, which is a task the Process Modeller cannot handle. Also in that stage, you will not need the multimedia and reengineering capabilities of the Process Modeller. This may affect your decision of which one to use for the Information Gathering stage.

Keep in mind that whatever your choice of diagrammer you can always use the other diagrammer to create a new diagram and include (with the **Edit→Include** menu option) existing elements, no matter where you first defined them.

The following discussion details some of the operational aspects of the Dataflow Diagrammer that differ from the common diagramming techniques mentioned in Chapter 2. This discussion also covers how the Dataflow Diagrammer differs from the Process Modeller in specific techniques or features.

Figure 8-1 shows a sample Dataflow Diagrammer session.

Basic Techniques

The Dataflow Diagrammer uses the same basic techniques as the other diagrammers for opening, saving, and creating a new diagram. When you select **File→New** from the menu, you have to choose a function on which to base the diagram, as you do in the Process Modeller. This function serves as a frame to contain all child functions (subfunctions) and is called a *frame function.* You can create a new function at this point with the Create

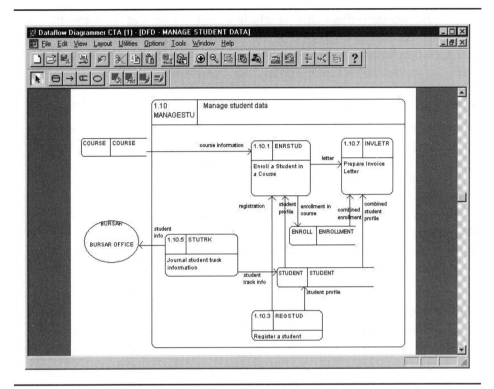

FIGURE 8-1. *Dataflow Diagrammer session*

Function button or choose an existing function from the list. The function you choose will appear as a rounded box on the screen (as do all functions) with a name, number, and description. Remember, Oracle Designer makes no distinction between a process and a function. Therefore, while you may think in terms of modeling processes in a dataflow diagram, Oracle Designer stores these processes as the Business Functions element type.

Drawing Objects

Except for the frame function, which Oracle Designer draws when you create the diagram, you draw all elements in the diagram by clicking the corresponding button in the drawing toolbar and clicking within the drawing area. With functions, you can just click the drawing area to create a default-sized box. If the element you want to diagram is already in the repository, you can select **Edit→Include** from the menu and choose the type of item and then one or more existing items of that type. If you are including functions, you can include the dataflows automatically by checking the With Dataflows check box in the Include Function dialog box.

TIP
Some of the Oracle Designer dialogs (like
Edit→Include *dialogs) have buttons such as*
Select All and UnSelect All. These will speed
up entry when you want to choose all or most
of the selections in the list. Remember that you
can usually deselect items one at a time, so it is
sometimes faster when you have a long list to
choose Select All and then deselect any items
you do not need.

Using the Symbol Set

The number of symbols in the Dataflow Diagrammer is quite small, consisting of only functions, dataflows, datastores, and externals, as shown in Figure 8-2.

FUNCTIONS   Functions in Oracle Designer are separated into the following categories according to their diagrammatic purpose:

- *Frame function* is the base function for the diagram that contains the child functions.

- *Common function* is a copy of a function from this or another application system. You define this function on the Common tab in its Properties dialog. This function copies the label of its source function. This type of function displays with a double line on the left side of the box.

- *Local function* (also referred to simply as *function*) is a function within the frame function.

- *Global function* is a function outside the frame function.

All categories of functions have the same basic symbol in the DFD, and you distinguish them mainly by position. The categories are distinct from the types of processes that the Process Modeller handles. In that tool, you can

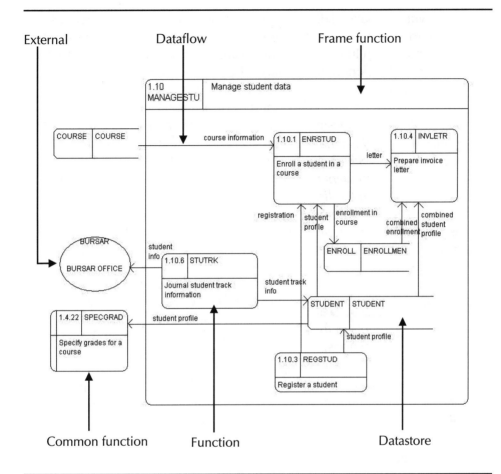

External   Dataflow   Frame function

Common function   Function   Datastore

FIGURE 8-2.   *Dataflow Diagrammer symbol set*

assign a process as one of the following types: Process Step, Decision Point, Data Entry, Internal, External, or Report. The specified type becomes a property of that process and further refines its meaning.

You can display a function's properties dialog by double-clicking on the function symbol in the diagram or by selecting Properties from the right-click menu. The Definition tab of this dialog has a check box for a property called *Elementary*. This property is important because the Application Design Transformer will create modules (screens, reports, procedures, and others) from all functions you designate as elementary. Think of an elementary function as a complete unit of code that represents a business process that cannot be stopped midway. An example would be the function of filling out a registration form. There is no benefit to the business in having a partially completed registration form. Thus, the function "Complete a registration form" would be elementary. The function Definition tab also includes a property called *Atomic*. A function with the Atomic property checked is at its lowest level of decomposition. Oracle Designer automatically places a check mark in this box if you have not broken the function down into any component functions. You cannot change this value directly. This property does not appear in the Process Modeller properties dialog.

If you have created functions on a lower level than a function on the diagram, that parent function will have an ellipsis (. . .) above the upper-right corner. The ellipsis indicates that, after selecting the function, you can choose **Open→Down** from the File menu to display a diagram with its subfunctions. It is not necessary to have an existing lower-level diagram. This operation will create one if it does not exist.

DATAFLOWS   *Flows* (or *dataflows*) in Oracle Designer (unlike some other CASE tools) are single directional, with one source and one target. You can represent a two-way flow in the Dataflow Diagrammer with two one-way flows in opposite directions. This technique enables you to specify separate names, properties, and data usages for each direction.

Resolved flows link elements on a lower level than the one in the diagram. You cannot create a resolved flow on the diagram, but you can include one from a definition already in the repository (entered using the Repository Object Navigator, for instance). Oracle Designer indicates resolved flows with a dashed line, as in Figure 8-3. The dashed line indicates that you have to choose **File→Open→Down** for the function to see the lowest level in which this flow appears.

The DFD makes a distinction between normal dataflows and *global flows,* which link to a global function. Therefore, when you choose **Edit→Include** from the menu, you see separate types for Global Flows and Dataflows, as shown here:

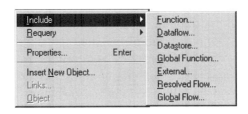

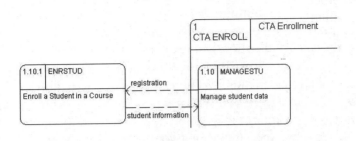

FIGURE 8-3.   *Resolved flows in the DFD*

The Dataflow Diagrammer also allows you to type in your own classification (type) for the flow in the Properties dialog. This is a free-form field and there is no fixed list to choose from. The Process Modeller also allows you to classify flows and to assign a flow a type from a fixed list of options: Flow, Data Flow, Temporal Flow, and Material Flow. The DFD and Process Modeller classification types are separate properties in the repository.

You can *split* flows to create new flows or elements from existing ones. You split a flow to add a new (or include an existing) datastore in a flow between a global and local function, indicating that the data is stored before the next process takes over. All you need to do is select the flow and the store (if there is one) and click the Split Dataflow button (or select **Utilities→Split Dataflow** from the menu).

You also can *divide* a flow to add a new flow to which you will assign part of the data usage. For example, you might have Dataflow1 to which Entity1.Attribute1 and Entity1.Attribute2 are assigned. You could create another flow from this one and assign Entity1.Attribute 2 to it (which would de-assign Attribute2 from the original flow).

For example, you create a dataflow between the function "Complete registration form" and "Review registration form." The flow contains attributes from the Student entity for First Name, Last Name, Company Name, Address, and Zipcode. Later on, you find that you need a parallel function to "Validate zipcode." The "Complete registration form" function should send it some of the attributes it is already sending to "Review registration form." You can split the dataflow and create a new dataflow with the Zipcode attribute. The Zipcode attribute will be removed from the first flow and attached to a new flow between the same two entities. You then move the end of the new flow to the new function.

This feature is useful when you want to send part of the data from one flow to another destination. The procedure is as easy as selecting the flow and clicking the Divide Dataflow button (or selecting **Utilities→Divide Dataflow** from the menu). You will see a dialog, where you can specify the elements that you want to move to the new flow, and then the tool will draw a new flow between the same two functions that you can move to another element. Figure 8-4 shows the Divide Dataflow Contents dialog box.

DATASTORES Datastores are simple elements with just a few properties. The only trick you can pull with them is to create them on the fly between functions with the Split Dataflow feature just mentioned. The Dataflow Diagrammer Properties dialog lets you assign one of the following types to a datastore: Computer, Manual, or Transient. Assigning a type is useful for grouping stores later and for reporting purposes. The Process

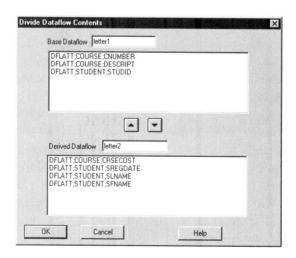

FIGURE 8-4. *Divide Dataflow Contents dialog*

Modeller classifies datastores using the following types: Store, Material Store, and Data Store. The Process Modeller store type and Dataflow Diagrammer datastore type are separate properties in the repository.

EXTERNALS   Externals also have only a few properties. You might want to designate the organization unit or data entity from this application system with which the external entity is associated. Externals may also be organization units or entities from another application system that are shared with this application system and so fulfill the definition that an external identifies something outside the scope of the hierarchy that will have data flowing to or from it.

Naming Elements

The way you name the elements on the diagram is up to you, but consistency is important, and you should start with guidelines when beginning the diagramming process. Most elements require a short name and a full name, both of which are displayed on the diagram. The short names are converted to uppercase, as are the names of datastores. Function names, by convention like process names, start with a verb (something other than "process") and are mixed-case phrases that indicate an activity, such as "Complete a registration form." Flow names can be lowercase words or short phrases that indicate the type of data flowing, such as "student profile" or "validated zipcode." Store names are usually one-word uppercase nouns that correspond, roughly, to entity names, such as "STUDENT." External names are also uppercase single-word nouns, such as "BURSAR."

Assigning Data Usages to Functions

One strength of the Dataflow Diagrammer is that you can identify the data source of processes, flows, and stores. There are actually four different ways to assign entities and attributes to a function as follows:

1. Fill out the Entity Usages tab of the function, then add the necessary attributes for each entity on the Attribute Usages tab. The attributes inherit the entity usage settings and you do not need to set them explicitly.

2. Fill out the Entity Usages tab of the function. Then fill out the Attribute Usages tab of the function with specific usages for each attribute.

3. Fill in the Entity Usages tab and use the Function/Attribute Matrix utility to assign all attribute usages for all entities of selected functions.

4. Use Matrix Diagrammer to assign usages.

You would use method 1 or 2 if you were just starting in Oracle Designer and wanted to be very careful when entering each usage. You would use method 3 if you wanted a head start on the attribute usages and were using a junior analyst to enter the entity usages; in this case, you could have that person run the utility and you could examine and refine the attribute usages at a later time. Method 4 would work best for entering usages that you know very well and you want to do more than what the default attribute assignments (from 1 or 3) will give you. Alternatively, you would use 4 to check the work done in the other methods.

The following discussion addresses techniques you need to perform methods 1 and 2; the section on the Function/Attribute Matrix utility following introduces that utility for method 3. Chapter 10 discusses method 4 and how the Matrix Diagrammer helps you assign or check CRUD (create-retrieve-update-delete) usages for functions.

In the Dataflow Diagrammer, you assign function data usages in the Properties dialog, as Figure 8-5 shows.

To assign a usage, you need to specify an entity that already exists in the repository. This means that you need to use the ER Diagrammer or RON to create the entities and attributes before or at the same time as you create the DFD's data usage assignments. Chapter 10 describes details on how to use attributes with entities although this is an activity you would perform to some degree in the Information Gathering step of Analysis as well. If you are not concerned with data usages yet, as may be the case in the Information Gathering stage of Analysis, you can leave this task for later. Assigning usages is a matter of choosing entities and attributes from drop-down lists in the Properties dialog and then filling in the usages for the entities—Create, Retrieve, Update, Delete, Archive, Other (which refers to a user-defined usage)—and for the attributes—Insert, Retrieve, Update, Nullify, Archive, Other.

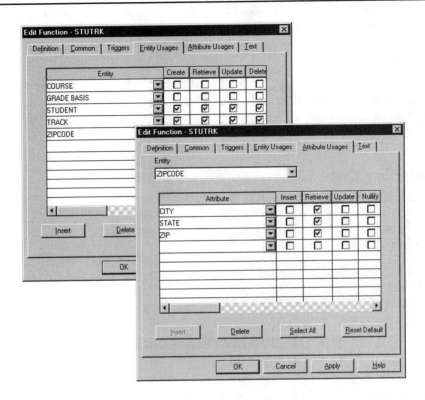

FIGURE 8-5. *Entity and attribute usage assignment for a function*

TIP
While it is quite possible to enter data usages in the diagrammer as you create the diagram, it may be easier to use the Repository Object Navigator to do this because of its element-grouping capabilities.

When assigning data usages to functions, you will save keystrokes if you enter the Entity with its CRUD on the Entity Usage tab before entering the attributes as in methods 1 and 2 above. When you switch to the Attribute

Usages tab, you can use the Select All button to load all attributes, or you can select one attribute at a time. The attributes will "inherit" the same usages that were set for the entity. Of course, you might still have to refine the CRUD usages on the Attribute tab. You can also use the Function/Attribute Matrix utility on the Utilities menu to assign attributes to functions, as described later in this chapter. Alternatively, you can also use the Matrix Diagrammer to assign the create-retrieve-update-delete usages for entities and attributes, as Chapter 10 explains.

Assigning Data Usages to Flows and Stores

The method you use to associate the data with flows and stores is a bit different from the one you use for functions. You perform this task in the Properties dialog as usual, but you use the Contents tab to assign both entities and attributes, as Figure 8-6 shows.

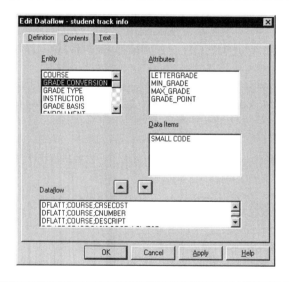

FIGURE 8-6. *Data usage assignment for a flow or store*

Notice that there is no place to enter usages, because the flow or store does not make changes to the data; it only transfers or holds it. Also notice that this dialog has a *Data Items* area. A data item is an element type you can create in the Repository Object Navigator; it has attribute-like properties (*Format, Maximum Length, Derivation,* and so on), but is not associated with an entity. These will then appear in the Data Items area on the flow and store Contents tabs so you can specify that a flow or store has an attribute that currently is not part of an entity. Naturally, you will create an attribute in an entity later in the analysis process and copy the data item's properties into that attribute using RON.

Function/Attribute Matrix Utility

The Utilities menu includes the Function/Attribute Matrix utility (also called Create Function/Attribute Matrix in RON), which presents a dialog box where you can select the function or functions you wish to act on. When you click OK, Oracle Designer adds attribute usages for all entities used by the selected functions. If the entities have CRUD usages, the utility will copy these to the attribute usages it creates. This is a fast and easy way to add all attribute usages to a set of functions. If you need to change the assignments, you can do so, but these changes should be less work than specifying all attribute usages from scratch. Remember that this process is not one you will necessarily need to do until the Requirements Analysis stage of the Analysis phase.

Other Techniques

Normally, the diagrammer numbers the functions in the order you create them. To change this order, select a function and click the Resequence button on the standard toolbar (or choose **Utilities→Resequence** from the menu). The dialog shown in Figure 8-7 appears, and you move the function names around using the arrow buttons. When you click OK, the function numbers will have the new order that you specified.

FIGURE 8-7. *Resequence dialog*

TIP
In all Oracle Designer diagrammers, if the button or menu choice you wish to use is disabled (dimmed), you have not performed the prerequisites for that task. Usually, all the diagrammer requires is for you to select an object on the drawing, but you may have to do something else as well. The quickest way to find out what to do is to click the Context-Sensitive Help button and then click the help cursor on the button (or select the menu item) in question. A help screen with information on that particular activity will appear.

Decomposing functions is another common activity in the Dataflow Diagrammer. This process is as simple as selecting the function you wish to further describe (by defining component functions) and selecting **File→Open Down** from the menu. To move to the diagram at the next level up from the one you are at, select **File→Open Up**. If that menu item is disabled, you are at the top level.

Dog-legs, as described in Chapter 2, are angled flow lines and are useful when you are moving functions around and do not want a flow to intersect another function or store. You can have as many dog-legs on a particular flow as you want, but the fewer dog-legs you have, the easier your drawing will be to read. You have to weigh this guideline against the guideline that says no flow lines should intersect a function or store. You create a drawing point for the dog-leg, as usual, by selecting the flow, holding down the SHIFT key, and clicking the mouse in the middle of the flow. To eliminate a dog-leg point, hold down the SHIFT key and click the mouse on that point.

You can specify triggered functions for each function in the Triggers tab of the function's Properties dialog. A triggered function is one that occurs as a result of this function's completion. For example, if Function2 starts as a result of the completion of Function1, then Function2 is a triggered function. To specify this relationship, you open the Properties dialog for Function1 and specify Function2 by moving it to the "Functions triggered" box. For example, the "Complete registration form" function triggers the "Validate zipcode" function so the properties dialog of the former would list the former function in its "Functions triggered" box.

You can also specify trigger information in the Process Modeller, and it will appear in the Functions/Events-Triggering node under the Business Function node in the Repository Object Navigator. This information will appear on reports for the function model, but will not generate any code in the modules derived from these functions.

Other Menu and Toolbar Functions

The Dataflow Diagrammer features conform closely to the features common to all Oracle Designer tools discussed in Chapter 2. The Window and Help menus and toolbars contain the normal choices, and the Tools menu has selections for standard repository utilities and other tools you might want to use in the Analysis phase. In addition, it offers access to the Design Editor, where you set up and manipulate all Design elements.

The File menu, too, contains all standard diagrammer features, including Open Up and Open Down to allow you to easily create or move to a lower- or higher-level diagram. Remember that you can delete an existing diagram using **File→Delete Diagram**. The Edit menu is also standard. The View menu contains the same zoom, grid, Toolbar, Tool Palette, and Status Bar choices as other diagrammers.

TIP

When you choose Open Up or Open Down to go to another diagram in the hierarchy, Oracle Designer keeps the original diagram open. A list of open diagrams will appear on the Window menu, and you can navigate back and forth by selecting the diagram names from that list rather than worrying about which function is the parent for which other function.

The Layout menu has items similar to those in all Oracle Designer diagrammers for AutoLayout and for applying Rescale Diagram (to fit it on a certain number of pages). The Utilities menu contains the Resequence, Split Dataflow, and Divide Dataflow functions mentioned in the preceding discussion. It also contains an option to load the Application Design Transformer. In addition, it provides a utility to convert dataflow diagrams from a repository migrated from version 5.0 or 5.1 of Oracle*CASE to Oracle Designer as well as the Function/Attribute Matrix utility described earlier in this chapter.

The Options menu contains the standard choices for Broadcast, Text Editor, and Diagnostics. It also has a selection called Customize, which opens the Customize dialog, shown in Figure 8-8. This is like the Customize dialogs in other tools, which allow you to change what you see in the diagrammer.

TIP

You can also use the Matrix Diagrammer, discussed in Chapter 10, to attach attributes. This diagrammer also helps you assign CRUD usages to functions for which you have already assigned data. In addition, the Matrix Diagrammer helps in the initial assignment of entities and attributes. However, if you will be using most or all of the attributes for an entity, the Function/Attribute Matrix is the fastest tool to use.

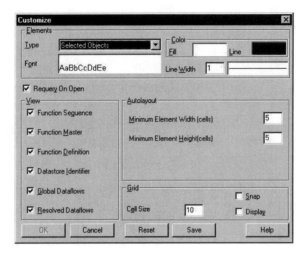

FIGURE 8-8. *Customize dialog*

Where Does This Information Go?

The element definitions you create or diagram in the Dataflow Diagrammer
show up in other phases as well as later in the Analysis phase, when you
create different diagrams, using Function Hierarchy Diagrammer or Process
Modeller. They also appear in the Repository Object Navigator as the
element types listed in Table 8-3. Notice that Table 8-3 is similar to the one
for the Process Modeller, discussed in Chapter 4, since the Dataflow
Diagrammer diagrams essentially the same objects but in a different way. In
addition to these elements, the Application Design Transformer converts
function data usages and flow data usages to module usages and module
parameters, respectively.

Dataflow Diagrammer Element	Repository Element and Future Use
Datastores	Datastores; used to cross-check data usage in functions
Externals	Externals; assigned to a business unit or entity and used on reports
Functions	Business Functions; used by the Application Design Transformer to create modules
Functions triggered and Functions which trigger this Function	Events, also called "Triggered By" and "Triggering" as subnodes of Business Functions; used to document which functions cause which others to begin
Dataflows	Dataflows (Source for Dataflows and Destination for Dataflows) subnodes under a particular Business Function or Datastores; used to cross-check data usage in functions and generate parameters to the modules derived from these functions

TABLE 8-3.   *Dataflow Diagrammer Elements and Repository Elements*

Legacy System ERD

The legacy system ERD consists of entities that represent tables in the current (legacy) system. You create the legacy system ERD in three basic steps, which each use a different Oracle Designer tool or utility:

I. Use the Capture Design of Server Model from Database utility in the Design Editor to automatically insert information on current tables and views into the repository. This means that you do not have to manually add the definitions—normally a time-consuming and error-prone activity.

2. Run the Table to Entity Retrofit utility in RON to automatically create entity definitions from the table definitions created in step 1.

3. Create an ERD with the Entity Relationship Diagrammer to represent the entities the utility created in the step 2.

This section discusses these steps and the utilities you use to perform them. As you create the legacy system ERD, notice how most of the work is automated when you use Oracle Designer. Instead of performing what is typically a time-consuming manual process, with Oracle Designer virtually all you need to do is check that the objects were created successfully.

1. Capture Design of Server Model from Database Utility

Design capture means loading the repository with objects that exist in the database or file system. This concept was called *reverse engineering* in Designer version 1. There are two types of design-capture utilities: database objects and front-end program files (specifically, Forms, Reports, Libraries, and Visual Basic code). This section describes the Capture Design of Server Model from Database utility, which for the sake of brevity is called design capture.

Oracle Designer can capture the definitions of database definitions from the following databases:

- Oracle8, Oracle7

- Rdb (v 7.0, 6.1)

- ANSI 92

- DB2/2 and DB2/MVS 4.*x*

- Microsoft SQL Server (v 6.5, 6.0)

- Sybase System 11

The support for some databases is more robust than the support for others with Oracle being the one that is most fully supported, of course. The details of which object types in which database is able to be design-captured are contained in a help system topic called "Database design capture - summary of support." This topic also lists the database objects that the utility can design-capture from a text file. That is, if you have a Data Definition Language (DDL) script in a text file, the utility can read that file and create repository definitions for the objects defined in the script.

To create the legacy system ERD, you will want to design capture just those tables needed in the system with views, snapshots, triggers, and indexes. Alternatively, you might want to design capture all tables and set the Table Implementation *Complete* property to "No" which means you will not be able to generate DDL for that table. This will give you better documentation on the legacy system and, if you have to include the table later, you set the *Complete* property to "Yes" and it will be ready for use.

The task is quite simple from the Oracle Designer point of view: start the utility, specify the database objects you wish to bring into the repository, and click the Start button.

Start the Utility

The design capture utility does not have a separate button in the Oracle Designer window, but you can start it from two places in the Design Editor: the **Generate→Design Capture of→Server Model From Database** menu item and the **Tools→Database Navigator** utility. The following describes the Generate menu item. The discussion of the Design Editor in Chapter 14 will explain the Database Navigator utility. This menu item displays the Source tab, shown in Figure 8-9.

In this dialog, you select which source type you will work with: Database, DDL Files, or ODBC (Open Database Connectivity). You also designate which user schema the objects will be assigned to. This is a user definition in the repository (not necessarily a real Oracle user in the database) associated with a database definition in the repository. You create both of these definitions using RON. All objects you capture the design of must be associated with a database and user in the repository. Objects like tables can actually be associated with more than one schema; this information is stored in the element Table Implementations association. This allows you to implement the same table definition in multiple databases or user schemas.

Table Implementations is an important concept and one new to version 2. For example, if you have a development and a production database environment with the same tables. Each environment might have different

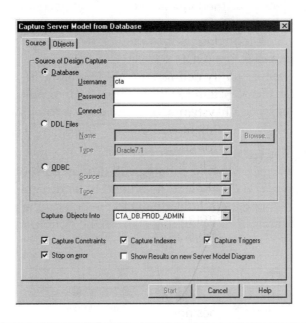

FIGURE 8-9. *Source tab of the Capture Server Model from Database dialog*

storage parameters for each table and you could create separate Table Implementations for the development and the production versions of the table. Each implementation would specify a different storage parameter set. Then, when you generate the DDL script, you would specify which user you want to generate for and the Server Generator would use the Table Implementations under that user's schema node in the repository.

If you choose Database as the source, you fill in the connection information: the login name, password, and database connect string. The login name should be the name of the schema that owns the objects. If you choose DDL Files as the source, you enter the name of the file and database type. If you choose ODBC as the source, for all databases other than Oracle, you specify the name of the ODBC source and its type.

After you set the source and its related information, you can select the check boxes at the bottom. The first three choices, if checked, automatically capture the design of the triggers, indexes, and constraints for the tables you select on the Objects tab. There are also check boxes to stop on an error and to show the results on a diagram when finished. If you don't need triggers, indexes, constraints, or a diagram, uncheck these check boxes so the utility will run faster.

The Design Capture utility will capture all definitions that are found in the specified DDL file. When you capture the design of objects in an Oracle or ODBC database, you must also specify the objects to be captured.

Specify the Database Objects

Clicking on the Objects tab of the dialog will display a list of objects, as Figure 8-10 shows. You then select the objects to be design-captured by clicking on them; move them individually to the box on the right by clicking the right arrow button or move all objects with the double-right arrow.

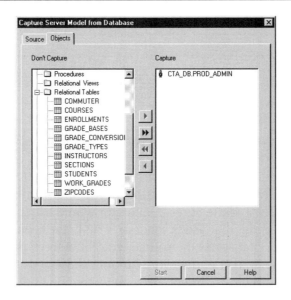

FIGURE 8-10. *Objects tab of the Capture Server Model from Database dialog*

NOTE
*You can capture the design of an object that
already exists in the repository. If you do that,
the utility will add any columns that are not in
the repository that are in the database. It will
not modify columns that already exist even if
they have different datatypes or sizes. It will
also not drop columns from the repository that
no longer exist in the database. To reconcile
the database definitions with the repository
definitions, run the Generate Database from
Server Model item in the Generate menu of the
Design Editor. Specify that you want the target
to be a Database. When you run this utility, it
will generate a script with DDL ALTER
statements as well as a reconcile report
(described in Chapter 20) that you can view
from dialogs in the utility. These files will show
you the differences between the repository and
the database so you can determine how to
synchronize them.*

Click Start

When you are done selecting objects, click Start to run the utility. The
Design Editor message window will appear and show the progress. When
the utility is done, it shows this dialog:

The dialog asks whether you want to browse the definitions before saving. If you choose to browse, you will be able to distinguish the uncommitted new definitions because their names are colored blue in the Navigator. Follow the prompts and messages in this and the next dialog to complete the design capture session. If you did not receive these dialogs at all, you may not have anything to design-capture.

Lay Out the Legacy System ERD

To create the legacy system ERD, you will want to reverse-engineer just those tables needed in the system with views, snapshots, triggers, and indexes. If you will be using other database elements in the system design or your objective is to create a complete set of repository objects that you can build from, you should choose all these objects and reverse-engineer them.

TIP

If the number of objects to design-capture is large, you may find it easier to run this utility more than once with subsets of objects. When you run subsets, however, be sure to include the parent tables for tables with foreign key constraints. Otherwise, the foreign key constraints will not be captured. If the objects are owned by different schemas (users), you will have to run the utility once for each user.

2. Table to Entity Retrofit Utility

Step 1 created table and other definitions in the repository for the existing legacy objects. If you want to use these objects for analysis tasks, you need to create entity definitions to match the table definitions you just design-captured. The Table to Entity Retrofit utility performs just this task. You follow three steps to run it: start the utility, select the object names, and click the Reverse Engineer button.

Start the Utility

You can start the Table to Entity Retrofit from the Utilities menu of either the Repository Object Navigator or the Entity Relationship Diagrammer. When you choose this menu option, you will see the dialog shown in Figure 8-11.

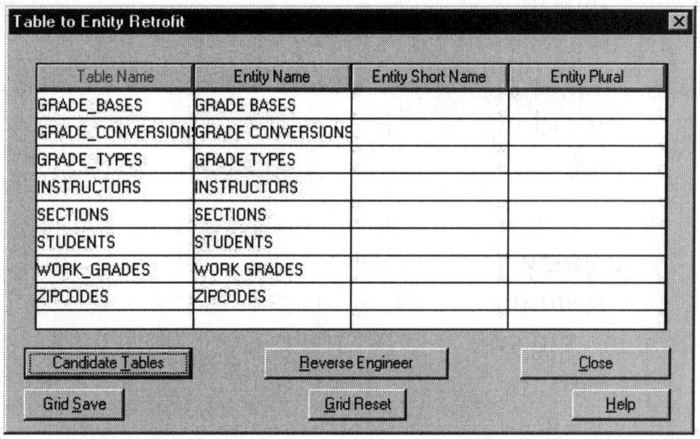

FIGURE 8-11. *Table to Entity Retrofit dialog*

Select the Object Names

Click the Candidate Tables button to display a list of available tables that do not have entities associated with them. Oracle Designer gets this information from the association called Usages: Mapped to Entities listed under the table definition. If a table is not mapped to any entities, it will appear as a candidate table. Note that views and snapshots cannot be retrofitted. Note also that you can name the entities differently than the tables. You can also supply a short name and plural. If you do not, the utility will fill these in for you.

Click the Reverse Engineer Button

After you select the tables, you click the Reverse Engineer button. Oracle Designer will create the definitions for entities from tables, attributes from columns, relationships from foreign key constraints, and unique identifiers from primary key constraints. These are the elements you need for the next step in the process of creating the legacy system ERD.

3. Entity Relationship Diagrammer and the Legacy System ERD

This section continues the discussion of the Entity Relationship Diagrammer begun in Chapter 4, and this tool is discussed further in Chapter 10, as you will use it frequently in the Requirements Analysis stage of the Analysis phase. Here, you will learn how to automatically create the legacy system ERD from the retrofitted tables created with the Table to Entity Retrofit utility. The real objective of the ERD in this part of the Analysis phase is to represent diagrammatically the data elements from the legacy system in an analysis format. However, the simple technique discussed here is useful even if you do not want to produce a legacy system ERD.

Since you have all the entity definitions, all you need to do is open the ER Diagrammer, create a new diagram, and choose **Edit→Include** to show the Include Entity dialog as in Figure 8-12. Here you select all the entities you design-captured and retrofitted. You can select all entities with or without relationships (in this case, you want entities with relationships), and you can choose where the layout will appear. Choose Whole Diagram to put the new objects anywhere in the drawing area, New Area to have the utility pause and wait for you to draw an area for the new objects, or Same Area if you have created a new area before and want to use this same area. If you want to see the layout area you are using, select **Options→Customize** from the menu and check the Show Layout Area check box.

TIP
Examine the preferences by choosing ***Options→Customize*** *and decide if you really need to see all the labels and elements. Depending on your audience, there may be some items you wish to omit from the diagram to make it look simpler. For example, Hidden Arcs—arcs that have only one relationship on the diagram—are normally displayed, but this symbol may be confusing to some viewers. You can turn off this symbol by unchecking its check box.*

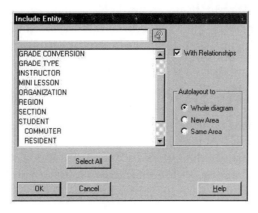

FIGURE 8-12.   *Include Entity dialog*

Another decision you can make at this point is how much detail about
the entities to display. You can show just the attributes which comprise the
unique identifier; all mandatory attributes; or all attributes. If you want an
overview of the system, which fits compactly onto a printed page, you can
choose not to show all attributes. Remember, you can always use a
repository report, or write a custom report, to give the entity details. If you
decide not to show all the attributes, you will want to resize the boxes,
making them smaller, before you refine the diagram's appearance.

A good thing to do the first time you display objects in the drawing is to
try some of the Autolayout combinations. Just click the Autolayout button
(or choose **Layout→Autolayout** from the menu), and the diagram will be
redrawn in a new layout. You can always go back to the old layouts
(except the first one) by using the Previous Layout button (or choosing
Layout→Previous Layout). Autolayout provides New Area and Same Area
menu options for placing the new layout; these act the same way as similar
options in the Include Entity dialog. Also, you can choose the objects to
which Autolayout applies by selecting them and then clicking the
Autolayout button.

At this point, you should spend some time with the layout and arrange it
to your satisfaction. Remember the tip from Chapter 4 about laying out the

entities without worrying about the relationship lines. When the entities are in place, you click on a relationship line, choose Select All from the Edit menu, and use Autolayout again to redraw the lines in an orderly manner. At the end of this process, you will have a legacy system ERD.

Tracking Report Audits with User Extensions

Another Oracle Designer deliverable in the Information Gathering step of the Analysis phase is a plan for tracking existing (legacy) reports using the repository. The creation of this deliverable consists of two setup steps:

1. Add a user extension to the module element type.

2. Create a module definition for each report.

These steps are detailed in the next two sections.

1. Adding a User Extension

In the Analysis phase, you need a way to store definitions for and assign priorities to the legacy reports. You can store the report definitions in the Oracle Designer repository module element. A *module* is a finished application, usually a form or report file, which acts as a distinct part of the system. Modules can also be menus or libraries and you can distinguish them with the *Language* property (such as Oracle Forms, Oracle Reports, or Oracle WebServer) and the *Module Type* property (Default, Menu, or Library). In the case of legacy reports, the module will probably have a *Language* of Oracle Reports and a *Module Type* of Default. A property called *Legacy Status* will be used to assign a priority level for the legacy report auditing process.

The problem is that Oracle Designer does not have a module property called Legacy Status. The Oracle Designer User Extensibility feature can solve this problem. You can define a new property for the module element type called *Legacy Status* and, as you create the definition for each report in the repository, assign a value of Keep, Discard, or Modify. Then when you list the legacy reports, each can include one of these values as its legacy status designation, and reports can even be grouped according to their legacy status designations. This process of entering and making choices regarding the status of the legacy reports is really part of the audit process itself.

The User Extensibility feature is provided by the Repository Administration Utility and is covered in Chapter 27. You should refer to that chapter for more information on the concepts and mechanics of user extensions. Briefly, you need to name a single unused user-defined property as *Legacy Status*. When you publish this extension, you will see it in the repository module's Properties dialog, which you use to assign a status to each legacy report. You can use RON, or the Matrix Diagrammer, or a utility of your creation to facilitate the data input. You can also write your own reports to show the legacy report definitions using the API views.

2. Creating Module Definitions for the Legacy Reports

Creating module definitions in the Repository Object Navigator is largely a manual process consisting of clicking the Create button after selecting the Modules node. You then fill in the name, purpose, and language of the report. If the language used is not on the list, you can add the appropriate language under the Languages node. You should also fill in the Legacy Status property that will appear in the module's Properties dialog. If your legacy reports are written in Oracle Developer Reports, you could also use the Capture Design of Report utility in the Design Editor Generate menu to create the module definitions from existing reports (.RDF) files.

If you have a large number of reports (a hundred or more), you might consider another way to insert the modules—using the Oracle Designer Application Programmatic Interface (API). Assume you have a table that stores the names of all the reports in your system. You could write an API procedure to read that table and create repository definitions for each module there. Chapter 28 describes how to use the API and provides some sample code to get you started. You should probably not consider this approach if you have only a small number of modules, because the coding work involved might take longer than manually entering the module definitions. Then again, if you did create an API routine, you could reuse it for the same purpose in other projects.

TIP
If you need to create multiple elements of the same type in the Repository Object Navigator, use the Fast Create dialog in the Design Editor's Edit menu. This is a way to get a list of definitions sketched out in the repository quickly and might be useful for entering the legacy reports list. You can call up this utility after selecting the Modules node, and it will show a list to fill in of module names and languages. This is the minimum amount of information needed to create a module. After you press the OK button, the utility will create the definitions, and you can fill in the other properties later.

CHAPTER

9

Analysis—Requirements Analysis

I've been in analysis for 15 years and it hasn't done me a bit of good.

 n Chapter 7, we discuss the information-gathering activities of the Analysis phase. This chapter will discuss how the information gathered is analyzed and organized a into a Requirements Document.

Overview of Requirements Analysis

Throughout the Analysis phase, as information is gathered we need to assemble this information and create a comprehensive image of the system requirements. We gather information from a variety of sources, namely, interview notes, preliminary ERDs, function hierarchies, report audits, and requirements extracted from the legacy system. From this mass of information, we need to design a coherent data model and function architecture to support these requirements. The traditional CASE method does not explicitly provide for a Requirements Document. This deficiency can cause user dissatisfaction and, ultimately, system failure. One resolution to the problem of how to deliver exactly what the user wants and needs is to team up with the users to produce a Requirements Document that includes process flows, Analysis ERDs, and function hierarchies. This document is the main deliverable in the Analysis phase.

The need for a Requirements Document is based upon a simple idea: a system designer must first have a clear and precise description of the business area's requirements before beginning to develop a solution. Then the designer can create a system that truly meets the user's needs. To successfully complete the Analysis phase, all of the business requirements must be documented. Only after this is done can decisions about the design of the actual system be made.

The primary deliverable of the Analysis phase is the Requirements Document. This is usually a very long, detailed document that includes all of the information gathered from various sources. Without a Requirements Document, analysts can only take their ERDs, functional models, and screen dumps and ask the user, "Does this work?" The ERDs, function hierarchy, and prototypes can be used to help validate the system with the user, but the knowledge transfer must also be verified in order for the system to be implemented successfully.

During Analysis, the focus continues to be on the user, coupled with both the new and old systems. The users have invaluable knowledge of the legacy system as well as information on how the new system should work. This information is elicited from the user, and then the focus shifts to analysis. The information is re-architected in the form of ERDs and function hierarchies, but a direct reference still is needed to the information the users provided regarding what they want in the new system. You will not be certain that the system will be built correctly unless there is a cross-check. The Requirements Document provides this cross-check.

The current system development process usually moves directly from knowledge acquisition to the placement of information into the Oracle Designer repository. Creating a Requirements Document provides a crucial control point in the CADM process when moving from knowledge acquisition to the generation of function hierarchies and ERDs. It also provides the client with a deliverable to verify that the knowledge acquisition occurred. Therefore, the Requirements Document must be designed to provide this verification.

The information elicited from the users should be structured to avoid simply listing one unrelated concept after another. First, information should be broken into categories based on business functions. Second, the document should be in a form that can be cross-checked against the models. The analyst must be able to say, "What we designed is something that makes sense." Verification of the models is the last part of the Analysis phase.

The existence of a Requirements Document does not mean that the user is not involved in developing and validating the ERDs, function hierarchy, and process flows. Indeed, users should be directly involved in all parts of the system development process. This may add significant time to the Analysis phase, but the alternative is running the risk of not meeting user needs. Failure to involve the users increases the possibility that requirements are incomplete and inaccurate and that the users will not take ownership of the system. Users will look at the proposed system as "yours," not "theirs," and will be more inclined to distance themselves from it. In other words, the developer should not complete the jobs in this phase alone.

The requirements portion of the Analysis phase is where the analysts bring together all of the collected material from users and extract the relevant system requirements. This process includes determining the appropriate ERDs to create and finalizing process flows that describe both the legacy system and potential changes to it as well as new process flows that may be relevant to the system being created. The goal is to create a coherent statement of all the system requirements for the proposed system.

Deliverables

The deliverable for the Analysis phase is the Requirements Document. For a very large project, the Requirements Document could consist of hundreds of pages. A Requirements Document outlines the needs of the users for the entire system. A carefully defined and prioritized list of requirements coupled with the business models and matrices result in a Requirements Document that gives the development team considerable insight into the business.

The various parts of the Requirements Document are

- System requirements: that is, a structured list of all requirements elicited from users, including the requirements for the legacy system

- Function hierarchy, cross-referenced to the system requirements

- Full documentation of the legacy system (discussed in Chapter 7)

- Report audit (discussed in Chapter 7)

- Business objectives and critical success factors for each business area that the system will support

- Analysis ERD

- Process flows for all business functions

Requirements List

The requirements list should be broken into several sections: one section at the global project level and one for each project subsystem. A *project subsystem* consists of the modules that projects are traditionally divided into so that work can be allocated. The difference between project-level and subsystem-level requirements is that a project-level requirement applies to the entire project. Examples of project-level requirements include project-level hardware requirements, overall business needs, and notes on the user interface. However, most requirements will be found in the module-level requirement lists. These lists contain specific requirements for such subsystems as sales and manufacturing. Many requirements will be included in more than one subsystem area.

After all of the necessary requirements have been collected, the information must be analyzed, organized, and documented for ease of reference. The information elicited should be structured to avoid lists of one unrelated concept after another. You do this by first dividing the information into categories based on business functions. You then organize these functions into a top-level function hierarchy.

Function Hierarchy

After conducting all the user interviews, JAD sessions, and legacy system walkthroughs, the analyst is left with a large binder of notes. These notes may be structured by functional area, but often requirements may span several areas, and there is no clear outline showing what requirements go where. The analyst should attempt to expand the function hierarchy from the Strategy phase. The goal is to end up with an Analysis phase function hierarchy.

Classifying the requirements will necessitate adding the next layer down on the function hierarchy. These additions are based on the requirements, tasks, and decisions of the users and the requirements retrieved from other sources. When addressing requirements from users, the users may be categorized by class. For example, all users involved in data entry of sales information might be in one functional group. Another group might be those who work with math functions—users from this functional group might want online screen calculators, for instance. An individual user may be a part of one or many functional groups.

Traditionally, Oracle Designer has been used to identify the navigation menu and modules used to build the hierarchy. Although this is not a basic capability, it also is possible to extend Oracle Designer to organize user requirements. At this point, the analyst can build the function hierarchy. Each person on the development team can read a few pages and try to sort the requirements into modules. As the process moves closer to the Design phase, it becomes increasingly important to be precise regarding which requirements go with which function or module. However, at this point the goal is simply to place each user requirement somewhere in the function hierarchy. General requirements go high up in the tree, with details attached to specific functions at the leaf level.

Once the user requirements are sorted and organized in the function hierarchy, the analyst needs to look at each function. Redundancies need to be eliminated. Sources of conflict should be identified and harmonized. If the requirements for a function are inadequate to build that function, the analyst needs to collect more information before proceeding. All of the collected requirements need to be detailed enough for the analyst to build a function that meets user needs.

Once it is completed, the function hierarchy needs to be summarized and organized into a more coherent diagram. Within each function, requirements can be broken down into specific requirements types:

■ Performance specifications, such as response time

■ Functional requirements: that is, what the function accomplishes

For each subject area, create a function hierarchy, sorting the users, user classes, and sources into topics. Keep in mind that some users will appear in more than one category. Boundary spanners cross more than one technical area. All other users should fall into specific areas. Each task that the user identified should become a function in the next layer of the function hierarchy. Everything else should become a requirement that pertains to one or more tasks in that area. Try to fit the rest of the requirements into the function hierarchy and into categories. When it is unclear where to put a particular requirement in the function hierarchy, put it higher on the tree.

Ideally, all requirements should reside in the CASE repository. Unfortunately, CASE does not easily support this. You can use user extensibility in Oracle Designer, as mentioned in Chapter 6, to store the requirements and map them to one or more functions in the function hierarchy.

Functions should be mapped to entities to ensure that the function hierarchy is complete and to identify redundancies. For example, if you find that there is no CREATE usage for a particular entity, then you obviously are missing a function. If an entity can have information deleted by several different functions, there may be a problem in the design.

You can then use this information to map the main functionality of the old system to the new system. You can also use it to make sure that no legacy-supported business function was missed in the design of the new system and to map legacy fields to the new system attributes.

Note that functions should usually not be mapped to attributes. The cost to determine that level of detail outweighs the added benefit. One possible exception to this rule might be allowed to support the report audit, to show users that multiple legacy reports can, in fact, be combined into one new report.

Business Objectives and Critical Success Factors

The purpose of the next section of the Requirements Document is to document the goals, objectives, and critical success factors of the business area. Goals are the broad themes, directions, and aspirations of the business area. Objectives are the measurable targets that are set to determine whether a goal is met. Critical success factors are those things that have to go right in order for the business to achieve its goals. These objectives and factors are usually identified during management interviews. It is important to include this strategy-type information in the Requirements Document, since everything that follows in the life cycle should support this section.

This section should also verify that the business importance of the system has been communicated to the design team. Without this high-level perspective, it is impossible to make intelligent design decisions on such basic features as fault tolerance and design flexibility.

The objectives and critical success factors can be directly obtained from user managers. If the users have not thought through their business objectives and critical success factors, the analysis team should guide the users through these important first steps in the development process.

Most of this work should have been done in the preparation of the Strategy Document. However, in Analysis, these objectives should be expanded and reconfirmed to include the perspective of rank-and-file users. In addition, success factors critical to the development of the system should be identified.

Analysis ERD

A picture is worth a thousand words; one ERD is worth a thousand requirements. The Analysis ERD stores many of the business requirements in one place. The ERD can then be used to communicate between the users and developers a common understanding of the data requirements and rules.

What is the Analysis ERD? It is a compact representation of most (often hundreds) of the data-related business requirements. The Analysis ERD should not be concerned with speed or performance. Its only goal is to capture as many business rules as possible. The more rules captured, the better. The Analysis ERD is the core of the Requirements Document.

Ideally, the ERD should reflect *all* of the data business rules. However, some rules may need to be expressed in text form. Therefore, the Analysis ERD is not complete unless it also contains written, explicit business rules not contained in the diagram. There must be clear and precise descriptions of each entity in the ERD. The process of creating the ERD is as follows:

1. Bring together the unit-level Analysis ERDs from the first stage of the Analysis phase. Build the ERD but do not fully attribute the model. Include some attribution information, but only to illustrate the entity. For example, a university database may contain an intersection table called "enrollment." In this case, show the class grade in the enrollment entity to illustrate what kind of information should be stored in
that entity.

2. Audit the diagram against the user requirements with a senior modeler who has not yet seen the diagram. Defending a model to someone else is one of the best ways to find flaws and problems. Even skilled modelers can make mistakes.

3. Fully attribute the model by scrutinizing all user requirements and reports to be implemented, as specified in the report audit. Important sources for attributes are screen shots of the new system, legacy system screen shots, old reports, and new reports. Users can also be asked to identify attributes. If the ERD cannot support the generation of a report, more work needs to be done.

4. Audit the logical ERD with the developer using real business transactions. For the sake of this walkthrough, assume that each entity is implemented as a table, without worrying about performance or possible denormalization. The purpose of this auditing process is simply to see whether all requirements are included and that there is a place in the model to store all the data or whether more work needs to be done.

5. Map the data-related requirements to the Analysis ERD entities or relationships.

During the creation of the Analysis ERD (just as with the Strategy ERD), the analysts needs to spend time creating good entity names and descriptions. However, without worrying about entity names, the diagram should be audited solely for entities, relations, and descriptions to make sure it encompasses all the requirements. This is not to diminish the importance of entity names, which are crucial. However, the question is when to come up with these names. Initially, it is more important to agree on the descriptions of what the entities represent. Then the entity names themselves can be determined.

After the ERD presentation, it must be clear to everyone what the ERD represents. The diagram serves as a logical model of the business area data requirements. Since it is still just a logical model, it cannot be critiqued for performance considerations at this stage.

Process Flows

The flow of work tasks within an organization is frequently not optimal. Duplication of effort is common. After someone spends the afternoon typing, printing, and submitting reports to other departments, the people that receive the information may reenter the same data so it can be printed in a different format or used for calculations. A process flow makes the duplication of effort apparent.

For example, the steps that a company takes in processing an application for membership can be tracked. Instead of viewing the process from the point of view of one user, you want to examine it from the perspective of the company. You may discover that after an application arrives, it is entered into the legacy system by the application processing group (the people who receive applications and retrieve the necessary information on the applicant, such as name and address). Then the application is entered again by the people who approve applications and again by the people who issue and track new members. By modeling the process flow, opportunities to reengineer business efforts can be identified.

Process flow modeling illustrates what an enterprise does and how it does it and when information systems are used to support business processes. User involvement in process flow modeling is essential. Users are the primary sources of information, and like other models, the process flow model will go through several revisions with the user before it is finalized at the end of the Analysis phase.

Processes are not usually neatly organized hierarchies. Some processes must precede other processes. Some processes may follow other processes. Still other processes spawn processes of their own. Some process flows are linear. Others loop back on themselves or support various degrees of parallelism. These process flows are integral system requirements that cannot easily be placed within the function hierarchy.

One of the main uses of process flow modeling is to determine the appropriate use of task queues or other workflow-related system modifications. To achieve this objective, every function that can be separated from another function either by time or by its users must be individually modeled. For example, answering a customer's phone call and entering a diary event on the system noting the phone call would not be two functions, because those two events always take place right after each other and are always done by the same person. However, taking a customer order and approving the order would be two tasks, because they are done by two people. Similarly, taking an order and shipping goods would probably best be modeled by two processes, even if these tasks were done by the same person, because the two processes might be separated by time.

Here is the technique for creating process flows:

1. Identify primary business processes. These are probably the top-level functions from the function hierarchy.

2. Identify subprocesses within each primary process. Each subprocess may be repeated in more than one primary process. Subprocesses are a collection of tasks or activities that support a primary process.

3. For each subprocess, identify the title of the person who performs it, the department in which the subprocess is performed, and whether the subprocess is manual or automated. If the subprocess is automated, identify the functional area (for example, sales, manufacturing, or shipping) that does the task.

Identify how the tasks relate to each other. Recognize that tasks can be ordered in more ways than by time. Note that a manual task usually *spawns* a computer task, and a computer task usually *precedes* a manual task. There may be other verbs required to reflect your process flows. You will probably need to use decision boxes to reflect the flow of tasks. Create dataflows among and between subprocesses to identify their sequences.

Assigning Requirements to Functions

Assigning system requirements to functions takes place during requirements analysis. Much of the checking has already been built directly into the process because you are building the functional model directly from the requirements list. However, as a safety measure, you should map the system requirements from the Requirements Document to the ERD and process flow models to determine where each requirement is met, why it is met, which function or process meets the requirement, and how the requirement is met. A report should be created in this phase listing all of the requirements with the areas and nodes to which they pertain and where they are met in the models. You can conclude that your analysis is complete if your ERDs and function hierarchies successfully capture all of your requirements.

Analysis allows you to span the boundary between discussions with the user and the design of the system. Adding a Requirements Document to the process gives the users and the development team more confidence in the process and a shared understanding of the business requirements that will be leveraged during the Design phase.

Table 9-1 shows the results of a Requirements Document after cross-checking.

Summary of Requirements Document Creation

In summary, take the following steps to complete the Requirements Document:

1. Create a detailed function hierarchy that is decomposed to the elemental level.

2. List all system requirements and map each requirement to zero or more functions.

3. Create the ERD.

4. Map each requirement to zero or more entities.

#	Pg	Source	Requirement	Area	Function Reference	Level of Importance	Completion Comments
1	88	Maggie Brown's interview	Report the number of sales per salesperson.	Sales	SAL1000 SAL2000 SAL3000	Done	Implemented in function hierarchy. Also, references SALES FORCE and UNITS SOLD entities.
2	3	Legacy system	No salesperson can sell to a customer outside his or her territory.	Pricing	PR10090 PR10100 PR10110	Done	Implemented in function hierarchy. Also, references SALES FORCE, CUSTOMER, and REGION entities.
3	15	Legacy system	Create and update a list of the current sales force.	Sales	SAL1050	Done	Implemented in function hierarchy. Also, references SALES FORCE entity.
4	10	Dan Fleece's interview	Provide online access to the customer database to help customers plan their orders.	Sales	None	Out of scope	This will be implemented at some future point.

TABLE 9-1. *Sample Results of a Requirements Document (After Cross-Checking)*

Note that a single requirement may be mapped to one or more functions, one or more entities, or, if out of scope, to no functions. Table 9-1 shows a report that maps requirements to functions. A similar report should be built to show the mapping of requirements to entities. Appropriate exception reports would include requirements that are not mapped to either functions or entities, as well as functions or entities that have no system requirements associated with them.

On one project the authors worked on, no Requirements Document was originally planned. The senior development staff felt that such documentation would be a duplication of effort, because the CASE tool provides for descriptions of each function. However, this was not enough for the user. The user wanted a list of everything that has been discussed in this chapter for the Requirements Document, from detailed requirements to process flows.

The user got tired of consultants coming on-site, taking information, and putting it directly into the functional models and ERDs. This approach made it impossible to cross-check the information. The project manager could not track who performed or authorized what functions (especially when information such as sources and topics was not noted in the CASE tool). Development funds were spent on complex ERD modeling when some of the data being modeled was not even required for the system. Furthermore, duplicated functions were hard to find, and it could only be inferred from the description of a function exactly who needed that function.

Using a Requirements Document, one of the authors was able to cross-reference requirements by entity model, function model, and source. A tool was created for the users and developers that validated the information transfer. By mapping system requirements to the CASE tool deliverables, the ERDs and function hierarchies were validated.

Without a Requirements Document, it can only be hoped that someone can remember all of the requirements while validating the ERDs and functional hierarchies. A better approach is for developers to obtain the user's approval of the requirements and then model them in a way that achieves the appropriate goal.

Often, there is a lack of consistent quality in CASE development efforts. Frequently, project leaders put the emphasis on generating a product rather than on satisfying the user's needs. The pressure to produce a product quickly encourages an informal approach to methodology and documentation. Perhaps the fault lies in not having a formal development strategy that would improve the chances of success. It is a key point of this chapter that except for very small projects, every project team should create a Requirements Document. This document is the main deliverable from the Analysis phase of the project.

Security

At this stage of the SDLC, you have noted and collected diagrams of different individuals' opinions regarding security. For analysis of this information, you need to determine the level of security requirements associated with each attribute in the logical database and each function in the function hierarchy. You will need a basic level of security for the whole application using roles, passwords, and user profiles. In addition, using the security requirements gathered from the users, you will need to identify a security level for each of the elements in the repository and assign each a security level on a scale of 0 to 3, as follows:

- 0 = Information for which no additional level of security is needed. Examples include mail-stop information and office locations.

- 1 = Information that would not cause a huge hardship to the organization if released but should, as a matter of policy, be kept reasonably secure. Examples include home addresses and telephone numbers of employees.

- 2 = Information that could potentially be damaging either economically or to the reputation of the organization. Examples include payroll information and personnel files.

- 3 = Competitive or strategic information whose unauthorized use or manipulation could seriously affect the organization. Examples include customer lists and contracts.

The deliverable of the security information requirements is the assignment of a security rating of 0 to 3 to each relevant repository element. You can assign these security ratings in two steps. First, define a user extended property called Security Rating for each relevant element type. Then assign the appropriate security rating to each element instance.

Executive Information System (EIS) and Ad Hoc Query Needs

EIS and ad hoc query needs must be considered separately, since they are different from other requirements. In the Analysis phase, it is not necessary to go into much depth, but the developer should have a reasonable understanding of these needs and where they will fit into the finished system. Any of these needs that can be met by the core production system should be included. Regardless of whether the project is a warehouse system, production system, or even a redesign of a legacy system, these requirements should be gathered.

How should the analyst gather the EIS and ad hoc query requirements? With ad hoc query requirements, the goal is the same as in requirements analysis: namely, to get a good set of requirements. Again, the analyst cannot rely on a single source for this information. Using multiple sources is even more important in this instance. There are four good ways to gather ad hoc query information:

■ Interview the users. Asking the users what they do in a general way is the least effective way to gather ad hoc query information, and asking what users would do with a tool they have never seen and perhaps can't imagine isn't likely to yield much useful information either. However, some information will be collected.

■ Every IS department receives requests to implement ad hoc reports. Many of these actually wend their way into the production reporting cycle. The developer should find all of the one-time special reports requested for the past six months to one year and analyze them.

■ Many systems have a utility report that runs to a file. Users take information from this report and generate their own report forms. The developer should find the actual reports generated and analyze them.

■ The most effective way to gather information on ad hoc user requirements is by using a query log. Ask users to imagine that they have their own perfect in-house systems person. Anytime they want a particular (imaginary) report, the systems person would produce the report in 10 to 20 minutes. Users can be asked to write down what they would ask such a person to do. They can write down all of their questions for a specified period of time, such as one week. This will help ensure that the new system has all the information needed to respond to the users' questions. Unlike user interviews, this query log is not created during an interview but during actual work. This type of information-gathering technique usually has a high compliance rate. It also gives the developer a good idea of who the high-end ad hoc query users will be. Some may come up with ten or more queries per day.

When all this information is gathered, the analyst should have a good idea of what the user ad hoc query requirements are.

For EIS requirements, the same techniques can be used. The executive group may or may not use the utility reports. However, the query log is even more important for executives. Because the number of information requests may be lower for executives than for other users, the executives may need to keep query logs for a longer period of time in order for you to gather enough questions.

Modifications for Smaller Systems

As mentioned in the discussion of the Pre-Analysis phase in Chapter 5, in smaller projects Analysis is less important. For smaller systems, you can use an informal analysis technique. An ERD is still necessary, but you can directly create module definitions bypassing the function hierarchy. Oracle Designer is so sophisticated that analysts can begin building and tinkering right from the beginning. The software being built acts as its own Requirements Document. Oracle Designer provides a rapid application prototyping environment that enables small projects to be completed without taking many of the formal steps of CADM, the modified CASE methodology.

Medium-sized projects still require careful analysis. For these projects, no aspect of the Analysis phase should be eliminated.

When Is Requirements Analysis Complete?

To determine when requirements analysis is complete, you must look at each of the deliverables individually.

Auditing the Analysis ERD

To fully encapsulate the business requirements, you must make sure complex business transactions can be stored in the model. Does the model have the capabilities needed to store all the information associated with the most complex business transactions? Does the data structure support the most complex questions? Asking these questions is called *trying to break the model.*

The best way to try to break the model is to formally present the model to other developers and, if possible, an outside auditor. This auditor should be a senior modeler, preferably from outside the development team, whose role is to ask the tough questions that others may not think of. This audit of the logical model should be considered a formal step in the system development process. The person defending the model should arrive with some of the complex transactions tested and demonstrate how the model supports those transactions.

Business rules that cannot be captured within the model should be discussed. Places where the model fails should be identified. There are always interesting decisions made during the modeling process. Frequently, earlier in the process decisions are made to explicitly not include some business rules in the data model because of the extra complexity they would add to it. All such modeling decisions should be revisited and defended during this audit process.

The audit of the ERD is one of the key factors in the success of a project, and it too often is overlooked. The development team should not just build an ERD with 200 or more entities and assume that it is correct. This is the last opportunity for easily implementing user requirements into the data model. Thus, it is important to audit and validate the thought processes that went into the creation of the model. This model will be used as the foundation for the rest of the system.

Auditing the Analysis-Level Function Hierarchy

The audit of the function hierarchy is far less critical than that of the ERD at this point in the system development process. There will be other opportunities to modify the function hierarchy in the Design phase. What is important at this point is to make sure that functions have not been generated excessively. Analysts must keep in mind what these functions will eventually be used for: that is, to generate modules. The function hierarchy should more or less correspond to application modules. For example, even though CREATE NEW EMPLOYEE, UPDATE NEW EMPLOYEE, and DELETE

NEW EMPLOYEE are three separate functions, there is no reason not to combine these within the function hierarchy. To do otherwise causes the function hierarchy to expand to an unreasonable size. For example, the authors worked on one system where the individual in charge of the function hierarchy created almost 300 functions for one business area of a system. After a review of the function hierarchy, that number was reduced to about 50.

As mentioned earlier, the main purpose of the function hierarchy is to help organize system requirements. So long as you can neatly organize and distribute system requirements, you can be reasonably satisfied that the function hierarchy is correct. However, you still need to have some confidence that the function hierarchy with its associated requirements is adequate. To ensure this, you should again use the process of explaining and defending the function hierarchy in front of the development team and an outside auditor. This review should be much quicker and less traumatic than the ERD review.

One important validation that the function hierarchy and ERD are complete is accomplished by mapping the way each entity interacts with each function. For each function, you should specify the impact of that function on each affected entity. Then you should specify whether that function can create-retrieve-update-delete instances. This CRUD matrix will help you validate whether there are sufficient entities to support all business functions and whether each entity has adequate functions associated with it. Exception reports can be run to indicate which functions are not associated with any entities and which entities lack functionality.

Auditing the Mapping of Requirements to Functions

Mapping all of the requirements is a big job, and it is often done by less-experienced members of the development team. Thus, the audit of the mapping process at this point is important. You should make sure that system requirements have been both correctly extracted from source notes and correctly mapped to the functions in the hierarchy. Sample checks of several source documents should be done for each developer. Even though monitoring should presumably occur during the information-gathering process itself, a final audit still should be conducted at the end of the requirements analysis phase.

Auditing the Process Flows

The process flows represent the development team's understanding of how business transactions occur within the organization. If BPR is performed, the reengineered process flows must also be audited.

The translation of a business process to a process flow diagram is straightforward, so process flows can be audited directly with users. Therefore, the defense of the process flows should involve users to a large extent. Again, you should present the process flows to a group of users and senior development team members for audit. For a complex system, it might be appropriate to have two defenses: one with the entire development team to iron out development issues, and a second with users and some development team members to handle user issues.

Auditing the Legacy System Review

You do not need to directly audit the legacy system review. Assuming that some of the existing system developers are still available within the organization, they can audit and sign off on the review. If more than one legacy system developer is available, have one help with the review itself and the second perform the audit.

Completing the Report Audit

The users can supply information on the report audit. Depending on how the information was gathered, results of interviews, questionnaires, and so on can be returned to the users for sign-off. When users agree that these items are correct, the report audit is finished.

Auditing Business Objectives and Critical Success Factors

As with the report audit, the records of the business objectives and critical success factors that have been collected can be distributed back to management at all appropriate levels for sign-off.

When this and all of the other parts of the Requirements Document are finished, then requirements analysis can be considered complete.

CHAPTER
10

Oracle Designer in
Analysis—Requirements
Analysis

To whom nothing is given, of him can nothing be required.
—Henry Fielding (1707-1754), *Joseph Andrews*

racle Designer supports many of the activities you perform in the Requirements Analysis step of the Analysis phase. The diagrammers and repository utilities will help you capture, analyze, manage, and process the information you have gathered about the business and represent it with repository definitions. Table 10-1 shows the diagrammers and utilities that you typically would use in the Requirements Analysis part of the Analysis phase.

This chapter discusses the functions of these diagrammers and utilities and the work you perform in the Analysis phase. This discussion relies on the basic information about the Oracle Designer tools introduced in Chapter 2. If you need extra assistance as you work in these tools at any point, the

Activity or Deliverable	Oracle Designer Tool
Analysis ERD	Entity Relationship Diagrammer
Synchronize all attributes in a domain	Update Attributes in Domains utility
Insert attribute usages for functions	Function/Attribute Matrix utility
Process flows	Process Modeller or Dataflow Diagrammer
Function hierarchy	Function Hierarchy Diagrammer
Assign CRUD to cross-check or assign entity usage	Matrix Diagrammer
Document the analysis objects	Repository Reports

TABLE 10-1. *Requirements Analysis Activities and Oracle Designer Tools*

Oracle Designer help system can answer specific questions and provide step-by-step instructions.

Here is one approach to the sequence of Oracle Designer work in the Analysis phase:

1. Use the ER Diagrammer to define the data side of the business.

2. Use the Process Modeller or Dataflow Diagrammer to refine the process flows.

3. Use the Function Hierarchy Diagrammer to refine the process hierarchy and attach entity usages to functions. You can also add attribute usages in this diagrammer, or you can use the Function/Attribute Matrix utility instead.

4. Use the Matrix Diagrammer to define CRUD for the entities. Applying create-retrieve-update-delete (CRUD) characteristics to attributes can wait until the module data usages are created in the Pre-Design phase or can be done in this phase.

5. Use Repository Reports to show the details of the work you completed.

This approach gives you the choice of filling in attribute usages for functions manually (in the Function Hierarchy Diagrammer or Dataflow Diagrammer) or accepting the default values from the Function/Attribute Matrix utility. You need these in the Pre-Design phase when you run the Application Design Transformer to create candidate modules. However, you spend time in the Design phase refining the table and column usages for the modules anyway, so you can consider accepting the default attribute CRUD in the Analysis phase and refine the usages in the Design phase. At that point, the design will be more stable, and you can pay attention to not only the data column properties but also the display column properties.

The following discussion uses this five-step framework to examine the tools you need in the requirements analysis stage of Analysis.

Entity Relationship Diagrammer

Chapter 4 covered the basics of the ER Diagrammer and its use in the Strategy phase. This chapter expands on that information and relates this diagrammer to the work you do in the Requirements Analysis stage of the Analysis phase. In the Strategy phase, you create a Strategy ERD that contains the entities but may or may not contain attributes. In the Analysis phase, it is important to completely identify entities for all "things of significance" as well as to fill in these entities with all known attributes and relationships. Therefore, the level of detail in the Analysis phase is much greater than in the Strategy phase, although you can use the Strategy ERD as a starting point for this work. If you versioned the application systems, you will automatically have separate ERDs for the two phases. If you did not version, you should keep a copy of the original Strategy ERD in case you need to refer to it. In addition, if you are performing business process reengineering, you should also create an ERD that diagrams the entities created or modified in the reengineering process.

Remember that the ER Diagrammer handles data-related elements only and that you need these when you assign entities and attributes to functions. Therefore, your work on entities and attributes has to be at an advanced stage of completion before you start defining function data usages. Of course, the process and data models are often developed and refined simultaneously and modified in an iterative way, so you probably should not create the final function entity usages until both models are as complete as possible.

The following sections describe tasks you perform to create domains and attributes in the ERD—elements that were not necessary in the Strategy phase. While you may have defined and used some domains during the Strategy phase, you should not spend much time and effort on this. You will have a more complete and accurate picture of the system in Analysis, and it will be easier to define the remaining domains and attributes at this point. While the physical implementation details are not that important to the Analysis deliverables, it is useful to know which properties on the element definitions you complete in this phase will affect the elements in the Design phase and beyond. The section "Where Does This Information Go?" provides general information on this subject, and Chapter 29 goes into more depth on the information flow from Analysis elements to Design elements.

NOTE
All properties available in the diagrammer's properties window are also available in the Repository Object Navigator (RON). You might consider using RON instead of the diagrammer, because once you understand the properties you will be able to work faster in the RON interface. You use the diagrammer, of course, for diagram changes and for fast changes that the right-click menus allow you to perform.

Using Domains

A *domain* is a set of allowable values and format rules for an attribute (or column). The Oracle Designer implementation of the relational database concept of domains is quite powerful and well integrated into the repository. You can attach a domain definition to an attribute in the Attribute properties window in RON or on the Attribute tab in the entity properties window in the ER Diagrammer. The attribute will then take on all the characteristics of that domain. If you change any attribute property that the domain is in charge of, such as the length, the domain name will be removed to indicate that the attribute no longer reflects values from the domain.

A benefit of this approach is that you can manage the characteristics of a group of attributes that are assigned to the same domain by changing the underlying domain definition and running a utility to synchronize the attributes for that domain. Another benefit is that you can enforce standards on datatypes for particular uses. For example, suppose two different analysts create two different entities, both of which have an EMPLOYEE ID attribute. Without a domain for this attribute, one analyst could make the datatype for the EMPLOYEE ID attribute VARCHAR2(6), and the other could make it NUMBER(10). With a domain called EMPLOYEE ID, each analyst can attach it to the attributes and not need to worry about the actual datatype and size.

Naming Domains

You might consider naming your domains the same as your attributes. For example, you would create ID domains to manage all ID attributes in all entities. The attribute may need a slightly different name, but you should name the attribute so it is not difficult to decide which domain to use. For example, you might create a domain for CODE but your attributes might use names like APPROVAL CODE or STATUS CODE. The domain name is a common suffix for the attribute names so the link between the two is obvious. Another example might be a domain called DATE. You will not give your attributes the name DATE but you might use names like APPROVED DATE, ENTERED DATE, or REGISTERED DATE. The names of these attributes all have a common suffix of the domain name. This technique provides standardization and clarity when reading through a list of domains or columns.

Defining Domains

Before attaching the domains, you have to create them by choosing **Edit→Domain** from the menu and filling in the Domains dialog, as Figure 10-1 shows. This dialog has variable-length entry columns that you can resize by dragging the edges of the labels left or right. The tool will remember the new setting when you return to this dialog. Alternatively, you can create the definitions in the Repository Object Navigator or the Design Editor, but the Domains dialog is easier to access when you are in the ER Diagrammer.

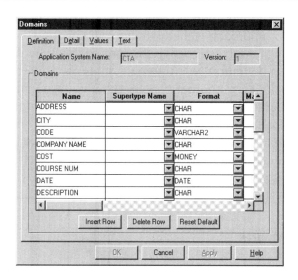

FIGURE 10-1. *Domains dialog*

The details you define for a domain include the datatype, size, and default value of the attribute. The same domain can describe both entity attributes and table columns, and you can have different datatypes and sizes for each. This distinction is required because a different set of datatypes is used to describe analysis-level attributes than the datatypes available for describing design-level columns. For example, the datatype (called *Format* for attributes) for an attribute may be MONEY, but such datatypes are transformed to NUMBERs in a table column and implemented as NUMBERs in an Oracle database.

The Detail tab of the Domains dialog has more information to describe the domain more fully, as Figure 10-2 shows. You can start filling in some of these properties now, or you can wait until the Design phase. The *Default* domain property copies to the *Default Value* property of the column or attribute that uses this domain. Another property in this tab, *Dynamic List* (called *Soft LOV* in version 1 and documented that way in the help system and API views for version 2.1), specifies how a text list or drop-down list item based on this domain will be generated. Check this check box (which sets the value to "Yes") for domains whose values are likely to change throughout the life of the application. Uncheck the check box for domains

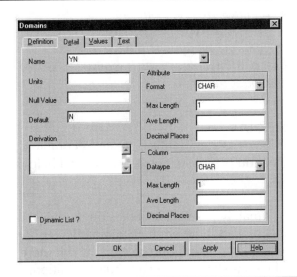

FIGURE 10-2. *Detail tab of the Domains dialog*

whose values are not subject to change—a Yes/No attribute or column, for example. The *Derivation* property lets you document the calculation or expression on which this value is based.

The Values tab of the Domains dialog is where you enter the values used to validate columns with this domain attached to them. For example, you might have an attribute called ACCOUNT STATUS that has a domain property of ACCOUNT STATUS. This domain has four Values defined for it on the Values tab: NEW, APPROVED, ACTIVE, and CANCELLED. Another example is an attribute called INCLUDE, which has a domain called YES NO attached to it. The YES NO domain has Values for Y and N. This information eventually ends up in reference tables for the finished application or in the application or database code to validate the value entered in the table.

NOTE
Domains can be based on domains. The Definition tab of the Domains dialog has a Supertype *property, which allows you to specify an existing domain name that is the parent of the one you are defining. This documents that the domain is a subset of another domain and has characteristics in common with it. The* Supertype *property is used for documentation only; you still have to specify the subset of allowable values in both the child and parent domains.*

Managing Domains

Before you add attributes to your entities, create as complete a set of domains as possible. You can make two rules that will help in your use of domains:

- **Rule #1** Ultimately base all attributes on domains, regardless of whether only one attribute pertains to a particular domain. Although this may seem like a lot of up-front work, it will more than pay for itself with the consistency of the attribute definitions in your data model and the ease of maintaining the model (via the Update Attributes in a Domain utility). Analysts may, however, temporarily assign datatypes, sizes, and values if no existing domain fits a particular attribute they are creating. You can even write a custom report, "Attributes Without Domains," and insert it into the Quality section of the Repository Reports.

- **Rule #2** Restrict the right to add, change, and assign new domains to the Oracle Designer administrator. You may actually want to do this with an API utility you create outside the Oracle Designer front end. Although you have to write such a utility, it could give you an easier-to-use front end for domains. In addition, the administrator might not need to install (or have a license for) the Oracle Designer product. Alternatively, you could allow analysts to temporarily define domains, which the administrator would inspect and move to the master application system.

When an analyst needs a new domain, the analyst can assign properties manually, without using a domain. The Oracle Designer administrator (or your data administrator if you have one) should periodically look at the repository to see if there are any attributes without domains. If so, the Oracle Designer administrator should create a domain using the sizes and types the analyst used for the attribute itself and attach the new domain to the attribute. A drawback of central administration of domains is that the person assigned to the task could be unavailable or reassigned and this could impact design work. While this may sound like a lot of administrative work, the API utility mentioned could ease the burden, and this arrangement will help enforce standards and consistency in attributes.

TIP
You can create one application system that contains master copies of objects commonly used in your company, like domains, storage definitions, and reusable module components. This allows you to share the definitions into new application systems but keep the administration of the objects in a central location. The administrator role, in the case of domains, would be the one that could change or add to those domains, but other roles would not have that capability.

Adding Attributes

An attribute is an atomic piece of information that describes an entity. Oracle Designer uses the following three symbols to show different types of attributes:

\#   Indicates a unique identifier that consists of one or more attributes that identify one instance of this entity. Specify this on the UIDs tab of the Entity properties dialog.

*   Indicates mandatory attributes that must contain values. Specify this by unchecking the Opt check box on the Attributes tab of the Entity properties dialog.

o   Indicates an optional attribute that can be null or unknown. Specify this by checking the Opt check box on the Attributes tab of the Entity properties dialog.

After you create the entity, you double-click the entity's symbol in the ER Diagrammer to open the Edit Entity dialog and then click the Attributes tab to display a spreadtable, shown in Figure 10-3. Here you fill in the name and domain of each attribute that describes this entity.

The Attributes tab lets you quickly enter the names and domains of all attributes. You can also look at a detailed view of each attribute in the Att Detail tab. This tab contains the same properties as the Attributes tab and some additional properties:

- **Derivation**   Used to enter an expression that supplies a value for this attribute

- **On Condition**   Used to document when non-mandatory attributes will contain a value

- **Null Value**   Used if this will be a non-Oracle database that needs something to represent null values

- **Default**   Used to supply an initial value for the attribute

- **Sequence in Sort**   Used to designate the position number that this attribute holds in the sorting of this entity (like the position of a column in a SQL ORDER BY clause)

- **Sort Order**   Used to designate if this is an ascending or descending sort

Some of these details may or may not be appropriate at this stage of development.

"Foreign Key" Attributes

In Oracle Designer, relationships contribute to an entity's description in the same way that attributes contribute. Therefore, to fully describe an entity, you need to specify all its attributes and all its relationships. Since the relationship is a key piece of information, there is no need to specify a separate attribute to hold the link between one entity and another. If you included an attribute link like this—a foreign key attribute—the Database Design Transformer would create a duplicate foreign key column.

This concept, while simple and flawless in logic, makes some people uncomfortable because they prefer to see the foreign key as an actual

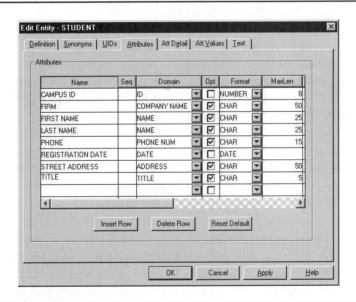

FIGURE 10-3.   *Attributes tab of the Edit Entity dialog*

attribute in addition to the relationship line. In reality, the whole concept of a "foreign key" comprised of "columns" is appropriate to a physical, but not a logical, design. It is a necessity for a relational database to contain a foreign key column to tie two tables together. Other database systems, such as object-oriented databases, are not based on the foreign key concept and do not necessarily need that physical representation of a link.

Relationships in entities become foreign key constraints and foreign key columns in tables. Therefore, the idea of a key, in general, is really a physical database concept. Although you may eventually convert a set of entities into physical tables, that physical representation is a detail that is inappropriate at the logical modeling level of the Analysis phase. Regardless of your views on this controversial subject, while working with Oracle Designer, you will get used to creating entities that do not have "foreign key constraints."

Unique Identifier Attributes

After defining the attributes, you can select the attribute or attributes that identify a particular instance of the entity. For example, you find in your information gathering that an employee can be identified by his or her entry badge number. The EMPLOYEE entity would contain an attribute for BADGE NUMBER, and you can specify that this is a unique identifier—no two employees will share the same badge number value. In addition, you may assign a combination of attributes to a unique identifier. For example, a SALARY HISTORY entity is uniquely identified by the START DATE and BADGE NUMBER, which indicates that an employee can have more than one salary rate and the identifier includes the date on which the salary began.

You can specify more than one unique identifier for a single entity, but you need to choose one to serve as the *primary unique identifier*. This is the identifier you have chosen to be the most common identifier for this entity.

The UIDs tab in the Edit Entity window, shown in Figure 10-4, allows you to assign attributes as UIDs. Note again that a UID may consist of one or more attributes and relationships. You can specify more than one UID for each entity by adding a row at the top of the dialog. You have to designate one of the UIDs as primary to create the primary key of the table based on this entity. The Attributes tab contains a *Primary* property that lets you specify which attributes participate in the primary unique identifier. As with "foreign key" attributes, the concept of a primary key is a physical

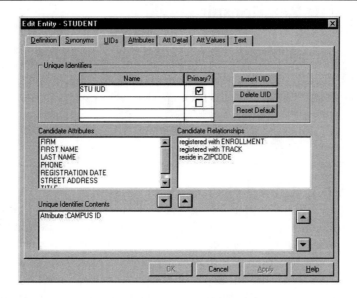

FIGURE 10-4. *UIDs tab of the Edit Entity dialog*

implementation—one that does not really belong in Analysis except for the knowledge that the primary unique identifier becomes the primary key when this entity is transformed into a table.

Attribute Text

The Edit Entity dialog contains a Text tab, where you can enter text on either entities or attributes. If you choose to attach text to attributes, a field appears where you can choose the attribute. You can then assign different types of text to the attribute—such as *Notes* and *Description*. You can enter the text using the edit box on this tab or, as in other tools, with your ASCII or HTML editor, by using the Text Editor and HTML Editor buttons, respectively.

Detailing Relationships

Relationships have a properties window that you display by double-clicking the relationship line. The Edit Relationship window contains places to change cardinality and optionality as well as the name of the relationship.

Primary UID Relationships

If a relationship is part of the primary UID, you can also specify that in the Edit Relationship window. You can specify a relationship as part of a primary UID only for the "many" side of a relationship; when you do, a crossbar will appear by the many (crow's foot) symbol to indicate that the relationship is part of the primary UID, as shown here:

Transferable Relationships

Oracle Designer uses another special symbol for relationships that are not transferable. The Database Design Transformer transforms the entities to tables and copies the *Transferable* property from the "many" side of a relationship to the foreign key constraint (on the "many" side of the foreign key relationship). When tables are joined by a transferable relationship, the generators create code that allows the foreign key value to be updated. If the foreign key is not transferable, the foreign key value cannot be updated, to point to (transfer to) another primary key value. For example, users would be able to change the DEPARTMENT ID value of an EMPLOYEE table to signify that the employee moved from one department to another, if the foreign key were transferable. If the entity this table was based on had a relationship that was nontransferable, the generators would create code to disallow the move from one department to another, if the foreign key was transferable. You define a nontransferable relationship in the Edit Relationship window by unchecking the Transferable check box. A diamond will appear by the end of the relationship you specified, as shown here:

Other Relationships

All combinations of optionality and 1-to-many relationships are available in the ER Diagrammer. You might consider not resolving many-to-many relationships at this stage of the SDLC; these cannot be implemented in tables of a relational database system, so you must resolve each such relationship into two 1-to-many relationships attached to an entity called an *intersection entity* or *associative entity* created just for that purpose. This is the classic technique for resolving many-to-many relationships; nevertheless, many-to-many relationships are valid logical concepts, and you can leave them in for now. Additionally, you might want to leave them because the business users you show these diagrams to may not understand the need for an intersection entity. You have to consider your audience in the decision you make here.

When the entities become tables in the next phase of development, you can resolve each many-to-many relationship into an intersection table and two 1-to-many relationships that can be implemented in the relational database. If, however, you find in the Analysis phase that there are attributes associated with the many-to-many relationship, you can create an entity in the ER Diagrammer for the intersection and put those attributes in it.

The same considerations apply to arc and subtype/supertype relationships. You cannot implement these directly in a relational database system (though you can diagram arcs on the Data Diagrammer and create triggers to enforce them), so you'll have to resolve them eventually. You can generally wait until you move to the Design phase. However, if there are additional attributes that the relationship implies, or if the relationships are confusing to those who need to understand them, you should consider resolving these relationships in the Analysis phase by creating extra entities.

TIP
You can quickly change the cardinality, optionality, or transferability of a relationship by right-clicking on the end you want to change and selecting from the popup menu.

Completing Entity Details

In this part of the Analysis phase, you need to fill in some properties on the entities that you have not needed before. You can assign *Initial*, *Maximum*, *Average*, and *Growth Rate* values on the Definition tab of the Edit Entity dialog. This volume information will help you in future phases to size the database. This tab also shows the names you gave the entity when you defined it, and you can change these if you want to. Another property indicates whether this application system owns this entity. If the entity is shared from another application system, you cannot change its properties.

The *Datawarehouse Type* property documents whether you will be using the entity as a Fact or Dimension table in the Design.

At this point, you should review the Synonyms tab, where you list the alternative names that the system uses for this entity. Since these names identify the entity, they must be unique in the system.

TIP

Although a short name for an entity can contain up to ten characters, it's better to use seven or fewer, especially if you'll be generating Oracle Developer forms from your application. The Database Design Transformer uses the short name as the table's Alias *property, which eventually becomes the block name in a generated form, and forms coding is easier if the block names are short.*

Using the Update Attributes in Domains Utility

The ER Diagrammer has a menu choice (**Utilities→Update Attributes in Domains**) for loading the Update Attributes in Domains utility. This utility is also available in the Repository Object Navigator (**Utilities→Update Attributes in a Domain**). It does what the name implies: for selected domains, it updates the attributes attached to them. For example, suppose you created three attributes and based them all on a domain called ADDRESS that you defined as VARCHAR2(25). You find out later that addresses can contain up to 35 characters, so you change the domain definition to accommodate the increased size. The attributes that have this domain attached to them are not automatically updated to the new size, so you run this utility to perform the update.

When you choose **Utilities→Update Attributes in Domains** from the menu, a dialog box with a list of existing domains appears:

You select the domains and click OK. The utility will scan the repository for all attributes that use the domains you selected and update their definitions to reflect the current state of those domains.

Using the Function/Attribute Matrix Utility

Filling in the attribute usage for functions at some level is important at this point in the development life cycle. Although you will need to revisit the assignments in the Design phase when you tune the module data usages, you need to at least assign attributes to functions and make a first pass at the create-retrieve-update-delete properties. The first step is to assign entities to functions in the Entity Usages tab of the Edit Function dialog for each function in the Dataflow Diagrammer or Function Hierarchy Diagrammer. Alternatively, you can use the Matrix Diagrammer, described in this chapter, to do this. Once this task is complete and you have specified CRUD for each function, you can run the Function/Attribute Matrix utility (as introduced in Chapter 8) to obtain a rough-cut set of attribute usages.

If you are moving through Oracle Designer into Design and final code generation, you will create modules based on these functions. The functions that really need data usages are those considered atomic, elementary, or common; these will become modules as the Application Design Transformer will copy their data usages to the modules. It may be desirable to specify usages for other functions to document the data used in the functions, but those will not create code.

This utility is available on the Utilities menus of the Entity Relationship Diagrammer, Repository Object Navigator, Dataflow Diagrammer, and Function Hierarchy Diagrammer. When you choose this item from the menu, the Create Function/Attribute Matrix dialog box appears:

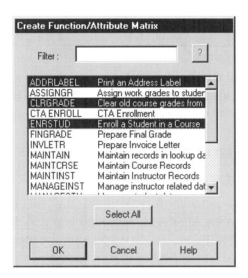

Select the functions for which you wish to generate attribute usages and click OK. The utility will look at each function you selected and add attribute usages for the entities attached to each function (with function-entity usages). Note that this process will load all attributes for the entity if they are not already defined as usages, but it will not remove attribute usages. When this utility is done, you can visit each function definition and remove attributes that are not applicable or modify the insert-retrieve-update-nullify characteristics (as with CRUD for entities). You may want to perform this task in the Matrix Diagrammer, as it is easier to navigate through a number of entities, but you can also do the work in the function diagrammers. As mentioned, you may consider not spending time on refining the attribute CRUD and instead spend time in the Design phase working on the column CRUD.

NOTE
The Other *property on the entity copies to the* Other *property on the attribute when you run this utility. The Application Design Transformer copies this property, called a "user-defined" usage in the help system, as the* Context *property for the module's column usage. This property is, therefore, not very important in the Analysis phase, where you are not really concerned with Design properties like* Context.

Where Does This Information Go?

The information you model in the ER Diagrammer, as with the information you model in all diagrammers, is available in the repository for other phases of the development process. You use the entity and attribute definitions when you attach entity and attribute usages to functions. Also, in the next phase, Pre-Design, you will create physical design data objects from these elements, as shown in Table 10-2.

Strategy and Analysis Data Element	Design Data Element
Entity	Table
Attribute	Column
Primary unique identifier	Primary key constraint
Nonprimary unique identifier	Unique constraint

TABLE 10-2. *Analysis Data Elements and their Design Data Element Counterparts*

Strategy and Analysis Data Element	Design Data Element
One-to-many relationship	Foreign key constraint and foreign key column
Many-to-many relationship	Intersection table and foreign key constraints
Arc and subtype/supertype relationships	Single tables or multiple tables with special columns to link them

TABLE 10-2. *Analysis Data Elements and their Design Data Element Counterparts* (continued)

Process Modeller in Requirements Analysis

Chapter 4 explains the Strategy phase and how to use the Process Modeller in detail. The process-diagramming activities you perform in the Requirements Analysis stage of the Analysis phase are no different from those you perform in the Strategy phase. However, at this stage you need to add and confirm more detail in the Process Modeller (or in the Dataflow Diagrammer) to ensure that you have represented all major flows and processes in the system that are driven by system requirements. Also, you need to decompose functions and processes down to atomic levels. That is, you need to reduce or decompose the function to a point where it can no longer be broken into subfunctions. If you can describe a particular function as being comprised of a number of other functions, you need to create another level diagram in the Process Modeller to represent these subfunctions.

To create this lower level, select the function and choose **File→Open Down** from the menu. This procedure opens a new diagram with the base process of the selected process. You place functions, flows, and stores on this diagram to describe the upper-level function. This is the essence of how you perform functional decomposition in the diagrammers. You will also use the function diagrammers when performing business process reengineering to show the new or modified flows resulting from the reengineering process. There may also be reengineered data elements that you represent in the ER Diagrammer to go along with the new flows.

You should exercise moderation in decomposing functions, since this is an area where "analysis paralysis" can set in. That is, you can get stuck in the Analysis phase, spending more time and effort than you originally budgeted and finding that the functions you analyzed first are no longer applicable because so much time has elapsed and the business has changed its policies since you began.

Another point to remember is that the functions and flows you created in the Strategy phase may not be fully applicable to the Analysis phase diagram. You may have to split or combine processes to more accurately reflect what the final system will accomplish. These are all activities you can perform in the Analysis phase in the Process Modeller. The Process Modeller is a logical choice for this phase, especially if you are performing business process reengineering, as the tool contains critical path and other time and resource analysis properties. You can also reorganize functions in the Function Hierarchy Diagrammer, as mentioned later. One approach is to partition the business area and focus first on decomposing and detailing the area you will implement first. Remember that you can define entity and attribute usages only in the RON, Matrix Diagrammer, Dataflow Diagrammer, or Function Hierarchy Diagrammer, so the Process Modeller in this phase is not the only process tool you will use and you may, in fact, not use it at all in this phase.

Dataflow Diagrammer in Requirements Analysis

Chapter 8 discusses the Dataflow Diagrammer for the Information Gathering stage of the Analysis phase. Most everything that you do in the Process Modeller to represent and analyze functions and flows is available in the Dataflow Diagrammer as well. Some analysts use this diagrammer instead of the Process Modeller to complete the process flows, and some use only the Process Modeller; each tool has a slightly different focus, as Chapter 8 discusses, and you can use either one or both.

All preceding cautions about analysis paralysis also apply to this diagrammer. You should temper your urge to be complete in modeling the business processes and flows with an interest in completing the task in a reasonable time.

Techniques and Properties

There are a few techniques and properties you should pay more attention to in this phase than in the Strategy phase. One of these is *reparenting*: moving a subfunction from one parent to another at the same or a higher level. For example, suppose that functions 1.1.1 and 1.1.2 describe function 1.1. You decide that function 1.1.2 really belongs under 1.2, so you perform reparenting: you drag the function out of the frame function and drop it outside the border. The New Parent dialog box will appear, as shown in Figure 10-5.

After you select a parent function, in this case the one numbered 1.2, and click OK, the Dataflow Diagrammer draws the function where you dropped it and renumbers it to reflect its parent; in this case, the function becomes 1.2.1.

You can make a frame function the parent of a global function (one outside the frame function) simply by dropping the global function inside

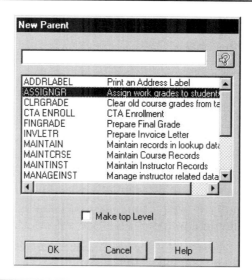

FIGURE 10-5. *New Parent dialog*

the frame. You will be asked to confirm this operation, but the New Parent dialog box will not appear, because the new parent is the frame function.

Properties you should pay attention to here more than in other phases appear in the Edit Function dialog. The Definition tab, shown in Figure 10-6, contains the *Label* and *Short Definition* specifications, both of which appear on the diagram as well. The Parent area of this tab shows the *Label, Short Definition,* and *Elementary* properties of the function that is at the level just above this one, but the parent properties are not editable here.

The Frequency area consists of the same properties as in the Process Modeller. Here you can assign the number of times and the time period in which this function occurs within the frame function. The Frequency area also has a key field called *Response*, where you can specify Overnight or Immediate. Overnight functions are those that do not happen immediately when started and become utility modules later in the development process. Immediate functions are those that happen right away when started and will become manual, screen, or report modules later in the life cycle. The Application Design Transformer also uses this field to determine which

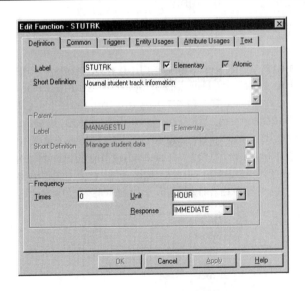

FIGURE 10-6. *Definition tab of the Edit Function dialog*

functions it can group together. Thus, the value you enter in this field is important at this stage.

You should also pay attention in the Analysis phase to the Elementary check box. You check this box if the function represents a logical unit of work that must be completed entirely to be useful to the business. The Application Design Transformer uses this value when it determines which functions it converts into modules for the Design phase. Therefore, be sure to be accurate here if you will be using that utility later.

TIP

Fill in the Elementary and Response fields in the Edit Function dialog's Definition tab if you plan to use the Application Design Transformer later in the life cycle to generate candidate modules for the final application. In addition, be sure you enter entity usages for the function; otherwise, Oracle Designer will treat the function as a manual function that will have a manual module created for it (one with no code generator and therefore no program code).

The last area to note in the Edit Function properties in the Dataflow Diagrammer is the Text tab. This tab appears in one form or another in all diagrammers, and many of the text types are the same for elements that may not even have diagrammers. The Text tab allows you to store information about the element in a multiline text area. The following illustration shows the drop-down list from the Text tab showing the types of text you can store for the function element. As in other tools, you can use the internal edit window, an ASCII editor, or an HTML editor to specify text.

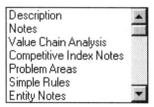

You can select these types one at a time and fill in the text area that appears below it. The text types are the standard ones that Oracle Designer defines for each element, and certain types appear only for certain elements. For example, *Value Chain Analysis*, where you store text about the added value that this process adds to the system, describes only functions, stores, and flows. Other elements may have fewer or more types of text, but *Notes* and *Description* are available for all. If you need more or different text types for any element (and not just those provided for the Dataflow Diagrammer), you can define them with user extensions to the repository.

The text here is only for your use in documenting the system, and although you can list the information in reports, the text itself does not have any additional effects in the Design phase.

Context Diagram

You can include a context diagram in your dataflow diagram set. This diagram contains only one function and one or more externals with flows to and from the function. Although you will decompose this function in later steps, you do not show subfunctions, internal flows, and data stores in the context diagram itself. This diagram is useful for showing the scope or boundaries of the system as a whole and the entities outside the system with which it interfaces. You do not show dataflows between externals, as those are outside the scope of the system.

The Dataflow Diagrammer allows you to construct a context diagram by using the top-level function (1.0) and drawing it by itself on a diagram. There are no other functions at that level, so the function numbers will start with 1.1 for the next level down from the context diagram. This diagram is useful in the Strategy phase as well, but as with the other dataflow diagrams, you expand and refine it in the Analysis phase.

Function Hierarchy Diagrammer

The Function Hierarchy Diagrammer (FHD) is the third diagrammer (along with the Process Modeller and Dataflow Diagrammer) that allows you to model functions (also called processes) during the Analysis phase. Although the Process Modeller and Dataflow Diagrammer are relatively similar in intent and you can use one in near exclusion of the other, the Function Hierarchy Diagrammer is quite a different tool, which you usually employ in conjunction with one or the other, or both, of its companion process diagrammers.

Why Another Function Diagrammer?

The objective of the Function Hierarchy Diagrammer is to display the functions in your system in a hierarchical or multilevel view. The functions themselves are the same as the Process Modeller process steps and the Dataflow Diagrammer functions, but the diagram itself (in one of its views) looks more like a typical organizational chart, as Figure 10-7 shows.

The activities you perform in the Function Hierarchy Diagrammer are similar to those in the other two diagrammers, but this diagrammer offers a view of the business that is primarily task-oriented, without any indication of user group, department, dataflow, or datastore. It allows you to manipulate the hierarchy itself. The lines between functions do not represent flows but parent-child relationships. The function at the top of the diagram represents the highest-level function that you are representing in this diagram. The next row of functions represents the decomposition of, or subfunctions within, that function. Each of those functions could, in turn, be decomposed into subfunctions, which would appear in the next row of the hierarchy.

This diagrammer is like the Dataflow Diagrammer in that you can attach entity and attribute usages to each function. Despite the differences between

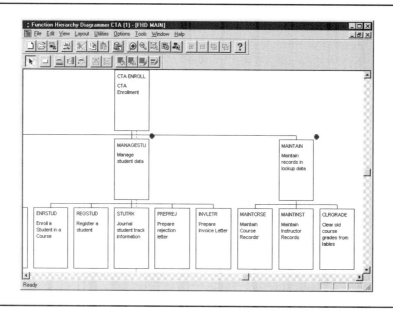

FIGURE 10-7. *Function Hierarchy Diagrammer session*

the Function Hierarchy Diagrammer and other diagrammers, the FHD is another tool for handling functions, which are among the most important elements in the repository, since they affect the finished application programs.

Basic Techniques

You use the same basic techniques in the Function Hierarchy Diagrammer as in the other process modeling tools. The Edit Function property dialog is the same as that in the Dataflow Diagrammer, for example. There are a few differences that make this diagrammer unique, however.

Creating a Diagram

The procedures for opening a diagram and creating a new diagram are the same as in the other diagrammers: you choose **File→Open** and **File→New**, respectively, from the menu. If you are creating a new diagram, the New Diagram dialog box appears, where you can choose a function on which to base the diagram. This operation is similar to that of the other two function diagrammers, as each function hierarchy has a root (or base) function that serves as the top level in the hierarchy for this diagram. You can also create a new function on which to base the diagram by clicking the New Function button, as in the other diagrammers.

The difference in the Function Hierarchy Diagrammer is that Oracle Designer automatically includes all child functions that describe the root function when you base the diagram on the root function. This happens because the diagram represents a hierarchy structure that does not make sense without a full layout of all child functions of the parent function.

You can include more than one root function when you create the diagram and so display more than one hierarchy structure in the drawing area. This enables you to view multiple structures at the same time and move or copy functions between them. The Edit menu also allows you to include another root function (**Edit→Include Root**) or remove one or more root functions from the diagram (**Edit→Exclude Root**).

Changing the Layout

The FHD is unique in the way it lets you view multiple levels of the function hierarchy at the same time. This feature enables you to see the functions that make up a particular function. The parent functions and all *branches* (its children and their children) will appear on the diagram. There is no practical limit to the number of levels displayed, although displaying too many levels on the same diagram may make the diagram difficult to read.

Once you have opened or started a new diagram, you can change the layout of the hierarchy (using the Layout menu) to one of the following three styles:

- **Horizontal Layout** is the default. This style shows each level of the hierarchy in a horizontal row.

- **Vertical Layout** displays each level of the hierarchy in a vertical line, with each level indented slightly to the right of the one above it.

- **Hybrid Layout** is a combination of vertical and horizontal layouts that shows parent functions in a horizontal layout and childless functions in a vertical layout. This style is the best of the three for reading multilevel hierarchies.

The three layout styles are shown in Figure 10-8.

In addition to setting the layout for the entire diagram, you can select one or more functions and cause the functions under them to conform to either a horizontal or vertical layout, no matter what the rest of the diagram is set to, by selecting Horizontal Layout Selection or Vertical Layout Selection, respectively, from the Layout menu. Thus, you can place functions on the diagram using a mixture of layout styles. The standard toolbar also provides buttons for these options.

TIP
The bulletins installed with Oracle Designer contain important information that may not appear anywhere else. You can view these files from the Start menu Designer Bulletins group. The bulletin for the Function Hierarchy Diagrammer, for example, contains this warning: "Hierarchies consisting of more than 1500 functions may require the user to reduce the node size (through the preference dialog) in order to display the complete hierarchy." The contents of these bulletins change with each new release, so be sure to look at the new bulletins that are installed when you upgrade the product.

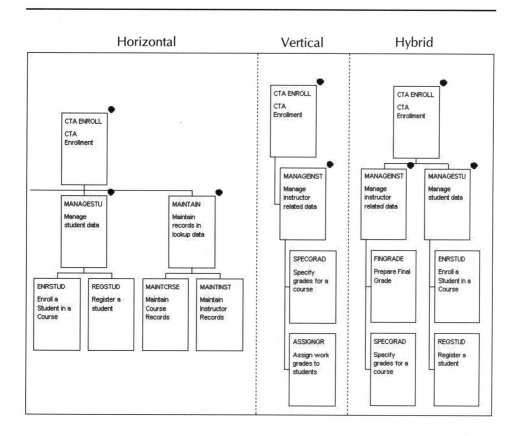

FIGURE 10-8.   *Horizontal, vertical, and hybrid layout styles*

You can also manipulate the function hierarchy views within these basic layouts in other ways. In the diagram, a red circle with a + sign appears next to a function if there are levels under it that are not shown. If you double-click the + sign, the diagrammer will show the child functions, and the red circle will contain a – sign, which you can double-click at any time to hide the child functions. This procedure is similar to the one you use to expand and collapse nodes in the Repository Object Navigator. The Layout menu contains selections that match these actions:

■ **Expand and Collapse** displays or hides, respectively, child functions of the parent functions you have selected (by clicking or drawing a selection box around them).

■ **Expand All and Collapse All** displays or hides, respectively, all child functions of the selected parent functions and their children.

■ **Expand Tree** displays all child functions of all parents in the entire diagram no matter how many root functions are displayed and no matter which functions are selected.

Another way to manipulate the functions you see on the drawing is to set the focus function. The *focus function* is the function at the top of the displayed hierarchy. Normally, the focus function is the one you have chosen as the base function for the diagram. If you have a diagram with a large number of functions, you may want to zoom in on a particular function and the branches under it. You do this by choosing **File→Set Focus** from the menu. This will display a list of functions you can use as the focus functions. You can select multiple functions as focus functions, and all will be displayed with their children. The File menu also provides several other focus options:

■ **Focus on Selection** uses functions you have clicked and selected as the focus functions (so you can bypass the function list dialog box).

■ **Focus Up** sets the next function up in the hierarchy (the parent) as the focus function.

■ **Focus on Root** sets the top-level function in the hierarchy as the focus function.

NOTE
Setting the layout style, expanding or collapsing the view, and changing the focus do not alter the functions in the diagram. These are only techniques for viewing smaller or larger parts of the diagram.

Drawing Objects

You can draw only one symbol on the FHD: the function symbol. Placing a function is slightly different from work in the other diagrammers, because all functions in the diagram are placed according to their positions in the hierarchy and are all sized the same. Thus, you do not have a choice as to placement or size; you can only specify which function is the parent of the function you want to create. You create a function on the diagram by clicking the Function drawing button in the toolbar and clicking the function that will be its parent. The prospective parent function will be selected as you fill in the Create Function dialog box, as shown in Figure 10-9. If you want to create a new root function, click an empty space on the drawing area (not on a function), and after you fill in the Create Function dialog box, the diagrammer will place the new function in a free area (not necessarily where you clicked).

You can include functions already in the repository with the **Edit→Include Root** menu selection. Since this is a hierarchy diagrammer, when you include the function, you will also include its children automatically. If you do not want to see the children, you can set the focus function or collapse the function branch as previously mentioned.

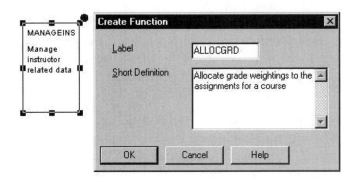

FIGURE 10-9. *Create Function dialog*

TIP
All diagrammers in Oracle Designer allow you to pin a drawing button so you do not have to reselect it if you are drawing multiple objects of the same type. If you want to draw three functions, for example, you can hold down SHIFT *when you click the function button. This pins the button so you can draw as many functions as you want without having to press the function button before drawing each one. When you want to stop placing functions, just click the Select toolbar button.*

Using the Symbol Set

The symbol set is really only the function box and the connector lines that are drawn automatically when you place a function. There are a few more techniques you can use other than those already mentioned to manipulate these symbols. These techniques consist of the following:

■ **Resizing functions**   All function boxes are the same size; if you resize one function, all others will automatically match that size. Alternatively, you can set the size and spacing between the function boxes by choosing **Options→Customize**, which opens the Customize dialog. This approach is particularly useful when you turn off the display of function definitions (using the same dialog), so the only text in the function box is the label. The small function boxes will reveal the structure better because you will be able to see more functions and their relationships at once.

■ **Reparenting functions**   You can reposition a function from one parent to another by selecting it and dragging and dropping it on the new parent. The mouse cursor changes to that shown in the following illustration when the mouse cursor is on top of a valid parent function.

- **Resequencing functions** Reparenting moves functions across hierarchical levels or from one parent to another, but sometimes you may want to move functions around within the same level. You do this by selecting the function to be resequenced and dragging and dropping it on the function you want it to precede. The mouse cursor changes to a symbol similar to the reparent symbol when you perform this operation.

- **Customizing the display** If you select one or more functions and choose **Options→Customize**, you can apply color, fonts, and line widths to the selections. You can also press the corresponding buttons on the drawing toolbar (as you can with other diagrammers). The Customize dialog box also contains other preferences that you can change, as Figure 10-10 shows.

TIP
You may find RON's Hierarchy view (as described in Chapter 6) a faster way to resequence and reparent functions.

Naming Objects

Since the functions you place in this diagram are the same functions you draw with the other function diagrammers, you can use the same naming conventions for their properties. The *Label* property is a one-word abbreviation for the action, and the *Short Definition* property is a phrase starting with a verb that describes the action.

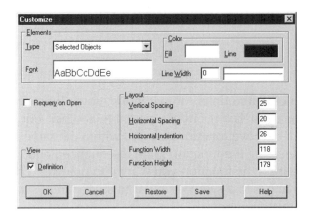

FIGURE 10-10. *Customize dialog*

Defining Function Properties

The Function Hierarchy Diagrammer presents exactly the same properties window as the Dataflow Diagrammer. You can double-click the function; select the function and choose **Edit→Properties** from the menu; or choose Properties from the right-click mouse menu to display this window. Chapter 8 and the preceding explanation of the Dataflow Diagrammer in this chapter describe these properties in detail.

TIP
When you print a function hierarchy diagram, what you see is what you get. Therefore, if you want to print different views of the same hierarchy, use the layout techniques described to create the layout before printing.
Additionally, what you save is what you get. If you save the diagram you have laid out, it will appear the same way the next time you open it.

Other Menu and Toolbar Functions

In addition to the menu and toolbar activities just discussed and those that are common to all Oracle Designer diagrammers, there are a few additional functions specific to this diagrammer:

- **Edit→Navigate** displays a list of functions on the diagram. If you choose a function from this list, the diagram will center on that function, although the selection and focus will remain unchanged.

- **Utilities→Application Design Transformer** loads the repository utility that creates module definitions from the function definitions you created. Chapter 12 discusses this utility in detail.

- **Utilities→Function/Attribute Matrix** creates default assignments of attributes to your functions, as explained in the discussion of the ER Diagrammer in this chapter.

- **Edit→Delete from Repository** removes a function from the repository. If the function is a parent, it will remove the parent and all its children from the repository, but will present a confirmation dialog that only contains the name of the parent.

The Tools menu contains items to call: the usual common Repository utilities, Repository Reports, RON, and Matrix Diagrammer; the other Systems Modeller tools, Process Modeller, Entity Relationship Diagrammer, and Dataflow Diagrammer; and the Design Editor, which gives access to all Design tools.

As with the other diagrammers, be sure to check the right-click mouse menus for quick access to selected actions. For example, the right-click mouse on a function allows you to delete a function or show its properties.

CAUTION

*The **Edit→Undo** menu item will not reverse layout changes. It will also not reverse any changes made to the definitions, as these are saved (committed) to the repository as you do them.*

Typical Function Hierarchy Diagrammer Tasks in the Analysis Phase

The features of the FHD enable you to identify a set of functions from the Information Gathering part of the Analysis phase and develop them into a complete function model in the Requirements Analysis part. The Function Hierarchy Diagrammer allows you to concentrate on the various levels and the structure of the functions of the business without being distracted by representations of dataflows or stores. You perform functional decomposition here as you do in the other function modelers, but the difference here is that you can actually see multiple levels of decomposition at one time so you can easily reparent and resequence functions. The ease with which you can visualize, move, and reparent functions is one of the strengths of this diagrammer.

Since visual representations of the dataflows and stores are also important, you will normally use this diagrammer in conjunction with either the Dataflow Diagrammer or Process Modeller. Those other diagrammers show you how information flows from one process and store to another, and this diagrammer shows you the big picture of how these functions relate to one another hierarchically.

CAUTION
Consider function hierarchy diagramming complete when you have decomposed functions down to the level where all requirements can be mapped. There is no sense, although there may be a temptation, to model functions that will not fulfill a business need. You should, of course, model functions that are manual if they fulfill a requirement. The driving force behind all you do in the life cycle should be the business requirements.

Where Does This Information Go?

The function elements in the Function Hierarchy Diagrammer are the same as those in the other function diagrammers. Table 10-3 summarizes their use as elements in the Repository Object Navigator as well as what happens to them later in the life cycle.

Function Hierarchy Diagrammer Element	Repository Element and Future Use
Functions	Business Functions. These are used by the Application Design Transformer to create modules.
Hierarchy connector lines	*Parent Function* property of the function element. These determine the atomic functions that are the functions without children.
Data usages: entity	Usages: Using Entities under the Business Functions node. These are the basis for choices the Application Design Transformer makes regarding the grouping of functions into modules and they become table usages for the module.
Data usages: attribute	Attributes node under a particular function's entity usages. These are used the same way as the entity usages but become column usages for the module.
No data usages	If a function has no data usages, the Application Design Transformer will create a manual module that will not have code generated for it.

TABLE 10-3.   *Function Hierarchy Diagrammer Elements and Repository Elements*

Matrix Diagrammer

In the Analysis phase, you create CRUD (or at least CUD) usages for functions at the entity level. This means you have to define the entity data usages for each of the functions in your system. You also need to examine each function to make sure there is a way to enter all the data in entities through existing functions or through functions or processes outside your system that you can explain. You must also ensure that there are create, update, and delete characteristics for each of the entities, or that you have a valid explanation of why there is not. For example, you may not have a create characteristic associated with an entity that represents data in an external system if you do not insert data into that entity but only retrieve data from it. In this case, the entity should have only a retrieve (R) characteristic associated with it, not CRUD.

The Matrix Diagrammer (MXD) is the easiest tool you can use to create, check, and modify data usages (CRUD) for functions. If you think of a diagrammer in Oracle Designer as a tool that lets you choose symbols and draw them on the drawing surface, the Matrix Diagrammer is really more of a repository utility than a diagrammer. As with the diagrammers, though, you can define a certain layout style and the contents of the matrix diagram and save it for later use.

However you classify it, the Matrix Diagrammer is an essential tool throughout the CADM life cycle, as it lets you quickly cross-check and modify the work completed in other tools using associations (called Usages in some locations) between elements. Figure 10-11 shows a sample MXD session with the Matrix window on the left and the Property Palette on the right.

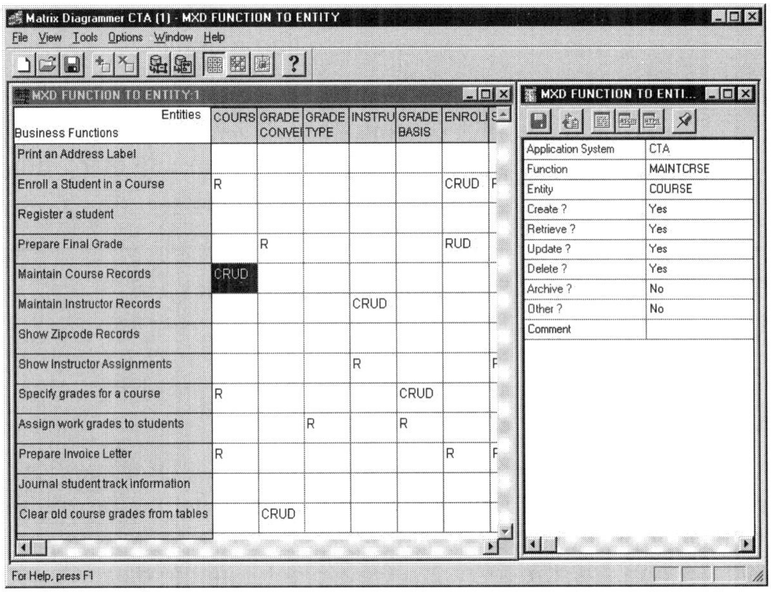

FIGURE 10-11. *Matrix Diagrammer session*

Creating a Matrix

The best way to see how the Matrix Diagrammer works is to step through creating a simple matrix. Assume that you need to check or modify the function data usage of entities during the Analysis stage. The Matrix Diagrammer lets you view a grid with the functions as the rows and the entities as the columns. The *intersection*, or *matrix cells,* of the rows and columns consists of the entity usages—CRUD. These matrix cells represent the association between one element and another (for example, functions and entities). There are three basic steps in creating this grid, or matrix, after you open the Matrix Diagrammer:

1. Select **File→New** from the menu. This step displays the New Matrix window:

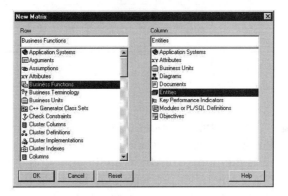

2. Choose the row and column elements and click OK. In this example, you select Business Functions for the rows and Entities for the columns, as in the preceding illustration. When you select an element type from the Row side, the Column side is automatically restricted to the list of associated elements.

3. Specify the row, column, and intersection properties in the Settings window, as shown in Figure 10-12. This step is further explained in the following discussion.

When you define a new matrix, the last dialog box you fill in is in the Settings window. The row and column properties specify the information used for the headings. The intersection properties designate which properties of the association are displayed.

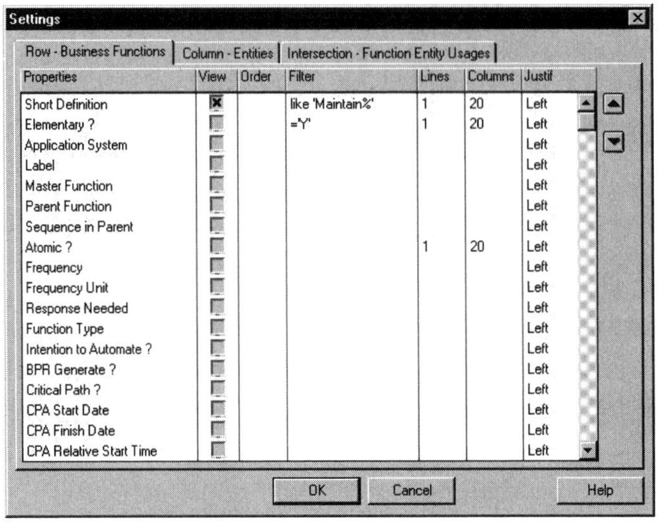

FIGURE 10-12. *New matrix Settings window*

For example, the functions appear on the row axis, so you would enter something to identify each row. A good choice here would be the *Short Definition*, as this is the name shown in all the function diagrammers, but you can also include any other property that describes the function.

All properties you choose will appear on the left side of the matrix as the heading (label) for each row. You can specify the format of rows by filling in the number of characters you will see of each property (the Columns field), the number of lines used for that value, and the justification format (left, right, or centered). There is also a setting for the ordering of the rows within the property values (ascending or descending). You can filter using a limited set of conditions to view only a subset of values by filling in the Filter item (such as ='Y' or like 'Maintain%'). Buttons on the right side of the window let you resequence the properties so you can see them in a certain order within the matrix.

After you have completed the row information, select the Column tab and fill in the same type of information for the column headings, which will appear at the top of each column. The *Name* property is the best choice for the entity labels, and you may want to specify a value less than the default of 20 as the number of characters.

Click the Intersection tab to choose the properties of the association between functions and entities that you want to see. A Displayed As area lets you specify the letter that will identify each property in the matrix. In this example, you can select Create, Retrieve, Update, and Delete for the properties and leave the default Displayed As area as is. You can also specify a separator character (like the | symbol) to separate the letters, so you might see something like C|R|U|D in a matrix cell for an entity that has all four usages for a particular function. The missing character will fill in a placeholder if a particular usage is not filled in. For example, if Function1 uses Entity1 in Create and Retrieve and you have specified a missing character of = and a separator character of | the intersection cell for these two would look like C|R|=|=. Being able to specify these characters allows you to show the CRUD in an easy-to-read way. Figure 10-13 shows this tab.

When you click OK on the Settings window, the diagrammer will build a grid with functions as rows and entities as columns. As with the other

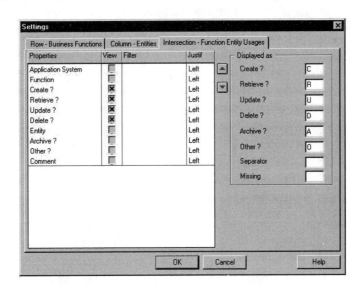

FIGURE 10-13. *Intersection tab of the Settings window*

navigator-style utilities, you select **Window→Tile Vertically** from the menu to arrange the windows in the utility. In this diagram, however, you probably want to make the Property Palette narrower because the matrix will potentially need a large working area. This is another place where it is good to use a large monitor and high-resolution setting.

Matrix View Modes

The intersection of the rows and columns shows the CRUD for the entities. You can display the matrix itself in several view modes. Each view mode can be selected using either an option on the View menu or a toolbar button. The view modes are as follows:

- *Standard view mode* (the default) displays the letters that you specify on the Intersection properties tab in cells that have the corresponding data usages.

- *Iconic view mode* displays only check marks where any properties (usages) exist for the intersection. This view is good for seeing where usages are missing, as you can see more columns and rows than in Standard view mode.

- *Micro view mode* (or *Micromap mode*) displays only a black box where usages exist. In this view, the diagram is collapsed into a smaller view, so you can navigate to an area quickly by dragging a selection box to the desired area and switching to one of the other view modes.

Modifying the Values

If you select one of the intersection cells (in the Standard or Iconic views), the Property Palette allows you to view and edit the properties of that intersection (the actual CRUD). You can group intersection cells together and edit their properties from one Property Palette. You can also insert or delete repository elements by selecting the header label for the row or column and clicking the Create or Delete toolbar buttons or selecting the corresponding Edit or right-click mouse menu items.

CAUTION
Remember that this is a live view of the repository, where you can modify element definitions directly. Anything you do to change the usages will change the repository data, and if you delete an object, there is no procedure for undoing the change.

You can also change a property of a row or column element by clicking its label. The Property Palette will show all properties of that element just as they are shown in RON, and you can edit them directly in this window. In the Matrix Diagrammer, however, you cannot see the subnodes and elements under this element as you can in RONs Navigator.

Other Techniques

There are some other techniques you can use to modify the view of the elements and their associations, as follows.

Resizing the Matrix

If the matrix is in Standard view mode, you can resize columns and rows by dragging the separator lines between them out or in. Resizing one column or row will resize them all at the same time. You cannot resize rows or columns (other than the row labels) in the other two view modes.

Property Palette Tips

The Property Palette acts much like the one in RON, and you can pin it in the same way. Note that only one Property Palette is available for each Matrix window. You can, however, open more than one Matrix window at a time for the same matrix (using **Window→New Window**). This lets you see different parts of that matrix at the same time if you want to compare properties or usages.

View As Web Page

The View menu choice As Web Page loads the HTML editor you set in the **Options→Text Editor Options** dialog. The editor will open with an HTML version of the diagram saved to a file that you can edit or save for later use. Figure 10-14 shows a matrix diagram loaded into an HTML editor.

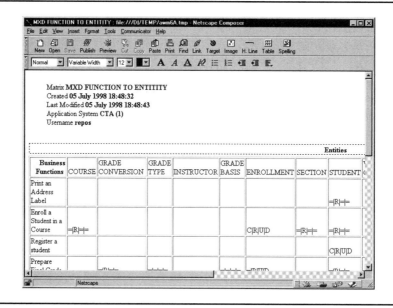

FIGURE 10-14. *Matrix diagram as a Web page*

Share and UnShare

If you use the application systems element as a row or column in a matrix, you can share the element on the other axis. For example, you set up a matrix of Application Systems and Domains. You can then choose a cell, like the intersection between the ADDRESS domain (owned by APPSYS1) and APPSYS2. If you select Share from the Edit or right-click mouse menu, APPSYS2 will receive a useable (but not modifiable) reference of ADDRESS though it is still owned by APPSYS1, and the intersection cell contents will change from being blank to "Shared". Unsharing works the same way. Both of these actions are also available in RON, though you use a different technique to perform them. Chapter 26 explains application system sharing in more detail.

3D Matrices

Some element matrix combinations allow you to display limited numbers of properties for a third element as well. For example, you can create a matrix with Business Functions for rows, Attributes for columns, and Function-Attribute Usages (CRUD) as the intersection cells. The settings dialog for this particular matrix has an additional tab called Intersection Axis – Entities. This tab allows you to define what property you will see from Entities in a tab folder interface at the bottom of the matrix. Figure 10-15 shows this 3D matrix.

Clicking an Entity name in the tab folder set on the bottom of the matrix changes the display so you see only the attributes belonging to that entity with their CRUD. This helps by letting you reduce the number of cells visible at the same time. The full list of available 3D matrices is available in the help system topic "Element combinations for 3D matrices."

Other Menu and Toolbar Functions

The Matrix Diagrammer uses the same File functions as the other Oracle Designer tools. The Edit menu has a selection for Properties that opens the Property Palette if it is not already open. A Settings selection opens up the Settings window you use to define the matrix when you create it. This

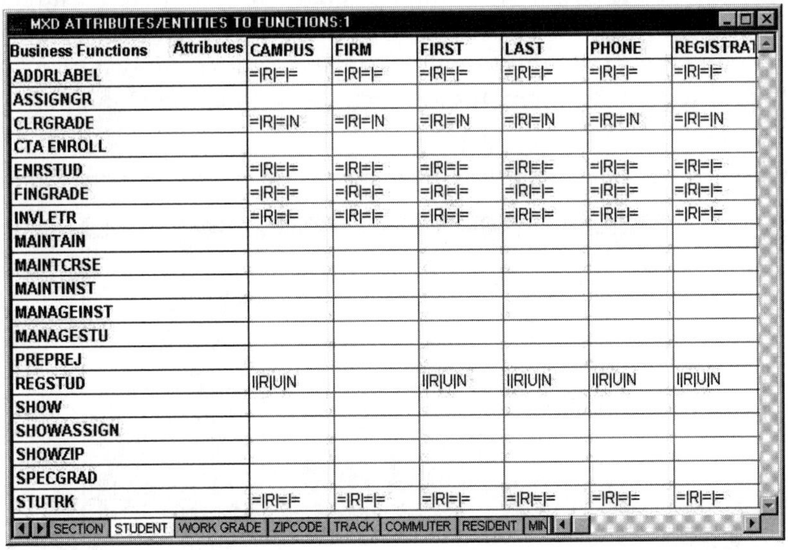

Business Functions	Attributes	CAMPUS	FIRM	FIRST	LAST	PHONE	REGISTRA
ADDRLABEL		=|R|=|=	=|R|=|=	=|R|=|=	=|R|=|=	=|R|=|=	=|R|=|=
ASSIGNGR							
CLRGRADE		=|R|=|N	=|R|=|N	=|R|=|N	=|R|=|N	=|R|=|N	=|R|=|N
CTA ENROLL							
ENRSTUD		=|R|=|=	=|R|=|=	=|R|=|=	=|R|=|=	=|R|=|=	=|R|=|=
FINGRADE		=|R|=|=	=|R|=|=	=|R|=|=	=|R|=|=	=|R|=|=	=|R|=|=
INVLETR		=|R|=|=	=|R|=|=	=|R|=|=	=|R|=|=	=|R|=|=	=|R|=|=
MAINTAIN							
MAINTCRSE							
MAINTINST							
MANAGEINST							
MANAGESTU							
PREPREJ							
REGSTUD		I|R|U|N		I|R|U|N	I|R|U|N	I|R|U|N	I|R|U|N
SHOW							
SHOWASSIGN							
SHOWZIP							
SPECGRAD							
STUTRK		=|R|=|=	=|R|=|=	=|R|=|=	=|R|=|=	=|R|=|=	=|R|=|=

MXD ATTRIBUTES/ENTITIES TO FUNCTIONS:1

SECTION | STUDENT | WORK GRADE | ZIPCODE | TRACK | COMMUTER | RESIDENT | MIN

FIGURE 10-15. *3D matrix*

selection, also available in the right-click mouse menu, is quite handy for making changes to a diagram's setup after you have worked with it.

The Tools menu contains items for all the diagrammers as well as the major utilities (RON, Repository Reports, and Design Editor).

The Options menu contains the normal choices for changing Text Editors and Broadcast options and Diagnostics. It also provides a Color/Font item that displays a dialog, shown in Figure 10-16. This dialog lets you change the colors and fonts separately for Rows, Columns, and Intersection cells.

Other Useful Matrices

You can create matrices to represent numerous combinations of repository elements. Business Units to Business Functions shows you which organization units perform which business functions. This information was entered in the Process Modeller when you created process steps (functions) in organization units (business units). You can then add other business unit assignments to that function in RON (the Usages: Performed by Business Units Usages node under a particular business function).

A matrix of Table Definitions and Modules shows which modules use which tables. If you want to show tables, views, and snapshots used in a module, choose the Relation Definitions element, as it includes all these. You can also create a matrix of a user-extension element Requirements to Business Functions in the Pre-Analysis stage to quickly view and enter the mapping of system requirements to functions. A Relation Definitions to

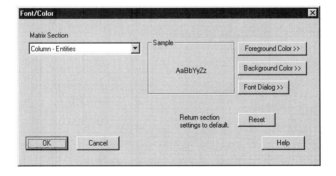

FIGURE 10-16. *Font/Color dialog*

Entities matrix shows which tables were created from which entities. If you decide to define function attribute usages, a Business Functions to Attributes matrix may be useful. Generally, you may matrix any two elements that have an association type linking them.

Where Does This Information Go?

As mentioned, the information in the Matrix Diagrammer is basic repository data that you are manipulating and displaying for the particular elements in a format different than that used by RON. The element associations that this utility represents appear in all phases of the life cycle, and you will find yourself using the Matrix Diagrammer throughout the design and development process.

Repository Reports in the Analysis Phase

As in all phases, Repository Reports are available to give you organized lists of elements and quality-check reports. At this point, you should concentrate on the following:

- **Entity/Relationship Modelling** The *Entities and their Attributes* report provides a full listing of the important properties of entities and attributes. You can also use the *Entity Definition* and *Attribute Definition* to see more properties for each of those elements. The *Attributes in a Domain* report is helpful if you want to determine which attributes will be affected by the Update Attributes in a Domain utility.

- **Function Event Modelling** These reports include the *Function to Entity Matrix* and the *Function to Attribute Matrix* reports from the work you do in the MXD and function modellers. The *Function Hierarchy* report will yield something like the diagram with boxes for functions and connecting lines between them. The *Function Hierarchy Summary* gives a text version of the previous report but with some more of the properties like *Response* and *Frequency*.

■ **Quality**   This group contains reports like the *Quality Checking of Relationships*, which shows relationships with potential problems. The *Entity Completeness Checks* report examines and reports on potential problems with entities. The *Function Completeness Checks* report does the same thing for functions. If you are fully documenting dataflows, the *Dataflows without Attributes or Data Items* will show potential omissions.

Remember, if you look at the Repository Reports hierarchy using View by Group, the same reports may appear in more than one group. Also recall that a fuller description of each report is available by invoking the help system while in Repository Reports. Chapter 6 explains how the Repository Reports tool works.

TIP
Another way to quickly get information on what a report does is to click the Context-Sensitive Help button in the toolbar. The cursor changes to the help icon. When you click with this cursor on the report you are interested in from the hierarchy, the help system opens up to the topic that describes that report. The F1 help keypress only shows an alphabetical list from which you choose.

CHAPTER
11

Pre-Design

His designs were strictly honorable, as the phrase is; that is, to rob a lady of her fortune by way of marriage.

—Henry Fielding, *Tom Jones*

he Pre-Design phase could be called the "speak now or forever hold your peace" phase. It is the last opportunity for users to add input to the project that will be reflected in the system design. System requirements are basically frozen at the end of Pre-Design. Thus, it is very important to think through both the application and database aspects of the system before the actual Design phase begins.

Overview of the Pre-Design Phase

In the Pre-Design phase, the various design standards, including GUI standards, coding standards, and design naming conventions, are determined along with the ways in which Oracle Designer will support these standards. Next, a conceptual design of the applications is generated; this design should include detailed storyboards and a list of the modules to be developed, with the system requirements mapped to those modules. Finally, the remainder of the Design phase is planned, including procedures for resolving design conflicts and criteria for determining when the design is complete.

The Design phase itself includes two broad subphases:

- **Physical design of the database** Remember that you will already have a complete ERD from the Analysis phase and a conceptual design of the applications from the Pre-Design phase.

- **Physical design of applications** Here you specify in detail exactly how the applications will interface with every field of the database.

At the end of the design process, you should have a fully specified database and associated applications. The design plan generated in the Pre-Design phase must keep this goal in mind.

Deliverables

There are several sets of deliverables in the Pre-Design phase:

- ■ **Design Standards**
  - ■ GUI design standards
  - ■ Coding standards
  - ■ Design-naming conventions

- ■ **Conceptual Design of Applications**
  - ■ Storyboards for applications
  - ■ Module structure for applications
  - ■ Map of requirements to modules
  - ■ Functional descriptions for each module

- ■ **Design Plan**
  - ■ Database design plan
  - ■ Application design plan

A high-level testing plan must be in place to determine, in principle, how design testing will be accomplished.

Design Standards

Three types of standards must be considered in the Pre-Design phase: GUI design standards, coding standards, and design-naming conventions.

Setting GUI Design Standards

Before setting GUI design standards, you need to decide how much work you want the generator to do in building applications. Compared to what is possible with a sophisticated application development tool such as Oracle Developer, the capabilities of the Oracle Designer generator are relatively limited. Therefore, you have two choices:

- Be satisfied with relatively basic GUI applications.

- Recognize that after Oracle Designer generates applications, there will be some amount of work required to complete development of screen modules.

It is now possible to have the full specification of a complex Forms module stored within the repository. However, the optimal method of determining this specification is by using Oracle Designer and Oracle Developer together with some work done in each tool.

The alternative is to set GUI standards independent of Oracle Designer and the screen module development platform, thereby greatly increasing the cost of building the applications.

GUI features fall into three categories:

- **Features built automatically using Oracle Designer generators** These include applications that require a basic layout of database fields, buttons, poplists, and other standard GUI items.

- **Features easily supported by the screen module tool but which cannot be generated directly by Oracle Designer**   In the Forms component of Oracle Developer, these include multiwindow applications and flexibility in using stacked canvases and tab controls. (Although Oracle Designer supports these interface objects, they can only be generated in limited circumstances.)

- **Features that cannot be easily built using a screen module design tool**   For Forms, for example, these include heavily graphics-oriented programming, of the type required to create an organization chart or dynamically create a PERT/CPM diagram, and complex manipulation of rich text objects.

As much as possible, you should try to restrict GUI features to the first type, using the other two types of features only when the benefits outweigh the costs. It is possible to achieve near-100 percent generation if you are willing to make some compromises in your design standards.

The ability of Oracle Designer to *design capture* a form (formerly called reverse engineering) is greatly improved in version 2.1. However, it is not yet complete. We still do not have the ability to build a form in Oracle Developer, design capture that form, generate it, and get the exact same form back. Record groups, LOVs, and user parameters are lost, and the layout of objects on the screen will not be exactly as created in Developer. If you want to use complex stacked canvases, some careful thinking will be required to get the desired results.

There are ways around these problems. The generator includes the ability to preserve the layout of a form previously produced using Oracle Developer. However, this option still entails making Oracle Developer changes to the form. (For example, if you need to add or delete a field.) And once you use it, you'd better remember to use it all the time and/or have a backup copy of your carefully developed form handy. A generic LOV can be created and placed in a template, which is modified with code at runtime. Rather than using hard-coded record groups, we can build our record groups at runtime using PL/SQL code. In the template, we can include a set of generic user parameters to support the passing of information to a form. Although we cannot create our form in any format we desire, it is now possible to have forms 100 percent specified in the repository. When generated, the form is completely and cleanly generated from the repository with no post-generation modifications required.

In this chapter, we will discuss how to design and build modules. Oracle Designer is not the appropriate tool for creating the optimal layout for a module. Designer is not a GUI tool. When trying to think through design, this work should be done in Oracle Developer. You can create the initial specifications in Designer, generate the module, check the results, and modify the layout in Designer or Developer. Before you can specify your module, you must know exactly how that module will be laid out on the screen and how it will function (i.e., storyboard). Later in this chapter, we will discuss how these storyboards are created.

You need not be particularly restrictive about the way the module should be laid out. Oracle Designer is much more sophisticated in its layout capabilities than many developers and designers are aware. A detailed discussion of how the generators work can be found in a future Oracle Press book in this series on the Oracle Designer generators. If you understand both Developer and Designer, it is possible to make Designer lay out your forms almost any way you want. Once you know what you want Oracle Designer to do, you can usually make the product comply. There is no reason to be satisfied with the forms that have traditionally been generated with Designer. Designer has been able to create reasonable-looking forms for some time. However, many people do not understand how to make the product work to its best advantage. By understanding and using the generator preferences correctly—particularly those concerned with form layout and the design of the user interface objects—only the most skilled observer would be able to tell the difference between the generated layout and a handcrafted one.

The steps that should be followed in creating a form are these:

1. Have a clear vision of the finished form.

2. Lay out the form in the Oracle Developer Forms product.

3. Specify the form in Oracle Designer.

Following these steps, you will have a form that looks just the way you want it to. Additional complex code and triggers can be written in Developer and tested immediately. Any code written for the form can be design captured and written back to the repository.

Oracle Designer and Oracle Developer together create the development environment. You need to be skilled with both products to get the best out of each individual product. In the first edition of this book, we advocated using a different template for each form, because Designer's ability to generate control blocks and non-base table items was limited. Code could not be attached to items. Since all of these limitations are gone in version 2.1, it is now viable to store the entire specification for virtually all forms in the repository. This is not to say that all of the work of designing and specifying a form is done within Oracle Designer. There are still places where development work should properly be done in Oracle Developer. When you are finished with the development process, it is still possible to 100 percent generate a form in Oracle Designer even though substantial portions of the module definition were done using Oracle Developer. You will still need to spend time thinking through the creation of or purchasing appropriate templates. Record groups and LOVs will have to be manipulated through PL/SQL code. But it is a relatively straightforward process to write library routines to make such manipulations easy for the novice to moderately skilled developer.

A complete discussion of GUI standards would fill a book. There is no way to thoroughly cover the topic here. However, the following paragraphs present some basic principles and strategies to keep in mind.

There is no industry standard for GUI development. Different companies have radically different standards of how screens should look. Thinking through how screens should be created helps avoid fundamental differences in the way screens look within the same application. In the old character-based environment, screens within the same company usually had a reasonably consistent look and feel. With GUI applications, organizations often have many applications that are grossly dissimilar. Look and feel standards should be determined for each type of application.

Application Types
Applications fall into five basic categories:

- **Navigation applications**   These include full-screen (menu) applications with many buttons. The user clicks the buttons to move to different parts of the screen. Typically, the first screen that the user sees in the application allows direct navigation to the appropriate place in the application.

- **Administration applications**   There are several choices for handling the administration of code description tables. The table structure for these must be decided upon first. For some developers, a clean approach works best, with a different table for each code description. However, this approach leads to a great number of tables. Other developers prefer to combine all descriptions in a single table. Choices can then be made about the look of the screen. A good strategy is to have one single administration module (or form) that supports the maintenance of all administration applications. Tables that don't fit on one screen can be grouped on tabs within the same application.

- **Master-detail applications**   A master-detail application is a standard application in which there is a parent-child relationship between two sets of records. For the current record in the master block, associated detail records are shown in the detail block: for example, departments and their associated employees or purchase orders (POs) and their associated PO details. The master record information can be displayed in several ways: in a single-record block, multirecord block, or poplist. The detail records can be displayed in single-record or multirecord blocks. The appropriate standards for each type of master-detail application must be considered.

■ **Locator applications** This common type of application allows you to quickly and easily locate a specific record. For example, in a PO system, you can easily find a particular PO if you know the PO number. However, if all that you know is which department initiated the PO and that the PO was issued in the past two months, you will have problems finding the correct information. Therefore, to make it easy for users to locate particular records, it is customary to build a separate application that helps users locate specific records. Such an application has an area at the top of the screen to set criteria and an area at the bottom of the screen to display query results. Double-clicking a retrieved record in the locator automatically opens the primary application associated with that record and retrieves the record into the application.

■ **Complex applications** These include applications with a lot of information and calculated fields. Because of the evolving Windows interface standards, the best way to handle these complex forms is with tabs. According to the tab selected, the user can display different stacked canvases. In Forms 5.0, the native tab object allows editing access to all tabs, even in design mode. This feature is very useful, since the developer won't have to worry about stacked canvases. The one problem with tabs is that they take up a full line that is the height of the tab, which can be a waste of screen real estate. A big canvas that scrolls or multiple pages accessed by Next Page/Previous Page buttons are alternative ways of handling a large amount of information; however, these are now considered outdated approaches and should not be used.

For each form, no matter what the type, certain decisions need to be made. The toolbar functions need to be determined. Insertion, modification, and deletion functions need to be made available to the user. Features should be obvious to the user and consistent on every form. The designer can assume that users have some training. Nevertheless, actions should be natural and designed from the user's point of view. An example of a user-unfriendly action is a procedure that requires the user to choose a button or item called "Clear Screen" to create a new record before inserting information in a new record and saving it. This selection is not logical from a user standpoint. Instead, there should be an Insert button. The user can then click the Insert button, which should display a prompt asking the user to "insert record and save" and then clear the screen.

Screen Fonts and Color

There are numerous books on GUI design standards. All recommend keeping the number of colors and fonts to a minimum. Many hours can be wasted thinking about appropriate fonts and colors. The best the developer can hope for is that no one hates the choices. It often pays to make boring selections, since different machines with different video boards (or different browsers for web-enabled applications) display things differently. The monitor used also affects the display. The developer should create samples and test them on the client machines with the users.

Screen Real Estate

Conservation of screen real estate is extremely important. Screen real estate is the designer's most precious commodity. It is very easy to waste screen space by not thinking about the layout of the application. The best way to minimize wasted screen space is to think carefully about every pixel.

For example, in a multirecord block, don't put any pixels between fields. Start at the top and fill the screen one layer at a time. Each block or area should be laid out horizontally to maximize the use of screen space.

Here are some suggestions for making the most of screen space:

■ Don't put titles on screens. Put titles on the windows.

■ Oracle Designer generators automatically place a frame around an area, with the label on the top-left area of the frame. Adjust the generator preferences to ensure that no space is wasted between fields. Stack the labels horizontally next to the fields laid out horizontally and move them two pixels away. The recommended space between horizontal fields is ten pixels. The trick to making this work is to change the cell size in Oracle Forms to 2 pixels × 2 pixels. (You can change it to 1 pixel, but then you will want to select preferences for the values that are too large.)

■ Since most preferences in Designer are measured in characters, the cell size that you specify in the form specifies how many characters high or wide to make things. For example, you can have a two-pixel gap between your prompt and your item by changing the Item/Prompt Gap to 1 with a two-pixel cell size in the form template.

■ It is important to decide how many rows are realistically needed for multirecord frames. If the user will be looking at a large table, you should try to place as many records on the screen as possible. A form that displays the names of as many employees as possible, for example, may be easier to use. However, for something like a list of the disk drives attached to PCs, where 90 percent of the users will have only one or two choices, and 10 percent will have three or four choices, it doesn't make any sense to display lots of records on the screen.

■ If there is a lot of information, try to let the user see as much as possible on one screen. Using a crowded screen is often better than using more than one screen or a simpler but less-useful screen. This is a stylistic decision that should be driven by the user. Through reengineering, you may be able to fit information from several screens on one screen without the use of tabs.

■ An efficient way to handle records with long text fields (such as fields for notes, comments, and descriptions) is to divide the screen into two parts. The top part can show the important fields (all records). The bottom part can show the note, comment, or description associated with the selected field.

BUTTONS   Buttons shouldn't be any bigger than necessary. They need to display the button label with a few extra pixels on each side. All buttons in a row don't need to be the same size. For example, an Exit button doesn't need to be as large as an Execute Query button.

Putting buttons across the bottom or top of the screen wastes less vertical space than stacking them vertically. Standard buttons take up 17 pixels. Buttons are most often placed at the top or bottom of a screen. Other, creative solutions are possible, such as placing buttons in a horizontal row in the middle of the screen. This placement enables easy use, and the row of buttons makes a natural divider for the screen.

POPLISTS   Poplists are a major space-saving device. The space of only one record is needed for a poplist, but the poplist can display as many records as needed when it is selected. Two hundred records is a practical limit for poplists. A user will not want to have to scroll through a list longer than this. However, if you need to include more records in a poplist, you can use an LOV (list of values) as a search facility. You can use a button to bring up the LOV.

LOGOS   In general, logos and fancy graphics are unnecessary. They take up a lot of space and have little use. Logos are not needed for internal forms within organizations. Employees don't need to see the company logo on every form. For forms going to those outside the company, place graphics and logos on a welcome screen rather than letting them consume memory, functionality, and space on the working forms.

Setting Coding Standards

Coding standards are essential to the readability and maintainability of your code. As with GUI standards, a complete discussion is well beyond the scope of this book. One of the best discussions of PL/SQL standards is contained in Steven Feuerstein's book, *Oracle PL/SQL Programming* (Sebastopol, CA: O'Reilly, 1995). Here is our "top-ten list" of important coding standards to follow:

1. **Use lowercase almost everywhere.** There may be some readability gained by using uppercase and lowercase; however, seldom are the two cases implemented consistently. Use uppercase for data values, for example, "TRUE."

2. **Use % type for all local variable declarations that correspond to database objects.** This will minimize the amount of changes to your code when changes occur in the data structure. And % rowtype is especially powerful and efficient.

3. **Use two spaces (not the TAB key) for indention in PL/SQL triggers.** By default, Oracle uses an eight-character indent for tabs. With this indent, after three or four levels of indenting, you won't be able to see the code on the right side of the screen.

4. **Use explicit cursors.** Explicit cursors decrease the number of database accesses.

5. **Generate functions and procedures and store them in libraries wherever possible.** Reusable code is one of the great benefits of PL/SQL. You should take advantage of this feature wherever possible.

6. **Within modules, implement global variables as local package variables.** This optimizes memory usage and helps prevent sloppy coding.

7. **Create a standard list of abbreviations for variable names.** This list can be as extensive as you want. However, the use of only these abbreviations and no others is crucial to the maintainability of the code, so the list should be as short as possible, including no more than 500 abbreviations. Just as in the Analysis phase-naming conventions, any words not on the list should be spelled out.

8. **Use CURSOR FOR loops to scan a set of records.** This syntax makes the code tidy and more readable.

9. **Store functions and procedures that require heavy database traffic in the database.** This will minimize the amount of network traffic when these programs execute.

10. **Use very robust exception handling.** One of the best features of PL/SQL is its exception-handling capability. One of the greatly underutilized features of PL/SQL is its ability to handle almost every abnormal condition and return to the user a meaningful alert informing them about what has occurred in the application.

A coding manual should be long enough to ensure consistency, but not so long that no one will read or follow it. Realistically, a few pages of tips are all one can expect developers to comply with.

Establishing Design-Naming Conventions

Naming conventions in the Design phase need not be significantly different from the standards used in the Analysis phase. Oracle provides relatively generous lengths for table, column, and PL/SQL variable names. However, particularly long table and column names can cause code readability problems. A better policy is to implement a slightly more aggressive naming convention in Design than was used in Analysis.

One approach is to develop a relatively extensive list of five-character abbreviations for all words used to name objects in the database. Consistent use of naming conventions is important to make development as straightforward as possible. If you use a formal, rigorous abbreviation technique where only approved words are abbreviated, you can—for example—automate the process of moving from Analysis entity and attribute names and other names to physical table and column names by writing a simple procedure using the API. This is done by first running the Database Design Transformer utility, which automatically generates tables and columns from entities and attributes, then writing a utility using the API. This utility should replace words in the table and column names with approved abbreviations from the abbreviation list, which will ensure that abbreviations are consistently applied through all table and column names. Because much of the code will be automatically generated, there is less of a need than you might think to aggressively abbreviate.

Oracle Designer lets you preface all column names with a table abbreviation; however, this is not recommended. It unnecessarily lengthens column names and makes generic procedures written for similar columns more difficult to use. It is easy enough to preface column names with the actual table names where appropriate.

Both table and column names should be descriptive. Under no circumstances should tables be named with obscure codes. Module definitions should also be named with easy-to-recognize descriptive names using the same abbreviation list as the tables and columns.

Conceptual Design of Applications

The conceptual design of applications must be created before the database can be designed. Tool selection, storyboarding, creating a user-friendly interface, modularization, requirements mapping, and the creation of functional descriptions are all part of this conceptual design process that will be discussed in this section. The conceptual design of the applications was performed as part of the Pre-Design phase, because database design cannot take place without a very clear picture of what the application will look like.

Selecting Development Tools

There are several choices for Oracle application design. Systems designers need to decide which tool to use for building applications, choosing from among the following: Oracle Developer, Visual Basic, C++ applications, JDeveloper and Oracle WebServer (using HTML). This section discusses how to make this decision and the pros and cons of each tool.

Oracle Developer is Oracle's flagship product. It provides tight integration with the database and is a great development environment regardless of whether you are using an Oracle database or some other database. Oracle Developer now supports both web-based and client/server deployment of both forms and reports. The primary reason not to choose Oracle Developer over other platforms is the availability of development talent within your own organization. If you have very strong Visual Basic, C++, or HTML talent, it might be sensible to choose one of these platforms instead.

Oracle Developer is the tool of choice for building applications. Because it is an Oracle product, Oracle Designer support is strong. An additional advantage to this choice is that it enables you to move between different hardware platforms, such as Macintosh and IBM, with few modifications. Some initial performance, memory-usage, and browser-compatibility problems have been reported with deploying forms on the Web, but many of these problems have been solved or are close to being solved as of this writing.

Visual Basic is a full-featured language with thousands of libraries of extensions available. However, it is limited to the Microsoft Windows platform. If this limitation is acceptable and your organization has strong Visual Basic resources, this may be a good choice. Also, if the standard for application development throughout your organization is Visual Basic, it makes sense to be consistent. It is possible to use Oracle's Oracle Designer to generate Visual Basic applications to run with an Oracle database or, with minor modifications, with any other relational database.

C++ is the flagship of third-generation languages. In the past few years, extensive libraries have become available to support C++ in a GUI environment. However, writing C++ code when modifications are needed is time consuming. Two to ten times as much C++ code must be written as what would be necessary in Forms. This can make developing applications costly. However, Forms is a fourth-generation language with limitations. In comparison to Forms, C++ gives the developer much more control over the application. Therefore, with C++ you can theoretically create applications that run much faster than those created with Forms.

Another advantage to C++ is that you can find good C++ programming talent relatively cheaply, whereas expert Forms talent is rare and expensive. C++ may not be a good choice, however, if you need to cross platforms, because C++ requires significant rewriting of applications to move from platform to platform.

JDeveloper is a Java-based development toolkit. It is especially suited to Web-based development.

HTML is one of the Web languages. Oracle WebServer applications are generated as PL/SQL packages that reside on the server. They are dynamically translated to HTML and are brought to the client machine only when invoked. The big advantage of HTML is in distribution, since there are no runtime worries. Applications are accessible to anyone with access to the World Wide Web.

Creating Storyboards for Applications

A storyboard is a nonfunctioning prototype that allows users and developers to assess the quality of the application design.

Once the GUI standards are implemented within Oracle Designer as preferences and templates, the quickest way to create a storyboard application is by following this procedure:

1. Generate a default database directly from the logical ERD.

2. Generate default modules based on the relatively crude function definitions from the Analysis phase.

3. Use those default modules to quickly generate sample data to populate the database tables, or use a simple data generator.

4. Begin the process of refining the default modules to conform to the physical process flows already designed.

5. Continue to manually modify those sample modules until they conform to the basic look and feel of the final application.

Physical Process Flows

During Pre-Design, you must lay out the physical process flows in the new system. These physical process flows look like those at the logical level drilled down to another level of detail. The processes should be detailed enough to represent the elemental processes in the function hierarchy. Each process will translate into a form.

Making the Application User Friendly

You need to consider a number of factors that affect the user friendliness of the application. In particular, the help system will play an important role in the way the user interfaces with the application.

Consider these factors:

- **Number of users**   The more users there are, the more carefully the help system must be designed.

- **Level of users**   A higher level of support must be designed for nontechnical employees than for systems people.

- **Complexity and flexibility of the application**   The greater the complexity of the system, the greater the attention that should be paid to software usability. For example, if the reporting system allows only the generation of simple, canned reports using default parameters, then little attention needs to be paid to the user interface. If, however, the reporting system allows dynamic selection of breaks, sorts, and filters, then much greater attention will need to be paid to the user interface.

- **Training**   The more training that is provided, the more corners that can be cut on the user interface. Building a computer-based training system can also be cost effective if the user population is very large.

- **Documentation**   Good manuals, tutorials, courses, and so on reduce the need for more sophisticated help systems. People don't usually like to look things up in a manual. With the availability of authoring tools, manuals and tutorials can easily be converted into online documentation.

- **Online help system**   Help can be made available all the way down to the item level in applications. Using Oracle Designer, this can be done relatively easily and cheaply.

■ **Actual design of the application itself**   It's possible, although rarely desirable, to put the instructions for the application right on the screen as text. Web applications frequently use this strategy.

You must consider all of these factors together to make applications user friendly. You cannot decide what to do in regard to one factor in isolation from the other six. In addition, the strategy you use to achieve user friendliness will be influenced by the tools you select and how easy it is to implement each of these. For example, in Oracle Designer it is very easy to implement item-level help when the application is being designed. As of this writing, there are no tools to cheaply create high-quality computer-based training. Your user-friendliness strategy will obviously influence the design of your applications—that is why the strategy must be chosen in the Pre-Design phase.

Of course, the cost of whatever user-friendliness strategy is used must also be considered; your goal is to minimize the cost of the overall system for its entire life cycle. You also need to consider the rate of user turnover and user expectations for user friendliness.

If your users are currently running character-based applications on dumb terminals, they will probably be thrilled by almost any consistent, well-designed GUI interface they get. However, as more and more users get PCs on their desks or at home or start to use the Web, user expectations can be a big problem. As soon as the users see a toolbar or menu on a GUI screen, they may expect an application that is as sophisticated as Microsoft Word, with every bell and whistle imaginable. These products have been through thousands of hours of user testing and refining and are mature versions. The best applications that you build are going to seem crude by comparison. However, your applications are not used by thousands or millions of different users. Most business software is built within a specific context. Also, although it can often cost the organization millions of dollars, your application will end up looking nowhere near as elegant as a commercially available word processing package available at the local computer store for a few hundred dollars or less. Unfortunately, there is no way for you to develop applications that are as sophisticated as commercially available software that still are cost effective.

In your designs, use the default behavior of the tools whenever possible. Avoid the temptation of trying to meet every user whim when designing the interface. Think very carefully about how to get the greatest user friendliness for the least cost and at the same time educate users as to what is reasonable to expect from the applications being built.

Determining the Module Structure for Applications

You must determine which storyboard modules will be used in the final application. You may combine some of the current screen modules into one module and decompose others into several modules. Finally, it may be necessary to manually build whole new modules. These modules can be implemented within Oracle Designer by design capturing the modules to generate base modules within Oracle Designer.

At this point in the CADM process, logical functions generated in Analysis exist in the function hierarchy. These were brought into the physical world as module definitions, and from these module definitions functioning module programs were generated. Using these functioning module programs, storyboards were created. Now you have determined the appropriate modules to use. In the context of Oracle Developer Forms, these modules correspond to .FMB files.

Your next step is to assess the correspondence between the set of appropriate modules and the information currently in the Oracle Designer repository. There is a three-step process to do this:

1. If a module in the repository is relatively close to one of the final modules, you can declare that this is the module that corresponds to the storyboard module.

2. If the storyboard module has no corresponding repository module, you should design capture the storyboard module to create a repository module.

3. Repository modules that have no analog as storyboard modules should be discarded.

Mapping Requirements to Modules

At this point, the requirements from the original function hierarchy must be remapped to the new modules. The modules should be closely related to the functions from the original function hierarchy, so this mapping should not be difficult.

Writing Module Functional Descriptions: Creating the Design Book

Each module needs design notes that describe in detail how that module will function. These notes will guide developers in designing the application and will form the basis of the design book. The design book (which will be fully described in Chapter 15) is a complete, self-contained specification of each module. It should include everything from screen shots and system requirements to column-level usages and pseudo-code for the triggers. It is the document from which the developer builds the module, and the tester uses the same document to make sure that the module meets design specifications. The conceptual design of the applications generates the first draft of the design book. The design book is completed in the Application Design phase.

Design Plan

The overall design plan addresses strategy, activities, and tasks necessary to design the two largest components of the new system: the database and applications.

Creating the Database Design Plan

Up until this point, it has not been possible to consider a plan for the database design; the conceptual design of the application must be complete before you can start thinking about building the database. The design plan for the database should include provisions for security, history keeping, denormalization, database instances, and capacity planning.

Security

Security can be handled in many ways within Oracle, such as through roles, profiles, login, and operating system and network security features. You will need to assess how security will be handled at the database level according to the application. Some applications, such as those involving money or personally sensitive or competitive information, will require much higher levels of security than those that concern information on internal business operations of a nonsensitive nature.

History Keeping

In the Pre-Design phase, you do not need to decide how to physically implement the system history; you simply need to decide what system history to keep. There are two types of history you can track:

■ **Data errors**   If, for example, the incorrect middle initial is printed on a check, this error needs to be changed, but is it necessary to keep a record of it? This depends upon the context. If the organization making the error is a bank, it may be useful to keep track of the error, but other businesses may not need to do so. You need to decide whether all errors, some errors, or only substantive errors will be documented. In the Pre-Design phase, issues such as what constitutes a "substantive" error can be defined.

■ **Real changes over time**   These changes are actual alterations in a record. You need to decide whether to keep track of this history. Examples of changes that should be kept track of include changes to an employee's name because of marriage, an employee's history within a department, and sales credited to specific departments. How to document these changes does not need to be decided at the attribute level at this stage. However, it is appropriate at this point to define just what history will be tracked.

Denormalization

In a perfect world, you would not have to consider the applications when building the database. However, machines are not infinitely fast, and all but the smallest databases will require some level of denormalization to make the applications run at an acceptable speed.

As with other issues at this stage, it is useful to include a policy statement regarding how to denormalize data. Databases that have a clearly defined policy on this issue are rare; however, a good policy is to normalize the data completely and cleanly until performance considerations demand a halt. A clean third normal form database should be generated and then denormalization should only occur when necessary. The policy should be used in all cases.

Instances of the Oracle Database

In working on a system, you need to have more than one copy of the
database since changes would have to be made to the existing production
system. In most cases, there should be one copy for developers to
experiment with, a second copy for testing, and a third copy for production.
These three database copies constitute a minimum. A fourth and fifth copy
can be used for additional testing. In this case, one copy would be used for
small-scale testing and another copy would be used for full production
testing.

Capacity Planning

A big mistake often made in database design is not allowing for indexes.
Indexes can be counted on without any careful analysis to add 50 percent to
estimated data size. In a warehouse, it should be assumed that adding
indexes will double the size of the database. (Bitmapped indexes may
reduce these requirements under some circumstances, but it's still a good
rule of thumb.) How much space is really needed? For example, if you have
10 gigabytes of data in a legacy system, in the development instance, you
first need to bring the legacy system into Oracle as is. This will require
roughly 15 gigabytes of space, since Oracle doesn't store data as compactly
as most legacy systems do. In addition, you will need 5 to 10 gigabytes for
indexing. In the test instance, you will need 5 gigabytes for the small test
instance and 20 to 25 gigabytes for the large test instance. Similarly, you
will need an additional 20 to 25 gigabytes in the production instance.
Therefore, the 10 gigabytes of legacy data requires 81 to 95 gigabytes of
disk storage.

The final aspect of database design planning is to have an auditor review
the final physical database design and ensure that the choices made by the
design team are appropriate.

Creating the Application Design Plan

The application design plan is relatively straightforward to create.
Application design involves identifying the detailed column usage for each
module and fully specifying the modules. Much of the final application
design work is done in the Build phase.

Application design is among the most tedious, time-consuming, and unglamorous tasks of the entire design process. Therefore, it is very important to plan to review the accuracy of the application design. This review is discussed in Chapter 15.

Creating the Testing Plan

At this point, you need to be able to determine your test plan. The design book will drive the test plan. It is beyond the scope of this book to discuss the automated test tools available, which may help in the efficiency of the testing process and should be integrated into the testing process.

Modifications for Smaller Systems

For small systems, the Pre-Design phase is unnecessary if standards are in place. Usually, the analyst can keep the small number of system requirements in his or her head and use sophisticated tools such as Oracle Designer to begin building almost immediately.

For medium-sized systems, you can cut some corners at this stage. Since the set of system requirements is relatively small, the designer does not need to map each requirement to the design book. It might be wise to perform a more global mapping: that is, to show which requirements map to which subsystem rather than to which elementary function. When in doubt, it is better to err on the side of more structure rather than less. No project ever failed because too much structure was imposed. For a medium-sized project, it shouldn't take you too much time to map requirements to functions.

Physical process flows may or may not be necessary for a medium-sized system, but it is usually a good idea to include them. Also, design standards and storyboards still should be completed for medium-sized systems. One big decision that needs to be made for these projects involves the use of templates and GUI design standards. The designer must ask these questions: Will this be a stand-alone project? Is it likely to be modified in the future? Should the system be built quickly and GUI design standards imposed afterward? For large projects, these decisions must be made before this point in the process. With medium-sized projects, designers may be using the software tools for the first time, and they may not know enough to design the GUI at this point. The project can then be used as a learning experience.

When Is the Pre-Design Phase Complete?

There are many parts to the Pre-Design phase for which to assess completion. Deciding when GUI standards are complete is a judgment call on the part of one or more senior developers. The question must be posed: Are GUI standards detailed enough to enforce consistency across screen modules? The answer will be apparent soon enough if GUI standards are inadequate since completed screen modules will be grossly dissimilar.

Any problems will also be evident during conceptual design of applications and coding standards. You also need to come up with as many guidelines as deemed appropriate to enforce consistency in PL/SQL routines; the fewer the standards, the greater the variability you will see in PL/SQL coding. However, if standards are too complex, you run the risk of overwhelming the developers so that they either do not comply with the standards or waste time adhering to standards that are not relevant.

Storyboards are complete when the users sign off on the designs. The users must spend sufficient time entering real transactions into the storyboard applications to make sure their needs are met. It must be made very clear to users that this is the final functionality they will see in the completed application; after this, no nonessential modification to the system will be allowed until after version 1 of the application is delivered. Be firm; you need to avoid the dreaded "creeping featurism," whereby requirements not originally specified seem to creep into the finished product. Stress that all your schedules and cost estimates are based on the requirements as currently stated and the storyboards as approved. If the users or developers later discover that a requirement was inadvertently misstated or misinterpreted, a formal change control mechanism should be in place to negotiate the scope of the change and, if appropriate, corresponding changes to the project schedule or cost.

Knowing whether functions have been correctly modularized is a judgment call on the part of the design team. If the individuals performing modularization are inexperienced, it is appropriate to temporarily bring in an individual capable of reviewing the decisions made during the modularization process.

The assignment of requirements and functional descriptions to modules is a straightforward process that can be reviewed by virtually any member of the design team. At this point, the designer needs to look at the design plan and ask the question: Will it be complete enough to keep testers happy? There must be sufficient detail in the design book so that the completed module can be tested. Without a detailed design book, a tester can only guess at the functionality of the module, and testing of the module will therefore be inadequate. It must be possible to ensure that the design meets the requirements. This can be done by mapping the requirements to individual modules.

What happens to this Requirements Document? Every requirement paragraph contains a separate and unique object to attach to tables, or a relationship, collection of tables, module, set of modules, or module connection. The only way to prove that the requirements have been met is to note where each and every requirement went, including the identity of the specific module and how the requirement was implemented. The whole point of a good design is that it meets the specifications laid out for it.

From this point forward in the CADM process, tasks are largely performed within the design team with little input required from outside sources. There is a serious temptation to turn over the remainder of the project to the development team with little outside review until the system is complete. However, the result of such a strategy will almost assuredly be the failure of the project.

The design plan *must* be reviewed throughout the remainder of the CADM process. This quality-control effort, involving people outside the design team, should continue to be an important part of the overall system development process.

CHAPTER
12

Oracle Designer in Pre-Design

Intelligence...is the faculty of making artificial objects, especially tools to make tools.
—Henri Bergson (1859-1941), *Essays on Time and Free Will*, 1899

racle Designer assists your work in the Pre-Design phase as you prepare for the Design phase. There are a number of deliverables that comprise this preparation: the design standards, conceptual design of application (storyboard), and the design plan. Table 12-1 shows the Pre-Design activities or deliverables that Oracle Designer supports and the tools that perform them.

Other than the GUI design standards, the main deliverable in the Pre-Design phase that Oracle Designer supports is the storyboard or

Activity or Deliverable	Oracle Designer Tool
GUI design standards	Module templates and the Design Editor: Generator Preferences
Storyboard (conceptual design of applications)	Database Design Transformer, Application Design Transformer, and Design Editor: generators
Integrate changes in tables from the storyboard	Design Editor: Capture Design of Server Model From Database utility
Integrate changes in modules from the storyboard	Design Editor: Capture Design of Form and Capture Design of Report utility, Module Diagram
Module structure for applications	Design Editor: Module Network Viewer
Map requirements to modules	Repository Object Navigator or API
Functional descriptions of the modules	Repository reports and the repository itself
Database and application design plan	Repository reports and the repository itself

TABLE 12-1. *Pre-Design Activities and Designer Tools*

conceptual application design. You can create the storyboard outside Oracle Designer and capture the design of files you create in Oracle Developer. This discussion, however, assumes you will create the storyboard from modules in Oracle Designer. The storyboard is really a prototype of the complete system that you can use to communicate your ideas to users or clients. It contains all, or some, of the modules (or program pieces) that you know you will need at this point in the development. The main steps in creating and processing this storyboard in Oracle Designer are as follows:

1. Create a first-cut set of table definitions with the Database Design Transformer.

2. Create a first-cut set of modules and a module network with the Application Design Transformer.

3. Run the Generate Database From Server Model utility to create scripts for the tables.

4. Accept all nonmanual candidate modules. Then generate screens, menus, and reports using the Form Generator and Report Generator.

5. Refine the forms and reports using Oracle Developer and rearrange the module network on paper—a non-Oracle Designer step.

6. Integrate changes in table design from the storyboard process into the repository using the Capture Design of Server Model From Database utility.

7. Integrate modified modules and the module network structure into the repository using the Capture Design of Form and Capture Design of Report utilities and the Design Editor Module Network Viewer.

8. Map requirements to modules using the API or RON.

The following sections discuss how to set GUI standards for the application modules and how to use the Oracle Designer tools that support these steps in the storyboard process. The discussion in this chapter centers around an Oracle Developer approach. Even if you are not implementing the system using Oracle Developer, you might still be able to use it to do the storyboard if your audience is able to understand that this is not what the final product will look like. You could be understandably wary about that approach. If so, and you are using another product that Oracle Designer generates, you can use that product for the storyboard instead of Oracle Developer. If you are deploying the system in a product that Oracle Designer does not generate, you would do the storyboard with that product. In the cases where you do not use Oracle Designer, you need to adjust the concepts presented in this chapter to be consistent with the tool you are using.

This chapter does not discuss the Capture Design of Server Model From Database utility, which was explained in Chapter 8, or the generators or module templates, which are explored in Chapter 18. The work you do in the generators in the Pre-Design phase is similar to the work you do in the Build phase, with one main difference: in the Pre-Design phase you accept all the default preferences for each module when you perform generation. This chapter also does not provide details on the Module Diagram and the Module Network Viewer, as these are discussed in Chapter 16.

Before creating the storyboard, however, you should work on your GUI design standards because the storyboard modules themselves will use them. The main Oracle Designer tool you use for standards in module creation is the Design Editor. This chapter discusses the basic operations of this tool. Chapters 14, 16, and 18 explain its functionality as related to tasks you perform in the Design or Build phases.

Design Editor

The Pre-Design phase task of setting GUI standards involves setting the generator preferences in the Design Editor (DE). Like RON, this utility uses the Navigator with Property Palette-style of access to the repository. The Design Editor Navigator window reduces the list of element types from RON to just those elements you need to manipulate in the Design and Build phases. In addition to the Navigator window and Property Palette, the Design Editor also allows you to open diagram windows to graphically represent the data and module information and to assist in the design process. Figure 12-1 shows a typical DE session with the Navigator, Property Palette, and diagram windows.

If you are using just the Navigator and Property Palette windows for an extended period of time, you can get a better view by using the technique

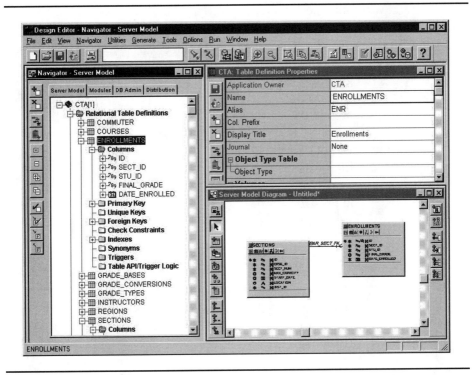

FIGURE 12-1.   *Design Editor session*

mentioned in the RON discussion to maximize the outer window, click on the Navigator window, and select **Window→Tile Vertically** from the menu.

The Oracle Designer Release Notes recommend using SVGA (800×600) resolution and 256 colors. You will find yourself to be more productive with this tool if you have a large monitor with higher resolution (1280×1024 or more). Figure 12-2 shows a similar DE session on a monitor configured to display 1280×1024 pixels. Higher resolutions often require more video memory, but you can set the number of colors lower (256 or higher) if your video memory is limited. You can see that there is more screen space for windows and you will find yourself rearranging the screen less often than if you used a lower resolution. Examples in this book use an 800×600 resolution for readability in the printed medium, but you should seriously

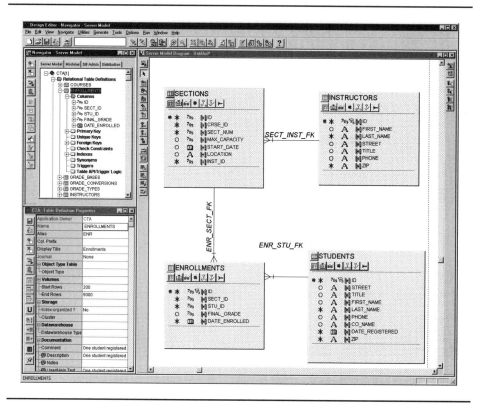

FIGURE 12-2. *Design Editor running in a high resolution*

consider the monitor resolution as a key factor in increasing productivity when using the Design Editor.

Basic Techniques

You start the Design Editor from a button in the Oracle Designer window or from the Tools menu of the other tools. When you first open DE, the dialog shown in Figure 12-3 appears. This dialog opens the desired tab page in the Object Navigator and, optionally, presents a wizard to help you through the next steps. You can turn off this opening dialog by unchecking the box to display this screen on startup. You can turn it back on again by choosing the **Options→General Settings** from the menu and checking the Welcome Screen check box. The opening dialog also allows you to open a diagram

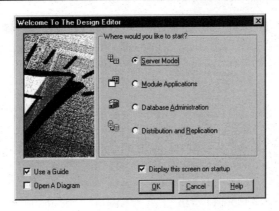

FIGURE 12-3. *Design Editor opening dialog*

for the Server Model and Module Applications choices and to run a *guide,* or wizard, to assist you in creating definitions for the Server Model, Module Applications, and Database Administration (but not Distribution and Replication) choices.

The Design Editor then opens into a standard Navigator window, like the one in RON. In this tool, however, you can work with only one application system at a time.

Working in the Navigator Window

You work with the Navigator window the same way you do with any other navigator in Oracle Designer, such as the one in RON discussed in Chapter 6. You can expand and collapse the nodes, use the Find field, copy properties between elements, create and delete element definitions, navigate to and from marks, query and requery, and switch between the Navigator and Property Palette.

The Navigator window has four tabs that contain the elements used in the Design and Build phases. Figure 12-4 shows the tabs and their top-level objects. The tool remembers which tab was open when you exit DE so that tab will be the active one the next time you open the tool. This tab interface partitions the information according to how you might use it and offers a faster method to navigate the large number of repository elements. You cannot customize the contents of these tabs as you can do in RON, but the

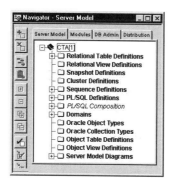

Server Model Design

Module Applications Design

Database Administration Design

Database Distribution Design

FIGURE 12-4. *Navigator tabs and their contents*

tabs give you predefined levels of organization that, like RON's customized groups, make it easier for you to find a particular element definition.

The logical grouping into four tabs helps you find objects because the number of top-level nodes is greatly reduced. You can switch tab pages by clicking on the tab or choosing it from the View menu. You can also display the tabs as icons, using **Navigator→Show Icons On Tabs** as shown here:

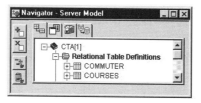

Conversely**, Navigator→Show Text On Tabs** changes the tab label to the text version. If you need more vertical space to show more nodes, you can select **Navigator→Vertical Tabs** to display the tabs on the right side of the Navigator window. Change back to horizontal tabs using **Navigator→ Horizontal Tabs**. **Navigator→Hide Tabs** and **Navigator→Show Tabs** cause the tabs to vanish and reappear, again, if you need more space. If you hide the tabs, you can only switch to another view using the View menu options or by right-clicking in a blank space in the Navigator and choosing from that menu.

USAGES AND DEPENDENCIES   It is often important to see which definitions are using a particular definition. This is important knowledge if you are trying to delete or change a design element and need to know what other elements are using it. This information appears in the Usages node under the element in the RON Navigator. DE has no Usages node but provides a dialog to show the element usages.

For example, you want to change the table definition for the ZIPCODES table and need to see which other elements might be affected. Select the table in the Navigator and select **View→Usages** from the menu. The results display in a dialog, as Figure 12-5 shows. This list does not contain the analysis element usages as RON does. However, it does contain some nodes that RON does not, for example the Used in SQL Query Sets node for a table element.

This dialog lets you browse the other definitions that use this one. It also lets you navigate to a particular definition by selecting it and clicking the GoTo button or double-clicking the icon to the left of the element name.

NOTE
As with RON, the Design Editor View menu changes depending on the window that you have selected. For example, if you click in the Navigator window, the View menu will contain items specific to Navigator views. If you click in the Property Palette, the View menu will contain items specific to that window. In addition, the top-level menus change from Navigator to Properties depending on the window you select.

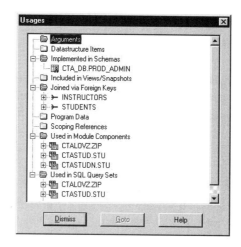

FIGURE 12-5.   *Usages dialog*

A related utility is the **Utilities→Analyze Dependencies** menu item. Choosing this menu item displays the dialog in Figure 12-6. This utility shows all definitions that the selected element depends on, all definitions that are dependent on it, and any text (written on any element) that contains the name of the selected element. This would be of use if you want to determine where your element fits in the big picture of the entire application system. The results appear in the Messages Window, described shortly. If you specify a file name in the Dependency Analyzer dialog, you will be able to view the output from this utility. The file contains something like the following:

L 12-1

```
Performing dependency analysis for Module...
MAINTAIN COURSE RECORDS(PROGDIR)
Objects that the analysis object references...
Language
     Developer/2000 Forms
Application System
     CTA
Objects that reference the analysis object...
Module Component
     MAINTAIN COURSE RECORDS(PROGDIR).COURSES
```

```
Window
    MAINTAIN COURSE RECORDS(PROGDIR).MAINTAIN_COURSE_RECORDS(PROGDI
Module Component
    MAINTAIN COURSE RECORDS(PROGDIR).COURSES
Objects that have text that reference the analysis object...
Module
    ENTER INVOICE (User/Help Text)
```

This utility thoroughly analyzes all element definitions in the same application system. It is more thorough than the **View→Usages** utility, which only displays the child elements (not the parents). After filling out the properties in this dialog, click the Start button. The utility runs and displays messages in the Messages Window. If you specify a file name in the dialog, you can press the List Actions button in the Messages Window and browse the file that was created. You are not able to navigate to the element definitions determined from that utility as you are in **View→Usages**. The Usages utility does not show where text with the selected element's name occurs, but the Analyze Dependencies utility does show this.

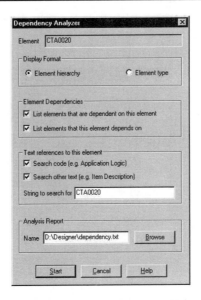

FIGURE 12-6. *Dependency Analyzer dialog*

MULTIPLE NAVIGATOR WINDOWS   You can actually open more than one Navigator window if, for example, you want to have both Server Model and Modules tab pages visible at the same time. Click on the Navigator window and select **File→New→Navigator** from the menu (or click the New toolbar button) to display another Navigator window. When you select an element definition in any open Navigator window, the Property Palette will update to reflect the selected element.

CUSTOMIZE YOUR DESIGN EDITOR!   Just as you can select the properties to view in the RON Navigator window, you can do the same in the Design Editor. Select **Options→Customize** and click the Show Properties tab to see the dialog shown in Figure 12-7. In this dialog, you select the element that you wish to customize on the left and specify the properties to show in the Navigator. Like RON, you will not be able to edit any properties other than the *Name* directly in the Navigator window.

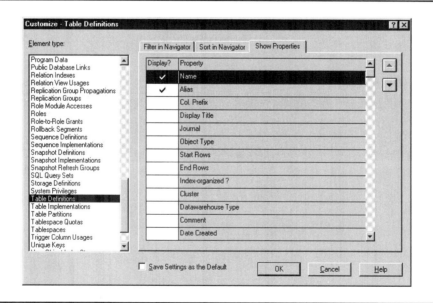

FIGURE 12-7.   *Show Properties tab of the Customize dialog*

TIP
*Select an element type node (such as Relational
Table Definitions) and choose Display
Properties from the right-click mouse menu to
quickly display the Customize dialog for that
node. This is faster than selecting the Options
menu item, as you do not need to find the
element type. The right-click mouse menu also
contains options for Sort and Filter, which work
in the same way for a particular object node.*

This dialog also lets you define sorts (with the Sort in Navigator tab) and
filters (in the Filter in Navigator tab), as in RON, to modify the list of
elements you see in the Navigator. The sorts and filters are also specific to
an element type, so you need to choose the element on the left before
modifying its sort or filter characteristics. The following illustration shows
the DE Relational Table Definitions node after specifying a filter of %GRADE%
in the Name field.

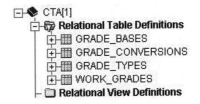

When the filter is in place, a funnel symbol will appear on top of the
Navigator node icon that is being filtered. The filter condition strings you
use become a SQL query, so you can use the wildcard symbol % but you do
not need the word LIKE or the single quote symbols. If you do not use the
% sign, the Navigator will filter using an exact match of whatever you type
in the Condition field. The query is not case sensitive, so you do not need to
worry about uppercase and lowercase. Check the Save Settings as the
Default check box if you want to use these settings the next time you open
the Design Editor.

If you want to remove the filters, reload the Customize dialog in the Options menu or choose **Navigator→Clear Selected Filters** (for Navigator nodes you have selected) or **Navigator→Clear All Filters** for all filters on all nodes. You can also choose Clear Selected Filters from the right-click mouse menu in the Navigator.

CAUTION
*If you remove filters that have previously been saved as the default, the next time you open the Design Editor, the filters will be in place. To remove the filters permanently, clear the filters, select **Options→Customize**, and check the Save Settings as the Default check box in the dialog.*

Working in the Property Palette

The Property Palette shows the properties for whatever element you select in the Navigator (or in the diagram window). The Property Palette has an interface similar to its counterpart in RON, and the toolbar buttons and menu items have the same effect as in RON (described in Chapter 6).

You can display the Property Palette window in one of three ways: by selecting Properties from the Navigator right-click mouse menu; by choosing **Tools→Property Palette**; or by pressing F3. If you perform any of those actions while a property window is pinned (using the toolbar button or **Properties→Pin Palette** menu item), another property window will open (as in RON). This is useful if you want to compare different element types without using the spreadtable view or have opened more than one Navigator window. The Properties toolbar button also switches focus to the Property Palette.

TIP
You can cause the cursor selection to jump to the referenced element definition. For example, with the STU_ZIP_FK foreign key properties displayed, click on the Join Table *property (which has a value of ZIPCODES) and select **Properties→Locate Object Definition** (or press the F12 key). The cursor in the Navigator will jump to the ZIPCODES table node. If your repository is large and complex, this could save you a bit of searching.*

As in RON, you can collapse property categories to save vertical space
in the window, but DE will not remember the collapsed state between
sessions. Nevertheless, collapsing is a useful feature because it may allow
you to do less scrolling in the Property Palette for that session, if you hide
properties in categories that you are not using.

Property dialogs are also available to assist you in filling out properties
for new elements or existing elements. The Options menu lets you choose to
Use Property Palette for the standard palette version of properties or to Use
Property Dialog for a wizard dialog version. (The DE toolbar also includes a
button to Switch to Palette or Switch to Dialogs.) The dialogs use the same
style of multitab property settings as those in the tools like the ER
Diagrammer. Data entry via the Property Palette is much faster if you know
the properties you want to set. If you are new to Oracle Designer, treat the
dialogs like training wheels on a bicycle: use them while learning and shed
them as you become more familiar with the vehicle. Figure 12-8 shows the
first tab of a property dialog for a table definition.

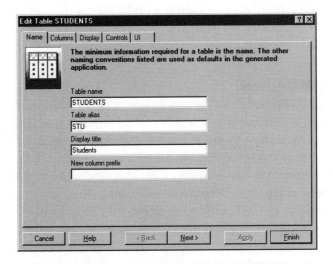

FIGURE 12-8. *Table property dialog*

TIP
Click on the help button in the top-right corner of the property dialog and click the help cursor on a property to show the help topic for that property. This same operation is available in the Property Palette, although you use the Context-Sensitive Help toolbar button instead of the top-right button.

Options→Customize Property Palette displays a dialog where you customize the palette's settings. These include the following:

■ *Show Application System Owner* to show a property line for the application system owner account name.

■ *Show Audit Properties* to show the user and date the definition was created and modified.

■ *Include Multi Line Text Properties* to allow you to select and copy the properties you edit in a text editor.

■ *Automatically switch to spreadtable mode on multi insert* to show the spreadtable property window automatically when you are creating more than one element definition at the same time. Use this option with care, because you may need to scroll far to the right in the property window to see some properties.

Messages Window

The Messages Window in the Design Editor appears when needed to show various messages generated when you run the utilities, such as the generators, analyze dependencies utility, and design capture utilities. The Messages Window (shown in Figure 12-9) appears, by default, in the bottom of the DE window. You can also explicitly display the Messages Window by using the **View→Messages Window** menu option.

This window contains a toolbar with the following buttons (going from left to right), which are enabled once a message has appeared:

■ **Copy** to copy selected text to the clipboard. You can then paste it into a text editor or word processor.

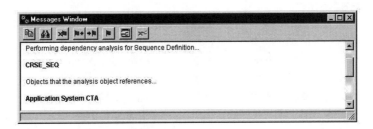

FIGURE 12-9.   *Messages Window*

■ **Show Help** to display a small help window with text about the selected message line. If the message line you select is a boilerplate label or header, there will be no help text for it.

■ **Clear** to clear the Messages Window.

■ **Previous** to navigate to the previous message in the Messages Window and display the right-click mouse menu for that message. This right-click menu allows you to get help on the message the same way as the Show Help toolbar button. It also allows you to navigate to the referenced definition in the Navigator.

■ **Next** to navigate to the previous message in the Messages Window and display the right-click menu for that message. This right-click menu is the same as the one for Previous.

■ **Goto Source** to navigate to the element definition in the Navigator that is referenced in the message.

■ **List Actions** to show a window listing actions you can perform, based on the output from the utility. For example, the Generate Database from Server Model utility creates a number of script files that create database objects. Use this button to show a list of actions (including browsing the files) in the Build Action dialog. You can then open each file in an editor by pressing the Run button.

■ **Abort** to stop the utility that is creating the messages before it is complete.

Fast Create

You can quickly create a list of element definitions by using the **Edit→Fast Create** menu option after clicking on an element type node in the Navigator. This is useful if you want to create the definitions as a group and refine the details at a later time. You can even do this for columns that have a number of required properties, such as datatype. The default column length is set to VARCHAR2(240). There is no fast create for primary keys, but there is one for foreign keys. This names the foreign keys with the table alias plus primary key table alias plus 'FK' (separated by underscores). For example, a new foreign key in the EMPLOYEE table that references the DEPARTMENT table (aliases of EMP and DEPT, respectively) would have the name EMP_DEPT_FK. Figure 12-10 shows the Fast Create dialog for table definitions. Other element types may have different dialogs for the Fast Create function.

Property Details

Clicking on a property name and pressing F5 displays property details as it does in RON. This helps if you are doing a query in another tool like SQL*Plus and need to find out the ID for an element or need to know

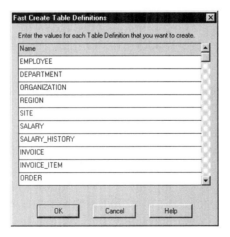

FIGURE 12-10. *Fast Create dialog for tables*

the name of the API view and column to which the property or
object corresponds.

Other Menu and Toolbar Functions

The Design Editor menu contains quite a few items. Chapters 14, 16, and 18
will discuss some of these as they relate to work in the Design and Build
phases, but there are some others that have a more general use that have not
yet been mentioned. As in other tools, the menu changes based on the
window you are working in. For example, if you are working in the Property
Palette window, the toolbar contains a Properties menu; this changes to a
Navigator menu when you activate the Navigator window.

File→Summary Information is also different depending on which
window you select. With the Navigator window selected, the summary
information contains the application system name, user name, and connect
string. These will print in a title box on the page if you print anything in the
Navigator. If you have selected the Property Palette or Messages Window,
the Summary Information will not be available. With a diagram window
selected, you can enter information such as a title and author.

The **Options→General Settings** dialog allows you to set (with Welcome
Screen) whether you want to see the welcome screen when Design Editor
starts up. You can also set (with Default Setting Dialogs) whether or not the
dialog box shown in Figure 12-11 will display after you create a database
object definition. This dialog lets you choose how you want to handle
assigning the new object to a database and user. This will be very important
when it comes to implementing the database, discussed in Chapter 18.

The Dialogs on Drag and Drop check box in the General Settings dialog
lets you specify whether DE will display a dialog when you perform a
drag-and-drop copy operation. This is useful if you are copying within the
same application system, as the copy operation might fail because an
element with that name already exists. This check box solves this problem.
General Settings also lets you specify what the default display of a module
diagram will look like: Data or Display (Default Module Diagram View);
whether you want to show dialogs when setting properties (Use Dialogs);
what the default date format mask will be (Date Format); what level of
messages will be displayed in the Messages Window (Generation).

Utilities→Force Delete works the same way it does in RON: it allows
you to remove a definition even though it has been associated to another

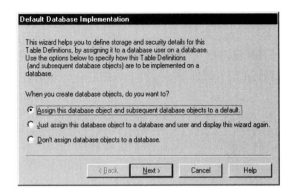

FIGURE 12-11. *Default Database Implementation dialog*

definition. If there are associations linking the element to another, those associations are deleted along with the element definition to which you apply the Force Delete.

The Tools menu contains some items for application and database definitions as well as for the common repository utilities: Repository Object Navigator, Repository Reports, Matrix Diagrammer, and SQL*Plus.

The Run menu allows you to open the Form Builder and Report Builder to check code you generate. It also contains options for the Forms Runtime and Reports Runtime so you can run the code you generate with the Form Builder and Report Builder.

Where Did All Those Design Tools Go?

If you used Designer version 1, you will notice that a number of Design tools appear to be missing from version 2. The Design Editor contains all the Design and Generator utilities that were separate tools in version 1. The following are some of the changed locations for the tools, utilities, and their components:

- Toolbar buttons common to the diagram windows appear in the standard toolbar at the top of the DE window. Specific drawing toolbars are included in the diagram window itself.

■ The diagrammers are generally available by displaying a definition and right-clicking to select the Show on New Diagram option. Alternatively, you can drag an element definition to a blank space in the Design Editor window to create a diagram. You can open a saved diagram with the **File→Open** menu item. Specifics for each type of diagram follow.

■ The Data Schema Diagrammer (DSD) is replaced by the Server Model Diagram. A Server Model Diagram opens when you select Show on New Diagram with a table or other server object definition selected in the Navigator window.

■ The Module Data Diagrammer (MDD) is reincarnated as the Module Diagram, when you right-click on a module definition and select Show on New Diagram.

■ The Module Structure Diagrammer (MSD) function available in the Design Editor node *Module Network* in the Modules tab. There is still a Module Structure Diagrammer, but it has limited functionality.

■ The Module Logic Navigator (MLN) is now a utility called the Logic Editor. To run it, you select the object in the diagram or Navigator and choose **Edit→Logic** from the menu or Add Logic or View Logic from the right-click menu or press the Edit Logic toolbar button.

■ The Preference Navigator is also part of DE. It is discussed in the next section on Generator Preferences.

■ Generators are available in DE by selecting the module and clicking the Generate button or choosing **Generate→Generate Module** from the menu or selecting Generate from the right-click menu. You can generate server object code by using the **Generate→Generate Database from Server Model** menu item.

Generator Preferences

One important process you go through in the Pre-Design phase is the examination or creation of the graphical user interface (GUI) standards for the application modules. Application code you generate from Oracle Designer automatically has a common look and feel and adheres to many recognized standards; however, you can also make some decisions to implement standards particular to your organization's environment. In addition, you can modify the way Oracle Designer handles many GUI issues. For example, you can set forms generation standards so all radio groups in your application system have a raised border with a line width of two points around them and a title for the radio group inside the box.

Settings such as these are called *preferences* in Oracle Designer, and there are preferences specific to the type of generator you will be using: Forms, Reports, Visual Basic, WebServer, and Help. Each of these products has different considerations, so you will set different kinds of preferences for each, but you can edit and view all of them in the Design Editor's Generator Preferences window.

In the Pre-Design phase, you will be setting up standards for the overall look and feel of all modules in the system. A *module* is a repository element that represents a program or part of a program in your final application. It can be a menu, screen, report, utility, or script that performs some task or provides a user interface to the database. There are different *languages* for modules that designate the tool used for the finished code. The module's *Language* property signals to Oracle Designer which generator it will use to create the code for a module.

There are hundreds of preferences, each with multiple levels of settings. You can have an almost unlimited number of combinations of settings among those levels, and it is essential when working with the generators to know how these levels relate to one another. This section discusses preferences in the context of the different levels on which you can set them, but during Pre-Design you are concerned with preferences mostly on the application system level, as these become your standards. Although you will actually generate prototype modules for the storyboard, those modules will not have individual preferences. In the Design and Build phases, other preference levels become more important.

Preference Levels

You can set preferences at many different levels. For example, if you set Forms preferences at the application system level and override the default values (called *factory* settings), all Forms modules will generate using the same set of preferences unless those preferences are overridden at a lower level. Figure 12-12 shows the hierarchy of levels for preference settings. The *module component* that this figure refers to is a piece of a module that is associated with no tables, one table, or set of tables. In a Forms module, the module component corresponds to a block; in a Reports module a module component corresponds to a group.

Two concepts are important here: *inheritance* and *precedence.* The preference settings at a particular level are inherited if they are not set at that level. Explicit preference settings at a lower level take precedence over a higher level setting and are in effect for all levels below. For example, a module, like CTAREGSTU, inherits the preference settings from the application level, if preferences are set there, or from the factory settings, if there are no application level settings. However, if CTAREGSTU has a particular preference set at the module level, that preference will override the application or factory setting at the module level and at all lower levels unless the lower-level preferences are set specifically. Inheritance and precedence can be simply stated in this way:

A preference level uses settings from its parent level unless it is set explicitly.

Application-level preferences are handy for setting standards for the entire application. Lower-level preferences are handy if a particular module or other object requires special treatment (still within the standards, of

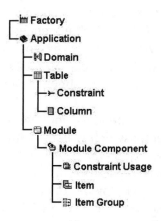

FIGURE 12-12.   *Preference level hierarchy*

course). Although you do not use preferences to generate server DDL code, you can set preferences at the Table, Constraint, and Column levels. These will affect the table, column, or constraint usage in any module that uses that element. If, for example, your ZIPCODES table would always have a certain set of block layout preferences in all modules, you could set those preferences on the table level and would not need to set them for each table usage of ZIPCODES in a module component.

You can read more about preference levels in the help system topic "About Generator Preference Levels," which you reach from an Index search for the word "preferences" in the Design Editor help system.

Showing Preferences

The Design Editor gives you quick access to preferences on any level. Once you identify the level on which you want to set a preference, you must find the node in the Navigator that corresponds to it. For example, if you are setting preferences on the application system level, select the application system name in any of the Navigator tabs. If you need to set preferences on a module level, find the module in the Modules tab and select it.

While Designer version 1 supplied a separate tool for preferences with its own navigator, Designer version 2 lets you use the Design Editor navigator to find the element to which you need to attach the preference. Once you have found the element, right-click on its name in the Navigator and select Generator Preferences. Some elements, like tables, may not provide this right-click mouse menu item, but you can select **Edit→Generator Preferences** or click the Generator Preferences toolbar button to display the Generator Preferences window. Your Design Editor session will now contain an additional window, which you can arrange using the **Window→Tile Vertically** menu item. Figure 12-13 shows a Generator Preferences window in the Design Editor.

Once the Generator Preferences window is displayed, you can select the product or generator set for which you are setting preferences. Each generator has distinct sets of preferences because different visual and operational aspects apply to each. If you select a module in the Navigator, its Generator Preferences window product will be selected based on the language assigned to the module. Figure 12-13 shows the Generator Preferences window with the Forms Generator product selected.

Filter field

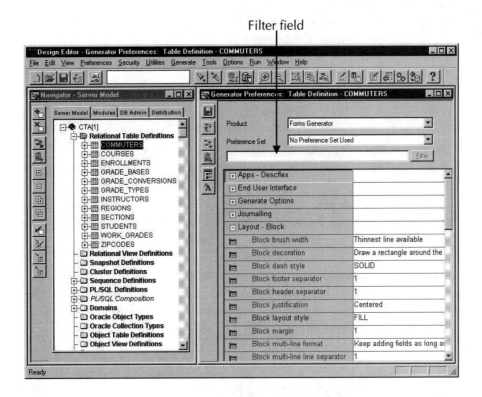

FIGURE 12-13.   *Design Editor session with the Generator Preferences window*

TIP
After you choose an element for which you want to set preferences, check that the Generator Preferences window title indicates the correct element. For example, if you choose the COMMUTERS table in the Navigator, the Generator Preferences window will show a title of Generator Preferences: Table Definition – COMMUTERS. It is possible to navigate to another tab and expand a node without changing the preference set that is loaded in the Generator Preferences window. That's why it's good practice to always check the window title.

CAUTION
Even though you can select multiple elements in the Navigator while the Generator Preferences window is showing, you can only modify preferences for one element at a time. Again, the window title will indicate on which element you are setting preferences.

The Generator Preferences window uses a standard property window-style interface that lets you expand and collapse categories of preferences and make settings directly next to the preference name. Preferences display as descriptive phrases or sentences, but you can also show them as six-character abbreviations by selecting **View→Show Name**. These abbreviations may be easier to read because they are shorter and in time you will come to recognize favorites like BLKDEC and LOVBUT, but when first getting used to working with preferences, the descriptions are more useful. Switch back to descriptions by selecting **View→Show Description**. The Show Name and Show Description functions are also available by clicking a toolbar button. The following illustration shows a few of these abbreviated preference names from the Layout – Block category.

⊟ Layout - Block	
BLKBWD	0
BLKDEC	LINES
BLKDST	SOLID

The preference categories are arranged in the Generator Preferences window in a collapsed state by default so you can read all the category names without much scrolling. You can reduce the list of displayed properties and categories by entering a word or phrase in the Filter field to the left of the Find button. The list of categories will reduce to those that contain preferences with that word or phrase somewhere in their descriptions. If you are displaying the preference names and not the descriptions, the Find feature works the same way but on the names instead.

Setting Preferences

After finding and expanding the category that contains the preference you want, you can set the preferences by entering the values as you do in the Property Palette. The Generator Preferences window uses the same color scheme for preferences as the Design Editor does for properties in the Property Palette. The default colors are: red for mandatory preferences, black for optional preferences, and blue for preferences that you have modified but not committed. You can change these colors using the **Options→Color/Font/Style** menu item.

It is quite useful to know the level at which a preference was set, and you can see this by pressing the Show Icons toolbar button. The display will change so you can see the level icons as they appear in the Navigator. (Figure 12-12 also shows the icons that correspond to each level.) Hide the icons using the Hide Icons button. These functions are also available in the View menu. The following illustration shows the level icons next to a few preferences.

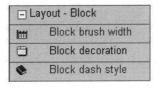

NOTE
You will not find all preferences and preference groups in all preference levels. For example, the Table preference level contains preferences in the Block – Layout category. These preferences are inappropriate and thus not available at the Column level.

If you want to copy a number of properties from one element to another, you can use the Copy button or select **Edit→Copy Preferences**. The preference you are copying must be set at that element. In other words, you cannot copy a preference set on the module level if you are viewing the table-level preferences. Also, you need to select the preferences using the mouse click, CTRL-click, and SHIFT-click. To view the properties you have copied, select **Edit→View Copied Preferences** from the menu. You can paste the preferences to another node using the Paste Preferences button or the **Edit→Paste Preferences** menu item.

Inheriting Preferences

If you find, after setting a preference, that the setting at the parent level was better, you can click the Inherit button in the toolbar, use the Inherit right-click mouse menu item or select **Edit→Inherit** to restore the parent-level setting. The Edit menu also contains Cascade Inherit All to inherit all preferences for preference hierarchy nodes under the selected one. For example, you might want to ensure that all preferences in a module were used for all levels under it, such as the Item and Item Group. This would be useful if you, or someone else, set some preferences at the item level but you don't want to search for them—you only want to set those preferences on a higher level. The **Edit→Cascade Inherit Selection** menu item does the same thing as the Cascade Inherit All item, except that it works only on preferences you have selected, not all preferences.

Preference Sets

You can create a set of preferences that you will always use together. This is called a *preference set,* because you select and manage it as a group. These named sets are useful when you generate modules, as you can attach a specific set of preferences to a module temporarily for that one session without changing the module preferences. Another use of named preference sets is that they allow you to attach the same set of preferences to different parts of the preferences hierarchy. Another good use of preference sets is to have different sets for different types of modules. For example, one preference set could be used for online queries, a second set for data entry programs, and so on.

   You create a named set by expanding the Preference Sets node in the Navigator's Modules tab, selecting a particular product such as Forms Generator or Report Generator, and clicking the Create button. Then click the name in the Navigator and display the Generator Preferences window to specify preferences for this set.

NOTE
*While you cannot assign a preference set to
another preference set, you can assign different
preference sets to different levels. For example, if
you have PREFERENCE SET 1 that you assign to
MODULE1, all module components, items, item
groups, and constraint usages under MODULE1
will inherit that preference set. If you want to
apply PREFERENCE SET 2 to that module as
well, you could attach it to all module
components for that module. In effect, you
would have two active preference sets governed
by the precedence and inheritance rules.*

The **Edit→Create As Preference Set** menu item allows you to create a
preference set from another element. Select the element in the Navigator,
select this menu item, and fill in the name of the new set when requested.
This is handy for creating a copy that you will modify for use in testing
some new settings.

Other Views of the Hierarchy

In addition to displaying the *Name* or *Description* or expanding and
collapsing the hierarchy nodes to modify what you see in the Generator
Preferences window, you can filter out some nodes to make the list easier to
read using the following View menu items:

- **Show All Values** to display the entire list of preferences. This is the
  default view.

- **Hide Default Values** to remove preferences with factory (default)
  settings from view. This is useful if you want to see what preferences
  have been modified.

- **Hide Application Level Values** to remove the preferences you set on
  the application level from view. This will also hide preferences with
  default (factory) settings.

■ **Show Modified Values** to remove all preferences except those that have been changed from the default for the element you are viewing. For example, if you have set preferences on the application and module level, but are viewing preferences for an item in that module, the only preferences you will see in this view are the ones that are set for the item.

These View menu items are only available when the Generator Preferences window is the active window. Categories that have no preferences that fulfill the conditions you set with the menu items and Filter field will also be hidden.

NOTE
When you reduce the list of preferences using the View menu options, the Filter field will still be applied, so you may not see everything you expect. Remove the filter condition if you do not want that to apply when using the View menu filters.

Preference Security

After spending some time examining and modifying the preferences, you might want to prevent others from changing them. As you can imagine, messy situations can develop if many developers work on preferences at the same time, particularly if they change application-level preferences or other preferences that are global in nature (like Table preferences). Since preferences are so powerful and can radically modify the appearance and actions of a generated module, you may want to put one person in charge of maintaining preferences on the higher levels (perhaps the data administrator or Oracle Designer administrator). Sometimes a developer may need to modify module-level preferences for a specific purpose, which could be allowed if the preferences do not violate higher-level standards. In any case, the issue of who sets the high-level preferences is worthy of consideration and a policy decision.

There are a number of built-in control facilities to help you manage changes to preferences. The first control is that you must have administrator privileges on the application system to set application-level preferences.

This is a privilege that an administrator of the application system grants to specific repository users using the RON Application menu. Other controls consist of actions you can select in the Security menu when the Generator Preferences window is active.

You can stop others from modifying preferences for a particular element. If you display preferences for an element in the Generator Preferences window and choose **Security→Lock Preferences**, a padlock icon will appear by all preferences for that element, indicating that no other user will be able to update the value. The following illustration shows some preferences that have been locked using this method.

Coding Style
🏷 🔒 Ignore first word when generating n
📋 🔒 Maximum length of a generated PL
📋 🔒 Use uppercase for PL/SQL packag
📋 🔒 How PL/SQL statements are code

You select **Security→Remove Current User Locks** to release all locks that you set (you cannot remove locks selectively). If you are the application system owner or an administrator, select **Security→Remove All User Locks** to release locks set by all repository users.

If you are the application system owner or administrator, you can freeze preferences for an element, which will disallow any changes to that element's preferences or to any child element's preferences. For example, if you freeze the preferences for a module component, all constraint usages, items, and item groups under it will also be frozen. You freeze an element's preferences by displaying them in the Generator Preferences window and selecting **Security→Freeze**. A pin icon will appear beside all frozen preferences, as the following illustration shows.

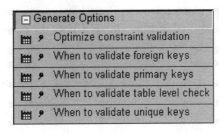

Generate Options
📋 📌 Optimize constraint validation
📋 📌 When to validate foreign keys
📋 📌 When to validate primary keys
📋 📌 When to validate table level check
📋 📌 When to validate unique keys

Security→Unfreeze All allows you to release the frozen preferences. You can unfreeze on an element-by-element basis but can only unfreeze the parent element. Therefore, if you have frozen MODULE1 and MODULE2, all child elements of those two will be frozen. You can unfreeze one of the modules without affecting the other, but you cannot unfreeze a child element like a module component or column.

NOTE
*The menu items for Remove Current User Locks, Unfreeze All, and Remove All User Locks are available in the **Utilities→Unset Preference Security** menu item if a window other than the Generator Preferences window is active.*

The View menu also includes an Unfreeze All option to unfreeze all nodes whether selected or not.

CAUTION
If you freeze an element's preferences but do not freeze a preference set that is attached to that element, someone can still change the preference set and the frozen element will use those changes. The best advice is to freeze the preference sets that are used by the elements you are freezing.

Where Does This Information Go?

The preferences you set here affect the way the generators run. When you set an application-level preference, it will affect all modules for that product you generate in this application system. If you set a module-level preference, it will affect the generation of only that module. The Oracle Designer generators use the preferences you set for a specific product to guide the generation process. Since you can have more than one preference set, you could attach sets one at a time to the same module (using the module's Preference Set property in the Generator Preferences window) and see how they affect the output. This is a powerful tool for testing how preferences affect generation and will assist you in using preferences productively.

The Pre-Design phase is the appropriate time to set standards, before any code is produced. The correct setting of preferences is a broad topic, beyond the scope of this book, and one that requires knowledge of how the generators work as well as detailed expertise on the products you are generating (for example, Forms and Reports). The discussion of generators in Chapter 18 provides many examples of preferences you might want to try out.

Database Design Transformer

One of the objectives of the Pre-Design phase is to create a working storyboard or prototype to show what the system will consist of. The first requirement of the storyboard is a rough-cut table structure. The Database Design Transformer (DDT) repository utility allows you to create tables for the Design phase from entities in the Analysis phase. At this point, you are concerned less with completeness and accuracy in the table designs than with the creation of a data repository that you can use as a basis for storyboard modules. You will spend the Design phase refining the rough-cut table and columns according to user feedback from prototype sessions and denormalization considerations that you, as the database designer, impose.

The Database Design Transformer is available from the Oracle Designer opening window as well as from the Utilities menus of the Repository Object Navigator and ER Diagrammer. Figure 12-14 shows the first tab of DDT. You use this tab to specify the run mode of DDT. You can run the transformer in default mode, where you accept all the standard settings for the mappings and run the utility on entities you selected in RON or on the full set of entities; or you can customize the Database Design Transformer. Selecting the customize option enables the other tab pages in this dialog. If you always want to run in one mode or the other, uncheck the box to show this tab at startup, and this tab will not reappear.

DDT is highly customizable but also has a good set of defaults and can be run with minimal intervention on your part. Although you can run this utility more than once to create column and table definitions, you should wait until the Analysis work is as complete as possible before you run it for the first time. The reason for this is that DDT cannot delete definitions, and if

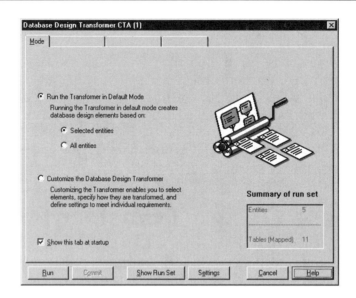

FIGURE 12-14. *Mode tab of the Database Design Transformer*

your entities are not fully formed when you run the utility the first time, table or column definitions may not correctly reflect the entities and attributes they should be based on.

TIP

Start the Database Design Transformer from RON, because if you select entities in the RON Navigator, those entities will automatically have the In Set *box checked when DDT starts. This could save a significant amount of time if you are running the utility for a subset of the entities. Starting DDT from RON is also recommended when you are just getting started with Oracle Designer or with a new team of developers, so you can check the output of DDT and make corrections to the analysis-level objects before all the design-level objects are created.*

Output of DDT

Table 12-2 shows the Analysis elements and the Design elements that DDT creates from them. Chapter 29 provides details about how properties are copied from Analysis elements to Design elements.

Generally, DDT creates tables and columns in a one-to-one mapping from entities and attributes, respectively. The tables and columns DDT creates will consist of properties copied from the corresponding entities and attributes, respectively. The entity *Plural Name* becomes the table *Name* with spaces converted to underscores. A column will have the same *Datatype*, *Maximum Size*, and *Optional* characteristic as the attribute it is derived from. The utility will create a foreign key column on the many side of a one-to-many relationship and also create a foreign key constraint from that relationship. It will create a primary key (a *surrogate key*) for the table

Analysis Data Element	Design Data Element
Entity	Table
Attribute	Column
Allowable values on an attribute	Allowable values on a column
Primary unique identifier	Primary key constraint
Nonprimary unique identifier	Unique constraint
Missing primary unique identifier	Surrogate primary key and sequence
1-to-many relationship	Foreign key constraint and foreign key column and index
Many-to-many relationship	Intersection table with foreign key constraints and foreign key columns
Subtype/supertype relationships	Single tables or multiple tables with special columns to link them
Arc relationships	Arc foreign key links

TABLE 12-2. *Analysis Elements and Corresponding Design Elements Created by DDT*

(with a *Display?* property value of "No") if the entity does not have a primary unique identifier defined.

NOTE
The DDT will copy an attribute Format *property of INTEGER to the column property* Datatype. *The Generate Database from Server Model utility will produce a CREATE TABLE script using a NUMBER(38) datatype for the INTEGER. If this is not your intention, change the column property before running the Generate Database from Server Model utility.*

The Analysis model may contain constructs that can't be implemented on a one-to-one basis in a relational database; DDT will resolve these issues. For example, if there is a many-to-many relationship, the utility will create a separate table called an *intersection* table, also known as an *associative* table. This table (named with a combination of the two table names, such as DEPT_EMP) contains the primary keys from both table generated from the entities in the many-to-many relationship. The many-to-many relationship becomes two one-to-many relationships between the two original tables and the new intersection table. This action agrees with the generally recognized method for handling many-to-many relationships in the Design phase. Another situation that must be resolved in the relational database implementation is the subtype/supertype relationship, and DDT provides four methods to handle this, as Table 12-3 shows. Chapter 29 explains these methods further.

In all cases you specify that you want to create tables (as described in the section later on the Run Options). You include an entity in the run set by checking the In Set option on the Table Mappings tab (also described later). The discriminator column mentioned for the supertype implementation identifies to which of the subtypes a particular record belongs.

Mapping Approach in DDT	Result	Settings in DDT
Supertype implementation (single table)	Single table for subtype and supertype; discriminator column added with one allowable value representing each subtype.	Include the supertype but not the subtypes in the run set; subtypes should have the Map Type set to Included; if not, they are not correctly defined supertypes.
Explicit subtype implementation (separate tables)	Separate tables for each subtype with supertype columns in each; no table for the supertype.	Include the subtypes but not the supertype in the run set.
Implicit subtype implementation	Separate tables for each subtype and for the supertype; subtypes have all supertype columns; the supertype does not have any subtype columns.	Include the supertype and subtypes in the run set.
Arc implementation	Separate tables for subtypes and supertype; subtypes do not have supertype columns; the supertype has a separate foreign key column for each subtype; foreign key constraints for each foreign key column.	Run DDT twice: the first time, include the supertype and subtypes for the run set but no columns or keys (on the Run Options tab); the second time, check the Arc check box for each subtype and specify the modification of tables columns and keys.

TABLE 12-3.   *Approaches to Mapping Subtype/Supertype Relationships*

Table Mappings Tab

The second tab you see in DDT is Table Mappings, as shown in Figure 12-15.

This tab is where you specify which entities you want to use as the basis for tables. It shows the current set of entities and any tables already created from them. You click the *In Set* check box if you want to create a table definition for this entity; or if a table definition already exists and you want to add extra columns from new attributes of the entity; or if you want to modify existing characteristics of the table and columns. If you manually fill in the table name by selecting an existing table from the poplist in the Table item, DDT will immediately create a table-entity usage, showing that the entity is *implemented by* the associated table, and the table is *mapped to* the associated entity. There is really only one association that shows up twice in RON—under the Table's *Usages: Mapped to Entities* node and under the Entity's *Usages: Implemented by Tables/Views/Snapshots* node.

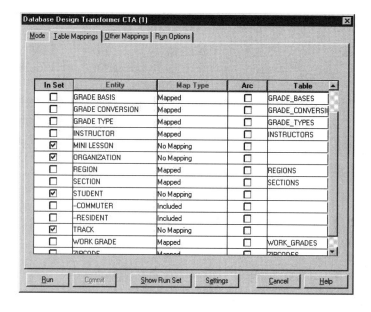

FIGURE 12-15. *Table Mappings tab of the Database Design Transformer*

You can choose all entities or no entities by choosing Include All and Include None from the right-click mouse menu. If you choose to include an entity, DDT will automatically include all its attributes in the run set. The Arc check box is where you specify arc relationships when implementing a subtype/supertype relationship or arc relationship, as mentioned in Table 12-3.

TIP
In the Table Mappings tab, as in other tab dialogs in Oracle Designer, you can reorder and resize the columns if you need to see more characters. For example, the values in the table name column may not be totally visible, but you can move the column to the left by dragging and dropping the Table column heading. You can then resize the column by dragging the side of the heading left or right. DDT remembers the new layout the next time it's used.

Other Mappings Tab

The Other Mappings tab allows you to individually control the way DDT handles the relevant elements. You can specify the mapping of entity information to table information (such as attributes to columns and primary unique identifiers to primary keys) and designate which of these individual elements DDT should include in the next run. The information on these tabs makes more sense after you run the utility for the first time, since the tables are mapped at that point to entities.

You can use this tab if, after you run DDT for the first time, you create additional attributes for a particular entity. You can choose to map columns or you can specify that you want to create new columns from these attributes. Alternatively, you can specify that these new attributes are associated with existing columns in the table definitions. This is useful if you created a table from an entity but modified the table definition (or the actual table in the database) without modifying the entity—a common situation when Analysis is complete and you move on to Design and Build. The decision of whether to keep the Analysis model current with the Design model is one you will have to make at some point. Assuming you wanted to keep the Analysis model complete, you would capture the design of the table (if it had been modified in the database only and not the repository), create the corresponding attribute for the entity, and map them using DDT.

Figure 12-16 shows the Other Mappings tab. The mapping field that contains the poplist of elements to map works the same way as it does from entities to tables on the previous tab.

Run Options Tab

The next step you take when you run DDT is to fill in the Run Options tab, shown in Figure 12-17. This tab presents a list of the elements you are implementing and allows you to customize the Create and Modify actions for tables, columns, keys, and indexes. Generally, you leave these set to the default choice, Create, when running the utility for the first time so you can create all elements. Then, on subsequent runs, you might choose to update certain element types. You can both create and modify the same type of

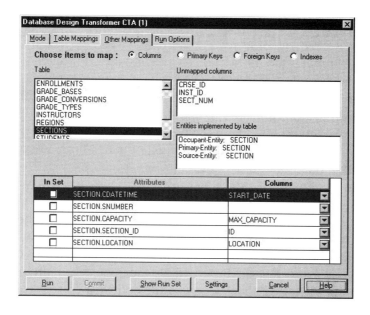

FIGURE 12-16. *Other Mappings tab of the Database Design Transformer*

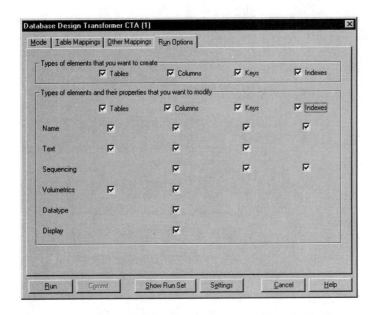

FIGURE 12-17. *Run Options tab of the Database Design Transformer*

element in the same run. This tab also has an area in the bottom for specifying which properties this run will modify.

Settings Dialog

The DDT utility will run correctly with other defaults after you fill in the Table Mappings and Run Options tabs. In the Pre-Design phase, this should suffice. However, you will eventually have to specify additional properties for the tables. You can specify some of these properties on the Settings dialog, which has various tabs, one of which is shown in Figure 12-18. You access this dialog by clicking the Settings button at the bottom of the DDT window.

Some of the properties you can set here are the database name and user that will be associated with the tables DDT creates. If you fill out these fields, you are specifying that in addition to a table element, DDT will create

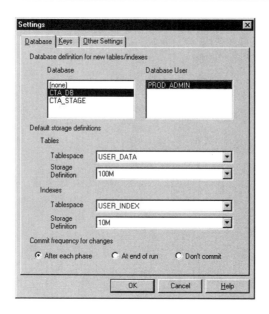

FIGURE 12-18. *Database tab of the Settings dialog*

table implementations that represent a table in a particular user's schema in a database. You can also specify the tablespace and storage definitions to associate with the tables and indexes. These all refer to element definitions that are in the repository, so a preparatory step to running DDT would be to create the database, user, tablespace, and storage definitions in the repository.

Specifying the associations in this tab provides an alternative to running the utility and manually changing these properties in RON or DE, which would probably be a more time-consuming process. Whether you use this tab or not depends on your development methodology and standards. For example, if your DBA insists that all CREATE TABLE commands contain an explicitly named tablespace and storage clauses, you should supply this information from the first time you create a table definition. Be sure to treat any properties specified as defaults, however, subject to change as you refine the table's storage requirements and the database layout. You should also be aware that if you use this feature fully, it means that you need to run the utility more than once. For example, you probably do not want all the tables in your system to be in the same tablespace; therefore, you would have to run this utility once for each tablespace definition you wanted to associate with a different set of tables.

At the bottom of the Database page, you can state when you want the commit to occur. Committing after each phase is the most efficient procedure, and if an unrecoverable error occurs in the middle of the run, you will still have definitions for everything DDT did before the last commit operation. Committing at end of the run will roll back operations to the state before the run if an error occurs. This procedure is useful if you want to ensure that if the run completes fully the results are written all at once or if it fails at some point all changes are reversed. If you use the option called Don't commit, DDT will validate the design but not insert the elements in the repository. This option is useful if you want to do a dry run to see what the utility will create.

There are two other tabs in this dialog: Keys and Other Settings. The Keys tab allows you to specify what update and delete rules you want to associate with the tables you are creating. For example, if you choose Cascades for the On delete option, the corresponding property will be filled in on the foreign key definition, and when you run the Generate Database from Server Model utility, the ON DELETE CASCADE clause will be generated. This means that if a row of the master table is deleted and that row has child records in the foreign key table, the rows in the foreign key table will also be deleted.

Use the other settings on the Keys tab to perform the following:

■ *Implementation level for constraints* to specify where the constraints are validated—on the client side, server side, or both. If you specify server or both, constraints (primary and foreign key) will be created in the repository. The database will validate these constraints automatically when you add, update, or delete records from the database. When you generate code on the client side, code will be generated to validate the value in the application module as well. This is double effort, because both database and client are validating the same value, but it may be necessary to present a friendly user interface.

■ *Create surrogate keys for all new tables* to create an extra primary key column for a table regardless of whether the entity has a primary unique identifier. All tables will then have a common primary key based on the domain in the next setting. This is good if you want all your surrogate keys to have a consistent datatype.

■ *Surrogate Primary Key Domain* to specify the datatype and size of the surrogate key.

■ *Maximum identifier length* to limit names to a certain number of characters. In an Oracle database, the limitation is that names must be 30 characters or less. DDT will create unique names within the number of characters you specify in this field. The default is 30.

The Other Settings tab contains settings for specifying prefixes for names of columns, foreign keys, surrogate keys, and tables. You can use the Table prefix (usually two or three characters followed by an underscore) to identify the application system to which the table belongs. This is particularly useful if your project or system uses many application systems.

If you check the Allow instantiable super-types setting, DDT creates an allowable value in the discriminator column for the supertype table. The setting handles the single-table implementation of subtype/supertype relationships, which creates a discriminator column to store a value indicating to which subtype a particular record belongs. Checking this option means that a value will also be generated for the supertype itself.

Another setting you can customize in the Other Settings tab is the Column component priority. This designates the order that the columns will be placed in the table definition. For example, a common standard is to list the primary key columns first, then mandatory columns and foreign key columns. You can move these groups around to specify this order.

Running DDT

Once you have completed all settings in the DDT and Settings dialogs, click the Run button. DDT will run and present the results in the Database Design Transformer Output Window, as Figure 12-19 shows. When the utility is finished, you close the output window, after scrolling up to see messages or copying the messages to the clipboard with the Copy button.

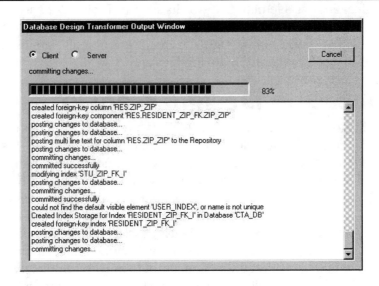

FIGURE 12-19. *Database Design Transformer Output Window*

Other Functions

At any point while you are specifying the run set, you can view the elements that will be created or modified by pressing the Show Run Set button. This action will display the Elements in the Run Set window. This nonmodal window is extremely handy if you just want to check the effect of some setting but do not want to go through a full run of DDT.

If you make changes in the mapping of any element, the utility will show the output window and display a message when it is finished. It will not commit those mappings, however, until you click the Commit button at the bottom of the DDT window.

Where Does This Information Go?

The element definitions you create here are stored, as usual, in the repository. Each element you create with DDT also has a link or association to the logical analysis element that was its source. Table 12-2 shows these mappings. The elements created by DDT form the basis for modules you create using the Application Design Wizard. These modules are used as prototypes for the storyboard in the Pre-Design phase.

Application Design Transformer

The Application Design Transformer (ADT) is a repository utility that works like DDT: it creates Design elements from Analysis elements—in this case, modules from functions. Your system analysis consists largely of the data model and function model, so after you finish translating the entity definitions to table definitions and the function definitions to module definitions, you can build a complete set of application files that you can use for the storyboard process. The process described here assumes you have run the Function/Attribute Matrix utility described in Chapter 10 or that the low-level functions have entity and attribute usages completely defined.

Remember that a module is a repository element that represents a program or part of a program in your final application.

ADT is available from the Oracle Designer window, the Utilities menus of RON, the Function Hierarchy Diagrammer, and the Dataflow Diagrammer. The interface is essentially simple but has an intricate set of rules it uses to create module definitions from function definitions and module structure networks (hierarchies) from business unit usages. Table 12-4 shows the Design elements this utility creates from Analysis elements and the final product generated by the generators.

Your function model should be as complete as possible before you run ADT, so it will give you a set of modules that closely matches your needs. You need to run ADT with two different settings for each function branch: first to create *candidate modules* (generated modules you need to explicitly accept) from functions and second to create a module structure from the function business unit usages. You cannot create a module structure without modules, so you must follow this sequence of first creating modules and then creating menus.

CAUTION
Unlike the Database Design Transformer, the Application Design Transformer is not intended to be run iteratively to modify the definitions of previously created elements.

Analysis Data Element	Design Data Element	Finished Product
Function	Module (and module component)	Form, Report, PL/SQL script, Visual Basic, WebServer code
Function business unit usages	Module network structure	Menu
Function entity usages	Module Component Table Usages	Tables used in generated code
Function attribute usages	Module Component Bound Items under the Table Usages	Columns (items) used in the generated code
Dataflow data usages	Module arguments	Parameters passed between modules

TABLE 12-4. *Analysis Elements and Corresponding Design Elements Created by ADT*

The ADT Window

When you start ADT, the dialog shown in Figure 12-20 appears. There are fewer entry fields to fill out for ADT than for DDT, and they are grouped into different categories: Generate Options, Common Parameters, Module Options, Merge Granularity, and Menu Options. Most of the defaults suffice, but you should pay particular attention to Generate Options and Start Function (in the Common Parameters area).

As is true with DDT, if you select a function in RON and choose **Utilities→Application Design Wizard** from the menu, that function name will be loaded into the Start Function field.

Generate Options

The Generate Options area is where you specify whether you are generating modules or menus. Remember that you cannot generate menus unless you already have modules that you have accepted (*Candidate ?* property is "No").

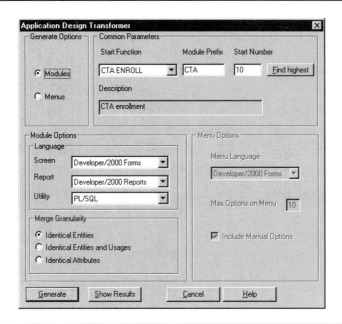

FIGURE 12-20. *Application Design Wizard dialog*

Common Parameters

The Common Parameters area is where you designate the Start Function. ADT generates a module for this and all other applicable functions under it in the function hierarchy. If you want to generate modules for all functions, leave this field blank. The Module Prefix field lets you specify a short prefix that ADT uses to name the modules. All modules will have *a Short Name* property value of this prefix followed by a four-digit number. The default prefix is the first six characters of the application system name for modules and the application system description for menus. Also, ADT inserts a value for the *Name* property of each generated module definition. The default for this property is the uppercase *Short Definition* property of the function, but you can modify the default by editing the value. You can also specify the number at which the module names will start. The Find highest button fills in a number based on the highest module number already generated. You need to enter a number between 10 and 9999 before clicking this button.

Module Options

If you are running ADT for modules, the Module Options area is enabled so you can indicate the language for screen, report, and utility modules that ADT generates. Part of the process ADT goes through when creating the candidate modules is assigning a module type: Default (whatever is natural for the language chosen, such as a form for the Oracle Forms language), Menu, or Library. This is assigned as a module property along with the language for the type that you specify here. Notice that the default settings—Developer Forms, Developer Reports, and PL/SQL—will work at this stage and that you can change individual modules in RON or DE at a later time. The Language area drop-down lists for Screen, Report, and Utility include other options besides the supported generators, so be careful to specify Forms, Reports, Visual Basic, or WebServer if you will be using one of these generators. The defaults should suffice for these Language options.

Merge Granularity

When creating modules, you can determine the rule ADT uses to group functions into modules. You choose one of three options for Merge Granularity:

- *Identical Entities* merges functions into one module if they have the same entities mapped to them.

- *Identical Entities and Usages* combines functions into one module if the functions have the same entities and same CRUD for those entities.

- *Identical Attributes* joins functions into one module if those functions have the same entities and attributes mapped to them.

Menu Options

If you generate menus in the ADT run, this area is enabled and the Module Options area is disabled. Here you choose the menu language (Developer Forms is the default). Max Options on Menu defines the maximum number of items you can have in each menu. If there are more, ADT creates another menu to hold them. The items that ADT groups on a particular menu are governed by the menu rules discussed later in the section on ADT Rules. The last setting in this area is Include Manual Options. If you check this, ADT will add the modules it determined to be manual (those without data usages) into the menu structure. You can use these for information screens that tell the user what to do manually, but this might not be useful for your system.

Running ADT for Modules

After choosing Modules under Generate Options and completing the other fields in the ADT window, you click the Generate button. ADT will run and display a message screen as it runs. Messages from this utility are stored in a file called SMADW.TXT (located in the Start In directory designated in the shortcut you used to start Designer—by default, the ORACLE_HOME/ bin directory). When ADT is finished, you can click the Show Results button to browse the file that will contain a report of the modules that were generated or error messages. You can also run a repository report called *Module Definition* to get more details. If you want to start over, you need first to delete the candidate modules using RON or DE.

TIP
*If you need to start over with ADT but have already created modules, you must delete the modules first or you will get naming conflict errors when you run the utility again. The fastest way to delete a group of modules is to select them in RON or DE and use **Utilities→Force Delete.** If you simply try to delete the modules, you might have to run the delete process a number of times, as the delete will fail on modules that are called by other modules.*

Running ADT for Menus

After generating candidate modules, you need to accept the candidates. You do this in RON or DE by changing the *Candidate ?* property to No. Remember that you can group definitions together (mouse click and CTRL-click) and change all of them by changing the value in the Property Palette. The icon for candidate modules is the same for all languages, as the following illustration shows.

When you accept a candidate module, the icon changes to one that is specific to the language assigned to the module. After you accept the candidate modules, you can run ADT again to generate the module hierarchy for menus. Fill out the same screen as you did for modules, but this time specify Menus under Generate Options and fill in the Menu Options area, as described above. Again, you want to specify an upper-level function in the Start Function field. The top-level menu module's *Name* is derived from the application system *Title* property.

When you have filled out the fields for menu generation, press the Generate button, and after ADT finishes, examine the results using the Show Results button. Remember to accept the candidate menu modules, too, or you will not be able to generate menu code.

CAUTION
Modules have dependencies that mandate a certain sequence for the tasks you perform in the design transformers. Be sure to run the Database Design Transformer or in some other way create table definitions before running the Application Design Transformer. Also be sure to run ADT to create module definitions before running it to create menu modules.

ADT Rules

ADT follows five types of rules in creating the module definitions:

- Function mapping

- Module categorization

- Module grouping for menus

- Module data usage

- Module arguments

If you understand the decisions that ADT makes to create modules, you can more easily interpret the results and get more out of the utility. There is additional information on these rules in the online help system. Follow the link from the topic on the contents page titled "Generating preliminary application designs" to "Introduction" to "The elements and usages created by the Application Design Transformer."

Function Mapping Rules

In general, one module is created for each function in the hierarchy under the one you specify as the Start Function when you run the utility. A function must be one of three types: a leaf (atomic) function with no elementary or common function parents, a common function, or an elementary function. A *leaf function* is at the end of the hierarchy tree (it has no children). A *common function* appears more than once in the function hierarchy. An *elementary function* is one for which you have set the *Elementary ?* property to Yes. You set this property on the function because you consider the function as a single unit of work that has no use to the business unless it is completed entirely.

ADT merges modules if they are not manual (that is, they have entity and attribute usages) and are associated with functions that have the same *Response Needed* property, input parameters, business unit usages, and similar data usages (based on the granularity you set in the ADT window).

NOTE
If ADT merges functions into one module, it will also merge the text (in the Description and Notes properties) from those functions.

ADT will duplicate a module if the function it is based on has more than one business unit usage. ADT will create one module for each business unit for that function.

Module Categorization Rules

The next step ADT takes after creating modules is to categorize them into types. It categorizes a module as manual if no tables are implemented for entities of the functions or if the function has no entities and attributes associated with it or if the function has entities but no attributes. It creates a report module if the function has read-only (retrieve) data usages. It produces a utility module if the *Response Needed* property of the corresponding function is Overnight. It creates a screen if the *Response Needed* property of the corresponding function is Immediate. If none of these conditions apply, the module becomes a screen type.

Module Grouping Rules for Menus

Just as there are rules for ADT to follow when it creates modules, there are also rules to follow when it creates menus. The application-level menu module is generated as the top level (main menu), and this module calls the first-level menu modules. ADT generates the first level of menu modules from the module business unit usages (derived from the function business unit usages). If the module is not associated with any business unit, ADT groups it in a Miscellaneous menu. The next level of menu hierarchy groups modules by module type: for example, reports or screens. The menu system therefore has the following structure:

Top level	Application system (main menu)
First level	Business unit grouping (top menu items)
Second level	Module type grouping (pull-down menu items)
Third level	Individual modules under the specific module types (menu items)

If you do not like this division of modules into menus, you can change it in the Module Network Viewer of the Design Editor, as discussed in Chapter 16. Remember that the menu modules that ADT creates are candidates as well and you have to accept them before you perform any generator work.

Module Data Usage Rules

Each module that ADT creates will contain one module component and a corresponding table usage from each entity usage in the function the module is based on. For example, assume that the REG_STUDENT module was created from the Register Student function, which has the INVOICE entity as a usage. If there is an INVOICES table that was created from or mapped to the INVOICE entity, ADT creates a module component called INVOICES with a table usage of INVOICES.

Column usages are similar; they are mapped to bound items in the table if the function has the corresponding attributes mapped to it. If DDT created a surrogate foreign key for a table, that key will be created in the module component usage even though there is no corresponding attribute. Another rule is that if a table has an INSERT usage on the module, ADT will add all mandatory columns as bound item usages whether or not there are corresponding attribute usages.

Module Argument Rules

ADT creates module arguments based on the attributes and data items in the dataflows associated with the corresponding function. If the dataflow is an input, the source must not be a datastore; and if the dataflow is an output, the destination must not be a datastore. The type of the argument for the module is IN if the dataflow flows into the function and OUT if the dataflow flows out of the function.

Where Does This Information Go?

The Application Design Transformer produces *candidate modules*—modules that are not ready for generation—that you can later accept as application modules in the Design Editor or Repository Object Navigator. After accepting a module, you can generate working code from it with the Oracle Designer generators. ADT creates modules with module data usages based on the functions and function entity usages. You diagram the module hierarchy or structure in the Design Editor to show and manipulate the menu system. Table 12-5 shows how these elements are used in future stages of development.

ADT can go a long way toward the creation of rough-cut modules. But before you generate prototypes for the storyboard, you need to accept the modules and then reorganize the hierarchy, define missing modules, and eliminate any extra modules ADT produces. The Design Editor Module Network Viewer, described in Chapter 16, assists in this reorganization and cleanup work.

Data Element Created by ADT	Future Use
Modules for screens, reports, and utilities	Used to generate code in Forms, Reports, Visual Basic, and WebServer
Module associations and menu modules	Application system menu structure and module calling structure
Module component table usages	Usages that specify how tables, columns, and constraints are used in modules
Module arguments	Parameters passed between a calling module and a called module

TABLE 12-5. *Future Use of Data Elements Created by ADT*

Integrating the Storyboarded Tables

The storyboard process produces the first, rough-cut set of tables that you can use as a starting point for the database design part of the Design phase. The next step is to integrate the changes you have made, or want to make, into the repository, based on information you gained in the storyboard process. These changes may be the result of modifications you make to the table definitions in the database or notes you take when you work on the storyboard. Table 12-6 summarizes the possible status of a table after the storyboard process and how you use Oracle Designer to integrate these changes.

Note that you can use the Reconcile Report feature of the Generate Database from Server Model utility, described in Chapter 20, to determine the differences between the database tables and the repository definitions of those tables. This feature is quite useful and powerful, but it cannot handle

Action on Table During Storyboard Process	Method for Integrating Table into Repository
Column information was changed, but the database table is similar to the repository table definition.	Delete extra repository columns manually in DE or RON; add columns not in the repository with the Capture Design of Server Model from Database utility.
Database tables were combined or split.	Delete the repository definitions and use the Capture Design of Server Model from Database utility.
New database tables were created.	Run the Capture Design of Server Model from Database utility to add the repository definitions; retrofit to entities if you want to keep the Analysis model in synch with the Design model.
Table was intentionally deleted in the storyboard process.	Delete the table definition using RON or DE.

TABLE 12-6.   *How Tables from the Storyboard Process Are Handled*

all changes (such as a deleted column). You can also use the Design Editor and Repository Object Navigator for manual changes to table definitions and the Capture Design of Server Model utility (introduced in Chapter 8 and explored further in Chapter 14) for automated modification of table definitions.

Integrating the Storyboarded Modules

After you generate the default set of modules in ADT and accept the candidate modules using the Module Network Viewer of the Design Editor, you use the Form Generator and Report Generator to create the screen and report files (as discussed in Chapter 18). Then you work with the modules as program files in the storyboard process to refine and revise them using Oracle Developer. When you are satisfied with the storyboard files, you need to restore them to the repository module definitions. During the storyboard process, you may have changed data usages, added code, merged program files, and eliminated unnecessary programs. You need to integrate these changes into the repository module definitions so you can further refine the definitions and create finished code. If you change the interface standards during the storyboard process, you can incorporate those changes into the preferences (or templates as described in Chapter 18).

The method you use to integrate files into the repository module definitions depends on the file status, as Table 12-7 shows. You should keep track of changes as you go through the storyboard process so you can determine the file status. When you are done with the storyboard integration, the repository should have one module for each program in the storyboard.

This discussion assumes that you perform the storyboard operation using Oracle Forms and Reports. As mentioned, you can use Oracle products for this work even if the finished modules will be in other languages, since all you need to do is change the language from Forms or Reports to the appropriate one before you perform generation. For example, it might be easier to set up a demo of a Forms module rather than a WebServer module. In this situation, you could generate the module using Oracle Forms as the language. After the demo, you could switch the language to WebServer on this module and use that generator in future work on the production system.

The parts of the Design Editor that you use to manipulate the module definitions in the repository are discussed in Chapter 16. The following section discusses how you capture the design of Forms and Reports when you develop modules outside Oracle Designer and need to create module definitions for them. Chapter 18 discusses these utilities further and explains how to incorporate extra application logic from outside the repository.

Capture Design of Form and Report Utilities

The Capture Design of Form and Capture Design of Report utilities are available from the Design Editor's **Generate→Capture Design of** menu.

Status of File after Storyboard Process	Method for Integrating Module into Repository
File is similar to the module in the repository (its tables did not change significantly).	Make changes to the existing module manually in RON or DE.
File is a combination of modules in the repository.	Delete the module in RON after moving the table and bound item usages to the other module.
File was created after generation and has no repository module definition.	Run the Capture Design of Form (or Report) utility to add the module definition based on the file you created in Oracle Developer.
File contains code that was not generated from Oracle Designer	Run the Capture Design of Form (or Report) utility to merge the changes into the module definition based on the file you created in Oracle Developer.
File was intentionally deleted in the storyboard process.	Delete the module definition using RON or DE.
File navigation (calls) was changed.	Manipulate the module structure using the Module Network Viewer of DE.

TABLE 12-7. *Handling of Modules from the Storyboard Process*

They are actually part of the generator utility set and are used to create or update module definitions with related table and column usages for existing Oracle Forms or Reports stored in the file system or database. The following discussion concentrates mostly on the Capture Design of Form utility, but the Capture Design of Report utility has similar features and methods. Chapter 29 discusses some of the properties that are copied from the form file into the repository. If you are design capturing a file, you need to complete the settings on the dialog shown in Figure 12-21.

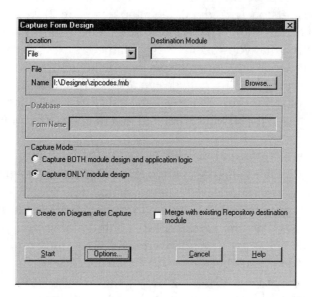

FIGURE 12-21.   *Capture Form Design dialog*

An important consideration here is that the table and column definitions that represent the tables used in your module must already exist in the repository. For your purposes in the storyboard process, this will not be a problem unless you added columns or tables manually to the database. If you did that, you need to run the Capture Design of Server Model from Database utility to add these definitions to the repository. This utility is explained in Chapter 8 in the discussion of the legacy ERD. Of course, you can always manually add the columns or tables using RON.

The settings on the Capture Form Design dialog require the location of the form (usually a file) and the destination module name into which you want to capture this form (only one file at a time). The destination module can be an existing module in the repository, which means the file definition will be merged with the repository definition. Use the Merge with existing Repository destination module check box to indicate that you want to do the merge. You can capture the design of Oracle Forms versions 4.0 (CDE), 4.5 (Developer version 1), and 5.0 (Developer version 2) without any conversion. If the location is a database, you have to supply a form name; if the location is a file, you specify the file name.

The Capture Mode area lets you specify whether you want to capture just the module design or both module design and application logic (trigger code and program units). You can also check the check box to Create on Diagram after Capture, to see the module depicted in a diagram when the utility is done.

Clicking the Options button displays the dialog in Figure 12-22. This dialog is also displayed when you choose the **Options→Design Capture Options→Forms** menu item in DE. In this dialog, you specify the database command and connect string if you are capturing a module from the database. You also can choose to capture control blocks, lists of values, and library links (attachments). The utility will add notes and comments to the module definition if you check the Add Notes check box. The Design Capture Log File area allows you to specify into which file the messages from this session will be written. Click OK to dismiss the options dialog.

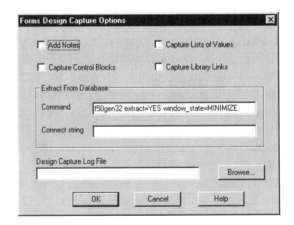

FIGURE 12-22. *Forms Design Capture Options dialog*

CAUTION
It bears repeating that you should be sure the definitions exist in the repository for the tables and columns used by the form or report you are design capturing. Otherwise, the design capture utility will fail.

After completing the fields in the Capture Form Design dialog, click the Start button. The utility creates (or updates) the module and module component usage definitions. The Capture Design of Forms utility creates the module, module component usages, and links (if there are links). It also sets the *Display Type* property of columns based on the item type in the form, although it does not capture values for list items or check box items. While it does not create definitions for boilerplate decoration or prompts, it does load the column name into the *Prompt* property of the detail column usage for the module. If the item was defined in Form Builder (Oracle Developer version 2 and beyond) with a *Prompt* property value, that value will be loaded into the column usage *Prompt* property.

The Capture Design of Reports utility contains similar settings, and you activate it in a similar way.

Repository Object Navigator and API in the Pre-Design Phase

As you work in the Pre-Design phase, you may want to check various features of the rough modules or tables. While you can write your own API utility (form or query script) to view repository definitions, the Repository Object Navigator and Design Editor provide the fastest built-in way to see most properties and related information on elements. You can navigate through the hierarchy and find the element you want to view and inspect and change its properties. In addition, you can group elements together and change properties of the group in one action.

Mapping Requirements to Modules

One of the last steps in Pre-Design is to synchronize the mapping of system requirements to modules. Although the Application Design Transformer creates modules from functions and copies the data usages, there is no utility to copy requirements from functions to modules. You need to associate these two elements, because one of the checks you perform in the Pre-Design phase examines whether all requirements have been addressed by modules in the system. If they have not, your system is not fulfilling some need, and you will need another module. Since not all functions are implemented as modules, you may lose functions and their associated requirements along the way. Therefore, you should be sure to copy the requirements from the functions to the modules derived from those functions.

Alternatively, you can create a report that shows the Requirements to Functions to Modules association. If you add to this report a list of Requirements to Functions for functions that were not implemented as modules, you will have a complete picture of where your requirements are implemented. Whichever way you handle the requirements to modules association, you will be able to let developers check for an existing function for a module they want to add based on further user needs. These approaches also document that there are a certain number of fixed requirements that the system was designed to handle and help guard against users claiming that a requirement was missed.

You create new repository elements in the Pre-Analysis phase with the User Extensibility feature, as mentioned in Chapter 6. In Analysis, you fill in instances of these new elements to provide the link between requirements and functions using the Repository Object Navigator, the Matrix Diagrammer, or a utility you write using another tool such as Oracle Developer.

In the Pre-Design phase, the requirements are already assigned to functions, so all you need to do is copy these assignments to the modules. Since each module definition also has a module function usage—the function or functions from which the module was derived—you can look at the corresponding function and copy the requirements assignment.

First you need to use the User Extensibility feature (described in Chapter 27) to create an association element that links requirements to modules as you did to link requirements to functions in the Pre-Analysis phase. Then you need to assign each requirement to one or more modules in RON or the Matrix Diagrammer. Alternatively, you can write an API procedure that looks at each function one at a time and determines the requirements associated with it. Then it finds the module or modules based on that function (using the Module's *Usage: Implementing Business Functions* association node) and assigns those modules the same requirements. This relatively simple API routine can save a lot of manual work in RON or the Matrix Diagrammer.

Repository Reports in the Pre-Design Phase

The reports you run in the Pre-Design phase are aimed at filling out the Design Plan with descriptions of the database design and the application design. As always, the repository itself plays a part in documentation, as it is a central place where you can find out organized details about your system design and analysis. That this is in an electronic, not printed, medium is secondary to the documentation requirement. If you absolutely require hard copy of the application and database design, you might consider running reports from the following groups:

■ *Module Design* These reports show different details on modules. The *Module Definition* report includes the Function to Module mapping that ADT performed as well as a listing of the table and column usages. The *Module Network* report provides a listing of the module structure that you refine in the Design Editor as part of the storyboard process. *Menu and Screen Definition* shows specifics on those types of modules including a representation of the menu calling structure.

■ *Server Model Definition* These reports focus on the database objects. The *Table Definition* report is the place to start. Although it is fairly long, it shows details on tables, views, and snapshots and columns including comments and constraints. *The Entity to Table Implementation* report shows the mapping performed by the DDT utility.

CHAPTER
13

Design—Database Design

I drink to the general joy of the whole table

—Shakespeare, Macbeth, III, iv, 89

n the first edition of this book, we wrote "Physical database design is a huge topic that can easily fill a book." That book has now been written. *Oracle8 Design Using UML Object Modeling* by Dr. Paul Dorsey and Joseph Hudicka (Oracle Press, 1998) covers data modeling, relational and object-relational data modeling, and physical database design. This chapter only briefly outlines the decisions that need to be made when designing a physical database but does not go into the details regarding how these decisions are made or the pros and cons of the various choices.

Overview of Database Design

Modifications to the underlying data structure needed to provide adequate application performance have a major effect on the database design. However, at this point in the process, the applications do not yet exist. The conceptual design of the applications exists, but the quality of the design of the database can't be tested until the actual applications are created.

You need to recognize, however, that you cannot consider physical database design independent of the applications associated with it. If denormalization is taken too far, you run the risk of making your applications difficult to maintain. Conversely, if not enough denormalization is performed, applications may be difficult to write and will run very slowly. Thus, you must perform a balancing act between performance and conceptual cleanliness.

The goal of good physical database design is a product with low long-term costs of development and maintenance that delivers acceptable performance. This goal requires that standards be set for performance. The designer's job then becomes to do what is necessary to achieve desired performance while staying as close as possible to a third normal form database.

What you need to do in this phase is to make the best educated guess at the appropriate database design. Only when the database has been built and populated and applications that operate on the database have been created can the quality of both the database and application design be tested.

The basic strategy of database design is to map entities to tables, making adjustments for subtype, denormalization, aggregation, and summary tables. Other considerations are the data-level system requirements. You need to ensure that these requirements are all taken into account during the design of the database. As you map entities to tables, you will also copy references to the associated data-level requirements. This procedure will maintain the link between the database and the data requirements.

This chapter emphasizes topics that frequently cause problems for novice database designers. It makes no claim to completely describe all of the issues surrounding physical database design. Chapter 14 discusses how to use Oracle Designer to design the database.

In general, you should start with a more or less clean third normal form database, add columns redundantly throughout the database, and use triggers to update the information. You may also need to build aggregation tables from the database in batch mode to make applications run in acceptable time frames.

The process of database design consists of the following steps:

1. Specify tables.

2. Determine the primary keys for the tables.

3. Implement dependencies.

4. Assign attributes to tables.

5. Implement complex business rules.

6. Create redundant columns.

7. Create summary and aggregation tables and views.

8. Create code description tables.

The following sections will describe each of the steps in the database design process.

Specifying Tables

When specifying tables for a database, you should not simply take the ERD and, with very little thought, generate a table for each entity, nor should you ignore the logical ERD as a major influence on the physical design. Either of these approaches will generate a poor database. In the first case, not only will applications probably run unacceptably slowly, but they will be difficult to maintain. In the second case, you may find it easy to build version 1 of the system, but this system will be completely inflexible and will be difficult for developers who did not work on the original system to understand. Therefore, you should try to stay as close as possible to the logical ERD in building the physical tables.

Entity Subtypes

Subtypes, such as hourly employees and salaried employees, cannot be mapped directly to tables. You can physically implement the subtypes in one of the following ways:

- Using a single table with a single entity and all subtypes

- Using one table for each subtype

- Using one table for each subtype and one table for the supertype

- Generically, accommodating any number of supertype and subtypes in the subset

Very Large Tables

Tables can become very large. It is not unusual for a main transaction detail table for an organization to contain 20 million rows. When you have tables with millions of rows, you should set up a test to see if applications will be able to run at all. You may need to decrease the size of the table by partitioning it.

Before Oracle8, tables had to be partitioned by physically creating several separate tables, each with its own CREATE TABLE syntax and storage parameters. Somewhat complex logic then needed to be implemented to ensure that records were inserted into or retrieved from the appropriate table. A view was typically used to retrieve data from all of the partitions.

With Oracle8, table partitions can be part of the table definition. Based on *partition keys*, the columns whose values are used to determine which partition the row is actually stored in, the database management system, and not the application logic, is responsible for inserting and retrieving data from the appropriate partition.

Tables can be partitioned in many ways. The two most common partitioning methods are:

- **By date**   Each year's transactions are in a separate table. The difficulty with this approach is that any applications spanning more than one year will have to access multiple tables or partitions.

- **By subject area**   A company may have multiple lines of business. Transactions associated with different kinds of business can be separated into different tables. However, again, applications spanning more than one business area will need to access multiple tables or partitions.

Partitioning increases the complexity of the application (prior to Oracle8) or of the DBA's backup and recovery strategies (for Oracle8). If not done correctly, it can actually hurt performance, for example, if a query is forced to retrieve data from multiple partitions. Partitioning should be done only if all other strategies fail to generate adequate performance, or if it is required by limitations of the physical storage media.

Prejoined Tables
Joining master-detail tables together, thus violating first or second normal form (depending upon how the join is done) was a common strategy throughout the 1980s. Experience has shown that storing prejoined tables in the long run costs more than it saves. Making any modifications to the system becomes a very complex procedure. This strategy should not be used unless absolutely necessary. A preferable approach that is very similar is to use redundant columns within tables. This strategy is discussed later in this chapter.

Determining Primary Keys for the Tables
This book assumes that you know enough about design to determine appropriate unique identifiers (UIDs). However, you need to decide whether

to use soft-key system-generated UIDs or logical UIDs. Under what circumstances should you use system-generated UIDs instead of logical UIDs? Using a system-generated UID for every table can be efficient. When writing code and procedures, the foreign key constraints are always known. Columns are neat and tidy. You need not worry about foreign key constraints becoming particularly large. The best reason for using system-generated UIDs is that otherwise logical UIDs can be cumbersome. For example, the logical UID for a telephone call consists of the originating number, date, and time. This sequence makes sense logically but does not provide an intuitively attractive UID. The allocation of that call to one or more accounts for billing purposes requires logistical work. If you use only system-generated UIDs, these problems disappear.

There are other benefits as well. If structural modifications are made to the database that affect the UID and system-generated UIDs are not used, the changes will propagate to other tables and constraint names, possibly affecting triggers, applications, and other work occurring after the UID is generated. When you use a system-generated UID, modifications can be made that do not propagate through the system. In addition, system-generated UIDs don't require as skilled a modeler to come up with complex UIDs such as the UID in the telephone example. Under what circumstances should system-generated UIDs not be used? In code description tables (lookup tables), it doesn't make sense to use system-generated UIDs. These tables typically don't change or change infrequently (unless, for example, a new phone system is installed). The UID in this case is the code.

System-generated UIDs waste space and add unnecessary columns. You will need to put a uniqueness constraint on logical candidate keys anyway. When an insert operation is performed, the sequence generator must be called. In addition to a column, a whole additional index must be stored.

Using system-generated UIDs, it is much easier to be lazy and create a bad database design. When you use logical UIDs for tables and they propagate, you can more easily spot logical inconsistencies in the database.

Implementing Dependencies

In a logical ERD, the horizontal bar crossing a relationship line connecting entities connotes logical dependency. This means that the child entity has no meaning outside of the context of the parent entity. Even at the physical design level, it is important to keep in mind that entities are dependent. For example, a purchase order (PO) detail makes no sense outside the context of a PO; it is a part of the parent entity.

Under what circumstances should a relationship between two physical tables be made dependent? The two associated entities don't have to be logically dependent. All that is of concern is what happens with UIDs: UIDs cannot change. The child entity can never move to another entity over time. (In Oracle Designer terms, it is not "transferable.") It must always be associated with the parent entity. The primary access method for the entity should be consistent with the primary key index. Dependent relationships are troublesome to use in the Design phase: the criteria for their use varies between Design and Analysis, so relationships that are not dependent in Analysis may become so in Design, and vice versa.

Assigning Attributes to Tables

At the end of the application design process, you will refine the database. At this point, you should err on the side of including attributes that may later be deemed unnecessary. The first step in assigning attributes is to map all attributes from the logical model. Then look at the conceptual design of the application and add any columns used in the conceptual model that are missing in the data model. Such columns may reveal omissions in the Analysis phase. These columns may also have to be added to the logical model. Add redundant columns in a separate step, discussed later in this chapter.

At this point in the system development process, it is important to be careful about the physical characteristics of the data. A lot of work involved in attribution is easily overlooked. Addresses are a common example. In Analysis, a field simply called "address" may be specified for an entity. However, as you move into physical design, you need to worry about how addresses work in the real world and how you can search and report on them. If you want to print mailing labels easily, you should probably store the entire address in a single field. For ZIP codes or postal codes, you need to consider different postal code conventions for different countries. Will you have a separate postal code column for each country with appropriate validation or will you store the postal code in a single column and then write a complex validation trigger? Some countries write addresses in an order different than that used in the U.S. Will you have an address and then an address label in a redundant column or will the application handle this situation?

Sometimes, it is important to be able to search on a geographic unit that is not normally part of the address. For example, in the U.S., the ability to display reports by county may be important in some applications. Will this be handled by storing county names with each customer or with a separate table showing which cities are in which county? For marketing purposes, do you need to be able to detect whether an address is for a single family dwelling, apartment, or office building? If you are interfacing address data with census data, such a question becomes very important.

These are some of the many questions that may arise during attribution. For each table, each column must be carefully considered to determine its physical representation in the database. Pay particular attention to addresses and phone numbers. They are some of the most frequently stored datatypes. They appear simple in the logical model but can be quite complex in the physical design.

Implementing Complex Business Rules

There are always data-related business rules that cannot be supported through the table structure and referential integrity constraints. You have to decide how to enforce such business rules. Some examples of such business rules are recursive rules. If you are implementing a hierarchical structure through a recursive relationship, you probably have a business rule that states that an individual cannot be his or her own grandparent. In other words, it is not possible for person A to manage person B, person B to manage person C, and person C to manage person A. Similarly, if you have a budget allocated to various accounts, you probably do not want the allocated amount to exceed the budget.

How can these rules be enforced? Here are five approaches:

- Rules can be enforced with a trigger on the database side by using BEFORE_INSERT, BEFORE_UPDATE, and BEFORE_DELETE triggers.

- Rules can be enforced on the client side in the application.

- Rules can be enforced on both database and client sides.

- Rules can be enforced in batch mode by running a periodic check of the database to identify violations.

- Rules may not be enforced at all.

Of course, enforcing business rules does decrease performance. The best way to handle rules is to enforce them on both the database and client sides. That way, the database is protected against applications with errors and updates through SQL*Plus or inserts through SQL*Loader. Enforcement on the client side allows you to alert the user to violations in business rules without accessing the database. If enforcement on both sides makes performance unacceptable, use one of the other approaches.

Creating Redundant Columns

The ease of writing database triggers enables you to create redundant columns that are automatically updated by operations on the database and do not require the application to update the redundant data. There are two different types of redundant columns worth considering:

- **Calculation columns**   For example, the total of a purchase order (PO) column should be a redundant column so that calculating the total does not require summing PO details each time. You just need appropriate triggers on the PO detail column to keep the total current.

- **Key fields**   These are best explained using an example. Your database has four tables: department, employee, sales, and employment history (which is an intersection table between employee and department). There is a 1-to-many link between employee and sales. The only way you can find out total sales for the department for a period of time is to first determine the appropriate employees for that department for that period of time. Then you must use a correlated subquery to determine the appropriate sales for each employee. Such a query would not execute particularly quickly. If, however, you redundantly store the department UID in the sales table as the key field, then you can calculate department sales for a period of time directly.

Creating Summary and Aggregation Tables and Views

Instead of using complex joins for a specific application, another approach is to create a redundant table. Just as with redundant columns, you can use database triggers to keep the redundant table correct and consistent with the rest of the database. An alternative approach, particularly if the summary table is accessed infrequently or only at specific times, such as a fiscal period-end or month-end, is to use a batch program to maintain the table.

Redundant aggregation tables are also useful, particularly for reporting. An example of a useful aggregation table is "Monthly Sales by Customer." For most reports, you are not interested in individual sales. You can have an aggregation table for monthly sales by customer. A handy trick when using aggregation tables is to store cumulative amounts rather than monthly amounts. That way, if you want to determine the total for a time period, rather than aggregating all records for a particular time period you need only to retrieve the first and last records for that period and subtract.

Summary and aggregation tables can be implemented as views. The advantage to a view is that it takes very little storage space in the database. Another advantage is that no increase in the overhead of transactions is required to maintain the table. A disadvantage is that performance when retrieving information from a view is much worse than when retrieving the information from an aggregated table.

Creating Code Description Tables

Some columns in a database will be associated with specific and reasonably constant lists of values: for example, male/female. Other lists of values are less stable. How can these two types of lists be handled within the database? One way is to place a check constraint on the field. This is appropriate for very small lists of values such as gender, Boolean variables (yes/no, true/false), and marital status (single/married/separated/divorced/widowed). However, check constraints are inappropriate for lists of values that change over time, such as the valid car colors for an automobile manufacturer. There may be dozens, or even hundreds, of colors over time.

For these less-stable lists of values, you need to store the information in code description tables. You can store all code description information in one big table or store each validation list in its own table. Which of these methods is better depends upon a number of factors. Having code lookup tables in memory is ideal. The best solution is to have all code descriptions in one table if all of this data will reside in memory. If you have many code description tables or lists with many values, however, all of the data will not fit in memory. Probably the best approach is to put all code description lookups in a single table but build views on top of the table so that the physical implementation is transparent to the application. That way, the underlying architecture can be changed if necessary without affecting the application.

DBA Issues

You won't know exactly how large the tables are going to be until legacy system data migration is complete. However, you can at least come up with a relatively good estimate of table size to determine whether you need to partition tables. You should be able to estimate the approximate number of rows in each table and how fast the table will grow. For each column in the table, you can make an educated guess regarding its size by looking at the legacy data and at how often a specific field is used. For VARCHAR2 fields, you can estimate the average length. This information will give DBAs the information necessary to determine tablespaces and physical locations.

Oracle Designer supports precise specification of storage parameters. You can now specify and define databases, tablespaces, and even storage parameters and partitions at the user level. Role-based security can be defined for each table and can be implemented on views in the applications. Server-side triggers and PL/SQL code can be stored within the repository.

Oracle can support very complex application environments. Using a distributed database environment implemented through Snapshots and Replication, it can support worldwide applications that would otherwise be impossible.

Object-Relational Databases

The relational database industry is undergoing a radical transformation. Oracle is beginning to incorporate object-oriented theory features into relational databases. With Oracle 8.0, we saw the beginnings of an object-relational database. Since Oracle8's initial release, there have been substantial improvements in Oracle's implementation of the object-relational model. Oracle Developer's latest release, which should be available by the time this book is published, should allow developers to build applications that will access and manipulate object tables.

The database modeling syntax for object-oriented databases is the Unified Modeling Language (UML). A subset of UML has been implemented in Oracle's Object Database Designer (ODD), which is shipped as a component of Oracle Designer 2.1. ODD supports the specification of Oracle8 object-relational structures, including object types, object tables, and nested tables.

Modifications for Smaller Systems

Modifications to the database design process must be made for smaller systems. However, there are different criteria for determining just what constitutes a smaller system in database design than in earlier phases. A large system in earlier phases was one with a large number of entities and applications. What makes database design complex is the size of the tables and, to some extent, the number of users. Database design becomes more complex when the overall amount of data increases and when individual tables are very large. Also, database design is complicated by volatile data (that is, hundreds of transactions happening every second). If none of the tables have more than 100,000 records, then you can probably use a third normal form database.

For these smaller systems, you will not need summary and aggregation tables and views. These items are generated to facilitate performance and are relatively unimportant in a small system. The bigger the tables, the higher their transaction load and the greater the extent of denormalization required to achieve adequate application performance.

When Is Database Design Complete?

Database design will not really be complete at the end of this phase. As you design applications, you will make modifications and refinements to the database. Therefore, you do not need to be particularly concerned about making the database design perfect at this point. You do need to be sure that every field on every screen in the conceptual application design created in the Pre-Design phase is in the database. Similarly, you need to be sure that all attributes in the logical model correspond to columns in the physical tables. You will, of course, add views and summary and aggregation tables where appropriate, but these decisions can be modified during application design. It is sufficient that the senior development team members approve the database design.

CHAPTER
14

Oracle Designer in
Design—Database
Design

It is not my design to drink or sleep,
but my design is to make what haste I can to be gone.
                    —Dying words of Oliver Cromwell (1599-1658)

he Design phase consists of two main tasks: database design and application design. The main objective of the Database Design part of the Design phase is to define the definitions for all database objects needed in the system. You need to have a good start on the database design before you can begin the application design, because the modules you work on in the Application Design stage rely on the tables you defined in the Database Design stage. This is an iterative process, though, so you will be defining and refining some tables as you define modules.

When the Design phase is over, you end up with a complete set of definitions for all database and application objects. The database objects you need to define in this part of Design include all tables and views that support the client code directly; all storage objects like tablespaces and data files; other administrative objects like databases and log files; and application programming interfaces (APIs) like the *Table API*—a package created for a table that provides a consistent contact point regardless of what application is accessing the table.

Therefore, your goal in the Database Design stage of the Design phase is to have as complete a set of database object definitions as possible to support the application design part of this phase. This chapter will discuss details of the major parts of the database design that you need to define to implement the logical business model. The Oracle Designer Design Editor (DE) and other Oracle Designer tools support this work through various features and utilities, as Table 14-1 shows.

In addition, there are some database design activities that the developer does in collaboration with the DBA to complete the database design. These are listed in Table 14-2.

This chapter discusses the utilities and tools you need to complete these tasks. Most operations using the Design Editor's Navigator and Property Palette can also be performed with the Repository Object Navigator (RON), discussed in Chapter 6, but the Design Editor contains links to the generators and other Design utilities and is the tool of choice for design work.

Activity or Deliverable	Oracle Designer Tool
Refine table design including views and snapshots and all storage clauses	Design Editor: Server Model Diagram, Server Model Guide, and Navigator—Server Model tab with Property Palette
Produce table diagrams	Design Editor: Server Model Diagram
Denormalize data structures	Design Editor: Navigator—Server Model tab with Property Palette
Define summary, journal, and code tables	Design Editor: Navigator—Server Model tab with Property Palette
Define the storage model: database, tablespaces, data files, and rollback segments	Design Editor: Database Administration Guide and Navigator—DB Admin tab with Property Palette
Create table implementations	Design Editor: Database Administration Guide and Navigator—DB Admin tab with Property Palette
Define Oracle8 types and objects	Object Database Designer and Design Editor: Server Model Diagram
Integrate existing tables not incorporated during Analysis	Design Editor: Capture Design of Server Model from Database utility
Synchronize columns belonging to domains	Design Editor: Update Columns in a Domain utility
Sketch out code for denormalization (aggregates and summary columns or tables) and server code	Design Editor: Logic Editor
Document the database design	Repository Reports

TABLE 14-1. *Design Database Design Activities and Designer Tools*

Activity or Deliverable	Oracle Designer Tool
Define the distribution model	Design Editor: Navigator— Distribution tab with Property Palette
Define replication structures	Design Editor: Navigator— Distribution tab with Property Palette
Define tablespaces and other storage objects	Design Editor: Navigator—DB Admin tab with Property Palette
Create table implementations	Design Editor: Database Administration Guide and Navigator—DB Admin tab with Property Palette
Define data security	Design Editor: Database Administration Guide and Navigator—DB Admin tab with Property Palette

TABLE 14-2. *Database Design: DBA Activities and Designer Tools*

This chapter does not mention the Database Design Transformer (DDT) or the Capture Design of Server Model from Database utility. DDT, described in Chapter 12, is used extensively in the Pre-Design phase to create the tables needed for the storyboard process. However, you will also find DDT useful if you refine entities in the Design phase and need to create or update the tables based on those entities. Similarly, the Capture Design of Server Model from Database utility, introduced in Chapter 8, may be useful for reconciling changes to tables made during storyboarding with the repository definitions of those tables, as explained in Chapter 20.

As mentioned for other phases, the following discussion of Oracle Designer tools assumes that you have reviewed the notes on the common interface for Oracle Designer in Chapter 2. In addition, be sure you are comfortable with the organization and access methods for information in the online help system, as this is the best facility to use when you have a question about an operation while using the tools.

Server Model Diagram

In the database design part of the Design phase, you refine, revise, and replace the tables you created for the storyboard process. The process of integrating the storyboarded tables into the repository occurs in Pre-Design, so in the Design phase you start with a rough draft of the table definitions already in the repository. The activities you perform on these definitions include checking the primary and foreign key relationships, denormalizing the tables for performance or other reasons, and creating definitions for as many views and snapshots as you know about. The Build phase may also include creation of more tables, views, and snapshots as needs arise in the application.

The Design phase is an appropriate time in which to outline the database triggers you know are needed. These triggers consist of PL/SQL code that runs automatically when the table is accessed with INSERT, UPDATE, or DELETE statements. They are a potential place to locate the code that supplies derivation or summarization values, which may result from denormalization. For example, you might want an AFTER INSERT, UPDATE, or DELETE statement-level trigger on an ORDER_ITEM table that sums the line totals and updates the NUM_IN_STOCK column in the INVENTORY table. Although you write and debug program code in the Build phase, you can define rough-cut versions of triggers as well as some of their functionality in the Design phase. You can also define triggers on views in Oracle8 as described in the section later on Triggers.

In addition, you should examine each table and column definition and fill in as many details as possible about how each will be displayed in the application modules. The more complete you are in this phase, the less frequently you will have to pause during the Application Design part of the Design phase or the Build phase to fill in missing details. Also, if you fill in the table and column definitions as completely as possible in the Design phase, whenever the tables are used in modules, the table usage will inherit some characteristics of the table definition. Similarly, the column properties will be inherited by the bound item properties in the module. Therefore, you can make choices at this point about the common way the tables will be viewed or used. For example, suppose you have a table definition that is used in four modules. If you complete the display properties of the table definition, all four modules will use those same properties. Of course, you can override the table settings and provide more details on the module level, but the table-level properties will give you a good set of defaults and reduce the amount of customization needed for the modules.

The Server Model Diagram window of the Design Editor allows you to diagram tables, views, snapshots, and clusters with their columns and any relationships that apply between them. You can show the columns, keys, and databases to which the objects belong. You can also edit and fill in properties for tables as well as columns directly on the diagram. This tool's functionality parallels that of the ER Diagrammer, which is used in the Analysis phase. Although the symbol set is different, both tools model data (logical or physical), show overall containers for details (entities or tables), display the details of those containers (attributes or columns), and diagram the relationships between containers (relationships or foreign keys). In fact, an entity relationship diagram and a data schema diagram may display the exact same data elements but at different stages of the development process. The logical and physical models are often different, however, and Oracle Designer provides the Server Model Diagram so you can represent the physical design model and still keep the logical analysis model intact. Figure 14-1 shows a Server Model Diagram session.

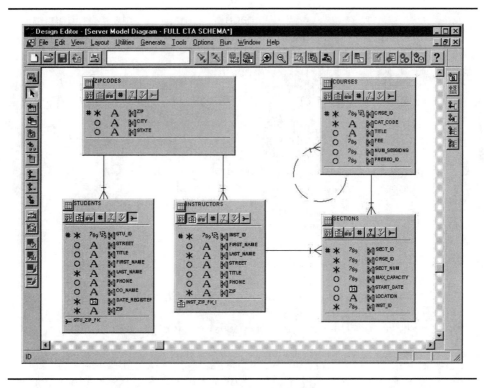

FIGURE 14-1. *Server Model Diagram session*

As mentioned in Chapter 12, Oracle Designer requires a large monitor displaying a high resolution so you can display diagrams, the Navigator, and the Property Palette at the same time. A large monitor will save much opening, closing, and moving windows within the Design Editor; all of these take valuable time away from your work and may interrupt your train of thought. Figure 14-1 shows the diagram window maximized in the Design Editor session.

Server Model Diagrammer— A Hidden Utility

You can also run a faster but leaner version of the Design Editor Server Model Diagram with a tool supplied with Oracle Designer 2.1 (at least with release 7.0.20), called the Server Model Diagrammer. This is a separate executable program, similar to the tool called the Data Diagrammer in version 1, which does not appear in the Oracle Designer opening window. You run it by double-clicking on DWFDD20.EXE in the ORACLE_HOME/ bin directory or by creating a shortcut for it using the Windows shortcut facility. (ORACLE_HOME is the directory in which your Oracle tools are installed, and this varies from one machine to another. It is usually named something like C:\ORANT or C:\ORAWIN95.)

This tool looks like the Design Editor version, but it has a subset of operations. You can open, create, save, and delete diagrams, as with the Design Editor. The drawing toolbar is smaller, though, and you need to choose **Edit→Include** from the menu to draw existing tables on the diagram rather than dragging them from a Navigator window—drag and drop from RON does not work. The following are some operations you can do and some you cannot do with this tool.

Some of the operations you can perform:

- **Open an old diagram** that has definitions no longer in the repository or that are still in the repository but have changes. The Design Editor version of this tool automatically updates the diagram, but this tool does not. This allows you to preserve old versions of a diagram even though the repository has changed.

- **Eliminate the red dots** that the other tools use to indicate that a definition has changed in another tool. For example, if you change a definition in RON, the Design Editor diagram shows a red dot next to the element that was changed. The Server Model Diagrammer does not show these update dots.

- **Open diagrams** created in the Design Editor and save diagrams you will open with the Design Editor.

- **Embed OLE objects** such as text and graphics in the same way as in other diagrammers.

- **Track associations** as in DE. This highlights the columns used by another element such as a foreign key constraint.

- **Show secondary element details** to display or hide details under the column list for each table.

Operations you cannot perform:

- **Create or delete definitions** from the repository.

- **View or change properties** on any element.

- **Drag and reorder columns** within a table to resequence them.

- **Drag elements in** from any Navigator or other diagrammer.

- **Use right-click mouse menus** on the diagram or on the elements in the diagram.

The menu is quite similar to the Design Editor toolbar that you use for the Server Model Diagram. Documentation on this tool exists in the DWFDD20.HLP help file in the ORACLE_HOME/cdoc70/help directory. This help file is accessible from the diagrammer's **Help→Help Topics** menu item. Think of this tool as a quick way to change the layout of diagrams or to create diagrams you will modify using Design Editor. The main benefit of this tool is that it does not automatically query the repository when you open a diagram, which makes it faster, especially for diagrams with many elements.

Basic Techniques

The Server Model Diagram tool closely parallels the ER Diagrammer, so many of the techniques are the same. Opening an existing diagram is accomplished in a similar way, by selecting the **File→Open→Server Model Diagram** menu option or by clicking the Open Component toolbar button when another Server Model Diagram window is the active window (the window title is highlighted).

As is true with much of Oracle Designer, the flexible user interface allows you to perform operations in multiple ways. For example, here are six different methods for creating a diagram:

■ Select a table or set of tables in the Navigator and click on the Open Component button.

■ Select a table or tables and choose Show On New Diagram from the right-click menu.

■ Drag the table or tables you have selected to a blank area in the Design Editor. This will create a new diagram that includes the selected tables.

■ Make an open diagram window the active window and click the New Component toolbar button.

■ Select the Server Model Diagrams node in the Navigator and click the Create button.

■ Select **File→New→Server Model Diagram** from the menu.

The point is that you do not have to worry about knowing the one and only way to perform an operation, as the one that is most intuitive to you will (probably) be the one that works.

Remember that although this discussion refers to diagramming tables, you can also diagram views, snapshots, clusters, and object types.

Including Existing Tables

You place existing tables on the diagram by selecting **Edit→Include** from the menu when the diagram window is active. The Include Tables/Views/Snapshots/Foreign Keys window appears, as Figure 14-2 shows.

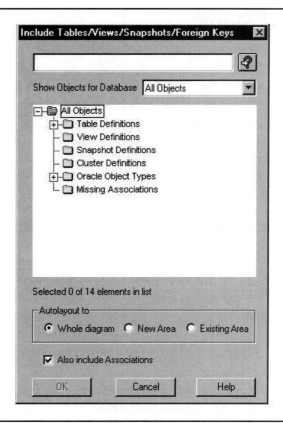

FIGURE 14-2.   *Include Tables/Views/Snapshots/Foreign Keys window*

You expand these hierarchy nodes and select the elements you want to include on the diagram. The list will not include elements already on the diagram. You can filter by entering a filter condition in the top field and pressing the filter button next to it. You can also filter according to the database(s) to which the objects are assigned using the Show Objects for Database poplist. Leave the default of All Objects to see objects in all databases and those not yet assigned to databases.

As with the ER Diagrammer, you can also specify whether you want to include the associations such as foreign key constraints. You can also select which area you want the diagrammer to use to lay out the new objects—Whole diagram, New Area, or Existing Area. After choosing the elements you want to include, you click OK, and the elements appear on the diagram.

An alternative to the Include procedure is dragging and dropping into the diagram from the Design Editor or RON Navigator window. You can also drag and drop from another server model diagram or a matrix diagram.

The **Options→Layout** menu item displays a window that lets you modify the minimum table box size in cells and specify the size of each cell. Nevertheless, when you include an existing table, Oracle Designer will ignore these settings and make the boxes for each table large enough to hold the column names (whether they are shown or not). You can resize these, of course, once they are placed on the screen. Layout options also allow you to display the grid and *grid snap,* or lock, a point or line you are drawing to the grid. When you move objects around on the diagram, particularly foreign key lines, grid snap will help keep your lines parallel. In addition, you can specify Connector Text Alignment to be Horizontal (so the name of the foreign key is always Horizontal on the page) or parallel to the line (so vertical lines will have vertically-arranged text).

TIP
Sometimes your drawing may contain a stray pixel or two of a line that remained when something was moved or when you scrolled the window. Since there is no redraw action in any of Oracle Designer's diagrammers, you have to force the tool to perform a redraw operation. The easiest way to do this is to use the window icons in the top-right part of the window to minimize the drawing window (not the MDI window) and then maximize it again.

Drawing New Objects
You draw a new object in the Server Model Diagram the same way as in other diagrammers: click the appropriate toolbar button and draw the element in the drawing area. Depending on the type of element you create, a property dialog or palette will open where you specify properties and save them. Drawing a new table creates a table definition in the repository.

You can expand the drawing to cover more pages by dragging a table outside the page boundaries, thus creating a new page. In this way, you can, if needed, represent your entire system in one diagram with as many pages as needed. Changing the layout of a large diagram is not a trivial matter, however, so a "subset" approach may be more appropriate in many cases. In this approach, multiple diagrams, each of which represents a portion of the application, can be used. For example, you can show a single business area in one diagram with all the tables that will be used to carry out a particular business process or set of processes. The choice of what to represent on a diagram is up to you. Any subset of tables can appear in any given drawing, and you can diagram a particular table in more than one drawing.

NOTE
The Server Model Diagram is essentially an ER Diagrammer for tables. It represents the physical (design) data model, which may differ from the logical data model you diagram with the ER Diagrammer. It is good to keep in mind the distinction between logical and physical objects (analysis and design, respectively) when working in Oracle Designer. It is also good to remember that the diagram represents what is in the repository but need not contain everything that is in the repository.

You can change the font of the text in particular objects, which may be helpful if you want to reduce the size of the table boxes to fit more on a single page. Select the tables you want to change and select **Options→ Color/Font/Style** from the menu to display the dialog as shown in Figure 14-3.

Click on the buttons in this dialog to change the line widths and the color of lines, fonts, and fills. You can set these options for selected, existing, and new objects. Alternatively, you can change the visual aspects by selecting the objects and using the toolbar buttons for fill, font, line color, and line width.

You can draw a dog-leg (angled) line by clicking intermediate points between the source and destination object. If you need to add a dog-leg

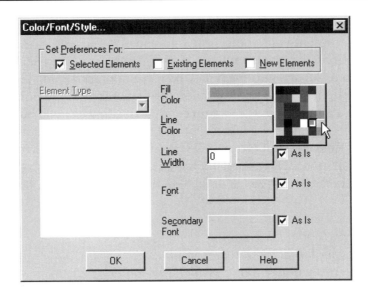

FIGURE 14-3. *Color/Font/Style dialog*

after a line is drawn, you can do so by holding down SHIFT as you drag out the middle of the line the same way as in the other diagrammers. SHIFT-click on the dog-leg point to remove the point.

TIP
To move a pig's ear (self-referencing) foreign key line, click it to select it and move the whole line by clicking the middle of the arc (not the end). You can drop it close to a corner, and the line will span the two adjacent sides.

Using the Symbol Set

The symbol set in the Server Model Diagram is somewhat similar to that of the ER Diagrammer. This diagram uses hard boxes (with right-angle corners) instead of soft boxes, and it uses only two types of foreign key relationships: mandatory and optional. It also has a symbol for an arc relationship, which indicates mutually exclusive columns in the table. This relationship is not implemented via database constraints. However, you can create check constraints to enforce it, or use the Table API (explained later in this chapter), which includes a validate arc procedure, to perform inserts and updates to the table rather than coding INSERT or UPDATE DML (Data Manipulation Language) statements. Some of the symbols used in this diagram are shown in Figure 14-4.

An ellipsis at the bottom of a table box means that the table contains more columns than are displayed. If you expand the bottom of the table box, those columns will be visible. This figure does not show the symbols for views, snapshots, and clusters as they are the same except for the default fill colors and for the buttons that appear in the upper-left corner of the box and the secondary element buttons underneath it. You can always tell the name of an object and its type by holding the mouse cursor over the

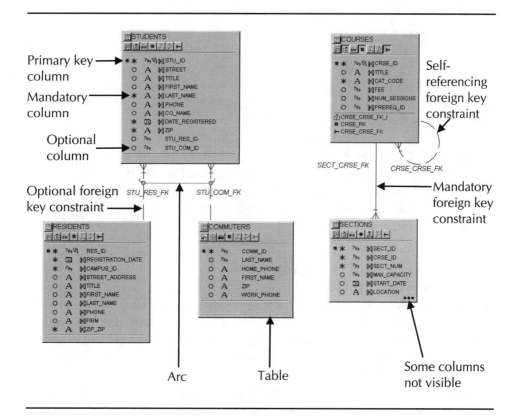

FIGURE 14-4. *Server Model Diagram symbols*

element for a second; its name and type will appear in a hint (or tool tip), as shown in the following illustration.

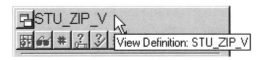

The icons in the upper-left corner are also indicators, since they are different for each type of object, as the following illustration shows.

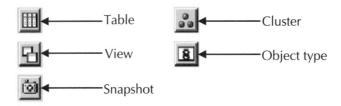

Other drawing features include the ability to open another window that contains the same diagram by saving the diagram, choosing **File→Open→ Server Model Diagram** from the menu and choosing the currently open diagram. This is useful if you want to focus on two different parts of a large diagram at the same time. Any update you make in one window of that diagram will automatically appear in the other diagram window. You can shift between diagrams by using the Window menu or pressing CTRL-F6. To close extra windows, choose Close from the drawing window menu in the top-left corner of the window frame.

Exploiting Layout Techniques

As with the ER Diagrammer, you can use the Autolayout feature (**Layout→Autolayout** or the Autolayout toolbar button) to let Oracle Designer place and size the objects. This lets you see if one of the random arrangements is close to your needs. Autolayout has the same menu items as the ER Diagrammer for a new area or same area layout. If the area you specify is smaller than the objects selected, the diagrammer will use only the shape of the area and lay out the objects in an area large enough for them to fit. The Same Area and New Area menu options are disabled unless you have something selected. The shape can be useful, though, if you want all or selected tables in a certain rectangular shape and in a particular part of the drawing area.

Autolayout will allow you to return to any previous layout if you do not perform any other operations between the layouts. Therefore, you can cycle through a number of layouts and decide to go back to one that was presented by pressing the Previous Layout toolbar button (or selecting **Layout→Previous Layout** from the menu).

TIP

*After initially laying out the existing objects, select **Layout→Minimize Number of Pages** to reduce the number of blank pages. Remember that you can change the page orientation in the **File→Print Setup** dialog box at any time if you prefer to use landscape mode to get more horizontal space on the page.*

If your foreign key lines ever get out of alignment, you can select the line (holding the CTRL key if you need to select multiple lines) and click the Autolayout button. If all foreign key lines are out of alignment, you can select one foreign key line (not its name) and choose **Edit→Select Same Type** from the menu to select all foreign key lines on the diagram before clicking the Autolayout button.

TIP

One strategy you can try when creating a new diagram is to include the tables you need without including the foreign key (associations), using Autolayout to create a layout that is close to the one you want. Once you've got a layout you like, include the foreign key constraint lines. The foreign key lines often clutter the display while you are creating the initial layout, so the last step is to include these lines. The diagrammer will draw the lines as straight as possible based on the layout of the tables.

There are shortcut keys you can use to speed up your work in the diagrammer. If you select a diagrammed object and press CTRL-X, you will cut the object from the diagram. CTRL-DELETE will delete it from the repository. Pressing CTRL-C while a table is selected in a diagram will copy it into the clipboard. Pressing CTRL-V in another diagram will paste the table into that diagram (if it is not already there).

TIP
Shortcut keys can make your work in the Design Editor much faster, as you can, for some operations, avoid searching the menu or grabbing the mouse to click a toolbar button. A full list of shortcut keys is available by pressing CTRL-K in the Design Editor or selecting **Help→Show Keys** *from the menu.*

Changing the Display

In addition to the font and color changes you make to the diagram, you can change the way the table symbols are displayed. If you select **Options→Show/Hide** from the menu when the diagram window is active, you will display the Server Modeller Show/Hide Options dialog, as Figure 14-5 shows.

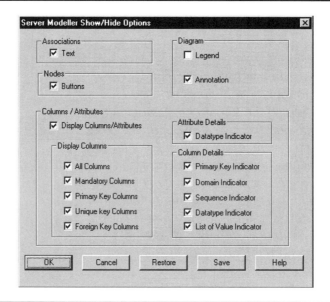

FIGURE 14-5. *Server Modeller Show/Hide Options dialog*

This dialog allows you to specify which elements will be displayed in the diagram. You set whether the foreign key associations will show names (the Text check box in the Associations area) and whether the tables will show the toolbar buttons (the Buttons check box in the Nodes area) for secondary elements. *Secondary elements* are definitions that are associated with the table, such as the triggers and primary keys, shown in the following illustration.

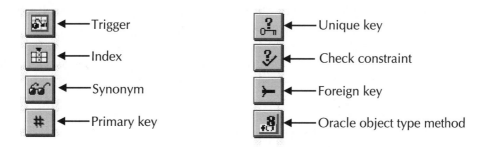

You can show the names of these secondary elements under the column names in the table's box. You do this by clicking the appropriate secondary element button so it is inset. To hide the display of the secondary element, click the button again. This will change the button to show as outset, or not depressed. The following illustration shows a table with secondary elements displayed for triggers, a primary key, and a check constraint.

You can also hide or display secondary elements when the diagram window is active by choosing **View→Secondary Element Details** from the menu. This displays a dialog that lets you make global settings for which secondary elements are shown. While the settings in this dialog affect all elements in all diagrams open in that Design Editor session, you can override the setting on an element-by-element basis by clicking the appropriate secondary element button in a table box.

The Show/Hide dialog also lets you specify whether the diagram will show columns (and attributes for object types) and what types of columns (mandatory, primary key, unique key, foreign key, or all) it will display. You can turn off the display of the Datatype Indicator, which gives a quick visual cue as to the database column or attribute type. Similarly, you can uncheck the check boxes for primary key (to show if the column participates in the primary key), domain (to show if the column contains a value in the *Domain* property), sequence (to show if the column contains a value in the *Sequence* property), and list of values (to show if the column or domain the column is based on has Allowable Values).

Other settings you can make in the Show/Hide dialog are diagram settings for a legend and annotations. The *legend* is a title block that contains information you set in the dialog opened with **File→Summary Information**. This will print with the diagram. An *annotation* is text or a graphic that you have pasted in by copying it into the clipboard from another application. For example, you could copy some text into the clipboard from your word processing program. When you choose **Edit→Paste** from the menu in DE, the text will be written on the screen as an annotation.

Working in the Diagram

The Server Model Diagram is a tool you use not only to communicate the database design, but also to you complete the details about the design. You can add and modify components of the tables you diagram as well as the table itself.

The right-click menu on the table button to the left of the table name on each table box holds the secret to quick manipulation of the element definitions. This menu allows you to create another table, generate the server DDL code, create another diagram, and show the usages of this table by all elements in the repository. You can also create any of the secondary elements (triggers, constraints, indexes, and synonyms) as well as add a column.

If you double-click on any object in the diagram (or select it and press ENTER), you will display the Property Palette (or dialogs, if you have switched to dialogs), where you can change properties on the existing element. If you are creating a new element, the properties will pop up automatically so you can complete the definition before saving the element. You can also choose Add from the right-click menu of any secondary element button to create a new element of the appropriate type. The section "Defining Design Elements" later in this chapter discusses the actual property values to which you need to pay attention.

While you will probably want to use the Navigator for some operations, you can think of the diagram objects as providing a different way to navigate to an element definition and display its properties. You can perform some actions in the diagram as easily as you can in the Navigator. For example, in both the Navigator and the diagram, you can drop a column onto an existing foreign key or primary key node. In the case of the diagram, you need to display the secondary element for primary key listings at the bottom of the table by clicking the primary key button. Dropping the column on the correct key node will add that column to the list of columns in that key.

Another operation you can perform quickly is to reorder the columns within the table. You just drag the column and drop it in the correct place in the list. Most element names in the table diagram allow in-place editing, which saves a trip to the property sheet if all you want to do is change a name. Just click on name (table, column, constraint, and so on), and an edit field will open up where you can change the name. Click outside the edit box or press ENTER to stop the editing.

If your diagram contains a large number of elements, you might have problems finding a certain element. While you can use the technique of moving the mouse over each item to see the name, there is an easier way. Selecting **Edit→Navigate To** from the menu displays a dialog like the one in Figure 14-6.

This dialog shows all elements in the current diagram. You can search for elements with a specific name by entering the name or part of the name in the find field at the top of the dialog and pressing the filter button. You can also just expand the nodes and browse for a particular element. If you select an element in the list and click OK, the diagram focus will shift to that element. If you want to select the element as well as focus on it, check the And Select check box before clicking OK.

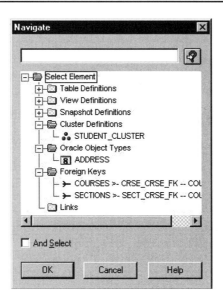

FIGURE 14-6. *Navigate dialog*

Naming Elements

One quality-control step you perform in the Design phase is to check the names of all data elements to be sure they match your naming standards. A decision you made in the Analysis phase early in the life cycle was whether to use plurals for table names. The table name derives from the entity plural name, so you can force a table name to be singular by defining the *Plural Name* property for the entity with a singular word. The Database Design Transformer (DDT) uses this plural name as the table name. If you decide to use plural names for tables, you can accept the default entity plural name, and DDT will create the table name as plural. You can also specify the table prefix that DDT will generate. A table prefix is a short identifier (usually three or four characters with an underscore) that identifies which application system or project the table is in. While this does add to the size of the

...me, it can assist in keeping the location and ownership of a table
...wn.

...ever system you use, it is important to be consistent, so if you add a
... after DDT is done, use your naming standard. One of the most
...standards is to use descriptive but short names for columns. This
name may or may not be the same as the attribute name, but there will be
less confusion if the names of attributes and columns are similar. Remember
that rules apply to column names that do not apply to attributes. For
example, column names may not start with a number and must consist of
one word of 30 characters or less (in an Oracle database).

Another decision you make when running DDT is whether you want a
column name prefix. DDT can create column names with a prefix of the
entity short name. The benefit of this approach is that each column in the
database will have a unique name that indicates the table it is in. The
drawbacks are that column names will be longer than if they had no prefix
and that foreign key and primary key names will be different. Also, the
means for joining tables will not be as obvious. As with the plural table
names, if you decide to use the column prefix, be consistent when you add
columns to tables after DDT runs. Therefore, if you use the column prefix
strategy, use it everywhere.

An exception to this rule is that, even if you do not use column prefixes
for all columns, you would use them for primary key columns that represent
a system-generated ID number. For example, the ORDERS table uses a
system-generated number as a primary key. This number column would be
named ORD_ID because it is an identifier for the table ORDERS which has
an *Alias* property of ORD. You would name foreign key columns that point
to this column with the same name. For example, the ORDER_ITEMS table
contains a foreign key that references the primary key in ORDERS. The
ORDER_ITEMS foreign key column would be named the same as the
primary key it refers to: ORD_ID. If you use this strategy for naming, you
have to be careful about not changing the table *Alias* property because the
ID column would then be out of sync with the alias.

DDT creates foreign key columns and foreign key constraints for
relationships, and it names the column and constraint based on the short
name of the entities involved in the relationship. For example, suppose there

is a relationship between the EMPLOYEE entity (short name: EMP) and the DEPARTMENT entity (short name: DEPT) that states that an employee must belong to one and only one department and a department may be composed of one or more employees. DDT will create a foreign key column from the relationship and name it either DEPTNO or DEPT_DEPTNO, depending on whether the Foreign key columns check box on the Other Settings tab of the Settings dialog is unchecked or checked. The foreign key constraint will have a name of EMP_DEPT_FK to show that it is in the EMPLOYEE table and references the DEPARTMENT table.

The other task that DDT performs is to create foreign key indexes that are named by adding the suffix _I to the foreign key name. The primary key constraints are named with the table alias (entity short name) with a _PK suffix. If you use different naming standards, you can change the names in the table property window as described later in this chapter. If you require additional indexes, you can use a naming convention without the FK and PK tokens to indicate a different purpose (for example, TABLENAME_ COLUMNNAME_IDX). If you can live with the Oracle Designer naming convention, though, you will not need to rename these elements.

Other Menu and Toolbar Functions

Other than the menu options detailed earlier and those that are common to other Oracle Designer tools, there are a few options worth mentioning. The **View→Track Associations** menu item, when checked, will automatically select an association element each time you select an element in the secondary element list at the bottom of the table box. For example, with the association tracking on, you select the foreign key EMP_DEPT_FK in the secondary element list in the EMPLOYEE table. The diagram will automatically select the DEPTNO column that is in the foreign key constraint.

It's important to remember in all work you do in the Design Editor (as well as other Oracle Designer tools) that the menu will change based on the active window. For example, if the diagram window is selected because you are working in it or have clicked somewhere in it, the DE menu will contain a Layout menu but not a Navigator or Properties menu.

A menu item that affects the diagram is actually available when the Navigator window is active. Use **Navigator→Track Diagram Selection** to select the element node in the Navigator that corresponds to the object you select in the diagram.

TIP

*You can select Print Preview from the File menu to show what the printed diagram or list will look like. However, settings like Fit to Page, X or Y (to designate how many pages the diagram should take), and Page Title (to print the summary information) are available only in the dialog opened with **File→Print**. If you set these in the Print dialog, you have to print to set them. The problem is that if all you want to do is preview what will print, you do not want to print and will not get the Print dialog. The workaround is to select **File→Print** and check the Print to File check box. Then make the other desired settings and press the OK button. A dialog will appear where you would normally enter the name of the file to which you wanted the list or diagram printed. If you press the Cancel button in that dialog, the settings you made in the Print dialog will still be set and used for your Print Preview.*

Where Does This Information Go?

All elements in a Server Model Diagram are destined to become database objects. Therefore, although the diagrammer includes various element types, all are the basis for DDL scripts that the Generate Database from Server Model utility (also called Server Generator in the help system) produces.

You run these scripts in the database to create the database objects that support the application modules. Table 14-3 shows the major element types represented in the Server Model Diagram and the use made of these elements by the Generate Database from Server Model utility.

Server Model Diagram Element	Future Use
Table, view, snapshot, cluster	CREATE TABLE, CREATE VIEW, CREATE SNAPSHOT, CREATE CLUSTER statements, respectively
Column definitions	Column clause in respective CREATE statement
Primary key and unique key constraint	ALTER TABLE statement to ADD the corresponding PRIMARY or UNIQUE KEY constraint to the table definition
Foreign key constraint	ALTER TABLE statement to ADD the FOREIGN KEY constraint to the table definition
Check constraint	Check constraint clause for column definition in the CREATE TABLE statement
Index	CREATE INDEX statement
Trigger definition	CREATE TRIGGER statement
Domain or column values list	Check constraint clause for column definition in the CREATE TABLE statement

TABLE 14-3. *Future Use of Data Design Elements*

TIP
The key to success in the Server Model Diagram (indeed, in all of Oracle Designer) is knowing what the result will be when you set or ignore a particular property. When in doubt regarding what DDL statement or clause a particular property will generate, create a test table or element and run the generator before and after specifying the setting to note the differences in the script that the Generate Database from Server Model utility creates. The extra time it takes to learn the properties will benefit you in the long run. Chapter 29 and the help system provides a starting point for some of these details.

Defining Design Elements

The previous section explained how to use the Server Model Diagram to create and find some of the commonly used element definitions you need for the database design. You can also use the Navigator in RON or DE to create element definitions. The objects discussed earlier all fall under the Server Model tab, where you define the building blocks and high-level objects for your database. This section will explain the details of how to complete the definitions for these database objects.

As the database design stage progresses, you will also need to visit the other tabs (DB Admin and Distribution) to specify details on database objects other than the basic ones. While the elements on the Server Model tab correspond roughly to the logical analysis model objects, the elements on the DB Admin and Distribution tabs have no real equivalent in the logical model. For example, a logical model does not include information about where a table is implemented (its database or tablespace) or how it needs to be replicated to support distributed processing. Although this section does not explain details about these elements, they are a necessary part of the database design stage of Design. You may need to consult with your DBA staff to get help on standards and best practices for elements like physical storage, distribution, security, and replication.

Table 14-4 shows the main element types available in two Design Editor tabs that are responsible for database design. Some element types appear in multiple tabs, but this table lists the most commonly used one. You will have to open the Navigator structure down multiple levels to reach some, but the locations should be relatively logical once you consult this list.

The following discussion examines properties for these elements. The section later in this chapter, "Designing Objects with Oracle Designer," explains how to create definitions to support Oracle8 objects. Although you can use property dialogs or the Property Palette (as mentioned in Chapter 12), the discussion here focuses on the properties themselves with notes on how the palette displays those properties. The property names are the same or very similar in both dialog and palette interfaces. The following assumes

Navigator Tab	Database Object
Server Model	Tables—Relational Table Definitions
	Views—Relational View Definitions
	Snapshots
	Clusters
	Domains
	Sequences
	PL/SQL Definitions—procedures, functions, packages
	Columns, Primary Key, Unique Keys, Foreign Keys, Check Constraints, Indexes, Synonyms, Triggers— under the Relational Table Definitions node
DB Admin	Storage Definitions
	Databases
	Table implementations—under Schema objects under a particular user
	Tablespace—Tablespaces node under the Storage node

TABLE 14-4.   *Standard Relational Database Objects and Where to Define Them*

that you are able to navigate to the correct element and show the property dialog or palette.

> **NOTE**
> *You can set up the Design Editor to display both dialog and Property Palette styles of dialogs. If you set the default for properties to the Property Palette (using the toolbar button or Options menu item) and display the properties, the palette window will open. If you then switch to Property Dialogs (with the button or menu item), when you double-click an object in the Navigator, the dialog will appear, even though the palette window is still open. Once you dismiss the dialog, you can set any properties in the Property Palette that were not in the dialog. For example, you prefer the dialogs but can only set text properties like* Description *or* Notes *in the palette, so you use the dialog to do what is possible there and enter the text using the Property Palette.*

Tables

When you create a table definition, you need only fill in the table name, as other properties have default values. There are properties for volume information that you can use to obtain a report on estimated database size. If that is of interest, you would fill in the *Start Rows* and *End Rows* (or fill in the *Initial* and *Maximum Volume* for the corresponding entity before running DDT) and run the *Database Table and Index Size Estimates* repository report. The *Complete ?* property must be set to Yes if you want to generate a CREATE TABLE script from this definition.

The *Comment* property is important if you want to document your table in the online data dictionary. If this property is filled out and you set the Generate Database from Server Model utility options to create comments, the utility will add COMMENT ON statements to the table creation script. You can consider this another way to document the table in the database. While you may feel that the Oracle Designer repository is documentation enough, the repository may not be universally available to those who can view the tables in the database. Online comments would assist those people in gathering information about the database design because they could, without access to the Oracle Designer repository, query the comments using the data dictionary views ALL_COL_COMMENTS and ALL_TAB_COMMENTS.

Table Journaling

The *Journal* property signifies if and how rows from this table will be handled on inserts, updates, and deletes. You can specify that, if a row is updated, the column values being updated will also be written into a table that has the same name as that table with a "_JN" extension. This table has the same columns with some additional columns to record who made the change, when it was made, and, optionally, the reason the change was made. The same kind of process occurs for inserts and deletes. This journal table will not appear as a definition in the repository, but the Generate Database from Server Model utility will produce a CREATE TABLE statement for it and the code generated by the Oracle Designer generators will handle the manipulation of this table.

If you set the *Journal* property to "None," no journaling will occur. If you set it to "Client," the client code generator will create code to insert records into the journal table and optionally require users to enter a reason for the change. If you set the value to "Server," the generator will create a trigger that calls a procedure in the Table API that does the journaling. This is useful if you are generating a non-Forms application or if it is possible for users to change the rows in the table outside the application, because the database trigger will always fire regardless of which application is performing the operation. You can also set the value to "Client calls server procedure." This value also causes a trigger and procedure to be generated, so operations not done from the client code will create the journal record. Operations done from the client side can record the reason and will also call the procedure but will disable the trigger call to that procedure so only one journal row is written.

Generator preferences in the Journaling category of the Forms Generator specify how the application will handle the journaling.

Table Property Dialog

In addition to using the Property Palette to view and manage properties, you can use the property dialog for this purpose. The Name tab page of the table property dialog is shown in Figure 14-7.

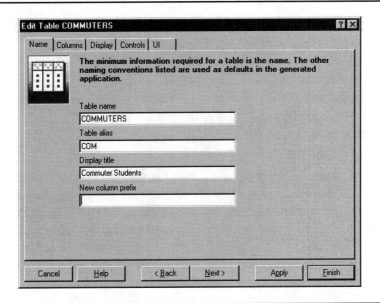

FIGURE 14-7. *Table property dialog*

This dialog contains the following tabs:

- **Name**   Used to enter general identifying information about the table.

- **Columns**   Used to define the columns in the table.

- **Display**   Used to define which columns will be displayed if this table is used in a module. You can change the display order by selecting the column name and pressing the up or down arrow to resequence it.

- **Controls**   Used to define properties for how the columns will appear in the module, such as display type and size.

- **UI**   Used to define user interface properties such as hint text, uppercase, alignment, and format mask.

TIP
If you create a table using the property dialog, you can specify an option to create audit columns. If you set the option to "Yes," the dialog will create columns for the user and date created and modified with appropriate values for the AutoGen Type property. This option does not appear in the Property Pallette.

Table Implementation Properties

So far, most of the table properties mentioned are independent of the way the table is actually stored in an Oracle database. The only exception is in the Database Design Transformer, where you can optionally specify the name of the database where the table will be stored and the schema that will own the table. Those properties are not listed under the Relational Table Definition for the table however, so you have to look elsewhere in an element called the table implementation.

The association between a table and a database/schema combination forms the basis for a *table implementation,* the way a table is actually stored within a database and installed in a user's schema. This association means that you can create a table that has the same basic definition (the same columns and constraints) but has different implementations in different databases or under different users in the same database. The implementation includes such information as which tablespace the table will reside in and how large it will be (its storage parameters). The table implementation is important when you generate the server DDL because if you run the utility against the table definition, the script will not contain clauses for the tablespace and storage parameters. The table implementation contains these extra pieces of information, and if you run the Generate Database from Server Model utility against those definitions, you will get CREATE TABLE clauses that specify storage and tablespace assignments.

DDT automatically creates one table implementation for each table. You can view table implementations or define new ones in the DB Admin tab of the Navigator (for a specific schema of a specific database). The process for creating a table implementation is the same as usual: select the node and click on the Create toolbar button. The following illustration shows the various implementations nodes, including Table Implementations node in the DB Admin tab. Table implementations are also available in the Distribution tab in the Tables node under a particular Schema node under a particular Database node.

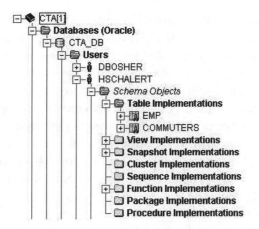

TABLESPACE One table implementation property you fill in is *Tablespace,* which indicates the tablespace this table will be created in. This property relies on tablespace definitions already in the repository, so you need to define the tablespace before you can use it in a table implementation. You do this in the Tablespaces node on the DB Admin tab (under the Storage node of a specific database), as the following illustration shows:

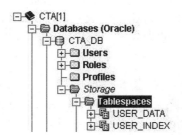

The tablespace definition contains properties that correspond to the SQL statement clauses that apply when creating a tablespace. There are subnodes for Datafiles and Rollback Segments, as those are objects owned by the tablespace. The Generate Database from Server Model utility will produce a CREATE TABLESPACE statement with the appropriate clauses based on the repository definition.

STORAGE DEFINITION The *Storage Definition* property of the table implementation refers to another repository element that you create in the DB Admin tab (a top-level node). This is a repository-only concept that has no physical implementation in the database. It is a way to group together tables or tablespaces with common storage needs. The storage clause of a CREATE TABLE, INDEX, or TABLESPACE statement defines the amount of space that object will take initially and how space will be managed as the object grows. After creating a Storage Definition element, you can attach it to a repository element with the *Storage Definition* property.

The table implementation definition also contains properties for entering storage parameters not covered by the storage definition, like initial transactions (*Init Trans*), maximum transactions (*Max Trans*), *Percent Free*, *Percent Used*, and *Cached.* Typically, values for these properties need to be determined jointly by the application developers, who know how each table will be used and accessed, and the DBAs, who can translate that knowledge into the corresponding storage parameters. There are other books in this series that discuss Oracle database tuning and administration in great depth and will help you make decisions when setting these properties.

Another area where developers and designers will need the assistance of a DBA is database replication. *Replication* involves copying data from one database to another or from one schema to another. Oracle Designer provides elements for snapshots and replication groups that are the database means to this end. The discussion of elements and particular properties requires knowledge of the internal database mechanisms and is beyond the scope of this chapter. As before, employ the assistance of your DBA to help you design the replication needed in your application and look under the Databases node of the Distribution tab for the elements that support this concept.

TIP

*Remember that you can enter a number of definitions for a particular type very quickly with the Fast Create utility. Run this from the **Edit→Fast Create** menu item after selecting an element type in the Navigator. You will be able to enter a number of definitions at once. In most cases, the only property you fill in for this dialog is the* Name, *so you will need to complete the definition later, but this will give you a starting point.*

Table Implementation Property Dialog

The property dialog for the table implementation actually contains more properties than its Property Palette. Figure 14-8 shows the Storage tab page.

The Storage, Data Blocks, and Generation tabs contain properties corresponding to the palette. If you select "Yes" for the snapshot question on the Generation tab, two new tabs will appear, Snapshot Log Storage and Snapshot Log Data Blocks. These also correspond to palette properties. The Security tab allows you to specify access privileges to this table for users and roles (as defined in the repository). This information is only available otherwise on the DB Admin tab in the Granted to Users node under the Table Implementations for a specific user in a specific database.

The Index Storage tab page lets you specify the storage definitions for the indexes on this table. Figure 14-9 shows this tab.

You can specify that the index use default storage definitions or a specific definition by clicking the appropriate button.

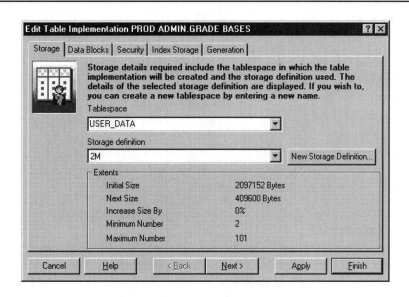

FIGURE 14-8. *Table implementation property dialog*

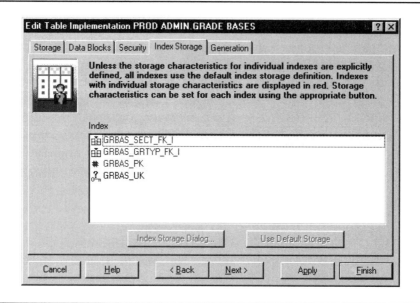

FIGURE 14-9. *Index Storage tab of the table implementation property dialog*

Columns

The column properties contain two sets of information. One set specifies the properties of the column when implemented in the database; these properties affect the DDL CREATE TABLE script produced by the Generate Database from Server Model utility. The other set specifies how the column will act inside an application module; these properties affect the code created by the client code generators.

Basic Properties

The most important properties of the column are: *Name, Datatype, Maximum Length,* and *Optional ?.* These are basic to the column specification in the CREATE TABLE script. Descriptions of some other properties follow. As before, refer to Chapter 29 for discussions on what properties flow from one definition to another and affect the final code generation.

■ *Domain* assigns the domain name to the column. If there are Allowable Values attached to this domain, the column will inherit them, unless it has Allowable Values attached directly to it.

■ *Average Length, Initial Volume,* and *Final Volume* assist in the database sizing report.

■ *Uppercase ?* is "Yes" if modules will convert input and output to uppercase characters.

■ *Default Value* is handy if you want the generator to create a default value clause for the column. This can be a fixed value with a matching datatype, such as ABC or 123, or a pseudocolumn or function, such as USER, SYSDATE, UID, or the USERENV (remember that USERENV requires a parameter, but the others do not). The value will appear as a DEFAULT VALUE clause in the column specification of the CREATE TABLE statement. It will also appear as a default for the bound item based on this column in the client code generated by the Oracle Designer generators.

■ *Sequence* will create code in the generated module or Table API to assign a number from a sequence database object. You need to define the sequence (which includes both a sequence definition and a sequence implementation) before you can use it here.

■ *Complete* is "Yes" if you want to include this column in the CREATE TABLE script.

■ *Sequence in Table* is the sequence in which the columns will be created in the CREATE TABLE script. A common practice is to put the primary key columns first in the list, then the unique key columns, then other mandatory (NOT NULL) columns, foreign key columns, and optional columns. However, partitioning into groups like this can be a lot of effort. Even if you decide not to do that, you should place the primary key columns first as that is a recognized standard. You then have to decide on an order within whatever strategy you use. The simplest is to list all columns in alphabetical order after the primary key column and, if you use the groups, you still need to alphabetize. Alternatively, you can order by something else that makes sense, like functions (for example, all address columns appear in one group).

Allowable Values

Each column in the table can have a set of valid values associated with it in the Allowable Values node under the column or under the domain attached to the column, as shown in the following illustration.

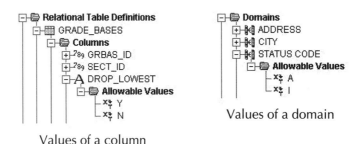

Values of a column   Values of a domain

The advantage of using a domain is that the same domain can be used for multiple columns rather than having to define allowable values for each one.

The Generate Database from Server Model utility will create table-level check constraints to enforce the values when it creates the DDL script for the table. You cannot specify the names of these constraints, but the utility will create a name consisting of AVCON_ (for allowable values constraint) plus the first five characters of the table name plus an underscore (_) plus the name of the column plus an underscore plus a three-digit number starting with 000 for the first constraint on this column (for example, AVCON_ COURS_TITLE_000). If you want to have control over the name used for this check constraint, you can use the Check Constraint node under the table to create a table-level constraint.

Display Properties

As mentioned, a number of other properties also affect the application module based on the column's definition within the table. If you complete the column definitions as fully as possible, you will have less to do when you define the bound items based on these columns for the module. Also, some properties on the column definition do not appear in the bound item definition but still affect the final code. As mentioned before, Chapter 29 details how some of these properties affect the generated code. Here are brief descriptions of some of the display properties:

■ *Display*   Specifies whether this column is displayed in the module. The table may generate key or other column values that the user does not need to see, and you can set the display property to "No" for that type of column. Surrogate primary keys that the ADT creates for tables with no primary keys are not displayed by default.

■ *Display Type*   Specifies which GUI control or datatype is used to show the column value. For example, you can specify an item as a combo box, check box, button, radio group, OCX control, OLE container, or any other control supported by the generator you will be using. The default of null will produce a text item.

■ *Template/Library Object*   Specifies the name of the object in the generator template or object library (for Forms) that will be the basis for creating the item in the module. For example, you might have a standard date item with a KEY-LISTVAL trigger attached to it that pops up a calendar window. The item and its code can be stored in a Forms object library file. If you type in the name of that object for the value of this property, the Forms Generator will copy the properties of the object library object as a basis for creating the item in the form.

■ *Display Sequence*   Specifies the order in which the items will appear in the module. This order may be different from the order in which the columns are arranged in the table. There is no need to assign a display sequence number to a nondisplayed column. This property may be useful if, for example, you want to always place your primary key columns first in the table but want a description column to be displayed first in the module.

CAUTION
If you drag and drop columns in the Navigator to change the order, it will change the order in which they appear in the CREATE TABLE statement. If you want to use a visual interface for rearranging the display order, use the property dialog for the table. This dialog contains a Display tab which you can use to move columns around.

- *Order by Sequence*   Is used only if this column contributes to the sort order or default ORDER BY clause for the table used in the module. For example, if the table is ordered by LAST_NAME as the first sort key and FIRST_NAME as the second sort key, the LAST_NAME column will have a value of 1 for this property and the FIRST_NAME column will use a value of 2.

- *Sort Order*   Is either Ascending or Descending if *Order by Sequence* is specified for this column. If *Order by Sequence* is not specified for the column, this property is meaningless.

- *Descriptor Sequence*   Specifies the order in which columns are used for this table's descriptor. A *descriptor* describes a row in the table to the user. For example, an EMPLOYEES table uses the column called "EMP_ID" to uniquely identify a row but a column called "LAST_NAME" to describe it to the user. The LAST_NAME column is descriptor number 1. If the FIRST_NAME column is also required to identify this row to the user, it would be descriptor number 2. Descriptors are used by the module to form table lookup usages. Placing a number in this column signifies not only the order of the column in the descriptor but also that the column is actually used in the descriptor.

- *AutoGen Type*   Facilitates table-level auditing. For example, you can define a column called USER_CREATED and give it an *AutoGen Type* property value of "Created By." The generators will create the code to load the current user's login name into that column at the proper time. Other *AutoGen Type* property values are "Date Created," "Date Modified," and "Modified By."

  Another *AutoGen Type* value is "Seq in Parent," which assigns the next unique sequence number within the same primary key (parent).

  For example, suppose you have an ORDER table that has a primary key of ORDER_NO. You also have an ORDER_ITEM table that has a primary key of ORDER_NO and LINE_NO. If you define LINE_NO with an *AutoGen Type* property of Seq in Parent, the generator will create the code needed to create a unique number for this column within the same ORDER_NO value (parent). Thus, order number 1 might have line numbers 1, 2, and 3, while order number 2 might have line numbers 1 and 2. Oracle Designer will produce the code to create a new sequential line number for each new line item record. The sequence in parent concept may not be able to handle multiple users updating the same master record at the same time, so if that is a consideration, you should examine and supplement the Table API code that handles the inserts and updates for the sequence within the parent. You might want to consider this update problem when using this property.

NOTE
Many of these properties also appear on the bound item definitions for module components. You define them for the table so the module will take its defaults from these settings. Therefore, if you need to set properties the same way for the same column in all (or most) modules, you can specify these properties in the table definition so you will not need to set them for each module that uses this column. This procedure can save much time and effort and allow you to implement standard ways to handle particular columns.

- *Derivation Expression*   Allows you to provide a source value to the column for denormalization purposes. The value in this property is a SQL expression (from the column list of a SELECT statement) like LAST_DAY(ENROLLMENT_DATE) + 1 or a function call such as cta_inv_date(ENROLLMENT_DATE). The property *Derivation Expression Type* is "SQL Expression" in the first case and "Function Call" in the second case. In addition, you set the *Server Derived* property to "Yes" if you want the database to populate the column value if no value is assigned by the client or "No" if you want the generated client code to populate the column value. Set the *Server Defaulted* property to "Yes" if you want to create server code that provides a default value if no value is supplied by the client. The *Server Defaulted* property should be "No" if the *Server Derived* property is "No."

NOTE
The column properties have a dramatic effect on the generated code. For example, if you forget to define prompts for the column and generate a data entry module from the definition, the form or Web page will appear with field items that have no labels (prompts).

■ *Dynamic List (Soft LOV)* The column and domain windows have a property called *Dynamic List* (called *Soft LOV* in Designer version 1 and still referenced as such in the help system and API documentation). If you set this property to "Yes," the generators use a special reference table, called by default CG_REF_CODES, which Oracle Designer creates and populates from Allowable Values of domains and columns. You can create and populate this table from the DE menu item **Generate→Generate Reference Code Tables**. You can name this table differently using an option in the dialog from the **Options→Generator Options→General** menu item. You cannot change its structure, however, which you may wish to do if you want to age lookup values or set them active or inactive as time goes on. Still, the basic reference table has many uses and is worth your consideration. If you set the *Dynamic List* property to "Yes," the generators will use this table to present a list of values for the column usage. The generators will also create code to validate the value entered in this item based on the reference table.

Column Property Dialog
There is no separate dialog for column properties. If you set up DE to display properties in the dialog interface and choose to view properties for a column, they will be displayed in the table dialog as described earlier.

Domains
Just as domains are useful for keeping attributes consistent, they are also good for keeping columns consistent. When you define columns, you can attach a domain name that supplies the datatype, size, and list of valid values to the column. The valid values can include a range, which can be

useful for validating numbers. For example, you could create a domain called NEGATIVE MONEY that is bound by a high value of 0 and a low value of minus 2 billion. This could be used for accounting double-entry programs that require expenses to be represented as negative numbers.

Chapter 10 contains some tips for using domains, in the discussion of the ER Diagrammer. One tip is to use domains to set the properties for all columns. This approach will make changing the column definitions easier, because you can change a domain and then run the utility as described here to synchronize all columns that have that domain attached to the new property values.

You can create and edit domains in DE as you do with other elements: by selecting the Domains node in the Server Model tab and clicking the Create toolbar button. You can also create and manage domains in RON's Reference Data Definition group.

Update Columns in a Domain Utility

Just as you use a utility in the Analysis phase to update attribute properties from domains that had changed, you can update columns in domains. This utility is available on the DE and RON Utilities menu and is called Update Columns in a Domain. If you change properties for a domain, you can run this utility to synchronize column properties for columns based on that domain. This utility works the same way as its counterpart does for attributes. You select the domain or domains whose columns you want to update in the Navigator window and select **Utilities→Update Columns in a Domain** from the menu. The utility will run and display a message window that disappears when the utility is finished. You can also run this utility by checking the Update columns in domain? check box in the domain property dialog.

You should perform this operation before running the Generate Database from Server Model utility and also before assigning tables and columns to module components. This will ensure that the definitions you use conform to the latest version of the domains.

Domain Property Dialog

The domain property dialog contains three tab pages to define the same properties as just described. Figure 14-10 shows the Name tab of this dialog.

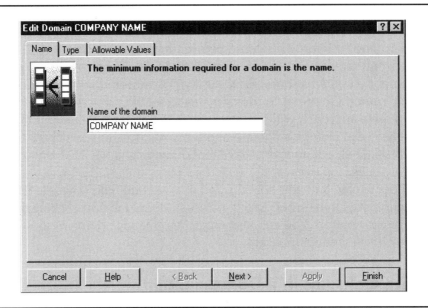

FIGURE 14-10. *Domain property dialog*

Constraints

The properties for each type of constraint—primary, foreign, unique, and check—differ slightly from one another, but all require that you specify the *Name* of the constraint in the database. When you create primary, unique, and foreign key constraints, the name defaults to the table alias with a suffix (_PK for primary key, primary key table alias plus '_FK' for foreign key, and _UK for unique key constraints). Other common properties are *Complete,* if you want to include this constraint with the table DDL statement, and *Validate In,* to indicate where you want the constraint enforced. Server validation places the DDL code in the database, Client validation places the code in each module, and Both places the validation code in both places. You also specify the *Error Message* property for the message that appears if the constraint rules are violated and *Enable,* which may or may not be useful in your environment but specifies whether the constraint is active (enabled) when you first create it.

Primary, Unique, and Foreign Key Constraints

You can create only one primary key constraint, but you can create many unique keys that are equivalent in purpose. The storage properties associated with the primary key in Designer version 1 have moved to the table implementation node in the DB Admin tab (User Object Index Storages mode).

Foreign keys can be defined as mandatory (a value is required in the foreign key column) and transferable (you can update the foreign key value when running an application module). You may define foreign keys that do not have foreign key constraints implemented in the database by setting the *Validate In* property to "Client." The module definition needs the foreign key constraint definition to link the tables or views.

TIP

You can create foreign key constraints by dragging and dropping in the Navigator. Drag the primary key table's node and drop it on the foreign key table's node. This will create a new foreign key in the table that was the target of the drop. You still have to assign columns to this constraint, but the constraint will be created. This drag-and-drop facility can be a problem if you accidentally drop a table on another table when you meant to drop it on a free space to create a diagram. While you can always delete the foreign key you accidentally create, it is best to exercise caution when performing drag and drop with tables. Another tip for using foreign keys in RON: click on the blue arrow to the left of the foreign key name in the Navigator. The selection will jump to the table definition of the table to which the foreign key points.

Check Constraints

As mentioned earlier, the Generate Database from Server Model utility will generate ALTER TABLE ... ADD CONSTRAINT ... CHECK statements to create check constraints for Allowable Values defined under the column or the domain attached to that column. This is basically a check constraint that has no Oracle Designer definition other than the implicit one of the Allowable Values. You can also explicitly define check constraints using the Check Constraints node under the table definition.

When you define a check constraint, use the text area's When/Validation Condition to hold the constraint text. For example, When/Validation Condition text on the GRADES table might be as follows:

L 14-1 START_DATE <= END_DATE

Any statement that you would place in an ALTER TABLE ADD CONSTRAINT statement is valid for this type of text when you define check constraints.

Adding Columns to Constraints

All constraints except for check constraints must be associated with columns. While you can associate a check constraint with a column or columns, it is not necessary for the generated ALTER TABLE syntax. For other constraints, you add columns using the Columns node under the constraint name. Figure 14-11 shows the Create Key Components dialog that displays when you click on Create after selecting the Columns node. In this dialog, you move the columns you wish to associate with the constraint

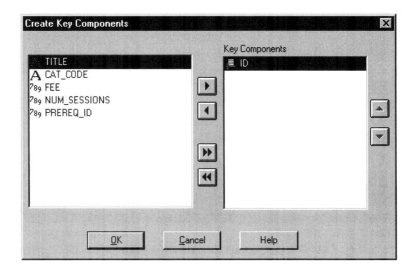

FIGURE 14-11. *Create Key Components dialog*

into the right-hand box by dragging or selecting and clicking the
arrow buttons.

NOTE
*Database procedures called from database
triggers are often a better way to do table-level
validation on column values than using check
constraints. You can easily perform most
validation with a check constraint because it
can use a database function as part of its SQL
expression. However, check constraints are not
a normal place to look for code; if someone
tries to determine where validation is firing for
a column, she or he may not find that code
easily. In addition, you can do operations in a
procedure that might not be possible with a
function that has SQL restrictions. For example,
writing a record to an audit table if validation
failed is straightforward in a database
procedure called by a trigger but may not be
possible using a function in a check constraint.*

Constraint Property Dialogs

Each type of constraint has a slightly different property dialog. Primary keys
and unique keys start with a Mandatory tab, where you specify the columns
in the key and other properties, as Figure 14-12 shows. Both types of
constraints also have a Validation tab to specify the validation level and
message information.

Foreign keys start with the Mandatory tab page too, as Figure 14-13
shows. The Validation tab is similar to the one for the primary and unique
keys. You use the other tabs to specify the foreign key column (or columns)
and cascade rules.

The check constraint property dialog shares a similar Validation tab with
the other constraints, but it has a different first tab, called Name, as Figure
14-14 shows. This specifies the name and the condition properties.

Indexes

In Oracle databases, creating the primary key constraint automatically
creates a unique index. The Database Design Transformer automatically

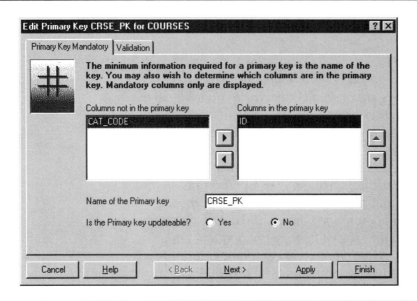

FIGURE 14-12. *Primary key property dialog*

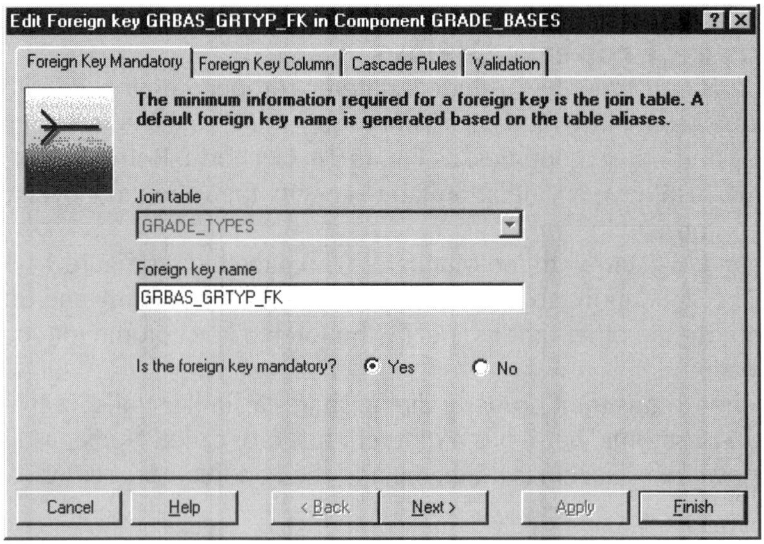

FIGURE 14-13. *Foreign key property dialog*

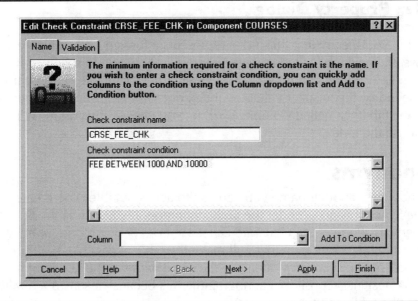

FIGURE 14-14.   *Check constraint property dialog*

creates indexes for all foreign keys. This is the recommended design for Oracle databases to guard against full table locks on the primary key table. If you create foreign key constraints outside the DDT utility, you should add indexes for them as well. The Indexes node is under the table definition, and it contains the expected properties if you are familiar with the CREATE INDEX syntax.

TIP

If you need extra information on what a particular property of a database object is intended for and cannot find the answers in the help system, check the Oracle server documentation, which is optionally installed with the server software. This is a set of HTML files (for Oracle versions 7 or 8) that contains all manuals describing the server. The HTML files are searchable and have sample syntax and descriptions of all clauses. A good document to start with is the "SQL Language Reference," since most of the objects you are creating from repository definitions will produce SQL CREATE syntax.

Index Property Dialog

The index property dialog Name tab lets you specify the name and type of index. If you specify that this index represents a foreign key, as Figure 14-15 shows, the next tab (called Foreign Keys) will allow you to specify which foreign key and the columns associated with that foreign key will be used for the index. If you specify that the index does not represent a foreign key, the next tab (then called Columns) will let you choose the columns that comprise the index.

Synonyms

A synonym is another name you can use to access a table. You create these in the Synonyms node under the table definition. If you define the *Scope* property as "Public," the Generate Database from Server Model utility will create a PUBLIC synonym that will make the table accessible to all users. In practice, public synonyms often use the same name as the table but the Oracle Designer repository cannot handle this because it senses a duplicate name (the table and the synonym).

If you want to create public synonyms for your tables, you can create this script from SQL*Plus by running the following statement as a repository user (or owner). This uses the API views (described in Chapter 28).

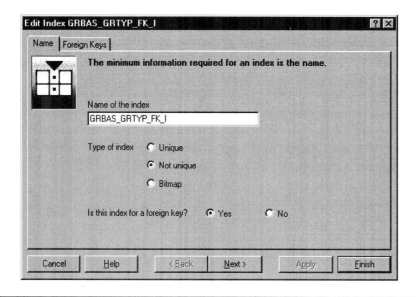

FIGURE 14-15. *Index property dialog*

L 14-2
```
SELECT 'CREATE PUBLIC SYNONYM ' || name || ' FOR owner.' || name || ';'
    FROM ci_table_definitions
  WHERE application_system_owned_by =
        (SELECT id
           FROM ci_application_systems
          WHERE name = '&1'
            AND latest_version_flag = 'Y') ;
```

Substitute the name of the table owner for the word "*owner*" in that statement. If you SPOOL ALL_TAB_SYN.SQL before the SELECT and SPOOL OFF at the end, you will have a script file called ALL_TAB_SYN.SQL with the synonym statements in them. You run this script while logged in as a DBA type account or as the account that owns the tables. You could add to this script if you do not want to create public synonyms for all tables by inserting a subquery to filter the tables to a subset by repository schema definition or database definition.

If you do not want to use public synonyms, you could use the same technique to create a private synonym script that you can run in each user's account. The Generate Database from Server Model utility will create private synonyms only for the owner of the tables. For example, if the CTA_ADMIN schema owned the STUDENTS table and you had created a STU private synonym definition, the generator would create a script that would create the STU synonym only in the CTA_ADMIN account. If you want other users to access the STU synonym, they would need to run a CREATE statement in their accounts after they were granted access to the STUDENTS table. This private synonym script could be generated with a query like the one earlier but without the PUBLIC designation.

Synonym Property Dialog

There is no synonym property dialog. Calling the property dialog for synonyms opens the Property Palette, which has only three properties for *Name*, *Scope*, and *Complete ?*.

Triggers

You define database triggers in the Triggers node under the table definition in the Server Model tab. The main required property is the name, but you need to check the properties that indicate on which operation the trigger will fire (INSERT, UPDATE, DELETE, or a combination of these), as well as the *Level* (row cr statement) and the *Time* (before, after, or instead of). Views must use the INSTEAD OF value, which indicates (for views in Oracle8) that the trigger will execute as a replacement for the DML statement (INSERT, UPDATE, DELETE) that is issued on the view. Fill in the *PL/SQL Definition* property with the name of the trigger logic that you have defined for the trigger. If you have not yet written the trigger logic, leave this blank. When you save the trigger, a PL/SQL definition will be created for you and named the same as the trigger. Triggers can share PL/SQL Definitions, which might be useful if you have common operations done on commonly named columns in different tables.

You define the actual code for the trigger in one of two places on the Server Model tab: you can use either the Trigger Definitions node under the top-level PL/SQL Definitions node or the Trigger Logic node under the Trigger node of the table definition. At this point in the Design stage, you do not need to write all the code for the trigger, but entering comments on what the trigger will do is appropriate design work.

Trigger Names

One suggestion for trigger names is to use the table name (or alias) with a suffix that indicates what kind of trigger it is (B—before, A—after, I—instead of) and which operations it fires on (I—insert, U—update, D—delete). For example, a trigger that fires before an update statement on the STUDENTS table would be called STU_BU. If the trigger fired on both inserts and updates it would be called STU_BIU. A trigger that fires instead of the insert, update, and delete on the STU_ZIP_V view would be called STUZIPV_IIUD. You could also add a designation for the level (S—statement, R—row).

TIP
Another common use for triggers is to populate audit columns (such as DATE_CREATED and USER_CREATED). The Table API, described later in this chapter, can generate code you would normally have to write to maintain audit columns (called "change history columns" in the help system). These are columns for which you specify an AutoGen Type, such as "Created By" and a Server Derived property of "Yes." The Table API will create the code to populate the columns with the values specified by the AutoGen Type.

You can delay the enabling of the trigger by leaving the *Enabled* property as "No." The *Old Alias* and *New Alias* properties specify the *correlation* names used in a row-level trigger to access the old and new values of a column. These default to OLD and NEW, but you can rename them with these properties. The following is a sample piece of logic that uses these correlation names:

L 14-3

```
/*
|| If the application did not supply a student ID, get one from the
|| sequence
*/
IF :new.stu_id IS NULL
THEN
    :new.stu_id := next_stu_id_from_seq;
END IF;
/*
|| If there was a last name change and no name change record was
|| written, create one. There must not be a foreign key
|| between the two tables, or a mutating tables error will occur.
*/
IF :new.last_name != :old.last_name AND NOT
    name_change_record_exists(:new.stu_id, :new.last_name)
THEN
    INSERT INTO student_name_change
    VALUES (:new.stu_id, :new.last_name, sysdate);
END IF;
```

The Columns node allows you to specify the columns that, if changed, will cause the trigger to fire. When you need to create the CREATE TRIGGER scripts, you use the Generate Database from Server Model utility to generate the tables to which the triggers are attached.

Trigger Property Dialog

The trigger property dialog contains the same properties as on the palette. Figure 14-16 shows the Name tab of this dialog.

View and Snapshot Definitions

The discussion thus far has focused on table definitions. Snapshots and views have similar properties. You can even define foreign key constraints

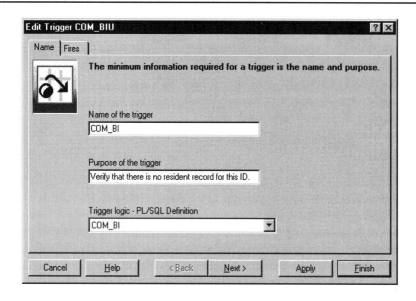

FIGURE 14-16. *Trigger property dialog*

between views (or between views and tables) that will not be implemented in the database but will document a relationship between the definitions. You can specify the enforcement of this type of foreign key constraint on the client side, and Oracle Designer will create validation code in the module it generates. You can also create a foreign key between objects in different databases, but again, the database will not support that code, and you will need to specify client-side validation or enforcement of the foreign key.

The main difference among views, snapshots, and tables is that a view is based on another table or tables. Therefore, for the view, you also need to specify the object (a table, another view, or a snapshot) this view is based on. The Base Tables node lets you enter this information. The Columns node allows you to specify the source column in the base table for each view column. Of course, you have to define the base tables first so that there are base columns to choose from. If the column is based on an expression (calculation or decode, for example), you leave the *Base Column* property blank and fill in the *Derivation Expression* property with the actual calculation or expression (such as UPPER(LAST_NAME)). The WHERE clause for the view statement is defined in the *Where/Validation Condition* property. When you define the base tables and columns in this way, Oracle Designer automatically constructs the text for the *Select Text* property from the base column names.

The view includes a property called *Free Format Select Text*. If this is "Yes," you enter the actual FROM clause as well as the WHERE clause for the view in the Where/Validation Condition text area instead of defining base tables and columns. Also, if the *Free Format Select Text* is checked, you need to specify the column list in the *Select Text* property. This option gives you the flexibility to include columns from any source, although you will not be able to determine the source of the columns as precisely.

Snapshots are separate database objects that are responsible for copying data from one schema or database to another. Snapshot definitions are nearly identical to view definitions, and Oracle Designer treats them similarly. The snapshot implementation (in the same node as the table implementation in the Distribution tab) contains snapshot-specific properties for refresh times and storage parameters.

TIP

If you're familiar with writing SQL VIEW statements using a text editor, it might be tempting to create most or all of your views using free format text. Try to resist this temptation. If you use free format text, the base tables and columns won't be available for doing an impact analysis, in case you have to change any of the underlying tables or columns during the development life cycle. Only use free format text when you have to, for example, to set up a view that is a UNION of information from two or more tables.

View and Snapshot Property Dialogs

The view and snapshot property dialogs are very similar and both display a similar tab page (called Name or Alias) when opened; Figure 14-17 shows the view property dialog. Once you choose tables on the Table Selection tab, a Columns tab will appear, where you can select columns that this view

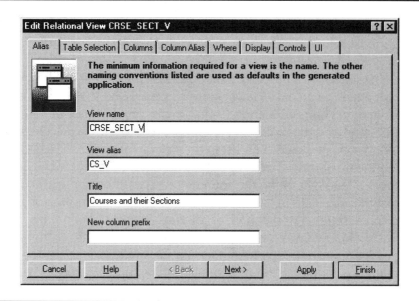

FIGURE 14-17. *View property dialog*

or snapshot uses. Once you select columns, another set of tab pages appears for Column Alias, Where, Display, Controls, and UI, where you specify properties to those categories.

Table API

The Table API (Application Programming Interface) is a component of the Server API, which manages DML operations on a table. The Table API consists of procedures to perform INSERT, UPDATE, DELETE, SELECT, and LOCK operations on the table. These procedures are called *table handlers* and are given full responsibility for all operations on the table.

One part of the Table API is a full set of database triggers that call the table handlers. It is through these triggers that full compliance is achieved. That is, the triggers ensure that no operation can bypass the table handlers. If a client application needs to call the table handlers to perform a similar function to the trigger, it can disable the trigger for that statement by setting a value to a package variable as a flag. In this case, the client code will execute, but the trigger code sees that the flag is set and will not execute the table handler call again.

The Form Generator and WebServer Generator use the Table API somewhat differently. The WebServer Generator requires use of the Table API to perform basic DML. The PL/SQL package generated for each WebServer module makes direct calls to the Table API procedures. Forms can operate independent of the Table API, because it connects to tables with its block mechanisms instead of with PL/SQL code, as does the WebServer module. However, Forms uses the other part of the Server API—the Module Component API (discussed further in Chapter 16) when the block it builds is based on a view or database procedure. The Module Component API calls the Table API to perform the DML operations.

Creating the Table API

You can create the Table API by selecting the table in the Server Model tab and choosing **Generate→Generate Table API** from the menu. This displays a dialog, shown in Figure 14-18.

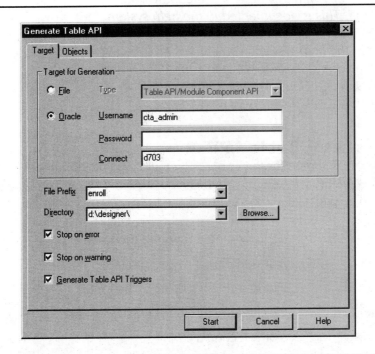

FIGURE 14-18.   *Generate Table API dialog*

This dialog is a variation on the Generate Database from Server Model utility dialog. You can run the utility to generate CREATE scripts into a file by selecting the file target, or you can generate directly into the database by providing login information. You also specify if you want to stop on errors or warnings and whether you want to generate the trigger code. This trigger code is necessary to fully utilize the table handlers for arc relationships. You click Start to run the utility.

When the utility is finished, you can examine and run the files in SQL*Plus, if you chose the file target. If you chose the Oracle target, you can examine the log files produced when SQL*Plus ran automatically using the login you provided.

TIP

*If the package installed by your Table API script does not compile correctly, be sure you have the CG$ERRORS package installed or accessible. The Table API procedures call this package, but it may not be installed into your schema. This is documented in the help system, but you may get the error before you see the note in the help system. You can install it by running the CDSAPER.PKS and CDSAPER.PKB scripts in SQL*Plus from the ORACLE_HOME/ CGENS70/SQL directory.*

What's in the Table API?

The scripts generated for the Table API create a package named CG$*table_name,* where *table_name* is the table for which you created the API. The package always contains the following procedures:

INS	For inserting a row into the table
UPD	For updating a row in the table
DEL	For deleting a row from the table
LCK	For locking a row for update or delete
SLCT	For selecting a row

Each of these (except DEL) takes arguments of two record variables: one is a PL/SQL record that has the same setup as a table record (same columns and datatypes); the other is a PL/SQL record containing one Boolean variable for each column in the table. The latter is the *indicator* variable that signals whether something has changed in that column. For example, if you wanted to update a record, you would load all updated values into the row variable and change the value of the Boolean in the indicator variable so that each changed column would have a value of TRUE. (This is similar to the technique used for the repository API, as described in Chapter 28.)

Other procedures, such as the following, may also be included in the Table API:

VALIDATE_ARC	For validating the arc constraint
VALIDATE_DOMAIN	For validating valid values list based on the domain by checking in the reference codes table
CASCADE_UPDATE	For updating all child tables when an update occurs to this table
DO_DENORM	For providing values to duplicate columns in another table

Such procedures are conditionally generated based on property settings. Other procedures that are available, based on the properties can populate a column derived from a sequence, default values, or from an *AutoGen Type* property, convert values to uppercase, maintain journaling information, and validate all other types of constraints.

Customizing the Table API

In addition to the package, the generator will also create another script containing CREATE statements for triggers that insert, update, delete, and lock in various combinations of statement, row, before, and after. You can supplement the Table API code by adding your own code before or after the generated trigger code. The method for doing this starts with creating a Table/API Trigger Logic element under the table definition, as in the following illustration.

A dialog will appear, in which you select when you want the code to occur (for example, After-Insert-row). Click on the Next button and click on the Add button to provide a repository name (not the procedure name) for the code you are creating. You can then add the actual code in the Logic Editor at that point, or you can click on the node later and invoke the Logic Editor with the Edit Logic toolbar button.

The code you write into the Logic Editor will be inserted into the trigger you specified. For example, if you added to the After-Insert-row trigger, your code would be filled in between the comments after the BEGIN statement in the following example.

L 14-4

```
BEGIN
--  Application_logic Pre-After.Insert.Row <<Start>>
--  Application_logic Pre-After.Insert.Row << End >>
---------- more generated code here
END;
```

Other Database Objects

In a book that you can easily pick up, it's not possible to review every single repository element in depth. This chapter covers the ones that will probably be used in all database development efforts, but you should consult the Oracle Server documentation for more information on other database objects. Table 14-5 lists some of the elements that this chapter has not discussed in depth yet, how they might be used in an application, and where you find them to work on them in the repository. As usual, some elements will appear in more than one tab for ease of use, but the table lists only one location.

Database Object	Usage	Definition Location
Clusters	Clusters physically locate table columns next to one another in the database files to increase performance.	Server Model tab, Cluster Definitions node
Data files	The files that comprise the physical storage for the tablespace data.	DB Admin tab, Datafiles node under Storage node under a particular database
Database	The parent structure for all stored objects. You can generate a CREATE DATABASE command from the Generate Database Administration Objects utility by checking its Generate Create Database statement check box.	DB Admin tab, Databases (Oracle) node and Databases (non-Oracle) node
Database links	A defined way to access objects in another Oracle database.	Distribution tab, Public Database Links node under a particular database
Database object privileges (grants)	Rights to access particular objects such as tables, views, and packages. These are granted to roles and users.	DB Admin tab, Database Object Privileges node under a particular role under a particular database and Database Object Privileges node under the Schema Objects node under a particular user in a particular database

TABLE 14-5. *More Database Objects and Where to Define Them*

Database Object	Usage	Definition Location
Log files	Files used to journal changes for database recovery and archiving purposes.	DB Admin tab, Logfiles node under Storage node under a particular database
Object tables	Tables that implement object types.	Server Model tab, Object Table Definitions node
Object views	Views that allow you to work with relational tables as if they were object tables.	Server Model tab, Object View Definitions node
Oracle collection types	A table of an object type. This is used for the nested tables or VARRAYs.	Server Model tab, Oracle Collection Types node
Oracle object types	A user-defined type consisting of multiple elements. Used to implement other object structures in Oracle8 databases.	Server Model tab, Oracle Object Types node
PL/SQL functions, procedures, and packages	Code stored in the database. These can be linked to each other to form packages.	Server Model tab, PL/SQL Definitions node
Profiles	A database object that sets limits to resources for the database and system.	DB Admin tab, Profiles node under a particular database

TABLE 14-5. *More Database Objects and Where to Define Them* (continued)

Database Object	Usage	Definition Location
Role grants (grants)	Roles can be granted all privileges from another role. This is a shortcut to granting individual objects, because by granting the role you grant all privileges that role owns.	DB Admin tab, Roles Granted node under a particular role under a particular database and Roles Granted node under the Schema Objects node under a particular user in a particular database
Roles	A group of privileges that can be assigned.	DB Admin tab, Roles node under a particular database
Rollback segments	A database object with physical storage requirements that is used for reversing changes before they are committed.	DB Admin tab, Rollback Segments node under Storage node under a particular database
Sequences	A number generator used to create unique values for columns.	Server Model tab, Sequence Definitions node
Snapshot refresh groups	A set of snapshots that are updated (refreshed) together.	Distribution tab, Snapshot Refresh Groups node under a particular database
System privileges (grants)	Rights to perform particular operations such as CREATE TABLE. These are granted to roles and users.	DB Admin tab, System Privileges node under a particular role under a particular database and System Privileges node under the Schema Objects node under a particular user in a particular database

TABLE 14-5.   *More Database Objects and Where to Define Them* (continued)

Database Object	Usage	Definition Location
Tablespaces	The logical grouping of tables that maps to database files in the file system.	DB Admin tab, Tablespaces node under Storage node under a particular database
Users	Accounts for login purposes. Users can own objects and are also referred to as "schemas."	DB Admin tab, Users node under a particular database

TABLE 14-5. *More Database Objects and Where to Define Them* (continued)

Property Palette properties and dialog properties may be slightly different, so it's best to check both when defining the objects. In addition, be sure to look in the implementations areas for physical properties like storage clauses and tablespace assignments. The implementation areas are found in the following places:

■ **Schema Objects node** in the DB Admin tab under a particular user and database, as in the following illustration:

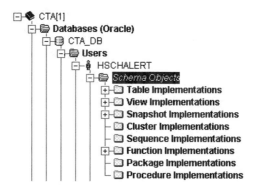

■ **Tables, Views, Snapshots, PL/SQL nodes** in the Distribution tab under a particular schema and database, as in the following illustration:

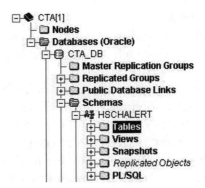

Design Editor Guides

The first part of this chapter discusses details on various database objects that you might define in the database design part of the Design phase. The assumption is that you know which kind of objects you need to create to have a complete database design. However, you may need some help or, at least, some reminders on how to make decisions like whether or not to use snapshots and what objects you really need to specify the database administration aspects of a system design. The Design Editor provides an easier way to fill out the somewhat intricate set of definitions needed to complete a design. It includes two wizards, or guides, called the Server Model Guide and the Database Administration Guide, which cover the basic database objects and the administration objects needed for the design, respectively.

TIP

These guides are worth looking at even if you consider yourself an expert, because they can help point out something you may have forgotten. You can use them as a checklist to review a design that you made outside the guide. Think of them as the interview mode that present-day tax preparation programs provide to step you through your income tax return. These programs take the answers you give to questions they ask and assign them to the correct location. You may know the process well, but having reminders never hurts.

Server Model Guide

The Server Model Guide is available from the Tools menu of the Design Editor. It can help guide you through the steps needed to define the basic database objects.

The first window you see is the one shown in Figure 14-19.

Checking the Track Selection in Navigator check box will let you see the definitions in the Navigator as you work in the guide. The guide is fairly self-explanatory, as is its intention. To get started, you click on the Create/Edit Database button, which displays the list of objects you need to create: Tables and Columns, Domains, Sequences, Advanced Objects, PL/SQL, and Oracle8 Objects. When you click on a button by one of these, you will get either a list of objects of the specified type (as is the case with Tables and Columns) or a list of object types (as is the case with Advanced Objects), which can in turn be expanded. At any time, you can go back to the page you were just on by clicking the left arrow button in the bottom left corner of the window.

If you need help or a reminder on what a particular object is, you can click on the object label to load the help topic for that element type. Also, as you go through the process, you can check your progress or jump to another

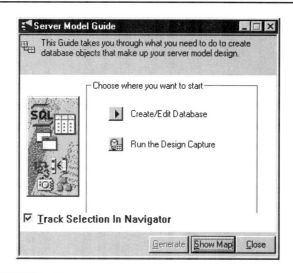

FIGURE 14-19.   *Server Model Guide opening window*

object quickly by clicking the Show Map button. This will display the hierarchy of definitions, shown in Figure 14-20.

You can navigate to another set of definitions by clicking the appropriate button. Dismiss the map by pressing the Hide Map button. The Generate button starts up the Generate Database from Server Model utility so you can create the DDL code. Whenever you see a list of objects on the left, you can edit it or create a new one by clicking the corresponding button. The Edit and Create functions will display the property dialog for the element. If the More button is enabled, you can show the next level of the object definition hierarchy (as shown in the map). Selecting one or more elements from a list on the left side and clicking the Diagram button will open a new diagram with those elements on it.

When you are done with the guide, you click the Close button, but at any time while you are using the guide you can work in the Navigator or any other Design Editor window. Lo and behold—instant database!

Database Administration Guide

The Database Administration Guide works in the same way as the Server Model Guide. You choose it from the Tools menu to start it up. The window shown in Figure 14-21 will appear. The navigation through this guide is much the same as the other guide, although you are manipulating different objects. The map you work handles these different objects, as Figure 14-22 shows.

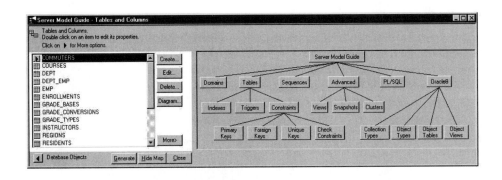

FIGURE 14-20.   *Show Map view of the Server Model Guide*

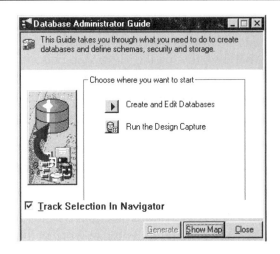

FIGURE 14-21. *Database Administrator Guide opening window*

Logic Editor

The denormalization process you perform in the Database Design stage includes creating summary and derived columns and tables. You can express your design thoughts on these elements as code using the Design Editor's Logic Editor. While you will spend more time using this utility in the

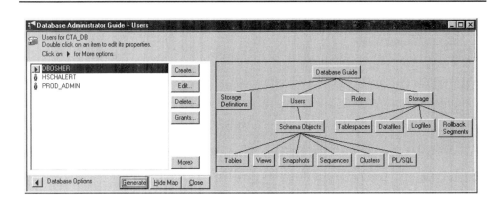

FIGURE 14-22. *Show Map view of the Database Administration Guide*

Application Design stage of Design, it is appropriate to mention it here for the denormalization process. The mechanism that performs the summarization or derivation consists of some PL/SQL code in the server (a trigger perhaps) or application module that calculates or sums values from one table or column to another. This PL/SQL code is stored in a repository node called PL/SQL Definitions in the Server Model tab, although internally the element type is PL/SQL Module and it shares some properties with the module, like *Candidate* and the Planning properties. The Logic Editor allows you to create the PL/SQL definitions that pertain to the Design phase and to fill them in more fully with code during the Build phase.

CAUTION

The Logic Editor makes creating PL/SQL code as easy as dragging and dropping constructs from one window into another. However, the unstated prerequisites for effective use of this tool are an understanding of programming logic and knowledge of how to build PL/SQL programs. The more experience you have with these prerequisites, the more effective you will be in writing PL/SQL definitions. If these subjects are new to you, you should get help with both logic and PL/SQL programming by consulting a knowledgeable person, studying these topics on your own, or pursuing formal training.

The Logic Editor assists you in defining new or editing existing PL/SQL definitions. While you can also use it to edit code from other languages (such as Visual Basic) and store that code as application logic in the repository, its main functionality is geared around PL/SQL.

This utility helps you enter correct PL/SQL syntax and gives you an outline menu of PL/SQL constructs and tools. It provides a built-in syntax checker. Figure 14-23 shows the Logic Editor within the Design Editor window with its main work areas. You can start the editor by selecting a PL/SQL definition in the Navigator and choosing **Edit→Logic** from the menu or clicking on the Edit Logic toolbar button. You can open multiple Logic Editor sessions on multiple PL/SQL definitions in the same Design Editor session. This is handy if you want to cut and paste between definitions.

Outliner

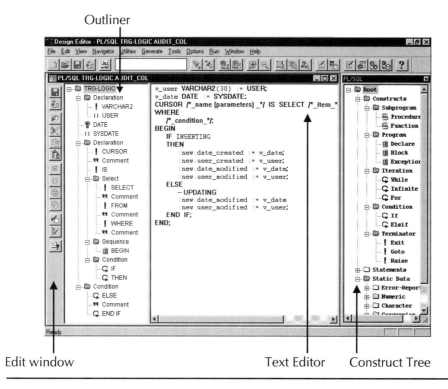

Edit window   Text Editor   Construct Tree

FIGURE 14-23.   *Logic Editor session within the Design Editor*

The triggers you create under the table definitions node are linked to PL/SQL definitions of type Trg-Logic that you can edit directly in this editor. The Generate Database from Server Model utility generates the trigger defined for a table and links the PL/SQL definition attached to the trigger to produce the CREATE TRIGGER code. There are other types of PL/SQL definitions you can create, and there are several methods you can use to define the code for these definitions.

Types of PL/SQL Definitions

When you create a new PL/SQL definition using the Navigator, you specify the *Type* property. There are seven types of PL/SQL definitions that determine what type of server code the Generate Database from Server Model utility will create:

- *Cursor* A SELECT statement that is not a server object by itself but can be contained in the other types. The benefit of the cursor type is that other PL/SQL definitions can share the same cursor definition.

- *Function* Generates a CREATE OR REPLACE FUNCTION statement. A function must have a return value and may be contained in a package or stand alone.

- *Package* Generates a CREATE OR REPLACE PACKAGE (and PACKAGE BODY) statement. A package can contain (or be the parent for) many cursors, functions, and procedures.

- *Procedure* Generates a CREATE OR REPLACE PROCEDURE statement. A procedure may be contained in a package or stand alone.

- *Trg-Logic* Generates a CREATE OR REPLACE TRIGGER statement.

- *Type Body* Flagged as "for internal use only."

- *<null>* Represents unassigned PL/SQL definitions.

Defining Code

When you work in the Logic Editor, you place PL/SQL block code (BEGIN...END) in the Text Editor either by typing it directly or dragging and dropping words and phrases from the Construct Tree area. The Edit window contains the Outliner area, where the Logic Editor shows the basic structure of the program you write in the Text Editor. This outline is arranged in a standard navigator format with nodes you can expand and collapse so you can quickly review the logic. It also allows you to jump to a particular spot by clicking the structure name to move the selection in the text editor to that structure. This feature is implemented by an option called Highlighting, which you can disable in the Logic Editor Options dialog (**Options→Logic Editor Options**).

Typing directly in the Text Editor is the same as typing in any other editor. The Text Editor tries to determine what you are typing and automatically indents each line based on the line above it. The Editor also recognizes keywords that you type and automatically capitalizes them. The automatic indention and keyword recognition are also options you can modify in the Options window. The Text Editor enables the Edit menu items (or standard keypresses) for accessing the cut, copy, and paste functions. Since you can edit more than one definition at a time, these functions allow you to transfer or copy code from one definition to another.

The Construct Tree window provides a drag-and-drop capability for keywords and logic structures. It too has a navigator-style arrangement, so you click a node to expand or collapse it. There is only one Construct Tree window, no matter how many definitions you have opened in different edit areas. The Construct Tree provides a complete summary of all PL/SQL language elements.

TIP

Turn on the icons for the Construct Tree nodes by making that window active and choosing **View→Iconic** *from the menu (or by checking Iconic Display on the* **Options→Logic Editor Options** *dialog). You can show icons for the Outliner area separately using the same methods. The icons give you an idea of the type of word or structure you are manipulating and can give you a quick picture of the logic in your definition.*

Performing a drag-and-drop operation is as easy as finding the words you want in the Construct Tree hierarchy, clicking them, holding down the mouse button as you drag them into the edit area, and releasing the button when the cursor is at the right line of code. This method gives you perfect spelling and structures (IF...THEN...ELSE...END IF) every time, but it may be faster in some cases to just type the words directly if you are used to the syntax.

If you drop a word or construct into the edit area, it will contain a note on what you need to fill in. This note will have the SQL comment symbols /* */ around it so it will not hinder the syntax check.

You can also perform a syntax check to verify that you have typed keywords correctly. Click the Syntax button or choose **Utilities→Check Syntax** from the menu. The syntax checker will review the code and report on errors in the Messages Window like the one shown in the following illustration.

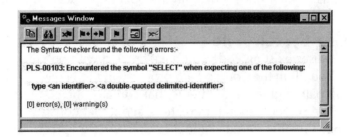

The syntax check checks the code only against repository definitions, not against physical database objects.

Methods of Defining PL/SQL

There are different ways of entering PL/SQL definitions. Since the Generate Database from Server Model utility processes all of them to produce code with the same results, the choice of which one to use is up to you. A brief description of each follows.

Free Format

You can set the property *Free Format Declaration* to "Yes" in the Navigator properties and write the code for the declaration section of the PL/SQL block yourself. In this case, you add the declaration section to the *Package Specification* property. You then fill in the PL/SQL text in the text edit area by typing it, pasting or importing it from another editor, or dragging and dropping constructs from the Construct Tree window. The PL/SQL text you write in the Text Editor shows up in the *PL/SQL Block* property of the definition.

Declarative

If you set the *Free Format Declaration* property to "No" (the default), you do not write code for the declaration section. The variable declaration, data structures (record and table datatypes), parameters, and return datatypes are all stored as separate elements in the repository. This type of detail is handy if you want to control the use of the various elements in your PL/SQL code

and list them on repository reports. The declarative method is well
documented in the help system (look for the topic "Program Data" in the
index), so this chapter does not detail the operations needed for this method.

Operating System File

This method uses existing code you have created with one file per
definition. You fill in the *Source Path* property in the Navigator properties
with the full path and name of the file that contains the complete CREATE
statement. The Server Generator creates a script that consists of comment
lines and one line that executes the file:

L 14-5 ▰▰▰ `@ filename`

The *filename* is the name and directory path you typed in the *Source
Path* field. While the Logic Editor can perform syntax checking with the
other two methods, no checking is performed on operating system files. If
you want to syntax check your PL/SQL, you can define the text and check it
in the Logic Editor. If you then save it by exporting it to a text file, you can
define that text file as the source for your definition.

Choosing a Method

The method you use is determined partially by your comfort with PL/SQL. If
you are comfortable with the language, you will find the free format method
faster and easier. If you need some help with PL/SQL or want to store as
much of the structures and components of your code as possible in the
repository (for reporting or impact analysis purposes, for example), the
declarative method may be more appropriate. If you have an extensive
library of files that you do not wish to move into the repository, the
operating system file method is best. You can also use a combination of all
three. Be careful when using the operating system file method, as you need
the external file in the file system. If you move the file, you have to be sure
to redefine the *Source Path* property in the definition properties.

PL/SQL Definition Properties

The *Implementation Name* property specifies the name you want to use to
create the object in the database. By default this field contains the definition
short name in lowercase. The *Scope* field specifies how this definition is

known if it is in a PL/SQL package. Procedures and functions in packages can have Private scope (known only to the other package functions and procedures) or Public scope (known to any user who is granted access to the package). A third scope choice, Protected, is not documented. The *Return Type (Scalar)* field lets you define the datatype this definition returns if it is a function.

Subnodes
The PL/SQL Definition has a number of nodes where you define or associate other elements with the definition. The subnodes are:

- *Arguments*   Where you define parameters used for input, output, or both.

- *Sub Program Units*   Where you list other program units that this one calls or includes. For example, a package's subprogram units would include all the cursors, procedures, and functions contained in the package.

- *Program Data*   Where you define the variables, constants, and exceptions used in the PL/SQL block.

- *Datastructures*   Where you define the composite datatypes that this block will use: PL/SQL tables, records, and cursors.

- *Synonyms*   Where you define an alternative name for the code.

TIP
Arguments, Program Data, and Datastructures can all use domains that you set up for attributes and columns. This is a good way to work the domains you use as standards into your code.

PL/SQL Implementation Properties
As with other objects that are created in the database, PL/SQL Definitions have implementations that you can find under a particular user in a particular database on the Distribution or DB Admin tab. The *Scope* property in the implementation indicates if this code will be used only

within the current database ("Database") or if it will be used outside the database ("World"), which means that database links and synonyms need to be created for this definition.

Defining Packages

PL/SQL package definitions require some additional considerations as they are potentially made up of many definitions. The important point to remember is that the package specification is one definition by itself, and all the subprograms (cursors, procedures, and functions) are individual definitions that are listed as *Sub Program Units* of the package. This link automatically sets the *Method of Use* property to "INCLUDE." This link also joins the subunits to the specification so the Generate Database from Server Model utility can construct one DDL statement from a number of definitions.

The work you do in the Logic Editor is modularized automatically, because even though you may be working on a large package of PL/SQL units, you have to think of them as individual definitions. Another important point about packages is that you can declare any or all subunits as private—without a calling interface from any outside code—or public—where everyone who has access to the package also has access to the subprogram. A setting of "private" will, in effect, exclude the subunit declaration from the package specification so the subunit becomes available only to the package body.

PL/SQL Composition Node

You can set up and modify the calling (or include) hierarchy in the *PL/SQL Composition* node of the Server Model tab, as shown in the following illustration.

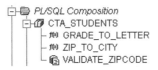

This node works like the Module Network node of the Modules tab (described in the Module Network Viewer section of Chapter 16). You can drag and drop subunits into the package and reorder the package contents by dragging and dropping or selecting Resequence Module Networks from the right-click menu for a subunit.

Changing Options

The Logic Editor Options dialog gives you control over some of the ways the Logic Editor works and looks. Choose **Options→Logic Editor Options** from the menu to display this dialog. There are two tab pages in this dialog:

- *Tree*   Allows you to set the fonts for the Outliner and the Construct Tree

- *Editor*   Allows you to set fonts for the Text Editor and change other aspects like the number of indentation characters and the automatic actions such as Highlighting and Keyword substitution

Another way to set some of these options is from the right-click menu in the Text Editor area or Outliner.

In addition, the View menu contains settings not in the Options dialog for changing what is visible in the Logic Editor session. For example, **View→All Logic**, when checked, displays all application logic (for modules, for example) regardless of the language. For example, if a module was specified as being an Oracle Form Builder module, code assigned to a Visual Basic module would be visible in the Navigator as well under that module. If you uncheck that menu option, only application logic appropriate to the language of the module will be displayed.

Creating PL/SQL Definitions with an External Editor

If you are comfortable with PL/SQL programming and have another favorite editor that is set up in a way to which you are accustomed, you might want to use it to create the PL/SQL text and copy and paste it into the PL/SQL Definition in the Navigator. You can actually automate this process by setting up your favorite editor as the one used in the Property Palette. Choose **Options→Text Editor Options** from the menu to show the Text Editor dialog, where you can set up your editor to be the ASCII Editor. After you display the Property Palette for a particular PL/SQL Definition, you can select the *PL/SQL Block* (or *Package Specification*) property and click the

Ascii Editor button on the toolbar. Your editor will be invoked and loaded with the text in the selected property.

Creating PL/SQL Definitions with the Capture Design of Server Model Utility

You can also create PL/SQL definitions the hard way. That is, you can create the code with a text editor and run it in the database to create the object. You can then run the Capture Design of Server Model from Database utility to create repository definitions for the code using the free format text method. The benefit of this approach is that if you have a good working knowledge of PL/SQL and are accustomed to the manual coding method, it will put the code you write in the correct place in the repository. In addition, if you are accustomed to working with an editor, such as Oracle Developer's Procedure Builder, you probably save code to the database directly from these editors. The syntax check occurs when you run the script in the database, so the code you capture into the repository should be bug free.

Using the design capture method, you will want to examine the definitions, change names, and possibly convert to the declarative method after the utility runs, but you will get a starting point by running the utility. The biggest drawback to this method is that you have to create all of the data objects that the code uses, which takes up additional storage space in the database. Another alternative is to capture the design from a CREATE script file that you have written, but unless you have tested the code by running the script against a database, you will not be assured that the code will be able to be reinstalled in the database.

Designing Objects with Oracle Designer

In previous versions, Oracle Designer has provided very strong support for design of relational databases. This version of the product extends this capability into the world of objects. It allows you to model objects you will deploy with an Oracle8 object-relational database. You can also generate DDL scripts for the object database structures based on your repository design definitions.

Object support manifests in two Oracle Designer tools: the Object Database Designer (ODD) and the Design Editor. These two tools contain specific features to assist you in completely and correctly defining the structures you need to implement an object design. The RON also contains access to element definitions that are object-based, but the methods you use to complete or review the definitions are the same as they are for other element types. Therefore, the following discussion focuses on the object support in ODD and DE.

The Subject Was Objects

It is not an objective of this book to explain object modeling and design for Oracle8, as there is another book in this series (*Oracle8 Design Using UML Object Modeling*) that fully explores that topic. It is useful, however, to put object concepts in context of the Oracle Designer work you do in the database design part of the Design phase. The concept of objects, at least in its current object-relational incarnation in Oracle8, closely parallels the extensions that most IS professionals have used over the years in their relational databases. Oracle has codified these concepts and integrated them into the Oracle8 database. This codification will guide the way systems are developed and implemented with the Oracle8 database.

You can decide to take advantage of the benefits of objects at many different levels. If you do decide to use object concepts, there will be a transition period while you learn the new language and techniques. However, your systems developed during this transition period do not need to demonstrate full usage of object concepts because the database still fully supports relational design. Moreover, you still need all the sound system development practices, like the CADM method this book describes and that many have developed over the years. Objects do not eliminate, or even lessen, the need for carefully planned software engineering.

The power and benefit of using objects is that they can more closely match the business entities that the users know. If you use objects for modeling and implementing the business area, you will find that those objects can closely parallel the actual business elements that you are modeling.

A simple example is the business object for Invoice. In relational design, this business entity exists as two entities: the invoice header and invoice line items. You would, no doubt, model this with two tables: INVOICES and INVOICE_LINES. There would be a foreign key in INVOICE_LINES that referenced the primary key in INVOICES. The problem is that this two-entity system is really only one business object and users are not accustomed to thinking about it as two things.

In object modeling, you can define a single table, INVOICES, which includes columns for what was the invoice header in the relational design. You would also define an *object type,* a template for objects you will create later, called Invoice Items. You then include a column that has a datatype based on Invoice Items. This approach allows you to represent with a single table a single business item that may have many "rows." Table 14-6 shows the Oracle8 syntax for implementing this table.

This example uses the *nested tables* approach to storing multiple rows with a single row. The DDL creates another table (INV_LINES) that you name in the statement, but the references to that table are internally maintained and you can treat the INVOICES table as a single entity. There are variations on this technique such as REFs, VARRAYs, and Object Views, but the definition of an object is the same for all.

Step	DDL Code

Define an object type	`CREATE TYPE line_item AS OBJECT (`
	`   Item_no   NUMBER(5),`
	`   Quantity NUMBER,`
	`   Price     NUMBER(10,2)) ;`

Define a table type based on the object type	`CREATE TYPE item_table` `AS TABLE OF line_item ;`

Define a table with scalar types and the table of object types	`CREATE TABLE invoices (`
	`   inv_no    NUMBER(8),`
	`   inv_date  DATE,`
	`   pay_date  DATE,`
	`   inv_items item_table)`
	`NESTED TABLE inv_items`
	`STORE AS inv_lines ;`

TABLE 14-6. *Sample Use of an Object Type*

This object type contains *attributes,* also called data members, which are properties that each represent an atomic piece of information for that object type. In the Invoice type example, the attributes would be item_no, quantity, and price. The object type is a template for objects you will create later. It is considered a *user-defined datatype* that, in most cases, includes multiple scalar (individual) attributes each with its own datatype.

The other important part of the object type is the operation that is an abstraction of the behavior of the object type. This translates to a method when the object type becomes instantiated as an object.

Additional Object Terms and Object Element Types

Before taking a look at how Oracle Designer supports object design and generation, we need to define some terms that the tools use to refer to objects. If you are familiar with these terms, you will be better able to make decisions when filling out definitions. These terms, which include some element types found in Oracle Designer, appear alphabetically in the following list.

- **C++ Class Sets**   A group of object types that you generate into a run-time context class. *A run-time context* class defines the interface between generated classes and database tables.

- **C++ Source Files**   Files containing code that the C++ Generator creates.

- **Collection Types**   User-defined types that are tables of object types. In Table 14-6 a collection type called line_item was created as a table of line_item (an object). The collection type can be used for an object that contains a number of records.

- **Generalization**   The association of a subtype to its supertype. This is represented on the type diagram as an arrow from the subtype to the supertype with the arrow head on the supertype. This is one view of the association from the standpoint of the subtype. A specialization looks at the same association in the other direction. Each subtype may only have one supertype generalization.

- **Method**   An implementation of an operation in Oracle8 as a stored PL/SQL function or procedure. It could also be implemented as C++ code stored in a file.

■ **Object** Instantiation of a type. For example, you could have a user-defined type called Student that contains attributes for First Name, Last Name, Address, and Enrollments. An object could contain another object, since you can use an object type to define an attribute of an object.

■ **Object Tables** Tables created by designating the object type alone. An undeclared and automatically maintained object identifier serves as the primary key for this table. A sample declaration follows using the object type line_item, as in Table 14-6:

L 14-6 `CREATE TABLE items OF line_item ;`

■ **Object Types** One form of user-defined datatype in Oracle8. They consist of multiple data members that may be scalar or user-defined (object) datatypes. If you define a column in a table using an object type, that column will be able to store discrete information for each of its members. You can specify that an object type is an interface object type, which is a collection of operations. If you create specializations from this object type, those object types can perform the operations in the interface object type.

■ **Object Views** Allow you to work with relational tables as if they were object tables. This allows you to take advantage of the benefits of object tables without converting existing relational tables.

■ **Operations** Abstractions of an object type's behavior. They represent code (methods) in the object.

■ **Packages** Groups of type definitions that you define as an organizational tool. You can put both object types and value types in the package. You can only put a type in one package.

■ **Server Model** The physical layer for object types, tables, and views. The Server Model tab in ODD and DE represents the elements from which you create database objects. The Server Model Diagram displays these elements graphically. You can transform the Type Model to a Server Model if needed.

■ **Specialization** The association of a supertype to its subtype. This is represented on the type diagram as an arrow from the subtype to the supertype with the arrowhead on the supertype. This is one view of the association from the standpoint of the supertype. A generalization looks at the same association in the other direction. Each supertype may have more than one specialization.

- **Type**   The high-level abstraction of entities in the business. There are two different types that are of interest to your work in Oracle Designer: Object Types and Value Types.

- **Type Models**   Allow you to define object types using UML concepts. The Type Model tab of the ODD Navigator is where you view the definitions for these object types and other object-based elements. The Type Diagram displays the Type Model objects and their relationships.

- **Unified Modeling Language (UML)**   A standard system of declarations used to describe a design that includes object concepts. UML includes various diagrams to represent the objects, their components, and relationships. The ODD Type Diagram implements a subset of UML and allows you to model the types you will use to define relational tables.

- **User-Defined Datatype**   An Oracle8 datatype other than the built-in datatypes provided by the Oracle database such as VARCHAR2, NUMBER, DATE, and LONG. User-defined datatypes can be object types or collection types. You use user-defined datatypes in the same way you use the built-in datatypes—by defining columns in tables (or objects) with their type.

- **Value Types**   Used to type attributes in object types. There is a set of predefined value types, but you can add your own and associate them with the predefined types. The value type is like a domain for object type attributes.

Object Database Designer

Object Database Designer (ODD) is included with Oracle Designer version 2.1 and installed using a separate installation CD. If you have the Oracle Designer repository running without ODD, you only need to install the client software to start running ODD. You use ODD as yet another repository tool to manipulate definitions in the repository that will document and provide DDL code for an Oracle8 implementation. You can define object types and Oracle8 objects using a repository installed in Oracle7, but you can only install those objects into an Oracle8 database with the Objects option installed.

Object Database Designer could easily have been called "Design Editor for Objects," as it presents the same interface as the Design Editor and accesses the same repository. There is much overlap between DE and ODD, because you can use both to manipulate Oracle8 table and object definitions. ODD is distinguishable from DE and other Oracle Designer tools in its ability to use UML to diagram the object types that you use to represent database objects. It uses a subset of the industry-standard UML to represent object types and their associations. The subset it uses is that required to support the design and implementation of a database persistent store (in other words, Oracle8 objects) and to implement a C++ class library which is the programming interface onto that store.

As you work in ODD, keep in mind that there is a distinction throughout Oracle Designer tools between UML modeling and traditional server modeling. In the case of ODD, the UML definitions are stored in the Type Model and the server definitions in the Server Model. While you can use the Type Model objects for analysis, the focus in this modeler is towards designing object types and objects for the Oracle8 database.

Therefore, it is best to think of the Type Model and Server Model as supporting different types of users. The Type Model is best for analysts and designers who know about the physical database objects and want to use the enhanced features of UML to model the object types used in the system. It is also good for those who want to represent their data structures in a more abstract, object-oriented, way. In addition, if you need to generate C++ code, you will create definitions in the Type Model as the source for this generator.

The Server Model is best for those who don't care about the enhanced definitions possible with UML but still want to be able to diagram objects in the database. It represents the physical mapping to the database in a more direct way than the Type Model. While you do not need to use the Server Model to create database objects, as you can also do this directly from the Type Model, the Server Model gives you more control over the database-related properties of the generated objects.

ODD offers a number of utilities that you can use to transform definitions from one model to another as shown in Figure 14-24. These utilities are discussed in the following sections.

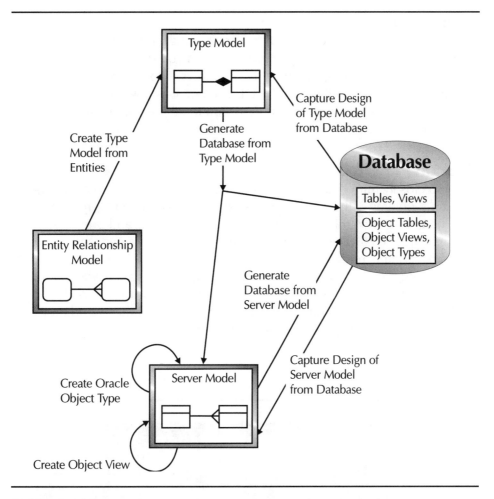

FIGURE 14-24. *Object Database Designer transformation utilities*

TIP
There is no utility to create Type Model definitions from Server Model definitions, but you can create DDL scripts from the Server Model using the Generate Database from Server Model utility. You can then use these DDL scripts as a source for the Capture Design of Type Model from Database. This will effectively create Type Model definitions from objects in the Server Model.

Running ODD

You start ODD using the Object Database Designer shortcut in the Start menu's Object Database Designer group. When you run this shortcut, the opening window appears, as Figure 14-25 shows. The choices in this window parallel closely those in the DE opening window. In fact, this tool contains the same Server Model and DB Admin tab pages. The additional modeling area is the Type Model, where you define the types.

Working in ODD

ODD so closely mirrors the workings of the Design Editor that you should have no problems with its standard operations—if you need to, refer to the operations described for the Design Editor in Chapter 12 and previously in this chapter. The Navigator, Property Palette, property dialogs, and Server Model Diagram windows work the same way.

Preferences include those for the two generators that are unique to this tool: the C++ Generator and the Generate Database from Type Model utility. There are a small number preferences for each of these, and they are arranged into two categories: General and Naming.

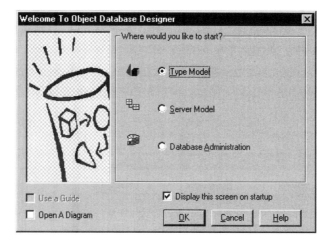

FIGURE 14-25.   *Object Database Designer opening window*

A number of property dialogs are tailored specifically to the object elements. Figure 14-26 shows one for the Oracle Collection Type element.

As with the property dialogs in the Design Editor, if you are familiar with the concepts of what you are trying to create, the Property Palette will probably be a faster method of entering the details about an element.

CAUTION

Drag and drop may not act the way you expect it to work. For example, if you drag and drop an object type into the Generalizations node of another type, it will create a Specialization association, not a Generalization association. It is possible, however, to click on the Generalizations node and press the Create toolbar button to pick the type you want to associate.

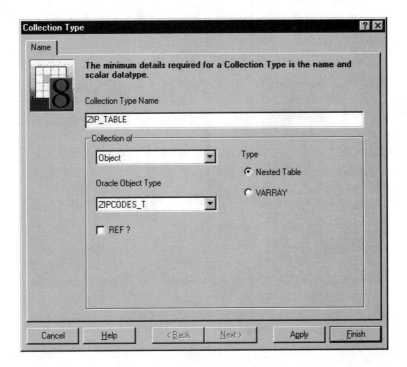

FIGURE 14-26. *Object Collection type element property dialog*

Objects in the Server Model Diagram

The Server Model Diagram has a set of toolbar buttons on the right side of its window for creating the object type and the links to other object types. In this version, you cannot diagram Oracle Collection Types, Object Table Definitions, or Object View Definitions. There are various forms of links to choose from: Embedded Link, Ref Link, Embedded Collection Link, and Collection of Refs Link. You choose one of these based on your needs for how the link will be implemented. Since the objects in the Server Model will translate into the physical database objects, this decision must be based on knowledge of the object features of Oracle8.

Type Diagram

The Type Diagram has a similar objective to the Server Model Diagram: to diagrammatically represent elements in the repository. In this case, though, the elements you model are abstracted from the physical layer. The following illustration shows some of the symbols for objects you create and modify in the Type Diagram.

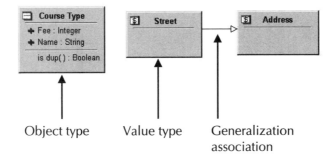

C++ Generator

The C++ Generator creates client code from the definitions in this tool. There are a number of well-defined and well-documented steps you go through to complete this process. Figure 14-27 shows a help system flowchart of the steps you perform to create the C++ class code. You can reach this topic from the "Where am I?" button in the topics that discuss the C++ generator or from the help Contents page "Generating and using C++ classes - About C++ Generation" topic.

Essentially, the generator creates C++ class files that you link with the ol8.lib and oci804.lib (installed into the ORACLE_HOME/cgenc20/lib/msvc50 directory). This combination allows your C++ programs to access database objects as it does other C++ classes. This eases the burden of C++

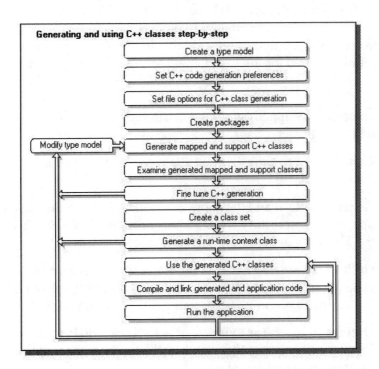

FIGURE 14-27. *Help system topic on creating C++ classes*

programming so you can concentrate on the front-end application and not worry about the database access. For example, as a C++ programmer, you normally have to worry about the mechanisms for coding an INSERT statement to the database. This SQL statement does not translate well into an object-oriented programming language, but, with the generated C++ classes, all you need to do is create an object of the desired class to accomplish this insert. Class manipulation is made easier because of the generated classes.

The C++ Generator uses the Type Model definitions to create a class for each type in the model. The generator creates two forms of classes: mapped classes and support classes. A mapped class has a direct association to a type. A support class is not tied directly to a type but provides ways, like collections and references, to manipulate objects. The generator creates class members from the attributes, operations, and associations of the type. The files it creates are implementation files (with a .cpp extension) and definition code (with a .h extension). The generator also creates run-time context classes for sets of types. These classes provide the interface between the generated classes and the database objects.

There are a number of utilities available in the menu that work with the definitions needed for the C++ Generator. Descriptions of some of these follow:

- **Generate→Mapped/Support Classes** runs the generator itself. This will generate the class for each type as described.

- **Generate→Run-time Context Class** creates the class files you need for the interface.

- **Generate→Re-scan Files** looks at the class code in the files and updates the repository with any locations that have changed since the files were generated.

- **Utilities→Validate** checks that the type model is complete for generating C++ code. You can also run this utility to check if the server model is complete for database DDL generation.

- **Options→Generator Options→C++** shows a dialog where you specify details on the file names and how the code will be partitioned or combined into files.

Generate Database from Type Model Utility

You can create Server Model definitions such as Oracle Object Types and Oracle Table Definitions using the menu option **Generate→Generate Database from Type Model**. The Target tab of the dialog is shown in Figure 14-28. This utility will create an Oracle8 object from a Type Model definition and link the server object to the type. You can implement this in three ways: select Create DDL Files Only to create files that contain the CREATE statements for the database structures; select Create on Database to create the DDL files and run them in the Oracle8 database; or select Repository held Server Model to copy the definitions from the Type Model area to the Server Model area and create Oracle8 definitions (but no DDL scripts). If you choose the Repository held Server Model option, you can

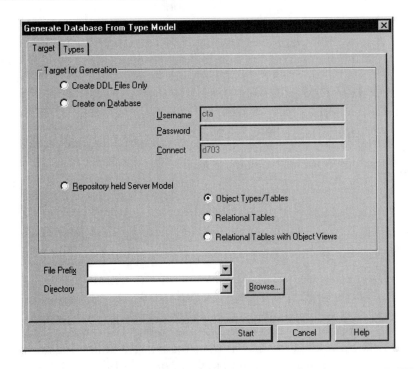

FIGURE 14-28. *Generate Database From Type Model dialog*

specify that you want to generate definitions for Object Types and Tables, Relational Tables, or Relational Tables with Object Views.

After choosing the objects on the Types tab page, you click the Start button. Depending on which target you choose for the generation, the utility will finish with the Messages Window or a dialog asking what you want to do next.

If you choose to generate Server Model definitions from the Type Model, an association is created between that Server Model and the Type Model. This association indicates to the repository that you have transformed the Type Model and you will not be able to generate DDL from it. If you want to remove the association for the entire Type Model, choose **Utilities→Remove Generated Server Model** from the menu. If you want to remove the association from only one Type Model definition, select it and choose **Utilities→Remove Server Model Mapping** from the menu.

These mappings also appear in RON under the Transformation Mapping Sets element in the Type Modeling group. This element stores the *Target Level* and *Source Level* for the mapping. You can create and delete mappings in this node. You can also make comments on existing mappings. The possible values for the *Target Level* and *Source Level* are: Abstract Type Model, Database Design, Object Database Design, and Relational Database Design. Each mapping consists of specific Mapping Elements that store the details of which elements were transformed.

These Server Model Oracle8 definitions correspond on a one-to-one basis with structures that you can create in the database. For example, if you have a Student object type (in the Type Model tab) that you want to create in the database, you can create the DDL to implement this type using the Create Oracle Object Type utility. Alternatively, you can run the Generate Database From Type Model utility to create a Student Oracle8 Object Type in the Server Model.

Other Menu and Toolbar Functions

The ODD menu contains many of the same options as the Design Editor menu. It adds options for object and C++ elements but does not provide options for the module elements as does the DE. The following are some utilities that you run from the menu to work on the object definitions:

■ **Generate→Capture Design of→Server Model from Database** loads definitions into the Server Model area of the repository from

structures that already exist in the database. This works the same
way as it does in the Design Editor.

■ **Generate→Capture Design of→Type Model from Database** loads
   definitions of relational tables and object types into the Object Type
   node in the Type Model. The following illustration shows the top
   part of the Objects tab page of this utility. This is useful if you want
   to represent tables in the database with a UML diagram.

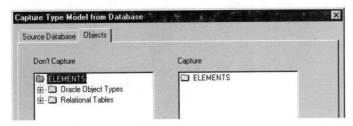

■ **Generate→Generate Database from Server Model** creates DDL
   scripts that you use to install database objects (relational or
   object-relational). It is the same utility that you use in the Design
   Editor.

■ **Options→Generator Options→Database** allows you to specify
   whether you want indexes, integrity constraints, and comments in
   addition to the objects you select for the Generate Database from
   Server Model utility. There is a check box for each of these objects
   as well as check boxes for generating triggers, valid value
   constraints, and grants and synonyms. These are a subset of the
   options you can specify in the Design Editor for the Generate
   Database from Server Model utility.

■ **Utilities→Create Oracle Object Type**, shown in Figure 14-29,
   creates an element under the Oracle Object Types node in the
   Server Model from an element in the Relational Table (or View)
   Definitions node. The resulting type definition includes attributes
   based on the columns in the table. The utility appends a _T suffix to
   the name of the table. This is useful if you want to transition an
   existing table to become an object type, since it copies the structure
   completely. Therefore, you have a starting point for building the
   object type.

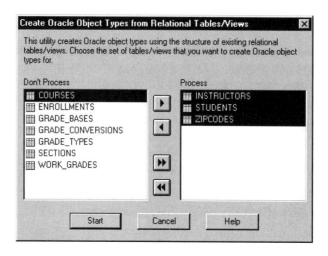

FIGURE 14-29. *Create Oracle Object Type dialog*

- **Utilities→Create Object View** creates object views in the Server Model from Oracle Object Types. This essentially copies the Oracle Object Type definition to an object view definition and copies the attributes into the *Select Text* property in the object view definition. The object view will have the name of the type with a _V suffix. The *Free Format Select Text* property will be set to "Yes" and the *Select Text* will have the column names list corresponding to the attributes of the type.

- **Utilities→Create Type Model from Entities** creates type model definitions from the entities and attributes in the same application system. Entities copy to object types and entity attributes copy to object type attributes. The utility creates value types from attribute allowable values and specializations or generalizations from entity relationships. This utility is useful if you need to use existing models you created for C++ generation in an earlier version of Oracle Designer. It is also useful if you want to create a type model from an entity model on a one-time basis.

■ **Utilities→Type Model Report** creates a set of HTML files into a directory that you specify. These HTML files contain the values of all properties and descriptions for elements in the Type Model. The files are tied together with hypertext links to make it easy to drill in and out of details for the element definitions.

■ **View→All Members** shows the all details of an Object Type under one node called "All Members." This is a check menu item like many of its companions in the View menu, and if it is unchecked, the details of an object type (in the Type Model) will consist of Attributes, Operations, and Association roles. The All Members view is useful if you want to see the entire list of details for that type, for example, if you are implementing this with a C++ class that has class members for the details. The different forms of members have different icons so you can distinguish them in the All Members list. In addition, if you create a new member while showing the All Members list, a dialog appears where you choose which member you are creating.

TIP
You can (with version 2.1 release 20) show a hidden Distribution model area that has the same elements as it does in the Design Editor. This is not available from the menu or tab display, but if you right-click on a tab (not on in the Navigator box below it), you will see an option called Distribution and Replication. Choosing this option will display the same element nodes as in the Design Editor's Distribution tab.

Design Editor Object Support

DE also supports object modeling to the extent of modeling the object elements in a standard Server Model Diagram and supplying their properties in the Property Palette or property dialogs. The Server Model Diagram as described earlier is the same in both tools. The DE menu also contains some of the same options needed for the object area of the Server Model. How do you choose which tool to use? If you are working with the Design Editor because you need to work with modules and all you want to do is define the Oracle8 structures that support object concepts, you can stick with the Design Editor. If you need to generate C++ code or want to create type definitions and diagram them with UML, then ODD is your tool of choice.

Database Navigator

The Design Editor contains a utility that allows you to browse and manipulate the online database. You can run this utility by selecting **Tools→Database Navigator** from the menu. After you provide login details for an Oracle or ODBC database, the window shown in Figure 14-30 will appear.

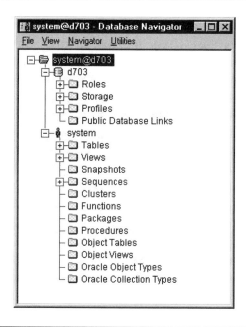

FIGURE 14-30. *Database Navigator window*

On the surface, this is a standard navigator. You expand and contract the nodes the same way as other navigators. The difference between it and the Oracle Designer navigators is that this one browses actual database objects instead of just the repository definitions. Once a particular database object is visible, you can select it and choose **View→Properties** from the menu. A dialog will open up, showing the properties of that element, as Figure 14-31 shows. If a property consists of multiple lines of text, you can select the property and click the Text button to display the text, such as trigger code or procedure code, in another window.

The Database Navigator is a separate window, and you can open up more than one at the same time by selecting **Tools→Database Navigator** from the menu and filling in different logins. This allows you to view the objects owned by two or more users side by side.

You can run the Generate Database from Server Model utility by dragging and dropping definitions from the Design Editor Navigator into the

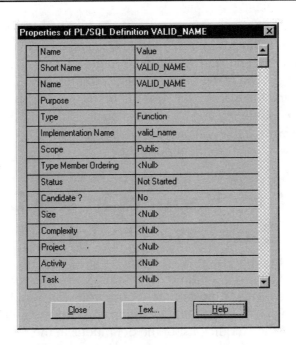

FIGURE 14-31. *Database object properties*

Database Navigator. This will open the Messages Window and run the utility to create the DDL from the elements that you dragged in. The generator is run in the mode that connects to the database (as described in Chapter 16) so you will get a message when it is done asking what you want to do next.

At that point, you can show the DDL scripts that were created, look at the reconciliation report that compares the repository with the online database, or execute the DDL scripts to create the objects. If you decide to create the objects, the generator will run the scripts in the user's account into which you dropped the objects. You will have to exit and reload the Database Navigator if you want to see the new objects.

Another utility you can run from the Database Navigator is the Capture Design of Server Model From Database utility. This is available from the **Utilities→Capture Design** menu item. This utility works the same way here as described in Chapter 8, but you do not need to log into the database because you are already connected when you are in the Database Navigator.

TIP

An alternative way to run the Capture Design of Server Model From Database utility is to drop a definition from the Database Navigator into the Design Editor Navigator. This runs the utility without an opening dialog and gives you a chance to browse the outcome before saving the changes it makes to the repository.

Repository Reports in the Design Phase: Database Design

You may want to run Repository Reports in this part of the Design phase to see the detailed table and column definitions. The Server Model Definition group of reports contains most of the reports you will want to run at this point in the life cycle. The *Table Definition* and *Column Definition* reports are handy for getting a quick list of the definitions in the repository. There are corresponding reports for views, snapshots, and most other database objects as well. The *Invalid Database Objects Quality Control* report lists database objects that are named with reserved Oracle words and Oracle7 database objects that are not in an Oracle 7 database. There is also an Oracle Type Definition report that shows object types and collection types.

There is a report in the Quality group called *Complete Status Quality Control* that lists database objects and problems that may exist as well as how complete their definitions are. This is appropriate at this stage of Design so you can get an idea of the completeness of database object definitions.

The Database and Network Design group also contains reports that apply to the objects you define in this phase. An interesting report (if you have filled in table volume information) is *Database Table and Index Size Estimates*, which provides storage requirement estimates for individual tables and indexes as well as a total size for these tables and indexes. If you set the value of the Include Help parameter to "Yes", the report will also include the formulae used for calculating the sizes. This group also contains reports on database administration elements like users, roles, and storage definitions.

CHAPTER
15

Design—Application Design

Fill in both sides of the application completely. Make no marks in the area labeled "For Office Use Only." Be sure to enclose your check with the application.

t this point in the system development life cycle, you have developed the basic database design and application storyboards. Upon completion of the Application Design phase of the Design phase, you will also have finalized the database design and will be prepared to build the database and applications.

Overview of Application Design

At the simplest level, application design is the design of software, including the creation of structures that address modules, programs, procedures, navigation, internal controls, and security.

Application design is where you finalize column level usages for each module. In addition to preparing the modules for generation, a major benefit for doing this is to validate that the database design was completed correctly. The conceptual application design was created in the Pre-Design phase. Then in the database design part of the Design phase, you built the best database possible using the logical ERD and the conceptual application design. Now in the Application Design portion of the Design phase, you will fully map the modules to the database. This will allow you to validate the database. You will be able to identify missed columns as well as extraneous columns not needed by the modules.

The reason for performing this mapping step in the CADM process before building the database is not just for the conceptual clarity of designing the system before building it. You cannot be sure that the database design is correct until you have fully mapped the columns to the modules. Therefore, not only does this mapping play a major role in the design of the applications, but it also validates the accuracy of the database design.

Complete the specifications for the modules using the following steps:

1. Completely map each module to the database at the column level.

2. Tune and complete the database design. At this point in the process, the database moves into the Build phase while the application design is being completed.

3. Refine and finalize the design book.

In parallel with completing the detailed module specifications using the previous steps, the application design phase must also include a study of security exposures evident in the proposed system and measures appropriate to reduce these exposures. Implementing some of these measures may entail changes to the module and/or database design. Such changes, of course, need to be incorporated into the design book.

Deliverables

The major deliverable for the application design phase is the finalized design book, including the complete and detailed module specifications from the Oracle Designer repository and first-cut generation to support the full screen layouts. All that has not been done at this point is the complex coding for the modules. Menus and Navigation are fully specified during application design. All of the navigation code to move from one screen to another must be implemented so that the full look and feel of the system design can be tested. PL/SQL packages must be specified, although they do not need to be written at this point.

Performing Column-Level Mapping of Applications

At this point, you need to return to the CRUD matrix. Each column needs to be carefully mapped to the modules. Recall that up to now, mapping has been performed only at the entity level. Now you must perform mapping at the finest level of detail to completely specify the interaction of the modules with the database. This is done by reviewing the conceptual design of the modules and determining how the modules will interact with each column in the database. This is a complex and tedious job, so quality control on this task is important. The mapping itself can be done by rank-and-file designers, but the work should be reviewed by senior team members.

View Definitions

The design of the modules cannot be created module by module. You need to look at the modules as a group, using views where appropriate. One of the limitations of views until recently was that insertions could not be made in views based on multiple tables or views that contained embedded functions. Starting with Oracle 7.3, this restriction was relaxed; insertions and updates in a multitable view are now possible so long as the changes modify only one table.

Before, views were useful mainly for reports and were of limited use for screen modules (such as Oracle Forms), but now they are useful for screen modules as well. For example, you may want to create views that bring lookup values into the data tables. This technique greatly reduces the number of tables or views required by each module. However, view creation needs to be carefully controlled to make sure that the minimum number of necessary views are created. The ability to create views should be limited to senior members of the design team.

Building applications and reports is frequently much easier if you build some intelligence into views. One powerful feature not often used in application design is the ability to embed functions in views. For example, in a PO system, a view in the PO table can store the total amount for the purchase order. Code can be written so that anytime users need to know the total amount of a PO, they can reference that column. Previously, in the "Creating Redundant Columns" section of Chapter 13, we discussed adding a denormalized column for the PO Total in the PO table. Perhaps a better solution is to calculate this information on the fly and display it using a view. This method is very efficient, since the code is stored in a shared SQL area. One of the nice features of Oracle is that if the same SQL code is called multiple times, the SQL code goes into a shared SQL area. When a user executes a SQL query, the application looks for the SQL statement in the shared SQL area. If the application finds the SQL statement, it doesn't need to reparse it. This feature makes the overall system much more efficient.

Tuning and Completing the Database Design

New fields will undoubtedly be discovered during the Application Design phase. When this occurs, columns must be added to the database design to support the application design. You need to continually revisit the database design to incorporate changes that result from the application column-level mapping process. You should produce a column-level report showing which columns are used in which modules. Pay particular attention to columns that are not referenced by any application. Such columns should be deleted where appropriate. When this is done, the database design is complete and you can enter the Build phase.

Defining and Finalizing the Design Book

The design book is the primary deliverable from the Application Design phase. It includes the full functional description of the application down to the detail level. It should also describe the overall structure of the system and the process for creating the desired structure. In other words, it should answer these questions: What should the system look like? How can the business requirements be satisfied? It should also include module-by-module design specifications. For each module, the following sections should be included:

- Mockups of screens or report facsimiles

- Mapping of each field displayed on the screen or report to a database field

- Relevant portions of the ERD showing tables and the relationships among these tables required to support the module

- Detailed description of the functionality of the module; some default functionality (such as insert and modify operations) will be built in

- All relevant requirements with respect to that module

- Encapsulation of all design-level analysis

The design book should be a self-contained document that the designer can use to build the application. If a design book is not prepared, then your system cannot be tested, because there is nothing to test against. Many automated tools are available to help testers perform testing. However, unless the tester is familiar with what the system is supposed to do at the detail level from both user interface and database perspectives, then the tester cannot audit the effectiveness of the application. The tester must look at the requirements and answer the questions: Does the application satisfy the requirements? Does the application work according to the design?

The design book should also present report specifications and describe navigation within applications.

Report Specifications

The design book should include an example of what each report looks like. The designer needs to know the underlying queries that will support the report. Any flexibility desired in the report (for example, filtering or sorting) needs to be declared at this point. Report distribution and security can be handled in the Implementation phase and need not be addressed here.

Navigation

Decisions must be made at this point regarding navigation within applications. The following options are available:

- Dedicated navigation application: that is, buttons on the screen

- Toolbar buttons

- Menu options

- Triggers on the form: for example, double-clicking the name of an employee in one application to display that employee's record in a second application

You need to establish the underlying functionality of navigation. You must decide for each application what other applications can be reached and determine how the user will move among and between these applications. Will the user be firing off database transactions or merely navigating to a different application?

There are two ways to document navigation:

- **Navigation flowchart**   Each module is a box on the screen with lines connecting applications to show the navigation paths. The lines themselves can also describe how the application path works: for instance, by using menu options, toolbars, buttons, or some other trigger.

- **Matrix**   All modules are listed on both axes of the matrix. Within the cells of the matrix, you can specify how navigation from one application to another is performed.

Although both methods work, the matrix is much more compact. The matrix enables the developer and tester to quickly and easily see which application maps to which other application, thus making it easy to verify whether or not applications meet the specifications. Matrices are less helpful to the designer, however. It is easier for a designer to use a navigation flowchart, since this also shows how the navigation paths function. Thus, you should use both approaches, as the system will require both development and design whether by the same or different people.

Internal Control and Security

The design of a high-quality internal control system requires the skills of two different groups. One group is the systems people who understand how roles, user profiles, passwords, grants, views, and other database techniques can be used to help make the application and the database secure. You also need the skills of the internal auditing group to help design an effective security system.

Security is not limited to computer controls. It encompasses not only the protection of the physical and monetary assets of the organization, but also the data that resides in its computer systems. When certain business processes of the organization are computerized, they must be considered within the perspective of the company's internal control system. Backup and recovery are also important parts of internal control and security and should be carefully considered toward the end of the Design phase. Decisions need to be made regarding how to protect the system against catastrophic events such as fires, floods, and hardware failure.

Sometimes, computer controls can help prevent human errors and fraud, and sometimes manual controls can help detect programming errors. For example, using an approved vendor list and approved purchase order items can help decrease data entry errors, just as periodically physically counting inventory can help detect a computer error in a purchasing system. All controls and all exposures (potential opportunities for harmful events) must be considered together.

It is important to remember that database controls, application-level controls, and accounting controls are not three separate topics. A coherent security strategy mandates integration of all three types of controls.

Traditionally, this has not been done. Database people, in general, do not understand accounting controls, and internal auditors have little understanding of database technology. Even now, the most common way that external auditors evaluate an internal control system is by first sending in a team of computer specialists to evaluate the computer controls and then sending in traditional auditors to independently evaluate the accounting controls. Such a strategy is conceptually flawed.

Designing an Internal Control System

This section describes how an internal control system should be designed. The first step is to establish all of the various exposures in the new system. Since both the application and database need to be designed to determine what all these exposures are, this step could not be taken until now. The key tools you will use to find exposures are the physical process flows.

After looking at all the exposures in the system and determining the appropriate controls for a particular application design, you may conclude that the design itself is flawed from a control standpoint and needs to be rethought. Such a situation, however, is rare. Usually, small module-level changes are sufficient to implement a control. It is not possible to determine the exposures in a system until that system is defined. Whereas some exposures are common to all systems, each system will have some unique exposures associated with it. You may want to identify general exposures and appropriate controls and add those to the system requirements prior to completing the detailed application design.

Exposures are of three types:

- **Hardware failure**   You should consider the possibility of every kind of failure, from the breakdown of a PC to a fire that destroys the computer room. Hardware failures that are the result of normal breakdowns, sabotage, accidents, and natural disasters should all be taken into account.

- **Human error**   This group includes errors ranging from data entry mistakes to the inadvertent reformatting of the hard drive by the night operator. Human errors can be quite serious. For protection, one midsized bank had all of its wire transfers entered twice, by two data entry people. By an unfortunate coincidence, however, both data entry people pressed the wrong button and mistakenly transferred $1,000,000 instead of $1,000 to the Philippines.

■ **Fraud** This is the most frightening exposure, particularly with respect to financial data, where diversion of funds is possible. However, fraud may also involve the improper use of competitive information or malicious destruction of system resources by disgruntled employees. In addition, fraud may be perpetrated by one individual, or it may involve collusion among two or more employees. Fraud involving collusion can be difficult, if not impossible, to protect against.

Every system has a different set of exposures. The physical process flows are useful for seeing what exposures may exist. For example, in a simple PO system, the process flow can be described as follows:

1. An employee in a functional area initiates a request for a purchase order by entering it in the system.

2. A manager approves the request online.

3. The Purchasing Department approves the request online.

4. The system automatically generates and sends the purchase order to the vendor.

5. The goods arrive at the Receiving department, which notes that these goods have been received and maps the shipment to the appropriate PO.

6. Goods are distributed to the employee.

Such a process flow reveals several exposures of each type.
Potential hardware failures in processing a PO:

■ Because this is an Oracle system, most of the potential hardware failures would not result in the loss of data.

■ The main hardware exposure occurs if the system is down for an extended period of time. In such a case, the needed goods might not be ordered.

■ The scanner in the Receiving department may incorrectly scan an item so that the correct item is not checked off, and the item may not get to the employee who ordered it.

Potential human errors include:

- The employee can erroneously enter the request.

- The manager may inadvertently approve a request that should not have been approved.

- The Purchasing department may make the wrong approval decision.

- Goods may be misdirected by the Receiving department or applied to the wrong purchase order.

- A programmer may accidentally create a bug in a program that causes transactions to be lost, altered, or mistakenly created.

Potential exposures to fraud include:

- A user may fraudulently create a preapproved purchase order record.

- A systems person may fraudulently create a purchase order record for himself or herself.

- Receiving department personnel may steal or misappropriate delivered goods.

Once exposures have been identified, controls must be developed to protect the organization from these exposures.

One of the hardest facts to accept about internal control systems is that it is not appropriate to protect against every exposure. After the bank in the example mentioned earlier discovered that two clerks both entered the same incorrect data, an error that sent $1,000,000 to the Philippines, the bank changed its procedure so that every transaction is entered by three different people. This increased data entry costs by 50 percent. The rationale used by the company to justify this expense was that the single error had cost it $999,000, which would pay for a lot of data entry security. The point is that controls cost money. For a control to be cost effective, it must cause at least a proportional decrease in the probability of an exposure.

The designers, working with the users, need to identify the appropriate controls to protect against the identified exposures. The best controls are those that protect against multiple exposures. For example, overnight backups of the data that are stored off-site limit exposure to any event that could cause destruction of information. A high-quality, periodic financial audit will uncover most blatant irregularities in the system.

Protecting against fraud, particularly fraud involving multiple individuals, usually involves very careful manual controls. For example, a managerial review and sign-off of all purchase orders above a specific amount limits the ability of any employee to defraud the company. Simple system controls can help detect employees with abnormally frequent purchase order requests.

Once the internal control system is designed, you will need to update the design book for the modules to reflect any changes in module design that occur as a result of internal control measures.

Specific Oracle Controls

Oracle provides specific tools that can assist in the building of system-level controls, including these:

- *Product user profiles,* which can restrict access to Oracle products

- *Passwords,* which restrict access to the system

- *Roles,* which help manage the rights of different classes of users

Security Deliverable

The deliverable for system security is a control/exposure matrix. Prepare a matrix where one axis lists all of the exposures that have been identified. Across the other axis, list all of the plausible controls. At the intersection of each control and exposure, rate how effectively that control decreases the risk of that exposure. If a control has no impact on the exposure, leave the cell blank. If the control decreases the risk of exposure, rate its effectiveness as low, medium, or high.

For the bank where the data entry error occurred, for instance, a control that restricts the amount that could be entered to a realistic range would decrease the risk of exposure by only a small amount and would thus be rated "low." A control that requires all wire transfers to be reviewed and approved would be rated "medium" because there is no way to guarantee how carefully the reviews are performed. The control that the bank eventually implemented, triple entry of all wire transactions, provides an exceptionally high degree of control and would be rated "high."

Once the matrix is complete, you can evaluate the quality of your internal control system by its ability to protect the system from each exposure. You may also find redundant controls that can be eliminated. In the banking example, once triple entry was implemented, no other control was necessary to prevent data entry errors for wire transfers.

After the design of the internal control system is complete, a report can be prepared and delivered to management on the level of security that is in place for the system. Management can then decide whether that level of protection is adequate. This formal approach to internal control system design is commonly used in many of the world's largest organizations but is almost unheard of in smaller companies.

Test Plan

One of the important aspects of the design book is that there is enough information in it to support system testing. Specifically, testers will check to make sure that applications conform to the system requirements associated with that application. At this point in the CADM process, we have sufficient information to develop our test plan. Indeed, one of the reasons for doing the test plan at this time is that it forces the designers to carefully consider whether the design book is adequate to support the Test phase. A complete discussion of Test will be postponed until Chapter 19, but it is at the end of the Design phase that the test plan should be developed.

Modifications for Smaller Systems

For large systems, application conceptual design completed in the Pre-Design phase is followed by database design and application design in the Design phase and then by the database Build phase.

For smaller systems, the entire Design phase can be simplified. After conceptual application design is complete, the process can proceed directly to the design and building of the database. Then the design and building of the application can be completed. This is a radical change in design methodology, but for small systems it is appropriate. For medium-sized systems, the team must assess which path to follow—the one for small systems or the one for large systems—using its best judgment. When in doubt, follow the same development path for both medium- and large-sized systems.

When Is Application Design Complete?

User acceptance of screen designs already occurred in the sign-off process in the Pre-Design phase. All that remains is for the system developers to perform an internal evaluation of the completeness of the design. Each application within the design book should be audited for completeness by a quality assurance (QA) person. Similarly, a random sampling of applications from each developer should be selected for QA. Specifically, several applications from each developer should be checked for accuracy and completeness. Of course, if any applications fail the audit, extra work will be required. The principle for determining completeness is an internal audit by another set of eyes. The design process should always include review by an internal auditor to ensure adherence to design standards in multiple places throughout the process.

Application design is complete when the users sign off on the design book and the development team completes its own internal sign-off based on the design book and validation of the information in Oracle Designer. Another way to ensure that the design is acceptable is to perform a system walkthrough with users.

CHAPTER
16

Oracle Designer in
Design—Application
Design

...It seems more designed to make people stumble than to be walked upon.
   —Franz Kafka (1884-1924), *Reflections on the Great Wall of China*

n the Application Design part of the Design phase, you fully define the modules (screens, reports, menus) that make up the finished application. Oracle Designer helps you enter these definitions in an organized and methodical way so you can completely specify the details. The Oracle Designer definitions serve as the program specifications from which you generate the final application in the Build phase. Another important activity in this part of the Design phase is the cross-check of the database design. You want to be sure that the data elements you defined in the Database Design part of the Design phase are fully utilized and included in the set of modules you produce. Oracle Designer facilitates this type of checking as well.

Table 16-1 shows the activities and the Oracle Designer tools you use for them in the Application Design part of the Design phase.

The work you do in this part of the Design phase with the Server Model Diagram tool is similar to the work you did in the Database Design part of Design, described in Chapter 14. The main reason to use this tool now is to add to or modify database definitions you created earlier. You may need to do this as a result of something you learned or thought of when defining modules. You also may want to review the properties for relational definitions (tables and views) to more fully specify the display characteristics of the columns. This activity is discussed in the "Module Diagram" section, as the display properties are similar to those in the table properties window.

The work you perform with the Logic Editor at this stage of Design consists of filling in properties for the PL/SQL definitions, as Chapter 14 discusses. You will also create additional PL/SQL definitions to support the application. You may need to supplement the table API to enforce business rules or to perform standard maintenance on data. In addition, you may want to build client-code libraries to use in the modules. While you will not write all the code for these needs in this phase, you will create the modules and PL/SQL definitions and connect them to the proper locations (module or network). The code definitions are *stubs*, code blocks to be filled in later, that allow you to document the need for a particular piece of PL/SQL without having to write all the code for it. You will complete the code in the Build phase before running the generators.

Activity or Deliverable	Oracle Designer Tool
PL/SQL module specifications	Design Editor: Logic Editor and PL/SQL Composition node
Supplement table definitions	Design Editor: Server Model Diagram
Define module components	Design Editor: Reusable Component Graphical Editor
Module component layout and data usage specifications for screens, reports, and charts	Design Editor: Module Diagram, Reusable Component Graphical Editor, and Default Links utility; RON: Create Default Module Data Usages
Restructure the module network (menu modules)	Design Editor: Module Network Viewer
Create reference, code, and help tables	Reference tables utilities
Exposure control matrix	User Extensibility feature and Matrix Diagrammer
Cross-check the module "CRUD"	Matrix Diagrammer
Document the module specifications	Repository Reports

TABLE 16-1.   *Application Design Activities and Oracle Designer Tools*

Remember, if you have questions about Oracle Designer operations or concepts, you can consult Chapter 2 or the online help system.

Module Network Viewer

The Module Network Viewer is a node called *Module Network* in the Design Editor Modules tab. It allows you to view and manipulate the calling hierarchy for modules, which is also called a *module network*. In the case of the Form Generator, it will create a menu system. In the case of the

WebServer Generator, the module network represents hypertext links from one module start-up page to another. The following discussion uses the Form Generator menu as an example of how the Module Network Viewer works. There is a similar network viewer for PL/SQL Definitions in the PL/SQL Composition node of the Server Model tab. Chapter 14 discusses that node and how you use it to create packages and procedure calls.

A menu is, essentially, a hierarchical structure. Each node of the network is a module itself. Each module can be either a menu module (where the *Module Type* property is "Menu"), Form (where the *Module Type* property is "Default"), or Report. You start with a top-level menu and create as many submenus as required to adequately structure the application.

The following illustration shows the Module Network Viewer with a partial set of menu, form, and report modules.

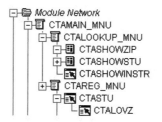

The nodes CTAMAIN_MNU, CTALOOKUP_MNU, and CTAREG_MNU are menu modules. The only function of these modules is to provide the pull-down menu items for the modules they call. It is also possible, in some cases, for one module to call another module. For example, the form module CTASTU calls another form module, CTALOVZ, which provides a list of values. Since, in the example of form calling form, there is no menu item to represent the call, something on the form, like a button, must contain code to perform the action. Since the menu system itself is made of menu modules, you work with that structure in the Module Network Viewer. The kinds of calls you use most frequently are menu to menu, menu to form, form to form, form to report, and report to report.

You first use the Module Network Viewer in the CADM life cycle when you produce the modules for the Pre-Design storyboard. At that time, you create *candidate modules* using the Application Design Transformer (ADT) and accept them with the Design Editor by changing the *Candidate* property to "No." ADT is the only tool that creates candidate modules automatically.

You then generate the prototypes and test the storyboard. When the storyboard process is done, you have notes on modifications to the calling structure. You incorporate these modifications using the Module Network Viewer and synchronize the repository definitions with the application modules you modified while storyboarding.

In the Application Design part of the Design phase, you return to this diagrammer and work with the rough-cut module definitions. In the Module Network Viewer, you can change the calling order, create new networks, move modules, and resequence the order of modules in the hierarchy.

Module Structure Diagrammer— A Hidden Utility

Another utility included with Oracle Designer 2.1 (release 7.0.20) lets you model the module network. It is called the Module Structure Diagrammer (as was a similar tool in Designer version 1), and you run it by double-clicking on the DWS20.EXE file in the ORACLE_HOME/bin directory or by creating a shortcut for it using the Windows shortcut facility. You can also run this diagrammer by selecting Open Diagram from the right-click menu on the diagram icon in RON's Diagrams node (in the Sets group) for a diagram created in version 1.

This tool shows the module structure in a hierarchy similar to that in the Module Network Viewer. The difference is in the symbol set, as Figure 16-1 shows. The symbols in the Module Structure Diagrammer are boxes that look slightly different for each type of module.

Screen, Report, Utility, PL/SQL, and Chart modules are all represented by boxes with slightly different borders. The diagrammer works in much the same way as the Function Hierarchy Diagrammer. You arrange the hierarchy using the toolbar buttons or Layout menu to create a horizontal, vertical, or hybrid arrangement. The **Edit→Preferences** menu item displays a dialog that lets you select which module types you see on the diagram as well as the color and fonts for the symbols. You can recolor or change the font of individual or selected modules with the toolbar buttons. You can open, create, save, and delete diagrams. The following is a list of some of the other operations that you can and cannot do with this tool.

Some of the operations you can perform:

- **Open an old diagram** that has definitions no longer in the repository. The Design Editor Module Network Viewer automatically updates the diagram, but this tool does not do that (unless you set the *Consolidate on Open* preference). This tool also allows you to view module structure diagrams created in a previous version of Oracle Designer.

- Print diagrams that you have arranged with different layouts.

- Embed OLE objects such as text and graphics in the same way as in other diagrammers.

Operations you cannot perform:

- Create definitions in or delete definitions from the repository.

- View or change properties on any element.

- Resequence or Reparent modules within the structure to reorder them.

- Drag elements in from any Navigator or other diagrammer.

- Use right-click mouse menus on the diagram or on the elements in the diagram.

You can view the help file for this tool by selecting the **Help→Help Topics** menu item or by double-clicking the DWM20.HLP file in the ORACLE_HOME/cdoc70/help directory. This tool provides an easy way to print an existing or new network layout in a variety of layout formats. It is also useful for those who are accustomed to the tool that this evolved from in Designer version 1.

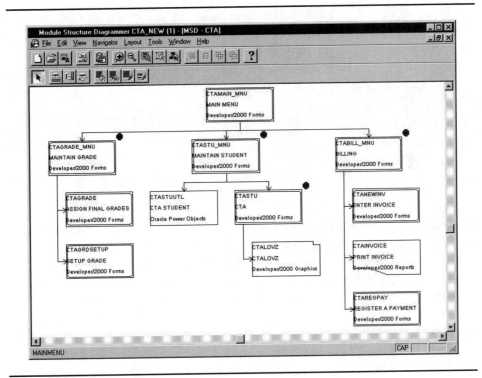

FIGURE 16-1.   *Module structure diagram*

Basic Techniques

The Module Network Viewer is just another part of the Design Editor Navigator window. It appears in the Modules tab as a node called *Module Network*. The elements you see in this area are parent-child associations between modules, not the actual modules. In fact, except for the root menu node, the Property Palette shows the properties only for the association. Therefore, when you create a module in the Module Network node, it will appear in the list under the Modules node as well. However, you can create a module in the Modules node and not have it appear anywhere in the Module Network node.

You can view this network in a vertical layout (the default) or horizontal layout by choosing the menu item **View→Display Network Horizontally**. The following illustration shows a sample network in its horizontal layout.

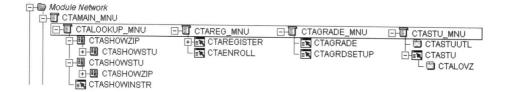

Since the Module Network is merely another way to display the module associations, you can work either in the Modules node or in the Module Network node when creating modules. You can actually build a module network using the Modules node, too, because the subnode Called Modules specifies the child modules. Seeing the entire structure this way is difficult, though, so it is best to use the Module Network Viewer to define the module.

NOTE
The Data view of the Module Diagram (described in the Module Diagram section later) also shows a subset of the network based on a single module. If you diagram a particular module, the modules that call it and those that it calls will be shown on the same diagram. This gives you an idea of the context of this module within the network, but you still need the Module Network Viewer to see the big picture.

The main actions you perform in this area consist of restructuring the module network created by the Application Design Transformer (ADT), building new menu network nodes from scratch, or a combination of those two.

Restructuring the Module Network

You can change the default menu structure that ADT creates. This structure consists of a main menu with submenus for each organization unit (Business

Unit). Under each of those menus are submenus for the various module types, and those submenus contain the actual module items.

Restructuring the module network is really just a matter of dragging and dropping modules from one node to another in the Module Network Viewer. You can also drop modules from the Modules node under the appropriate node in the network. When doing either of those drag-and-drop operations, you can choose a drop location to the left or right (top or bottom using the default view) of an existing node. A small indicator appears, as the following illustration shows, to the right (or under) an existing module when you select a module, click the mouse, and hold the mouse button as you drag it over the network.

When you release the mouse button, the module will appear in the position in which you dropped it. This makes reorganizing a module network relatively fast and painless.

You can also resequence the modules using a dialog. Right-click on a module or menu node and select Resequence Module Networks from the right-click mouse menu, or use **Utilities→Resequence** when a module network node is selected. You will see a dialog with the module you selected and all its siblings. For example, a menu module MAINREG calls two Forms modules, REGISTER and ENROLL. When you select Resequence Module Networks from the MAINREG module, you will see a list of other menu modules that are on the same level as MAINREG. If you select Resequence Module Networks from the right-click menu on REGISTER, you will load the dialog with the REGISTER and ENROLL modules. This dialog lets you resequence the modules by moving them up and down with arrow buttons. It is faster than drag-and-drop if you have major restructuring to do on a particular branch of the hierarchy.

Building New Module Networks

When you build a new module network or a new branch of an existing network, you add menu modules. A menu module is a module that calls other modules. You create new network modules from the right-click menus in the Navigator. The right-click menu on the Module Network node contains a selection for Create Module Network. Choosing this opens a property dialog (or Property Palette) where you specify properties for a new module with a *Module Type* of "Menu." You can change the module type and specify the language and name at that point. You can also create a network by creating a module in the Modules node with a *Module Type* of "Menu."

The right-click menu on a module network (menu) node contains options to accomplish the following:

- **Create Entry Below** creates a new menu module that is a sibling of the selected module (if it is in the top two levels of the hierarchy) or a child of the selected module (if it is under the first two levels). The new module appears after the selected module in the hierarchy.

- **Create Entry Right** creates a new menu module that is a child of the selected module if the selected module is lower than the first two levels of the hierarchy. It creates a sibling if the selected module is the second level in the hierarchy.

- **Copy Menu Structure** copies the entire network under the selected module and places it under another module. This utility will create a menu module with the name "MOD_*nnnnnn*" where *nnnnnn* is a number.

- **Go to Module Definition** causes the cursor to jump to the definition in the Modules node.

- **Called Modules** displays a dialog where you select a module to call, as Figure 16-2 shows.

This dialog is the one you see if you have the property dialogs selected as the default (**Options→Use Property Dialogs**). If you are using the Property Palette instead, the Create Module Networks dialog looks slightly different but allows you to do the same thing: add modules to the module network of the selected module. The property dialog version contains the descriptive *Name* (not *Short Name*) of the modules that are appropriate to call from the selected module. For example, if you select a Report Builder module and call this dialog, it will only show the Report modules in the application, as these are the only modules that can be called from a report module. If you check the *Show all modules?* check box, the list will expand to show all modules regardless of whether a call makes sense.

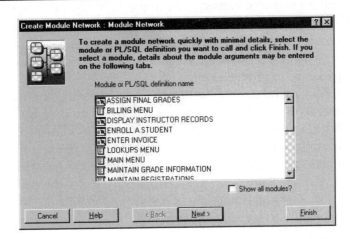

FIGURE 16-2. *Create Module Network dialog*

Selecting a module and pressing the Next button in this dialog allows you to specify passed values. *Passed values* represent data that flows from the calling module to the called module. There are two types of passed values: Argument Passed Values, for user-defined arguments in the called module, and Named Passed Values, for predefined arguments for the module. For example, you could create an Argument Passed Value that would pass a value from one report to another (in a drill-down report, for example). You would give that argument a name and a value. However, you might also want to pass values to built-in Report parameters like DESTYPE or DESFORMAT. You could do that using a Named Passed Value for DESTYPE and DESFORMAT. The Property Palette version of the Create Module Network dialog does not contain an area to define arguments; you must do that from the Modules node in the Navigator if you use the Property Palette.

NOTE
The Called Modules menu choice is the best way to show a module under two parents. For example, if you wanted Module 1 to appear under Menu Module A and Menu Module B, you could add Module 1 to Menu Module A's branch and right-click on Menu Module B to define another call to Module 1.

Some standard menu options appear in the right-click menu as well, like **Show on New Diagram**. If you create a module diagram from a module network node, you will see the selected element and its parent and children, as Figure 16-3 shows. You will not see any siblings or other branches in the network outside the selected module.

The right-click menu also allows you to delete modules or module networks. Be careful with this, as you could delete a module by mistake when you meant to delete just the module network (module association), or you could just delete the module network and leave a module that's not used. When in doubt, read the confirmation dialog carefully when you specify a delete. This dialog shows the type and name of the definition that you are deleting. You can press Cancel if you see the type is Module when you intended it to be Module Network.

CAUTION
Remember that deleting elements such as modules from the repository is not reversible. There is an implicit commit associated with a delete operation, so you cannot undo it.

Property Dialogs

When you create a module network, the Property Palette will be active if you have chosen to display properties in the palette. You need to enter the

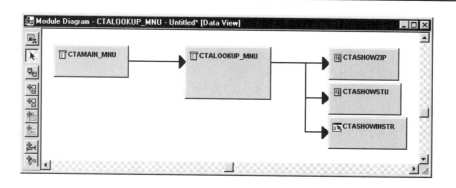

FIGURE 16-3. *Module Diagram of a module network branch*

name before committing. If you have chosen to show properties using the dialog, the module dialog will appear. This dialog will create a new module with the module type you specify. You can also view and modify the properties of a module after it is created by selecting Properties from the right-click menu after selecting a module. The property dialog shown in Figure 16-4 will appear.

This dialog appears regardless of whether you select the module in the Modules node or the Module Network node. Therefore, you can set up the network and modify the properties of the module without leaving the Module Network Viewer area. This shows the main set of properties for the module. The Property Palette is still important because it allows you to specify properties of the module association, such as whether the *Method of Use* property is set to "CALL" or "INCLUDE." The Include value is intended specifically for PL/SQL packages, as described in Chapter 14, and does not make much sense for modules.

The Property Palette is important for other module properties, like *Short Title*, which is used for the label of the menu item that calls the module. You

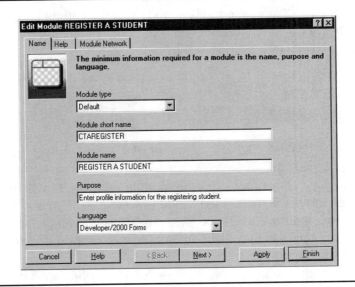

FIGURE 16-4. *Module property dialog*

have to navigate to the Modules node definition to display the Property Palette for a particular module.

Naming Modules

The Application Design Transformer assigns names to modules based on the functions they represent. The name of the module is the same as the name of the function it is based on. ADT forms a short name using the prefix you specify in the ADT window and a numeric suffix (such as 0040). These names have no special meaning, and you will want to change at least the suffix. File management will be easier if you give all modules from one application system the same prefix. Therefore, one of your naming conventions could be that module short names start with two or three letters that indicate the application system and end with up to 12 characters that are abbreviations indicating the purpose or use of the module. You can also use suffixes for special modules like menus (for example, "_MNU") to make searches by module name easier. If you are deploying into an operating system that has a file name size limitation, adjust your standard accordingly.

Creating a Recursive Call

A recursive module calls itself, and a recursive module loop consists of more than one module where the last module in the calling chain calls the first one. The Module Network Viewer represents a recursive call with a turnaround arrow, as the following illustration shows.

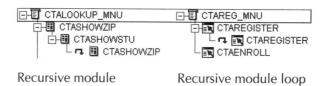

Recursive module   Recursive module loop

    To create a recursive call, click the module node under which you want to place the module. Select Called Modules from the menu and select the module that started the call. The viewer will create the recursive symbol automatically. You may find that you have no need for this, but Oracle Designer does support it.

    Recursive calls are not an issue in WebServer applications, but in Form Builder modules they could present a problem. For example, many applications allow users to freely navigate from one form to another without traversing any menus. The problem would occur if the built-in you use to invoke the form (via the *Command Line* property) were CALL_FORM; this built-in does not exit the calling form; it just adds the called form on top of the calling form. The user could call many forms in succession and eventually run out of memory. Also, unless you have coded around it, a user exiting the called form will return to the calling form. If there were many recursive calls in that session, the user would have to exit each form in turn to exit the application. If you use NEW_FORM as the built-in, the problem of recursive modules does not occur.

Other Module Properties

You can refine or further specify the properties of the module in the Property Palette or property dialog. The help system has detailed information on how most of these affect the generators. Click on the Context-Sensitive Help button and drop the help icon on the property in the Property Palette to view the help text. The properties that are important to set or check at this stage follow:

- **Language** This property defines which generator will create the final code for this module. It also interacts with the setting of the *Module Type* property.

- **Implementation Name** This property specifies the name this module will have when it is built. Forms, reports, and menu modules are all generated to the file system. If this will be a file, be sure to enter a valid file name. If you do not fill this in, the generator will use the module's *Short Name* as the file name.

- **Module Type** This property indicates what kind of file the generator will create. For example, if the *Language* is set to Developer/2000 Forms (Oracle Developer Forms) and the module type is "Default," the generator will create a form file. If the module type is "Library," it will create a library file. Some types do not make sense for some languages. For example, if the *Language* is set to Oracle WebServer, a "Library" module type will not be generated. These inappropriate values use a different color (the "Universal" values color) that you set in the **Options→Color/Font/Style** dialog.

■ **Titles** This area supplies fields for Top and Bottom titles that appear in the margins for Reports modules. The Top Title appears at the top of Web pages generated from WebServer modules. You can create generator items (such as CG$M1) in the template form to display these for Form Builder modules. The Short title property, which becomes the label of the menu item that calls this module, also appears in this area.

■ **Layout Format** This property specifies the layout of the form or report and contains choices such as Master Detail, LOV, Matrix, Control Break, and Label. This specifies the style that the generator will use to lay out the form or report. Most of these correspond to default layouts in the individual tool.

■ **Status** The generators will change this from "Not Started" (the default) to "In Progress." If you set the value to "Completed," the generator will issue a warning that the module is considered complete.

■ **Candidate** When ADT creates modules, it sets this property to "Yes." You will not be able to generate the module until you set this to "No" (the default for modules you create outside ADT). This property forces you to examine the modules that ADT creates and make decisions on whether to use them.

■ **Prevent Generation** This property, if set to "Yes," will stop the module from being generated. You can set this when you are finished with a module so someone does not generate it by mistake.

■ **Runtime Path** This field specifies the name and path of the file that contains the executable code for this module. Any module calling this module will hard-code this path into the call. This is usually not desirable because it makes the files nonportable between file systems with different directory structures. Leave this one blank.

■ **Command Line** This field contains the full command string that you would use to run the module from the calling module or environment command line. This is language-specific. For example, the default command line for a form is:

```
CALL_FORM('<MODULE>', HIDE, DO_REPLACE);
```

The generator will replace the '<MODULE>' string with the name of the file, so this line serves as a generic command for all forms. As mentioned before, you might want to change this to NEW_FORM for recursive calls.

■ **User/Help Text** This is text that appears in the online help system that you generate with the modules. If the module *Language* is set to Developer/2000 Forms (Oracle Developer Forms), you can generate help text to a table that is displayed via a help form. You can also specify the MS Help Generator for the help text to create a file you can compile into a .HLP file for file-based help in an Oracle Forms or Visual Basic module. WebServer Generator places this text on the opening page of the application.

■ **Help File Name** This property specifies the name of the MS Help .HLP file in which help is generated. This is usually set only in the top-level root module, with all child modules using the same file name. The MS Help Generator uses this property when it generates the help file.

■ **Graphic File Name** Generated help files can have an embedded graphic (.BMP) file, and this property lets you indicate the graphics file you want to use for the help contents topic on this module. The MS Help Generator uses this property when it generates the help file.

■ **Context Id Prefix** This optional property specifies the prefix number the help system uses to reference the module help text in the HLP file. This three-digit number must be unique among all modules in your system so the Help Generator can create links for the design elements in the module. The MS Help Generator uses this property when it generates the help file.

■ **Module Generation History** This property lets you track changes made to the module (if the developer enters information when the change is made). The Form Generator writes notes into this text area each time it generates the module, unless the preference *Add module history comment on generation* (MODCMT in the Commenting category) is set to "No."

■ **Release Notes** This property holds information you write on version numbers and descriptions of those versions.

Using RON to Enter Module Definitions

The Repository Object Navigator offers another way to create new modules. You can create the module and assign its properties fully in the properties window of RON, but the associations appear only in the Usages: Called by Modules node of the module. You can view and modify the module network using the RON Modules node in a hierarchy view (**View→ Hierarchy**), but the Module Network Viewer offers more features. The Design Editor should be your tool of choice for module network activities because it contains all that RON contains and also provides the more menu choises. The DE Modules node contains a Called Modules node that represents the opposite information from the subnode in RON. That is, it shows the child modules rather than the parent modules.

Where Does This Information Go?

The modules and module structures you work with in the Module Network Viewer form the basis for the code you generate in the Build phase, as Table 16-2 shows.

Module Network Viewer Element	Future Use
Module definition	Basis for Forms, Reports, Library, Visual Basic, and WebServer Generators
Module structure	Basis for the menu system for the Form Generator and start-up page for Web Server Generator
Module association (both call and include)	Appears in the Modules-Usages: Called by Modules node in RON for the child module; also the Modules-Called Modules node in DE; used to create the menu
Call association	Module generator adds code to call one module from another (for example, from a menu to a form)

TABLE 16-2.   *Future Use of Module Network Elements*

Module Diagram

The Module Diagram is an important tool you use to refine modules in preparation for generation. It allows you to assign the data sources (tables and views) used in each module and define much of how the finished application will look. You refine the menu system with the Module Network Viewer, and you refine the module components and data usages with the Module Diagram.

In planning your Design work, you may ask, "Which do I do first—the module network or the module layout and refinement?" The real answer is that it doesn't matter. The menu is an important part of the storyboard, so if you completed a storyboard you will already have a start with the module network. You will also have a first cut of most modules from the storyboard. Since design work, in general, consists of multiple refinement cycles, you will probably work on the module definitions and the module network at the same time, but most of the work will be in refining the module definitions.

In the Module Network Viewer, you set up the links between modules and set the main module-level properties. In the Module Diagram, you can designate what data elements are used for each table or view and how they will appear in the generated layout. When you get to the Build phase, a typical module generate session starts by reviewing the visual and data aspects of the module in the Module Diagram, then generating the module, making notes about what needs to be changed, and making the changes in the Module Diagram or Navigator properties. This cycle repeats until the module is working as required. All you really need to do in the Application Design part of the Design phase is to enter the definitions as completely as you can based on your knowledge of the system. You stop short of generating modules in this phase and perform the iterative generate and refine cycle in the next phase.

Figure 16-5 shows a Module Diagram session. All information in the diagram centers on the module itself. There are also symbols for the parent and child modules, that is, this module's calling and called modules.

Module Components

An important element to understand when building modules in Oracle Designer is the module component. You can think of the *module component* as something that will generate into a block in Forms, a group in

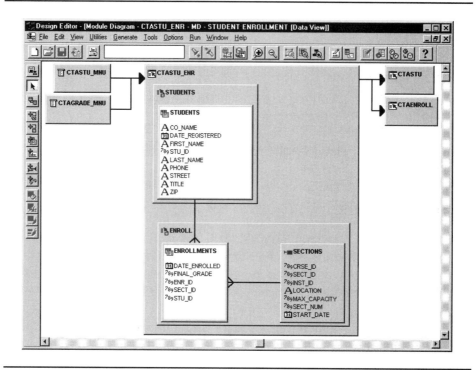

FIGURE 16-5. *Module Diagram session (in Data view)*

Reports, a zone in Visual Basic, and a record list in WebServer. The idea is that you group table usages and other objects and give the group a name. This is the module component.

The module component is one of the main ingredients of a module, and modules consist of one or more module components. The module components in turn consist of zero, one, or many database objects like tables or views; these are called *table usages.* A module component with no database objects, called a *control block,* will generate into something that is not linked to the database but that contains items needed in the application to do some processing or display information to the users. The module component also consists of unbound items that are not linked to a table but appear within the module component and outside a table usage; SQL Query Sets that define additional tables you will use to UNION with the base table in the resulting SQL statement (only for module components with a

Datasource Type of "Query"); Item Groups that combine items so they are treated as a layout unit by the generators; and Action Items that are used by Form, Report, and VB generators (but not the WebServer generator) to provide the user with a method to perform some function (like navigation within or outside the form).

Some important properties of the module component include the following:

- **Language** This specifies whether this is Forms, Reports, WebServer, or another language.

- **Insert ?, Update ?, Delete ?, Query ?** These indicate what operations will be allowed on this table in this module. The generators will create code based on these properties to allow only those operations for which the usage is set to "Yes." These usage settings must be appropriate to the module type. For example, a module component on a form may allow insert, update, delete, and select operations, but only query makes sense on a report.

- **Datasource Type and Datatarget Type** These specify where the data is read from (a table, view, query, or PL/SQL procedure) and where data is written to (a table, PL/SQL procedure, or transactional triggers). A Form module can read and write to any of these. If the source is a view or PL/SQL procedure and the target is a PL/SQL procedure, you can generate the module component API. A WebServer or Visual Basic module uses Query as the source; WebServer uses Query as the target; Visual Basic uses Table as the target. Chapter 18 explores this topic further.

- **Placement properties** This includes the *Window* this module component will appear on and *Placement* to specify where the module component is placed within the window—new content canvas, same content canvas, new stacked canvas, or same stacked canvas size. It also includes *X Position* and *Y Position* to define the location of the window on the screen or of the canvas on the window. Placement properties are used by Form and Visual Basic generators only.

- **Display** These properties are used differently by the different generators. The *Title* of the module component forms the block title in Forms. *Layout Style* indicates the presentation style for Reports, Visual Basic, and WebServer modules. *Rows Displayed* indicates the number of records on the screen. *Overflow* (for Forms modules) designates what happens if a single row exceeds the width of the canvas on which the items are placed.

Table Usages

Another important concept to understand when constructing modules is the table usage. You place table usages within the module component. Table usages designate which tables appear in the module as part of that module component. As before, this chapter uses tables as the example of a source for the table usage, but you can also create usages for views and snapshots. You can use a particular table in many module components. For each table usage, you designate the *Usage Type* property as follows:

- **Base**   This usage specifies the main table that this module component represents. The operations (Insert, Update, Delete, and Query) allowed for this table are stored on the module component itself. You can only have one base table usage per module component.

- **Lookup**   Linked to a base table, this usage shows values from other tables. For example, a STUDENTS table usage might require the city and state information, which is stored in the ZIPCODES table. You would create a ZIPCODES lookup usage to supply that value to the STUDENTS base table usage. If you generate a form, the columns specified in the lookup table usage become nonbase table items in the base table usage block. Lookup usages are query-only regardless of the operations allowed on the module component base table.

- **Single row SQL Aggregate**   Applicable for Report generation only, this usage designates a table that needs to be summarized in the base table usage. For example, to report on the number of enrollments for each student, you create a single row SQL aggregate usage for ENROLLMENTS that is linked to the STUDENTS usage. You also create an unbound item in the STUDENTS usage, with the

Unbound Type property, as "SQL Aggregate" and the *Derivation Text* property as the function (in this case, COUNT(enr_id)) that you use to perform the aggregation.

■ **Sub-Query**   Applicable for Report generation only, you specify this usage for a query that is contained within another query. For example, if you only want to display STUDENTS records that have no enrollments, you create a subquery table usage for ENROLLMENTS and fill in the *Usage Type* as "Sub-Query" and *Not Exists ?* as "Yes." The SQL generated for the report will be something like the following:

```
SELECT stu_id, first_name, last_name
  FROM students stu
 WHERE NOT EXISTS
       (SELECT NULL
          FROM enrollments enr
         WHERE stu.stu_id = enr.stu_id
       )
```

This is just one type of query possible with the Sub-Query type. The help system can guide you through other subqueries, for example, using the *Where Clause of Query* property.

The following illustration shows the symbols that will appear in the diagram and Navigator when you assign the *Usage Type* property.

Base

Lookup

Single row SQL Aggregate

Subquery

Untyped

You should assign the *Usage Type* as one of the other values if you will be generating the module.

Once you define the table usage, you add the following as elements associated to that usage:

- **Bound Items**   This is for columns in the table. You can set operations for each column with properties such as *Insert ?*, *Update ?*, and *Query ?*. In forms, these become base table items. You cannot add nonbase table items inside the table usage; these are unbound items.

- **Key Based Links**   This is for the associations between table usages, for example, between a base table and lookup table. Key Based Links can extend between module components but must start and end at a table usage.

- **Constraint Usages**   These are the foreign and primary key constraints for the particular table that the table usage represents. Constraint Usages are automatically created from the constraints on the table and are used to set Form Generator preferences. You cannot change, delete, or add Constraint Usages.

These elements are discussed further in the following sections.

Basic Techniques

Opening an existing module diagram and creating a new diagram are accomplished as they are in the Server Module—through the toolbar buttons, File menu items, right-click menus, or drag-and-drop. There are two views of the module—Data and Display—that you use for different purposes.

Data View and Display View

The *Data view* (as in Figure 16-5) shows the module with its calling and called modules. It is a database-centric picture of the information manipulated by the module. The main elements are the tables and columns that the module uses and the links between the tables. Other elements are the module components, which group the table usages. The Data view shows all bound items used in the module in alphabetical order within the table usage. Each bound item displays an icon indicating its datatype. This view is good to use when you are refining which elements are used in the module but do not care what the layout will look like.

The *Display view*, shown in Figure 16-6, represents the module in a form that is closer to how it will look when generated. This view contains the same module components and table usages, but with a difference—it only shows those items that have the *Display ?* property set to "Yes." It does not show the table usage links. This view also shows the bound and unbound item display types (such as text, button, and check box) instead of the datatypes. It includes unbound items inside the table box.

The main use for this view is to provide a rough picture of how the finished application will look. The bound items appear in the order in which they will appear in the module, and you can drag and drop them within the table usage to resequence them. You can also resequence using the right-click menu on an item called Resequence Items in the Navigator. This menu is available in the diagram as well, but the results will not be shown unless you show the Display view.

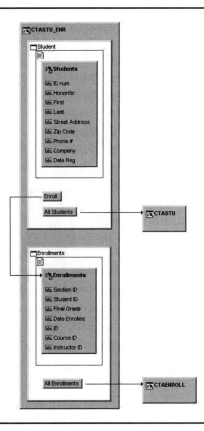

FIGURE 16-6. *Module Diagram Display view*

You can control the property values shown in these views using the Show Property tab on the **Options→Customize** dialog. Select a Display view element type (like Module Components) on the left and click the Module Diagram Display View radio button at the bottom of the dialog. You can place a check mark by the properties you want to see in the Display view. Clicking the Default radio button allows you to select properties to show in the Data view.

TIP
Closing or minimizing the Navigator when working with the diagrammer can save space on the screen and allow you to make the diagram window as big as you need it. If you need to change properties on an element, you can open the Property Palette window and click on the element in the diagram to load its properties.

Using the Symbol Set

The symbols in the Module Diagram are basically boxes and links, as in most other diagrams. Some symbols used signify module-specific elements. Figure 16-7 identifies the symbols in the Data view. The bound items have symbols to represent the datatype of the column. The columns are arranged in alphabetical order. The links represent foreign or primary key constraints. Symbols indicate the table usage type, as discussed earlier in the "Table Usages" section.

The Display view contains different symbols for the same module, as Figure 16-8 shows. You can see that unbound items appear as part of the table usage. Also, the Course ID bound item in the Enrollments module comes from the SECTIONS lookup table usage. The ordering of columns is different and reflects the order the items will appear in the form or report. The symbols next to the items designate the display datatype, not the column datatype. Also, some columns do not appear on this diagram because they are not displayed. The reusable module component (discussed later) has the same symbol as the other (specific) module component with a small curved arrow (to indicate reuse). The placement is a property of the

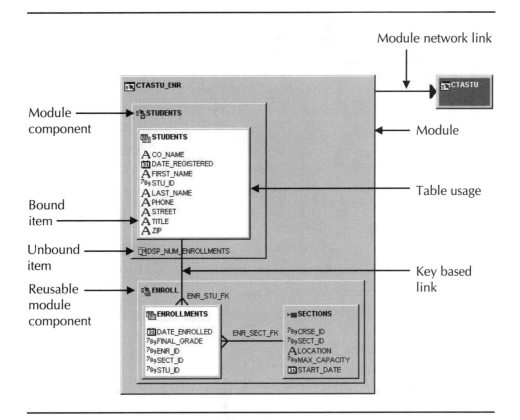

FIGURE 16-7. *Data view symbols*

module component within the window (as described earlier in the "Module Components" section).

Building a Module

If you ran ADT to create candidate modules, then accepted these candidate modules, you will already have modules and module components. At this point, you work with the Module Diagram and Navigator to refine the existing elements and define new elements for those modules. You might also create new modules by using the techniques outlined earlier in this chapter for creating modules and setting their properties. In the Module Diagram, you work with the details of the module, and regardless of when

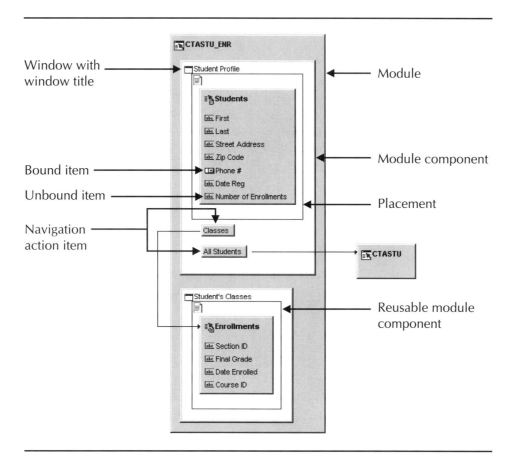

FIGURE 16-8. *Display view symbols*

or how the module was created, the techniques for modifying an existing module and building one from scratch are the same. The steps in building a module consist of creating module components; adding table usages to the module components; specifying additional elements, like unbound and action items; linking the table usages; and changing the layout.

Creating Module Components
Since modules consist of module components, you need to define module components before you add table usages. There are many ways to do this:

■ Use the standard method of clicking on the Module Components node under the module and clicking the Create toolbar button in the Navigator. You then fill out the name and usage properties of the Module Component in the Property Palette and save it.

■ If you have a module diagram window open, you can select the Create Specific Component toolbar button in the diagram window and drop it on the appropriate module in the diagram.

■ Alternatively, choose New Module Component from the right-click menu in the diagram or the Create Module Component right-click menu item for the Module Components in the Navigator.

The next step is to add table usages and their related bound items. You can do this by selecting the Create Table Usage button in the diagram toolbar and dropping the mouse on a particular module component. You can also use the Create button in the Navigator to add table usages and bound items.

If you find the previous methods of adding table usages too tedious, an alternative is available. Use the property dialog that you activate through the **Options→Use Property Dialogs** menu item or the Switch to Dialogs toolbar button (if you are currently switched to the Property Palette). When you ask to create a module component, you will see the Module Component Data Wizard dialog, as in Figure 16-9.

This dialog, also available by selecting **Tools→Module Component Data Wizard** from the menu, steps you through creating the module component and loading a table usage, bound items, bound item usages, and links. The last step in this dialog is to create the module component. At that point, you have the option of also setting the display properties for the module component through the Module Component Display Wizard. This dialog, shown in Figure 16-10, steps you through the properties you need to set to affect how the bound items are displayed in the module.

Using the wizards (dialogs) is potentially much faster than the Property Palette method, because the dialogs let you specify a number of elements and then create all of them for you when you click the Finish button. The Property Palette method commits each element definition as you move to the next definition, and the commit times can add up.

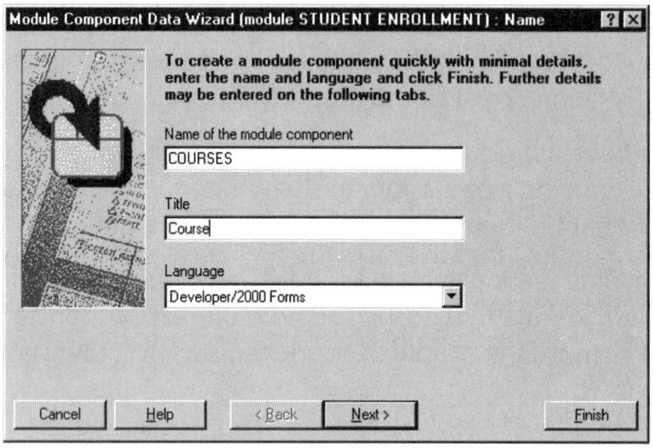

FIGURE 16-9. *Module Component Data Wizard dialog*

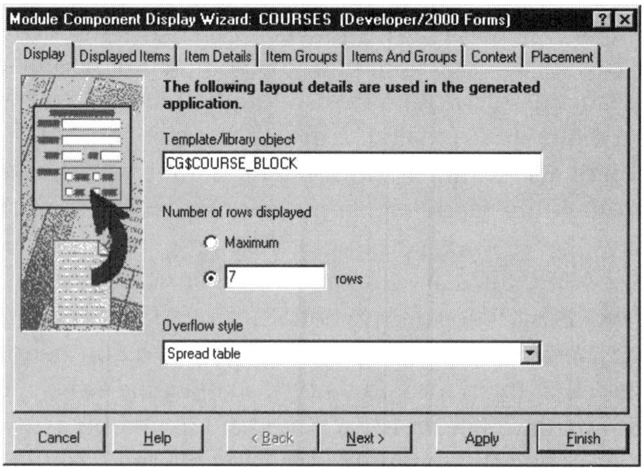

FIGURE 16-10. *Module Component Display Wizard dialog*

TIP
The Module Component Display Wizard is available for editing existing module component properties, too. If you use this wizard to create the module components, you may find it easier to use it to modify them, as you will be familiar with the location of certain properties in the dialog. Select the module component in the Navigator and choose the **Tools→Module Component Display Wizard** *menu item.*

Perhaps the fastest method for creating module components is to drag a table definition to the diagram or Module Components node in the Navigator. You can open a second navigator window (**File→New→Navigator**), select the Server Model tab, and find the table you want to use as the base table for the module component. Dragging that table definition over the Navigator and dropping it on top of a specific module will display the dialog in Figure 16-11. Be aware that this drop operation is possible only onto the module node (not under the module component node).

The following illustration shows this same drag-and-drop operation onto a module diagram.

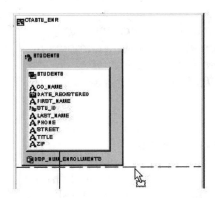

You will be able to tell where you can drop the table because the dashed line will appear above, below, or to the right side of an existing element.

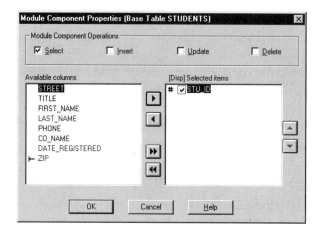

FIGURE 16-11. *Drag and drop table to module dialog*

Whenever you see that dashed line, you know that you have reached a valid drop point. You have to be a bit careful here, because the location of the module component designates its function in the module, as discussed in the "Linking Table Usages" section later.

NOTE
When you create a module component in a module, you are creating a module component inclusion. *This element indicates that a particular group of table usages is associated to a module.*

Specifying Special Items

After building the module component (by whatever method) and creating table usages and bound items, you are ready to define extra items like unbound items and action items. It is probably more appropriate to fully define special items in the Build phase, but you can still include them in rough format in this phase to be as complete as possible for the module definition.

UNBOUND ITEMS   An example of an unbound item would be a display-only item in the Student form that displays the invoice date that, according to a business rule, is 30 days after the date the student registered. There is no need to store this date, as it will always be calculated based on the value of the DATE_REGISTERED column. Therefore, you would create an unbound item in the STUDENTS module component and assign the *Unbound Type* property as "SQL Expression." The *Derivation Expression* property is set to: "DATE_REGISTERED + 30." When you generate this into a form, it will create a nonbase table item in the STUDENTS block that has a *Calculation* property of "Formula" and a *Formula* property of :STUDENTS.DATE_REGISTERED + 30. The form will maintain the value in this item for all queries and updates of DATE_REGISTERED.

Creating an unbound item is a quick operation in the Module Diagram. Select the Create Item button, hold the mouse button, and drop the item outside the table usage symbol. Dropping the item inside the table usage symbol will create a bound item. A property dialog (or palette) will open, where you can specify the name and other properties.

You can run a utility to associate an unbound item with a column in the base table. This effectively transforms the item into a bound item. This might be necessary if you created the unbound item and found out that it was really (or later became) a column in a table definition. Select **Utilities→Map Unbound Items** after selecting the unbound item or items you want to map. Follow the dialog to select a column for the unbound item. This utility also appears in RON.

CAUTION
Not all elements appear in both Data and Display views. If you can't find a particular element on the diagram, step back and think whether it is data related or display related. Then look in the appropriate view. You can switch back and forth between views without losing anything.

ACTION ITEMS Action items are user interface elements that allow you to include special actions within a module component. There are three main types:

- **Navigation** This is used to move the cursor to another part of the module or to another module. A navigation action item can be implemented either as a push button (the default if you create the button using the dialog), or a menu item. For example, a Form module has two module components that appear on different windows. A navigation action item can be created (with the *Create Button ?* property set to "Yes") between the windows with code to move the cursor to the other window. You can create your own action items and set the *Navigate to – Module Component* property to the module component you want the button press (or menu selection) to navigate to. Alternatively, you can set the *Navigate to – To Module* if you want the button to call another form or a report. You need not write any code for these buttons or menu items. They only apply to modules with languages of Form, Report, or Visual Basic.

- **Generator** This is used to execute a piece of code that the generator creates. These are used for Visual Basic modules only for operations like Delete Record, New Record, and Query.

- **Custom** This is used to execute a piece of code that you create. These are used for Form or Visual Basic modules only. You specify the code in the *Application Logic* node under the item in the navigator. For example, you might want to select all the records in the block. You could create a custom action item as a button with code to call the procedure that navigates the records, changes the display color, and stores the key values in a table variable.

Linking Table Usages

When you include table usages on the diagram, Oracle Designer will determine the links and create Key Based Links for the appropriate foreign and primary key constraints. If you need to add links after this you can do so by drawing them in the diagram with the Key Based Link toolbar button or in the Navigator with the standard creation procedure. It is important to know what types of links are possible and what they can be used for. The following is the

list of links that you can create within a single module component. The first
two of these are described earlier in the "Table Usages" section.

- **Lookup** The base table usage appears on the left and the lookup
  table usage on the right. This is shown in the following illustration:

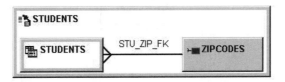

- **Single row aggregate and Sub-query** These appear as a base table
  usage on the top and aggregate or subquery table usage under, as
  shown in the following illustration. Remember that these only work
  for Report modules and module components.

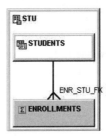

- **Treewalk** The table references itself as represented by the pig's ear
  link, as the following illustration shows. If two tables are involved in
  the treewalk link, they will appear as base table to lookup table with
  two key links (one for the lookup link and one for the treewalk link).

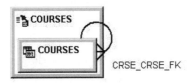

In addition to the single-module component layouts, the following
layouts provide links between module components.

- **Master-Detail**   The detail table appears under the master table, as in the following illustration. Use this to represent the classic header-lines or master-detail module.

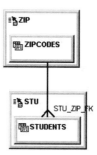

There is also an inverted master detail where the detail appears on top of the master. The only difference in the diagram is that the link line has the "many" (crow's-foot) side on the top. This is an unusual type of link, but it is possible to create it.

- **Same Table Links**   The same table appears in both module components and the link represents the primary key, as shown in the following illustration.

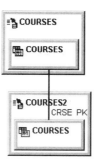

When you lay out this type of link, a dialog appears asking which link you want to use. In this case, you choose the primary key link. Use this for modules where you need to split the table usage between two windows or pages.

■ **Different module**   The link occurs between a table usage in one module and a table usage in another module. It could be based on a primary key (same table) or a foreign key. This is used to pass values to another module. The following illustration shows this link.

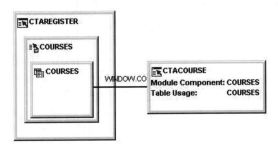

You can also chain the links together if needed. For example, a lookup table usage can link to another lookup table usage. In all cases, the types of links shown here are position-sensitive and you cannot change the size or positioning of the module, module components, or links. You can drag and drop table usages in certain places, depending on the table usage layout. The dashed line will tell you when the mouse has dragged a table usage over a valid drop spot.

TIP
The order that elements appear on the diagram determines how they will generate on the form. Most Display view elements are geared towards this end, but there are also some Data view elements like links that affect the layout and functionality.

Layout Elements

The Module Diagram uses layout elements to define how the generated module will be partitioned to the user. The three layout items are: Window, Content canvas, and Stacked canvas. All appear in the Display view of the module diagram. Windows are containers for all elements on the screen, and canvases are one of those elements. Both windows and canvases have

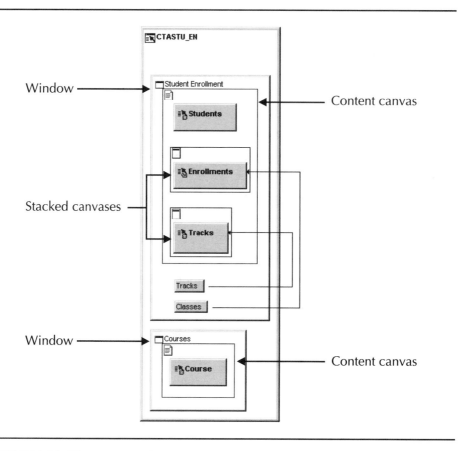

FIGURE 16-12. *Layout elements*

position and size properties. Figure 16-12 shows these three elements in the context of a module. For clarity, this diagram does not show the items.

- **Window** This appears in the diagram as a raised rectangle. For a Form module, objects assigned to different windows in the module will appear in different Forms windows when generated. If the module is a Report module, a separate window means a report within a report. For Visual Basic modules, a separate window appears as a different form. For WebServer Generator, separate windows appear as separate pages. Figure 16-12 shows two windows for a Form module—one for Student Enrollment and one for Courses.

- **Content canvas**   This is used for Form generator modules only and appears as a red box around the table usage. This represents a content canvas that has layout items on it in the form. A content canvas is an area that fills the window. There can be only one content canvas visible on a window at once (although there can be many stacked canvases visible on that content canvas as well). Figure 16-12 shows two content canvases—one for each window.

- **Stacked canvas**   This is used for Visual Basic and Form generators and appears as a blue box around the items in a module component. This will generate into a stacked canvas in Form Builder code and a stacked zone in Visual Basic. There can be many stacked canvases visible at the same time, if they do not overlap. Figure 16-12 shows two stacked canvases in the Student Enrollment window. Each has a button in the Student Enrollment window that navigates the cursor and pops up the canvas.

If you want to combine module components in a window but they are on separate windows, resize one window box around both module components. This will merge the two windows into one. The same technique works for canvases. To split elements out of a window into a second window, draw a window around the second element or drag it into another existing window.

The layout items are a powerful way to define the visual layout of the tables in the generated module. Try out different arrangements of placement items and generate each one to test the effect; your time will be well spent. This process will increase your understanding of the way the generators interpret the symbols on the diagrammer and speed up your work later.

TIP
*You can use the diagram as a navigation tool for the properties window. If you select an object in the diagram and have the Property Palette open, the properties for that object will appear in the Property Palette. You can also turn on tracking using the **Navigator→Track Diagram Selection** menu option. When this option is checked and you select an object in the diagram, the corresponding element will also be selected in the Navigator.*

Item Groups

A feature you can use in defining the bound and unbound items for a particular module component is the *item group.* This is a set of items that have a name you specify. The generators treat an item group as a unit, and all items in it are displayed together in the generated module. For example, you can define an item group called Customer Profile that contains the name, address, and phone number of a customer. All these items will be treated as a group, and when the generator decides to place items in different windows or different parts of the screen, it will keep the set of items together. You can even specify a prompt for the whole group. Several preferences exist for customizing the layout of the items within the group. You can place item groups within item groups, but you cannot place action items in item groups

If you set the *Stacked ?* property to "Yes" the generator (Forms and Visual Basic) will create a tab canvas for each stacked item group in that table usage. This is handy if you need to save screen space or have many items in one table usage. For example, you have a STUDENTS table usage that contains 10 items for general information, 12 items for the student's home information, and 15 items for the student's work information. There is only enough room on the window for the 10 items of general information and one of the other two sets of items. You can create item groups for HOME and WORK and assign the items to them appropriately. If you generate the module as a form, the form will contain two tab canvases—one for home and one for work. The user can click on each tab to view and edit the item values. The Help generator also uses the *Stacked ?* property to determine how to assign text to the topic pages.

You create an item group by selecting the columns you want to include in the group and choosing the **Utilities→Group Items** menu item or the Create Group toolbar button (in Display view). The item group will be created and a box will appear around the items, as the following illustration shows.

You can remove a column from an item group by selecting it and choosing **Utilities→Remove From Group**. If all items are removed from the group, the group will still be seen in the module component. You can delete it using the Navigator Item Groups node under the module component.

TIP
In most diagram elements, you can edit the names in place. For example, the item group prompt has a default when you first create it, but you can click once and then click again on it in the diagram (two slow clicks, not one double-click) and open up an edit box to change it. This works for the window title as well.

Reusable Module Components

One of the most powerful features of a module component is that you can make it reusable. You can create a module component that you can share with other modules in your application system and even with modules in other application systems—a *reusable module component*. This has the same effect as *referencing* an object group in Oracle Developer Form Builder, which makes a nonmodifiable copy of a set of objects from one form to another. The copy points back to the source, so if you change anything in the source group, the referenced group changes as well.

Reusable module components are handy for setting up standard data blocks that will appear in a number of forms. For example, you may use a module component with WORK_GRADES and GRADE_TYPES in a Form module that shows the grades for a particular course and also in a Form module for entering grades for a particular student. In both modules, you want the module component to look and act the same. Therefore, you create a reusable module component for those two tables and use that module component in each module. If you need to change the way the WORK_GRADES block looks, you can change the module component, and both Form modules will "inherit" those changes. You need to generate the modules again to update the files, but the definitions in the repository will be automatically updated when you update the reusable module component.

You can create a reusable module component in much the same way that you create a specific module component. You can use the Navigator and Property Palette, which means you also need to enter the table usages and bound items through the Property Palette. You can use the property dialog for the module component node by switching property dialogs from the Options menu and clicking the Create button when selecting the Reusable Module Components node.

Once you have created the reusable module component, all you need to do to include it in a module is drag and drop it from the Navigator to the diagram or to the module node in the Navigator. You can also right-click on the module and select Include Module Component from the menu. This dialog is for reusable module components only and allows you to either use the reusable module component in a specific module or to copy the component to create a specific module component.

Reusable Component Graphical Editor

You can view and change a reusable module component using a diagram tool. If you select **Tools→Reusable Component Graphical Editor** from the menu after selecting a reusable module component in either the Navigator or the Module Diagram, you will load that module component into a diagram window. You can also drag the reusable module component to a blank area in the Design Editor window to create a diagram. This window mirrors the functionality of the Module Diagram, but it centers on one reusable module component instead of the entire module. This diagram window has its own data view and display view so you can work with it in the same way.

Converting to and from Reusable Module Components

You can convert an inclusion of a reusable module component within a module to a nonreusable, or *specific,* module component within that same module. Right-click on the module component name in the Navigator (or symbol in the diagram) and select Make Private Copy from the menu. This creates a local copy that you can modify but that starts with the same parts as the reusable version. Remember, when you do this, the module component is no longer linked in any way to the reusable module component from which it was created. Therefore, if the reusable module component changes in the future, that change will not automatically be propagated to the specific inclusion that this process creates.

You can also convert a specific module component to a reusable module component by right-clicking on the module component name in the Navigator (or symbol in the diagram) and selecting Make Reusable from the menu. Another way to do this is by changing the *Module Component Type* property from "Specific" to "Re-usable." This might be useful if you created a module component that you thought would never be used again, then you found that you needed the same module component in another module. Instead of copying the module component into the other module, you could make it reusable and specify it in the second module.

When you make a module component reusable, the local (specific) copy of that module component is copied to the Reusable Module Components node and the specific copy becomes linked to that reusable module component. This is the same effect as if you had included the reusable module component in the module in the first place.

TIP

As with other Oracle Designer diagrammers, the Module Diagram tool does not save the zoom (magnification) setting with the diagram. Therefore, after opening a diagram you need to use the toolbar buttons or View menu to zoom in or out and restore your preferred zoom setting. Doing this right after the diagram opens and you have maximized the windows will save you time later in adjusting the view.

Other Techniques

You can resequence the bound items in a table usage by dragging and dropping them in the Display view. You can also select Resequence Items from the right-click menu after selecting a bound item in the Navigator or diagram. This shows a dialog where you can reorder the bound items. The Data view always shows the items in alphabetical order, so resequencing items while viewing the diagram will not make a change in the diagram, although you will see the change in the Navigator.

After you have created a new module, the diagram takes care of the layout for you. Any element that is part of that module will be displayed automatically. You cannot resize or move the elements around on the screen without changing the definitions. The tool calculates the sizes automatically based on the displayed elements. Although you can reorder elements, such as bound items in the display view, those changes write directly to the repository and affect the base definitions. This is slightly different from the Server Model, where you can resize and move elements without affecting anything in the repository other than the way the diagram looks.

You can change the fonts and colors of elements on the diagram in the usual way—by selecting the element or elements and clicking the toolbar button for Fill color, Font, Line Color, and Line Width. You can use the Key Based Link toolbar button to create the links from foreign key definitions, or you can use the Default Links utility to place the links, as discussed later. The Link Module toolbar button assigns the module's calling and called modules. This button accomplishes the same task that you perform in the Module Network Viewer, but only for the scope of a single module.

Show/Hide Options

As with the Server Model Diagram, you can hide some elements displayed on the screen by choosing **Options→Show/Hide** from the menu when the Module Diagram is the active window. This dialog, shown in Figure 16-13, lets you turn on or off the display of bound items (columns) as well as other diagrammed elements and properties. This might be useful if you had a large number of table usages in one module and wanted to print a summarized version of the module's data usages. If you hid the bound items, the table usages boxes and the module itself would become smaller.

These settings become part of the diagram, so when you open the diagram again, you will see the same Show/Hide setup as when you saved

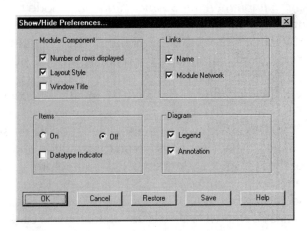

FIGURE 16-13.   *Show/Hide Preferences dialog*

it. This allows you to save different views of the same module in case you need to represent different details.

> **NOTE**
> *Unless you need to save the exact view of the module (Show/Hide options), there is no need to save the diagram. Any time you add something to the diagram or change the elements, the element definitions shown on the diagram will change automatically. You can actually define everything you need for a module by using the properties windows and the Navigator. Diagrams are easier to manipulate for many concepts, though, and are quite useful in setting the display aspects of the module.*

Create Default Module Data Usages Utility

The Utilities menu in RON provides the Create Default Module Data Usages item, which lets you load table and column usages for a module from the functions on which the module is based. The module must have at least one entry in the *Usages: Implementing Business Functions* node to tie it to one or more functions. In addition, those functions must have entity and attribute usages. Since ADT already does this for modules that it creates, you would need to run this utility only for modules you create outside ADT that can be associated with existing functions.

You run this utility by choosing the menu item after selecting the module name in RON. The utility will display a progress window as it runs. The utility checks all functions with which the selected module is associated. It creates a table usage for each entity usage on the function and assigns the appropriate operations from the function CRUD. Therefore, if the function Register a Student used the entity STUDENT for Create, Retrieve, and Update, the associated REG_STUDENT module would have a module component for the STUDENTS table (assuming that the STUDENTS table had an association to the STUDENT entity). This STUDENTS module component would be assigned operations of Insert, Query, and Update based on the function's CRUD usages.

Default Links Utility

The Default Links utility in the Design Editor creates table usages links between tables in your diagram. It uses the foreign keys you have defined in the repository for the tables to link tables on the diagram and provide descriptors. To run the utility, select a module in the Navigator or diagram and choose the **Utilities→Default Links** menu option. The following dialog appears:

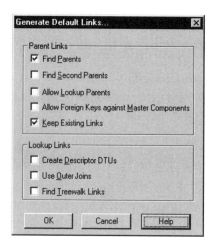

The Find Parents and Keep Existing Links check boxes are probably the most universally useful selections; if you need more information on each check box, click the Help button in this window. Note that you can also create the links quickly by drawing them in the Data view with the Key Based Link toolbar button, if the foreign key already exists.

TIP
You may define foreign keys against lookup tables or views that do not have foreign key constraints implemented in the database by setting the Validate in property to "Client." The module definition needs the foreign key constraint definition to know how to link the tables or views.

Where Does This Information Go?

The main elements you use in the Module Diagram are the module component table usages and the layout itself. These definitions are core components for code generation. To generate most code modules in Oracle Designer, you need the module definition with its module component definitions, the specific generator utility for that module type, preferences (either default or customized), the module template (for most generators), and the template object library. The particular generator combines the properties and associations of the module with the preferences and predesigned template to create the finished application module. As mentioned, code generation in the Build phase is an iterative process, and the Module Diagram is a perfect place from which to start the generator utilities.

Module Component API

The Server API helps provide a consistent interface to the database tables. It consists of two parts: the Table API or table handler (discussed in Chapter 14) and the Module Component API, or module handler. The Module Component API (MCAPI) is a set of PL/SQL packages that call procedures in the Table API to insert, update, delete, lock, and query the data. You create the MCAPI by selecting the module in the Navigator and choosing **Generate→Generate Module Component API** from the menu.

The MCAPI is used only by Form modules that are based on views or procedures. Form Builder can base a data block on a procedure, but the default Form processing must be supplemented by customized PL/SQL code, which requires a good knowledge of complex datatypes. The MCAPI creates these PL/SQL procedures for you and hides the apparent complexity of this feature.

For the module component for which you want the API, be sure the *Datasource Type* is "View" or "PL/SQL Procedure" and the *Datatarget Type* is "PL/SQL Procedure." These are not the defaults but are required for the MCAPI to generate. Before running the scripts created from the Generate Database from Server Model utility, you have to generate and install the Table API for the table involved.

When you generate the form based on this module component, the Form generator will create triggers with names like INSERT-PROCEDURE, UPDATE-PROCEDURE, DELETE-PROCEDURE, QUERY-PROCEDURE, and LOCK-PROCEDURE. These triggers, in turn, call the Module API that has procedures for the insert, update, delete, query, and lock operations on either the view or the procedure. This provides another layer but reduces network traffic, because a multirecord DML operation passes across the network using a PL/SQL table of records. This saves round-trip processing from the client to the server. The "Module Component Properties" section in Chapter 18 provides details on the various settings for source and target.

You can customize the MCAPI just as you can customize the Table API. You do this under the Module Component in the Navigator in a node called API Logic. When you add a definition here, you specify which event will contain the code (such as Pre-Insert or Post-Delete). You also name this code segment and decide whether to open the Logic Editor to enter the code. At this point, it is a good idea to enter some code because you can then test that the code is complete enough to run in the database. When you choose **Generate→Generate Module Component API** from the menu, the utility will insert your API Logic code in the proper place in the generated PL/SQL package.

CAUTION
If you get an error when generating the MCAPI that says "CGEN-03385 Language differs from Save Language; repository definition not updated," you are not using a procedure or view as the basis for the table usage or you have not set the Datasource Type *property of the module component to "View" or "PL/SQL Procedure" and the* Datatarget Type *to "PL/SQL Procedure." After you make the corrections, the MCAPI should generate correctly.*

Module Application Guide

The Module Application Guide steps you through the process of creating modules. Its interface is similar to that of the Server Model Guide and Database Administration Guide, as discussed in Chapter 14. Figure 16-14 shows the expanded opening window that you load when you select **Tools→Module Application Guide** from the menu.

The interface is set up so that you can step through the process in a "wizard" fashion. That is, you define what the window presents and it "interviews" you to get properties needed for module definitions. You still need to know about all the elements that a module requires, but there are links to the help system to give you information on concepts you do not understand. After you finish the series of screens (pressing the next arrow button), the module definitions will be complete. You can generate the modules from this interface by selecting the module from the list and clicking the Generate button. You can also run the design capture utilities to create module definitions from existing forms and reports (as described in Chapter 12).

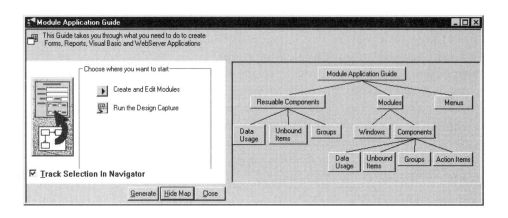

FIGURE 16-14. *Module Application Guide*

Reference Tables

The applications work you do in the Design phase includes some database activities. One of these is revising the tables your modules are based on to work in the most efficient way. The decision to make some changes to the database design for the application can only come during the Application Design part of the Design phase. Another database activity you perform in the Design phase is defining reference code, code control, and help tables. These tables are database objects but are used heavily by the application modules. The Application Design stage is the first time you will have enough information to be able to make the decisions about these tables. Once you create the reference tables, the code, reference, and help tables are automatically populated when you generate a module.

Reference Code Table

The *reference code table* stores the allowable values you attach to a column or domain. *Allowable Values* are elements associated with an attribute, column, or domain that identify what values the user can enter in the columns. Allowable Values are characterized by properties such as *Value*, *High Value* (for range validation), *Abbreviation,* and *Meaning* (the description of the value). All properties but the *Value* are optional, but it is practical to provide, at least, a *Meaning* for each value so the user can more easily understand what the *Value,* which is often a short code, represents.

If the domain or column has the *Dynamic List* property set to "Yes," the Allowed Values are stored in a database table from which the generated code retrieves the valid values when the application runs. The *Dynamic List* property should be used whenever the values are subject to change over the life of the application. The main alternative to using a code table is to hard-code the valid values in the application code. This alternative provides a slightly faster response time with less network traffic and may be appropriate for domains whose allowable values do not change, such as Yes-No values. However, it means that you need to change application code, possibly in many modules, if a code changes.

The generator examines the Allowed Values for all columns in the module and all domains used by those columns. If there are Allowed Values, the generator inserts them into the reference code table. The generator also creates the program code to check the table and to display lists of values of the reference codes. The *Dynamic List* property of the Domain and Column, if set to "Yes," specifies that the column will be generated with code to look up the values in the reference code table. The Table API will contain the lookup and validation code.

The standard name of the reference code table is CG_REF_CODES, which refers to "CASE Generator Reference Codes." This table stores the allowable values for domains referenced in all applications in the repository. You can change both the table name and its scope by selecting **Options→Generator Options→General**. This dialog, shown in Figure 16-15, allows you to specify the Scope of Reference Code Table field as one of the following:

- **Single Table** to create one CG_REF_CODES table.

- **Application System Wide Table** to create a single reference code table for each application system. The table name will be *application system name*_REF_CODES, where *application system name* is the application system for which you are generating modules.

The reference code table in Oracle Designer does not provide space or facilities to deactivate unused codes but keeps them in the same table for historical records. There is a fair amount of functionality in the default

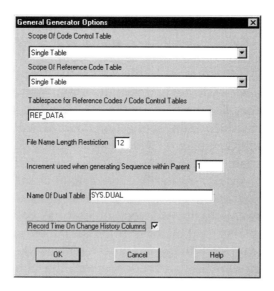

FIGURE 16-15. *General Generator Options dialog*

method, though, and this simplifies or eliminates code you would need to write yourself to maintain the values in the column.

TIP
A single reference code table is better if application systems share table definitions that have allowable values on their columns or domains on those columns. In this situation, if you define separate code tables, you have to update the individual reference code tables if an allowable values set changes. With one reference code table for multiple application systems, there is only one place you need to make changes if the allowable values change.

Generate Reference Code Tables Utility
You create the reference code table by clicking on the module for which you want the code values, choosing **Generate→Generate Reference Code Tables** from the menu, filling out the dialog (which looks the same as the dialog in

the Generate Database from Server Model utility), and clicking the Start button. You can also generate the DDL code with the **Generate→Generate Database from Server Model** menu option by selecting tables on which the Allowable Values exist. Oracle Designer creates DML like the following listing, which handles the YN domain on the DROP_LOWEST column in the GRADE_BASES table.

L 16-3

```
DELETE FROM CG_REF_CODES
WHERE RV_DOMAIN = 'YN'
/
INSERT INTO CG_REF_CODES (
RV_DOMAIN, RV_LOW_VALUE, RV_HIGH_VALUE, RV_ABBREVIATION, RV_MEANING)
VALUES ('YN', 'N', NULL, NULL, 'No')
/
INSERT INTO CG_REF_CODES (
RV_DOMAIN, RV_LOW_VALUE, RV_HIGH_VALUE, RV_ABBREVIATION, RV_MEANING)
VALUES ('YN', 'Y', NULL, NULL, 'Yes')
/
```

The Generate Reference Code Tables utility will create a .SQL file with statements like the preceding. The Generate Database from Server Model will create a number of files related to the table you select. One of these will be the .TAB file with the CREATE TABLE statements. One of those CREATE statements will be for CG_REF_CODES. A file with a .AVT extension will also be created with statements like those in the preceding listing.

Whichever utility you use to create the script, the RV_DOMAIN column in the CG_REF_CODES table will contain the name of the domain on which the columns in the module were based. If the Allowed Values were created on a column instead of the domain, the RV_DOMAIN column will contain the name of the table and column, for example, "GRADE_BASES.DROP_LOWEST." This RV_DOMAIN is used in the WHERE clause for LOVs and validation code. For example: WHERE rv_domain = 'YN'.

After you create the reference code table (in the database schema that will own the application tables), you refresh the reference code table using the same utilities. Since the first step in the script that these utilities produce is a DELETE statement, you can refresh a newly updated list of Allowed Values by running the scripts these utilities produce.

Code Control Tables

Code control tables supply columns with unique values from a table. While the traditional way to do this in an Oracle database is with a sequence, you may be implementing a non-Oracle database. In this case, you use a code control table to store a number. Each time you need another number, the code created by the Table API retrieves the number and increments it for the next use.

The *Sequence* property of the Column definition allows you to designate the name of the sequence definition that will populate the column when a row is inserted. The *Server Derived* property is set to "Yes" if you want the server code to generate the sequence number (if the client application does not supply it) or "No" if you want the client code to generate the sequence number.

You create a sequence in the Sequence Definitions node of the Server Model tab. If you want to use a standard sequence database object for the unique number value, set the sequence property, *Code Control,* to "ORACLE Sequence." If you want to specify a table-based sequence generator, set the value to "Code Control Sequence."

The code control table is named CG_CODE_CONTROLS by default. You can change the scope and name of the code control table in exactly the same way as you do for the reference codes table. Use the **Options→Generator Options→General** menu item. This dialog, shown before in Figure 16-15, contains a Scope of Code Control Table field. In addition to the options for a single table and a table for each application, you have an option to use one table for each code control. The table name is *table name*_CC (where *table name* is the name of the table with the columns defined using the sequence) for each table that has code control sequences.

CAUTION

Before going too far into design, if you are using the Table API, after checking the sequence creation scripts, run the **Generate→Generate Table API** *utility and examine the package body to see if it will use the _CC or CODE_CONTROLS tables you think it should use.*

The Generate Database from Server Model utility will create scripts for the sequence creation based on the type of sequence. If the sequence is

a standard Oracle one, you generate a CREATE SEQUENCE script. If it is a
code control sequence, you generate the INSERT statement into the
CODE_CONTROLS table (remember, its name will depend on the scope
you picked). An example follows:

L 16-4

```
INSERT INTO CG_CODE_CONTROLS
     (CC_DOMAIN, CC_NEXT_VALUE, CC_INCREMENT, CC_COMMENT)
VALUES
     ('ZIP_SEQ_CC', 1, NULL, NULL)
/
```

You generate the DDL for a table that uses the sequence if you want to
generate the CREATE TABLE script for the code control table itself (CREATE
TABLE CG_CODE_CONTROLS). The Generate Database from Server Model
utility will create statements for all tables you select as well as for the
CG_CODE_CONTROLS table.

The Table API (if you set the *Server Derived* property to "Yes") will create
code to populate the column using the sequence. When you generate the
Table API, you produce a package and triggers that call procedures in that
package. You generate the API using the **Generator→Generate Table API**
menu option after choosing a table or tables. If you create the Table API for
a table containing a column with a standard Oracle sequence, the package
body will contain code such as the following:

L 16-5

```
SELECT  CRSE_SEQ.nextval
INTO    cg$rec.COM_ID
FROM    DUAL;
cg$ind.COM_ID := TRUE;
```

If you specify a code control sequence, you will produce Table API code
like the following:

L 16-6

```
SELECT  CC_NEXT_VALUE
INTO    cg$rec.COM_ID
FROM    CG_CODE_CONTROLS
WHERE   CC_DOMAIN = 'CRSE_SEQ_CC'
FOR UPDATE;

UPDATE CG_CODE_CONTROLS
SET    CC_NEXT_VALUE = CC_NEXT_VALUE + CC_INCREMENT
WHERE  CC_DOMAIN = 'CRSE_SEQ_CC';
```

Help Tables

You can implement a help system for your generated code (Form and Visual Basic) using the MS Help generator (described in Chapter 18). You can also use table-based help for Form modules. This type of help stores the text in a table that is queried into a separate form when the user views the help system. This kind of help is context-sensitive based on the cursor location in the form, but it does not contain some standard help system features like hypertext links to other topics, graphical images, or any kind of text formatting other than the standard font.

If you decide to use the table-based help system, set the preference for *Type of Help System used* (HLPTYP in the End User Interface category) on the application level to HELPFORM. Set the preference *Name of form that displays user help* (HLPFRM in the same category) to the name of the form that will display the help text. The default is the form supplied with Oracle Designer, OFGHLPF. You can also set the application system-level preference *Scope of online help table* (HPTABL in the DBA category), to one of the following:

■ **GENERIC** to specify that you will use the CG_FORM_HELP table to serve as a single table for all application systems.

■ **APPSYS** to specify that user help text for each application will be stored in a table with the name *application system name*_FORM_ HELP (where *application system name* is the name of the application system where your modules are defined.

If you use APPSYS, you will have to modify the help form (OFGHLPF) to reference a table with an application-specific name instead of CG_ FORM_HELP.

You create the help table using the Generate Help System dialog (called the Update Help Tables Utility in the Oracle Designer help system). This dialog is run by selecting a module in the Modules node and choosing the menu option **Generate→Generate Module As (Help System)**. The dialog in Figure 16-16 appears.

After selecting the Update the Form Generator Help Tables button, you can specify that you will generate help only for the module or for the tables associated with the module (or both). You set options here only if you are

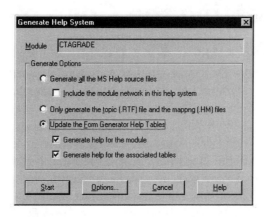

FIGURE 16-16. *Generate Help System dialog*

generating an MS Help file by clicking the Options button. When you click the Start button, the generator will run, create the table if it has not yet been created, and load the help table from the *User/Help Text* property defined in the module, table, or bound item help levels.

When you generate a form, Oracle Designer will insert rows for help based on the help text in the form or its tables and columns. This occurs only if the property *Module Generation History* is null; you can set a preference, *Add module history comment on generation* (MODCMT in the Commenting category) so the generators will not load text in this property.

NOTE
The help table is created in the repository user's schema. It is best to make that table shared, especially when there are many developers using the same application system. One option is to create the table in the application table owner's schema as soon as possible when working with modules. Then create grants and synonyms (public or private) to that table so developers and users can access the help system.

Implementing the Control Exposure Matrix

One of the tasks in the Design phase is constructing a control exposure matrix. You can implement the system of controls and exposures with user extensions in Oracle Designer. You can run the Matrix Diagrammer to cross-check the assignments and include the control exposure plan in reports.

All you need to do is to create user extension elements for exposures and controls. These elements should allow you to enter all details of those parts of the security system. You also need an association element with a property called *Evaluation* that relates the exposures and controls. You can then associate exposures to controls by placing a numeric *Evaluation* value in the association element.

Creating the user extensions is a job you complete in the Repository Administration Utility, discussed in Chapter 27. Filling in the association between exposures and controls is easiest in the Matrix Diagrammer, although you can also use the Repository Object Navigator. You can run reports on the new elements and associations by printing the matrix diagram or creating your own reports with SQL*Plus or Oracle Reports.

Matrix Diagrammer in Application Design

Toward the end of the Application Design part of Design, you should cross-check the design. One of the tools you use to perform this check is the Matrix Diagrammer, introduced in Chapter 10. Three matrix diagrams are useful at this stage in the life cycle to ensure that the design is as sound as possible.

Modules and Columns

The first matrix you create in this phase cross-checks data and modules. You want to be certain that all data elements you defined are being used correctly and completely in the modules you designed. You can set up a 3D matrix of Modules (as the matrix diagram row) to Columns (as the matrix diagram column) to check the insert-delete-update-query properties. The

Intersection Bound items settings for this matrix include the Insert, Update, and Query properties. You can determine whether any columns are missing from modules or some operation (Insert, Update, and Query) is not being performed anywhere in the system. If such exceptions exist, the matrix diagram will help you identify them so you can fix the usages.

This review may also point out a module that repeats the data usage of another module and therefore may not be essential to the application. It may also reveal that you need another module to handle some operation on a particular table or set of tables. Once you have a sense of where the trouble spots are, you can modify modules, add modules, and delete modules before running the matrix again to check the design. You also need to run a report (not a matrix diagram) on the table usages for modules to be sure you are providing delete capabilities in the desired modules. This report is one you will have to construct with the API views, as Chapter 28 describes.

Requirements and Modules

Another matrix you may want to run at this point shows requirements and the modules that fulfill them. In Pre-Design, you created a user-extension element of Requirements and a user-extension association of Requirements to Modules. The requirements linked to functions during the Analysis phase were passed on to their respective modules during Pre-Design so that each module has the same requirements as the functions from which it derives. The matrix you create at the end of Design shows these elements and associations and allows you to check that all requirements have at least one module. By carefully examining the matrix, you can determine whether there are any requirements without modules or modules without requirements. In the former case, you may need another module to fulfill the requirement. In the latter case, the module either was not assigned requirements or is unnecessary and should be deleted. You can also use the alternative mentioned in Chapter 12 to show the Requirements to Functions to Modules associations and check for lost requirements.

Exposures and Controls

As mentioned above, you may want to develop user extensions for Exposures and Controls with an association between them. You can then create an Exposures and Controls Matrix using the Matrix Diagrammer. This matrix enables you to check whether all exposures have at least one control.

This matrix would be one of the tools you used to enter the information in the first place, so you just need to open it again at the end of the Design phase and check whether there are controls for all exposures and exposures for all controls. If you find that you are missing controls, you have to add them. If you have controls without exposures, you can probably delete these extra controls.

Repository Reports in the Design Phase: Application Design

As usual, at the end of a phase (or part of a phase), you can run reports to show and check the work you have done in that phase. The major repository reports you run at this point are in the Module Design group of the Repository Reports tool. The *Module Definition* and *Module Network* reports provide detailed information on the modules and menus, respectively. The *Module Component Definition* report shows the properties and table usages for module components and which modules use them. The *Non-Default User Preferences* report lists, by product, the preference settings that you have changed from the factory (default) values.

The Impact Analysis group contains the *Column Change Impact Analysis* report, which gives a list of all modules that use specified columns. This is useful if you need to drop or modify a column and need to know what modules contain a usage for that column. The Analyze Dependencies Design Editor utility (in the Utilities menu) provides some of this information too.

A useful report that is not within the Group view of Repository Reports is the *Access to Modules by Roles* report. This report lets you check the module access you have assigned to roles in the repository. You can reach this by viewing the Repository Reports list as a hierarchy (in the Role node) or by name (in alphabetical order).

You also need to check whether module security has been applied to implement part of the exposure control system. Another check is user or role access to tables, but this report is one you need to write yourself using the API views (as described in Chapter 28), as there is no such repository report.

CHAPTER
17

Build

Which of you, intending to build a tower, sitteth not down first, and counteth the cost, whether he have sufficient to finish it?

—*Bible*, Luke 14:28

n the Build phase, we build both the database and the applications. If all the activities and deliverables identified in the previous phases have been completed carefully, building the proposed database should be a relatively straightforward process. However, building the modules to support the database still requires quite a lot of work, because you need to use the Oracle Designer module generators. The Oracle Designer generators are very powerful utilities that, when used correctly, can automatically generate nearly perfect production applications. Incorrectly used, however, generators can increase development time and provide little benefit to the project. The key to Build phase success is correct use of the generators.

Overview of the Build Phase

In the Build phase, you build the database and applications, but there is also other work to be done. These are the steps in the Build phase:

1. Build the database. This work includes physically configuring its location and creating instances.

2. Build a quantity of test data and perform data migration. Applications cannot easily be built with an empty database.

3. Build applications and implement the internal control system. To build and validate the application, you will use the design book as a blueprint to ensure that all specifications are met. The developer should meticulously check off each system requirement in the design book as it is met during the building of the module.

4. As the application is built, you must perform tuning and unit-level testing to ensure functional and technical accuracy. This is a crucial step in the Build phase. This quality assurance process is perhaps the most critical part of the building process.

Each application must go through this build-test process to ensure that it is built correctly. In addition, you must consider the help system and user documentation.

Deliverables

The Build phase deliverables consist of the following:

- Unit tested application system
- Populated databases
- System documentation
- User documentation
- Help system and online documents

Building the Database

The actual building of the database is a relatively straightforward process. There is only one minor detour: you have been specifying the tables' physical characteristics, such as the storage requirements and tablespaces, to fit the production system requirements. However, if you generate DDL from these production-ready table implementations, the generated table and index sizes will be too large for development, and they will not be placed in the correct tablespaces.

The detour consists of creating another set of schema objects for the development database. You have to create table implementations specifying smaller storage parameters and different tablespace names for the tables and associated indexes. You can then have Oracle Designer generate the data definition language (DDL) scripts based on these table implementations to create the tables.

You will actually want to have three versions of the database:

- **Version 1** Small tables populated with dummy test data. Dummy test data is unrealistic-looking test data that has been carefully constructed to validate the correctness of the applications and reports. You should use data that allows you to easily see whether the applications and reports are running correctly.

- **Version 2**   Small tables populated with realistic-looking data. This version shows users what the application will actually look like. For this version, the developers and testers build the test data at the same time as the application. The creation of this sample data is then part of the testing process.

- **Version 3**   Full-size database populated with real migrated data. This version is used for stress and performance testing.

You can create the first two versions using the table implementations you created for development. You can then use the original production-specific table implementations to create the full-size database.

Building Unrealistic Dummy Data

How much dummy data should you use in the first version of the database? Each core main table will require 200 to 1,000 records. For example, a sales database might be set up using 10 to 20 regions. Each region might have 0 to 20 customers, each customer might have 0 to 20 sales, and each sale might have 0 to 20 items. On the surface, it might seem like a lot of work to create dummy data for this many records. This process cries out for automation.

The purpose of the dummy data is to support the application and report building process by providing an easy way to validate that the application and reports are performing correctly.

Fortunately, several products exist that automate the generation of sample data. Such utilities are relatively inexpensive and can save hundreds of hours of developer time. When working on a system with inadequate sample data, it is common for report writers to spend a significant portion of their time populating the database with sample data to ensure that their reports have been correctly developed. These products should be used with caution. Some adopt the philosophy of complete automatic generation with little or no setup. Such products may save time but also generate very unrealistic-looking sample data. Other products require extensive setup but pull their information from sample data fields to provide realistic-looking data. For example, a sample list of city and street names are supplied so that address data will look realistic. A balance between these two approaches must be achieved for sample data to be useful and not too time consuming to generate.

Dummy data should be published and not changed by the developers. After using the dummy data to check applications, a restore operation should be performed to bring the dummy data back to its original state. Otherwise, one developer's manipulation of the dummy data may cause another developer to think that the applications are not working.

Another reason for using dummy data rather than production data is that because the amount of data is relatively small, it enables applications and reports to run very fast.

Building Realistic Sample Data

Realistic sample data for the second version of the database can be built as part of the developer's testing process for the applications. Initially, the developer can use the dummy test data version of the database to make sure that the basic functionality of the module is in place. Then the developer can shift the module to the second version of the database by logging in as a different user and use the module itself to generate sample data, using real business transactions supplied by the users. Additional realistic sample data can be generated by the module testers in a similar fashion.

Performing Data Migration

Data migration can consume a large portion of the total development effort. Migration strategies are discussed in detail in Chapter 25.

Auditing the Database

It is important to know that the database has been built according to the data requirements. The module design and cross-checks helped to validate the database design, as did the legacy system migration. You must assume that during the building of the modules, further modifications will be made to the database. Therefore, you will need to audit the data structure during the Test phase.

The question then remains: what level of audit of the database design is appropriate prior to the building of the modules? If you performed a legacy system data migration, there is probably little need to fully audit the database. However, you do need to ensure that the Design and Build phase processes have been completed correctly. Therefore, as a minimum, you should randomly spot-check each developer's work in the Design and Build phases. If problems in the work of one or more developers become evident, or if there was no legacy system to migrate, a more thorough audit may be necessary.

Building the Modules

Module building is an iterative process. You generate the modules and then assess how different the generated modules are from the desired modules. Here, developers take different approaches. Some developers prefer to make changes to the Oracle Designer repository and then regenerate the module; others make all of their modifications within the screen module and run Designer's Design Capture utility to reverse engineer those features which can be stored in the repository. The approach the developer uses depends, in part, on what tool the developer prefers. However, regardless of the approach, the resulting application should be the same.

You don't need to explicitly worry about internal control system implementation at this point, because you have already made the necessary modifications to the design book required by internal control systems. The control requirements are simply another feature or function in the modules that you must build and test.

In Chapter 11 on Pre-Design, we briefly discuss the strategy for building modules. In the Build phase, these modules must be created. The entire specification of the Forms modules should be contained in the Oracle Designer repository. However, some of the work of building the modules will be done in Oracle Developer as well as in Designer. There are several basic steps in building the modules:

1. Create the development environment by setting preferences in the Oracle Designer Forms generators and create one or more Forms templates.

2. For each module, create the storyboard and module specifications.

3. Generate the module.

4. Make modifications to the forms.

5. Design capture, regenerate, and test.

Each step will be described separately.

1. Setting Preferences

The setting of the preferences and the creation of the Forms template(s) must be done together, since this is the way the development environment is set up. Extensive testing is required. Once the preferences are specified, they should not be modified. One technique that can be used is to create different sets of preferences for different module types. Many development teams have different sets of preferences for different types of blocks. We have not found this to be necessary. We use one set of preferences for all forms. We do, however, use a few different Forms templates, one with tabs and one without tabs. In our Forms templates, we must make allowances for the limitations of the Designer generators. Therefore, we include generic user parameters, three generic LOVs (one for each icon type), and an attached library. The template should also include an object library for the purpose of subclassing. Virtually every object in the template form is subclassed, providing precise control over all properties of an item.

2. Creating Storyboards

In order to create storyboards, you need a very precise understanding of how the module will be laid out and how it will function. The storyboard must be realized as a module in Oracle Designer.

3. Module Specification and Generation

When the module is generated, it should look exactly the way you want the final form to look. To accomplish this, you will need to specify not only fields that will appear on the form but hidden fields as well. Generation must be a part of this step, since the form rarely looks exactly right the first time. An iterative process should be used to achieve the desired result.

The form is not complete at this point but does include all blocks, items, basic poplists and LOVs. For many forms, this may be all that is necessary. For complex forms, additional coding is required.

4. Making Modifications

Next, you need to refine the module. You need to make the generated module conform to the system specifications. The easiest way to do this is

probably by using the development tool—for example, Oracle Developer—
rather than making modifications within Oracle Designer and generating the
module again. Keep in mind that modifications must be made in such a way
that they will not be lost when a design capture in Oracle Designer is done.
There are several ways to accomplish this. You can write code anywhere.
Program units can be created. Code can be attached to triggers or items with
impunity without losing anything during design capture.

There are several things you can and cannot do when modifying forms:

- You must be careful if your code references items on the form. If the
  names of those items change, you will have to make manual
  modifications and the code will not be automatically updated. You
  can usually avoid this problem if you make package variables for all
  items that you want to reference in the form. Then use the COPY
  and NAME-IN commands for all form variable interactions.

- If fields do change, you can always update the references to forms
  fields in code using the Forms API. Another way to update references
  is to convert the form to text format, make string substitutions on
  Forms' name calls, and convert back to binary format. This last
  approach is not recommended by Oracle.

- You can easily add blocks and items to a previously generated form
  if these are not to be displayed. If you are adding items to be
  displayed, you will have to manually manipulate the layout
  properties in Designer before the form will generate correctly. You
  will also need to manually copy any subclassed information, since
  design capture misses this property.

- We do not recommend that you generate using the "Preserve Layout"
  feature. This essentially means that the specification of your form is
  no longer in the repository. This is a feature that should be avoided,
  if possible.

- Because of Oracle Designer's limited ability to design capture a
  form, care must be taken with what is done with the form in
  Developer. You cannot create record groups, LOVs, alerts, and user
  parameters or attach additional libraries to a form and design
  capture. There are some ways to overcome these limitations:

a) You can create record groups programmatically.

b) You can alter the generic LOV at runtime to provide all necessary functionality.

c) You cannot add new alerts but you can use alerts already existing in the template.

d) The template library should contain the appropriate generic code for alerts, LOVs, etc. in order to minimize the amount of hand-coding required.

The best overall strategy is to take the time to make sure that your templates are correctly architected.

5. Design Capture, Regenerate, and Test

If you have been careful in how your form was developed, nothing will be lost in the design capture process. After design capture is complete, you should then immediately generate and test the form. If modified in Developer, forms should not be passed along for unit testing until they have been design captured and regenerated in Oracle designer.

Postgeneration Work

The next step is to decide whether enough of the postgeneration work for this module can be embedded within Oracle Designer in such a way that future changes in the data structure will be reflected in the generated modules. If you decide you can achieve nearly 100 percent generation, including the modifications, then you should take the next step.

You need to implement all postgeneration work in such a way that changes automatically occur when the module is regenerated or generated again. There are three basic strategies for accomplishing this:

- Place the information in the Oracle Designer repository. This is the best approach. This way, all requirements are stored in the repository and any changes are automatically applied to the generated modules.

- Embed the changes in a form-specific template.

- Make selective changes to modules and regenerate.

Using One or More Templates

You need to decide at this point whether to use one template or many. Forms generated by Oracle Designer include predefined features, triggers, code, and so on. The developer can generate an underlying, base template that acts as a foundation for the generated module.

This base template should include the following:

- One or more object libraries

- Help application

- Sample menu

- One or more attached libraries

You need to decide if one template for all forms is adequate or if you need different templates for different types of forms. We currently use two templates—one for simple forms and one for multi-tab forms.

Tuning and Unit-Level Testing

The application and database cannot be tuned completely separately. You cannot simply tune one and then the other. Both components must be tuned together. This means that developing the tuning strategy requires both a skilled DBA and a skilled developer. Of course, some tasks, such as tablespace striping and RAID storage, will fall exclusively to the DBA. Some tasks, such as minimizing screen refresh operations that require access to the database, can only be addressed by the application developer.

Though some tuning problems can be solved exclusively by either database or application tuning, others require a combined approach. Each tuning problem must be considered individually to devise the best solution strategy. If the application is built according to standard development practices (that is, using explicit cursors and appropriate indexing in the database), tuning is an engineering issue. It involves establishing what is adequate performance for each process in the application. Once the application meets those standards, the development team can move on.

The initial unit testing procedure in the Build phase should proceed as follows:

1. Generate the application.

2. Develop the application using the dummy test data set.

3. Work with the application until you are satisfied that it runs properly.

4. Test applications and reports using a database populated with a small sample of realistic data. Make sure the layout makes sense for real data. It is easier to validate the system by running a test of business transactions with realistic data.

5. Run the application using a production-size test database that will ensure adequate performance. If data migration is not complete, the production-size test database can be generated using a sample data generation utility.

The next step is performance tuning. A complete discussion of performance tuning is beyond the scope of this book. However, the following is a list of standard classes of tuning problems and some possible techniques for solutions. (Note: Examples are specific to Oracle Forms, chosen here because of its wide use.)

1. **The form takes too long to open.**

   - **Technique A** Have the form DLLs load when Windows starts. This approach moves the delay from the form to Windows start-up. Having the delay occur when Windows starts is not as noticeable to the users.

   - **Technique B** Have a very small welcome form that calls the first main form.

   - **Technique C** Delay initialization routines until necessary. For example, record groups that don't need to be populated until someone accesses a poplist do not need to be populated initially. Population can occur the first time the record group is selected.

2. **The query takes too long.**

- **Technique A**   Make sure there are appropriate indexes for the joined columns in the database.

- **Technique B**   Tune the SQL using standard SQL tuning techniques such as hints.

- **Technique C**   Don't perform the query very often. Bring the results of the query back locally if multiple accesses are required. One common problem with Forms is that postquery triggers are essentially correlated subqueries, which generate a query for each row fetched. One possible technique is to bring the results of the query back to the form in a record group and then, for postquery triggers, perform all accesses using the local record group.

- **Technique D**   Use views. Since it is now possible to update multiple-table views in a limited fashion, avoid using postquery triggers at all by using views.

3. **Insert/modification/delete takes too long.**

- **Technique A**   Reduce the number of indexes. There may be too many on the table.

- **Technique B**   Tune and rethink the database triggers.

- **Technique C**   Rather than directly inserting all data modifications, pass them to a transaction log and perform data modifications in batch mode.

4. **A specific program unit is too slow.**

- **Technique A**   Minimize database accesses. It is necessary to minimize the number of cursors; you may be able to combine information retrieved on one cursor. Don't perform any unnecessary fetches. Avoid the repeated use of system variables that require database access. For example, a call to SYSDATE in Forms actually executes SELECT SYSDATE FROM DUAL, even though you don't need to explicitly use that syntax. If a call to SYSDATE is in a loop, it can greatly slow the loop. Even if you need an up-to-the-second, accurate SYSDATE value, you can get this by executing one fetch to SYSDATE and then incrementing the SYSDATE value locally in the client.

■ **Technique B**   The developer needs to intelligently decide whether the program unit should reside in the client or server. Program units that have little or no database access should reside in the client. However, program units that require extensive database access should, in general, reside on the server. For example, a program unit that performs complex string validation but requires no database access should certainly reside on the client. On the other hand, a complex function that calculates the amount owed by a client, possibly requiring hundreds of rows to be fetched into the procedure but returning only one value, should reside on the server. By moving that function to the database, you can perform the function by simply passing the function call to the database and receiving the return value in the client. If that program unit resides in the client, however, it may require hundreds of network round trips. Judicious placement of functions and procedures on either the client or server side can greatly enhance performance.

These are just a few examples of common problems and their solutions. There are books written exclusively on the subject of database and application tuning.

After a form is tuned during the Build phase, it should immediately be passed to unit testing. This enables developers to get immediate feedback regarding whether the forms meet the design specifications. Such an approach allows you to catch problems in the Build phase before they propagate through all applications.

Once the developer is satisfied that the system is functioning properly, a crucial part of the Build phase is unit-level testing. Ongoing testing is very important in the Build phase. You cannot consider a module successfully built until it passes unit-level testing.

A tester should be designated to perform unit-level testing. This individual does not need to be highly skilled. The tester's goal is to find out when the program doesn't act as the user expects it to. Just because it works in the way the developer intended does not necessarily mean that it will perform as the user expects. The tester acts as a surrogate user. The tester should "click all the buttons" and log any problems with the system.

Unit-level testing consists of answering the following questions:

- Does the module meet design specifications as laid out in the design book?

- Does the module conform to GUI, coding, and reporting standards?

- Is performance in a realistic environment across all user machines and network configurations adequate? This question is a bit tricky to answer because it requires the simulation of multiple users; however, it is important to try to catch problems early, so put the module on a number of different machines and run minimal tests on the different configurations.

System problems should be logged in a systematic way. There should be a simple way built right into the application for a user to log bugs and comments. For instance, you could provide a toolbar icon that the user can click to open a dialog box for logging a comment or bug. This approach is ideal for testers and developers since the log can be linked to a bug-tracking system. In this way, bugs can be automatically passed back to the developer for modification or correction. If the developer disagrees with the tester's suggestions, the issue can be submitted for arbitration by a senior QA person.

Documentation and Help

Both system and user documentation are important parts of the Build phase. Because of the way the system has been built using CADM, the system documentation is almost complete at this point. It should include all of the deliverables from the previous phases, reports generated by Oracle Designer, and notes from designers and developers describing the decisions made throughout the process. All that is left to add are design notes made during the Build phase and testing results.

User documentation should include manuals, tutorials, possibly even computer-aided instructional programs (for large organizations), training materials, and courses. To some extent, abundant training can make up for any gaps in user documentation. Similarly, a good help desk system can make up for less comprehensive training materials. Users should be involved in the documentation process to ensure that its level is appropriate for successful knowledge transfer. A complete discussion of user documentation is beyond the scope of this book.

A good online help system should be built into all screen modules. In most systems, help is an afterthought and not even considered until the system is in the Test phase. Often, only then does the lack of a Help system become painfully apparent. Adding Help to a system in Test is quite expensive. However, if Help is added to the system as it is being designed, it can be done in a cost-effective manner.

There are two strategies for creating Help systems:

■ Build separate and independent Help documents using a third-party tool.

■ Store Help in the Oracle Designer repository and generate the Help documents.

Each approach has its own pros and cons.

Using a third-party tool, you will be able to generate more sophisticated help. Help can be developed independently from the rest of the system; however, all of the Help will then exist outside of the Designer repository.

Generating Help from the repository is more cost efficient if done while applications are being developed. Help will be stored in the repository along with the module specifications and system documentation.

Having all of the system components stored in the Oracle Designer repository is a tremendous benefit. This strategy should be used whenever possible. To this end, setting your Help standards should be done in a way that is consistent with what Designer can generate.

Modifications for Smaller Systems

For small systems, the Design and Build phases may occur simultaneously. For medium-size systems, the Build phase process should be followed just as described in this chapter.

When Is the Build Phase Complete?

The Build phase is complete when all the applications pass unit testing, the user and system documentation are both nearly complete, the database is populated, and all elements have passed your company's initial quality review.

Conclusion

The system is nearly complete at the end of the Build phase. You have a database, migrated data, and unit-tested modules. All that remains to be done is to perform additional testing, finalize user and system documentation, and train users. The Build phase is probably the most complex from the Oracle Designer point of view. The true challenge in using Oracle Designer is the effective use of the generators.

There is a great temptation to generate applications and make all modifications using the client-side tool. However, this breaks the link to Oracle Designer and makes it impossible to regenerate the modules. In rare cases, this strategy is appropriate because of the complexity of the design. However, you should strive to use the Oracle Designer generators to build as many of your modules as possible. Where feasible, you should design capture any postgeneration changes back to the repository. In this way, you can realize the full potential of Oracle Designer.

Although you have used Oracle Designer as much as possible to create the finished application, the life cycle is not over. The post-Build phase steps in the life cycle and the activities that you need to perform before placing the system in production are covered in Chapters 19 and 20. This next step is called the Test phase. Chapter 21 discusses what happens when changes occur at various points in the CADM process and outlines the change control process.

CHAPTER
18

Oracle Designer in Build

The youth gets together his materials to build a bridge to the moon, or, perchance, a palace or temple on the earth, and, at length, the middle-aged man concludes to build a woodshed with them.

—Henry David Thoreau

he Build phase is the time when everything comes together. All the careful analysis and design work you did before feeds into the Build phase and results in your final database and application. The exact activities you perform in Oracle Designer depend on your choice of products for the application modules. If you decide to use Oracle Developer—Forms and Reports—or Oracle WebServer, the Oracle Designer generators in conjunction with other Oracle products can give you a complete set of working modules. If you use the Visual Basic, MS Help, or C++ Generator, you will have to use non-Oracle products to perform some tasks, such as compilation after Oracle Designer generates code from the repository (although some of this work is automated in Oracle Designer). Whichever front-end source code you generate, Oracle Designer also produces the Data Definition Language (DDL) scripts that create the database objects for Oracle or other databases.

Table 18-1 lists the deliverables and activities that occur in the Build phase and the Oracle Designer tools that support them. The tools with a "DE" prefix are contained in the Design Editor.

Many subjects in this list appear in other chapters. Chapter 14 introduces the Logic Editor, which is used to complete the code definitions in PL/SQL and other languages. Chapter 16 covers the Module Network Viewer and the Module Diagram. It also explains how to create and maintain the control code, reference code, and help tables. Chapter 14 explains how journal tables are managed and created. Chapter 20 discusses how to perform unit testing to ensure that modules fulfill requirements. That chapter also details the documentation set that you start in the Build phase.

Chapter 20 also explores the subject of problem tracking in the Build and Test phases. The section "Setting Form Generator Preferences," later in this chapter, discusses some specific preferences as examples, but for a full explanation of the Design Editor's Generator Preferences, see Chapter 12. The Object Database Designer (ODD) is the tool you use to create object definitions to support the C++ Generator. Chapter 14 gives an overview of this subject. Further discussion of this generator is out of the scope of this

Activity or Deliverable	Oracle Designer Tool
Complete PL/SQL definitions and application logic code	DE: Logic Editor
Data definition language scripts	DE: Generate Database from Server Model utility
Table API scripts	DE: Generate Table API utility
Refine module definitions	DE: Module Diagram
Refine module network	DE: Module Network Viewer
Application-level standards	DE: Generator Preferences
Screen code: Oracle Forms	DE: Form Generator
Module-level standards	Generator templates and object libraries; and DE: Generator Preferences
Module component API scripts	DE: Generate Module Component API utility
Report code	DE: Report Generator
Screen code: VB and WebServer	DE: Visual Basic and WebServer generators
Help system	DE: MS Help Generator or help table system loaded by module generators
C++ class code	Object Database Designer: C++ Generator
Code control table, reference code table, and help table	DE: Generate Database from Server Model utility and module generators
Journal tables	DE: Generate Database from Server Model utility
Unit-test documentation	Repository Reports
Problem tracking	Repository Object Navigator or API
System documentation	Repository Reports

TABLE 18-1. *Build Activities and Oracle Designer Tools*

book, although you can consult the ODD help system for detailed steps including a flow chart of the process of C++ generation.

A complete discussion of the Oracle Designer generators would fill an entire book, not just one chapter. While this chapter offers an overview and some technical details on this subject, you will, at some point, be ready to move to another level and will need to refer to other books, such as one in this series, or third-party training for more details on the generators.

One of two primary objectives of the Build phase is to complete the database scripts and run them to create database objects and test data; the other is to build the application modules using the generator products. The creation of test data is outside the scope of the Oracle Designer tools, but the other main activities are fully supported.

Generate Database from Server Model Utility

You need to create database objects as the first step in the Build phase because the tables and other supporting objects must exist in the database before you can successfully generate code for a module. The Generate Database from Server Model utility is a repository utility that produces SQL*Plus text files you can run to create database objects. The code it produces includes the SQL DDL statements, as well as SQL*Plus comments and commands to document the objects and provide messages as the script is run. It can produce code to create every type of database object defined in the repository.

The definitions for each of these objects should be as complete as possible before you create the code for them. In addition, you might want to run the Update Columns in a Domain utility from the Design Editor Utilities menu so that all columns have up-to-date domain information.

The properties for database objects and PL/SQL code definitions are best filled in using the navigator (or Server Model Diagram) and Property Palette (or dialogs), as Chapter 14 describes. You can also examine these definitions using the Property Palette in RON or DE.

Running the Generate Database from Server Model Utility

You can access the Generate Database from Server Model utility (also called Server Generator in the help system) from the **Generate→Generate Database from Server Model** menu option of the Design Editor. You can also click the Generate DDL toolbar button. In addition, as Chapter 14 mentions, you can start this utility from the Database Navigator. The interface is similar to that of the Capture Design of Server Model from Database utility, discussed in Chapter 8.

Target Tab

The first tab you see is the Target tab as shown in Figure 18-1.

You fill in the destination of the generated output: DDL Files (for Data Definition Language files), Database, or ODBC.

- **DDL Files Only**   Fill in the type of database (for example, Oracle7 or Oracle8) and the generator will create a script specifically for that syntax.

- **Database**   Fill in the standard connection information for an Oracle database accessed with SQL*Net 2 (or 1). Oracle8 databases need SQL*Net version 2 for database versions 7.3 and later.

- **ODBC**   Fill in the data Source, which you set up with the ODBC software, and the Type for the type of database (such as DB2, RDB, SQL Server, or Sybase).

The Database and ODBC selections connect to the specified database and run the Reconcile Report in addition to creating the DDL scripts. (Chapter 20 provides details on this report.) If any database objects are out of synch with the repository definitions of those objects, the utility will also create "alter" scripts. While the DDL Files Only target selection does not produce the Reconcile Report, it does not, by definition, need a database

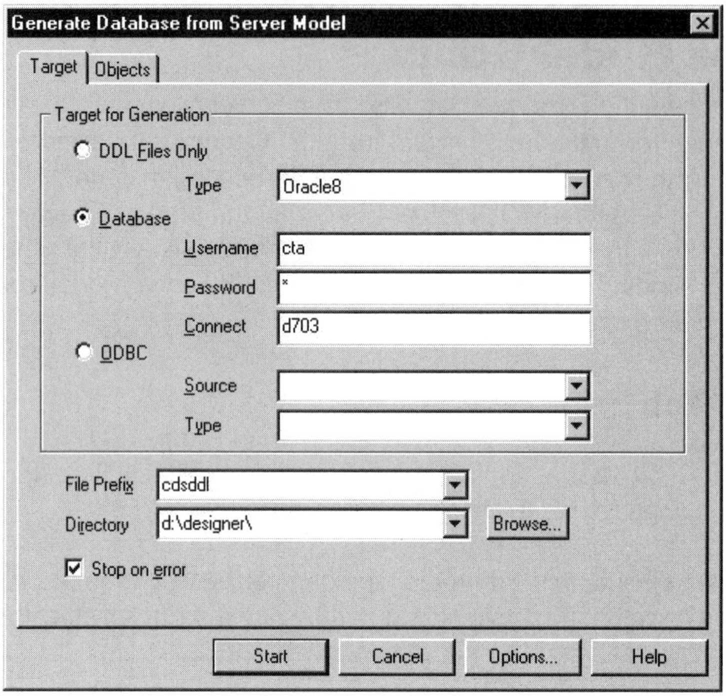

FIGURE 18-1. *Target tab of the Generate Database from Server Model utility*

connection to the repository other than the existing one, and is faster as a result.

Another field you fill out on this tab indicates the File Prefix, which is the base file name for the scripts that the generator creates. DDL produced for each type of object will be written to a file named with this file name and a different extension, specific to the object type. For example, if you generate code for a table definition and specify that the file prefix is "projddl," the generator will create files such as projddl.tab (for creating tables), projddl.con (for constraints), and projddl.ind (for indexes). It also creates a file with a .SQL extension that runs all the files in the correct sequence. The generator creates these files into the directory you specify in the Directory field. To avoid problems resulting from the utility not being able to find a script, be sure the files are generated into the same directory as you designated as the Start In directory for the Oracle Designer icon.

The Stop on Error check box indicates whether the generator will abort the generation session if there is an error. You would leave this unchecked if you wanted to generate scripts for as many objects as possible, even if some objects have errors. Even though some objects do not generate correctly, you would still have scripts for those that did generate correctly.

Objects Tab

After selecting the target, you click the Objects tab to select the elements to generate. Figure 18-2 shows this tab.

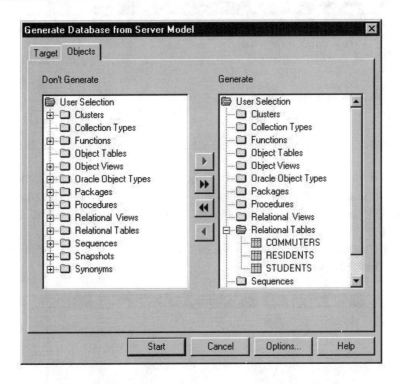

FIGURE 18-2.   *Objects tab of the Generate Database from Server Model utility*

In this tab, you expand nodes on the left "Don't Generate" box to reveal the definitions and select and move them to the right with the arrow button. You can select multiple definitions using the SHIFT-click and CTRL-click techniques. The elements in these lists are the primary elements, such as tables. Other elements, such as constraints, indexes, triggers, and comments, are generated automatically with the primary object. When you are done selecting and moving elements into the "Generate" box, you click the Start button to start the generator. As the generator runs, it writes messages into the Messages Window.

If you choose the DDL Files Only target, there is no closing dialog, but the Messages window will stay open. You can click the List Actions button to view a list of files that were created. The Build Action dialog will appear as shown in the following illustration.

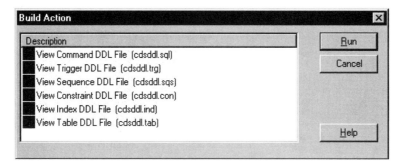

In this dialog, you can select a file and click the Run button to show its contents. If you want to run the files in the database to create the objects, open SQL*Plus (from the Oracle Designer launchpad window) and start the file with the .SQL extension.

If you choose Database or ODBC as the target, the generate session will end with a closing dialog as shown in the following illustration.

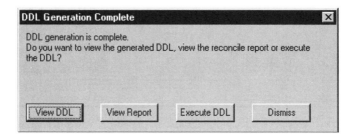

The View DDL button opens all files so you can browse their contents. The View Report button shows the Reconcile Report. The Execute DDL button runs the .SQL file using the login you specified in the Target tab. If you click the Dismiss button, you can still use the List Actions button in the Messages Window to view the files. These files are also available in the directory you specified in the Target tab.

Specifying Options

If you click the Options button in the utility dialog, the Options dialog appears. This lets you choose whether to generate indexes, integrity constraints, and comments with the objects you have selected. It also lets you choose Oracle-specific objects that will generate with the selected object, such as triggers, valid value constraints, grants and synonyms, and distributed capability (for remote synonyms and database links). There is also an option to assign the database objects to a replication group if you are using replication features.

Automating the Object Selection

An easier way to select the objects to generate is using the Navigator or Server Model Diagram windows. If you select objects in either of these tools and run the Generate Database from Server Model utility, the Objects tab's Generate list will be pre-loaded with the objects you selected. It is not even necessary to show this tab, unless you just want to check the selections. This can save time when running the utility.

The code you generate depends on how you select the objects. If you select a table definition, for example, from the Server Model tab, the table creation script will not contain any implementation-specific clauses like the tablespace assignment and storage parameters. This is because these details are recorded for the table implementation. If you select the table implementation in the DB Admin tab, the CREATE TABLE statement will contain the storage and tablespace clauses if you assigned them. This means that, if you want the full CREATE syntax, you need to create an implementation where you assign the object to a database and user schema.

For PL/SQL definitions, if you choose an individual function or procedure in the navigator and run this utility, you will generate a script for a stand-alone function or procedure, even if it is a subprogram unit of a package. If you select a package in the navigator and run the utility, you will generate the network of functions and procedures that are part of that package.

Other Utilities to Generate Database Objects

In addition to the Generate Database from Server Model utility, other utilities share the same interface and can be used to create database scripts. These utilities, which are all available in the Design Editor, concentrate on objects in a certain category, such as database administration. The following is a review of these utilities.

GENERATE DATABASE ADMINISTRATION OBJECTS This utility (run from the Generate menu of the Design Editor) works the same way as the Generate Database from Server Model utility, but has a different Target tab, as Figure 18-3 shows.

The File Prefix, Directory, and Database Type fields work the same way as the Generate Database from Server Model utility. The Generation Options area allows you to specify other objects that you will generate, such as the database itself (for the CREATE DATABASE script), system privileges (as assigned to roles and users), space quotas (as assigned to users), and replication statements (to create replication groups if you select a master replication group definition).

GENERATE TABLE API This utility (available from the Generate menu) creates the table part of the Server API as described in Chapter 14.

GENERATE MODULE COMPONENT API This utility creates the module component part of the Server API (as described in Chapter 16). It is available from the Generate menu.

GENERATE REFERENCE CODE TABLES This utility, available in the Generate menu after selecting a module definition, creates scripts to generate or load the reference code table. This is described in Chapter 16.

NOTE
When you determine a strategy for access to tables and views, whether through public grants and synonyms or private grants and synonyms, you need to include in this strategy the plan for access to the packages in the Table API and Module Component API. The schema in which you create your application system tables will also hold these packages and users will need execute privileges on the packages if they are to run the application.

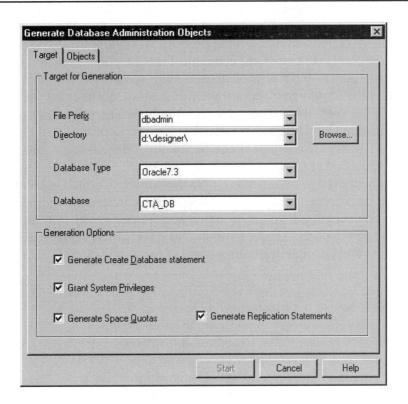

FIGURE 18-3. *Target tab of the Generate Database Administration Objects utility*

Generating Modules

The general procedure for creating code from module definitions is to run the appropriate generator, examine the resulting application module by running it, make changes in the module definition, and then repeat the entire process. When you are done with this iterative procedure, you have both the refined definition in the repository and the finished code module (source and runtime or executable module). If the module design changes, you simply run the generator again to re-create the program file.

After you generate code from a module, you should test that code to be sure it works as you expect. Then you give it to the QA group, where a unit test is performed to ensure that the module fulfills the requirements assigned to it. Chapter 17 discusses the techniques for unit testing and Chapter 20 mentions the Oracle Designer support for this unit test.

The next sections discuss how to produce working forms using the Form Generator. The Form Generator is the most mature and complete of the generator products and this book gives it more space than the other generators in order to give you a start with the tool. Subsequent sections also introduce the WebServer Generator and briefly describe the other code generators that Oracle Designer provides: Library, Report, Visual Basic, and MS Help. The C++ Generator is another major code generator, but it is not discussed outside of Chapter 14.

All generators are documented in the help system, which you can access from any help Contents page in the Design Editor by expanding the node for the desired generator. If you are looking at a Contents page from any other tool, expand the node "Access to other Designer help systems" and select "Designing and generating databases and client applications."

TIP
The best way to approach learning the generators is to budget some "training" time to examine the preferences, templates, and object libraries. The help system provides a wealth of information on these and other aspects of the generators and your learning process will be more rewarding if you can check the effects of various property and preference settings by generating and testing the code. This time will pay you back when you do real development work as you will not be frustrated by having to learn and produce at the same time.

Using the navigator, Property Palette (or dialog), and Module Diagram, you can designate what data elements are used and how they appear in the layout. A typical generation session starts by reviewing the visual and data aspects of the module in the Module Diagram, then generating the module, making notes about what needs to be changed, and making the changes in the Module Diagram or navigator properties. This cycle repeats until the module is fully refined and working. This iterative method is appropriate to the Build phase. All you really need to do in the Application Design part of the Design phase is to enter the definitions as completely as you can based on your knowledge of the system. You stop short of generation in this phase and pick it up in the Build phase.

Parts List

The generators pull information from many parts of the repository and file system as Figure 18-4 represents. You can construct a parts list from this diagram and use this list to gain an understanding of what you need to generate a module. Each generator requires different parts as this chapter explains. The following briefly describes each of the required parts.

Table and Column Definitions

Some properties on the table and column—for example, *Display Type*—are copied to the table usage and bound item when you create those elements

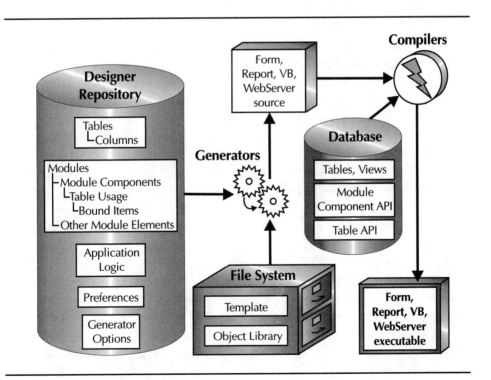

FIGURE 18-4. *Parts modules*

of the module component. These properties are not linked to the table and column, so you can set them differently for each specific module. However, some properties can be set only on the table and column definition, such as the *Journal* table property and *AutoGen Type* column property.

NOTE
Be aware that some properties, for example, Width, *appear on both column and bound item. Normally, the generator uses the* Width *property on the bound item to determine the width of the item. However, if the bound item has no value for* Width, *the generator will use the* Maximum Length *property on the column that is the basis for the bound item. Thus, when you look at the properties that affect the generated module, you also need to examine the columns and table that the module's bound items and table usages represent.*

Objects in the Online Database

If you want to test the code that you generate, you need to have tables and other database objects installed in the online database. If the database objects referenced by the module component table usage do not exist, you will see an error message when you try to compile the generated source file. With the database objects in place, you can run the module in the same way the user would run it, which allows you to perform an accurate test of the functionality you intended. In the Build phase, you also must be sure to complete the server-side PL/SQL definitions required for triggers, procedures, packages, and functions.

Table API

Modules that access the database through the Table API (TAPI) need to have the API generated and installed in the database. WebServer Generator code requires the TAPI, and Developer Forms use it in some cases, as discussed in Chapter 16. Unless the TAPI is installed and working, the code that the generators create will not compile, and you will not be able to test the module. Fortunately, you do not have to do extensive testing on the code in the Table API. This code should be bug-free if you have all supporting objects in the database.

Module Component API

For Developer Form modules, you can generate the Module Component API (MCAPI) that serves as an interface between a module component (block) based on a view or PL/SQL procedure and the base tables. The MCAPI is a package that calls the TAPI and is called by generated Form code, so both TAPI and MCAPI must be installed in the online database for the Form Generator code to compile correctly.

Module Definitions

The module definition includes the module properties, module component properties, table usage and bound item properties, module component placements (such as new canvas and same canvas), windows, called modules, and all other details about the module. Much of the work you do to refine code is done in the module definition and the other definitions under it.

Preferences

Preferences manipulate how the generator handles the visual or behavioral aspect of items and tables. When you get to the Build phase, you have already worked out all standard application settings. In the Build phase, you change these on a module level or below to create a module-specific variation on the standard.

Application Logic

You create stubs (or placeholders) for the application code you know about in the Design phase, but, in the Build phase, you need to fill in the stubs and actually write the working code for the final module.

Templates and Object Libraries

The generators use template files as starting points from which they create code. This provides a way to define default mechanisms and "look and feel" standards that all generated modules will share. The Form Generator uses object libraries to provide archetypes for individual Form objects like text items, buttons, and check boxes. You can modify the templates and object libraries to enforce standards or to alter the visual or behavioral aspects of generated applications.

Generator Options

There are specific settings that affect how the generator runs. These settings are not specific to a module or application system, but are used for all modules you generate in all application systems. The settings deal with the operation of the generator and specify things like the destination for generated code files and whether you want the code to be compiled automatically.

The discussion on each generator later in this chapter provides details on how these parts affect the specific generator.

Writing Application Logic

A major part of the development work that you perform in the Build phase is filling in the application code definitions. This is traditionally the place where developers spend most of their time. While the Oracle Designer generators ease the burden on the developer by creating as much as possible in the way of default operations and layout, there will still be a need to write code to handle business rules. Generally, you will write as much code as possible on the server side, using stored PL/SQL packages (procedures, functions, and variables) and trigger code that calls those packaged program units. This should leave you with a small amount of application code to write, probably to perform actions specific to the tool. For example, a Developer Form module might need application code to navigate through the block and set record properties based on the value of a particular item. This code is not appropriate, or possible, as server code so you would create application logic to do this in a library or form. There are two main techniques you can use to create application code. The end result, though, is the same with both techniques—you create code (tested or not) that is stored in the repository. The techniques follow.

Write and debug the code in the deployment product

In other words, if your application module were deployed in Oracle Developer Forms, you would write and debug the code using the Developer

Form Builder. Once the code is working to your satisfaction, you copy and paste it into a repository application logic definition. Alternatively, if the code is non-specific to a particular form, you can put the code in a Form Builder. PLL library and design capture the library into the repository.

If your module is deployed in Oracle WebServer, you will write package code to supplement the code that this generator creates. In this technique, you write and debug the package code using Developer Procedure Builder or your favorite database package editor and design capture the package as server code (a PL/SQL definition), not application logic.

The benefit of this technique is that you can fully debug the code before you generate. You know that the code is syntactically compatible with the target product and has been tested in that environment. The drawback is that you are working outside the repository and need to design capture the code back into the repository in the correct location.

Write the code in Oracle Designer

You can use the Design Editor's Logic Editor to enter code. You define the text as a PL/SQL Definition (if it is server code) or as an Application Logic node (or Named Routine under a Library module).

The benefit of this approach is that you store the definition in the repository immediately, so there is no need to design capture the logic. Another benefit is that you can use the enhanced editing features of the Logic Editor—drag and drop of constructs, automatic fill-in of syntax, color highlighting of various types of text (like comments), and syntax checking. The drawback, and it is a big one, is that you cannot check how the code will run or whether it will even compile. This means that no matter how well the code passes the syntax check in the Logic Editor, you will debug the code after the module is generated.

NOTE
Once you record application logic for a module, the module symbol in the navigator will be joined on its left side by the attached logic symbol, as the following illustration shows.

⓪ 🖿 CTAGRADE

Copying Modules and Menus

There are three Design Editor menu items that allow you to copy modules. This is a useful thing to do if you have spent time defining a module and are satisfied that it is complete, but need to base another module on the same design. In this situation, you copy the module and make the changes in the copy. This has a different effect than that of using reusable module components in different modules because the reusable module components do not own module-specific objects such as Windows and Arguments. When you copy a module, the process copies everything including Windows and Arguments; it even copies preferences. A brief description of the copy utilities follows.

COPY OBJECT   Selecting a module and choosing **Utilites→Copy** from the menu (or choosing the Copy Object right-click menu item) will display the Copy Objects dialog where you specify the new name and short name. After you click the Copy button, the utility will copy the object using those names. You can then edit the definition and change the properties, add objects, or remove existing components.

COPY WITH NEW LANGUAGE   Another reason to copy modules is if you want to generate code for that same definition into a different language. For example, you create a working Developer Form module and want to create a Developer Report that looks like the form and contains the same data. Another example is that you have an Oracle Form module that you want to generate for the Web. In both situations, you could use this utility to create the new module and switch the language automatically.

Selecting **Utilities→Copy With New Language** from the menu, after selecting a module, shows a dialog where you specify the language which you want to use for the new module and the new module name. Clicking the OK button copies the module. The copy utility makes some intelligent choices about what to copy and what not to copy. For example, if you copy an Oracle Form module to a WebServer module, any application logic defined for the form will not be copied as this logic does not apply to the new module.

TIP
*A quick way to generate to another language without creating a new module definition is to choose **Generate→Generate Module As** from the menu. This will display the Generate Module As dialog, as shown in the following illustration. You click on one of the language buttons in the radio group on this dialog and click the OK button. The appropriate generator dialog will then appear and, from that point, you follow the normal path to generate the code. This is a powerful utility that lets you create reports from a Form module definition or WebServer code from a Form application. However, since you are not setting properties for the module specific to the new language, the generated code may not look the way you want. This is useful for the times you need to quickly generate a report from a Form definition.*

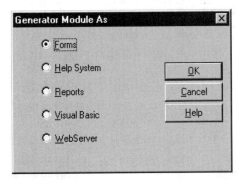

COPY MENU STRUCTURE   The Copy Menu Structure utility copies module networks from one node to another. This might be useful if you

want to create two menus that are similar for most of the menu choices, but different enough to warrant a separate menu. If you copy one menu network to the other, the second will contain copies of the same menu modules and associations to the other modules.

Select **Utilities→Copy Menu Structure** from the menu after selecting a module. Choose the module or module network node under which you want this network copied and click the OK button. The module network is copied into the selected modules node. You can view the entire structure by expanding the module's node in the Module Network Viewer. The utility will copy module network (menu) nodes and give them a unique name. It will create associations for all elements under the module network, as well.

Form Generator

The Form Generator creates screen and menu application files based on definitions in the repository. It creates blocks and items on the form based on table usages and bound items associated with the module. This section first details some of the requirements and then describes how to run the Form Generator.

The result of a Form Generator session is a standard Forms binary source (.FMB) file and, optionally, a runtime (.FMX) file as used in the Developer Form Builder. If you are generating menus, the source binary file uses a .MMB extension and the runtime file uses a .MMX extension. You can open the source files in the Form Builder to check the code or make changes to the file.

The Form Generator needs all of the parts listed earlier, although the TAPI and MCAPI are optional, depending on the source of the module components in your form module.

You can run the forms you create with the Form Generator on the Web (called *Web Forms*) if you install and configure the Developer Server. The code you create with the Form Generator is contained in standard .FMB and .FMX files. The same .FMX files can be run on an application server if the server is running the same operating system as the machine that created the .FMX files. If the operating system is different, you need to recompile the .FMB file to create a new .FMX file on the server. This solution imposes a greater overhead on the client and the server side than generated WebServer Generator applications, but it is an alternative when you are thinking about deploying on the Web.

Using Module Definitions

Some of the important properties that the Form Generator requires to generate modules follow. Refer to "Other Module Properties" and "Building a Module" in Chapter 16 and "Information Flow" in Chapter 29 for more information on specific properties.

- *Short Name*, which is a character string used as the name of the generated .FMB file. Be sure this name creates a file that can be stored in the operating system, although the 32-bit MS Windows family can handle long file names.

- *Name*, which is used as the window title if there is no top title or short title specified.

- *Module Type*, which identifies the type of finished module and may have a value of Default (for a Form), Menu, or Library.

- *Language,* which specifies the use of the Form Generator and must have a value of Developer Forms (Developer/2000 Forms).

In addition to the module properties, the properties of elements that make up the module affect the generated form. Some of these are discussed in the sections just cited, as well as in the help system. If you click the Context-Sensitive Help button in the Design Editor and drop the cursor on a property in the Property Palette, you will see a help box, such as the one in Figure 18-5, that may have links to other topics specific to a generator.

There are also properties on Module Components, Table Usages, Bound Items, and Unbound Items that have specific meaning in a Form module.

Module Component Properties

When you define a module component, you need to state where the data is coming from and where it is going. These are the *Datasource* and *Datatarget* properties, respectively. The default is Table for both the source for queries and target for insert, update, and delete statements. If you generate a form based on Table-Table, source-target, the generator will create a block for the module component. Since you can also base a module component on a view or package, there are more possible combinations of *Datasource* and

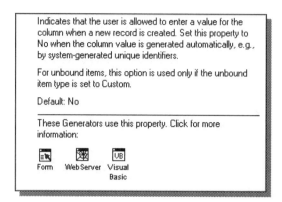

FIGURE 18-5. *Help box for a property in the Property Palette*

Datatarget. There are some values combinations, such as Procedure as a source and Procedure as a target, that require another layer, the Module Component API, to do their jobs.

These target properties correspond roughly to the Developer Form Builder properties *Query Data Source Type* (and *Name*) and *DML Data Target Type* (and *Name*). Table 18-2 shows the combinations of *Datasource* and *Datatarget* and how these combinations affect the Module Component API (MCAPI) and the Developer Form code. For these examples, a table was the base table object in the module component (not a view) and all attempt to use the MCAPI.

When deciding which of these combinations to use, remember that the Table-Table combination is the easiest to read and requires no MCAPI. The PL/SQL Procedure data source choice is potentially more efficient as it passes a block of records at the same time, which reduces network traffic. Views are more efficient if your module component contains a lookup table since the form does not need a POST-QUERY trigger to fire after each retrieved row to query the lookup values.

Module Component Usages link the module to the database objects by specifying the table operations allowed for the tables—insert, update, delete,

Designer Datasource Type; Datatarget Type	Developer Query Data Source Type (Name)	Developer DML Data Target Type (Name)	MCAPI Notes	Form Notes
PL/SQL Procedure; PL/SQL Procedure	Procedure (name of MCAPI package.qry)	Procedure (name of MCAPI package.qry)	Ignore the 3385 error for MCAPI—MCAPI is package spec and body	Form will have triggers INSERT-PROCEDURE, UPDATE-PROCEDURE, and so on; Query by example (QBE) does not work.
PL/SQL Procedure; Table	Procedure (name of MCAPI package.qry)	Table (table name)	Warning 3385. Only qry procedure created	QUERY-PROCEDURE trigger only. QBE does not work.
PL/SQL Procedure; Transactional Trigger	Procedure (name of MCAPI package.qry)	Transactional Triggers (<null>)	Warning 3385. Only qry procedure created	Triggers for ON-INSERT, ON-UPDATE and so on. Compile error in form—form is created but not compiled.
Query; PL/SQL Procedure	FROM clause query (SELECT statement)	Procedure (MCAPI package.qry)	Package spec and body	Query by example works for this combination.
Query; Table	FROM clause query (SELECT statement)	Table (table name)	"Unsupported data source/target"	Form compiles. QBE works.
Query; Transactional Trigger	FROM clause query (SELECT statement)	Transactional Triggers (<null>)	"Unsupported data source/target"	Triggers for ON-INSERT, ON-UPDATE and so on. Compile error in form—form is created but not compiled.

TABLE 18-2. *Designer and Developer Data Properties and the MCAPI*

Designer Datasource Type; Datatarget Type	Developer Query Data Source Type (Name)	Developer DML Data Target Type (Name)	MCAPI Notes	Form Notes
Table; PL/SQL Procedure	Table (table name)	Procedure (name of MCAPI package.qry)	Package spec and body	Form will have triggers INSERT-PROCEDURE, UPDATE-PROCEDURE, and so on. QBE works.
Table; Table	Table (table name)	Table (table name)	"Unsupported data source/target"	Standard block. No MCAPI needed. QBE works.
Table; Transactional Trigger	Table (table name)	Transactional Triggers (<null>)	"Unsupported data source/target"	Triggers for ON-INSERT, ON-UPDATE and so on. Compile error in form— form is created but not compiled.
View; PL/SQL Procedure	Table (view name)	Procedure (name of MCAPI package.qry)	View, package body, package spec generated	Form will have triggers INSERT-PROCEDURE, UPDATE-PROCEDURE, and so on. QBE works.
View; Table	Table (name of MCAPI view)	Table (table name)	Package spec and body and CREATE VIEW script	No special triggers. QBE works.
View; Transactional Trigger	Table (MCAPI view name)	Transactional Triggers (<null>)	Error 3385— Warning CREATE VIEW script only, no package	Triggers for ON-INSERT, ON-UPDATE and so on. Compile error in form— form is created but not compiled.

TABLE 18-2.   *Designer and Developer Data Properties and the MCAPI (continued)*

and select. These settings greatly affect the code that the generators create and it is worthwhile taking some time to ensure that they are correctly set.

The Placement properties, discussed in Chapter 16, let you tell the generator how to place the module component in the form (such as on a new content canvas, on the same content canvas, or in some other location). Normally, the generator will lay out all items in a table usage on one line in the same canvas. You can also set the *Overflow* property to the following values to specify what the generator does with items that extend beyond the width of the canvas.

■ **Wrap Line**   The generator will continue laying out items below the line until that line is filled. It will then continue wrapping to multiple lines until there are no items left. This works the same way that word wrap does in a text editor.

■ **Overflow Area Right**   This setting displays the overflowed items in a single record "area" on the right side of the main block. This is especially useful for multirecord blocks where you cannot fit all items in the multirow area. As the user moves the cursor from one row to another in the multirecord block, the single overflow area updates to reflect the values for that row.

■ **Overflow Area Below**   This setting is similar to the previous one, except that the overflow area is underneath the multirecord area, not to its right.

■ **Spread Table**   This setting creates a scrolling stacked canvas so all items are on the same line, but the user only sees the ones that fit within the canvas width. The user must scroll the canvas horizontal scrollbar to reveal the other items in the block.

There are also generator preferences (in the Layout-Block and Layout-Overflow categories) that manipulate the overflow area. Specifically, the *Default block overflow action* preference (BLKOVF in the Layout-Block category) sets the overflow style if the *Overflow* property is null. In other words, the module component *Overflow* property overrides the preference setting.

Table Usage Properties

Also called *module component table usages,* these elements specify the details for how a table appears in the module component. As discussed in Chapter 16, there are properties to define the *Usage Type,* such as Base, Lookup, Single Row SQL Aggregate, and Sub-Query. If the table has a *Usage Type* of Lookup, you can set the title of the LOV (list of values) window that the Form Generator will create from this usage.

Window Properties

A module component becomes a block in the form and its items are placed on canvas inside the window. You can define more than one window for each module and place different module components in each.

The window's *Title* property value will appear as the form's window title when you run the form. This window title defaults to the module *Top Title* property. If that property is not set, the module *Short Name* becomes the window title. If neither of these is set, the window title will be the module *Name* property value.

Module components become blocks in the generated form. Blocks are placed on canvases, which are placed in windows. In addition to the placement items and properties, you can specify preferences that affect the layout, such as the decoration of objects. These are discussed later in this chapter, in the section "Setting Form Generator Preferences."

Link Properties

A lookup table usage is a usage for a table that is used by another table (block) in a generated form to retrieve values into nonbase table display-only fields. Therefore, there will not be a separate block on the form for the lookup table usage, because the columns will become nonbase table fields in the base table block. Before you can create a valid lookup table usage, at least one base table usage must already exist, and a foreign key constraint must exist between the base table and the lookup table. Remember that you can define a foreign key link for the purposes of the module table link and set the *Validate in* property to Client so the link is not implemented in a database constraint.

A base table (or master-detail) link defines the interaction between a parent (master) and child (detail) tables. The Form Generator will create a block for each table and generate code to synchronize the rows between the two blocks. Therefore, if you have a base table link between INVOICES and

INV_ITEMS, with INV_ITEMS as the detail, you can query a particular master record, and the corresponding details will be shown automatically.

The link for a lookup table will create an LOV for the foreign key item(s). This LOV will display the rows in the lookup table in the order you specify in the *Order By Sequence* and *Sort Order* properties of the bound items for the table.

Bound Item Properties

A bound item specifies that a particular column is used by the module and provides details regarding the operations allowed for that column—insert, select, update, and display. A bound item is always part of a table usage.

The properties for the bound item greatly influence the decisions the Form Generator makes about how to create the finished module. You can change the order in which the bound items will appear by dragging and dropping to resequence them in the navigator. The *Prompt* and *Display Type* properties show up on the form as well. If you include columns in an item group, the generator will keep the items created from those columns in the same area on the generated form.

Unbound Item Properties

You can create nonbase table items in the Unbound Items node under the Table Usage node. These items are not associated with a particular table, but they appear in the same block as the base table for the module component for which they are defined. There are several types of unbound items that you can use for different purposes. Chapter 16 contains an example of one type, a derived item based on a SQL Expression.

You create the unbound items by clicking on the Create button while selecting the navigator node Unbound Items under a module component. When creating unbound items, be sure to set the *Display Type*, *Datatype*, and *Width* properties to appropriate values. The value of the *Unbound Type* property indicates the type, which, for Form modules, can be SQL Expression, Computed, Client Side Function, Server Side Function, and Custom. You can also generate unbound items from these types for the following uses:

SUMMARY ITEMS   These act on a group of detail block records but appear in a master block. Create the unbound item and set its *Unbound*

Type to "Computed." Set the *Derivation Text* property to a function (SUM, MAX, VARIANCE, COUNT, MIN, AVG, or STDDEV). The function must act on a single bound or unbound item, but this will summarize all rows in the table. For example, you might want to show the maximum value of the course fees. Set the unbound item *Derivation Text* to MAX (crse.fee). The expression inside the parentheses references the table usage *Alias* and item *Name* (not the *Column Name* property). You may be able to succeed without the table alias, but it is best to use it. This *Derivation Text* value sets the *Calculation Mode*, *Summary Function*, and *Summarized Item* properties in Developer Forms to appropriate values.

FORMULA OR DERIVED ITEMS   These take their values from other items in the block. A derived item acts on one row, and the expression contains single row references. Set the *Unbound Type* to SQL Expression, and the *Derivation Text* to the single row expression. For example, to create a line item total that is a calculation of price * qty in an ORDER_ITEMS table, you add an unbound item called LINE_TOTAL in the ORDER_ITEMS module component. The text you enter in the *Derivation Text* property is price * qty. This text is validated with a SELECT *expression* FROM *table_name* statement, where *expression* is the text you place in the *Derivation Text* property, and *table_name* is the table usage table name. Therefore, the table must exist in the database and be accessible to the user's account in order to compile the module.

Another type of text that you can enter is an expression such as:

L 18-1   `calc_line_price(product_id, qty)`

In this case, calc_line_price is a function you have defined to query the price from a product table and return the price multiplied by the quantity for the product_id passed in. Product_id and qty are bound items in the table usage. The function can be defined in the template form, attached library, or database. This text is validated when the generator compiles the form. When entering other item names in the *Derivation Text*, it is best to use the item *Name* property that is unique within the module.

Instead of specifying derivation expressions in the unbound item, you can place a *Derivation Expression* and *Derivation Expression Type* on the table column definition. This will generate client code for the appropriate column that loads the value into the base table item. This feature might be desired for denormalization of a value that you need to maintain in a column, but is not normally required in a normalized database design as you can obtain the same effect with an unbound item.

NOTE
Derivation expressions cannot use columns other than those in the same module component. In other words, a derivation expression in an EMP bound item cannot directly reference a value in a DEPT bound item if those tables appear in different module components.

BUTTON ITEMS   An unbound item used as a button is similar to a derived item usage except that you use the display datatype Button for the item and execute a procedure instead of a function or SQL Expression. One example of a button is one that issues a message and then executes a database procedure. Set the *Unbound Type* property to "Client Side Function" and set the *Derivation Text* to "." (no quotes, this just needs some value but it is not validated unless the *Unbound Type* is "Server Side Function"). Set the *PL/SQL Block* property to:

L 18-2
```
message('Note: We are about to update all student grades '||
    ' in the database.');
message(' ');
db_update_student_grades;
```

The second call to the Forms message built-in issues the previous message in an alert box. Set the *Prompt* to the label you wish to display on the button and *Display Type* to "Button." The generator will create a WHEN-BUTTON-PRESSED trigger that will execute the code in the *PL/SQL Block* property.

There are many other types of buttons you can generate, including action items as described shortly. All are outlined in the help system topic "About generated buttons."

CURRENT RECORD INDICATOR ITEMS   You can create an unbound item that visually indicates the row of a multirecord block that contains the cursor. The generator creates an item with the code needed to change the visual attribute of that item when the cursor moves into a new record. Set the *Unbound Type* to "Custom," the *Display Type* to "Current record," and the *Width* to 2 (or so).

EMPTY ITEMS   You may sometimes want the generator to create an item but not attach code to it because you will do so after generation. This is considered an *empty* nonbase table item, and you define it by specifying an *Unbound Usage* of "Custom," a *Display Type* of something other than "Button," and a blank *Derivation Text*. The generator will take this item into consideration when it lays out the form, but will not create any code to load or maintain it.

TIP
Oracle Designer ships with a calendar window, as shown in Figure 18-6, that you can attach as a list of values for date items. This will appear when the user clicks the LOV button or key to obtain a list of values when the cursor is on the date item and will assist the user in choosing a date. To define this action, set the preference for Add call to calendar window for date *(USECAL in the End User Interface category) to Yes, create a derived bound item for the date column, and specify display_calendar as the PLSQL Block. Display_calendar is a procedure in the OFGCALL.PLL library, which you need to attach to your template. You also have to load the calendar objects into the template by dragging and copying (or subclassing) the STANDARD_CALENDAR object group from the OFGCALT.FMB form file to your template.*

Action Item Properties

Another type of nonbase table item you can create in Designer is an *action item*. Chapter 16 provides an overview of the different types: Navigation, Generator, and Custom. You create action items in a similar way to other unbound items except that these are located either under the Window node for the module, or under a particular table usage. These items have specific navigation purposes such as to navigate to another block on the form or to

FIGURE 18-6. *Calendar LOV window*

navigate to another form. Action items always appear as a button (iconic or text) or a menu item. If you specify an action item for a window, you can define whether it navigates to a module component or module.

You specify the navigation to another module component (in the *Module Component* property) or another module (in the *To Module* property) and the generator will create the WHEN-BUTTON-PRESSED trigger for the button or menu item. If the action item is attached to a window, you do not need to write code to execute these default actions. If the action item is attached to a module component or you have something else you need to do with the action item, you have to define code in the Application Logic node under the action item.

Action Items Vs. Unbound Items

One difference between action items and unbound items is the range of types: action items appear as either a menu item or button but unbound items can be virtually any type. Another difference is the location of the item on the canvas of the generated form. Action items are generated into a location after all items in the block, whereas bound items are part of the block and can be sequenced among the other bound items.

Figure 18-7 shows a module node expanded in the Navigator. The unbound items and bound items appear in separate nodes at the top, but are grouped into the Displayed Items and Groups node. You can move these items around by dragging and dropping them into a different sequence in this node's display. You can also select Resequence Items from the right-click menu and resequence the items in the window that appears.

Action items can be assigned to a window whereas unbound items are assigned to the module component only. Action items assigned to a window are not generated into the same block as another module component. They generate into a control (nonbase table) block which has a name indicating the window (such as CGNV$WINDOW_1).

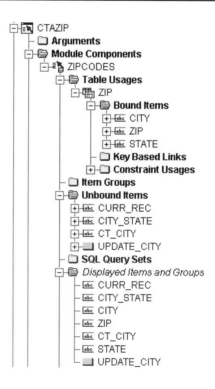

FIGURE 18-7. *Expanded module node*

TIP
Action items and unbound button items both need a Prompt *to act as a button label. In addition, if you specify an* Icon Name *(icon file name with no extension) for an action item, the generator will create an iconic button and the label is not required.*

Running the Form Generator

Once you have all the required components completely identified and defined, you can proceed to the generation process. The Form Generator is available from the Design Editor menu option **Generate→Generate Module** after you select one and only one module in the navigator or select the Module Diagram window. You can also click the Generate toolbar button. When the generator starts, it presents the dialog shown in Figure 18-8.

The short name of the module appears in the top of the dialog. Under it are three sets of options to fill in:

- **Generate Option**   This area allows you to specify whether you want to generate a form or a menu. If you do not want to generate application logic that you have defined for this module, check the Ignore User Application Logic check box. If you want to generate all forms that this one calls, check the Include Module Network check box. This will also generate a small menu with Show Keys and Exit items—if you have the preferences to show the exit option and keys on generated menus (MNUEXI and MNUSKY in the Menu – Gen Options category) set to Yes—and attach that menu to the generated form. To generate the menus associated with this form module at the same time you generate the form, check the Generate Associated Menus check box. Check the Generate Attached Libraries check box to generate, in this same generation session, Form library modules that you have associated with this module using the Called Modules node. These libraries will appear in the Attached Libraries node in the Form Builder file.

- **Preserve Layout**   This is where you specify whether you want to generate into an existing .FMB file. You fill in the file name (or find it using the Browse button) and the generator will use that file as a

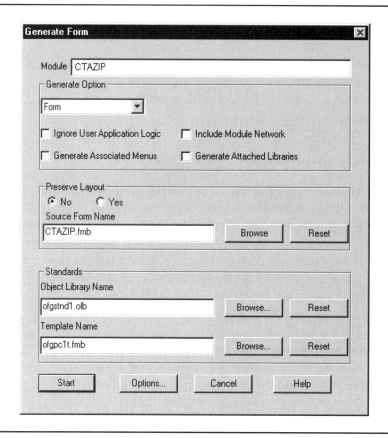

FIGURE 18-8. *Generate Form dialog*

starting point for the new layout. This technique is fully explained in the section later on "Preserving Layout." The Reset button restores the file name if you change it.

■ **Standards** This area lets you specify which Object Library and Template file you will use for this generator session. The Object Library and Template are discussed later in this chapter. As with the Preserve Layout option, you can use the Browse button to find a file and the Reset button to restore the file name set in the Standards preference category (STOOLB for the Object Library, STFFMB or STMMMB for forms and menus respectively).

TIP
If you want to generate more than one form in the same generator session and those forms are not linked in a calling hierarchy, create a menu (module network) module that calls all forms you want to generate. When you want to generate the entire set, generate the menu module and check the Include Module Network check box. If you use that menu module only for that purpose, it will not affect other modules or menus.

Setting Form Generator Options

You can set the Form Generator options to modify how the generator itself will run. Press the Options button in this dialog or choose **Options→ Generator Options→Forms** before displaying the Form Generator dialog. The dialog shown in Figure 18-9 will appear.

You should review these options if you have not done so before or if you want to modify the settings. The defaults will work sufficiently, but you might want to make your generator session run differently. This dialog is divided into a number of tabs as follows:

■ **Form Option**   This tab lets you specify the location of the form files you will generate. You can store the forms created by the generator in the file system or in the database (if you have the Developer tables installed). If you store the files in the database, you supply the connect string to connect to that database. You also specify the command lines to Insert, Extract, and Delete this file from the database.

■ **Menu Option**   This tab has the same fields as the Form Option tab, but for menu generation. It allows you to specify locations and commands for menus that are different from those for forms.

■ **Compile**   This tab contains settings that tell the generator whether you want it to produce executable forms and menus (.FMX and .MMX files, respectively) and where those executables will be stored. You can also have the generator add a line to the Action List in the Messages Window so you can compile the form after the

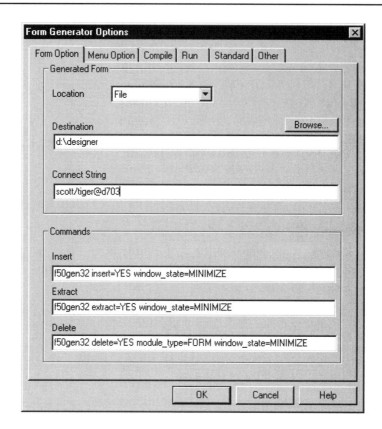

FIGURE 18-9. *Form Generator Options dialog*

generation process. You specify the connect string for form and menu compilation. This allows you to log in as a different user to compile the generated source file. This option is handy if the tables that this form uses are owned by someone other than the repository user who is generating the form. An alternative is to have the table owner grant the repository user access to the tables and to also create private or public synonyms for those tables.

■ **Run**   This tab allows you to state what you want to happen after the form is generated and compiled. You can run it automatically or have the generator add an item to the Messages Window's Action List to let you run it on demand. As with the compile options, you can log in with a different user account name when the form runs.

■ **Standard**   This tab lets you specify the directories where the form and menu templates reside so the generator can find them. The *form* names are specified by file/preferences: *The name of the template form* (STFFMB-Standards category) and *The name of the menu template* (STMMMB-Menu-Template category). There is a connect field if you store the templates in the database.

■ **Other**   This tab contains the library path—the location for attached library files and the terminal definition (a .RES file in the Forms directory). You probably will not need to change these, so the defaults will suffice.

Click OK to dismiss the Form Generator Options dialog.

Starting the Form Generator

After you have completed all the information in the tabs, you click the Start button to begin generation. The generator runs and displays messages on the status of various settings and preferences as it progresses. It may stop to ask for input if something is unclear, and noncritical warnings may appear if a setting or preference is confusing or wrong. If an error occurs that stops the generation, you can examine the Messages Window, shown in Figure 18-10, to view the messages.

If the generation session is successful, you will see a confirmation dialog box stating that generation is complete. If the generator needed to change a property value in the repository to successfully generate, it will show a message to that effect and, when the session completes, show you the changes by presenting a dialog that asks if you want to save the changes or browse. The changed elements will appear in the navigator in blue with the background color changing to gray. If you want to browse before saving, you can examine the element definitions, but you need to click Save to make the change permanent.

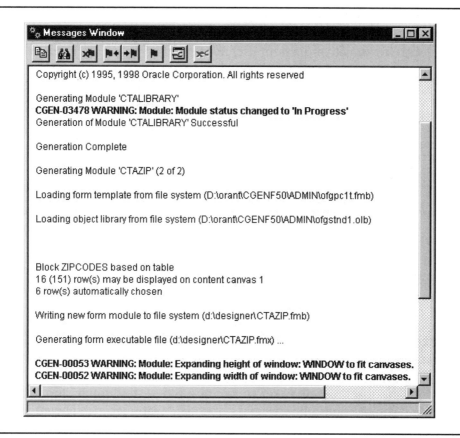

FIGURE 18-10. *Form Generator messages in the Messages Window*

TIP

*Since generating forms is an iterative process, you might consider keeping Forms Builder open at all times. Be sure the Windows Start menu icon has the same Start In directory as the Designer session. You can open the form you generate with Form Builder (or select the appropriate action from the Action List in the Messages Window). After examining or running the form, you can generate it again in the Design Editor and choose **File→Revert** f rom the Form Builder menu to open the newly generated file.*

Setting Form Generator Preferences

One of the required parts that the Form Generator uses is the preferences that you set in the Generator Preferences window of the Design Editor. Chapter 12 introduces this window and discusses the various levels of preferences, precedence and inheritance, and how to set the values. This section builds on that information to provide advice on how to use the preferences as well as some specific examples of preferences and their effects. This discussion can serve as an example, too, of how to work with the preferences of other generators.

TIP

*When first learning preferences, it is best to perform a quick test by changing a preference value or two and generating a form to see the effect of that change. This process takes a bit of time, but it will help you understand the effects of changing a particular preference. Also, remember the techniques of showing the preference descriptions (**View→Show Descriptions**) to see an easier-to-understand list. Another technique that you will find useful is clicking the Context-Sensitive Help button and dropping the mouse cursor on a preference to display the help topic for that preference.*

During module generation, preferences influence many aspects of the finished form such as coding style and content, layout, generation settings, environment, and end-user interface. Each preference is shipped with a realistic default value, referred to as the *factory value*. It is possible to generate forms using only factory values, but you can get more out of the generator by spending time carefully considering which preferences to change. You will save time you might otherwise spend in modifying the forms after generation. In addition, preferences allow you to establish and enforce code standards within a single application system, as well as for the entire enterprise.

CAUTION
Do not change the settings of too many preferences at the same time while you are still in the learning process. Create named sets and apply those to the modules instead of modifying all factory settings. This approach provides a more controlled and reversible way to test the effects of the settings.

Testing Preference Values

Each preference has a short name of up to six characters and a longer, descriptive name. You can display either the name or the description when using the Generator Preferences window to view the preference settings. Preferences are grouped into preference categories according to their functions. For example, all preferences that control the decoration of a block are members of the Layout-Block preference category. The BLKDEC preference, in this category, determines the style of line used to surround blocks on the generated forms. The poplist includes such choices as LOWERED RECTANGLE, OUTSET LINES, and RECTANGLE.

The best strategy is to create a named preference set as a group of preferences that you attach to the application level. (Preference Sets appear as a node on the Modules tab of the Design Editor.) You can test this Preference Set on individual modules to see if it works before attaching it to the application level. Use the module-level preference only for special purposes, and use the application-level preference to set the standards. All modules will have the benefit of these standards if you do this. You can copy, transfer, and share the Preference Set between application systems just like any other element, using the Repository Object Navigator. This will allow you to set the same standards among all applications that share or copy that named set.

Sample Preferences

The list of preferences is so extensive that you might want to concentrate on a small subset while you are learning how they work. Some of the most widely used categories of preferences are those that handle Layout, because the layouts of forms generated with default preferences usually do not have the desired look and feel.

SAMPLE BLOCK PREFERENCES   Suppose you generated a
multiple-row block in a form such as that in Figure 18-11 using default
preferences. You can change some of the default preferences that create this
form with the Generator Preferences. Open the module preferences node for
the module (by selecting the module and choosing **Edit→Generator
Preferences**) and expand the Layout-Block preference type node to display
the preference names. Then change the values in the Generator Preferences
window as in Table 18-3.

The form generated with your new preference settings will look like the
one in Figure 18-12. Changing these few preference values produces a
noticeable visual difference.

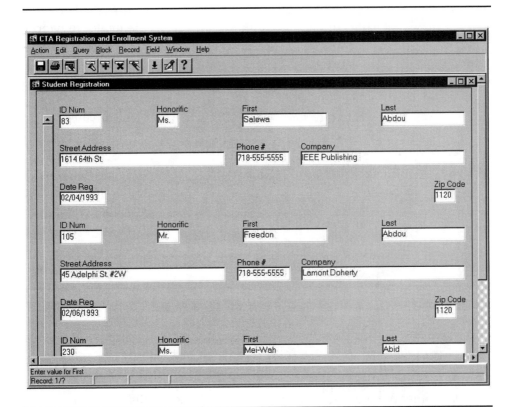

FIGURE 18-11.   *Generated form with default and preference settings*

Preference Name	Description	New Setting	Effect
BLKBWD	Block brush width	1	Wider line for border so the raised effect is more prominent.
BLKDEC	Block decoration	RAISED RECTANGLE	Border line around the block has lines with a raised look.
BLKOVF	Default block overflow action	SPREAD TABLE	The default value, WRAP LINE, causes the Form Generator to wrap rows that are too wide to the next line. Spread table creates a scrolling stacked canvas with one line per row.
BLKSBP	Block scrollbar position	RIGHT	Indicates where the vertical scrollbar will be positioned relative to the items in the block.

TABLE 18-3. *Sample Block Preferences and Their Effects*

SAMPLE ITEM PREFERENCES   You can continue this experiment to test some other preferences that affect the way items are displayed in a block by making the changes listed in Table 18-4.

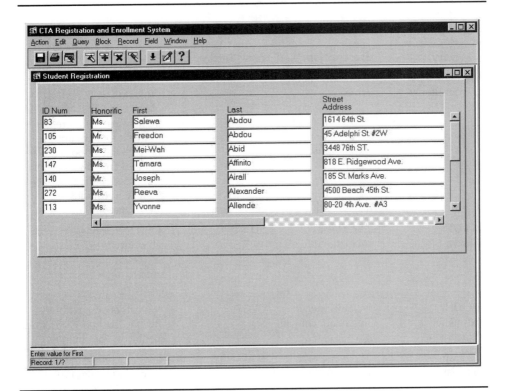

FIGURE 18-12. *Generated form with new preference settings*

Preference and Generator Tips

The following tips will help when you are using the generator and preferences:

■ You can attach only one Preference Set per level in the Generator Preferences window. If you want to use more than one Preference Set, attach one at the module level and the second one at the level of one of the module components. Both sets will affect that module component in that module. Use the same technique, this time attaching a Preference Set to the module and another to the application, if you want all module components in the module to use both named sets. Remember to restore the application level after generation if this is not a permanent change.

Preference Name (Preference Category)	Description	New Setting	Effect
BLKTAB (Layout-Block)	Block tabulation table	5.25.45.65	A normal setting has the format *tab1.tab2.tab3.tab4*, where *tab1*, *tab2*, and so on are numbers. This creates a grid with four columns at those character positions and as many rows as fit on the canvas. Note that only character positions are used, not points or pixels.
BLKUTT (Layout-Block)	Use block tabulation table	SD	If this preference is not set, tab stops are not used. SD means to use the tab stops to align the start of the items.
MODLIB (Form/Libr Attachment)	Module-specific library attachment	CUST	You can choose a library .PLL file, such as CUST.PLL, specific to your module.
STFFMB (Standards)	The name of the template file	MAINFORM.FMB	You can change the default template, OFGPC1T.FMB, to a template created specifically for your application: for example, MAINFORM.FMB. Do not include the path name.

TABLE 18-4. *Sample Item Preferences and Their Effects*

■ If you have two triggers of the same type (such as WHEN-NEW-ITEM-INSTANCE) at both the item and block levels, you want to control their execution. Set the *Item level trigger execution style* preference (ITMTGS in the Generate Options category) so that the item-level trigger fires BEFORE or AFTER the trigger with the higher scope, depending on which one should fire first. (OVERRIDE, which suppresses the block-level trigger, is the default.)

■ If you want the same field displayed on pages 1 and 2, set the column *Context* property (in the bound item for the table usage). This creates a *mirror item* in the Form Builder code that automatically copies values back and forth with the item it is mirroring. You can also explicitly create a mirror item by creating a bound item based on the same column as an existing bound item. The generator sets the *Synchronize with Item* Form Builder property on the mirror item to reference the first bound item.

■ Document your post-generation changes (if any) in the Notes text area of the module definition.

■ Create *tab canvases* by setting up stacked item groups and Native Tabbed Canvases (CANNTC in the Layout-Canvas category) to "Y." Each item group will have its own tab area and you will be able to switch back and forth between them by clicking on the tabs.

How to Proceed with Preferences

The preceding discussion should get you started with preferences. When learning preferences, experimentation is a key task. As mentioned, you should consider budgeting some research time into the Pre-Design phase to learn which preferences to use for which purposes. This research will greatly enhance the work you do in the Build phase as you will not have to stop in the heat of the coding and determine what effect a particular preference will have on the finished application. The earlier in the life cycle you can make changes to standards, the less expensive those changes will be.

The combination of preferences, the template, object library, and module definitions is quite powerful. Add the PL/SQL libraries you can attach to the template, and you have an extremely flexible way to define the form. In addition, after you develop your first project with the Oracle Designer generators, you will know how the generators work and so be able to quickly and efficiently produce finished code.

Using Object Libraries

Object libraries work with the template to provide default visual and functional properties for most objects the generator creates. Object libraries in Oracle Designer contain objects that serve as archetypes (or patterns) for how the generator creates objects. An object library is an Oracle Developer

Form (with an .OLB extension) file that contains form objects like blocks, items, trigger code, visual attributes, property classes, windows, and canvases. Virtually any object you can create in the Form Builder is potential material for an object library. If you create an object group in the Form Builder, you can include any set of objects inside it and then copy that object group to the object library. The sky's the limit!

The benefit of using object library objects in Form Builder is that you can reuse prebuilt objects that have been developed and proven. The reuse can occur as a copy operation into the form or a subclass into the form. The copy operation creates an exact duplicate of the contents of the object library object and there is no link between the source object and the target object.

The subclass operation creates a referenced copy in the target form, so that when the source object changes in the object library, the target form will pick up the changes the next time it is compiled. In previous versions of Oracle Designer, developers used referencing to accomplish the same type of reuse and automatic updates. You can modify properties of a subclassed object and the subclass link will not be broken for the other properties. This makes subclassing different from the old concept of referencing, which created an unchangeable, linked copy.

Another benefit to using object libraries is that the object library object, or *source object* contains all properties that the final generated item will have. Therefore, you have minute control over the entire object, which you do not have with the repository properties and preferences.

Types of Source Objects

The object library contains objects that fall into two categories: standard source objects and implementation source objects.

STANDARD SOURCE OBJECTS These are the "archetype" objects that the generator uses, in conjunction with the repository definitions, to create its objects. The source objects have three-part names:

- A mandatory CGSO$ prefix

- A mandatory name corresponding to the type of object

- An optional suffix denoting the context or purpose for which the object is used

For example, the standard source object named CGSO$AIBUTTON is used to generate an Action Item button; the object named CGSO$CANVAS is used to generate a canvas. The optional suffix can further distinguish the purpose for which the source object is used. These suffixes, which may be combined, are _MR (for multirecord block or item), _CT (for a control block), _DO (for a display-only item), and _MD (for a mandatory item). The combination of names is documented in the help system topic "Standard source objects and object libraries."

For example, assume the generator wants to lay out a multirecord, display-only check box. If your object library contains a CGSO$CHECK_ BOX_MR_DO object, it will use that source object as the "template" for the generated check box, and the generated check box will have all the property values specified in the source object.

All you need to do is create these source objects in the object library with the appropriate names and the desired property settings. The generator looks for them as it generates, and uses the source object with the closest match. With the combination of names, you gain nearly full control over the properties that the objects will include. The hierarchy of generator objects is documented in the help system, under the topic "Hierarchy of standard source objects." Figure 18-13 shows an excerpt from this hierarchy.

Forms searches from the bottom of this hierarchy up, so, if there is a source object on a low level, that will define the object. Otherwise, the generator will navigate the hierarchy until it finds an object which has a name matching what it wants to accomplish.

IMPLEMENTATION SOURCE OBJECTS These are object library objects that are referenced by the *Template/Library Object* property of the element definition. You can create and name these yourself (with any name other than one that begins with a CGAI$) or use objects with default behavior (named with a CGAI$ prefix). The CGAI$ items are placed below the other items in the block. These button items have triggers attached, so the item will be fully functional without code defined in the repository. A number of these implementation source objects are already created in the default object library as Figure 18-14 shows.

You use these objects when generating an action item or an unbound item that has the *Display Type* property set to Button. In addition, you can use the implementation source objects for windows, module components, items, and item groups.

```
CGSO$CANVAS_POPLIST
CGSO$CANVAS_HTOOL
CGSO$CANVAS_VTOOL
CGSO$LOV
CGSO$DEFAULT_ITEM
     CGSO$DEFAULT_ITEM_MR
     CGSO$DEFAULT_ITEM_CT
     CGSO$DEFAULT_ITEM_DO
     CGSO$DEFAULT_ITEM_MD
          CGSO$BUTTON
                    CGSO$AIBUTTON
                    CGSO$AIBUTTON_CT
                    CGSO$BUTTON_MR
                    CGSO$BUTTON_CT
          CGSO$CHAR
                    CGSO$CHAR_MR
                    CGSO$CHAR_CT
                    CGSO$CHAR_DO
                    CGSO$CHAR_MD
          CGSO$CHECK_BOX
                    CGSO$CHECK_BOX_MR
                    CGSO$CHECK_BOX_CT
                    CGSO$CHECK_BOX_DO
                    CGSO$CHECK_BOX_MD
```

FIGURE 18-13. *Standard source objects hierarchy*

NOTE
Implementation source objects take precedence over standard source objects. That is, if a repository definition contains a Template/Library Object value, the generator will try to find that object in the object library file. If it is not there, the generator will use the standard CGSO$ source object to generate the object.

TIP
When you define your modules, use action items instead of explicitly defined unbound items with code if possible. This will save you from having to write and debug code. It will also save a bit of clutter in the repository definition.

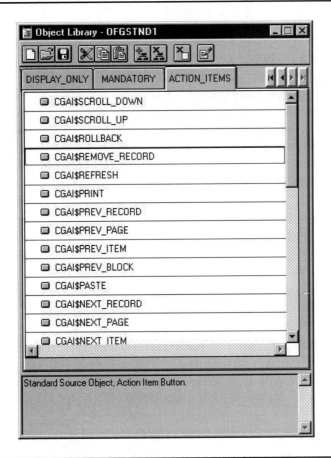

FIGURE 18-14. *Action Items tab of Object Library*

Designer Object Library

The standard object library file, OFGSTND1.OLB, located in the
ORACLE_HOME/cgenf50/admin directory, contains all standard and
implementation source objects as described earlier. It is divided into six tabs
as the following illustration shows.

The first tab lists the base, or parent, source objects (the top level of the source objects hierarchy), such as CGSO$BLOCK and CGSO$RADIO_BUTTON. The second through fifth list the suffixed variations on the parents. For example, the MULTI_ROW tab contains the CGSO$BLOCK_MR and CGSO$RADIO_BUTTON_MR source objects. The DISPLAY_ONLY tab contains the CGSO$BLOCK_DO and CGSO$RADIO_BUTTON_DO source objects. The last tab contains the ACTION_ITEMS objects as shown in Figure 18-14.

NOTE
A limitation of object libraries is that their objects cannot subclass themselves. That is, you cannot have a single parent object in the object library that has multiple subclassed child objects. You can make copies, but they will not be linked to the parent. This is another way of saying the hierarchy within the object library is flat—all objects are on the same level. For example, the CGSO$BUTTON source object has certain properties that it could share with the CGSO$BUTTON_MR source object. However, regardless of whether you create the CGSO$BUTTON_MR object as a subclassed object in the form, when you drag it into the object library, that subclass will convert to a copy. Therefore, if you are maintaining the four variations on a parent object (_MR, _DO, _CT, and _MD) you need to make the same change to all four as well as the parent.

Custom Object Libraries

You can create your own object libraries. However, there is a lot of setup work involved with creating a full set of source objects. Therefore, it is better to save the OFGSTND1.OLB object library file as a different name and make changes to that new file. Even if you are not adding to the object library but making changes to the existing standard objects, it is a good idea to work on a backup copy and keep the original handy in case there is a problem with the file you modify.

How the Generator Uses the Object Library

Several preferences can manipulate how the generator uses object libraries. Previous versions of Oracle Designer used some preferences that set a property in the form object—for example, the *Block vertical scrollbar* (BLKVSB in the Layout-Block category) and *Set automatic help for all fields* (AUTOHP in the End User Interface category). If you use the object library, this functionality could be included with the source object. These type of preferences are still supported for backwards compatibility and you can set the *Library Keep Old Preferences* preference (OLBOLD in the Standards category) to "Y" if you want to use the old preferences. This makes sense for systems that were developed using previous versions of Designer and do not want to change over to the object library facility right away. However, new systems should use the object library as it offers more flexibility and a better inheritance model.

Other preferences in the Standards category affect the generator's use of the object library. The *Name of Object Library for Generation* preference (STOOLB) specifies which object library file is used. This property is just the file name and you can also change that in the Generate Form dialog for a specific module. The *Object Library Subclass or Copy* (OLBSOC) preference determines whether the generator will subclass or copy the source object into the generated form. Subclassing is a powerful feature and one of the main benefits of object libraries, so you should leave this set at the default of SUBCLASS. The OLBOLD, STOOLB, and OLBSOC preferences are available on the application level as well as the module level, so you can set different interactions for specific modules, if needed.

Properties in the repository will override subclassed properties from the object library source object. For example, say you defined the *Title* property of the CGSO$WINDOW source object to be "General Information," but also defined the Window *Title* property in the module you were generating to "Show Invoice." The generator would subclass the CGSO$WINDOW object onto the window it created for the form. However, the module window property would override the subclass property and the window title would be "Show Invoice."

The generator will copy trigger code on source objects into the generated form. If the repository module definition also includes trigger code, that code will be merged with the source object trigger code. You can add your code before or after the generated code by placing special comments in the code. For example, if you had a KEY-CLRREC trigger on the CGSO$BLOCK object that issued a commit and you wanted this to execute before the generated code (which handles actions like recalculations) you would add a comment to the source object code as follows:

L 18-3

```
/* CGAP$OLES_SEQUENCE_BEFORE */
BEGIN
   commit;
END;
```

If you wanted your code to occur after the generated code, you would use

L 18-4

```
CGAP$OLES_SEQUENCE_AFTER
```

as the keyword in the comment.

Form to Object Library Utility—FORM2LIB

If you used a master reference form in the previous version of Oracle Designer and want to switch over to the object library method, you can run a utility called the Form to Object Library utility, form2lib.exe, that is located in the ORACLE_HOME/bin directory. This utility will create an object library from your template form. It is documented in the form2lib.txt file in the ORACLE_HOME/cgenf50 directory. There are some registry entries you have to set. To update your registry with default values for these entries, import the file form2lib.reg, also located in ORACLE_HOME/cgenf50, into your registry. This creates a registry key under HKEY_LOCAL_MACHINE/SOFTWARE/ORACLE/ CGENF50/form2lib. You should then, of course, review the entries, and change them if you want to use different tab names.

This utility also provides an easier way to make changes to the objects defined in the library. Make copies of all the object library objects into a form file and, when there are changes to make, you make those in the form file. You then run FORM2LIB to create the object library from the form. This is easier than the usual process, which consists of dragging the object library object into a form, making the change, and dragging it back into the object library.

Using Templates

Another important part of form generation is the template form. This is a normal Oracle Forms .FMB file that serves as the foundation for the finished form. It contains standard objects, that you want in your final application, as well as objects that the generator uses to influence the items, blocks, canvases, and windows it places in the form. Although the Form Generator technically does not require a form template, you will find it is easier to control the generation process and you will get better results by using it.

Typically, the template form is used to define objects that are standard requirements for the generated forms, but that have no place in the repository module definition. This allows you to set up a file with standard objects that all developers will use for generating forms with a consistent look and feel. While the object library also provides much in the way of consistent look and feel, and is, perhaps, more important to generation, the template can make a contribution to implementing application standards. It is useful for specifying standard alerts, editors, form-level properties like the *Coordinate System*, LOVs (that you load programmatically), and standard canvas sizes and positions. The template contains two classes of objects: *user objects* and *generator objects*.

CAUTION
Most of the discussion in this section on the template supports work you would do in Oracle Designer version 2 for a system that needs to be compatible with a system generated in Oracle Designer version 1. Much of the functionality and flexibility of the version 1 template has been moved to the object library and you would rely on this paradigm for code you generate for new systems using the Form generator.

User Objects

The Form Generator uses the form template to determine the coordinate system and other form-level properties and to copy blocks, items, canvases, and windows, called *user objects*, to the generated form. These user objects are form objects that the generator copies exactly into the finished form. The generated form will contain an unaltered copy of any object that is not named with a CG$ prefix. Therefore, you can name user objects anything you want as long as the name does not begin with CG$.

If you also add the comment CG$IGNORE_ON_DESIGN_CAPTURE to the *Comments* property of the user object in the Form Builder, the Design Capture utility will ignore the object. This keeps the template objects in the template, where they belong in order to ensure standardization and proper functionality, and keeps them from cluttering up the repository.

The template file can contain the following types of user objects.

WINDOWS AND CANVASES   You need these defined in the template to hold the user-defined blocks and items you want copied into the generated form. The Form Generator will not generate repository objects into a user-defined window or canvas. The *Order template canvasses at end* preference (OTCAEN in the End User Environment category) controls the sequence of the user-defined canvases within the form (before or after generated canvases).

BLOCKS AND ITEMS   You define blocks and items for specific functionality that you want to include in the final form. If you include a CG$ item in a user-defined block, the generator will move that item to the control block when the form is generated or create boilerplate from the item if it has a reserved name like CG$AT (for application title). You can also attach triggers to user-defined blocks and items and those triggers will copy into the generated form with the blocks and items. The Form Generator will not copy user-defined blocks and canvases into generated windows and canvases, so you need to have user-defined windows and canvases, as well. However, if you place user-defined items on a generator (CG$) toolbar canvas or header or footer canvas (such as CG$STACKED_FOOTER), the generator will generate the item into that toolbar, header, or footer.

FORM-LEVEL TRIGGERS   You can create form-level triggers in the template that will execute logic needed in each generated form. However, if the generator creates a trigger, it will overwrite a trigger of the same name in the template. Therefore, you have to be sure to place your logic in triggers that the generator will not touch. Alternatively, you can give your triggers user-defined names but you will have to issue EXECUTE_TRIGGER statements in the code to fire those triggers. Another alternative is to reference the form-level trigger from another form. The generator will not touch that code, but will also not add its own code, if it would normally do so. This means you might lose a piece of functionality that the generator would create if it normally generates to that trigger.

AN EXAMPLE OF USER OBJECTS   The calendar window, described in the previous tip, is a good example of a set of objects (items, blocks, canvases, and windows). These are standard objects that you do not need to attach to the repository definitions and that do not belong in the object library because you do not generate other objects from them. When you think of what functionality to put in the template, think about the calendar window. If the objects you want to place in the template are a complete unit like the calendar window, they probably belong in the template. If they are examples of how you want something to generate, you probably will put them in the object library.

Generator Objects

Generator objects are template form objects that serve as the basis for certain types of generated objects in the form. The generator uses generator objects in the template form to create special objects in the generated form and to set the attributes of generated objects. Generator objects have special names with a CG$ prefix (as listed in the help system). If the generator does not recognize the name of a CG$ object in the template, it ignores the object with no warning message.

SPECIAL OBJECTS   Special objects can create form objects that could not normally be defined within the repository. For example, the template form has a CG$AT generator object that creates an item with the application system title. You can place that item in any header or footer canvas, and the generator will create the item and then add the code to populate it with a value.

The following lists some examples of these special generator objects.

Name	Meaning
CG$AT	Application system title
CG$CN	Company name (as set in the CONAME preference)
CG$MN	Module name
CG$DT	Current date

TEMPLATE BUTTON ITEMS   There are also template items you can create for Forms functions, such as EXIT_FORM and PRINT. When the Form Generator finds one of these in the form, it creates a button item with the proper WHEN-BUTTON-PRESSED trigger code to call the appropriate Forms function. The following lists some examples of these button items.

Name	Action
CG$CM	Commit
CG$EQ	Enter query
CG$EX	Exit form

NAMED VISUAL ATTRIBUTES   The template can contain visual attributes with special names that the generator uses to assign the *Visual Attribute Group* property of the objects it creates. In Designer 2.1, the ability for a generated object to inherit properties, such as visual attributes, from a template object has been largely superceded by the use of object libraries, which support the inheritance of many more properties. You can continue to use the named visual attributes, however, for compatibility with systems initially developed using Designer version 1.

The Problem with Generator Objects

The problem with generator objects is that they are copied into the generated form. While there is a certain amount of referencing you can do from the template (or a master template) to the generated form, the inheritance model is limited. Most of the generator objects used in previous versions of Oracle Designer have been replaced with object library objects and exist in the template for backwards compatibility with older versions of Oracle Designer.

The benefit of using object libraries is that, if you are subclassing, the base objects can be changed in the library and the forms based on those objects merely need to be recompiled, not regenerated.

Attached Libraries
Generator libraries of commonly called PL/SQL procedures are shipped with the Form Generator. Whenever a form or menu module is generated, the attachments to these libraries are also generated. You can define additional library modules to be used by generated form or menu modules.

In earlier versions of Oracle Designer, you placed attached libraries and standard PL/SQL code in the template. You can now attach libraries as called modules in the Navigator and can place PL/SQL code in libraries or directly on the module as Application Logic. While the old methods still work, you will find more flexibility with storing as much as possible in the repository and stripping the template down to a minimum number of objects.

Standard Templates
Oracle Designer includes two templates that support generation in Windows for deployment on Windows systems:

- **OFGPC1T.FMB** contains an iconic toolbar with bubble help (tooltips), a set of visual attributes, a method for loading the application name into the window title, and the real coordinate system, in inches.

- **OFGPC2T.FMB** is the same except that it contains navigation buttons in a stacked footer for inter-form (Called Modules) navigation. Action items are an easier and more repository-based method for implementing navigation buttons, though, and you would probably want to use action items instead of this template.

CAUTION
If you are generating Web-enabled forms, one of the caveats is to avoid form timers as they incur excessive network traffic. The toolbar in the standard template form implements bubble help using timers and you would want to modify this in a Web deployment environment. In this situation, you might consider using the bubble help built into the SmartBar toolbar you create from a menu. This does not require form timers.

Oracle Designer includes other templates as well as sample forms. All are located in the ORACLE_HOME/cgenf50/admin directory. Templates include:

- **OFGCHRT.FMB**, which uses character cells for character mode deployment.

- **OFGHLVF.FMB**, which is a template for a form that will display allowable value ranges as an LOV.

- **OFGLOVT.FMB**, which is a template for generating LOV forms.

- **OFGMF1T.FMB**, which is a template for deploying into Motif environments.

Forms include:

- **OFGCALT.FMB**, which is a file that includes the calendar window objects. You drag and drop these objects into your template to include them in generated forms.

- **OFGEXPT.FMB**, which is a form that can serve as a comprehensive source of generator items examples. It is not used as a template; instead you copy these objects into your template.

- **OFGHLPF.FMB**, which is the default help text form that displays text stored in CG_FORM_HELP.

- **OFGLOVF.FMB**, which is a form used as an LOV form for allowable values.

The previous version of Oracle Designer used different names for some of these forms and the old files are still distributed in the same directory.

Custom Templates

If you decide not to use one of the templates Oracle Designer provides, you can create a custom template and cause the Form Generator to use it by changing the *The Name of the template form* (STFFMB in the Standards category) preference to the name of your new template file. If you also change the template location, be sure to specify the new location on the Template tab in the Form Generator options.

The best way to create a custom template is to modify an existing template using Oracle Developer Form Builder (available in the Design Editor Run menu if you have installed Oracle Developer). Be sure to select **File→Save As** from the menu as soon as you open the template file and supply another name so you don't overwrite the base template file. You might need this in case you need to rollback to an older version because you made a change that causes some problem.

TIP

The more you know about the way Developer Forms works, the more effectively you can use the Form Generator. The Form Generator does not substitute for knowledge about Forms unless you are willing to be satisfied with default behavior. You should find the best Forms developers you can (who are also enthusiastic about performing repository-based development using Oracle Designer) and let them control the work performed with the Form Generator. The skills of knowledgeable Forms developers are important in all aspects of forms generation, but especially when you start modifying the template form.

Process Form Utility—PRCFRM50

You need to upgrade Designer template files from version 1 to version 2 if these templates include any program units or triggers. This is because Oracle Designer release 2 relies on comments within the code to allow it to differentiate between generated code and code you placed in the repository definition or added to the form. To perform this upgrade, you would normally need to go through the manual steps of adding the appropriate comments. If you have a number of template files, this could take more time than you'd like. Oracle Designer ships with a utility called the Process Form Utility, prcfm50.exe, located in the ORACLE_HOME/bin directory. This utility will automatically perform the required updates and also convert Forms 4.5 templates to Forms 5. The utility is documented in the prcfm50.txt file in the ORACLE_HOME/cgenf50 directory.

Generating Menus

The Form Generator can also generate standard Windows-style pull-down menus. You don't need to generate a custom menu for your forms. If you do not use a custom menu, the form will use the default menu, which consists of a set of standard Form functions for manipulating items, records, blocks, and queries. This is the default for the Form Generator, although you can change it in the *Name of menu module if not implicit menu generation* preference (FNMDMA in the Form/Menu Attachment category).

The menu generation session starts the same way as a forms generation session. That is, you start the Form Generator from the Design Editor **Generate→Generate Module** menu item (or the Generate toolbar button) after clicking on the parent node of the menu. It is easiest to understand which module is the parent module by looking at the Module Network Viewer in the navigator. The parent will be a top-level module in this viewer. Remember that a single menu file consists of the parent menu module and all of its child modules. When you start the generation session, the Generate Form dialog appears as shown in Figure 18-15.

Other than the Template Name, all options are disabled as they do not apply to a menu. Once you have identified the type of generation to perform, you click the Start button, and the Form Generator creates the menu module.

NOTE
You can implement menu security which allows you to manage which users or roles can get to which menu items. This is a matter of defining roles under the Roles or Users node of a particular database, attaching the roles or users to the module under it in the Security node, and generating the DDL to create the roles and role grants in the database. You also need to set the preferences Generate menu security (MNUSEC in the Menu–Roles category) and Enable Use security flag (MNUEUS in the Menu–End User category) to "Y." During development and unit testing, you want to leave MNUEUS as "N" so developers are not hampered by the roles. Version 2 of Developer and Designer use database roles, not menu roles, to implement menu security.

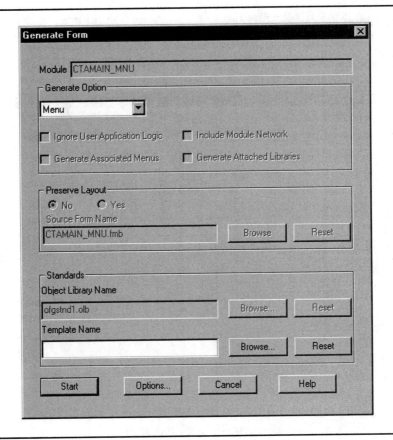

FIGURE 18-15. *Generate Form dialog for a menu module*

Attaching the Menu

You can only run a menu module by attaching it to a form, so you have to test the menu by running the form to which it is attached. The menu attachment is in the FNMDMA preference where you specify the file name (without path and file extension) of the menu module. Be certain that the generated menu module (.MMX) file is in a directory in the FORMS50_PATH (in the Windows registry) or in the directory which is the Start In directory as specified in the Runtime or Builder shortcut.

If you are using the default menu, which does not require a separate file, you can specify that you want the standard menu toolbar, or *SmartBar*, included with Forms 5. You do this by setting the FNMDMA preference to

"DEFAULT&SMARTBAR." The module you generate will use the default menu as well as a toolbar under the menu. The SmartBar buttons are a subset of the menu options. The following illustration shows this menu.

Other than the CLEAR_FORM, CLEAR_RECORD, LIST, and EDIT functions, the menu toolbar contains the same items as the template toolbar and more. While you cannot control the SmartBar buttons and menu choices, you can develop your own template menu and specify that particular menu items also appear in the SmartBar. In Form Builder, you change the menu item property *Visible in Horizontal Toolbar* to "Yes" for those menu items that you want to appear on the toolbar. You can also set an *Icon Filename* property to the name of the icon file (without the extension or path).

NOTE
An alternative to a pull-down menu is a navigation form with buttons that run the main forms in the system. You can generate this by creating a Form module with navigation action items that call other forms. Each form, in turn, has a set of buttons at the bottom of the screen made of action items as well. These buttons call other forms that relate to that form and return to the navigation menu. If you use the NEW_FORM Forms built-in in most calls, you will not stack many forms into memory (as you do with CALL_FORM). This type of navigation system may make sense, too, for a Web deployment environment where pull-down menus are not an interface standard.

Template Menus

The generator can merge a template menu with the menu module definitions in the repository to create the menu. You can store the template menu in a file or in the database. All the objects in the template menu (menus and menu items) are copied to the generated menu along with the menu module hierarchy from the repository. You set a preference on the menu module level to specify *The name of the menu template* (STMMMB in the Menu–Template category).

If you use the standard menu template OFGMNUT.MMB included with Oracle Designer (in the ORACLE_HOME/cfgen50/admin directory), you will be able to eliminate the toolbar and toolbar canvas and code from your form template. This template contains the same toolbar buttons (derived from menu items) as in the form template toolbar. You attach this template using the STMMMB preference mentioned or in the menu generate session by entering the name in the Template Name field in the Generate Form dialog.

You can also construct your own menu template. As with the form template, it is easier to make changes to the Oracle-supplied menu template and save it as a different file name. If you set the *Visible in Horizontal Menu Toolbar* property on a menu item to "Yes" in Form Builder, that item will appear in the toolbar. Clicking that button will execute the same code as on the menu item. You also need to set the *Icon Filename* property to the name of the icon file (no path or extension). Icons need to be located in a directory in the registry FORMS50_PATH, TK25_ICON path, or the Start In directory for the Form session. In this way, you can construct a menu and menu toolbar that will replace the form template toolbar.

Menu Item Labels

Menu generation creates menu item labels from the *Short Name* property unless you filled in a *Short Title* property value. If you did not do that, the menu could easily look like the one shown in the Form Builder menu edit session in Figure 18-16, where the menu item names are the short names of the modules.

This is not quite as friendly as it should be. If you specify the *Short Title* property, you will get something like the menu in Figure 18-17,

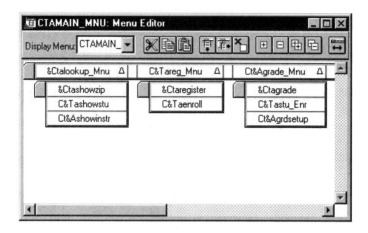

FIGURE 18-16. *Form Builder Menu Editor session—no Short Titles*

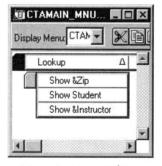

Menu in Menu Editor

Runtime menu pull-down

FIGURE 18-17. *Form Builder Menu Editor and runtime menu—
Short Titles specified*

which shows both the Menu Editor layout and the runtime menu with underscored letters.

The pull-down menu for the Lookup menu in this figure shows menu choices for Show Zip (with the "Z" underscored), Show Student (with the first "S" underscored), and Show Instructor (with the "I" underscored).

Normally, Forms runtime will place an underscore under the first uppercase letter in the menu label. This allows the user to press that key (after pressing ALT to activate the menu) and navigate to the menu item without using the mouse. In a Form, this automatic mouse-less navigation is called the *access key* and is similar in concept.

You do not need to specify the access key character for an item unless you want it to be something other than the first letter in the module *Short Title*. If you want something other than this default, you place an ampersand (&) character before the letter (upper or lowercase) that will be the access key. You also need to change the default setting of the preference *Unique letter or capital letter as menu access key* (MNUULC in the Menu–End User category). This specifies whether you want the generator to use a unique uppercase letter as the access key. The results of the generator setting this access key are often jumbled-looking menus, so it is best to take control and just say "No."

Form Generation Utilities and Techniques

No matter what you've heard from whichever source, creating code in the Build phase is never as simple as defining the modules and generating finished production-level code. This is not to say that you cannot achieve the goal of 100% generation (or even "0% Post-Generation Change"), but there is serious planning involved with getting the most you can out of the generators. Chapter 17 mentions some of the tasks and strategies you can use to do just that. There are a number of utilities or techniques you use in the Build phase outside the generators themselves to help with this work.

The main utilities and techniques that you use to assist with moving back and forth from the repository definition to the code files are: Capture Design of Form, Capture Application Logic, and Preserve Layout.

CAUTION
Consider the maintenance of your application when determining a strategy for maximizing the use of the generators. It is easy for developers who are Form Builder experts to squeeze the generators to the maximum by using generic coding, module-specific templates and libraries, sophisticated Forms PL/SQL, and complex objects. You will find that Developer and Designer can do virtually anything, but the cost of all these complex techniques is readability and maintainability. Regardless of the level of documentation, when the expert developers leave the project and the code goes to maintenance, those who take over will need to decipher and understand the complexities and then supplement or work around them to implement the enhancement or bug fix. These considerations must be factored into the generation strategy.

Capture Design of Form

This utility reads a Form Builder .FMB (source code) file and inserts or updates repository definitions based on the contents of the file. Chapter 12 explains the operation and the main screens you access when running this utility, but it is useful here to examine how the utility works.

Essentially, this utility creates or modifies definitions for the module, module component, table usages, items, windows, and lookup table usages for tables in an LOV query. If the Destination Module you specify does not exist, the utility will create it. If the module already exists, the utility merges the contents of the form being captured by inserting new objects, deleting objects in the repository that do not exist in the form, and updating properties of the existing objects based on the form objects.

DESIGN CAPTURE LOG FILE   You can obtain a report of what objects were captured by filling in the Design Capture Log File field on the Options dialog of the utility. Viewing the log file is possible from the Build Actions list after the utility runs. You can also find the file in whichever directory you stated in the log file name. (If you did not enter a directory path, the file will be in the directory listed as the Start In location for the Oracle Designer shortcut.)

There is a series of help topics on what objects and properties in the form are design captured. These topics are called "*Repository [object] properties set during design capture*" (where [*object*] is the type of object, such as module or module component).

WHAT DESIGN CAPTURE DOES NOT CAPTURE   There are a number of objects that are not design captured. The following list summarizes these objects:

- Blocks or items with a CG$ prefix and items on a TOOLBAR canvas
- Boilerplate text or graphics (including block titles and Forms 4.*x* item prompts)
- Forms built with SQL*Forms 3.0 or before
- Global variables
- Menu modules and popup menus
- Module Network (called forms)
- Object libraries object references
- Objects with a *Comments* property of CG$IGNORE_ON_DESIGN_CAPTURE
- Parameters
- Property classes
- LOVs and record groups
- Visual attributes
- Allowable values for check boxes
- List elements for pop lists

The Form Generator adds special comment to objects it copies or subclasses from the object library. This means that the objects you generate from Oracle Designer will not be design captured.

You can choose to capture the design of the application logic—code you write—into the module by checking the "Capture BOTH module design and application logic" check box on the Capture Form Design dialog.

Capture Application Logic

The Capture Application Logic utility lets you capture just the code you placed in the form. This screen is virtually the same as the Capture Design of Form, as Figure 18-18 shows, but has a different focus—to capture just the code. Therefore, this utility is more streamlined in its operation because it does not need to read extensive property lists from the form and create module objects.

You select an existing form module to which you want to attach the logic. You then select **Generate→Capture Application Logic** from the menu.

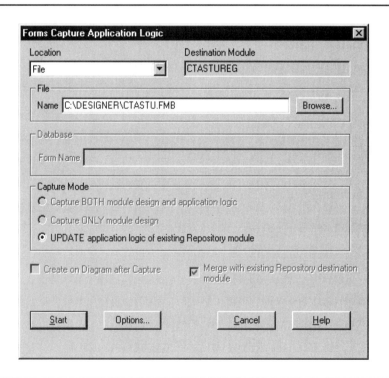

FIGURE 18-18. *Forms Capture Application Logic dialog*

The only modifiable fields are the Location to specify where the existing form resides (database or file) and the name of the file (or Form Name if you choose "Local Database" or "Other Database"). The Options dialog you see when you click the Options button is the same as the Capture Form Design but it only allows you to change the Capture Library Links check box and the command and connect string if you need to retrieve the form from the database.

A similar utility is available for Reports, as Figure 18-19 shows. This utility has only one input area: the file name.

There is also a similar utility for Visual Basic modules.

Preserve Layout

After you generate a form, you might make layout changes in Form Builder. If you then want to generate the module again, but keep the layout changes you made in Form Builder, there is a Preserve Layout option in the Form

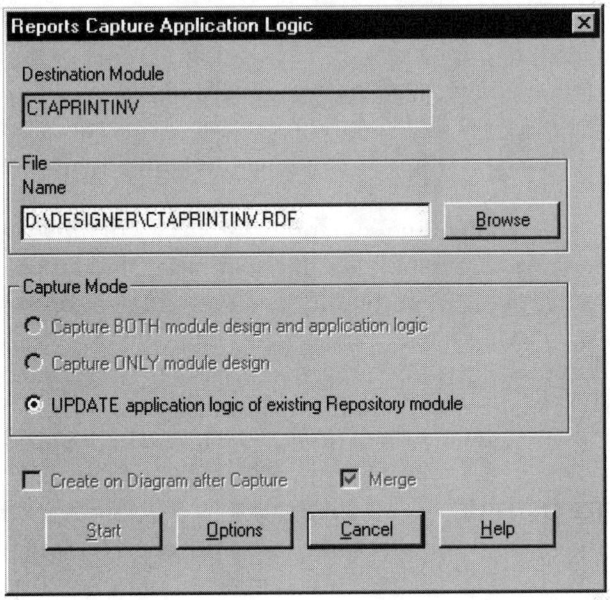

FIGURE 18-19. *Reports Capture Application Logic dialog*

Generator window, as the following illustration shows. This was called "Regenerate" in previous versions of Oracle Designer, but has greatly expanded functionality and documentation in this version.

CAUTION
Think twice or three times about whether you really need to use the Preserve Layout feature.

If you only added application logic (triggers and program units) that you want to preserve, you can run the Capture Application Logic utility to bring that logic back into the repository. Then, when you generate the form, you do not need to preserve layout as the module definition will contain all the code it needs.

If you only want to change the form by adding a block or item, you can probably define a new module component in that module and generate the module directly from the repository. This saves time in Form Builder and gives you a module that you can repeatedly generate with a consistent layout.

If the form doesn't look the way you want, do a final investigation of the capabilities offered by the template, object libraries, layout preferences, and item groups. Item groups, in particular, can do a lot toward improving the appearance of a form layout.

If you need to make layout changes and want to preserve those changes but still be able to generate the module to include new or changed repository definitions, you can use the Preserve Layout feature.

THE EFFECTS OF PRESERVE LAYOUT If you specify that a generation session will preserve the layout, the generator will add any new objects to *transfer canvases*. These are canvases not defined in the repository that the generator creates just to hold new objects. These canvases must be empty or missing. If they are not, the preserve layout option will fail. Once you have preserved the layout, you open Form Builder and transfer the objects to their proper locations. You can either delete the transfer canvases (which have names like CG$TRANSFER_n, where "n" is a number) after transferring their objects to other locations. Alternatively, you can leave the transfer canvases empty.

Preserve Layout adds objects from the repository definitions for objects missing from the form. If items were deleted from the repository or added to the form in Form Builder but not to the repository, those items will not be deleted from the form, nor will their code or layout be modified. You are responsible for deleting them from the form.

If an object has changed in the repository, Preserve Layout updates only those properties that do not affect layout and visual aspects. It does not affect item properties like *Display*, *Prompt*, *Display Type*, *Width*, and *Height*, but will replace any application logic attached to the object. If you have customized code on objects that will be updated, you need to move that code into the repository (through the Capture Application Logic utility).

The overall advice on this feature is to be careful with it and use it as little as possible.

Library Generator

A library is a collection of PL/SQL program units: packages, procedures, and functions. You attach a library to one or more forms or reports, and the code is available to those forms or reports as if it was written locally in the file. This implements a type of code-sharing which makes maintenance on common code easier. If something changes in the way the code should work, you make the change in the library and all application files that use it will automatically have access to the new code, sometimes without recompiling. It is a dynamically linked file that must be available in the FORMS50_PATH (for a Form library), REPORTS30_PATH (for a Report library), ORACLE_PATH (for Common Library files or Forms or Reports) or the Start In directory for the runtime shortcut.

There are three types of library files, each with a different extension: .PLL, .PLD, and .PLX. The .PLL file is the binary source file that you open and work with in Form Builder; you can also use the .PLL file at runtime. The .PLD file is a text version of the .PLL file that you use for examining or documenting the code you write. The .PLX file is a compiled, executable version of the .PLL file and is therefore smaller (and more secure, too).

CAUTION
The Forms runtime engine looks for .PLX files first. Therefore, if you have .PLL and .PLX files in the same directory, or if the files are somewhere in the FORMS50_PATH directory list, you may have versioning problems where the library being attached is actually a .PLX file that was compiled before the .PLL file you meant to attach.

You can define, generate, and design capture libraries in Oracle Designer. Creating a library is the same as creating other modules and you assign a *Language* (Oracle Developer Forms for Form code, Oracle Reports for Report code, or Common Library for either Developer products) and *Module Type* of Library. Also, set the *Implementation Name* property to the name of the file (without directory information so it is more portable).

Once you create the module, you can add code to its Named Routines node using the Logic Editor. In general, you put all code that is generic to a module in a library. In addition, you should use packages as much as possible to take advantage of the benefits of shared variables, hiding of internal procedure code, and organization of program units. The earlier section on "Writing Application Logic" provides some guidelines for the actual process of writing code.

Generating the Library

Once the library is fully defined, you can generate it by selecting the module in the Navigator and selecting **Generate→Generate Module** from the menu (or by clicking the Generate toolbar button). The dialog shown in Figure 18-20 will appear.

The only option in this dialog is to Generate Attached Libraries. If you check this check box, the generator will create files for all libraries in this module's Called Modules node.

An alternative method for generating a library is to generate the module that has the library in its Called Modules node. You can generate that library at the same time as the module by checking the Generate Attached Libraries check box in the Generate Form (or Generate Report) dialog.

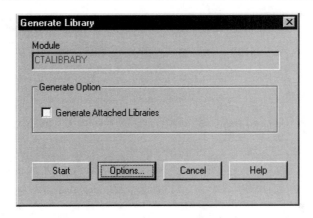

FIGURE 18-20.   *Generate Library dialog*

The Options button in the Generate Library dialog loads the dialog shown in Figure 18-21.

You can also display this dialog from the Design Editor menu selection **Options→Generator Options Library**. These options specify the type of files you are generating and the location of the generated code. There is a field for the destination of the .PLL, .PLD, and .PLX library files, which means you can place these in separate directories to guard against the version problem mentioned in the previous Caution. You can also specify if you want the .PLD file created. The radio group defines whether the .PLX file will be created at the same time or whether the generator will place an item in the Action List of the Messages Window that allows you to compile the file after generating the .PLL.

To run the generator, click the Start button. The generator will show its output in the Messages Window as usual and you will see the standard completion dialog if the generator made changes to the repository.

Attaching the Library

Once the library is generated you have to perform one other step. The module referring to the library code cannot use that code until you attach the library to it. You attach a library to another module by defining it as a Called Module under that module. You can also attach a library to the

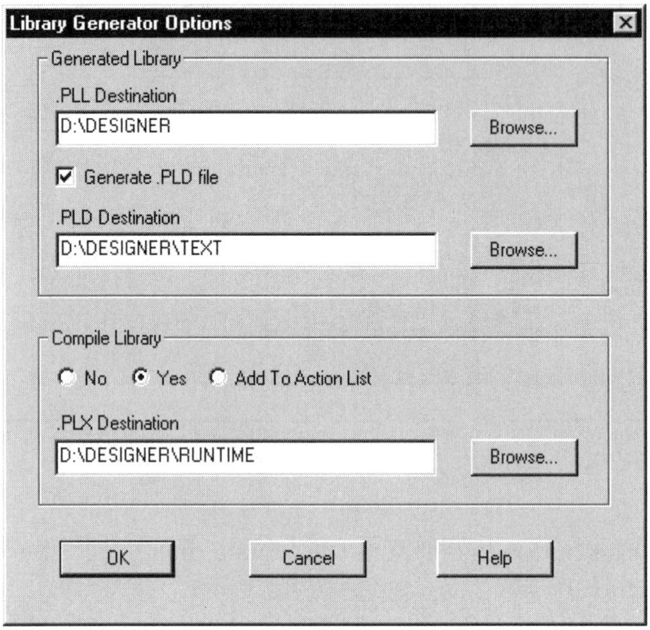

FIGURE 18-21. *Library Generator Options dialog*

template form and the attachment will be copied to the generated form. You can also use the *Module specific library attachment* preference (MODLIB in the Form/Libr Attachment category) to specify the name of the library file. You can attach a library to another library in the same ways; you may want to do this if you have utility routines that a number of libraries use. The utility routines would be placed in a separate library that you would attach to the other libraries.

Design Capture Library

In addition to generating library code from the repository definitions, you can capture the design of existing library files. This works like the other client code design capture utilities. You select **Generate→Capture Design of→Library** from the Design Editor menu. The dialog in Figure 18-22 will appear.

In this dialog you specify the module name and the library file name (.PLD or .PLL) you want to load into that module. You can choose not to

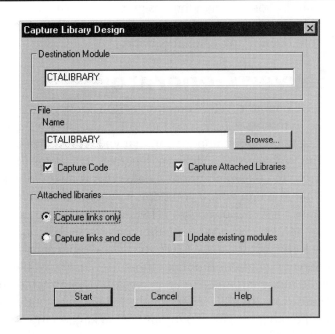

FIGURE 18-22.   *Capture Library Design dialog*

capture the code by unchecking the Capture Code check box. This will just
create a module definition of the proper type, but will not create Named
Routines or Called Modules elements under it.

You can also choose not to capture the design of any libraries attached
to this one by unchecking the Capture Attached Libraries check box. If that
check box is checked, you can fill in the Attached Libraries area at the
bottom. One of the options here specifies whether you want to "Capture
links only," which means you will add a module to the repository for each
attached library, but that module will have no code recorded for it. This is
useful if you just want to have a definition in the repository for the attached
library but want to store and maintain the file outside the repository. The
module definition for this file will contain a *Source Path* property with the
value of the file name where the code is located.

The alternative to "Capture links only" is to "Capture links and code,"
which adds a module for each attached library and records the code in that
module under the Named Routines node. Another check box specifies that
you want to update existing library module definition code with that in
the file.

Click the Start button to begin the design capture. The utility will issue messages into the Messages Window and allow you to browse the repository before committing when it is done.

WebServer Generator

The WebServer Generator (WSG) creates PL/SQL packages from modules that you define in the repository. You then run these PL/SQL scripts on an Oracle database to create an application that you can run on the World Wide Web. The WebServer application dynamically creates the HTML code needed to present the page and queried data. This is a very different environment than the one where you deploy generated Developer forms on the Web because the WSG pages are HTML-based and have simpler client and server requirements. The WSG method creates simpler-looking and simpler-acting forms but this may fulfill your requirements in some cases.

The WebServer Generator produces three files that have file names consisting of the module name and an extension. The .PKS file contains the package specification, the .PKB file contains the package body, and the .SQL file runs the other two files to install the package in the database. Installing the package in this case means running the script that contains the CREATE PACKAGE statements in the database. There is no design capture utility for this generator.

TIP
You can use the Design Capture of Form and Report utilities to create module definitions from existing forms and reports and use the **Utilities→Copy With New Language** *utility in Design Editor to change the language to WebServer and convert properties so they are appropriate to WebServer. Alternatively, you can choose* **Generate→Generate Module As** *in Design Editor to create a Web application from a module you have used for the Forms or Reports (or other) Generator. This method, however, does not convert the properties intelligently and is really only good for a fast look at the module with a different language.*

The Web pages that result from the generator sessions can be categorized into the following types:

- *Startup Page*, which is generated as the first page for each module and displays a set of links to other pages or modules in the application.

- *About Page*, which provides information on the module's version. One About Page is generated for each module and a link is normally placed on the Startup Page.

- *Module Content*, which contains links to the module components for the module. It also contains links to other called modules.

- *Query Form*, which is generated for each module component and is used to enter criteria for a database query and to execute that query.

- *Record List*, which displays, for each module component, a list of queried records in an HTML table or bulleted list.

- *View Form*, which is generated for each module component and which displays form-style details for a single record.

- *Insert Form*, which provides the user with insert capabilities for a module component if the module component's base table's *Insert ?* property is set to "Yes."

- *Delete Form*, which allows the user to delete the record, if the module component's base table's *Delete ?* property is set to "Yes."

Required Components

The WebServer Generator uses the following parts:

MODULE DEFINITION   You create the module definition for this generator with "Oracle WebServer" as the *Language* and *Module Type* as "Default." You must also define the module component table usages and bound items. You can specify the *Formatting* property for the bound item to designate how it will appear on the Web page (for example, as BOLD, ITALIC, MAILTO, or URL). The *User/Help Text* property values that you define for the module and its components will appear as boilerplate text on the Web page. This text can include any of the WebServer PL/SQL functions available in the Oracle database which provide HTML formatting such as htf.bold and htf.MailTo.

PREFERENCES   The WebServer Generator provides separate preference categories for the types of pages mentioned earlier, in addition to other categories such as Document Template and Frames. These give you individual control over the specific types of pages, as well as a way to enforce and create standards across all your WebServer pages.

TEMPLATES   You may optionally associate a template page with each of the Web pages to be produced based on the module definition. The template is used to override the default display characteristics of the standard HTML tags and the WebServer PL/SQL functions which are dynamically translated to HTML. Create an HTML page which contains definitions for all the tags you wish to customize and save the page as an ASCII file. Then specify the file name in the Document Templates category of the WebServer Generator preferences.

TABLE API   The WebServer Generator packages call procedures in the Table API to perform DML. Therefore, before you install generated WSG packages, you need to generate and install the Table API for the tables used in that module.

ORACLE APPLICATION SERVER   You must obtain and install a separate server product, the Oracle Application Server (OAS), which allows you to access an Oracle database from Web applications. The OAS consists of three main components—a Web listener, a Web Request Broker, and WebServer Toolkit packages—which are discussed in the following section. Some authors use the term WebServer as a synonym for the application server. In addition, versions before OAS 4.0 were referred to as Oracle WebServer (versions 1 and 2) and Oracle Web Application Server (version 3).

WEB BROWSER   You need to purchase a separate Web (HTML) browser (such as Netscape or Internet Explorer) to run the application modules.

The Application Server Architecture

Before further discussion on the generator, it is important to review the way that the application server handles requests from the client as well as the mechanics of how it communicates with the database.

Figure 18-23 shows the interaction between the user's browser and the database through the application server components.

The numbers on this diagram correspond to the following actions:

1. The client browser sends a Hypertext Transfer Protocol (HTTP) request via the Uniform Resource Locator (URL).

2. The Web listener provided with the application server determines whether the request is for a static page, a Common Gateway Interface (CGI) program or a PL/SQL routine. (Technically, you can use a different Web Listener than the one supplied with OAS.) If the request is for a static page, the Listener retrieves that file from the file system on the server. If it is a CGI program, it runs that program from the file system. If it is a PL/SQL request, the Listener extracts applicable portions from the URL and sends the request to the Web Request Broker (WRB).

3. The WRB sends a request through a PL/SQL agent (which you specify as part of the OAS configuration) to the database. A procedure named in the URL and contained in the application package you create with the generator calls the WebServer Generator Library (WSGL) packages that in turn call the WebServer Developer Toolkit packages. The application package connects to the database through the Table API you generate from Oracle Designer. The application procedure creates an HTML (Hypertext Markup Language) page that is sent back to the WRB.

4. The WRB sends the HTML back to the Listener.

5. The Listener sends the HTML back to the client browser.

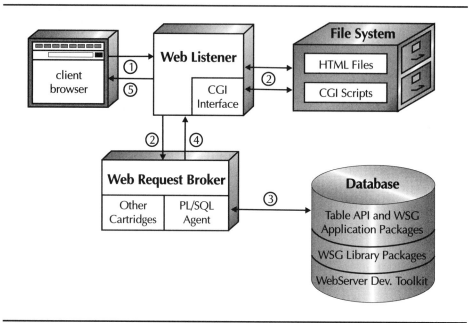

FIGURE 18-23. *Oracle Application Server Communications*

The client initiates all action by sending the URL that acts, in essence, like a command line command. Therefore, the construction and contents of this URL are quite important.

Running the WebServer Generator

You start the WebServer Generator from the Design Editor's **Generate→ Module** menu selection or Generate toolbar button after selecting a module in the Navigator or Module Diagram. The dialog shown in Figure 18-24 appears when you start the generator.

If you check the "Include the module network?" check box, you will generate all called modules for the selected module. The other field in this dialog is the password for the installation user. Once you create the package that makes up the WebServer application, you need to install it in the database, which essentially consists of compiling the generated package;

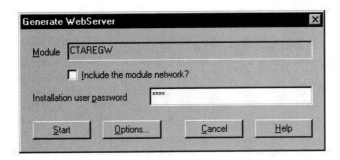

FIGURE 18-24. *Generate WebServer dialog*

this field lets you enter the password for the user account you define in the Options dialog.

Options Dialog

Clicking the Options button in this dialog loads the dialog shown in Figure 18-25.

This dialog needs careful attention as it contains values that link to the OAS installation. You only need to fill out this dialog the first time you generate WebServer code, or whenever the WebServer values change. You can also load this dialog by selecting **Options→Generator Options→ WebServer** in the Design Editor menu before running the generator. A brief explanation for each of the fields in this dialog follows:

- **Location of Generated Files** specifies the directory into which the package code scripts will be generated.

- The **Install Generated PL/SQL** area lets you enter the username and connect string (database alias) into which you will install the WebServer Generator packages.

- The **Auto-install after Generation** check box, if checked, allows you to specify that the packages will be automatically installed in the user account you filled in using the preceding option.

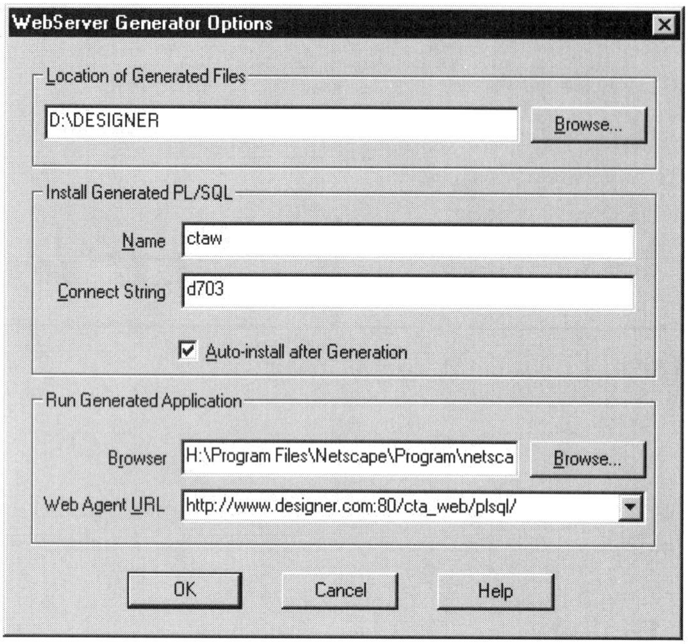

FIGURE 18-25. *WebServer Generator Options dialog*

- **Browser** specifies which Web browser you will use to run this application after it is generated and installed.

- **Web Agent URL** is the URL of the Web agent serving this application. It consists of an address with the protocol, machine name and port, agent, and service (plsql). An example of a valid URL for OAS version 3.0 is

  ```
  http://www.designer.com:80/cta_web/plsql/
  ```

  This URL indicates that the OAS is accessible via port 80 (the default), and the application is using a PL/SQL cartridge named cta_web. For version 2.1, replace plsql with owa. For OAS version 4.0, use the application and cartridge names instead of the agent and service, respectively, for example:

  ```
  http://www.designer.com:80/student/cart1/
  ```

This URL indicates that the OAS is accessible via port 80 (the default), and an application called student is using a cartridge called cart1. When you run this application from the Build Actions dialog, this URL will be suffixed with the name of the application module startup page. If the module is called CTAREGW, the full URL, for the OAS 3.0 example, would be

```
http://www.designer.com:80/cta_web/plsql/ctaregw$.startup
```

When you have completed the Options dialog, click OK. Click the Start button to start the WebServer Generator. The generator will display its messages in the Messages Window and, when it is complete, you click the List Actions button to show the Build Action list as shown in the following illustration:

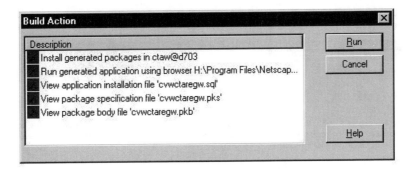

This dialog offers choices to install the packages (if you did not check the Auto-install option); run the module in your browser; and view the three source files (.SQL, .PKS, .PKB). As with the other generators, you would make changes to the module definition based on how the application works and looks and follow this cycle to generate and test.

NOTE
Read the warnings that are written into the Messages Window as the generator runs. Some of them may indicate problems in your module definitions that you should fix for the next generator session. This is true regardless of which generator you use.

Some Properties and Preferences

The values of properties and preferences for WebServer Generator modules, as for other modules, greatly affect the code. This section examines some of these and the effects they have on the generated application.

Figure 18-26 shows the startup form for a module based on a module component with a single base table (STUDENTS) and a lookup table (ZIPCODES). This module was generated without any changes in preferences. You can see the module *Top Title* ("Registration"), the module *User/Help Text*, the link to the About page, the module component *Title* ("Students") and items and prompts for each bound item.

This looks fine, but there is a lot of wasted space and all fields do not fit on one page without scrolling (in an 800×600 pixel resolution). To remedy

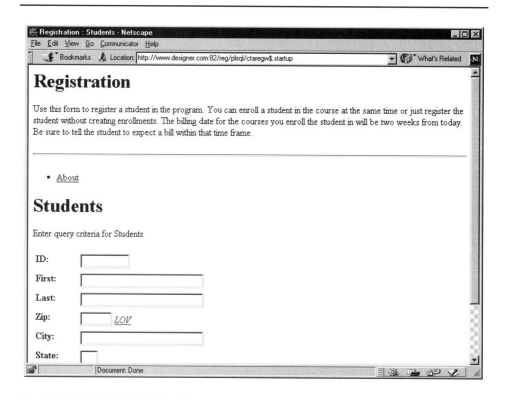

FIGURE 18-26. *Typical startup page for a WSG module*

this situation you can set the module *Top Title* property to null and change the *Startup Page: About Page Hyperlink Required* preference (MODALR in the Startup Page category at the application system level) to "No." You also need to set the *Short Title* property to null as the generator will use this if there is no *Top Title*. These simple changes create more room on the page as Figure 18-27 shows.

Other Settings

Table 18-5 describes a few more preferences and properties you could set to make this module act and look a bit better. The objective with these settings is to show the Query form when starting the module and, when the user clicks the Find button, to display a page with three frames: a header across the top and a Record List and View Form next to each other beneath the header.

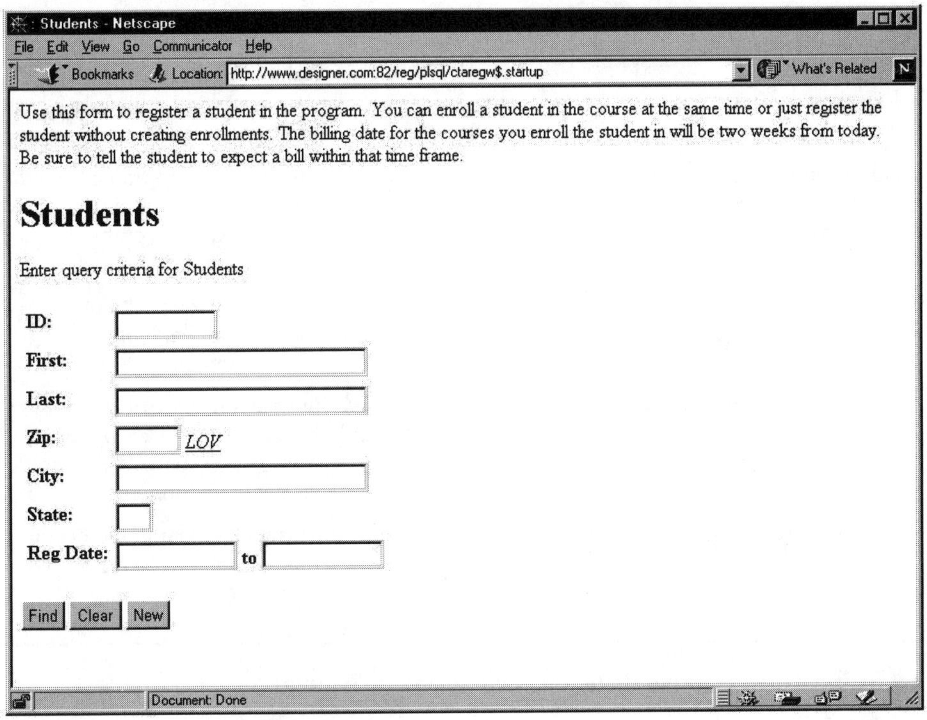

FIGURE 18-27.   *New page with modified property and preference*

Property or Preference	Value	Notes
Module Component *Layout Style* property	List/Form	Needed to display in frames. Also needed are the LFROWS and LFCOLS preferences. This replaces the property for *Presentation Style* used in Designer version 1.
Module Component *Rows Displayed* property	> 1 (for example, 6)	Default is 1. This affects the number of records displayed in the Record List page.
Preference LFCUST in the Custom Frames category	No	So the generator does not create customized frames (which you need to set values for).
Bound item *Context* property for context identifiers (like name)	Yes	The default is that the context column (displayed in the Record List) is the primary key column. If you set context columns, you can display descriptive columns in addition to or instead of the primary key.
Default Frames: Row Heights (LFROWS in the Frames – Default category)	25%,75%	The top (header) frame takes 25% and the bottom two (body) frames take 75% of the vertical space.
Default Frames: Column Widths (LFCOLS in the Frames – Default category)	*,2*	Use half of the width of the page for each of the bottom frames.
View Form: Display Context Header (ZONVCH in the View Form category)	"Display Context Values in Bold" or "No Heading"	Suppress display of context headings on the View Page to save screen space. This display is usually redundant.
User/Help Text on the module component	Some descriptive text	This will appear in the header frame for the Record List/View Form page.

TABLE 18-5. *Sample Preference and Property Settings*

Figure 18-28 shows the second page of the module based on these new settings.

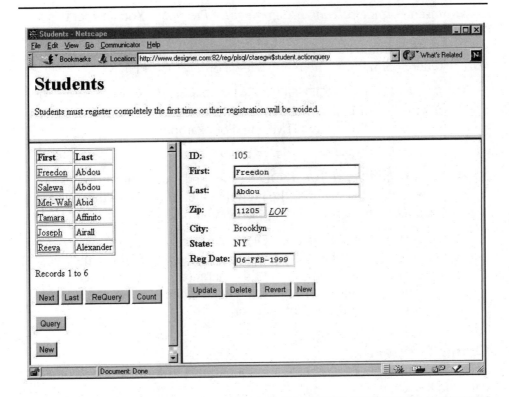

FIGURE 18-28. *Record List/View Form frame page*

Other Preferences

Some other preferences that you can use to enhance the generated module follow:

- *Startup Page Title Format* (MODFTF in the Startup Page category)
  If you decide that you really want a heading on the startup page, but do not like the large font that the generator uses, you can add a WebServer Toolkit call to make the Top Title smaller. For example, set this preference to:

```
htf.htitle('Query Student Records', 3)
```

  This will set the title of the page to "Query Student Records" in an HTML heading 3 tag.

■ *Insert Form: Horizontal Alignment for Prompts* You can set this preference to "Right" to specify that the item prompts are right justified in the Insert Form. The same preference is available for the Query Form (ZONQPH) and View Form (ZONVPH).

■ *Standard Header* (MODSHD in the Headers and Footers category) This sets the text or image that appears in the page header. You can use a PL/SQL function or an HTML tag. For example:

```
htf.center(htf.img('/img/co_logo.gif'))
```

■ *Background Image File* (MODBGR in the Document Attributes category) This specifies the graphic (.JPG or .GIF) file that will be used as the background for all generated pages.

■ *Default Prompt Separator* (ITMDPS in the General Layout category) This sets the character that is used to separate the prompt from the item. The default is a colon (":") but this character is really not needed to visually separate the prompt and the item because the item's border already accomplishes that function.

Other Properties

There are some other properties worth mentioning as they have a significant effect on the generated code:

■ *Prompt* on bound items sets (as it does in a generated Form) the label of the item. Since this is highly visible to the user, you need to set that with care.

■ *User/Help Text* for the module is displayed on the startup page and for the module component is displayed on the Record List/View Form pages (or in the top frame).

■ *Query ?, Insert ?, Update ?,* and *Delete ?* on the module component determine which pages are generated. For example if *Delete ?* is set to "No," the generator will not create a Delete Form.

■ *Datasource Type* on the module component should be set to "Query." *Datatarget Type* should be set to "PL/SQL Procedure."

Static Text Properties

Another set of properties you can set defines the text that appears in the top and bottom of the various pages. You access these properties from the property dialog for a module component or a module.

MODULE COMPONENT   Figure 18-29 shows the module component dialog with the User Text tab displayed. You can select a type of text on the left and enter the text in the *User text* property on the right. There are separate types for the top and bottom of the Record List, View Form, Query Form, Insert Form, and Delete Form. There is also a selection for Default Area which is the *User/Help Text* property.

MODULE   The module property dialog contains a similar interface to manage text for the module's Startup page and About page. The properties you set in this dialog follow:

- Default Area (*User/Help Text*)
- Top of First Page
- Bottom of First Page
- Top of About Page
- Bottom of About Page

You can set the values of these properties to be plain text, and that text will be written into the appropriate spot in the pages for which it is defined. You can also place HTML tags around that text to apply styles such as bold (<B>) or italic (<I>). In this case, you need to set the *Substitute HTML Reserved Characters* (MODSUB in the Text Handling category) to "No" so the generator will not put escape characters around the text. The last type of text you can use in these fields is a database function call. The function must return a character string. Also, you need to set the *PL/SQL Package List* preference (PKGLST in the Text Handling category) to the name of the package if you are not using the WebServer Toolkit functions in the HTF package or the WebServer Generator Library packages in the WSGL and WSGLF packages.

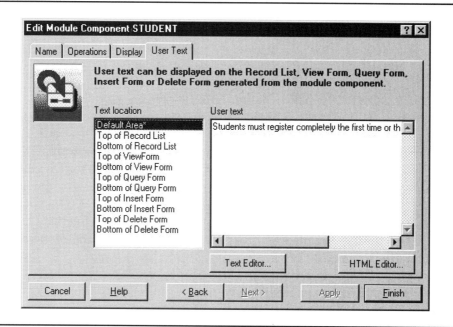

FIGURE 18-29. *Module Component dialog User Text tab*

Here's an example. You might want to include the username and date in the footer along with the company logo. You could locate the logo in a directory mapped to a virtual directory in the OAS listener configuration pages (like ows-img). Create a package in the WSG toolkit user's schema containing the function to construct a string with the name and date and return the proper HTML string. Be sure all DAD users have access to that package through public grants and synonyms. The package would look like this:

L 18-10

```
CREATE OR REPLACE PACKAGE co_page
IS
    FUNCTION standard_footer
        RETURN VARCHAR2;
END;
/

CREATE OR REPLACE PACKAGE BODY co_page
IS
```

```
FUNCTION standard_footer
   RETURN VARCHAR2
IS
BEGIN
    RETURN '<IMG SRC="/ows-img/co_logo.gif" ALIGN="RIGHT">'
           ||'<B>USER: </B>' || USER
           ||'<B> - DATE: </B>'||to_char(SYSDATE, 'MM/DD/YYYY');
END;
END;
/
```

You also have to set the module-level *PL/SQL Package List* preference (PKGLST in the Text Handling category) to be "co_page." Add a call to the function in the *Bottom of First Page* text property for the module (co_page.standard_footer). When you run this application, the first page text will include the string: USER: *username* – DATE: *system_date* with the company logo .GIF file on the right.

The properties and preferences presented here give some ideas to help you get started, but this short discussion does not exhaust the topic. The best way to learn the results of preferences and properties is to consult the help system and generate modules to test the effects.

TIP

The WSG creates Javascript code to validate input values on the client side. This saves network traffic and server activity for simple validations like mandatory columns. You can add your own Javascript code to the module using the application logic nodes on the module, module components, and items. The help system topic "About user application logic in WebServer applications" (under the Contents page topic Generating WebServer applications, Using application logic for WebServer generation) has a full description of the method. There is another help topic called "SQL to Javascript conversion tables" (under the Contents page topic Generating WebServer applications, WebServer Generator Reference) that can help you relate to this language if you know SQL.

WSG Templates

Using templates (also referred to as "stylesheets"), you can override
WebServer default display characteristics. When you designate templates in
a preference set, you are essentially redefining the specified display
characteristics for a type of page. For example, you might redefine serif
fonts, such as Times New Roman, to non-serif fonts, such as Arial for all
occurrences of a particular tag on all pages except the About page. You do
this by specifying an HTML tag with a particular setting. You also specify
whether the setting is for the head or the body of the page.

The steps to accomplish this are fairly simple, but they require you to
know some HTML. First you define a template HTML page or "style sheet."
This page will contain the tag mapping information. Second, you associate
that template file with preference set and page type(s). Third, you generate
your WebServer application.

Define a Template HTML Page

HTML tags define styles on an HTML page. For example, any text between
the tags <B> and </B> will be displayed in bold in the browser. Below is
part of an HTML page displayed by an application that was produced by the
WebServer Generator. It is a simple query page based on the students table.

L 18-11
```
<HTML>
<HEAD>
<TITLE>Student Query : Query Student</TITLE>
</HEAD>
<BODY>
<H1>Query Student</H1>
<P>
<H2>102</H2>
<P>
```

The heading at the top of the page, Query Student, is of Heading 1 style
(indicated by the <H1> </H1> tags). If you want to change Heading 1 from
its default style, which is 16-point black Times Roman, to Arial, 14pt and
blue for all query forms in your application, you could create a template that
contains the following:

L 18-12
```
<STYLE>
     H1 (font: 14pt Arial; font-weight: bold; color: blue)
</STYLE>
```

To create the style sheet, enter the style information just shown into a plain text editor and save it to a file with an html extension.

> **NOTE**
> *To keep the standard location of WebServer Generator templates in the same kind of structure as the Forms templates, you may wish to save them in ORACLE_HOME/cgenw20.*

Associate the Template File with a Preference

To use this template for all of your applications, define a preference set and associate it with each of your modules. In the Generator Preferences window expand the Document Templates category and fill in the full path and file name of each of the template preferences such as *Insert Form Template Filename* (DOCTIF). For example the *Query Form Template Filename* (DOCTQF) described earlier would be C:\ORANT\CGENW20\TEMPLATE.HTML. Save the preference set information.

Generate the WebServer Application

In order for the WebServer application to use the changes in your template you need to generate the application again. After generation, the HTML produced by the WebServer application includes the style tag.

L 18-13
```
<HTML>
<HEAD>
<TITLE>Student Query : Query Student</TITLE>
</HEAD>
<BODY>
<STYLE>
    H1 (font: 14pt Arial; font-weight: bold)
</STYLE>
<H1>Query Student</H1>
<P>
<H2>102</H2>
<P>
```

Report Generator

The Report Generator creates finished Report files (for Developer version 2) from information in the repository. You can approach working with the Report Generator components in the same way you do the Form Generator, as both generate Developer code, have preferences and templates, and require similar module definitions. Modules used for report generation have a value of "Developer Reports" as the language. There are a number of standard report types that the generator can create, as follows:

- **Tabular** shows multiple columns with one row of the query for each line of the output.

- **Form** displays records with more than one line for each row.

- **Address Label** arranges labels in a mailing label style output. This is also good for form letters.

- **Group Left** shows a break report with columns on the right and non-repeating (master) information on the left.

- **Group Above** contains two or more groups and can be a Master-Detail report.

- **Drill-down** generates two reports, one master and one detail, with a button for each master record that will "drill down" and query the detail report.

- **Matrix,** also called *crosstab*, is used when you don't know the number of columns ahead of time. One set of rows goes down the page on the left (rows), the other set of rows goes across the page on the top (columns). The rows and columns form a grid and the values are shown in the "matrix" or intersection of these two.

The help system includes a formula for the construction of each of these report styles. From the Contents tab page, select "Generating Report Builder applications, Defining report structure, Basic reports."

Output Formats

The Report Generator can create its output in a number of formats. The Report Preference *Report Output Type* (DSPFMT in the Report Level Objects category) specifies what type of output the report will produce. It sets the Reports DESFORMAT system parameter to one of the following:

- **RDF** uses the Report runtime to present the report on the screen or print it to a printer.

- **HTML** creates a set of HTML pages readable in a browser. These files correspond to the report output, bookmarks, and frames.

- **HTMLCSS** creates the same output as HTML, but uses cascading style sheets.

- **PDF** produces a portable document format file readable from most browsers with the Adobe Acrobat Reader.

Regardless of the value you select here, the generator will also create a .RDF file that you can open in Report Builder.

Generating Reports

You can invoke the Report Generator from the Design Editor menu selection **Generate→Generate Module** after selecting a module in the Navigator or Module Diagram. When you start this utility, the dialog in Figure 18-30 appears.

You fill in the name of the template and the password you use to run the report. In addition, if you set the *Role Name* preference (ROLENM in the Report Level Objects category) to the name of a database role, you can enter the role password in this dialog. Users of that report will be required to enter a password before accessing the report.

This dialog contains the standard generator option for Include Module Network to allow you to generate the modules that the selected module calls. The dialog also offers an option to Generate Attached Libraries which, if checked, will generate the libraries that are attached to the module. If you check this option, you also have to check the Include Module Network option.

If you have not yet set the options, or need to change preexisting options, you click the Options button. Alternatively, you can select **Options→Generator Options→Reports** from the Design Editor menu before you load the generator dialog. The options dialog appears as shown in Figure 18-31.

This dialog contains the following fields:

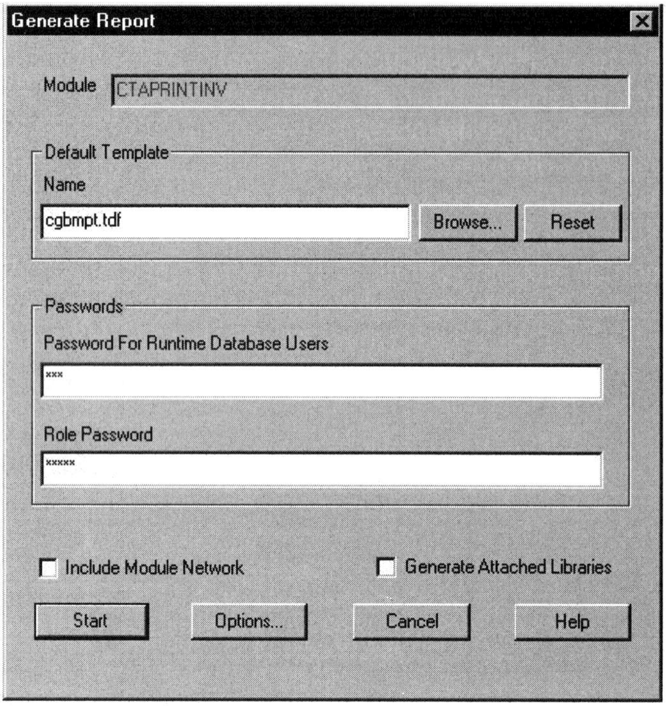

FIGURE 18-30. *Generate Report dialog*

- **Generated Reports** to specify the directory where the report will be generated.

- **Templates** to specify the location where the Report Generator looks for template reports.

- **Runtime Database User** to specify the database name and connect string (SQL*Net or Net8 alias) to use when running the report in this session. The password for this connect information is the one you enter in the Generate Report dialog.

Once you have completed the options, click the OK button and then the Start button in the generator dialog to begin generation. The generator will run and display messages in the Messages Window. When it is done, you can click on the List Actions button and select from the Build Action dialog as shown in the following illustration.

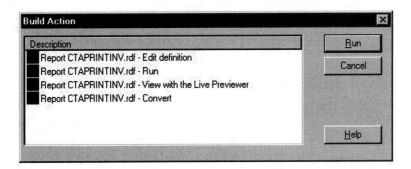

You can run the report as the user would run it or view it in the Live Previewer to make layout changes. You can also convert it to a .REX (text) file or .REP (runtime) file, or save it in the Developer tables in the database. If you set the *Report output type* preference (DSPFMT—in the Report Level Objects category) to something other than RDF, there will be a choice in the Build Action list to view the report output in the special format (such as PDF or HTML). If you want to run that option, be sure you select the Run option

FIGURE 18-31. *Report Generator Options dialog*

first to create the file to view. You can also just open the definition (.RDF) file in Report Builder to check the results of the generation.

Report Templates

Report templates are predefined reports that the Report Generator uses to determine how to display the information in the generated report. These are files with a .TDF extension that contain boilerplate text and graphics, parameters, objects that affect the layout and visual aspects of fields and frames, and application logic.

Standard template reports shipped with Oracle Designer are CGBMPT.TDF (for portrait layout reports), CGBMLS.TDF (for landscape reports), and CGBMDT.TDF (for drill-down detail reports). These are located in the ORACLE_HOME/cgenr30/admin directory. While you can customize these templates, it is best to follow the same strategy as working with the Form templates: Make a copy and modify the copy. That will ensure that you can restore a working template if you make accidental changes that affect some functionality.

One of the modifications you might make on a report template is to add user objects like boilerplate or text to the header and trailer pages. You may have a different standard for how the header and trailer pages should look and the report template is the place to implement it so that look will be used in all reports.

Generator Objects

Another modification you might want to make to the report template is to include extra *generator objects*. These are specially named objects that will generate into some functional item or area in the final report. You can create the objects in the Report Builder and name them appropriately based on the information in the help system. The names and functions of some generator objects follow:

- **CG$AT** shows the application system *Name* property value.

- **CG$MB** shows the module *Bottom Title* property value.

- **CG$MT** shows the module *Top Title* property value.

- **CG$US** shows the username.

TIP
You can write the name of your company into your report using the Company Name *preference (CONAME in the Field Layout category) for the value and the CG$CN generator item as the item on the report. This preference and item are also available in the Form Generator.*

Capture Design of Report

The Capture Design of Report utility reads a Report Builder .RDF (source code) file and creates or modifies module definitions. The utility is available from the **Generate→Capture Design of→Report** menu selection in the Design Editor and shows a dialog like that shown in Figure 18-32.

You specify the module name and file name for the target and source of the design capture. In the Capture Mode area you select a radio button to capture only the module design or to capture both module design and application logic. You also check a check box if you want to create a new Module Diagram when the utility is done. The Merge check box indicates whether you want to add the definitions in the .RDF file to those in an existing module. If you do not check this check box, the module named in the top field of this dialog must not yet exist or you will get an error message.

The Options button shows a dialog where you specify the name of the log file. These files are handy if you want to check which objects this utility changed or added to the repository. When you are done with Options, click OK and, when you are ready to design capture the module, click Start. The utility will run and display the Messages Window. When the utility is finished, you will be able to select from the build actions as with the generators.

Visual Basic Generator

The generator for Visual Basic (VB) creates the code for Visual Basic projects from module definitions. You then load the generated code into the VB development tool so you can create a finished executable file. A VB project consists of one or more forms (windows) that contain zones for tables

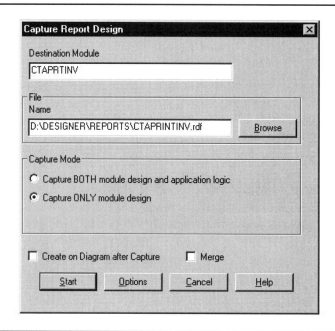

FIGURE 18-32. *Capture Report Design dialog*

(similar to blocks in an Oracle Forms application). The generator creates controls (such as items) from the bound items and the correct VB code to access the data in the tables. You define modules the same way you do for the Form Generator. You can supplement the generated code using the Logic Editor, which displays VB constructs for a VB module.

Required Components

The VB Generator requires the following components:

MODULE DEFINITION   You can create this module in the usual way and assign a value for the *Language* property of Visual Basic. As with other modules, you define the module component table usages for the module and the links between the table usages. One module can be generated to more than one VB form window.

PREFERENCES   The VB preferences contains a number of interface and environment preferences you can use to modify the standard look and feel of the GUI. The Controls category of preferences allows you to map a particular VB control to a *Display Type* (item property). As usual, the default factory preferences will get you started.

TEMPLATE PROJECT   Oracle Designer ships with standard VB template projects (.VBP files) that you can use to generate the code. You can also modify or replace these templates with your own. As with Form templates, the best strategy is to copy and modify the template files shipped with Oracle Designer. The standard template files reside in the ORACLE_HOME/cgenv20/cvbtmpt1 directory. You set the *Template project* preference (TFPROJ in the Templates category) to the name of the directory (from the cgenv20 directory root) and file that you will use as the template project. The shipped templates are written in VB version 4.0. If you are using VB version 5.0, you must open and resave the files before generating. The VB Generator System Release Bulletin (SRB) provides some details on this operation.

TIP
Read the System Release Bulletins for the generators. The file for VB contains some hints and "limitations" on how to use DAO and ODBC. These are not documented in the help system.

MICROSOFT'S VISUAL BASIC PROFESSIONAL EDITION   This is a separate non-Oracle product. You need this product to compile and create executable files from the files that the VB Generator creates. You can also use this product to modify the files the generator creates or to customize the template projects.

ORACLE OBJECTS FOR OLE OR DATA ACCESS OBJECTS
These are separate products that the generator relies on for access to database objects.

TIP
You can add your own controls, or third-party controls, to the set that the VB Generator uses by modifying the control definition file, called ctldef.txt (in the ORACLE_HOME/cgenv20/cvbetc directory). This file contains a description of the functionality of each control.

Generator Output

The VB Generator creates four different types of zones as follows:

- *Context,* which is a query-only view of a single record displayed as a poplist of values. A separate property sheet window supplies insert, update, and delete functions.

- *Form,* which also displays a single record, but in this case the record can be updated.

- *List,* which displays a number of records in query-only mode. You can delete records in this type of window but not update them. The update and add functions for this type of window are supplied by a separate property sheet window.

- *List/Form,* which displays a record list box in the same window as the single-record view of the record selected in that list box.

You can generate a query form for items in List, Form, and List/Form windows by setting the item property *Query ?* to "Yes." The look and feel of this window is contained in the CGTWQd template form.

For all zone types, default function and navigation buttons are automatically generated to enable basic actions within the record. The generator will create LOV windows for lookup table usages in a similar way to the Form Generator. It can create tab controls in the same way as the Form Generator if you define item groups with the *Stacked ?* property value of "Yes." Also, the *Use Tab control for Stacking Area* preference (USETAB in the End User Interface category) must be set to "Y."

Running the Visual Basic Generator

You start the VB Generator from the Design Editor **Generate→Generate Module** menu option after selecting a Visual Basic module in the Navigator or Module Diagram. The dialog shown in Figure 18-33 appears.

In this dialog, you specify whether you are creating a new project or adding to an existing one and whether you want to generate all modules that are called by this one as well. You also specify the database connect string for Oracle Objects for OLE or Data Access Objects. Click Start when you are ready to generate. This will create the .FRM form files that contain the code and controls, as well as a .VBP project (make) file.

Click on the Options button in the generate dialog (or select **Options→Generator Options→Visual Basic** from the menu before loading the generator dialog) to show the Visual Basic Generator Options dialog as shown in Figure 18-34.

Specify the Location of Generated Files. You must also indicate the Data Access Method as Oracle Objects for OLE or Data Access Objects (DAO);

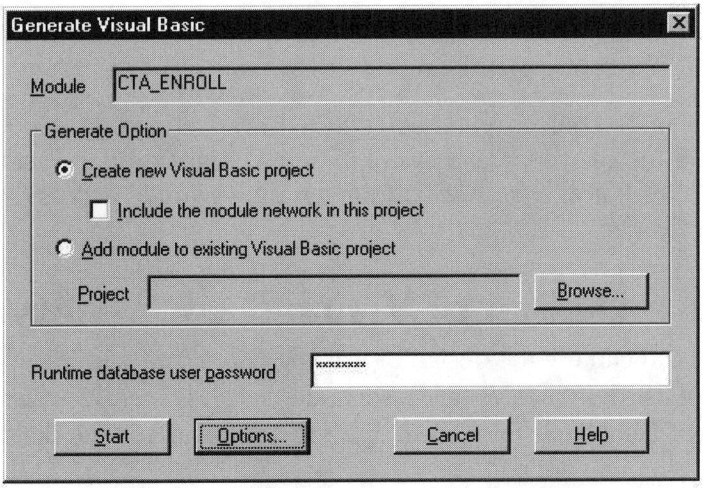

FIGURE 18-33. *Generate Visual Basic dialog*

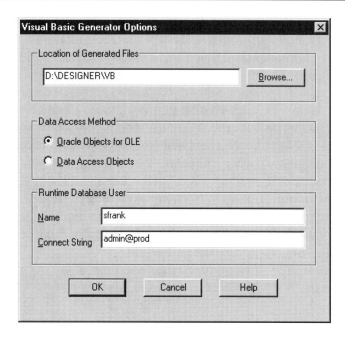

FIGURE 18-34. *Visual Basic Generator Options dialog*

for either of these choices, you need an ODBC driver and data source. Both products are installed separately from Oracle Designer and are set up in the ODBC Administrator. Data Access Objects allows you to access databases other than Oracle.

Capture Design of Visual Basic Utility

Just as you can capture the design of existing Forms and Reports code, you can capture the design of Visual Basic code. Select **Generate→Capture Design of→Visual Basic** from the Design Editor menu and the dialog shown in Figure 18-35 will appear.

The top field is where you specify the project file name. You also have to set the radio group to indicate how you want to map modules to forms: one module for each form, one module for the project, or a specific mapping of

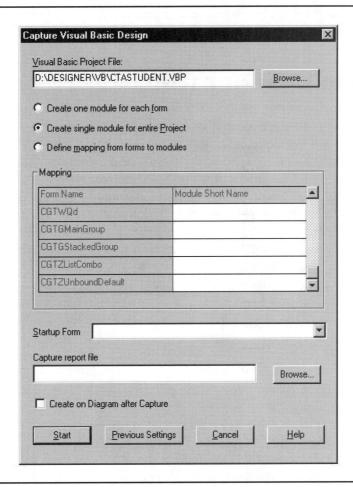

FIGURE 18-35. *Capture Visual Basic Design dialog*

forms to modules. If you choose the last option, you must specify which module should be created for each form.

In addition, you specify which form is the starting one for the application. The generator will create the code to present this form first when the application starts. The results of the generate session are available in the file name you specify in the "Capture report file" check box. If you want to create a diagram of the modules generated, check the Create on Diagram after Capture check box.

MS Help Generator

The MS Help Generator creates help files in MS Help (WinHelp) format that attach to your Forms and Visual Basic applications. It provides support for the standard MS Windows help system with text links, embedded graphics, multiple topics, a keyword index, a glossary, and a contents topic. The help system created by this generator is context sensitive. Therefore, if a user requests help when the cursor is in a particular item, the help file will open and automatically navigate to the topic that contains help on that field. This is standard operation for most Windows programs, and the MS Help Generator makes it easy to add this feature to your Form and VB applications. The Help Generator is a bit different from other generators because it does not create a database-aware interface, but is just a static file called by the form or VB program. There is no design capture for help files, although some third-party utilities will convert .HLP files to .RTF files readable by most word processors.

NOTE
The help file this generator creates is viable, as the name implies, only in MS Windows operating systems. You will not be able to run the files created by this system in character mode or Unix windowing environments. In addition, since deployment of Forms code on the Web means that the form actually runs on the application server, even if the application server is an MS Windows machine, the MS help system called from the form on the server will not show on the client. Be sure these restrictions are clear before jumping into this work.

The MS Help Generator provides an alternative to the help table system described in the section on "Help Tables" in Chapter 16. The following are the main components needed for help generation.

MODULE DEFINITIONS   The Help Generator requires one or more modules for which you want a help file. A help file is specific to a module or set of modules. Properties for these definitions are summarized in the following section.

FORM GENERATOR PREFERENCES   The Form Generator *Type of Help System used* preference (HLPTYP in the End User Interface category) specifies how help is displayed for modules. Set this preference to MSHELP if you want the form module to use the help file system, and the Form Generator will create the code required to do this.

HELP GENERATOR PREFERENCES   You can set additional Help Generator preferences to cause the generator to perform in a certain way. For example, the *New Topic for each Module Component* preference (TUPLCT in the Topic Structure category) specifies whether you want a new help topic (page) for each base table usage.

HELP COMPILER   The help compiler is a separate, non-Oracle Designer program that creates compiled .HLP files from the help source files that the Help Generator produces. This compiler is distributed with most Windows programming toolkits (for example, C++ and Visual Basic) and is also distributed in a package called Help Workshop available from Microsoft.

TIP
Be sure to read the online Oracle Designer SRB for the MS Help Generator as well as the help system for compatibility limitations on the Help compiler.

Repository Properties Used by the Help Generator

Table 18-6 shows the main repository properties that this generator uses.

As noted in the table, the *User/Help Text* property is the main source for the text that appears in the help file. A standard MS Help file contains an index of keywords that helps users in finding a topic. If the *Use Prompts as Keywords* preference (CAPKEY in the General category) has a value of "Y,"

Element	Property	Help System Result and Notes
Module	Top Title	Contents topic heading
	User/Help Text	Description on Contents topic
	Help File Name	File system name (without .HLP extension)
	Help Graphic File Name	Graphic file shown in the Contents topic header. Located in the working directory or in the directory set in the *Graphic Locations* preference (GRHLOC in the General category, application system level)
	Help Context ID	An optional property of the prefix number that the help system uses to reference the module help text in the .HLP file. This three-digit number must be unique among all modules in your system so the Help Generator can create links properly.
Module Component	Title	Hypertext link word from the Contents topic; Heading of the topic page
	User/Help Text	Description on the topic page for the module component
Item Group	Prompt	Paragraph heading on the topic page for the item group
	User/Help Text	Description of the group under the heading
Item (bound and unbound)	Prompt	Paragraph heading on the topic page
	User/Help Text	Description of the item under the heading
Business Terminology	Name	Glossary lookup word (forms hypertext link) and glossary entries
	Comment	Description of the glossary word

TABLE 18-6. *Main Property Values to Set for MS Help Generator*

the Help Generator constructs the keywords using the item prompts. You can supplement this keyword list by adding @@ symbols on a new line in the *User/Help Text.* For example, you can enter the following *User/Help Text* on the module level for the CTASTUREG module:

L 18-14

```
This form is used to enter registrations and student profile
information. You can enter and query both types of information
as well as update the student profile.

Use this form when a student first registers for the program.
Be sure to be complete when entering the student's first and
last names. Students with only one name will require a birth
certificate stating their given name.

@@Student Registration Main Topic

@@Registration

@@Student Registration
```

The main body of the text will be written to the help topic. Each line starting with @@ will become a new entry in the keyword topic list (without the @ symbols).

Running the MS Help Generator

You can run the MS Help Generator from the Design Editor window by selecting a module (in the Navigator or Module Diagram) and choosing **Generate→Generate Module As** from the menu. You will see the language dialog box where you select Help System to generate the help text. The dialog shown in Figure 18-36 will then appear.

Select the "Generate all the MS Help source files" option. Check the "Include the module network in this help system" check box if you want to generate help for all modules called by the selected module. You can specify options at this time by clicking the Options button. Alternatively, you can set the options before you get to this dialog by selecting **Options→Generator Options→Help System** from the menu. The Help System Generator Options dialog will appear as shown in Figure 18-37.

In this dialog, you set up the directory into which the generator will generate help files. You also specify the name and location of your help compiler. As mentioned, the Help Generator bulletin and help system provide some details about this compiler. If you leave the last field, Help

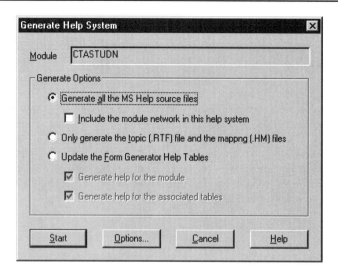

FIGURE 18-36. *Generate Help System dialog*

Executable, blank, the generator will use the standard Windows help engine (WINHLP32) to run the file. All three of these fields are used by the List

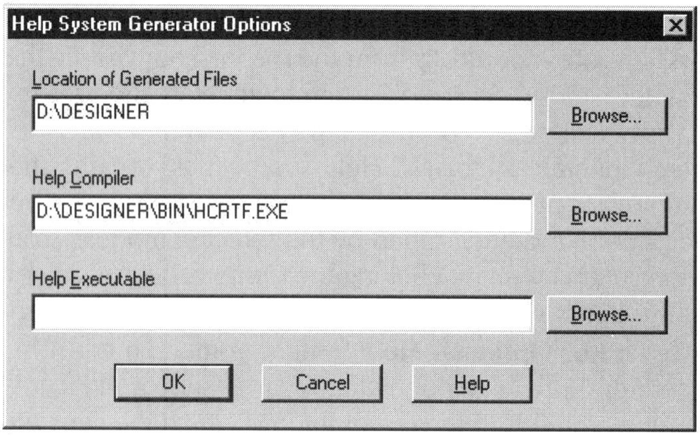

FIGURE 18-37. *The Help System Generator Options dialog*

Actions window to compile and run the file the generator creates. After you close the options dialog and click the Start button, the generator will create the help file and show messages in the Messages Window. When the generator is finished, you can click the List Actions button in this window to display the Build Action dialog, as the following illustration shows.

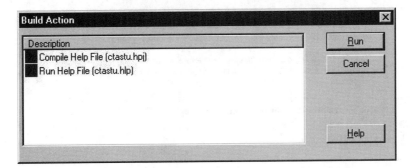

You can choose to compile the files that the Help Generator produced into a .HLP file. After the .HLP file is compiled, you can run it to test it from this dialog as well. Figure 18-38 shows the main Contents page of a module with the graphic file symbol in the header (non-scrolling region) and hypertext links to the module component topics.

Figure 18-39 shows a module component help topic that would appear after clicking on one of the hypertext links from the Contents page.

This help topic shows the item group for Student Name as well as individual entries for each item in the module component. If you were running this from a Form or VB program and pressed the F1 key when in a particular item, the help file would appear and jump to the item help that applies to that item.

Repository Reports in the Build Phase

Other than the repository reports you will need for unit testing as discussed in Chapter 20, there are no repository reports that are crucial to the completion of module code in the Build phase. Your system documentation (one of the deliverables in the Build phase) consists of the repository itself and any of the element definition reports you feel are needed. There are also

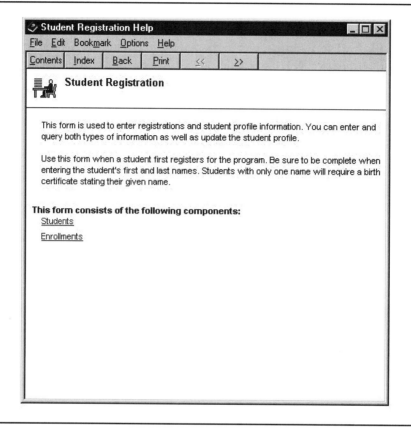

FIGURE 18-38. *Contents page of a help file*

some reports that can be useful at this stage to check the database object and module definitions. In addition, the process of creating user documentation starts in this phase. This is also covered in Chapter 20.

For the database side of the Build phase, you can run the *Database Table and Index Size Estimates* report in the Database and Network Design group to recheck the estimated size of your complete database system. In addition, the Server Model Definition group contains a report called *Invalid Database Objects Quality Control* that you can use to check database objects for problems. You may want to run two reports from the Impact Analysis group at this point. The *Column Change Impact Analysis* shows which modules use a specified column in case you want to see which modules would be affected by a change to a column. The *Column Display Usage (by Table)*

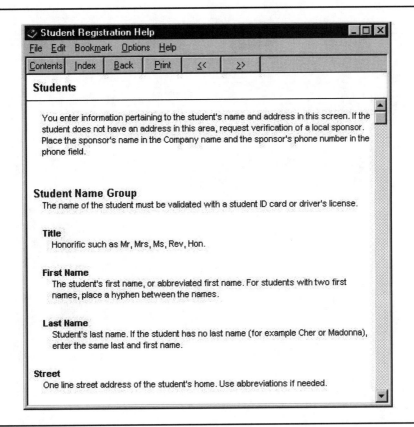

FIGURE 18-39. *Module Component page of a help file*

report in that group shows the display properties (module, module component, module component table usage, and bound items that use a particular column). This is useful for impact checking as well as for getting a picture on how this column is displayed in different modules.

For the application side of the Build phase, you can run reports in the Module Design group to obtain full details of the finished module for documentation or cross-checking. The *Module Definition* report is an example of a report from this group that provides documentation on the module. Another report in this group that is useful if you change the module network is the *Module Network* report, which shows the calling and called module hierarchy for a specified module. The *Non-Default User Preferences* report shows what preferences have changed from the factory settings (defaults) for each module specified on the module level and below.

CHAPTER
19

Test, Implementation, and Maintenance

This is a test of the Application Development System. Had this been an actual application, your data would already be corrupted and your organization would be plunged into chaos. This is only a test.

t this point, the system has been built, unit tested, and passed on from the developers to the test team. If you have followed the CADM process carefully, the Test phase should run smoothly.

Some of the activities and quality control executed during earlier phases that contribute significantly to the success of the Test phase include the following:

- Users approved the Requirements Document at the end of the Analysis phase.

- After the logical ERD was created in the requirements analysis portion of the Analysis phase, you worked with one or more senior modelers to carefully audit the logical model.

- The system storyboard went through a formal acceptance testing process with the users.

- Requirements were mapped to functions and modules.

- Column-level usages were specified for each module and reviewed by senior team members.

- The design book was audited against the system requirements.

One of the most important features of CADM is that as you move into the Test phase you have a complete audit trail that allows you to logically follow a system requirement gathered in the Analysis phase all the way through to the completed system. Because of the way the system was built, you know that it meets the stated system requirements as you understand them. Every step in the process has been checked and audited throughout the system life cycle. Theoretically, all that is left in the final Test phase is to conduct integration, system-level performance tests and user acceptance testing for the application.

However, as you have proceeded through the CADM process, everything undoubtedly has not gone completely smoothly. User requirements may have changed over time. Users may have changed. The scope may have changed. The business may have changed. In the course of the project, your thinking about how the requirements should be distilled into an Analysis Document may have changed. The design evolved as you moved through the Design and Build phases. For these reasons, many of your earlier audits and deliverables may not still be valid. In the development of the test plan, you need to carefully consider each of the major deliverables and decide what level of testing is appropriate.

Various system tests must be performed. Unit-level testing was already performed in the Build phase. However, you need to ensure that the new system interacts smoothly with existing systems, handles business transactions adequately, and performs adequately with the organization's full production load. The goal of user acceptance testing is to help uncover problems in the user interface and inadequacies in the GUI design. User acceptance testing should not be performed until after the system testing is mostly complete and the development team is confident that the system is basically sound.

Overview of the Test Phase

The Test phase is the point at which the new system is formally tested. In the Test phase, you develop a test plan that should describe not only tests to be run but also how test failures or variances will be handled. Especially for a large system, it is not practicable to wait until the end of the Build phase to start developing this test plan—there must be some overlap. As each module is tuned and passes unit-level testing, it is stable enough so that formal tests can be planned.

It is not necessarily true that every test failure or variance leads to modifications to the system prior to production. Within the Test phase, it will be necessary to reaudit the design process, perform system- and user-level tests, audit the quality of the documentation, test the internal controls and backup and recovery procedures, and in all ways ascertain the fitness of the system to move into a production environment.

Test Plan

The lead QA person needs to develop a test plan. Users need to be involved to identify the test cases, and they can write the test scripts and expected outcomes. There are two components to a test plan: the approach and the design. The approach includes the testing techniques, testing tools, roles and responsibilities, method of error detection and logging, change control process, retesting process, and testing environment. The design part of the test plan includes the test objectives, cases, and scripts. The test plan is the framework in which the different levels or types of testing are performed, i.e. system testing and user acceptance testing. You should develop a test plan for each type of testing.

The test plan must encompass the following elements.

- System tests:

  - **Audit of major CADM deliverables**   Make sure early phases were completed correctly.

  - **Integration tests**   Make sure applications work together smoothly.

  - **Transaction flow tests**   Make sure business transactions meet business requirements.

  - **Stress tests**   Make sure the system can handle a realistic production environment.

  - **Data migration validation**   Make sure the legacy system data is moved accurately into the new system.

  - **Backup and recovery tests**   Make sure the system is adequately protected against potentially catastrophic system events.

  - **Internal control evaluation**   Make sure the new system is secure.

- User acceptance tests:

  - **Small pilot lab tests**   Have a few users try out the applications in a controlled environment.

  - **Training sessions**   Conduct training sessions that also serve as user feedback sessions.

- Training and documentation:

  - **User training**   Finalize the training material and train the trainer(s).

- **User documentation** Ensure that user documentation is accurate.

- **System documentation** Finalize the system operations manual and the disaster recovery manual.

- **Help desk** Make sure the help desk personnel have the documentation and training necessary to support customer problems.

System Testing

System testing must validate two aspects of the system: the database and the applications. However, there is not always a clear distinction between the two. For example, are database triggers part of the database or the application? For the purposes of this discussion, the database will be defined to include all tables, table structures, and database constraints. Since the Analysis phase included a logical audit of the ERD and the Design phase included an audit of the physical database design, you do not need to test the structure of the database at this point. The physical structure has already been checked. However, if modifications are made, these will have to be tested.

With regard to the application, several testing issues must be addressed. The integration of the applications must be clean and seamless. The most complex and failure-prone portions of the application are the interfaces between parts of the new application and the existing systems. Even though all systems have passed unit testing, you need to ensure that all of the interfaces are correct. The essence of system testing is not to test the individual modules; that has already been done. Instead, entire business transactions must be processed through the system.

You can probably assume that not all of the business rules have been implemented as triggers and constraints. Not all of them could be, or the system would not run, would take years to code, and would never deliver adequate performance even if it were coded. It is therefore necessary to write some procedures that validate the business rules not implemented as constraints. For example, in an insurance company, a policyholder is not allowed to have two policies in force for the same coverage at the same time. A business rule set up as a trigger to test for this condition might make any modifications to the insurance policy coverage table unacceptably slow.

The application must also be tested at full production loads—not just at today's production capacity but also at projected levels of capacity for the life of the system.

There are many ways of checking the application portion of the system (that is, the code). The principle behind good testing is the one auditors use to find errors in large accounting systems. Many tests are run looking for the same errors in different ways. The logic is that if errors are not caught one way, they will be caught in another. Therefore, applications can be tested by running lots of little tests and looking for evidence that shows how well the system is working.

Auditing Major CADM Deliverables

During each stage of the CADM process, some tests will likely fail, new requirements will crop up, there will be scope creep, realignment of priorities, and new areas may need to be added to the system being built. Managing and controlling these changes in a thoughtful and systematic way can mean the difference between system success and failure.

At this point in the system development process, it is important to take another look at all of the major deliverables in the CADM process to decide what auditing is necessary.

STRATEGY DOCUMENT   If the system being delivered is significantly different from the proposed system, that difference needs to be documented. All that can really be done is to identify where objectives have not been met or where other valid objectives have been added. You may find that some portion of the system was overlooked and more work needs to be done. At this late point, anything missed will probably not be incorporated until the next version of the product.

REQUIREMENTS DOCUMENT   A full audit of the Requirements Document was performed at the end of the Analysis phase. However, as mentioned earlier, the Requirements Document has probably changed significantly since the Analysis phase. There are two alternatives:

- Audit the process used to allow changes to the Requirements Document.

- Reaudit the Requirements Document in the same way as at the end of the Analysis phase.

If you were careful in your original audit of the Requirements Document and have controlled and documented all changes to the Requirements Document, you can be reasonably confident that your Requirements Document reflects your best current understanding of the system. The only part that would remain to be checked is whether or not the user requirements themselves have changed during the System Development Life Cycle. If they have, you may need to modify major portions of the system to make the system useful. One of the most difficult decisions to make is whether to go back and make substantive changes to the system before delivering version 1; however, it is better to delay a system than to deliver a grossly inadequate system. Of course, such an action should be undertaken only if absolutely necessary. In general, it is better to deliver something than nothing.

If your audit of the procedure used to change the Requirements Document indicates that changes were not carefully controlled, it may be necessary to redo significant portions, if not all, of the Requirements Document audit, as discussed at the end of Chapter 9. However, if such an action is necessary, the entire system is at risk. This is tantamount to acknowledging a lack of confidence in the foundation of the system. If the Requirements Document audit fails, everything done after Analysis may need to be redone.

DESIGN BOOK   Of course, the design book will change a lot over the project life cycle. It has had periodic reviews and updates and remains a working document from the Pre-Design phase through the Build phase. The most important point of your audit is to make sure that the design book is up to date. You cannot test the new system without an accurate, up-to-date design book.

THE SYSTEM   The final deliverable is the system itself. Testing the system is what people traditionally think of as the work of the Test phase. As when testing other aspects of the CADM process, the key to good testing of the system is to perform multiple tests using different individuals and approaches to try to determine that the developers were careful and conscientious in conforming to standards and satisfying the system requirements.

Performing Integration Tests

As business transactions move through modules, they usually need to interact with other modules. For example, in a PO system, when a PO is initiated, it should show up in the approver's module for approval. To test this, you can enter a PO into the system to verify that it shows up in the approver's module.

You need to identify every such interface point in the system. In general, such interface points are easily identified through physical process flows. Modules naturally flow from one to the next. However, sometimes such interface points cannot be identified in this way. For example, some information may be gathered in a human resources system, and that same information may feed into an Equal Employment Opportunity (EEO) system that doesn't track human resource information but does report and manipulate it. Therefore, the interface between modules in the human resources system and the EEO system also needs to be identified and tested.

The testing of interface points involves the entry of information into one module and the retrieval or manipulation of that information by another module. The test should involve not only observation of the data through the modules, but also direct observation of the underlying database tables using SQL.

Performing Transaction Flow Tests

Transaction flow tests are an extension of integration tests. In this process, you walk entire business transactions through the whole new system. For example, in a PO system, you can follow the progress of a specific PO filled with sample data from its initiation through the approval process and the receipt and distribution of the goods. Transaction tests can be performed using only the interface with the modules, assuming that module-level tests and interface tests have been performed. The transactions must simply be walked through the entire process.

To adequately test the system, a small amount of sample data also needs to be used to test the entire process. This allows you to test not only the flow of transactions through the process flows, but also the interaction of those process flows with each other.

Performing Stress Tests

Just because a system works on sample data with one user on a dedicated machine does not mean that the same system will perform adequately in a true production environment. The system needs to be tested using realistic production loads to simulate the actual number of users in their actual locations, with production-level database sizes and realistic transaction rates (transactions per second). The stress testing should be done not only on current production loads but also on projected future loads.

Another type of stress condition that must be tested is multiuser locking. Sometimes locking problems are not discovered until several users are simultaneously trying to interact with the system. You need to either simulate or test a multiuser environment. However, it is likely that until the system is in the early stages of Implementation, it will be difficult to do this.

Validating Data Migration

Making sure that data migration is accurate is a very complex step that should be performed table by table, subject area by subject area as data migration takes place. This process is discussed in detail in Chapter 25.

Performing Backup and Recovery Tests

Backup and recovery procedures are crucial parts of any organization's system, and the testing of the backup and recovery system is just as crucial. If the system is supposed to support operation 24 hours a day, seven days a week, with no more than 20 minutes of consecutive down time, then a tester should be able to walk into the computer room and pull the plug, and the personnel on-site should be able to bring up the system again within the allotted time.

Realistic backup and recovery tests should be conducted without allowing the operations personnel to prepare for the tests. Real disasters rarely occur with prior warning. You can't realistically test a backup and recovery system by scheduling the test at a convenient time for systems people two weeks in advance. Each exposure that the backup and recovery system is supposed to protect against should be individually tested.

Evaluating Internal Controls

Testing the internal control system is much like testing the backup and recovery system except that there are many more exposures, most of which are, in general, less severe. The principle is the same: you should simulate each exposure, from incorrect data entry to fraudulent transactions, to make sure the system is protected.

Handling Test Results

Some of the results of the system tests will indicate that there are problems with the system. The test results that uncover problems should become system modification requests. Depending on the sophistication of the testers, you may or may not want to give the testers the authority to approve a system modification request for action before the new system goes into production. Only problems that prevent the system from going into production should be acted upon.

The most important point to remember is that only those requests that would prevent the system from going into production should be approved. It is easy to start making dozens of trivial formatting or data validation changes to each module that do not substantively affect the ability of the system to support the needs of the organization.

Determining Who Performs Testing

Testing can be done by people who do not have particular technical expertise. In fact, nontechnically oriented people are frequently better than systems professionals. Not only are they less expensive to hire, but they also better approximate the user population. In addition, automated testing tools are available that can help with many aspects of the testing process.

User Acceptance Tests

User acceptance testing involves putting the application in front of the users and making sure the users are satisfied. It also includes testing the documentation and training available. User acceptance testing helps identify any glitches in the user interface and inadequacies in GUI design. User acceptance testing should not be performed until the system testing is mostly complete and you are confident that the system is basically clean. The goal of user testing is not only to find any problems in the system; it also serves to generate user excitement. If the system has significant and obvious flaws, users will lose confidence in the quality of the system.

Performing Small Pilot Lab Tests

Small pilot lab tests involve bringing in a small number of users and extensively training them on the new system. The strategy here is largely the same as in transaction flow tests: the users should do real work on the system in a controlled environment. Users can identify problems and provide feedback.

Training and Documentation

The review of documentation, training, and help desk functions should first be done internally within the IS department. It is far too common to assign a technical writer to build a manual and then start making hundreds of copies before anyone reads it. After the IS review is complete, show the documentation to a small group of users for feedback. Also get a small group of users to provide feedback on training sessions and the help desk system. Then repeat these tests with a larger group as part of initial user training.

Good-quality documentation and training are critical factors in user acceptance of the new system. Testing this vital portion of the system should not be overlooked.

Conducting Training Sessions

At this point, if the system has passed all other tests and is close to implementation, users can begin real training on the new system prior to the Implementation phase. The first group of users brought in for training should be carefully observed. In addition, users should do real work to provide a full test run of the new system while they are under observation.

Modifications for Smaller Systems

For small systems, if the development team has a close enough relationship with the new system users, you can employ users as testers in the Test phase. This approach can also be taken if other testers are unavailable. However, users may not test as thoroughly as dedicated testers. What is required are individuals who will click every button, try every function, try every combination of buttons and functions, and find as many bugs as possible. Waiting until the system is in production to find bugs means those bugs might not show up for weeks or even months—certainly long after the people who developed the code are gone. Even if developers are still around, they may well have forgotten the intricacies of the code.

Of course, most of the process auditing, verifying of the strategy and requirements documents, and so on is irrelevant for small systems. Testing small systems may merely consist of making sure users are happy with the new system.

For medium-size systems, careful verification of the early phases is not as important as for large systems. However, all system and user acceptance testing should be performed as described in this chapter.

The deliverables for small and medium systems are just as important as those for large systems. The reason that testing is less imperative for small and medium systems is that the time frame and number of system elements associated with the projects is small enough that there is a greater probability of doing it right the first time, perhaps making the final reaudit unnecessary. However, you may want to take small and medium systems through the entire Test phase for one of the following reasons:

- You have less confidence in the quality of the process due to test failures.

- The system is mission-critical for the organization.

- A higher level of QA is desirable.

- Organizational policies and procedures mandate a quality review of the entire system upon completion.

When Is the Test Phase Complete?

The key to completing the Test phase is to not try to fix every little problem that comes up. As many as possible of the system modification requests generated by the Test phase should be shifted to version 2 of the system.

NOTE
One of the main deliverables of the Test phase is the version 2 specifications that address all the system modification requests.

To get the new system up and running, it is often necessary to "just say no" to more system modification requests. The system is complete when all type 1 bugs have been fixed. Type 1 bugs are bugs that prevent the system from going into production. For example, bugs that corrupt the data or prevent basic system functionality are type 1. Type 2 bugs represent a failure to meet a system requirement. Examples include inadequate performance or a bug in a noncritical system feature. Type 3 bugs represent previously undiscovered system requirements that would significantly improve the effectiveness of the system. Type 4 bugs are any other desirable modifications to the system. Whether type 2 bugs will be fixed for the first system production release or not is a decision to be made by the project leader. Type 3 and 4 bug fixes are typically deferred to later versions of the system.

Before the Test phase is complete, the Strategy Document, Requirements Document, and design book should be validated for correctness. Either amend or document any differences between the delivered system and the system proposed in the Strategy Document. This report must be signed by both the senior project leaders and the chief user.

System and user testing, documentation review, and training are complete when you have taken care of all type 1 bugs. Anything that is not a type 1 bug is deferred until version 2 of the system.

Implementation

Once the system is complete, it must be implemented and maintained. The concepts associated with implementation and maintenance are quite different, so each topic will be discussed separately.

Overview of the Implementation Phase

One of the most important factors in a successful implementation is adequate user support. If you roll out a system to an untrained, confused, or resistant user population, the system, no matter how good, is doomed to failure. Providing high-quality user training and documentation, maintaining positive public relations, and managing user expectations are frequently overlooked steps. Reducing user apprehension, fear, or distrust of a new system, however, cannot be done entirely during the Implementation phase.

The best way to overcome user fear or resistance is to adopt an approach that keeps users involved in the entire system development process. Users must believe that the system is being built to their specifications to meet their needs and improve their jobs. Ideally, the system belongs to the users. The absence of user involvement often results in resistance, which can even manifest itself in sabotage. A number of years ago, the U.S. Postal Service attempted to implement a system without the support of the user community, and users went so far as to "accidentally" destroy electronic data-gathering devices. Granted, usually user resistance to new systems is not so blatantly destructive, but a resistant user community makes system failure inevitable.

Another key to successful implementation is the ability of the project team to migrate the new application to the production environment. This process involves a transition period where the system is closely monitored and support is transferred from the project team to the system operation group.

You should have chosen an implementation strategy at the end of the Analysis phase: either to use phased implementation or to implement the entire system all at once (the "big bang" approach). Your strategy also should specify whether to keep the legacy system running in parallel with the new system for a trial period. It is important that you make these decisions before the Implementation phase begins.

Implementing the Entire System at Once

If the big bang approach is used, developers have to be very sure of the system. Any systematic bug is going to be multiplied by the amount of load on the system. Even trivial errors that don't show up in a controlled testing environment can become catastrophic when the big bang approach is used. The only rational justification for using a big bang approach is that the architecture of the new system demands it. For example, in a manufacturing environment, replacing one portion of an automated manufacturing process may not be feasible.

Frequently, the big bang approach is chosen for political reasons. It certainly can be cheaper, although much more dangerous, to implement the entire system all at once. Also, if the system is going to succeed, it will succeed much faster with this approach. There are certainly benefits to a big bang implementation. However, the question remains: Is a big bang approach worth the risk?

Big bang implementations are very risky. You need to recognize that there is a material probability that the implementation will fail. Therefore, complete implementation failure would have to be planned for. You should not burn all of the bridges of the old system, since you might have to bring it back up in the event of a big bang failure. With the cost of an implementation failure being fairly low, there would seem to be very few cases where a true big bang implementation is a viable approach.

Phasing in the System

If phased implementation is used, you need to decide how the new system will be phased in. The first option for phasing is on a functional basis. If an application contains several functionally distinct groups of modules (for example, sales, purchasing, and human resources), then it may be possible to isolate those module groups and implement them individually. The second option is to phase in the new system organizationally, perhaps implementing the system for only a portion of the organization, prior to rolling it out to all of the users. Phased implementation can be performed on a functional basis or an organizational basis, or both of these options can be used and the new system can be implemented a portion at a time to a subset of the user community.

The longer the phase-in process, the more expensive the Implementation phase becomes, but the lower the risk. Whatever implementation strategy is employed should be carefully thought out and have the support of the user community prior to its initiation.

Paralleling

Another important decision made prior to the Implementation phase is whether to keep the legacy system running in parallel with the new system. Paralleling is a very expensive strategy. It requires all data entry to be performed twice. Users will have a sense that half of the work they are doing is a waste of time. If parallel implementation is chosen, it will be necessary to go to some lengths to support and help users get through this process. Hiring temporary help to reduce some of the burden of duplicate data entry on the users may be a wise investment.

If the organization cannot take the risk of any even temporary system shut down or failure, then paralleling may be the only option. Paralleling is frequently combined with a phased implementation. Also, it may be possible to parallel only key areas until the new system is performing adequately.

Developers may want to consider using a parallel implementation for a longer time with a small subset of the organization followed by a parallel implementation of the full system for the entire organization for a short period (one or two days) to verify that the new system can run with full production loads.

Handling Implementation Problems

Problems that arise in the Implementation phase should be handled in the same way as problems in the Test phase: documented, analyzed, prioritized, and resolved. System modification requests should be used to document problems and enhancements. Any serious problems may necessitate aborting implementation until the problems are corrected.

Implementation Modifications for Smaller Systems

Implementation issues of small and medium-size systems are not greatly different from the issues associated with implementation of large systems. You still need to pay close attention to the effect of the implementation on the perception of the users. Flawed small- and medium-size systems can harm organizations just as much as flawed large systems. However, because a smaller system is easier to test, you are more likely to be able to successfully implement a small system using a big bang approach.

If a phased implementation is necessary for a small system, the duration of the implementation period will likely be shorter and the implementation plan will be simpler than that of a large system. One of the great dangers of small systems is to underestimate the importance of a careful, well-thought-out implementation phase.

For medium-size systems, you should use the same strategy as for large systems. For these systems, a shorter phase-in period is often used.

It is easier to support the users of small- and medium-size systems. For these systems, running the legacy system in parallel for a limited period of time may be appropriate.

When Is the Implementation Phase Complete?

Implementation is complete when the following three criteria have been met:

- In phased implementation, the phasing has been completed and implementation has been done throughout the entire organization or whatever portion of the organization is appropriate for that application.

- All parallel processing with the legacy system has been discontinued.

- A suitable period of monitoring has passed that allows you to be confident that the new system is up and running.

The last step is the most critical. Significant effort should be devoted to monitoring system performance, system resource usages, and user perceptions for the first few weeks after implementation. It is only after this intensive monitoring period is over that you can declare the Implementation phase complete.

Maintenance

Maintenance is a process that continues throughout the life of the system. A predefined process must be put into place to handle ongoing problems, modifications, and enhancements.

One interesting aspect of maintenance is the way requests are viewed. Many maintenance requests are not necessarily a bad thing. Some companies use the number of maintenance requests as a primary measure of system success or failure. Some companies may consider a large number of maintenance requests as an indication that the system is full of bugs and not meeting user requirements or expectations. Other companies may view a large maintenance queue as a sign that users want to fully exploit the system's potential.

Earlier chapters discussed how users log requests and problems through the system modification request process. In the Maintenance phase, these requests are ranked and decisions made as to when they will be addressed, if at all, and assigned to an appropriate version of the system.

Versioning

Changes to production systems should never be made on an ad hoc basis. Modifications need to be prioritized, grouped, approved, applied to the system, and then thoroughly tested before the next version of the system is implemented. The approval and prioritization process should be handled by a steering committee made up of both developers and users. When requests are approved, they should be assigned to an upcoming version of the system to indicate when these modifications will be implemented. After all of the scheduled modifications for a version have been applied, the new version must be tested prior to implementation.

Of course, certain system modification requests cannot wait for a new version and must be implemented immediately. For example, a bug that corrupts underlying data cannot wait for a new software version but must go through an immediate testing and implementation process.

Version Testing

Version testing need not be as comprehensive as the original testing of the system. You are making changes to an already thoroughly tested system, so you do not need to repeat the full testing process for each new version release. However, you do need to perform incremental unit testing for each affected module. Not only should the changed portions of the module be checked, but a full retest of any affected module should be performed unless the modification was cosmetic.

In addition, all integration tests associated with all affected modules should be performed again, as should transaction flow tests for each physical process flow that includes an affected module.

Since this testing process is the same no matter how many changes are made to a module, it is much more cost effective to group as many system modification requests together as possible and implement them together.

Modifications Necessitated by Software Product Changes

When the underlying application software, DBMS, operating system, or platform changes—for example, when a new Oracle Developer version or the next version of any software is released—you must not assume that the system will still operate correctly. Whenever you want to change to a new product or version, the transaction flow and stress tests should be repeated prior to implementation to ensure that the system operates correctly with the new architecture. Coexistence testing is also necessary if new systems that interface with the existing system are brought online.

Maintenance Modifications for Smaller Systems

For small systems, versioning may not be necessary in the early phases of the project until the system is stable. After the initial Implementation phase, small systems should be versioned just like large systems.

For medium-size systems, maintenance should be handled just as for large systems.

When Is the Maintenance Phase Complete?

Of course, the flippant answer to this question is that Maintenance is never complete. However, the reality is that systems do have a finite lifetime. One of the most difficult questions to answer is: when is it time to stop all but essential modifications to the system and begin designing its replacement?

There is an economically rational way to make this decision. You can carefully analyze the amount of money you are spending on maintenance versus the amount of money it would take to develop a new system. Of course, when you build a new system, you have the opportunity to reengineer the business processes. In practice, systems frequently stay in production long after it is economically rational to keep them in production. Maintaining legacy systems remains a fixed, if not increasing, cost over time. As the business grows and changes, the ability of the system to keep pace with those changes decreases.

Systems are usually only replaced when failure to do so would cause great distress to the organization.

Conclusion

Implementation marks the last of the CASE Application Development Method phases. However, once the system is complete, the developer's work is not finished. No system can succeed without competent maintenance. The ongoing satisfaction of the users depends upon how well the system can respond to requests for changes.

Following the CADM process does not guarantee that a project will proceed completely smoothly or that it will be on time or under budget. However, if you follow the CADM process throughout system development, you can be assured that your system requirements are coherently gathered and that you can track any system requirement from its point of origin to its eventual system impact, if any. All of the audit and quality control portions of the CADM process virtually guarantee that the final system faithfully fulfills the system requirements as the developers understand them. By carefully following the methods outlined here, you will have sufficient documentation of the process to be able to defend your decisions throughout the process.

All of this does not guarantee that you will build a good system; however, CADM does guarantee that you will build the best system that can be generated by the development team. Good systems require not just a sound development process, but also skilled, creative developers and good luck.

Throughout all phases of system development, you need to perform tasks to administer the repository as well as its application systems. You also need to manipulate and query data in the repository in ways particular to your needs but not provided for by the Oracle Designer tools. Chapter 20 discusses the role of Oracle Designer in the Test, Implementation, and Maintenance phases. Parts III and IV describe other Oracle Designer activities performed throughout the phases. They also discuss some additional tasks that may be integrated into the CADM methodology.

CHAPTER
20

Oracle Designer in Test, Implementation, and Maintenance

Computer Thesaurus entry for "bug": see undocumented feature, documented feature limitation, unanticipated feature, unexplained behavior, uncooperative user.

fter the Build phase, the majority of the development effort is completed. However, the critical life cycle phases of Test, Implementation, and Maintenance must still be completed. This chapter discusses the way that Oracle Designer supports work in each of these.

In the Test phase, Oracle Designer provides support for verification of database objects and system requirements. Since your system is made up of the database objects and program modules you created from definitions in Oracle Designer, complete system design documentation is built into the repository. From the repository definitions, you can check whether the application you have created fulfills the known business needs and other system requirements.

In the Implementation phase, you work in Oracle Designer to supplement the documentation you started in the Build phase for the help desk and for users. Since this documentation is derived directly from repository information, the only real work is choosing the format or developing reports.

While Implementation marks the last of the CASE Application Development Method phases, once the system is complete, the developer's work is not finished. No system can succeed without competent maintenance. The ongoing satisfaction of the users depends on how well the system can respond to requests for changes. Oracle Designer supports the Maintenance phase in the same way it supports all other phases, since a maintenance effort should use a subset of the phases you went through to create the system in the first place.

The Test Phase in Oracle Designer

Most of the Test phase tasks are outside the scope of Oracle Designer. However, there are some key activities that the repository can help with. These are listed in Table 20-1 along with the supporting Oracle Designer tools and utilities.

Activity or Deliverable	Oracle Designer Tool
System test documentation	Matrix Diagrammer
Problem tracking	Repository Object Navigator, Matrix Diagrammer, or the Application Programmatic Interface (API)
Database audit	Reconcile Report of the Generate Database from Server Model utility
Document problems and requirements mapping	Repository Reports

TABLE 20-1.   *Test Activities and Oracle Designer Tools*

This section focuses on how you can use the Oracle Designer tools and utilities for these Test phase activities. If you need to review details on using these tools, the Repository Object Navigator and Repository Reports tools are discussed fully in Chapter 6; the Matrix Diagrammer is explained fully in Chapter 10; and the API is explored in detail in Chapter 28.

Unit and System Test Documentation

Generally, your quality assurance (QA) group handles the test phase. These people perform similar tests in both the Build and Test phases to ensure that the application performs correctly and as designed. The Build phase consists of unit- or module-level tests that concentrate on each module, while the Test phase is concerned with system-level tests that check groups of modules or the interaction between modules.

Unit Testing

The objective of the finished application is to fulfill the business needs that were stated in the form of system requirements. In the Pre-Design phase, you attach these requirements to modules by creating a user-extended association type (as discussed in Chapter 12) and assigning individual requirements to each module. In the Build phase, you create the module code itself, and the QA group performs module-level unit tests to make sure the attached requirements are actually implemented by that module. QA performs a requirements audit of the design book to ensure that all requirements stated in the Analysis phase are assigned to modules. QA also needs to revisit the mapping of requirements to modules and ask the question: Does the module that now exists actually fulfill the requirements it was intended to fulfill?

The tool used for this testing is the Matrix Diagrammer. You can set up a matrix of modules and requirements that provides, at a glance, a list of the requirements for all modules in the system. This utility makes it quite easy to look at a module in a particular row (or column, depending on how you set up the matrix) and quickly see which requirements are assigned to it. If you print this list, QA can use it as a reference when checking modules to determine if all requirements are indeed mapped to and fulfilled by modules. In addition, it may discover modules that do not implement any requirements and that you may be able to delete.

System Testing: Module Design

The module-level requirements checking was done in the Build phase. All that is left in the Test phase are cross-module tests, also called system-level tests. These check whether requirements that use more than one module are fulfilled by the final code. The method used in this phase is the same as in the Build phase: check the requirements mapped to modules using the Matrix Diagrammer. In this case, however, since you have already tested the module-level requirements, you, as a QA person, need to concentrate on the cross-module requirements.

First, you need to know which requirements fall into the cross-module category. This is where the Matrix Diagrammer comes in. If you look at the Modules and Requirements matrix you created in the Pre-Design phase to assign this mapping, you can easily tell which requirements are fulfilled by more than one module. If you set up the matrix so that the requirements are rows and the modules are columns, a cross-module requirement will have more than one intersection cell filled in for that row. Table 20-2 shows an excerpt from such a matrix.

Requirements / Modules	CTAGRADE	CTAREGISTER	CTAZIPLOV
Provide entry of student's first registration		X	X
Provide entry of student's subsequent registrations		X	
Enter valid address for student			X
Assign grades to student work	X		

TABLE 20-2. *Cross-Module Requirement Example*

In this matrix, the requirement to "Provide entry of student's first registration" appears in two modules, which means that the requirement is only fulfilled by the results from both modules. Something to check as you do this is whether the requirement appears in more than one because it crosses modules or because there is more than one way to fulfill the requirement.

You can check the matrix visually by scanning across each row to see if more than one module fulfills the requirement. Instead of creating the matrix, you could write an API utility (or query) to perform the checking in an automated way. This might be useful for a complex system that might create a large diagram that would be difficult to analyze in a matrix.

You need to check all modules in each row to see if there is a dependency between them and to ensure that, together, they fulfill the requirement. For example, one requirement may state that a complete transaction needs actions from more than one module before it is considered complete. This kind of requirement cannot be tested on the unit level because one unit alone cannot fulfill the requirement. However, if you test all modules involved with the requirement by attempting to complete this transaction, you have a true test of the requirement and can verify that it is fulfilled.

System Testing: Database Design

In the Test phase, you also test the database design itself. First you have to ensure that the database objects that were actually created match corresponding definitions in the repository. A discrepancy may occur if a developer or someone else modified or added a database object without changing the Oracle Designer repository—which could easily happen in the heat of the Build phase. You can run the Reconcile Report of the Generate Database from Server Model utility discussed later to check whether the database and repository are synchronized.

Another test you have to perform on the database in the Test phase consists of checking whether the requirements fulfilled by tables are truly fulfilled. Some system requirements may not be linked to modules but to tables. These would require another association type called "Requirements to Tables" that tracks the link between those two elements. You would create this association type in the Pre-Design phase and fill it in during the Design phase. Column and constraint definitions may impact the system requirements (for better or worse), and you include notes in the table requirements for these objects. The Test phase is the time to test whether these requirements are met properly by the tables. The Matrix Diagrammer is the tool to use to show a Requirements to Tables matrix.

REPOSITORY REPORTS FOR SECURITY DEFINITIONS   The last category of database testing that is appropriate in the Test phase is the security test. You need to check whether the roles and user accounts in the actual database agree with the definitions in the repository. A repository report called *Role Definition* in the Database and Network Design group can help here. If you run this report, you will see a list of all properties of the role, including system privileges and database object privileges. You can compare this list to a list you get by querying the database data dictionary views ROLE_SYS_PRIVS and ROLE_TAB_PRIVS. Comparing the repository report and the data dictionary query results is largely a manual process, although you could automate it by querying both the data dictionary and repository with one SQL statement. The API views of the repository can assist in extracting the pertinent Oracle Designer information.

Problem Tracking

One of the activities you perform in the Test phase is ensuring that the modules work together with each other and fulfill the system requirements. During this activity, problems will surface that were not uncovered during unit testing. You need to keep track of these problems so they can be fixed before the Implementation phase. In the Build phase, you performed unit testing to check whether the individual modules work, and you need to track problems that arise in that phase as well. You need a single system to handle problems revealed by the tests in both the Build and Test phases. The ideal system would be contained in the repository so you can easily associate a problem with one or more modules.

Using the Repository Object Navigator for Problem Tracking

Oracle Designer has a *Problems* node (in the Enterprise Modeling group) that the help system states is for "...a business event or state that inhibits the progress of the enterprise towards its objective (e.g., personnel disputes, market moves, procedural or statutory changes, unresolved issues or unmade decisions)." This stated purpose sounds more like a requirement, because it tracks a business problem rather than an application problem. Since you already defined a user extension for Requirements, you can use the Requirements element instead of the Problems element to track business problems. The Problems node is then available for you to use to track problems that are found in testing. Although Oracle Designer does not provide a specific tool to handle problems, you can use the Repository Object Navigator to enter and modify the problem definitions. Also, the Matrix Diagrammer lets you enter and access these elements because they are linked to other elements such as Modules. Figure 20-1 shows the Problem Properties window for a sample problem definition in RON.

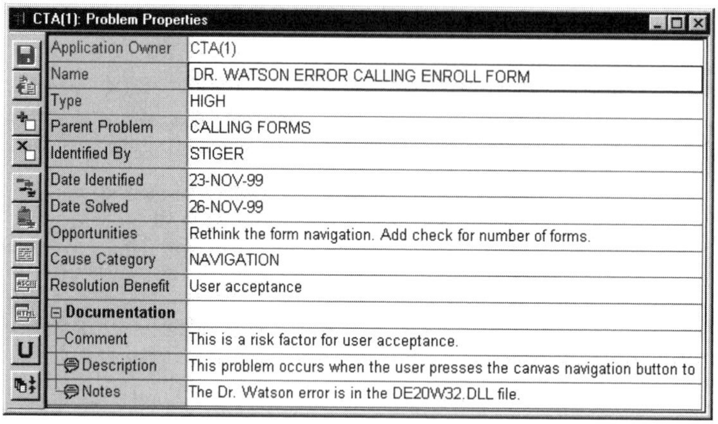

FIGURE 20-1. *Problem Properties window*

The properties include normal tracking fields for the name of the person who uncovered the problem and the date, and you may want to define user extensions for *Solved By* (the person who solved the problem) and *Solution* (a description of the fix). Other possible candidates for user extensions include *Status* (for example, to track the release status of a problem) and *Test Number* (if the problem was detected by running a formal test). The Problem properties also include a number of descriptive fields—*Comment, Opportunities,* and *Resolution Benefit*—that you can use to organize the details of the problem. There are also flexibly defined properties for *Type* (a property that you could use as a priority level) and *Cause Category* (a classification of the problem). You can tailor these to your needs and use them to report on categories or types of problems. There is no input validation for these properties, although the fields force the entry into uppercase.

Once you define a problem, you can link it to the module or modules where that problem occurs through the *Usages: Resolved by Modules* node under the specific problem instance, as the following illustration shows. This link gives you a way to create reports and matrix diagrams linking modules to problems.

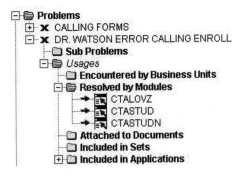

The *Usages: Encountered by Business Units* under the Problems node is another association element that links the problem to the business unit that experienced it. Creating these associations does not further the cause of tracking system problems, so you can ignore it for this purpose.

NOTE
Oracle has implemented the element type Problems, as well as the association types Business Unit to Problem *and* Problem to Module, *as user extensions to the main set of types. This does not really affect you, although it does reduce the number of additional element and association types that you can create.*

You can extend this problem tracking system to other repository elements such as tables, views, and snapshots. This will allow you to track problems in those objects in the same way as you track problems in modules. You will need to define a new association type for each element type you want to link to Problems. These new associations are managed the same way as Problems to Modules—with the Repository Object Navigator.

The problem-tracking system you use in the Build and Test phases of the life cycle is also suitable for tracking bugs or problems that arise in the Maintenance phase. Inserting a problem definition in the repository can be the first step in the problem-tracking procedure when bugs are detected. It can also be the first step in your system change request procedure when enhancements are needed. When the problem fix or enhancement is put into production, you fill out the applicable properties in the problem definition. This kind of tracking lets you store information on all bugs and problems in one place in the repository, whether they are from the Test, Build, or Maintenance phases.

Using Matrix Diagrammer for Problem Tracking

Another utility that can assist in problem tracking is the Matrix Diagrammer. You can create a matrix of Problems and Modules to see which problems occur in which modules. This matrix is most useful if you have multiple modules in which multiple problems occur, or if you want to see all problems as rows or columns in a grid. If you want a "big picture" overview of problems and modules, the Matrix Diagrammer is the correct tool. Otherwise, RON is faster and more efficient to use for handling individual problems and their associated modules.

Using the API for Problem Tracking

Instead of using RON for problem tracking, you can write your own front-end system with Oracle Forms or another tool, as outlined in Chapter 28. You can use the Application Programmatic Interface to build your own front end to insert, update, and delete problems and the associations of problems to modules or other objects. The drawback of this front end is that it requires a bit of work to code, test, and maintain. The benefits of this front end are that you can more easily enter and modify the problems and more easily associate modules to those problems. In addition, you can provide item-level validation in your code to restrict values entered, for example, to the *Type* and *Cause Category* properties.

Using an External System for Problem Tracking

You can design and create your own tables and front end for problem tracking. This system could still link to the Designer repository using the names and internal identifiers of the element definitions that experience the problems. The benefit with this system is that coding a front-end interface is easier than coding an interface to the repository. The drawback is that there is only a soft link to the repository definitions (the name and id columns), so it is easy to get out of synch if a repository definition changes.

Reconcile Report of the Generate Database from Server Model Utility

The Reconcile Report is a feature of the Generate Database from Server Model utility in the Design Editor (as described in Chapter 18). It is not so much a separate utility as it is an option when you run this utility for a target of the database or an ODBC connection. It allows you to determine what differences, if any, exist between the objects that are currently in the database and the repository definitions for those objects. It is possible that someone has modified an object in the database but not made the corresponding change in the repository. Or, conversely, someone could have changed the repository but forgotten to alter the database. This means that your repository is out of synch with the database. In this case, moving forward into the next phase, Implementation, may cause you problems, because the underlying data structures are wrong for additional applications you create.

For example, you create a ZIPCODES table, which contains columns for ZIP, CITY, and STATE. You then create your modules from this table and, as you are working with your modules, you find that you need another column for SUBZIP. You alter the ZIPCODES table and add the column but do not make that same change in the repository. If you create a new module using the ZIPCODES table, the SUBZIP will not be available in that module because you have not added it to the repository. Conversely, if you added a column to the repository but not to the database, you can define the module with the new column, but it will fail to compile or run.

The Reconcile Report can help you synchronize the repository with the database. You run the Generate Database from Server Model utility, which you reach from the Design Editor **Generate→Generate Database from Server Model** menu item. The Target tab of the dialog appears, as shown in Figure 20-2.

For the Reconcile Report, you select a target of Database (for Oracle databases) or ODBC (for non-Oracle databases). This option instructs the generator to produce a number of files: a DDL script that can be run to alter the database objects to match the repository definitions; scripts to create the objects if they do not exist; and a report on the differences between the database and the repository—the Reconcile Report.

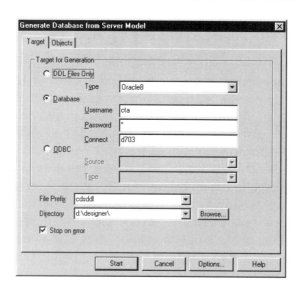

FIGURE 20-2. *Target tab of Generate Database from Server Model*

TIP
Select the tables or other objects you wish to reconcile in the Navigator or diagram before starting the utility. The selected objects will appear automatically in the Objects tab's Generate list. You do not even need to check that tab if you select the objects in the Navigator.

The Target tab also contains selections for the output file name and file location, as well as a Stop on error check box, which indicates that you want the utility to stop if it encounters an error. You might not want the utility to abort if you have many elements you want to work on and you need to save as much as possible of this information regardless of the success of all the objects.

If you select Database, you fill in the database connection information and click the Objects tab. The dialog shown in Figure 20-3 appears.

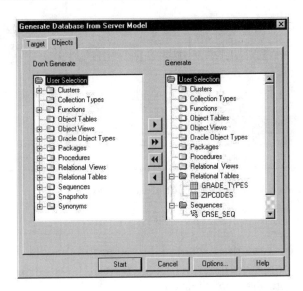

FIGURE 20-3.   *Objects tab of Generate Database from Server Model*

You can run this utility on any of the elements listed in this dialog by moving the names to the Generate list on the right-hand side. The element definitions that you selected in the Navigator window will already be selected, but you can add to that list by moving elements from the left to the right. If you select the elements in the Navigator before running the utility, those elements will appear in the Generate list and you do not need to visit the Objects tab.

After you have selected the elements to reconcile, click the Start button. The Messages Window will open and show the progress of the utility. If you have chosen Database or ODBC as the target, the dialog in Figure 20-4 will appear when the utility is done.

For the purposes of the Reconcile Report, you click View Report. This will show the file with a .LIS extension generated from this session. The report lists the differences between the repository and the online database. The scripts generated provide the ALTER statements needed to synchronize the database with the repository. You can run these scripts in the database to

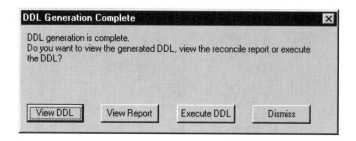

FIGURE 20-4. *DDL Generation Complete dialog*

effect the changes using the Execute DDL button in this dialog. In addition, if you changed something that affected a constraint, the dialog in Figure 20-5 appears before the final dialog.

This dialog indicates that a database change has affected an index or constraint; for example, a table no longer contains a column that was previously part of a foreign key constraint. The only way to add or remove a column from an index or constraint is to drop and re-create the index or constraint. The dialog in Figure 20-5 allows you to specify how you want to handle this change. You can specify (in the DDL Generation Complete dialog shown in Figure 20-4) that you want to generate the code for dropping the object, not to drop the object, or to abort the session. If you chose to drop the object, the code will not execute until you click the Execute DDL button. You will be able to view the code before executing it by clicking the View DDL button in the final dialog. After you dismiss this final dialog, you can still view the scripts or Reconcile Report by clicking the List Actions button of the Messages Window.

Options Dialog

You can change the way this utility works by clicking the Options button in the Generate Database from Server Model dialog; the resulting dialog is shown in Figure 20-6.

The General area in this dialog allows you to specify whether you want to generate the indexes, integrity constraints (foreign and primary key), and comments (for creating the COMMENT ON statements) for the tables you

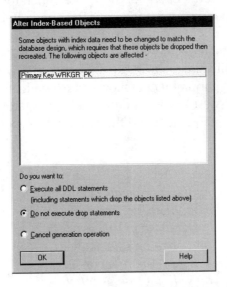

FIGURE 20-5. *Alter Index-Based Objects dialog*

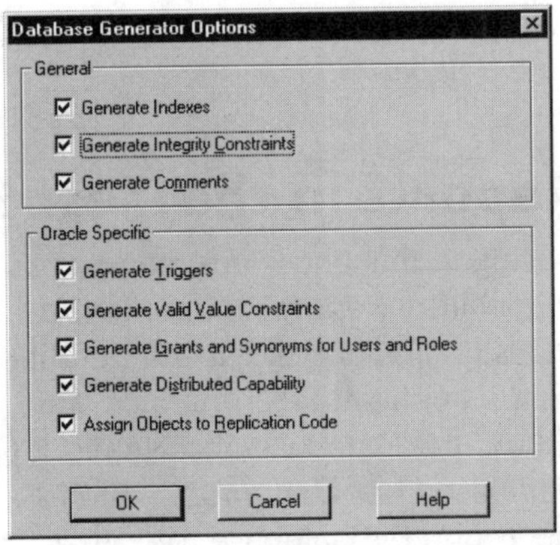

FIGURE 20-6. *Database Generator Options dialog*

have specified. If you deselect any of these, the generator will ignore all objects of the corresponding type and your Reconcile Report will not include them.

The Oracle Specific area allows you to specify whether you want to generate Triggers, Valid Value constraints, Grants and Synonyms, Distributed Capability, and object assignment to replication groups for the selected tables. If you deselect any of these, the generator will not build code to create or alter the object and the Reconcile Report will not contain the objects.

TIP
If you have a large number of objects (a hundred or more) to reconcile, consider running the Generate Database from Server Model utility more than once on selected groups (of 50 or less). If a problem occurs in the middle of the run, you will not lose as much work as you would if you were working with a larger group. Also, you will have smaller files to examine at the end. Keep in mind that PL/SQL objects take longer to reconcile because of the additional parsing needed. In addition, if you use a remote database, this utility may take longer because of the database link.

Repository Reports in the Test Phase

The elements you are using in this phase are modules and various database object elements. The Repository Reports utility offers a standard set of reports in the Module Design and Server Model Definition groups that can provide information on the application's programs and database elements you are testing. In addition, the Database and Network Design group offers *Role Definition* and *Database User Definition*, which show the security plan by listing database objects and the database roles that have access to them. The *Access to Modules by Roles* report is not in a group but available by switching to the Report Name View. This report lists the roles, users in those roles, and modules they are given access to. As with all other phases, there may be reports specific to your environment or documentation needs that you need to construct using the API (as described in Chapter 28).

The Implementation Phase in Oracle Designer

Although there are no Oracle Designer tools that uniquely support the Implementation phase, you can produce huge volumes of documentation of all sorts using the Repository Reports utility as well as reports you develop based on the Oracle Designer API views. This documentation from the repository, started in the Build phase, can become part of the help desk reference material or even serve as part of the user documentation. The help table or files you produce in Oracle Designer can also be sources for material in this documentation. Suitable repository reports, available in the Module Design group, list the definitions of objects, such as the *Module Definition* report, or the associations between elements, such as the *Module Program Data Usages* report. These reports may be useful for help desk personnel when answering questions about the modules.

The Oracle Designer activities and deliverables for the Implementation phase are summarized in Table 20-3.

If you have created detailed explanations when defining help text for various repository objects such as tables and modules, you can supplement user documentation with that text. This help text is contained in the CG_FORM_HELP table (as described in Chapter 16) if you are using Form help. If you are using MS Help, the help text appears in the MS Help file you generated (as described in Chapter 18). This help text also appears as part of various object definition reports; however, you may wish to write your own report of just help text using Oracle Reports or SQL*Plus to query the data in

Activity or Deliverable	Oracle Designer Tool
Finish help desk reference material	Repository Reports
Finish user documentation	Repository Reports, API view reports, help table, MS Help, or help file printouts

TABLE 20-3. *Implementation Activities and Oracle Designer Tools*

the CDI_TEXT view with a text type (txt_type) of "CDHELP." You need to join this view with other object views to retrieve the name of the object that the text describes. This type of query is described in Chapter 28.

Depending on the level of knowledge of your users, descriptions of the tables and columns that hold the data may be of use in the user documentation. The *Table Definition* report and *Column Definition* report (in the Server Model Definition group) are appropriate for this purpose. As mentioned in Chapter 6, you may wish to add to or modify the reports that Oracle Designer provides to suit your needs. If you do this, you should give the task to someone who knows Oracle Reports well.

Reports on the Analysis phase elements are probably not as useful for user or help desk documentation, but you might want to maintain current sets as system documentation for designers and developers who do not have access to the repository. The only problem with those reports is that they become out of date once you make changes to the repository. The best documentation for the system is always the repository itself if it is well maintained. If you have a strong need for reports, you could set up a Report Builder report to query the current contents of the repository and display it. Alternatively, you could create Web pages for the required reports and generate these from Designer.

Another set of reports that you probably do not need to run for the documentation purpose are the reports in the Quality group. Otherwise, it is worth examining the full list of reports to see which ones might serve as system or help desk documentation in the Implementation phase.

The Maintenance Phase in Oracle Designer

Essentially, the Maintenance phase in Oracle Designer consists of the same kind of work as performed in the other phases, from Strategy to Test. Depending on the particular change or upgrade, you may need to revisit each phase of the life cycle and work in the Oracle Designer areas appropriate to those phases. The typical Maintenance activities and the tools that support them are shown in Table 20-4.

Activity or Deliverable	Oracle Designer Tool
Version the application system	RON
Maintain repository data	RON, Reconcile Report of Generate Database from Server Model utility, Capture Design of Server Model from Database
Track module changes	RON
Create new or modify existing elements	Design Editor: Module Diagram, Design Capture of Form and Report utilities, and other tools appropriate to the element
Perform impact analysis	Repository Reports
Track problems	RON

TABLE 20-4. *Maintenance Activities and Oracle Designer Tools*

Versioning the Application System

The first step after you completely implement the system and before you make changes is to version the application system. This will freeze the version of the system that was implemented and create a new version you can use as the basis for upgrades and enhancements. The frozen version may not be changed, but you can, at any time, query the elements to see what the original system was like before changes were made in the Maintenance phase. Chapter 6 discusses how to perform versioning using the Repository Object Navigator.

Maintaining Repository Data

You should keep the repository up to date as you make changes or add new functionality to the system. This will ensure that the repository serves as detailed documentation for all aspects of the actual system. Changes to the system are easier to make if the repository is up to date because you can use Oracle Designer to drive them. That is, you can update or add the repository definitions needed for the change and generate the code required to implement it. If you use this tactic, the repository will always be in synch with the system. However, since you also will need to make manual changes on the fly, you need to use the design capture utilities to synchronize the repository with the database or application objects in the system. You can also use the Reconcile Report to identify any inconsistencies between the database and the repository. You can use this information as a basis for the work you do to synchronize the database design definitions in the repository.

An alternative to the design capture utilities is making manual changes to the repository, an approach that is practical if you are making only a few minor changes. In general, you should use the Oracle Designer utilities whenever possible and consider writing an API utility if there is a job they cannot accomplish. Always weigh the potential work you intend to do manually against the development work needed for an API utility. For a single, small project, you may find that the manual work is less time consuming and can be done by a more junior member of your team. On the other hand, a well-written API utility can serve you well for future work.

Tracking Module Changes

You can use RON to assign module change information. RON provides a subnode under the module, called *Module Change History,* where you can keep information on the different versions of a module. Each version or revision can have a separate element definition with properties such as the developer's name, date of revision, version number, directory name, and other change control information. This node is a good place to record details regarding the changes that you make to the modules during the Maintenance phase.

In addition, two text properties of the module, *Release Notes* and *Module Generation History*, are available in the Property Palette. You can store free-form text here to describe the different releases or versions of the module as well as notes on the generation such as the date and changes made. The generators write to the *Module Generation History* property automatically if you have the *Add module history comment on generation* preference (MODCMT in the Commenting category) set to "Y".

Creating New or Modifying Existing Elements

The Maintenance phase involves supporting the system and making changes, fixing bugs, and even adding enhancements. You need to make these changes in the repository as well, either before or after you make changes in the system. Whenever you decide to make these changes, you should use the appropriate tool in Oracle Designer.

For example, if you decide to add a function and a requirement to the system, you should insert the function using RON or the appropriate function diagrammer and the requirement using RON or the Matrix Diagrammer. You will need to decide whether to follow a miniature version of the life cycle and go through all Oracle Designer tools to assign data usages to the functions and produce the modules from functions. You will need to add new modules to the menu hierarchy and generate the code. This process may be appropriate for some changes that need the analysis support of Oracle Designer; however, minor changes are better done in the Design Editor.

If you implement the changes using the design tools, you have to decide whether the analysis elements are useful for full documentation of the system design. Since, for full documentation purposes, you should have both an accurate analysis model and an accurate design model, you should consider keeping these up to date. Remember that you can create entity definitions from table definitions using the Table to Entity Retrofit utility. There is no corresponding Module to Function utility, however, so keeping this information current will be a manual process that you can automate by writing an API utility.

Repository Reports in Maintenance

A repository report you might want to run before making changes to the existing modules is the *Column Change Impact Analysis* report in the Impact Analysis group. This report shows the element definitions that use the selected column. You can also check these dependencies using the Design Editor feature loaded with **Utilities→Analyze Dependencies** (as discussed in Chapter 12). Both of these are useful if you make changes to tables or modules and want to know the dependencies in other parts of the system.

Tracking Problems

The last category of activities that you perform in the Maintenance phase is problem tracking. You need to store information on problems that users experience with the system so you can map solutions to those problems and implement fixes. This activity is an extension of the problem tracking you did in the Build and Test phases and is discussed earlier in this chapter.

CHAPTER
21

Change Control

Just say "NO" to new requirements.

key feature of the CADM process has been the ongoing quality reviews. Sometimes quality reviews have been explicit, such as the audit of the logical ERD in the Analysis phase. At other times, the audit has been implicit, such as the automatic cross-checking of the physical database that occurred as a result of the migration of the legacy data. The point is that the CADM process is not linear; it can be spiral. At any phase in the process, you might discover information that, had you known it earlier, would have caused you to do something differently in an earlier phase. Unfortunately, if you tried to incorporate every new piece of information found throughout the CADM process into the new system, the system would never be built. Therefore, you need to carefully weigh the costs and benefits associated with the incorporation of each new piece of information into the application. In each phase, with the obvious exception of the Strategy phase, you must consider what happens when new information is discovered that is relevant to prior phases. Keep in mind that the later in the process that a new requirement, or change in scope is discovered, the more work that will be needed and the higher the cost of the change.

Who decides what will get done and when? Throughout the system life cycle, there should be a management team made up of the project leaders, a representative of upper-level management, one or more functional area users and, perhaps, a DBA (if no one else on the team has DBA experience). This small management team controls the CADM process and either performs all of the review tasks or delegates them to appropriate individuals. The process of review and quality assurance (QA) is critical to the success of the CADM process and should be handled by the best talent available. Of course, a key principle is that no one can perform a QA review of his or her own work.

As you progress through each phase of the CADM process, you have more and more to worry about with regard to changes to earlier phases. In the Analysis phase, you only have to worry about changes to the Strategy phase, whereas in the Design phase, you have to worry about changes to system requirements and changes in scope from the Strategy phase. At each phase, we will identify all the major deliverables from the earlier phases and discuss the impact of changes to any of those deliverables. This information can be thought of as a giant matrix with all of the deliverables lined up on one axis and all the phases on the other in order to clearly see the impact of changing each deliverable for each phase.

Guarding Against "Scope Creep"

It is important to prevent the onset of "scope creep" on a project. There will always be new requirements to support, slightly better ways of modifying your data model, and better ways to design an application. Unless you set a formal rule that prevents the majority of well-meaning suggestions about improvements from "creeping" into the system, the system will never be completed. Once you freeze a deliverable at any phase in the CADM process, it should not be altered. The only exception to this rule is when a mistake in the design of the system is uncovered that will prevent the system from going into production. If you do not enforce hard-and-fast rules about what changes are acceptable and when changes can be made, the system can be delayed for weeks or months or never come up at all.

Systems are not like works of art that, once completed, are hung in a gallery. They are inherently evolving structures that will inevitably need enhancements and subsequent versions. Every requirement does not have to be included in version 1. It is much better to have a system that is adequate and running than a perfect system that is never delivered.

Change Control During Each Phase of the Process

In the following sections, we will move through the entire CADM process, one phase at a time. Within each phase, we will discuss how you should respond when information leads you to reassess how well each of the preceding phases were done.

Changes During the Pre-Analysis Phase

During the Pre-Analysis phase, any changes you discover should be relatively easy to make, because the only stage completed thus far is the Strategy phase.

Strategy

If you discover changes in scope that affect the Strategy phase, little real work has been done yet, so changing the scope of the project at this point is not particularly costly. However, the modified Strategy Document will need to be reissued and the sign-off process for the Strategy Document repeated. If the organization in question is highly political, this may be a nontrivial cost.

One way to minimize the cost of amending the Strategy Document is not to reissue the entire document but instead to add an amendment that outlines the change in scope independently without opening up the entire Strategy Document for review.

Changes During the Analysis Phase

The Analysis phase is where you attempt to collect and analyze all of the system requirements through interviews, JAD sessions, questionnaires, and so on.

Strategy

As long as requirements are still being gathered, changes in scope do not have a particularly severe effect. You may even decide that many of the requirements that have already been gathered should be declared out of scope. At this point in the system development process, you should not hesitate to modify the scope of the project. The same issues apply here that applied to changes to scope in the Pre-Analysis phase.

Pre-Analysis

The two main goals of the Pre-Analysis phase are to set standards and formulate the Analysis Plan. Depending on how far you are in the information-gathering process, the effects of changes to the requirements-gathering standards can be quite severe. For example, changes to the document used for structuring interviews may require a great deal of repeated work. Do you go back and restructure all earlier information or leave the existing information and gather more in the new format? Another option is to reject the change in the standard altogether. The project leaders must carefully weigh the pros and cons of each alternative. However, given that at this point you are in the middle of requirements gathering, any decision that needs to be made should be made immediately.

Changes During the Pre-Design Phase

In the Pre-Design phase, standards are set and the design plan is created along with the conceptual design of the application.

Strategy

Scope shifts in Pre-Design necessitate redoing the entire Analysis phase for the expanded scope. Any scope shift will require redoing some portion of Requirements Analysis. Such changes are not unusual, since once Requirements Analysis is complete you have a very clear picture of what is needed in the new system. The narrowing of scope, although a rare occurrence, merely means that you can ignore portions of the system requirements for version 1.

In fact, it might be worthwhile to include a quality check at this point, in which the scope is reviewed to make sure that the development team's understanding of what is needed in the new system hasn't made the original Strategy Document obsolete. Some maturing of your understanding of the project scope is bound to take place as the project progresses. It is common to find that when the finalized Requirements Document is compared to the scope, the scope has already drifted. This is acceptable, but the Strategy Document needs to be amended to be consistent with the new and improved vision of the end product.

Pre-Analysis

Once Analysis is complete, changes to the whole structure of the Analysis Document should be made only if the project will otherwise fail.

Analysis

Incorporating new requirements during the Pre-Design phase is more expensive than it may seem. Not only does each new requirement need to be documented, you must also ensure that it is appropriate and update all relevant portions of the Requirements Document. From this point forward, new system requirements cannot be added by the developers without authorization from the project leaders. New system requirements should be filed as "system modification requests" and periodically reviewed to be either included in the current design or deferred for a later version. This rule must be enforced. Developers must not be allowed to respond to user requests for additional requirements.

Not putting some controls on this process puts the entire project at risk. This is one of the primary reasons for "analysis paralysis." This is not to say that essential new system requirements will not arise throughout the CADM life cycle. However, it is crucial that the addition of new system requirements be handled in a controlled fashion. The process of adding new requirements should be made very clear to the users early in the CADM process so they are not surprised by the enforcement of new rules later on. The method for adding new requirements outlined here should remain in effect through the end of the project. However, because the cost of adding new system requirements increases exponentially as you move into the later phases of CADM, the rules for accepting new system requirements will become increasingly strict the further along in the process that new requirements are discovered or suggested.

A system modification request should contain an impact analysis section. Before approving or denying the inclusion of a new requirement, you need to analyze its cost.

Anything that requires you to modify the Analysis deliverables will not affect anything being done in Pre-Design. Thus, such changes should be allowed, if necessary, with relatively minor restrictions.

Changes During the Design Phase: Database Design

The Database Design part of the Design phase is where everything begins to be put into place in preparation for the Build phase.

Strategy
During Database Design, modifying Strategy is very costly. Scope changes at this late date should be allowed only if the system will fail if the scope is not allowed to change. Scope changes here will require the reworking of all previous phases and should be avoided whenever possible.

Pre-Analysis
Any changes affecting your work in the Pre-Analysis phase should be handled as described for the Pre-Design phase.

Analysis

Any changes affecting your work in the Information Gathering part of the Analysis phase should be handled as described for the Pre-Design phase.

Changes to process flows have no effect on database design; but any changes to the logical ERD from this point forward are very costly and should be handled with the same system modification request process as used for newly discovered system requirements. Physical database design is a very complex step. Changes in the ERD should be made only if they are truly necessary to avoid system failure.

Pre-Design

The area to avoid changing in Database Design is naming standards. It is necessary to closely audit how well naming standards are working early in the Database Design part of the Design phase so that any necessary changes to the design conventions can be made early. It is a good idea to hold a meeting early in the Database Design process to review the current level of comfort with the design method. Any changes that show up with conceptual design of the application done in Pre-Design have little impact during Database Design and should be freely allowed.

Changes During the Design Phase: Application Design

The Application Design part of the Design phase is where the detailed column usages are defined for each module and the database design is validated. Changes that are made during Design may appear simple and straightforward; however, they usually have a "ripple" effect. Each individual change may have a minimal cost or impact, but the overall effect of many such changes can be substantial. The project manager must evaluate the changes to determine if they could effect time, budget, or quality. Careful prioritization and impact on users/customer/client is paramount.

Strategy

Any changes affecting your work in the Strategy phase should be handled as described for the Database Design part of the Design phase.

Pre-Analysis

Any changes affecting your work in the Pre-Analysis phase should be handled as described for the Pre-Design phase.

Analysis

Any changes affecting your work in the Information Gathering part of the Analysis phase should be handled as described for the Pre-Design phase.

At this point in the SDLC, the Analysis Document needs to be frozen. Any changes must now go through the same system modification request process used for changes that affect the Strategy phase and the Information Gathering part of the Analysis phase.

Pre-Design

Modifications to the database portion of the design plan need to go through the system modification request process. However, changes to the conceptual design of the application or the application part of the design plan can be made freely.

Design: Database Design

Changes to the database design during the Application Design process are to be expected. This is the main reason for creating the application design at this point in the CADM process. As column-level mapping is performed, columns that were omitted may be discovered, as well as columns that were never used, which can be deleted.

Changes During the Build Phase

Making changes during the Build phase is something you want to avoid. The cost of change is very high and usually has an unpredictable "ripple" effect. If changes are made during Build, they should be documented and reflected as modifications or amendments to prior Analysis and Design phase deliverables.

Once you reach the Build phase, all potential changes to any phase, with the exception of the physical database and application design developed in the Design phase, must go through the system modification request process.

Design: Database Design

The database design needn't stay fixed during the Build phase. Indeed, the legacy system data migration will probably uncover some changes that need to be made to the database design.

Design: Application Design

The application design is still in flux as the application is being built. It is to be expected that there will be many changes. You need to make sure that changes don't cause individual modules to diverge from a consistent user interface. Constant monitoring during the unit testing of the modules is necessary.

Changes During the Test Phase

Any test failure should automatically initiate a system modification request. Just because a test failure occurs does not mean that this failure must be corrected in this system version. Changes can be very costly. Any change to the completed system should be thoroughly evaluated before it is incorporated into the new system.

PART III

Additional CADM Activities

CHAPTER
22

RAD-CADM

The oracles are dumb.

—John Milton (1608-1674)
Hymn on Christ's Nativity, 1629

 ADM represents the conceptual foundation for how to build and design systems. Within it, we identify a way of thinking about systems design, the objectives associated with each phase, and how the development team can prove to itself and the user community that the project is moving forward successfully. CADM is not, and should not, be considered a road map that is slavishly adhered to for every system.

Any project development strategy should manage four criteria for determining project success. These criteria and their corresponding goals are shown in Table 22-1.

These criteria interact with and influence each other. The most important thing to recognize is that it is not possible to achieve all four goals simultaneously. In the best of all possible worlds, you can at most manipulate three variables, thus determining the fourth. For example, as long as cost is constrained on a project (as it almost always is), you must accept that either you will not have a firm completion date or settle for a lesser quality system. If both fast development time and high quality are required, the likelihood of project failure is greatly increased.

In CADM, we take the approach of minimizing risk and maximizing quality at the expense of cost and development speed. Realistically for most projects, of the four factors involved only two goals can be achieved. The RAD (rapid application development)-CADM method discussed in this chapter applies to small- to medium-size projects with the main goal of the

Criterion	Goal
Cost	Low cost
Time to complete system	Fast development time
Quality (features, bugginess)	High quality
Failure risk	Low risk of failure

TABLE 22-1. *Project Development Strategy Criteria and Goals*

fastest possible development time and, sometimes concurrently, lowest cost. However, this assumes more risk and the likelihood of accepting a lower quality end product than with a traditional systems development approach. Figure 22-1 demonstrates the relationship among the criteria.

Of course, this is a generalization. Overall, what will be described in this chapter is an approach that optimizes development speed.

What Is RAD-CADM?

The RAD-CADM approach greatly abbreviates the Analysis phase of system development. Instead, an iterative development process is used to determine the requirements. This assumes that the development cost is low enough to justify building a substantial portion of the system two or three times for a lower cost than that of doing a full Analysis phase. Thus, instead of performing a full-blown Analysis phase, RAD-CADM amounts to building a series of system prototypes.

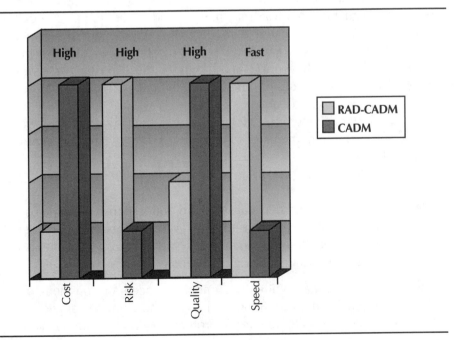

FIGURE 22-1. *Comparison of RAD-CADM and CADM criteria*

One of the problems with traditional Analysis Documents is that when you ask users what they want the system to do, they tell you, but there is no guarantee that what they tell you is really what they need. It isn't until users can actually see and feel the system in prototype that they can intelligently assess whether the system will meet their needs. RAD-CADM overcomes this problem.

When Can a RAD-CADM Approach Be Used Effectively?

RAD-CADM is effective when the system being built is not very large or complex. You cannot intelligently use a RAD approach with multiple complex systems interacting over a centralized generic data model. Where a RAD-CADM approach is best applied is for small- to medium-size systems when doing a "rehost," that is, porting a legacy system on a different platform to an Oracle system where equivalent functionality in the new system is acceptable.

Another instance where RAD is appropriate is when a project to develop the new system has been recently attempted and has failed one or more times. In this situation, Analysis may have already been done. Although the existing Analysis documentation is inadequate, the users and any remaining developers who already worked on the failed system have just been through the process. They will have thought through the difficult Analysis issues. The quality of the user resources has therefore been enhanced. Their knowledge can act as the Analysis Document.

Another instance where RAD is useful is for small systems with a small number of users. Again, the users themselves can act as surrogates for the Analysis Document.

RAD-CADM is a high-risk strategy for a number of reasons:

■   The system requirements are not laid out on paper. When a user rejects a prototype, there is no way to determine how much of that rejection is due to either inadequate gathering of requirements in the first place or users changing requirements on the fly.

■   Without a formal, written document to place limits on them, user requirements may continue to change. The ultimate danger is building an infinite number of prototypes with no external standard by which to measure system completion. Since system scope and standards have not been clearly defined or documented, the project can go on indefinitely.

■   Since there is no written Analysis Document to refer to, requirements can be easily forgotten. If an omitted requirement can't be easily added to a completed system, fundamental changes to the data model will be required, adding both time and cost to the entire project.

In order to avoid this situation, the following steps can be taken:

■   Place a hard-and-fast time limit for users to sign off on prototypes. For example, in one project we worked on, a vendor needed to deliver software to customers by a specific date. This guaranteed that our clients would not be motivated to keep asking for additional features.

■   If developers (either internal or external to the organization) are working on a time and materials contract where the users are paying for each iteration, the users will be motivated to complete the project more quickly.

■   If the project is a legacy system redesign, it can be declared that the developers need only equal or exceed the functionality of the existing system in order to consider the new system's first version complete.

It is possible to limit the time allowed for the project by defining a finish date, using cost to limit the number of prototype iterations, and providing a model (the existing legacy system) for the expected quality of the new system. These constraints will help to reduce the risk of project failure when using a RAD-CADM approach.

Limitations to RAD-CADM

Because the RAD-CADM approach does not capture requirements in written form and instead relies on informal notes and quick application development, developers will invariably forget things that users have told them. This means that users may have to be reinterviewed about the same material multiple times. The development team may discuss a particular requirement with users and inadvertently omit it from the system. Also, users will occasionally make decisions about requirements and limitations that they are willing to accept that they will later deny. Such disagreements are inherent in the RAD-CADM approach and should be anticipated.

Critical Success Factors for Making RAD-CADM Work

The following factors are necessary if a RAD-CADM approach is to be successful:

- **Careful management of user expectations**   Make sure that users are aware of the strengths and weaknesses of the approach and the reasons for using RAD-CADM. Users should especially be aware of the risks inherent in this type of system development. It is possible that the system will be brought to completion, at which point a critical missing element is discovered. Users should also be warned about the dangers of forgetting requirements and arguing about them later, as discussed earlier. This management of user expectations is the key critical success factor for RAD-CADM development. It is vitally important that users are fully engaged in the development process. If the relationship between developers and users becomes less than cordial or even antagonistic, the probability of project success is greatly diminished.

- **Use of highly skilled and experienced developers**   RAD development should not even be attempted by an inexperienced team. This is inherently a "fly by the seat of your pants" approach. Developers must have a clear sense of the steps required to bring a project to completion. Without a certain level of developer maturity and experience, the project will lack focus, get sidetracked, and not reach completion.

- **Application of formal GUI, coding, and development standards** For a RAD approach to be effective, it is crucial to have formal GUI, coding, and development standards in place before the start of the project. Otherwise, developers must spend time making coding, user interface, and similar design decisions while trying to build prototypes. This cancels out any time gains from using a RAD methodology in the first place.

■ **Knowing when to declare version 1 of the system complete**   The whole point of RAD is to achieve version 1 of the system quickly. It is very important not to use a particularly high user acceptance standard. When prototypes are acceptable and functioning, the project must move forward. As long as all critical functionality has been implemented, version 1 is complete. At this point, user comments and suggestions should be deferred and placed into a system modification log to be used for future versions. They should not be analyzed or prioritized. Version 1 should be deployed as quickly and efficiently as possible.

Details of the RAD-CADM Process

The RAD-CADM system development process differs slightly from a full CADM approach. This section will detail the parts of a RAD CADM project.

Abbreviated Strategy Phase

Even though we are attempting to work as quickly as possible, we still need to prepare a basic Strategy Document outlining the scope, problem, approach, and team roles of any project. This Strategy Document is just as critical in a RAD project as any other. The CADM concept is that the Strategy Document acts as a contract between all interested parties.

Analysis

In a RAD-CADM approach, we do not prepare an Analysis Document. Instead, we go directly to building the logical data model. For this to be effective, a highly skilled data modeler must be a part of the development team. Ideally, the data modeler should be able to accurately model 20 or more entities (unattributed) per day. A 100-table data model should be completed in approximately one week. The attribution of such a model should take an additional week.

It is crucial to be able to complete this model quickly, since it is the first deliverable presented to the users. There have been many debates about whether a data model should be delivered to a nontechnical user. Users should not simply be shown the data model and asked to comment. The data model should be used as a guide for discussion of the system. Developers can describe how various business entities relate and what the limitations of the model are. They can also discuss the kinds of information that can be stored.

Finally, the data model is derived from a process flow. Even if the process flow is not drawn (for time constraint reasons), it can be described to the users.

As the last part of Analysis, you will also want to create the first set of screen prototypes. This will let the users see firsthand the kind of user interface they can expect. It serves as a cross-check that the GUI standards you have set up are appropriate for this project and gives you time to adjust them before the prototype cycle is in full gear.

Physical Data Model

In CADM, we create a full prototype of the system prior to doing the physical design of the database. In RAD-CADM, we use our intuition about what the ultimate system design will be to move directly to the physical database design. Since we actually prototype the application, we may do further database tuning and denormalization. However, if the RAD project is going to stay on schedule, it is necessary to create an accurate data model at this point in the process.

Legacy Data Migration

If the project is a legacy system redesign, legacy system migration should be started concurrently with Analysis so that the forms and reports will have some data to use as sample data. You must be careful not to get too far ahead with data migration. Migration analysis can be performed on the legacy data during Analysis. As the data model is developed, you should start creating the migration maps as soon as possible. If the project is not a legacy system redesign, no sample data is generated at this stage. Sample data will be created by prototype applications as part of the testing process. Again, it is key to be able to migrate the legacy data quickly using some type of data migration tool.

Prototyping

Both forms and reports must be prototyped. If there is no legacy data, forms modules should be prototyped first. If the project is a legacy system redesign, forms and report modules should be prototyped in tandem, since this will validate both the data model and the data migration. And sometimes legacy system users will look at the forms and realize they don't need some of the reports they thought they did, for example, if converting a batch system to an online system.

There are two alternatives for generating prototype modules:

- Specify within Oracle Designer and generate
- Build directly using the Oracle Developer tool suite

Both approaches have merit and can be used effectively. The decision about which approach to use should be based upon the skills of the development team.

Developers should be able to build a form or report prototype in a few hours to one day. The idea in the early prototypes is not to include extensive functionality in modules until user feedback is obtained. Usually, the approach should be to develop a very primitive prototype without much functionality. If users are not satisfied with the first prototype, a second primitive prototype should be developed. Once users are satisfied with the basic functionality, the prototype should be built to production. Users should then be allowed a maximum of one more opportunity to critique the module. After this point, the only work that should be done is debugging.

Testing and Implementation

Testing in a RAD-CADM environment is no different from that of a traditional system development life cycle with the inherent risks and decisions to be made.

Conclusion

RAD-CADM provides an effective alternative to a full CADM process for small- to medium-size projects, as long as the development team is skilled and has a good understanding of what the system should do before the project is started and the risks are understood and willing to be assumed. If all of these conditions are met, then RAD-CADM can be used to bring a system to production relatively quickly at a lower cost than a traditional SDLC.

CHAPTER
23

"Start in the Middle"

*The worst and best are both inclined to snap like vixens at the truth; But, O, beware
the middle mind that purrs and never shows a tooth!*
—Elinor Hoyt Wylie (1885-1928), Nonsense Rhyme

 arely is there a project that you participate in from its very
beginning. Most of the time, when you start work on a
project, some work has already been completed.
Development projects can fail at any point in the System
Development Life Cycle. What you will be left with depends
upon how and why the project failed and where in the life cycle the failure
occurred. Further, you may or may not know if any particular methodology
was used up to the point of failure.

In order to "start in the middle," you must first assess where you are with
respect to the CADM process and its deliverables. Second, a project plan
should be created to complete the project. Finally, the project plan must be
executed to achieve the desired project goals. Assessing where a project
stands begins with auditing all of the work done up to that point. This is a
project in and of itself and may have its own share of political problems.
The scope and goals of the audit must be carefully defined.

Starting with a Failed Attempt

When you are beginning work on a project that has previously failed, there
are many factors to consider outside of simply following the CADM
methodology. The sponsoring organization may be interested in assigning
blame for the failure of the previous attempt. If this is the case, you will need
to document the process used, assessing both the soundness of this
approach and the quality of its execution. Auditing for culpability is very
different from trying to get a project back on track. In this chapter, we will
not provide information about how to audit a failed attempt in order to
assign blame but will discuss how to finish a project.

Although you would logically like to start with an inventory and
assessment of work previously performed, this might not be possible.
Because of the political ramifications, you may not be able to make a
rational assessment of where the project stands until some observable
progress is achieved. It may therefore be necessary to generate one or more
deliverables to satisfy users, even though focusing on these deliverables
might not be an optimal first step.

Top management support is a critical success factor for any project. If a project has lost this support, regaining it must be the first priority. Showing a successful semifunctional prototype of the system may be useful in regaining lost support. In one case where we entered a large project in the middle, we scheduled two interim JAD sessions within the first few weeks. We viewed these sessions as important opportunities to regain user support. In the first session, users were very antagonistic and the project was close to cancellation. We showed completely nonfunctioning storyboard screens not hooked to any data. Users were tolerant about seeing some results but still not supportive. In the second JAD session, a revised set of storyboards displaying mostly nonrealistic data was shown. After this session, where users could see applications bringing back data from the database, some support was generated. From a development perspective, taking the time to make these applications return data was premature. However, from an overall project perspective, it was a critical step, necessary for regaining user support.

Assessing a Partially Completed Project

With a partially completed project, you must review each of the deliverables and not only evaluate the quality of the work done but, even more important, also determine whether any initial audit for completeness or correctness was done. You also need to find out if any user acceptance was obtained on any portions of the work completed. Although it is useful to have a large, detailed, and precise Strategy Document detailing the scope of the project, the document is meaningless if the users never signed off on it.

It is likely that no matter where you enter a project, no one phase (as we define them in CADM) may have been completed adequately. If you do not have accurate documentation of the information sources and deliverables themselves, you may need to reaudit all existing deliverables. You may not have confidence in the Analysis Document or the determination of the scope of the project and believe that more analysis should be performed. This may not be a realistic option, because it may not be politically possible to do so. The environment surrounding a failed project attempt is very sensitive. Neither top management nor users may be willing to retrace their steps and redo work that was not done properly or at all in the first place.

For example, you may be brought into a situation where the existing Requirements Document has been declared to be complete. You can then either accept that this is the case and move forward or create a plan to audit the Requirements Document and complete it in accordance with the findings of the audit. If you accept the existing Requirements Document or any other form of compiled work already completed, then when the system is built you can warrant that it satisfies the needs of the Requirements Document and nothing else. This is a dangerous situation. Before getting involved in a project situation like this, you need to convey to management how risky this strategy is. If the Requirements Document is flawed, the final system will fail.

Depending upon where you enter a given project, different tasks, audits, deliverables, and strategies must be used to assess what has been completed and what still needs to be accomplished. We will discuss how to accomplish this for each phase of CADM.

Strategy

If entering a project in the Strategy phase, the first step is to make sure all of the deliverables outlined in Chapter 3 for this phase are in place. Many may not exist. It is critical for there to be a clear definition of the scope of the project at this point.

If entering a project late in the Analysis or Design phase, major portions of the system have already been developed or are in production. Some Strategy phase deliverables may not exist but we can say that the scope normally covered by these documents is implicitly articulated through other deliverables or vehicles. An example of a surrogate deliverable that could supercede a missing Strategy Document is an extremely detailed function hierarchy with good descriptions of the functions. Scope must be adequately defined in some way. Even with a bad data model and a set of accepted functions or storyboards, it is possible to implicitly define the project scope without an explicit Strategy Document.

Analysis

This phase tends to be the most successful and least prone to failure. Gathering information is something analysts have been doing for many years. However, the information obtained may not be documented in a coherent manner, if at all. In one dramatic case on a large project, many analysts had been collecting data for many months; but almost nothing had been written down. Many of their original notes were lost or so disorganized that they were useless. Nevertheless, the analysts had gathered the relevant information about what the system needed to do. Against our better judgment, we redesigned the data model and designed the applications by interviewing the developers rather than the users. Eventually, we were able to generate a reasonable Requirements Document. But this was done after the data model had been completed and the applications had been designed. We were not happy about using this approach, but the project was able to move forward and the system was eventually built.

Requirements Document and Analysis Plan

Emphasis should be placed on the importance of completing the Requirements Document. You also need to create an Analysis Plan. This may or may not have already been written. If it hasn't, it is critical to go back and write an Analysis Plan based upon the work that has already been done. Then, this plan can be audited to see if any requirements were missed. Missing major sources of requirements is a common cause of project failure. Even if the project you are entering includes storyboards, a data model, and partially completed applications that users have signed off on, it is common when building a large system for users to miss whole areas of what tasks they perform. These will need to be included in the new system requirements. Careful analysis of the legacy system and user interviews is needed to uncover all of the business processes that the new system needs to support.

Naming Conventions and Standards

A coherent naming conventions and standards document for all repository elements and usages must be formulated. This deliverable must be created. Unless the system is very close to completion, you must have consistent naming conventions applied throughout. If, as the new development team, you already have a set of naming standards you are comfortable with, using this set will make your team much more productive. This is especially true for a consulting team working on multiple projects.

If no naming conventions exist, the first step is to look at the work completed and figure out what the naming conventions are or should have been. Second, you will need to take into consideration how much development work has been done; changing names can be very expensive unless most of your applications have been generated from the repository. Even with significant development work, if you are not going to use the work, then any existing naming conventions are irrelevant.

The only reason to forego developing a set of naming standards consistently applied throughout a project is if the political costs are too high. Economically, it will almost always be important to have consistent naming standards. Inconsistent naming standards will create ongoing problems throughout the life of the project and for future maintenance.

Data Model

The data model is the foundation of the system. In systems that are failed attempts, the data model is usually flawed. However, even a flawed data model does provide a useful encapsulation of the developers' understanding of the data-related business rules. These rules are usually adequately represented in the data model.

The existing data model can act as a starting point for a new data model. It is possible that most, if not all, of the attributes on the existing model are correct. However, entities and attributes may need to be restructured, since the design decisions made in implementing the business requirements are often misguided. For example, the original data model may have different types of organization units (Division, Department, Group) that could be replaced with a single recursive "Org. Unit" entity. You might find old-style Address Line 1, Address Line 2, etc., which in most environments can be replaced with a single address column that will store multiple lines of information.

If you are going to try to use the existing data model, it should be audited to ensure that all of the system requirements are included. This audit is rarely done in failed projects. A formal data model audit must take place regardless of where in the project you are beginning. Even if an audit was performed, an additional audit can be used as a knowledge transfer vehicle from the old development team to the new one.

Pre-Design

If development work has already been done and you have assessed that this work is worth preserving, you still need to assess the quality of the development method. The probability of keeping any developed applications is low. From Pre-Design forward, it is likely that work will either need to be redone or done for the first time. If personnel from the first attempt are still working on the project, it might be helpful to use a development method similar to what these developers are used to.

Application design is an art. It is common for different application designers to have very different ideas about how to support a data model. If application design standards are in place, a decision must be made about whether to adhere to these or develop new ones. In one project we worked on, initial screen designs were done in a traditional "single screen for each function" method, popular in the mid to late 1980s. This resulted in 200 to 400 modules being necessary. By redesigning the system using more modern multitab techniques, the application was created with approximately 40 multitab screens. Even counting each tab as a screen, the total was less than 200 screens. Because we were able to greatly decrease the amount of work required to develop applications and improve the usability of the interface, it was more practical to discard all of the earlier work.

Some decisions must be made about using earlier work. If the data model was flawed, it is likely that screens will have to be redesigned. If screens have been audited and accepted by users, these screens can serve as a good source of system requirements, much like the flawed data model.

Design

Assessing the quality of system design need not be a concern unless you have decided to accept all of the work previously done up to this point and the work was so clean that a new team could come in and continue development. In this case, developers are in the uncomfortable position of using others' philosophy of development, data model, and designs. If this is the situation and there are no development standards documents to code against, these documents will have to be created.

Project Plan

There is an almost overwhelming desire to plunge headlong into development. However, creating a detailed project plan that tries to preserve as much of the previous work as possible while still delivering a quality system is the most important critical success factor in making a "start in the middle" project succeed. The fact that the political environment is still very sensitive makes this task even more difficult. Creating a practical plan to get to the end of the project in the fastest, cheapest way is the first step.

In creating the project plan, ask the following questions:

- Will this plan satisfy top management?

- Is it necessary to produce some interim deliverables to recapture user and/or top management support?

To demonstrate the look and feel of the applications:

- Produce storyboards that access realistic-looking sample data to create among users the feeling of progress being made.

- Demonstrate basic functionality of Inserts/Updates/Deletions and other basic operations on one tab of one form. This helps users get a sense of the possible look and feel of the new system and shows that the project is moving forward.

Decisions must be made about when to shore up holes to complete prior phases and where new work can begin. In earlier phases, where more work may be preserved, deliverables should be redefined and a plan created to either complete partially done deliverables or create missing ones. An additional document should be created outlining the risks associated with using work done in the failed attempt. There will be considerable risks using work done on a failed system. You can only guess at the quality of this work.

"Start in the Middle" Deliverables and Methodology

Although we're working in the CADM methodology, starting in the middle means you have additional or slightly altered deliverables. It may also mean slightly changing your development methods to maximize the value of previous deliverables worth saving.

Assessment Report

After you have examined all of the existing work, a deliverable document must be assembled, consisting of your analysis of the work done to date. This Assessment Report should be the first formal deliverable during your involvement with the project. In this Assessment Report, you should describe what work has been completed and what is missing up to the point of intervention.

The Assessment Report may have described a completely different development methodology from CADM. From this point forward, CADM will be used. How can these two different approaches be fused into a single, coherent plan? There are cases where the old methodology should be continued. For example, if a team skilled in the use of object-oriented techniques was working on the project, detailed use cases and scenarios may be available. These can serve as a major portion of the Requirements Document. If these use cases and scenarios were carefully done, it would be a waste of time to reformat them.

Project Plan

The goal of creating a "start in the middle" project plan is the same as any other project plan. Tasks, deliverables, and time lines are still needed. The difference is determining what deliverables are missing from previous work, what previous work needs to be completed or redone, and all of the new tasks and deliverables for completing the project. Again, politics is a major factor here. Managers may not approve funds to redo work that has already been paid for once. What can you do if additional critical work needs to be done? There is no easy solution. One answer is to defer work to a later phase of the project. After some visible progress is made and credibility is reestablished, management may be more willing to approve additional work. In a consulting environment, if a client doesn't want work performed, that work does not get done. Either you can carefully document the fact that critical analysis work was missing and not approved for completion or walk away from the project. This is another example illustrating the importance of top management support for project success.

Starting a project in the middle almost always requires more time than in a project with one development team used all the way through. The project plan is still critical and needs to be given adequate attention.

In "start in the middle" projects, the project plan will be a "living" document with many changes made as the project moves forward. This is particularly true initially, because you may have to do assessment while producing deliverables for political reasons.

Executing the Project Plan

As you are executing the project plan, you should be sensitive to any information that leads to a change in your earlier assessment of the deliverables. Your understanding of the system is not as complete when you enter a project in the middle. Users must be thoroughly questioned to ensure that what is being developed meets their needs. Be particularly careful in an environment where there is no user-accepted Requirements Document. Until storyboards from the Pre-Design phase are accepted by users, the project is still at risk.

Once the project plan is in place, you are likely to have redefined a new "hybrid" methodology only appropriate for this specific project. You will need to go through each phase, adjusting the plan as needed and auditing deliverables. Once you move one phase beyond where you entered the project, CADM can be followed more stringently. With CADM, when Analysis is complete, you can be more certain of project tasks having been done correctly. If you have to rely on other methodologies and other people's work, there is less certainty. For this reason, user acceptance testing should be even more rigorous. User involvement in every aspect of the project is also especially important.

Conclusion

The middle is never a comfortable place to start, but this is often the reality for developers on many projects. The most difficult issues on this type of project are regaining management and user support and dealing with the politics of a failed project environment. If you do a careful assessment, create a detailed project plan, and execute that plan paying particular attention to user involvement and acceptance testing, then project success can be achieved.

CHAPTER
24

Business Process
Reengineering

For 'tis sport to have the engineer hoist with his own petar.
—William Shakespeare, *Hamlet*, III, iv, 206

usiness process reengineering (BPR) is a radical redesign of the underlying way an organization performs tasks. When redesigning a system, it is frequently a good opportunity to not just replace an existing legacy system or automate a manual process, but also to think about what changes can be made to the underlying business processes in order to make them faster, more efficient, and better equipped to meet the needs of the organization. BPR is not a phase of the traditional system development process but can be added to broaden the scope of the proposed system.

What Is Reengineering?

Reengineering was first touted by information technologists. In the 1991 and 1992 annual *Computerworld* surveys, technologists reported that reengineering was the issue of main concern to them. Since then, many seminars, consulting houses, and senior managers have sprung up to meet the demand for reengineering knowledge.

Reengineering strives to achieve an order-of-magnitude increase in performance. It asserts that work should not be organized by vertical functions, such as purchasing, manufacturing, or sales, but that it should be organized by value-added, horizontal processes that cut across the traditional functional areas.

Reengineering has the following key themes:

- It involves radical redesign and restructuring of work.

- It uses information technology as an integral part of that redesign.

- It attempts to achieve dramatic improvements in performance.

- It emphasizes the cross-functional, horizontal processes of work.

- It may emphasize increased quality of the product.

Why Reengineer?

The current method of doing business may be grossly inefficient. The time when a system is being designed provides an excellent opportunity to rethink the way that business is done. Successful business process reengineering efforts purport to achieve a dramatic increase in productivity by radically changing business processes and their supporting information technology infrastructure.

There are several important reasons to justify a BPR effort:

- The existing system is already at its limits and at risk for catastrophic failure. Any new requirements may not be able to be supported by the current system.

- Accommodating any changes to the current system is very time consuming and expensive. Key pieces of information that are currently not being gathered would require days/weeks of effort to collect.

- The existing system is lacking core functionality.

In any project, one very important issue that must be considered carefully is how much the new system being built will change the existing system and the way business is done. For example, the automated teller machine (ATM) fundamentally reengineered the way people interact with banks. World Wide Web (WWW) applications have reengineered the way customers interact with companies.

A wide variety of factors are driving organizations, and financial services firms in particular, to reengineer, including the following:

- Cost pressures

- Fragmentation

- Technological change

Cost Pressures

For a variety of reasons, organizations may become highly motivated to cut costs. For example, in the late 1980s in the banking industry, defaults on loans and a recessionary economy motivated firms to cut costs, and in the early 1990s the pressure to reduce costs stemmed from the corporate culture. Although 1993 was a profitable year for the banking industry, particularly from trading operations, the corporate culture continued to emphasize the importance of cutting costs. Consequently, financial firms began reengineering their operations to achieve cost savings.

Fragmentation

In the first half of the 1900s, managers designed organizations by dividing work into the smallest tasks possible and then coordinated those tasks in a hierarchy. Firms were organized by vertical functions. This structure was based on scientific management, which stipulates that an employee would be the most efficient and productive, and thus the entire workflow would be the most efficient and productive, if work were organized into as many small, different tasks as possible. The underlying idea was that specialization was good: the more one performs a task, the better one performs it.

This organization of work maximized the number of hand-offs from one individual or functional area to another. In today's business language, scientific management advocated the fragmentation of work.

Excessive fragmentation, together with a functional organization, can lead to a number of problems. First, the time required to produce a product or service in a fragmented and vertical environment may be too long. Each time a hand-off occurs, the work is passed to the next person. There, the work waits in the person's in-box, where it may spend a short time (several minutes) or a long time (several hours or even days). In some cases, the work may actually spend more time waiting in the in-box than actually being attended to. For example, IBM Credit Corporation found that the financing process took an average of two weeks, yet the actual work totaled only 90 minutes.

Today, it is no longer acceptable for work to sit idly in an in-box: Customers take their business to organizations that do the job quickly. Fast cycle time is not simply an added benefit to products or services; it is a requirement to remain competitive.

Excessive fragmentation and a vertical structure may lead to a second difficulty: the lack of a strong customer orientation.

A third difficulty is that responsibility for the entire process is diffused across several managers and departments. Thus, any errors that occur in the process are difficult to account for because no one person is responsible for the process as a whole. There is a strong focus on increasing the quality of work in today's business environment.

Suboptimal performance on an enterprise-wide basis is another potential problem resulting from fragmentation. Different departments are responsible for different pieces. Each department may be evaluated on its own functional measures, but these measures may not lead to enterprise-wide optimization. Opportunities to improve performance occur when work goes from one department to another.

Technological Change

Information technology is continually advancing, providing almost continual opportunity to reengineer work. For example, the increase in object-oriented technology has led many financial services firms to rethink and reengineer the way they build financial instruments. Dr. Katherine Duliba has studied the way that companies reengineer their business and has developed the taxonomy shown in Table 24-1. She notes that when a new system is built, reengineering is not an all or nothing proposition. There exist gradations of reengineering reflecting the amount and types of changes made to the existing system. In the table, the X's represent what is being reengineered at each step.

The columns in this table provide a list of the elements that can change in the reengineering process:

- **Process**   The way business is done

- **Software**   The software used to perform the task

- **Interface**   The user interface, such as changing from text to GUI or WWW

- **Hardware**   The hardware used to perform the task

- **Data**   The data, such as restructuring data from flat files into a relational database

- **People**   The individuals who perform various parts of the task being reengineered

	Process	Software	Interface	Hardware	Data	People
Reaffirm						
Repackage			X			
Rehost				X		
Rearchitect		X	X	X	X	
Reengineer	X	X	X	X	X	X

TABLE 24-1.   *Business Process Reengineering Taxonomy*

The rows of the table indicate the amount of change from smallest to most radical:

- **Reaffirm**   Make an explicit decision to do nothing, an alternative that should always be considered.

- **Repackage**   Change the user interface, for example, from a character interface to a GUI or web-based interface.

- **Rehost**   Fundamentally change the hardware platform, for example, by moving from a centralized mainframe environment to a client/server environment.

- **Rearchitect**   Change everything within the core technology not explicitly affecting the way business is done.

- **Reengineer**   Change all of the factors just mentioned while moving from the old system to the new one.

Not only does reengineering have the potential to add value through increasing productivity, but it adds value in other ways as well. For example, reengineering can add value to the firm by increasing revenues through higher contribution margins, by increasing the output price through superior quality, or by increasing technological flexibility to provide the basis for achieving higher margins in the future. These benefits are known as *price recovery*, which is defined as the ratio of the prices of outputs to inputs. In Figure 24-1, the American Productivity Center (APC) profit variance matrix shows the effects of input quantities, output quantities, input prices, and output prices on profitability. Reengineering can achieve a dramatic increase in both productivity and price recovery. Value can accrue to the firm that invests in Information Technology (IT) change efforts through increased scalability, flexibility, customer satisfaction, quality, and reduced cost and cycle time. The profit variance matrix facilitates multicriteria evaluation of technological change by relating these disparate sources of value to profits through productivity and price recovery.

A confluence of factors, including technical and managerial factors, is now leading organizations to change.

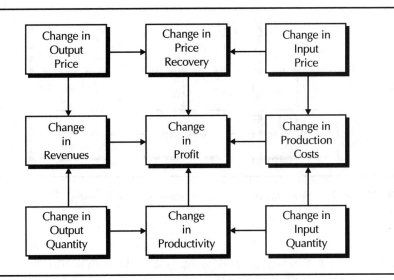

FIGURE 24-1. *American Productivity Center (APC) profit variance matrix*

Decision-Making Framework for Re-action

The components of a decision-making framework are shown in Figure 24-2. This framework integrates a number of ideas to help senior managers who want to make decisions about what their technology platform should be and what re-action strategy would be appropriate for them to undertake. *Re-actions* are the series of change mechanisms, such as rehosting or reengineering, for moving from the current IT platform to a new IT platform, as discussed earlier. Three sets of variables influence the re-action strategy that the manager selects: change drivers, the current IT architecture platform, and IT platform redesign moderators.

Change drivers, such as cost pressures and fragmentation, were discussed in the earlier section, "Why Reengineer?". For managers to change the IT architecture, there must be some description of the architecture itself. Changes in the IT architecture as discussed earlier in this chapter have been classified according to the scope and target of the change (such as reengineering affects on hardware, software, data, people, and process).

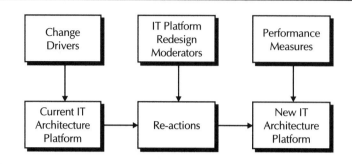

FIGURE 24-2. *A framework for re-action decision-making*

Senior managers also use the following IT architecture platform descriptors when describing their platforms:

- **Flexibility**   The ability to easily add functionality or services or customers

- **Interoperability**   The ability to easily add and remove modules, incorporating "plug and play" philosophy; also, the ability to communicate with all manner of databases and operating systems, incorporating open standards and portability

- **Scalability**   The ability to easily increase the volume of transactions by 50 percent or 200 percent; expandability

- **Reliability**   The ability to achieve fault tolerance and availability

- **Security**   The ability to safeguard the information system resources

These characteristics are used to describe both the current IT architecture platform and the new IT architecture platform.

IT platform redesign moderators are the constraints that every organization faces. These constraints include the following:

- The budget constraints for the re-action effort

- The length of time within which the re-action effort must take place

- The skill set of the people involved (critical when the re-action effort uses new technologies, such as object-oriented development)

Performance measures are key in this model. It is no longer sufficient to invest only in re-actions; managers require some analysis of the worth of investing in the change.

Re-Actions: Strategies for Technological Change

Reengineering is at the high end of a spectrum of technological change strategies, or re-actions, that managers can undertake to maximize the value of their firm. This discussion of IT change strategies focuses on the components of an IT architecture. An IT architecture consists of interfaces, operating systems, hardware platforms, software, databases, telecommunications, and human resources.

This section looks first at the strategy that requires the least amount of change, rehosting, and ends with the strategy that requires the most amount of change, reengineering (see Table 24-1).

IT managers can change the underlying processing power and cost structure of the IT platform through rehosting. Rehosting is the change effort that, from the user's perspective, involves the least amount of change. Rehosting typically involves migration from a mainframe platform to a minicomputer, workstation, or PC network platform. For example, General Electric moved its financial transaction processing from an IBM 3090 mainframe to a networked Intel 486 PC. The Intel platform uses the same data files and file formats that were used on the IBM mainframe. With rehosting, software applications retain their functionality. Indeed, the users may not even notice the change in hardware, because there is no change in the applications. Firms rehost to reduce cost and increase flexibility. Business value accrues directly from the reduction in the hardware cost, and indirectly from increased flexibility. It is much quicker and more cost effective to scale up a workstation-based platform than a mainframe platform.

IT managers can also change the interface, and thus part of the operating system, through repackaging. One common repackaging effort that many organizations are undertaking is moving from a text-based interface, such as DOS, to a graphical user interface, such as Windows.

There is more to the IT architecture than the interface and the hardware. The IT manager can change the way information is gathered and data is organized by rearchitecting the system. Rearchitecting makes some change in the functionality of the system, although the underlying business process remains the same. For example, changing a database from a network structure to a relational structure is a rearchitecting effort. The relational structure will allow the user to ask questions about the information that could not be asked under the network structure.

Data integration is a second type of rearchitecting effort. Organizations that want to make coordinated, enterprise-wide decisions find that they cannot do so because data fields that should be the same in two different databases are not the same, because different code is used in different parts of the database. Moving to a client/server architecture consists of two re-actions: rehosting and rearchitecting.

Reengineering is the re-action that causes the most change. The primary goal of reengineering is to change the business process. Because the business process will be changed, the IT platform will also most likely need to be changed. Reengineering seeks to radically change business processes to achieve dramatic improvements in performance.

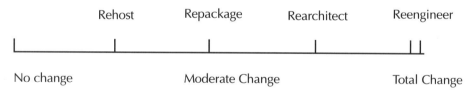

Keys to Successful Reengineering

The keys to successful reengineering include the following:

- Senior management must be committed to the reengineering effort. There is a lot tied to the status quo. To get people to accept changes, management needs to support the reengineering effort and make this support visible. The management team must have the will to make the necessary changes and lead the process. This means that senior management needs to be committed to the future environment.

- The scope of the effort must be large. Because reengineering occurs across multiple product lines, the opportunity to achieve the greatest gains from reengineering occurs when reengineering efforts are undertaken across broad functional areas.

- Reengineering is a cross-functional activity and therefore support by many groups is essential. This support can be achieved through an interactive workshop. All the groups need to be integral parts of the reengineering effort. The change in culture needs to be managed.

In conclusion, reengineering has the potential to improve the productivity and price recovery of cross-functional processes. By reducing redundancy, it can reduce costs. By increasing flexibility, it can facilitate the inclusion of new products. Successful change requires senior management commitment, management of the change in the company culture, and a large scope that extends across functional areas or products.

CHAPTER
25

Data Migration

As men say, there is a change and migration of the soul from this world to another.

—Plato (428-348), *Apology*

ata migration is a broad term, used differently by different people. We use the term *data migration* to refer to the entire process of moving data from one system (source) to another (target). Usually, the structures of the source and target systems are different; sometimes they are radically different. This means that the migration process also requires some level of "data transformation." It is also common for the source data to have errors. These errors are frequently significant enough that the data cannot be migrated as is, since it violates database constraints set up in the new structure. The process of removing the errors is called data *cleansing* and is performed prior to the actual migration.

Data migration, as we have defined it, can take up a significant portion of the entire systems development project. We have seen cases where data migration consumed as much as 80 percent of the resources of the entire project. Although this was an unusually high percentage, a reasonable rule of thumb is to estimate that data migration will consume 10 percent to 30 percent of the total resources of a given project.

A full treatment of data migration could easily fill a book. In this chapter, we will provide a brief overview of our data migration methodology and show how it fits into the overall CADM method.

Overview

The right way to think about data migration is as an independent project with its own phases and deliverables. These phases do not entirely parallel the CADM phases of the overall project. Specifically, data migration should be completed much earlier than the overall project because the migration process will invariably uncover changes that need to be made in the data model. You cannot declare that the data model is complete until migration has been done. Therefore, the data migration process must be substantively completed by the end of the overall project Pre-Design phase. As the project moves into the Design phase, data migration should be moving into its own Test phase.

In this chapter, we will lay out the migration portion of a project using most of the same phase names as those used in CADM. To avoid confusion in referring to phases, we will add the prefix "Migration" to the phase names to distinguish them from the overall project phases.

Using two parallel time lines, Table 25-1 shows how the migration phases correspond to the overall CADM phases.

There are two major types of projects where data migration is necessary:

■ Standard legacy system redesign projects where the legacy system is discarded when the new system is implemented. (For example, legacy system redesigns of OLTP systems.)

■ The new system being built will accept data from and/or pass data to another system on an ongoing basis. (For example, data warehouse projects.)

CADM	Data Migration
Strategy	Migration-Strategy
Pre-Analysis	Migration-Pre-Analysis
	Migration-Analysis
Analysis	
	Migration-Design
Pre-Design	Migration-Build and Unit Test
Design	Migration-Test
Build	Migration-Revise
Test	
Implementation	Migration-Implementation

TABLE 25-1. *Relative Timeline of CADM Phases and Migration Phases*

Why Data Migration Can Be Difficult

There are a number of reasons why data migration can be a complex and difficult process. First, the structures of the old and new systems are different. If you are migrating from a non-relational to a relational system, the structures will probably be radically different. When measured against the standards of a modern relational database design, files from legacy systems routinely violate the rules of normalization. Even moving from a relational legacy system to a new system can be a challenge. Second, data is often "dirty" (contains errors) and must be cleansed. This dirty data is usually the result of lack of constraints in the source system. For example, if we are tracking projects, the source legacy system may have allowed users to enter the project manager's name without being validated against a valid list of employees. In the new system, the same field will be populated from information stored in the Employee table. In order to migrate the data, all of the names typed into the legacy fields must be checked and validated against the Employee file. Names may have different spellings, nicknames may have been used, or errors in typing could have occurred. All of these discrepancies need to be resolved before moving the data to the new system. If the number of projects is small, this is not a big problem. With a large number of projects, cleansing the data becomes a difficult task. You can either remove the constraints in the new system or, using Oracle8, you can use "novalidate" constraints (where constraints are ignored for records added to the database before the constraint was enabled).

The most significant problem with data migration projects is that people really do not understand the complexity of data transformation until they have gone through a number of arduous migration projects. Given these issues, it is obvious that there is a desperate need for a sound methodological approach with which organizations can tackle migration projects.

The Phases of Data Migration

The ideal data migration project plan should be broken down into phases that mirror the overall project development phases. These phases and the deliverables or milestones for each are summarized in Table 25-2.

Migration Phase	Deliverable and/or Milestone
Migration-Strategy	Data Migration Scope Document, including Objectives High-level Data Migration Project Plan Data Migration Strategy Document
Migration-Pre-Analysis	Migration Plan, Test Plan
Migration-Analysis	Identify fields to be mapped
Migration-Design	Data mappings
Migration-Build	Conversion code
Migration-Test	Debugged conversion code
Migration-Implementation	Production-ready data

TABLE 25-2. *Data Migration Phases and Deliverables*

Each of these phases will be defined in further detail in the following sections. The life cycle of this methodology closely parallels the CADM phases. However, at some points in the project, the phases of the data migration effort may not be exactly in synch with the overall project development phases.

Some may argue about the necessity of dividing the migration process into this many discrete project phases. However, as Table 25-2 illustrates, each of these phases requires critical milestones to be achieved and deliverables to be prepared. These milestones mark strategic points along the project's time line. Any successes or failures in a given phase will significantly impact the start of the next phase and the outcome of the entire project. Each of these phases will be discussed in further detail in the following sections.

Migration-Strategy

The migration project planning process begins with the Migration-Strategy phase. In this phase, the focus of the overall project is determined. In the first part of the Strategy phase some simple tasks such as identifying the number of source systems and interfaces must be done. Although simple, if not done carefully, a source system or interface might be missed and could cause serious problems later in the process.

Data migration projects do not happen independently. Rather, they are spawned from other development efforts such as the implementation of new OLTP and/or OLAP systems. This is where the first fundamental mistake generally occurs. The project manager is focused on determining the requirements that the new system must satisfy, and pays little or no attention to the data migration(s) that must occur. It is quite common to review a project plan for a new system and discover that data migration is listed as a single task item, if at all. If you've ever worked with such project plans, in hindsight you realize that a separate project plan entirely devoted to the data migration effort should have been included.

One focus of the Migration-Strategy phase is to determine the scope of the migration. In other words, to answer the question, "What are we trying to migrate?" This is the time to identify the number of legacy systems requiring migration and a count of their data structures. Interfaces are another critical factor that should be identified at this time. Interfaces are no different from other data sources, except that they may receive data from the new system, as well as supplying data.

At this point, we are not only identifying the number of data files, but also the number of different *systems* from which data will be migrated. Multiple data sources are a common occurrence. Data sources are not limited to actual data processing systems. Inevitably, analysts will find employees who maintain files on their own workstations that they use to accomplish tasks that cannot be supported by their existing systems. Word processing documents, spreadsheets, desktop RDBMS packages, and raw text files are just a few examples of data sources you can expect to uncover in the Migration-Strategy phase.

The Migration-Strategy phase should be scheduled to occur concurrently with the Strategy phase of the core OLTP or OLAP project. Unfortunately, in most cases, the same people are expected to work on both efforts. This can be done, but these people need a clearly defined set of tasks for which they are responsible.

Another focus of the Migration-Strategy phase involves examining the actual data you plan to migrate. Remember, at this point in the project you have no idea if the data is even of high enough quality to consider migrating. In order to get a better sense, build or obtain a set of canned data quality reports. The reports can provide row counts, column counts, distinct values, and other statistics pertaining to your source data such as distinct values, and unique identifier checking. For example, 500 rows in a table and only 400 unique IDs indicate that a serious problem exists. This kind of information gives you a rough idea of just how much data there is to migrate and the quality of this data. You may find that the overall cost of migration is prohibitive relative to the business value of data that needs to be moved.

If this occurs, the most common solution is to migrate the source data to the new platform into data structures that are constructed identically to that of the source system. Doing so allows you to shut down the old system and bring up the new one with confidence and without losing historical data. The cost of developing a set of reports to access the historical data on the new platform tends to be far cheaper than the cost of migration in many cases.

The deliverable of the Migration-Strategy phase is the Data Migration Strategy Document, which outlines the intentions of the overall migration effort. In the Data Migration Strategy Document, we outline the reasons for our conclusions about whether data migration is worthwhile. The data quality research performed in this phase is still at a very high level, and in no way suggests that the team has gained a thorough understanding of the specific data cleansing issues it will face later in the project.

Migration-Pre-Analysis

The Migration-Pre-Analysis phase expands on the migration goals that were determined in Migration-Strategy, and generates a preliminary, detailed migration plan. At this point, the Migration Test Plan must also be developed. The Migration Test Plan lays out the measures that will be used to ensure that the migration is successful.

Next, we must determine who will perform the data migration. We also must perform more comprehensive data cleansing research, extending the knowledge of our findings in the Migration-Strategy phase. Developers must begin rolling up their sleeves and proceed to write and execute SQL statements against legacy data.

Early in the Migration-Pre-Analysis phase, someone should be appointed to port the legacy data from its current environment into an Oracle *staging area*. A staging area is merely a database account that contains tables that essentially replicate the data structures of the legacy system. (The datatypes may have to change, to accommodate different database management systems, but all the columns and tables should be there.) One benefit of porting the uncleansed legacy data to the Oracle environment is the ability to have your legacy expert staff begin working with Oracle very early on in the project development stage, thus spreading the learning curve out as much as possible.

After you have decided upon the legacy data sources and have conducted thorough data research, you must begin the roster selection. This involves going through the list of data elements from each and every source data structure, and deciding whether or not each one must be migrated. We differentiate roster selection from the overall mapping process. Roster selection involves the process of identifying candidate source data elements. These are not mappings because this roster selection will be fed to the OLTP CADM task of completing the ERD. This roster will definitely identify data elements not yet incorporated into the data model. This process should begin while in the CADM Analysis phase.

Migration-Analysis

The Migration-Analysis phase also happens largely in parallel with the Analysis phase of the core project. This is because each data element identified as a candidate for migration must be incorporated into the emerging data model of the new system.

The Analysis phase is not intended to thoroughly identify the transformation rules by which historical data will be massaged into the new system; rather, it involves making a checklist of the legacy data elements that we know must be migrated.

Analysts can rely on three sources in compiling this checklist:

- Legacy data analysis as conducted in previous phases.

- Legacy report audits: A complete set of legacy reports from the old OLTP system is reviewed. A comprehensive list of field usages should be compiled from these reports.

- User feedback sessions: These sessions should be scheduled for topics such as data model audits, reviews of interview notes, and the results of the legacy data analysis and legacy report audits.

Migration-Design

The Migration-Design phase is where the bulk of the actual mapping of legacy data elements to columns takes place. Like many development tasks, data mapping will be iterative—it does not happen in a single phase. The mapping portion of a data migration project can be expected to span the Design phase through Implementation. The reason for this is quite simple. The most important resources for validating the migration are the users of the new system. Unfortunately, they will be unable to grasp the comprehensiveness of the migration until they view the data through the new applications.

The maps to move data from one system to another are frequently too complex to be easily stored within the Oracle Designer repository. However, if the maps are not stored in a repository when code is generated, you will have to write your migration script in a coding language such as PL/SQL. For a one-time migration, this is a time-consuming task. In an ongoing migration environment (data warehouse) where source and target systems are periodically altered, the migration scripts must also be modified each time there is a change.

We have concluded from experience that developing the new reports prior to new forms allows for more thorough validation of the migration earlier on in the project life span. For instance, if some sort of calculation was performed incorrectly by a migration script, reports will reflect this. A form typically displays a single master record at a time, whereas reports display several records per page, making them a better means of displaying the results of migration testing. Also, the data model will change significantly while reports are being developed. Screen designs are easier to fix after reports audit migration than forms are. Reports are a better tool for evaluating the success of migration, because many rows can be evaluated in a single glance.

A popular misconception about data mapping is that it can be performed against logical data models. Unfortunately, logical data models do not include foreign key columns. This essentially means that you cannot map any of the connections between data structures while you are working with the logical design. Therefore, it is necessary to perform data mapping to the physical data model.

With the physical data structures in place, you can expand the mapping process, to explicitly map the foreign key columns and the relationships between tables. Mapping is generally conducted by a team of at least three people per core business area. The first should be a business analyst, generally an end user possessing intimate knowledge of the historical data to be migrated. The second team member is usually a systems analyst with knowledge of both the source and target systems. The third person is a programmer/analyst who performs data research and develops migration routines based upon the mappings cooperatively defined by the business analyst and the systems analyst. The programmer/analyst may have to delve into source code and/or DDL copybooks to figure out precisely what data (that the business analyst sees on the screen) is stored where in the legacy files.

Migration-Build and Unit Test

Since coding and unit testing are practically inseparable, they are often combined into one phase. In coding, you have to deal with both logical and physical errors. Physical errors are typically syntactic in nature and can be easily identified and resolved. Physical errors have nothing to do with the quality of the mapping effort. This level of testing deals with writing quality code in the scripting language used in the transformation effort. As in the core development effort, appropriate coding standards must be applied, and the code reviewed to ensure that these standards are met.

It is harder to identify and resolve logical errors. The first step is to execute the code that implements the mapping. Even if the code runs successfully, we must still ask questions such as:

- How many records did we expect this script to create?

- Did the correct number of records get created? If not, why?

- Has the data been loaded into the correct fields?

- Has the data been formatted correctly?

The first real test of data mapping is providing the populated target data structures to the users who assisted in the analysis and design of the core system. Invariably, the users will begin to identify other historical data elements to be migrated that were not apparent to them during the Analysis/Design phases.

Unfortunately, data mapping often does not make sense to people until they can physically interact with reports and/or forms in the new, populated data structures. Frequently, this is where the majority of transformation and mapping requirements will be discovered. Most people simply do not realize they have missed something until it is not there anymore. For this reason, it is critical to unleash users on the populated target data structures as soon as possible.

Migration-Test

The Migration-Test phase must be reached as soon as possible to ensure that it occurs concurrently with the Design phase of the core project. Otherwise, months of development effort can be lost as each additional migration requirement slowly but surely wreaks havoc on the data model, which, in turn, requires substantive modifications to the applications.

The migration script is tested in the same way as any other PL/SQL script with code walkthroughs, etc. With migration scripts, you can also do some level of user acceptance testing using reports built in the main CADM project. This ability to run reports against the migrated data is the key test to perform during the Migration-Test phase. Reports run against the migrated data should be carefully compared to reports run in the source system. Even using these tests, you still will not know that the migration testing is complete until all of the applications are built and running against the migrated database. Even then, there will be occasional problems that crop up during the project Implementation phase. Migration is an extraordinarily difficult task and almost impossible to accomplish flawlessly, no matter how much care is taken.

Migration-Revise

In the Migration-Revise phase, we have tentatively completed the migration. However, migration activity will not entirely stop because the main portion of the project is in Build and Test. During this time, the data model is being tweaked. Therefore, the migration script will need to be adjusted as well. If any parts of the migration failed during Migration-Test, the scripts can be modified and rerun during this phase.

Migration-Implementation

The Implementation phase is where all of the mappings are validated and successfully implemented in a series of scripts that have been thoroughly tested. Debugged code is moved from the development system to the production system. Users must stop doing work in the legacy systems long enough for you to get a consistent extract of all the legacy system data. The data is loaded into the new system with the goal of being production-ready. As already mentioned, there is a high probability that small migration errors will surface during implementation.

Migration-Maintenance

The maintenance phase differs depending upon whether you are migrating to an OLTP or a data warehouse.

If the migration is to an OLTP system, you are working within the "one and done" paradigm. Your goal is to successfully migrate the legacy data into the new system, rendering the migration scripts obsolete once the migration has been accomplished. Therefore, for all intents and purposes, there is no maintenance phase.

If the migration is to a data warehouse system, you will most likely be reloading or refreshing the new system in timely intervals. As new information is recorded in the source OLTP system, you need to transfer it to the warehouse system. Script performance is a critical issue in warehouse migrations, while OLTP migrations pay little or no attention to script performance since they will only be run once.

Data Transformation Tool vs. Programmer

How does an organization decide whether to use a data transformation tool to manage its data migration effort, or simply employ a group of willing and able technical experts to accept the bulk of the workload?

Typically, the decision is made based upon the comparison of the cost of a transformation tool and the cost of employing a few extra pairs of hands. Unfortunately, because of the high cost of most migration products, most projects attempt to perform their migration without the aid of a tool. This can greatly increase the time required and costs associated with migration.

This is not to say that the purchase of a transformation tool is the only solution. However, we believe that many people do not truly understand all of the benefits that a data transformation tool can deliver.

Data Transformation Tool Features

A data transformation tool offers a central repository to support the storage and ongoing maintenance of data mappings, lending itself to teams of all sizes. The most commonly used alternatives tend to be spreadsheets, which invariably fail when you need to map one source data element to one or more target elements. Spreadsheets typically prevent more than one person from making modifications at one time, resulting in a great deal of unnecessary administrative overhead. Spreadsheets are two-dimensional tools, and mapping is without question multidimensional to the nth degree.

A good data transformation tool should include the features discussed next.

1. Flexible Reporting

Reporting is easily accomplished, and serves as a comprehensive communication device between the systems and business analysts.

2. Code Generation from Mapping Rules

Systems analysts can generate the migration scripts directly from the mappings they have defined, reducing the overall programming staff requirements.

3. Script Scheduling Utilities

Some tools provide far more sophisticated options such as script compilation and scheduling utilities. Scheduling utilities can cut the overall script execution time of a migration project by more than one-third in almost every case, by processing scripts in parallel as opposed to sequential order.

4. Automatic Integrity Violation Detection

Another important and useful feature of a data transformation tool is the automatic detection of integrity violations. On one migration project, we uncovered 4.5 million data integrity violations. It certainly was not humanly possible to manually identify all of these violations in months, let alone days. However, we were able to develop a utility to automatically detect these violations, and had the results within four days.

Manual Data Migration

The manual approach to data migration is still a valid method. In fact, there are many small data migration projects that have very little data to migrate, and as a result do not require a major investment in a data migration tool or large amounts of effort by one or more programmers.

Decision Factors in Selecting a Data Transformation Tool

Inevitably, a decision about whether to perform data migration manually or purchase a data transformation tool must be made. Though the cost of a transformation tool is indeed recognized up front, most project leaders simply cannot foresee the complexity of the data migration aspects of a systems development project. This is an observation that we have found to be true at several organizations around the country.

A typical data migration project, assuming one legacy data source and a target system of 400 tables, requires a minimum three-person team, as described earlier. With a team of this size, the data migration will likely take about six months. However, with the use of a transformation tool, the overall project time line can be cut in half.

Conclusion

Data migration is a necessary evil, but not an impossible one to conquer. The key is to prepare for it very early on, and monitor it carefully throughout the process. Project time lines tend to become more rigid as time passes, so it really makes sense to meet migration head on. A devoted team with a clearly defined project plan from project inception, armed with automated tools where applicable, is the formula for success.

PART
IV

Additional Oracle Designer Activities

CHAPTER
26

Application System and
Repository Management

Do not administer this product without consulting your physician if you are currently taking prescription medication.

he goal of using CADM is to produce a finished application that meets business requirements. The Oracle Designer activities you perform to reach that goal are centered around entering information in the repository and getting output from the repository in the form of code and reports. While it is most important to complete the deliverables for a particular project, there is also essential work that you need to do to set up and maintain the application systems, and the repository itself, during the development life cycle.

This chapter describes how to manage and administer the Oracle Designer repository. Repository administration consists of two main sets of tasks.

On the physical level, the repository consists of a set of Oracle database tables and other objects contained in an Oracle database. The tasks involved in managing the repository at this level are similar, but not identical, to those typically performed by a database administrator. A *Repository Administrator* is given responsibility for activities such as installing and maintaining the repository instance; installing and maintaining the repository; setting up repository user accounts; backing up the repository (and restoring it if required); and performing product upgrades. You use the Repository Administration Utility (RAU), in conjunction with some typical database administration tasks and procedures, to perform these activities.

On the logical level, all of the information in the repository is divided into different applications. Each application generally corresponds to a particular business area or data processing subsystem. Tasks that must be performed to administer and maintain application systems include creating new versions of the application; sharing, copying, and transferring ownership of repository elements among applications; and granting and revoking users' privileges to select, insert, update, or delete element definitions from one or more applications. All application system administration occurs in the Repository Object Navigator (RON), which you use to create and manipulate the application system element definitions.

Figure 26-1 provides an overview of the relationship between the different participants in Oracle Designer repository maintenance.

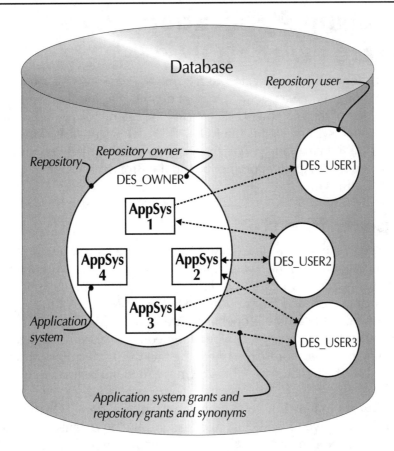

FIGURE 26-1. *The repository and user access*

Oracle Designer provides some repository reports not discussed in the other chapters that can help you administer and view the repository. These give you information on the repository itself, which you can use to document the setup of the repository at your particular site. This chapter discusses these reports and how to run the individual programs that make up the Oracle Design tool set. Finally, this chapter tells you where to look for more information on Oracle Designer.

Managing Application Systems with RON

The Repository Object Navigator (RON), introduced in Chapter 6, is the main tool you use to manipulate element definitions, and the application system is one of those elements. Therefore, the main tool you use to manage the application system itself is the RON. This tool has the following areas for managing the application system: the Property Palette, the File menu, the Utilities menu, the Application menu, and the Broadcast Options choice from the Options menu.

Property Palette

The Property Palette for an application system appears when you select the top-level node that has the name of the application system. Although you cannot change the application system *Name* property, you can change or enter any of the text and description properties. The *Status* of the application is also not enterable on the Property Palette. It will appear as blank (meaning that the application can be modified by any user who has the appropriate privileges) or frozen (meaning that the application cannot be changed). The Rename and Freeze/Unfreeze menu options manage these two properties.

The *Parent* property is used to group application systems. One parent application can have several child applications, but no parents. Grouping the application systems in this way facilitates manipulating multiple applications that share elements. The advantages of assigning a parent application are discussed in the section of this chapter on the New Version option.

File Menu

The **File→New Application** menu option provides the way to create a new application system. Alternatively, you can create a new application system by clicking on the New Application toolbar button.

Utilities Menu

The Utilities menu includes options relevant to application management, organized in three groups. The Share, UnShare, Transfer Ownership, Copy

Object, Copy with New Language, and Force Delete utilities create or delete element definitions or create or delete references to an element definition owned by another application system. The Load and Unload utilities are used to move element definitions from one repository to another. The Check Out, Check In, Lock Set, and Unlock Set utilities allow you to control changes made to application system definitions.

These functions work on individual definitions or groups of selected definitions in the application system. They are discussed in the following sections.

Share

The Share utility allows you to create a reference to an element definition owned by one application system in another application system. This is handy because normally you cannot create a link, such as a foreign key reference, between definitions in different application systems. Sharing definitions from other application systems solves this problem. If you have connected to the sharing application, you cannot modify the shared definition. It is important to note that the shared definition is a reference to the original definition, and not a copy; the shared definition will change whenever the definition in the owning application changes.

There are numerous productive uses for sharing definitions. First and foremost, it prevents duplication of work. An element definition developed in a previously implemented application can be reused in new development efforts; since the sharing application cannot change the element definition, change control is provided. Or, you might want to share preference sets between application systems, to ensure that all applications have a standard look and feel. You can put standard reference sets like domains and storage parameters into a "library" or "master" application. Sharing domains in this way allows all the application systems in an enterprise-wide environment to pick up domain changes.

NOTE

As mentioned in Chapter 10, the Matrix Diagrammer can also share element definitions between application systems.

One way to share a definition is to open both the source and target application systems, select the definition or definitions to be shared, and drag them from the source to the target. Alternatively, using the Utilities menu will allow you to better refine the sharing process. You select the definitions to be shared from the Navigator window hierarchy and choose **Utilities→Share**. The Share dialog is displayed, with the definitions previously selected listed under the Select List, as shown in Figure 26-2. You then specify the target application in the Share with Application field and click the Share button. The original application retains the ownership of the definition, but the target application will have a shared reference copy (which is locked from changes).

In addition to the Select List tab, this dialog has tabs labeled Share Rules, Expanded Share List, and External References. The Share Rules tab allows

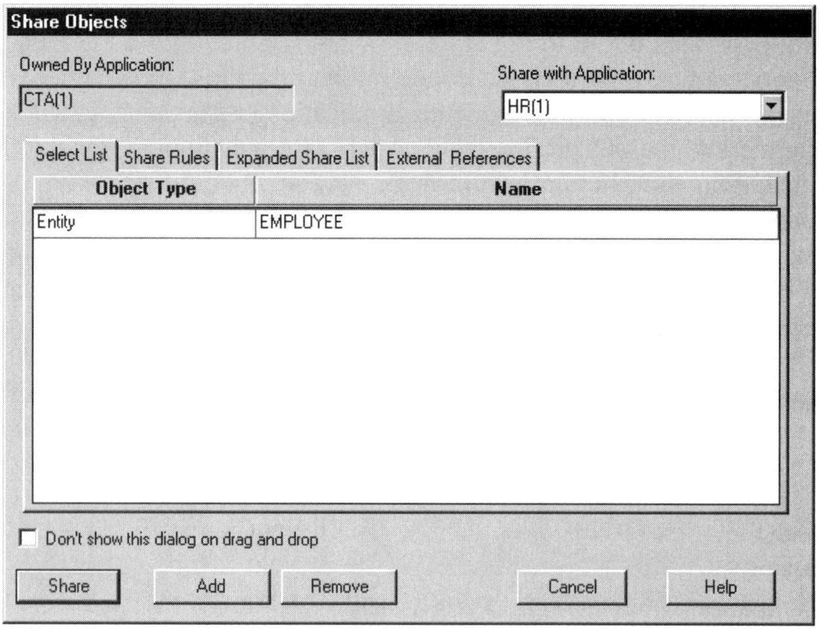

FIGURE 26-2. *The Utilities—Share Objects dialog*

you to choose which types associated with the definition will also be shared. For example, if the Share Rules specified that Sub Entities were to be shared, any subtypes of a selected supertype entity would be shared. The Expanded Share List allows you to see all of the definitions that will be shared based on the Select List and Share Rules choices you have made. The Expanded Share List also allows you to deselect individual definitions from the Share List. The External References tab lists the definitions that are referenced by the definitions to be shared. You can see the source of the reference by clicking on the Referenced By button.

TIP

When you share a definition, an open hand icon will appear on the shared copy to designate that it is shared. If you click that icon, the source application system will open and the source element definition will be selected.

UnShare

The UnShare utility reverses the share process and removes the shared reference from the sharing application system. Select the definition, choose UnShare from the Utilities menu, and click UnShare in the confirmation dialog box that appears. You can also simply select the shared element definition and press the DELETE key.

Transfer Ownership

The Transfer Ownership utility lets you move definitions from one application system to another. Select the elements in the Navigator window, choose **Utilities→Transfer Ownership**, and specify the target application system in the dialog window that appears. The definition will appear in the target application system but will leave a shared reference copy in the original application system. In addition, all subnodes of the definition (such as columns for a table) will be transferred, but the ownership of any associated definitions will not be changed; these will show up in the target application system only as shared definitions.

For example, suppose application system CTA owns the EMPLOYEES and DEPARTMENTS table definitions. EMPLOYEES has a foreign key that references DEPARTMENTS. You want to transfer ownership of EMPLOYEES to HR, so you select EMPLOYEES in CTA, choose **Utilities→Transfer Ownership** from the menu, and specify HR in the Transfer Ownership to Application field. EMPLOYEES will appear in HR as an owned definition with a shared reference in CTA. Also, DEPARTMENTS will be shared into HR, because the foreign key in EMPLOYEES needs to refer to a definition in the application system.

You can also transfer ownership by opening the source and target application systems, pressing and holding the SHIFT key and mouse button, dragging the definitions from the source to the target application system, and releasing the mouse button.

Copy Object

The Copy Object utility allows you to make an exact copy of a definition in one application system and place it in another application system or in the same application system. You can also open both application systems, select the definition, hold down the CTRL key, and drag the definition from one application system to another. Copy Object creates a complete copy of the definition with all its subnodes. With either method, a dialog window appears where you can enter the name of the new object. If you are making a copy of the definition in the same application system, you must assign it a new name. The Copy Object dialog has four tabs each with a definition similar to their respective tabs in the previous discussion about Share. The Copy Object dialog tabs are Context List, Copy Rules, Expanded Copy List, and External References.

TIP
You can get more information about the Share and Copy Objects utilities in RON's help system by doing a Find for Refining a copy or share operation.

Copying gets tricky when the definition you are copying has references or associations to it. For example, assume that the EMPLOYEES table has a foreign key reference to DEPARTMENTS. When you copy EMPLOYEES, a shared copy of DEPARTMENTS also needs to be created so the reference is not left open. You can specify this in the External References tab. A problem occurs if the target location has an existing definition with the same name as an associated definition. In this case, you have a chance to change the name of the associated definition before it is created. The Copy Objects dialog will present you with a system generated Name and Short Name for the associated definition. Unfortunately, the name is somewhat cryptic, consisting of the short name for the ` type and a sequence number. For example, a typical name for an entity would be ENT_6398. It does, though, give you the opportunity to adjust the names prior to completing the copy process. You can avoid this problem entirely by renaming the definition with the duplicated name in one of the application systems before performing the copy operation.

Copy with New Language

The Copy with New Language utility creates a new module with a different *Language* property. For example, you could use an Oracle Developer module as the basis for a WebServer module. This is discussed in more detail in Chapter 18.

Force Delete

The Force Delete utility lets you delete an element definition even if it has associations to other definitions. For example, suppose MODULE1 has a table usage of TABLE1. If you try to delete TABLE1, an error message will appear indicating that deletion is not possible because a module component table usage references that table. You could open the definition for the module, but the error message would not tell you which module contained the references. Also, even if you know that MODULE1 includes references, there may be other references elsewhere. Instead of trying to find all usages of the table definition, you can select the table and choose **Utilities→Force Delete**. The element definition and all associations or references will be deleted. This menu option is quite powerful, and it is not reversible, so be careful when using it.

TIP

Be sure to consult the other tabs in the Force Delete dialog before you delete. The Delete Rules tab will tell you precisely what action Oracle Design will take in order to remove references to the element to be deleted, based on the type of element which is referenced. For example, if you delete a tablespace definition, the reference to it in all table implementation definitions is nullified. If you delete a column from a table, bound items and key components based on the column will be deleted. You can also consult the Expanded Delete List and Expanded Nullify List tabs, to see precisely what elements will be affected.

Load and Unload

The Load and Unload utilities allow you to move element definitions between repositories using a file. You select any number of definitions and choose the **Utilities→UnLoad** menu option. The Unload utility creates a plain ASCII text file with a .DAT extension containing the definitions of those elements, all applicable subelements (such as column definitions for a table definition), associations from that element to other definitions, and *skeleton definitions* (which have a name but no other details) for any associated elements that were not included in the unload set. These skeleton definitions are listed on the Skeleton References tab.

This file can then be loaded into another application system in another repository using the **Utilities→Load** menu item and specifying the name of the unload file in the Control File field. Definitions that are in the load file but not in the target application system will be loaded as is. You specify in the load process how you want Oracle Designer to handle element definitions that are in the file and also in the target application system. If you specify Insert mode, the load process will not load the conflicting definition but make an entry in the load log file that a conflict occurred. If you choose Update mode, the existing definition will be modified to match the element definition in the file. It will update, but not delete, existing definitions based on the file element definition. Figure 26-3 shows an Unload dialog with the Expanded Unload List tab active.

CAUTION
If you click the Load button and nothing seems to be happening, move the window down to reveal the Load Progress dialog. This will tell you when the utility has completed. This effect can occur if you clicked on the dialog after clicking the Load button.

TIP
An Oracle white paper, "Oracle Designer Application Programmatic Interface," contains documentation on the structure and contents of the loader file. Check the Oracle Web site or contact your sales representative to obtain a copy of this white paper.

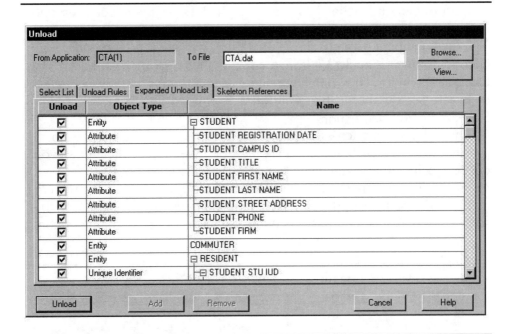

FIGURE 26-3. *The Utilities—Unload dialog*

Check In and Check Out

The Check In and Check Out utilities use a concept similar to the Load and Unload facility to store element definitions in a file. These utilities are designed more for source control because checking out a definition locks it. The utility moves definitions from a *source application system* (which owns the elements) to the *working application system* (where you work on the elements). This procedure is handy when an application developer needs some definitions from the main application system. The developer can check out the definitions (which locks them from changes in the source application) and check them into another application system in the same or a different repository. Then the developer can work on the definitions, make changes as needed, check the definitions back out of the working application system, and check them back in to the source application system, which unlocks them.

The Check In and Check Out utilities use another repository element, called a *User-Defined Set* (UDS). You use RON to define a UDS and associate existing definitions with it as *Set Members*. A definition can be a member of more than one UDS at a time. The UDS element type is used for locking definitions, as well as for the check-out process.

When you perform a check-out operation, you select a UDS and choose **Utilities→Check Out** from the menu. This displays the Check Out dialog window shown in Figure 26-4. The four tabs on the Check Out dialog are Set Members, CheckOut Rules, Expanded CheckOut List, and Skeleton References.

The radio buttons across the top of the Check Out dialog are used to specify the source UDS, intermediate files, or a working application. If you check Specify Intermediate Files, the utility will create a repository check-out file with an .RCO extension that you can check in to the working application system. This file contains the ID numbers of all elements in the source application system that the utility will use to identify changes upon

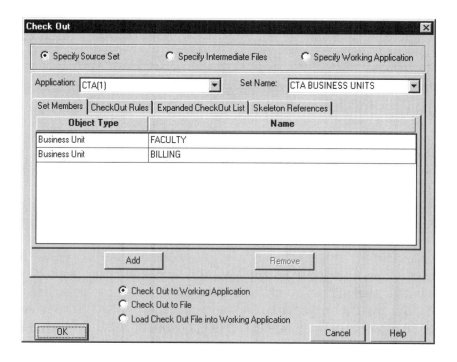

FIGURE 26-4. *Check Out dialog*

check in. Alternatively, you can check out the UDS directly to a working application system. You can even specify that you want the working application system to be created as part of the check-out process. This utility will also lock all definitions in the UDS for the source application system. (Lock icons appear next to the definition's node in RON to flag this lock.)

After creating the file from the source application, you can check it in to another application system using the **Utilities→Check In** menu item. In the dialog window that appears, you specify whether you are checking in to a working or source application system. You can also create a new application system to hold the elements you are checking in with a choice in that dialog window. The four tabs in the Check In dialog are Set Members, CheckIn Rules, Expanded CheckIn List, and Skeleton References.

When the check in occurs, the Check In utility matches the ID numbers of elements in the UDS of the file with those in the working application system. If the file contains new definitions, the utility creates definitions. If the elements in the file have been updated, the utility updates the repository definitions accordingly. If definitions are missing because they were deleted from the UDS in the working application system, the utility deletes them from the source application system.

After making changes in the working application system, you check out the UDS to a repository check-in file that has an .RCI extension, or you can check the UDS directly back in to the original source application. Only the user who checked out the UDS can check it back in.

Lock Set and Unlock Set

The Lock Set and Unlock Set utilities lock and unlock members of the specified User-Defined Set (UDS) without checking them out. Locking a set prevents others from making changes to any of its members. To reverse the lock, choose **Utilities→Unlock Set**. The Unlock utility is also useful if you check out a UDS by mistake or have a problem during the check-in process and need to unlock the UDS without checking it back in.

Application Menu

The items on the Application menu allow you to manipulate the application system definition itself. The user account you are logged in as must have the Manager role (as granted in the RAU) to enable the Application menu. The Application menu provides the following options: Freeze/Unfreeze,

Rename, Transfer Ownership, Copy, New Version, Delete, Grant Access by Appl, Grant Access by User, Archive, Export, Restore, and Reset.

Freeze/Unfreeze

You can use the Freeze/Unfreeze option to protect an application system from changes or to remove that protection. Repository users can view, but not change, a frozen application system. This option is handy if the application system stores information on a static set of definitions that should not be changed. The Freeze menu item allows you to freeze more than one application system at a time. To unfreeze an application system, choose **Application→Freeze/Unfreeze**, select the frozen application system from the list and click the Freeze/Unfreeze button. To freeze an application system, follow the same steps, but choose an unfrozen application system from the list.

Rename

The Rename option displays a list of application systems so you can change their names.

Transfer Ownership

You can use the Transfer Ownership option to switch the ownership of an entire application system to another repository user. This option is useful if all your shared application systems are owned by the Oracle Designer administrator and you want to move an application system defined and owned by another user into the Oracle Designer administrator's account.

Copy

The Copy option allows you to copy an entire application system to a new application system in the same repository. To copy into another repository, you archive and export it and then import it into the other repository.

New Version

The New Version option creates a copy of the application system or systems you select, as Figure 26-5 shows. The version number will be incremented by one to

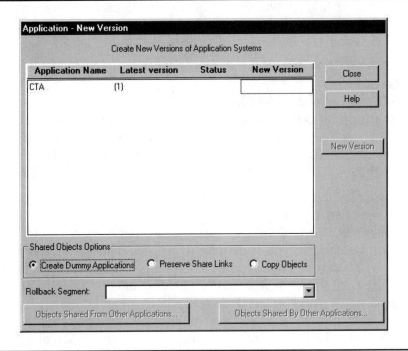

FIGURE 26-5. *Application—New Version dialog*

identify it. The old version will be frozen so it cannot be changed. This option was discussed in Chapter 6.

PARENT APPLICATION SYSTEM   If your development effort includes multiple applications that share definitions, you should version all of the application systems simultaneously. The Shared Objects Options provide some alternatives, as discussed under the help topic, "Creating a new version of an application system." However, these options can lead to maintenance issues in later versions of the applications.

If you have multiple applications sharing elements, one approach is simply to select all the applications to be versioned. An alternate approach is to create a parent application for all of the sharing applications. This way, you only need to specify the parent application system name, and the children will be versioned as well.

Parent application systems cannot have any objects or a parent; they exist only for organizational purposes. The *Parent* property serves to group application systems for deleting and archiving as well as versioning.

Delete

Use the Delete option to delete an application system. Be aware that Oracle Designer checks all dependencies when you use this option, which can take a considerable amount of time for a large application system. This action is not reversible, so you may wish to archive and export the application system before deleting it.

Grant Access by Appl

The Grant Access by Appl option lets you give other users access to application systems that you own or for which you have administrative rights. This option is helpful if you want to grant a number of users rights to a single application system. The dialog window contains a poplist of application systems and an area below to add user names and change privileges. Select, Insert, Update, and Delete rights are the same access rights as in a standard SQL database and apply to all individual element definitions in the application system. Share rights allow the grantee to share elements from the application system with another application system. Admin (administrative) rights can be granted only to users defined with the repository Manager role (in the RAU). Admin rights allow these users to grant access to the application system and perform all other options on the Application menu.

Grant Access by User

The Grant Access by User option accomplishes the same task as the Grant Access by Appl option but in a slightly different way. This option displays a drop-down list for users and an area below to grant rights to more than one application system. This option is useful if you want to grant a particular user rights to more than one application system at the same time. This might be needed when, for example, you add a new repository user to the system. Figure 26-6 shows a Grant Access by User dialog window. Here you see that the user MAYA is being given all rights to the CTA application system, but only Select rights to the HR application system.

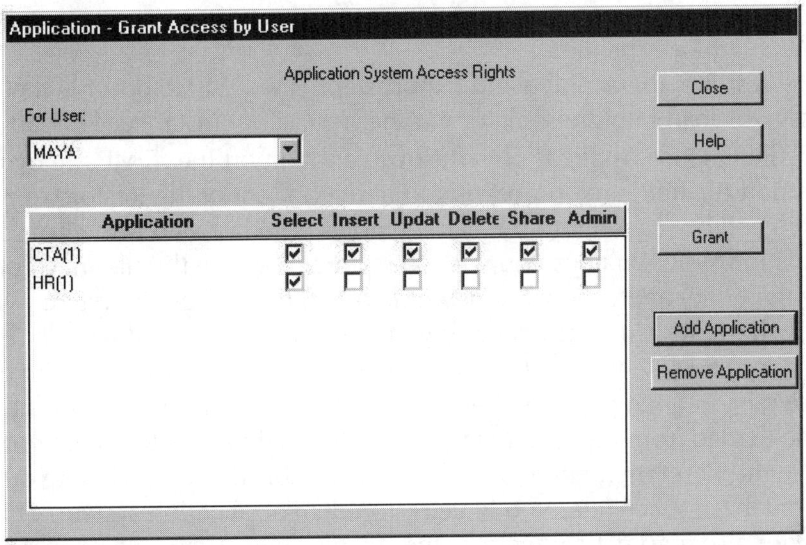

FIGURE 26-6. *Application—Grant Access by User dialog window*

Archive, Export, Restore, and Reset

The Archive, Export, Restore, and Reset options apply to operations you perform to create or load an external file containing all definitions in one or more application systems.

You can create a standard Oracle .DMP export file that contains one or more application systems. This file serves as a backup of the application systems and can be loaded into any repository instance as a copy of the original application systems. You can also use it to make a copy of an application system in the same repository instead of using the versioning facility. This type of copy is different from the copy you get when creating a new version, because the original application system is not frozen and there is no version number link between the original and the copy. The archive process consists of choosing Archive from the Application menu and choosing the application system or systems to archive. This loads all the repository elements, including diagrams, from those application systems into a set of temporary archive tables, also called *extract tables*, that have names starting with XT_. The next step is to export the extract tables to a .DMP file that you can store or load in another application system. You choose Export from the Applications menu and fill in the fields in that dialog to perform the export and create the file.

The result of the Archive and Export steps is a .DMP export file that you can save or load into the same or another repository instance. To load the .DMP file, choose **Application→Restore**, and import the .DMP file by using the Import file field and Import button at the bottom of the Restore dialog. The file will be loaded into the extract tables. The last step is to choose the application system names you wish to restore (because the file may contain more than one) and supply the new name of the application system (which can be the same as the old name if you are restoring into a different repository). Be sure to select an application system by clicking it with the mouse cursor. Then press the Restore button, and the application system will be loaded from the extract tables into the main repository elements.

Use the Reset menu item to clear the XT_ tables, which will let you reuse their database space after you have restored an application system. Oracle Designer also automatically clears these tables when you select the Archive menu item.

Most of the Application menu options display a dialog window like the one in Figure 26-5 in which you specify the application system you wish to affect. The dialog windows are self-explanatory and well documented in the help system. Some have a field for entering a rollback segment name. This is handy if the application system you are working on is large and the operation you are performing may exhaust your default set of rollback segments. If you specify the name of a large rollback segment (that has a size of 5MB, for example), the operation will use that as the rollback segment, and the "Out of extents" message should not appear.

Options

The Options menu in RON is mainly used for RON-specific settings and setup. There are two exceptions to this. The first is the Broadcast Options menu selection, which is discussed next. The second is the Diagnostics menu selection, which is discussed in Chapter 29. A setting in either of these will affect the way that other Oracle Designer tools work on your workstation.

Broadcast Options

The broadcast mechanism provides a means to notify Oracle Designer tools of changes made to repository definitions by another Oracle Designer tool in the same application system. The change notification, which appears as a red dot in a navigator or diagram item, is called a *broadcast indicator*. This is an extremely useful utility since it lets you and others in your development team know if you are all looking at the most up-to-date version of the definitions. The notification will occur between different tools connected to the same application system on the same machine, and if configured to do so, will notify users on other machines connected to that application system. The user who receives the broadcast indicator must perform a requery to see the changes in their tool.

Three broadcast levels can be set from **Options→Broadcast Options**: Disabled, Desktop Only, and Network. Disabled turns off the broadcast option; you will neither send nor receive broadcast information. Setting the level to Desktop Only tells the broadcast mechanism to send and receive broadcast information to and from tools running on the same machine and connected to the same repository. Network specifies that you want to send the broadcast message to all tool users on the same network.

NOTE
You cannot set the broadcast level differently in different tools running on the same machine. For example, if you set the level to Network in RON, it will also be changed to Network in Design Editor.

If you plan to use the Network level you first need to install and configure the broadcast server—a service similar to the Oracle listener. You also need to be using TCP/IP. The broadcast server runs by default on the same machine that is running the RAU to configure it. Alternatively, you can set it up to run on another machine. You may wish to do this if you are not running RAU on the machine that supports your repository database. The **Tools→Configure Network** menu option in RAU allows you to set the proper host and port. You can also set locations for trace and log files in the ORACLE_HOME/network/admin/notifier.ora file. After setting those, you start the broadcast server using:

L 26-1

```
ORACLE_HOME\bin\notifctl.exe
    repository_owner/password@respository_sid start
```

all on one line in an NT DOS command window (with ORACLE_HOME as the drive and directory where the Oracle executables are located) or:

L 26-2

```
$ORACLE_HOME/bin/notifctl
    repository_owner/password@repository_sid start
```

all on one line in UNIX. If the broadcast service starts correctly you will see a message similar to:

L 26-3

```
Starting cwbss10..
Notification service now running using
SOC:(DESCRIPTION=(ADDRESS=(PROTOCOL=tcp)(HOST=popper)(PORT=4966)))
```

After the service is started you can issue commands to the notification utility similar to the ones that you would issue to the SQL*Net (Net8) listener control program. For example,

L 26-4

```
notifctl repository_owner/password@repository_sid status
```

will show a list of users who have set their broadcast level to Network after the time that the broadcast server was started.

Once you have the service running and users connected, you will want to test the configuration. Start RON on two different machines and connect to the same application system. Make sure the broadcast level on both is set to Network by choosing it in RON's **Options→Broadcast Options** menu option. Update an attribute definition on one machine, then check RON on the other machine. You should see a red dot broadcast indicator as that attribute's icon.

TIP
You can get more help on setting up the broadcast server by doing a search for "Configuring the broadcast server" in the help system.

Multiple Application System Projects

Your project or business setup may require multiple application systems. The best approach is to determine the number of application systems to use before entering data into the repository for a project, but you can also partition the elements later, if necessary, by using a combination of the copy and transfer ownership operations.

For example, you may have an application system that represents the current production environment, where all existing database objects and code modules have definitions. These definitions are maintained so that whenever a new object is put into production, the repository definition is also entered in the production application system. In this case, you will probably also have a development application system where you do your work on the objects before you put them into production.

You may also want multiple application systems if you have a common set of tables (for instance CUSTOMERS or EMPLOYEES) that are shared by multiple applications and that are relatively stable. These tables could be contained in a separate application system, and new systems could reuse the definitions by sharing elements from this common application system. This would allow you to link new elements to existing elements and, at the same time, prevent modifications to the original element definitions. Although you can lock individual elements or sets of elements using a User-Defined Set, if you have a large group of elements that need to be locked, locking the entire application system will make management easier. You will also need multiple application systems if you want to specify a parent application that has elements shared by other application systems. The *Parent* property of the application system can store this hierarchy information, and you can share or transfer ownership to and from the children on a temporary or permanent basis. Separate application systems are needed to make up the hierarchy. There may be other considerations for your particular environment, so the best thing to do is budget some time in the Pre-Analysis phase to create a strategy for dividing up application systems.

Managing the Repository with RAU

When you install, upgrade, or make changes to the repository itself, you use the RAU. The repository consists of tables and PL/SQL code packages that are owned by a specific user. When you are working in this utility, you must log in as this user (the repository owner). Other users may have access to the screen, but they will not be able to perform most of the activities.

CAUTION
Anything you do to the repository will affect all existing and future application systems in that repository; therefore, you should be careful when using this utility.

The RAU is available from the Oracle Designer window or the RON Tools menu. After you start it from one of these locations, the main RAU window appears, as shown in Figure 26-7.

FIGURE 26-7. *Repository Administration Utility window*

As stated previously, the repository consists of a set of Oracle objects (including tables, views, packages, and role grants) installed in an Oracle database instance. You will need to have your database administrator (DBA) create a database with sufficient capacity for your repository. You will also need to have the DBA create Oracle database user IDs for all users who will be working with Oracle Designer. One of these user IDs will be the *repository owner,* the schema that owns and controls the objects which comprise the repository.

Repository users have normal Oracle database user accounts and are also registered (in the RAU) as having privileges to access the repository. The process of maintaining repository users creates private grants and synonyms for each user to the repository owner's database objects. This step ensures that the repository users can access the repository in a controlled way through the Oracle Designer front-end tools. In addition to that high-level access privilege, each repository user is given specific grants on a more granular level to the application systems themselves (as discussed previously).

The easiest way to see how the RAU manages the repository is by examining the six main work areas, which correspond to groups of buttons in the RAU window. Install/Upgrade is what you have to do first. Repository Maintenance includes options to grant users access to the repository. The Deinstall option may rarely, if ever, be required, but the Check Requirements and Backup procedures should be performed periodically. The User Extension options are not covered here, but are discussed in detail in Chapter 27.

Install/Upgrade

The Install button lets you create the repository tables, packages, and other database objects. You perform this installation after installing the Oracle Designer front-end software, because the scripts that this install process runs are part of the front-end software installation. When you run the RAU for the first time after installing the software, the Install button will be enabled, which signifies that you have not performed the repository installation. You click that button to install the repository database objects. Chapter 2 of the *Oracle Designer Installation Guide* provides more information on the installation process and the checks that you need to perform before you embark on the repository installation. It also gives routines to follow if you are upgrading or migrating repository data from older versions of Oracle CASE or Oracle Designer.

NOTE
There is a product called CASE Exchange that lets you migrate data from other CASE products into the Oracle Designer repository.

Before installing Oracle Designer, you should spend some time planning the administrative tasks that will be needed, as well as planning what your repository structure will be. For example, if you need multiple repository instances, will you create them in the same database in different user accounts or in different databases? The main issue to consider is that these repositories cannot share elements; although you can use the Archive facility to copy application systems, or the Unload facility to copy elements. The installation manual contains some guidelines and strategies for repository setup.

The Upgrade button installs new features for the latest software upgrade of the repository. The upgrade process is similar to the install process because you need to install the front-end software (upgrade) first. It is different in that this button does not fully reinstall the repository, but just applies the changes or additions to the database objects.

Repository Maintenance

The Repository Maintenance group of buttons contains procedures for working with the database users and objects for the repository. These buttons allow you to Maintain Users, Recreate any invalid database objects, View Objects, and Compute Statistics on the database tables and indexes.

Maintain Users

Once the repository database objects are installed, you have to grant access to users. The Maintain Users button lets you add, grant access to, and remove repository users. As mentioned earlier, a repository user is an Oracle database account that also is allowed access to the repository. You or your DBA has to create the database account before you define it as a repository account. When you click the Maintain Users button, you will see a hierarchical list of all current repository users, and you can add a user as a Manager or User by clicking the Add button and choosing an existing user account from the Oracle User Name poplist. The other required fields in this window are filled in by default, but you need to consider what type of user you are adding.

You can grant only one of two types to a repository user: User (the default) or Manager. A repository user with the User type has access to all elements in the repository but cannot create application systems or access other functions in the Application menu in RON. A repository user with the Manager type can access all elements, as well as create new application systems and perform the functions on the RON Application menu.

After creating and specifying a type for the repository user, you click the Reconcile button in that dialog to re-create or synchronize the synonyms and grants for the modified or added users. You then click the OK button to exit the dialog. The last step in granting access to the repository is actually granting access to application systems using RON, as mentioned before.

Recreate and View Objects

The Recreate button allows you to recompile invalid repository database objects or re-create the objects. Figure 26-8 shows the Select Recreate Option dialog that appears when you press the Recreate button. You will see that the Full Reconcile button is selected. Among other uses, Full Reconcile is a required step in producing user extensions, as discussed in Chapter 27. The Recreate feature is also handy when unexplained errors occur that point to a problem in the database packages or views that compose the repository. If such an error occurs, you can click the View Objects button in the Repository Maintenance group and select the Object Status radio button. If the list that appears has any invalid or missing objects, you can use the Recreate function to recompile or re-create those objects. Figure 26-9 shows a list that is produced by the View Objects button. You can also choose to view Object Sizes from the View Objects button.

Compute Statistics

The Compute Statistics button provides you with the ability to analyze the repository tables and indexes. This will assist Oracle's cost-based optimizer in choosing the best execution plan.

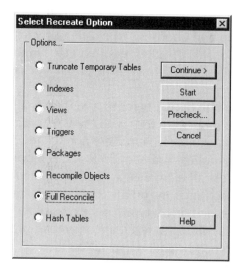

FIGURE 26-8. *Select Recreate Options dialog window*

TIP
Another performance-tuning action you can take in RAU is to pin the repository packages by clicking the Pin toolbar button. This loads all API packages into memory for faster access.

Deinstall

The Remove Repository button lets you remove all repository database objects belonging to the repository owner. You can use this button to prepare to import data from a repository export file or to redo an aborted installation.

The Remove All Objects button also removes all repository database objects belonging to the repository owner, but, in addition, it removes other objects that were created outside of RAU, such as application tables or views created in SQL*Plus. You would use this button if, for example, you are preparing to import a .DMP file that contains both repository and non-repository objects.

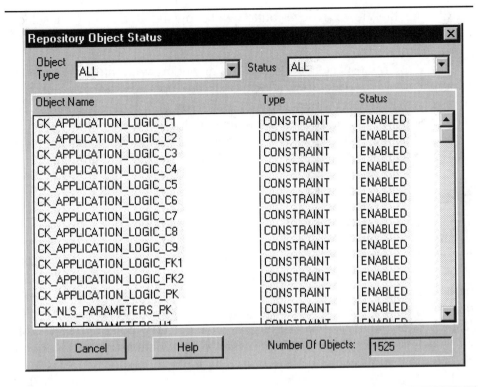

FIGURE 26-9. *Repository Object Status dialog*

CAUTION
The effect of executing one of the remove procedures is severe and not reversible.

Check Requirements

The Check Requirements buttons allow you to verify the state of the repository database. The View Privileges, View Tablespaces, and View Parameters buttons in this group let you check the status of the database objects in the repository. The information available by choosing any one of the buttons can be useful when preparing to install a new repository instance or when troubleshooting repository problems.

Clicking the View Privileges button will show a dialog where you select to view the Oracle database roles and privileges that have been granted to the repository user.

The View Tablespaces button displays a window with information on the tablespaces (sizes, space used, allocation to the repository user, and other parameters). The data will give you an indication of potential problems in the repository that you may be able to fix with the Recreate button.

View Parameters provides you with a look at Windows registry entries that can affect the configuration of your Oracle Designer installation.

Backup

The Backup group of buttons lets you export and import the repository database objects to a standard Oracle .DMP file. The Export button creates a file with the contents of the repository and the database structure definitions. You can use this file as a backup of the repository in case there is a hardware or software problem. You can also use this backup to move the repository to another database or user account. You can export either just repository database objects, such as the repository tables and views, or all objects owned by the repository owner, which includes other tables and objects created outside of the RAU, such as application-specific tables in addition to the repository.

You can restore the repository .DMP file using the Import button after using the Remove All Objects or Remove Repository button in the Repository Management group.

Repository Reports for Administration

Some repository reports can assist you in your administrative work. The Repository Reports Global group contains reports on the application system itself. The *Elements and Their Application Systems* report lists element names and descriptions for each specified element type. This group also contains a set of reports on elements shared from one application system to another: for example, the *Elements Shared into An Application System* report. Other reports list elements that do not easily fit into one of the other categories: for instance, *Document Definition*, which reports on the Documents node objects in RON, and *System Glossary*, which shows all entities, their synonyms, and business terminology definitions that you entered in RON. Another interesting report is the *Changed Elements* report, which shows which primary access controlled elements changed between one date and another and which user changed them.

The Function Point Analysis group gives you another method for evaluating the complexity and size of an application system. An example is the *FPA MKI (Design Level)* report, which examines the repository definitions in an application system and provides measurements of various aspects. Another example of this type of report is the *FPA MKII (Design 2)* report, which provides a measurement of the technical complexity of the system so you can determine the cost and time needed for a particular application system.

You can run reports on some of the user-extensibility objects that Oracle Designer provides, such as Assumptions, Key Performance Indicators, and Critical Success Factors. These elements can track information that you determine early in the System Development Life Cycle and want to capture in the repository. To list Critical Success Factors, or any other element type, for that matter, you can run reports in the User Extensions group. The *<Element> Definition* report shows the properties of the elements of a certain element type, and the *Detailed <Element> Definition* report provides more information on those elements, including their associations with other elements.

TIP

*Some repository reports that are appropriate for repository administration are not listed in the Group view. In order to see a list of all repository reports, choose the **View→Report Name View** menu option. One report you will find this way is the* Area Metric *report, which calculates a number for the application system that shows the complexity of the design. This number allows you to compare one application system design with another.*

Bypassing the Oracle Designer Window

One of the administrative tasks you may want to perform is to set up faster methods for accessing the tools and utilities than those provided with the product. You can set up a program icon for some of the tools or utilities to bypass the Oracle Designer window. This is useful if you find yourself using a particular tool for most of the work and do not want to load the Oracle Designer window to navigate to it. Many of the Oracle Designer tools and utilities have separate executable program files that you can use to create a program icon. If you are using Windows NT (4.x) or Windows 95, you should add a folder to the desktop or to another folder and create program icons within that folder. Consult the operating system help file if you need information on how to do that; however, that help file does not tell you the command line string to use when setting up the program icon.

You can determine the command line string for most of the Oracle Designer tools and utilities if you know the executable file name and the calling syntax. The executable file names are listed in Table 26-1.

In this table, other than the normal username, password, and database connect string, the known command line parameters are

- **/a:** Specifies the application system name and, after a comma, the application system version number.

- **/d:** Specifies the diagram ID. To find this, open the Sets node in RON, open the Diagrams node, show the properties for the diagram, click on a property, press F5, and look at the object ID. That is the diagram ID. Some syntaxes in Table 26-1 refer to this as diagname, diag_id, or diagram_id, but these are all the diagram ID.

- **/s:** Specifies that you will not see the Designer splash screen (silent mode).

- **/u:** Specifies user mode (expert or novice) for some diagrammers; although, this effect is subtle, if not invisible.

Oracle Designer Tool	Executable File Name

Dataflow Diagrammer	`awd30.exe [<username>/<password>[@<database>]]`
	`[/a:<appsysname>,<version>]`
	`[/d:<diag_id>]`
	`[/e:<element>]`
	`[/r]`
	`[/s]`
	`[/u:{E│N│EXPERT│NOVICE}]`

Design Editor	`dwfde20.exe [<username>/<password>[@<database>]]`
	`[/a:<appsysname>,<version>]`
	`[/d:<diagram_id>]`
	`[/s]`

Oracle Designer window	`des2k20.exe [<username>/<password>[@<database>]]`
	`[/a:<appsysname>,<version>]`
	`[/s]`

Entity Relationship Diagrammer	`awe30.exe [<username>/<password>[@<database>]]`
	`[/a:<appsysname>,<version>]`
	`[/d:<diag_id>]`
	`[/e:<element>]`
	`[/r]`
	`[/s]`
	`[/u:{E│N│EXPERT│NOVICE}]`

Function Hierarchy Diagrammer	`afw30.exe [<username>/<password>[@<database>]]`
	`[/a:<appsysname>,<version>]`
	`[/d:<diag_id>]`
	`[/e:<element>]`
	`[/r]`
	`[/s]`
	`[/u:{E│N│EXPERT│NOVICE}]`

Matrix Diagrammer	`awm30.exe [<username>/<password>[@<database>]]`
	`[/a:<appsysname>,<version>]`
	`[/s]`

TABLE 26-1. *Executable File Names and Command Line Syntax*

Oracle Designer Tool	Executable File Name

Module Structure Diagrammer	`dws20.exe [<username>/<password>[@<database>]]`
	`[/a:<appsysname>,<version>]`
	`[/d:<diag_id>]`
	`[/e:<element>]`
	`[/r]`
	`[/s]`
	`[/u:{E|N|EXPERT|NOVICE}]`

Object Database Designer	`dwo20.exe [<username>/<password>[@<database>]]`
	`[/a:<appsysname>,<version>]`
	`[/s]`

Process Modeller	`bpmod20.exe [<username>/<password>[@<database>]]`
	`[/a:<appsysname>,<version>]`
	`[/d:<diagname>]`
	`[/s]`

Repository Administration Utility	`ckrau20.exe [<username>/<password>[@<database>]]`
	`[/a:<appsysname>,<version>]`
	`[/s]`

Repository Object Navigator	`ckron20.exe [<username>/<password>[@<database>]]`
	`[/a:<appsysname>,<version>]`
	`[/s]`

Repository Reports	`ckrpt20.exe [<username>/<password>[@<database>]]`
	`[/a:<appsysname>,<version>]`
	`[/s]`

Server Model Diagrammer	`dwfdd20.exe [<username>/<password>[@<database>]]`
	`[/a:<appsysname>,<version>]`
	`[/d:<diagram_id>]`
	`[/s]`

TABLE 26-1. *Executable File Names and Command Line Syntax* (continued)

If the command line you try does not work, you may want to try a different case (upper or lower). The application system name, for example, is case sensitive in some syntaxes and you need to enter the name in uppercase.

For example, to start a session of the Entity Relationship Diagrammer loading the diagram with an object ID of 303 and suppressing the Oracle Designer startup screen, enter:

L 26-5 `awe30 repos/pwd@d703 /a:CTA,1 /d:303 /s`

The calling syntax is actually available in an error message that appears when you run the program at a command line with the wrong syntax. The easiest way to see this message is to use the operating system file manager or file explorer utility. Navigate to the BIN directory under ORACLE_HOME. Then drag the program file to a new folder or program group. Open the properties for that new icon and type an entry for the command line like the following for the Process Modeller:

L 26-6 `c:\orawin95\bin\bpmod20.exe scott/tiger@orcl /abc`

"scott/tiger@orcl" is the necessary login information, and "/abc" is an invalid command line parameter that will cause the error message that gives the correct syntax when you double-click the icon.

Additional Sources of Information

No matter how experienced you are with the various aspects of Oracle Designer, there will be times when you have questions about how to perform a task. The more you know about the repository and the various strategies for using the tools, the better you will be able to handle these types of questions. There are, however, sources of information that you can use to assist you as you work and as questions arise.

Oracle-Supplied Documentation

As mentioned throughout this book, the most important way to obtain information is to take full advantage of the help system. This online guide can get you started with Oracle Designer in general as well as help you with particular operations. It can also remind you about the meaning of seemingly obscure or forgotten properties. In addition, the help system contains a section for error messages and codes as well as a topic on "Getting Started with Designer," available from the Contents tab. A handy help system facility you can employ with the 32-bit Windows operating systems is the Find tab in the Help System window. This operating system facility allows you to create an index of words that appear throughout the document. It essentially lets you perform a word search on the whole help file and is useful if a keyword is not defined in the Index tab for the topic you are looking for.

TIP
If you perform a keyword search in the help system for the word "tip" you might find, depending on the help file you are looking at, a topic of hints for more productive use of the tool. If you need to see the tips for a particular tool, access the help file in that tool and perform the keyword search. If you have navigated to another help file (they are linked together), navigate back using the Contents topic "Access to other Designer help systems" and look there for the tips.

Another recommended source of information when you are learning Oracle Designer is the printed material included with the product—particularly the installation guide and tutorial. The tutorial, in particular, will help you get a sense of the objectives and scope of the tools. There is an online HTML version of this tutorial that you can load from the Start Here icon in the Oracle Designer start menu group. This Start Here icon also links to the Product Overview, which is a valuable introduction to the entire product. Chapter 2 provides more information on the help system and online documentation in the "Help System" section.

Tip:
The Release Notes are also critical reading material. These are printed pages that are included with the product and are last-minute supplements to the documentation and help system. They often contain necessary information on installation, restrictions, and workarounds.

SRBs

Oracle ships System Release Bulletin (SRB) files with Oracle Designer, and these will be installed when you install Oracle Designer on the client PC. There is a separate program group in the Start menu for these bulletins. When you select one of these entries, a text editor will open with the text of the file. The bulletins contain information not in the online help or other printed documentation, such as documentation available, dependent products, known restrictions (including bugs), bug fixes (from previous versions), and hints and tips. An example of a hint or tip is the following from the SRB for RON: "If you navigate to an object definition using the blue arrow, menu, toolbar, or function key, you can now return to the previous position in the tree using the return to object reference menu, toolbar, or function key. The Goto Object definition is also available from the Property Palette." Often the SRBs contain information that is otherwise not easily found or just does not exist in the online help system.

The SRBs may also report existing limitations, such as functions that do not work as you might expect them to (or as they are supposed to). Sometimes the SRBs provide workarounds for these limitations.

Getting Connected

Even if you have mastered all the material in the Oracle Designer help system and documentation, your education is not complete. You can take courses from Oracle and third-party vendors on Oracle Designer subjects. In addition, you may have mastered the basics, but you will be working in a void unless you get input from other people using the products.

One source for this information is Oracle Corporation itself. Oracle issues support bulletins like the one mentioned before on repository administration, and white papers such as "Oracle Designer WebServer Generator Technical Overview." These, like the SRBs, often contain information not in the manuals or help system. Some have been created in response to the most frequent user problems and questions addressed to the Oracle Support personnel. Others help get you started on new features or give hints on how to best use a product. In addition, Oracle Support personnel can look up bug fixes and workarounds if you run into problems. Oracle support also maintains useful reference material, including patches and bug fixes, on their website.

The best source for detailed information on how people use the product for real-world system development are other Oracle Designer users. There are local, regional, and international Oracle user groups with special interest groups, or SIGs, for Oracle Designer and Oracle CASE technology. Membership in these groups gives you access to their list servers and conferences where you can network by e-mail and in person with other members. The conferences are also helpful because they give practical presentations on how designers and developers are using Oracle Designer, as well as provide some advanced techniques that others have implemented.

As the popularity of Oracle Designer grows, so will these additional sources of information. The best advice is to tap in now and keep up with the flow of information. You will benefit from the experience of others and find yourself contributing your own advice.

CHAPTER
27

User Extensibility

Teacher, can I please have an extension?

he Oracle Designer repository has an enormous scope and allows you to enter almost everything you need to about a system. There will be a point, though, when you say, "How in the world do I enter this key business fact in the repository?" Often there is an answer to this question waiting for you if you scan the nodes in the Repository Object Navigator (RON) and use the help system to determine what each node represents. Inevitably, however, you will find something that is not supported.

For example, there is no place in the repository or Oracle Designer tools to enter system and user requirements. To accurately produce a system based on business needs, you have to capture the needs and requirements (not just processes and data) in some tool. Often the documentation for these requirements is kept in interview notes or a paper system or word processing document separate from the repository.

The problem with a non-repository approach is that you are not able to map the functions and entities (as well as the finished code modules and database definitions) to the requirements of the system. The intent of the system can easily be lost and key requirements missed because they are not accurately tracked. Oracle Designer contains an element that might serve the purpose—Objectives—but this is really a different concept altogether and its properties do not lend themselves easily to storing requirements. What you really need is a Requirements element that you can associate with other repository elements to help ensure that everything you do for the system is requirements-driven, or at least requirements-based.

User Extensibility is the Oracle Designer feature that allows you to add user extensions to the repository and solve the problem of missing elements. This chapter explores the methods and features of User Extensibility.

What Are User Extensions?

User extensions are additional properties or element types that you add to an existing repository. You use the Repository Administration Utility (RAU) to add, view, export, and import these extensions. This allows you to customize the repository to hold any elements you really need that are not included by default.

The example used in this chapter is that of the Requirements element and its links to the Functions element. You can use this extension to track all of the requirements gathered in the Strategy and Analysis phase and create mappings to functions and entities that you enter as usual in the Analysis phase. You can also map Requirements to Modules and Tables in the Design phase so you can cross-check that the design elements handle the stated requirements of the system.

To be effective with user extensions, you have to understand two related concepts. You need to be familiar with the high-level architecture of the repository so you can prepare to make changes to it, and you have to learn to use the RAU User Extensibility features.

Elements, Associations, and Text Types

You will find it useful to start by reviewing the repository architecture. These discussions refer to the metamodel, or the "model of the system model," and how to relate it to elements and associations in RON. Keep in mind that the discussion pertains to element and association types, not instances. For example, it refers to the Entity element type, which RON represents as the Entity node in its hierarchy. This type can have many instances, which RON represents as the entities themselves: for example, PERSON, PHONE, and ORGANIZATION. Also keep in mind that the discussion does not pertain to the tables or views where Oracle Designer stores or presents these items, but only to the concepts about and structures for the data.

All structures for the data in the repository can be divided into three main conceptual types:

- *Element types*, which include Functions, Modules, Entities, Tables, and Columns. These are both the high-level nodes (for example, Tables) and some lower-level nodes (for example, Columns for those tables) you see in RON. Each element type consists of a set of properties, discrete facts about the element type. For example, the table *Name* and *Display Title* are properties of the Table element type. RON represents properties as the rows that appear in the Property Palette.

- *Association types*, which include Function Entity Data Usage, Module Function Usage, Table Entity Usage, and Tables Implemented in Schemas. These relationships are defined between particular element types and are represented in RON's Usages nodes. Association types, like element types, are composed of a set of properties, which appear as rows in the RON property sheet.

- *Text types*, which include Description, Notes, Select Text, and Where/Validation Condition. Unlike element and association types, text types do not include discrete properties, but consist of one area which can contain multiline text. Text types appear in RON as properties of an element or association, but they are conceptually separate types.

Each repository type can be defined as a combination of properties and text type usage. Text type usage indicates the kind of text you are storing for an element or association—such as Description, Notes, or Where/Validation Condition. RON also shows the text type usages as rows in the Property Palette even though they are stored apart from the element instance. Text types use text type usages to indicate which element types use them.

Table 27-1 shows the symbols that the RAU User Extensibility window uses to represent each type.

Figure 27-1 shows this system of types and properties.

Type	User Extensibility Window
Element	
Association	
Text	

TABLE 27-1. *Repository Types*

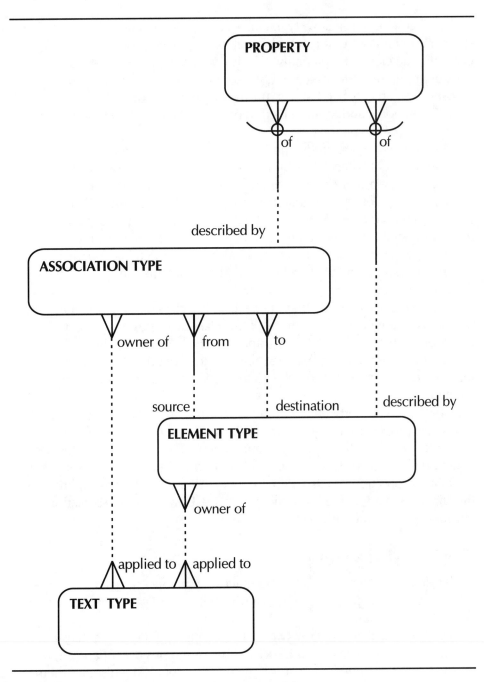

FIGURE 27-1. *The repository types metamodel*

This figure represents the type classes and property class which serve as structural definitions of the actual repository type and property. For example, the element type entity on this diagram represents the class or category of all repository element types. This class is instantiated in the repository as objects like Entities, Business Functions, Table Definitions, View Definitions, and Module Definitions. All of these are members of the same class: the element type.

Similarly, the association type serves as a class for all relationships between element types. For example, the association type on this diagram represents the class or category of all repository association types. The association type class is instantiated in the repository as objects like Function Entity Usages, Module Network, and Table Entity Usage. All of these are members of the same class: association type. Since there are multiple instantiations of the association type, implicitly there are multiple instantiations of the relationship lines that link the element type to the association type.

The text type on this diagram represents the class or category of all repository text types. Instantiations of this class are repository objects like Description, Notes, PL/SQL Block, and User/Help Text. As with the association type relationships, the relationships from the text type are instantiated in the repository when a text type links to an association or element type.

Finally, the Property entity on this diagram represents the class of all repository properties. Instantiations of this class are properties of repository types like *Name* for the Function element type, *Short Name* for a Business Function element type, and *Prompt* for a Column element type. Since there are many properties for each element type, the single relationship lines on this diagram that link the Property class to the Element and Association classes represent multiple instantiations.

Element Types

The User Extension area in the RAU makes these concepts clearer. Figure 27-2 shows the User Extensibility window with a portion of the element types node expanded.

The RAU displays only the Name, Comment, and the user-extensible properties (such as Usrx0 and Usrx1). Other properties do not appear, as they are system-defined and cannot be modified, but RON displays them for each instance of the element type as in Figure 27-3.

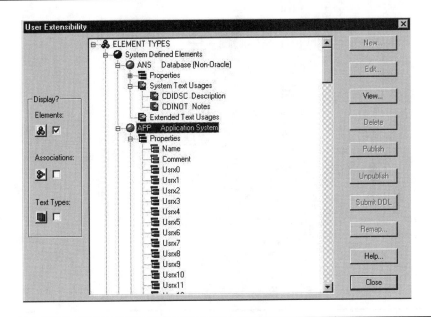

FIGURE 27-2. *Element types and properties in RAU*

The properties and element types in Figure 27-3 are *published* items—meaning they have been fully incorporated into the repository with views and procedure packages to represent them. If you create a new element type, you automatically assign *Name* and *Comment* properties and can also define some or all of the Usrx properties that are not normally displayed in RON. Once you publish the definition, the element type and properties appear in RON. You'll see an example of this later.

The RAU uses different colors and symbols to represent repository types in different states of completion. The colors are:

■ **Blue**   Used for the parent node only (element type, association type, or text type)

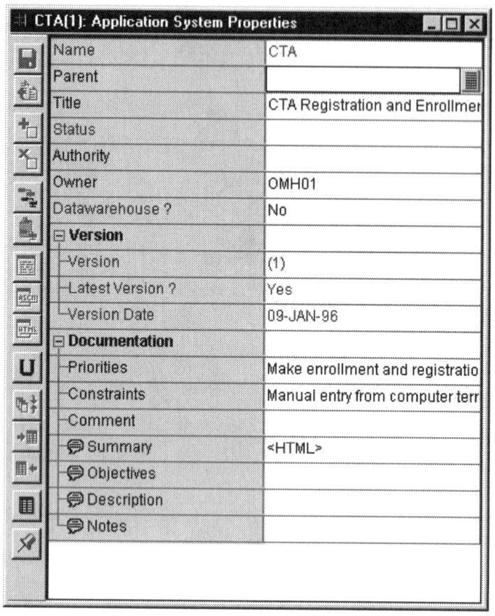

FIGURE 27-3. *Application system properties in RON*

- ■ **Green** Used for published extensions
- ■ **Red** Used for unpublished extensions

Table 27-2 lists the symbol used for each repository element type.

In RAU, you can also look at the details of element and property definitions. Figure 27-4 shows the Application System element type definition, and Figure 27-5 shows the *Name* property definition of the Application System type. These figures show examples of the details you will fill in when you create your own element types and properties.

Any element type may have one or more text type usages, as shown by the many-to-many relationship between text type and element type in Figure 27-1. Figure 27-6 shows the Application System element with its text type usages (CDISUM, CDIOBJ, CDIDSC, and CDINOT). You can extend the definition of an element by adding text type usages. The new usages will appear in the RON properties window as properties although each really represents a one-to-many relationship with the specified text type.

Type Subnode Symbol	Repository Element Type
	Element type
	Association type
	Property type
	Text type
	Text type usage

TABLE 27-2. *User Extensibility Dialog Symbols*

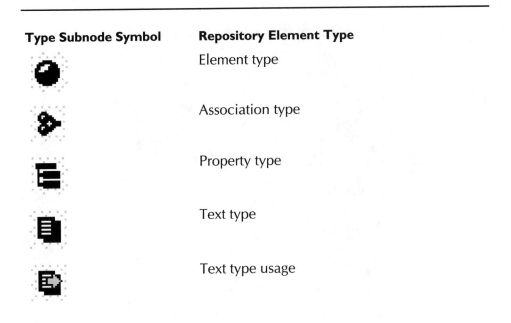

FIGURE 27-4. *Application System element definition*

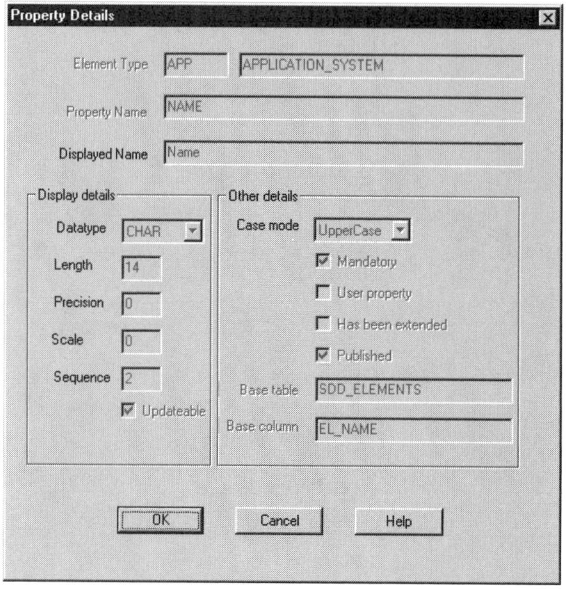

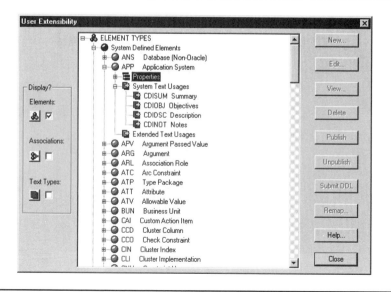

FIGURE 27-5. *Name property definition*

FIGURE 27-6. *Application System element with its text types*

Association Types

Association types denote a relationship or link between two element types. Like element types, association types may have both properties and text types usages. Figure 27-7 shows the definition dialog for association type Function Entity Usage, and Figure 27-8 shows the corresponding RON Property Palette.

Text Types

Text types differ from element and association types in that they have no properties, only text type usages that indicate which element and association types use the text type. Text types are at the end of the many-to-many relationships in Figure 27-1. For example, Figure 27-9 shows that the CDIDSC Description text type has many usages, which are element and association types. Figure 27-10 shows the Details dialog for the

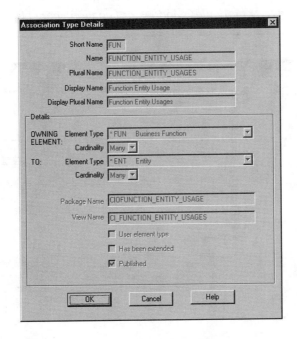

FIGURE 27-7.   *Definition of the Function Entity Usage association type*

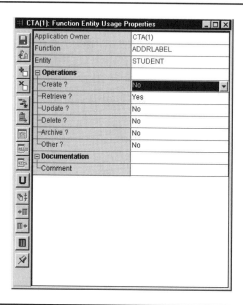

FIGURE 27-8. *RON properties window for Function Entity Usage*

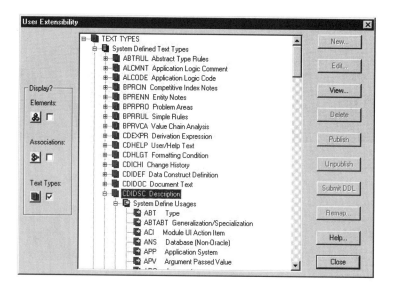

FIGURE 27-9. *Text type CDIDSC and its usages*

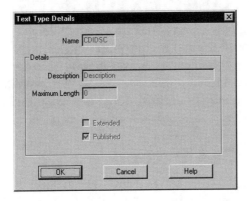

FIGURE 27-10. *Text type definition*

Description text type. Figure 27-11 shows the dialog for specifying the usage of a text type.

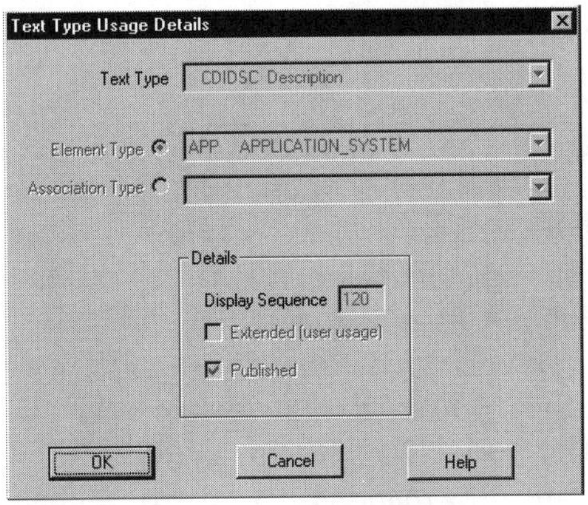

FIGURE 27-11. *Definition of a text type usage*

Creating User Extensions

The task of creating user extensions has a deceptively easy learning curve. If you follow the steps described in this chapter in conjunction with reviewing the Oracle Designer help topics you will be able to extend your repository and support your additional repository needs with very little effort. Heed all the cautions, tips, and notes because some of the actions you take in extending the repository cannot be easily reversed.

What You Can Extend

Using this system of repository types and their properties, Oracle Designer provides all the nodes in the hierarchy that you see in RON. You can customize the repository with RAU's User Extensibility feature to add up to 500 new element and 500 new association types or an unlimited number of text types and usages; you can also add up to 20 new properties for each type. Adding element and association types uses one of the predefined but unassigned types named E0 to E499 and A0 to A499, for elements and associations, respectively. Adding text types defines a new type with any unused name. Adding properties is just a matter of defining a new name and datatype for one or more of the 20 unassigned Usrx properties (called User-Defined Property 0 through User-Defined Property 19) already attached to each element type but not shown in RON.

CAUTION
Be careful when defining properties of existing elements. If you make a user-extended property mandatory, you will be unable to insert the definition through a property dialog or other tool that does not display the extended property. For example, assume that you add a user-extended property called Table Usage and make it mandatory. If you try to draw a new table in the Server Model Diagram, the action will fail because the new mandatory property has no value and there is no way to fill it in using the property dialog.

If you decide to define extra properties for an existing element or association, remember that the properties you see in RAU are only the extensible ones (and *Name* and *Comments*), so be sure a property whose name matches the one you want to create does not already exist.

TIP
The repository stores audit information on each definition. However, audit-related properties are not displayed by default. In RON, choose **Options→Customize Properties Palette** *from the menu. Then click the check box for* Show Audit Properties. *Once that is checked, you will be able to see the name of the person who created and last changed any properties of the element type and when these actions occurred.*

How to Define User Extensions in RAU

When reviewing the User Extensibility window you will see that each repository element type can contain definitions that are either System or User Defined. System-Defined types are included as part of the standard Oracle Designer repository. User-Defined types are created as extensions to the repository.

As shown here,

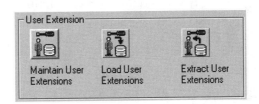

RAU provides three tools in its User Extension area to accomplish the following:

- *Maintain User Extensions* for creating, changing, and viewing user extensions

- *Load User Extensions* for bringing user extensions into the repository from an export file created with the Extract User Extensions utility

■ *Extract User Extensions* for creating the export file that stores the user extensions

The last two tools are used only for importing and exporting the extended definitions and are well documented in the help system. You use the first tool to perform the main work of creating and modifying user extensions, so the following discussion will focus on this tool.

Steps for Creating a User Extension

There are four major steps to creating a User Extension property or type.

1. Make a plan.

2. Define the new objects.

3. Publish the extensions.

4. Reconcile grants.

Remember that you can press the Help button to get more information on the process and details on particular steps as you work.

I. Make a Plan

Make a plan of the steps you will take and, if desired, draw an ERD of the new items like the one in Figure 27-12. If you have elements that have a relationship or link, you'll need to define an association type (for example, REQUIREMENT FOR FUNCTION).

CAUTION
When you publish a new type or property,
you will change all application systems
in the repository.

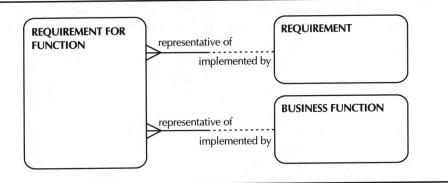

FIGURE 27-12.   *ERD of proposed element and association*

TIP
Perform a full user export of the repository to create a .DMP file via RAU before you start working on the extensions. In addition, try to work on the extensions when no one else is using the repository. If you make a serious mistake, you can delete the repository and import the .DMP file to restore the original state of the repository or you can unpublish the extension as described next.

2. Define the New Objects

Click the Maintain User Extensions button in RAU. If you want to create a new type (element, association, or text), expand the hierarchy so that the User Defined node is available. Choose that node. Click the New button (or choose New from the right-click menu) to display the Details dialog for the selected type and fill in all items there. Click OK. Note that the new type's symbol on the User Extensibility window is red, indicating that it is unpublished. Do not publish yet.

The element and association types are automatically named with a letter and number (like E7). If possible you should not change these names; they will help you clearly identify these items as user extensions. This reference name will not be visible anywhere other than in this utility (and in the base table, of course). Elsewhere, you will refer to the new item by the name you assign. Be sure to define properties for the new element. Figure 27-13 shows the Details dialog for the Requirement element type.

For the Requirement example, you also need to define a new association type for User Req to Function. The Association Type Details dialog requires you to specify the cardinality of the link between the associated elements. Specify the cardinality carefully—you usually want many-to-many associations so the link will appear under both elements. Figure 27-14 shows the Details dialog for the new User Req to Function association type. The Business Function (FUN) has an asterisk to its left. This indicates that FUN is a published element. Conversely, REQ, the extended element, does not have an asterisk to its left, indicating that the REQ extension has not yet been published.

After defining the element and association types, you can assign names to the extensible Usrx properties. Expand the new element and its Properties

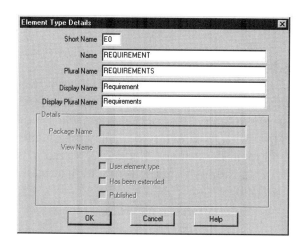

FIGURE 27-13. *Definition of the Requirement element type*

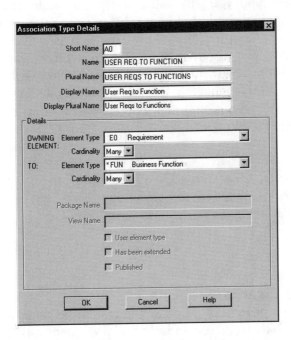

FIGURE 27-14. *Definition of the User Req to Function association type*

subnode. Then, select the Usrx property you want to use and choose Edit.
Fill in the items on the Property Details dialog and click OK. Do not
publish yet.

   If you want to create a new text type usage, expand the node of the type
you want to add it to until you see the Extended Text Type Usages node.
Choose that node, click the New button (or select New from the right-click
menu), and fill in the Details dialog that appears. Click OK and do not
publish yet.

3. Publish the Extensions

Even though you can unpublish later it is a good idea to back up the repository
before publishing so you can restore it if needed after the extension process.
Click the Publish button for each type after you have checked your work. If you

are defining a new type, you will be prompted to indicate whether you also want to publish unpublished properties. This means you are confirming that you want the Usrx properties for the new extension as well as the new extension; normally you would click OK because you do want properties as well as the extension. Then you will be prompted as to whether you want to run the data definition language (DDL) script to generate the views and packages. This is not an optional step, but you can perform it later with the Submit DDL button if you wish.

NOTE
Running the DDL is not necessary if the only change you have made is to add properties to an existing element type, but you do have to perform the Full Reconcile described in step 4 next.

4. Reconcile Grants

The last step in the process is to update the grants and synonyms for repository users so they can see and use the new extensions. Click the Recreate button in the RAU Repository Maintenance area. Choose Full Recompile, and RAU will run scripts to update user grants and synonyms so users can use the new elements or properties.

Unpublishing the User Extension

If you want to delete or edit the user extension, you first need to unpublish it. You can unpublish the extension only if you have not used it to add element definitions to the repository. In other words, if you start using the extension by defining elements, you will not be able to unpublish until you remove those element definitions. In addition, if there are other element or association types that reference the one you want to remove or change, you must remove the association before unpublishing. Once those conditions are met, you click on the element, association, or text type you wish to unpublish and click the Unpublish button in the User Extensibility dialog. If there are user-defined properties, a dialog will appear where you will make a choice whether to unpublish those properties. If you want to edit the extension, you can do so at this time by clicking the Edit button. If you want to delete the extension, click the Delete button. If you get an error message, you may still need to break the links to whatever element type is linked. If the delete is successful it will also remove the supporting API view and package.

Remapping the User Extension

If you wish to change the Short Name of an extension, you can use the Remap facility. You might use this, for example, if you need to rename the element E0 to E8. This would be necessary if you were importing an extension from another repository (see the "Import/Export" section later in this chapter) and that repository already contained an element E0.

To perform the Remap, choose the item that you want to change and click the Remap button. A dialog will appear similar to the one in the following illustration. When you have entered the new name click the OK button. The change is now complete, and there is no need to publish or Submit DDL.

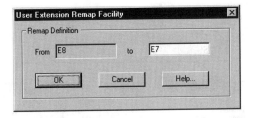

How to Access the User Extension

Your repository will now have new elements and properties. You will be able to view all of the new extensions in RON, while only some extensions are available in the Matrix Diagrammer and the Design Editor. The extensions are not available in any of the other Oracle Designer tools.

In RON be sure you specify that you want to see user extensions in the Hierarchy window by selecting the User Extensions check box in the **View→Include Navigator Groups** dialog before you open the application system.

When you open a new diagram in the Matrix Diagrammer you will see your element types on either side of your extended associations. Of course, if you did not add an extended element into an association you will not be able to see it in the Matrix Diagrammer.

After extending the repository you will want to view the extensions in RON, Design Editor, and the Matrix Diagrammer. If during the publishing process the tool you are going to use to check your extension was open, you should close it and reopen it before proceeding so that it picks up the repository changes. Start by checking RON for the new node or property in an element. It will appear if you have set the view as just described. The Property Palette will show the new Property as in this illustration (*Last Designed By*).

If you also defined an association, you will not see that node until you create an element of one of the types. Figure 27-15 shows the new Requirements element with an association node under one of its instances.

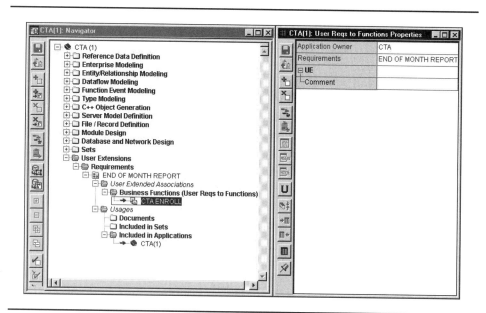

FIGURE 27-15. *New Requirements element*

What's Next?

After following the previous steps to define an extension, you can report on definitions you create in the new extended types using Repository Reports in the User Extensions group, such as the following:

- *Text Definition*   Report for definitions and usages of text types

- *Detailed <Element> Definition*   Report for properties of a specified element's use

- *Element Type Definition*   Report for the definition of a given element type including associations in which the element participates

- *All Text Held against an Element*   Report for details about the element

While the RON and Matrix Diagrammer (and Design Editor for properties) are the only Oracle Designer front-end tools you can use to access your new elements and properties, the API allows you to write your own front-end in an appropriate tool such as Oracle Forms or SQL*Plus. You can make this as flexible as you want. Although your tool will not be accessible from the Oracle Designer menus, the information you are manipulating is contained in the repository so you can query and update data from other elements as well as the new ones, if needed. The publishing process creates a package (for example, CIOREQUIREMENT) and a view (for example, CI_REQUIREMENTS). You would use these in your API work to manage the new elements.

API for User Extensions

You can actually affect the definitions of User Extensions before they are published using API packages. The online API help documentation includes a topic called "User Extensibility Support" that describes how you can call the INS, UPD, and DEL procedures for packages that manage User Extensions. These packages also allow you to publish the extension through an API call. The packages have names like CIOUE_ELEMENT_TYPE and CIOUE_ASSOCIATION_TYPE and allow you to change or insert definitions of pre-published extensions.

This might be useful if you wanted to create and publish a large number of User Extensions through an API script instead of the RAU front-end tool. There are views that correspond to these packages with names like CIUE_ELEMENT_TYPES and CIUE_ASSOCIATION_TYPES, which display the contents of the user-extended types.

Import/Export

If you need to export an application system from an extended repository into an archive file (through **Application→Archive** in RON), the user extensions require special handling. If the user extensions you created in the source repository do not exist in the target repository, you have to export them from the source repository using the RAU function *Extract User Extensions*. This creates a .DMP file that you can load into the target repository with the *Load User Extensions* RAU function. You can then proceed with the Archive and Restore as usual and your extended elements will be loaded.

CAUTION
A conflict will occur when the target repository already contains the same named extension (say E3) as the source repository but these elements are used for different purposes. The same type of problem applies to extended properties that exist in both repositories but are used differently. The rule-of-thumb here is to be sure the repository you are importing into has exactly the same extensions as the repository from which you are exporting.

CHAPTER
28

Application
Programmatic Interface

Beneath the Planet of the APIs

s you work in the CADM life cycle, you may discover activities you wish to perform that cannot be done with the supplied set of Oracle Designer tools and repository elements, despite their sophistication and scope. One of the key benefits of Oracle Designer is its capability of storing all information regarding a system design in the repository, but you may find something particular in your situation that has no default place in the repository. The way to solve the problem of not being able to store a particular type of data is to employ the User Extensibility feature as Chapter 27 describes. However, once you add properties or elements to the repository, you need a way to put information into them and query them. While RON and the Matrix Diagrammer serve as ubiquitous overseers of all repository data, including extensions that you add to the default properties and elements, sometimes you need a tool that's faster or easier-to-use than these to access the extensions you created.

No CASE tool could be written to handle all possible variations of requirements in all environments. However, Oracle Designer provides the Application Programmatic Interface (API) to help you handle these variations. The API opens the repository so you can write your own extensions to the tools and safely manipulate virtually any element in the repository. The API allows you to input and output information from the base repository elements as well as the ones you add with the User Extensibility feature. Although you need to write some code (or have Oracle Designer write it for you) to access the repository through the API, you can use it to do almost anything with the repository elements. The API allows you to manipulate the meta-data in a way that makes sense for your project and compensates for a wide range of problems that arise because of limitations in the built-in Oracle Designer functionality.

Thus, you should seriously consider learning and using the API, although it may seem like an advanced feature. As you work with Oracle Designer, you will surely need some functionality specific to your working environment or project that was not designed into the tools. In addition, you may be able to perform a task with the Oracle Designer tools, but the task may be extremely repetitive and prone to error. The API can help you here, too. For all of these reasons, learning about the API is really a required step toward full understanding and optimal use of Oracle Designer.

The first step toward using the API is to dig as deeply as you can into the documentation and other sources to determine whether the function you want to perform really is missing from Oracle Designer. Working with the API is not difficult, but there is a learning curve, and you will have to spend time creating program code to access the repository. Therefore, planning not only what to do, but the best way to do it, will save time in the long run. Just as you would take time addressing any application development need, take time for analysis and design before you jump in and begin building an API routine.

This chapter explores the components of the API, how to get started using the API, and what the API can and cannot do. In addition, it discusses a sample front-end application that uses Oracle Forms and the API to access and update repository elements.

What Is the API?

The API is a set of database views and PL/SQL packages in the repository owner's schema that allow safe access to the repository data (or meta-data). The repository consists of a relatively small number of tables that store the actual data. These tables have complex (undocumented) relationships, and Oracle does not support direct access to them using standard Data Manipulation Language (DML) SQL statements. There are, however, many views of these tables that represent actual repository objects, such as entities and attributes. These views are an important part of the API because they allow you to examine the definitions you create in your application systems.

The API also consists of the PL/SQL packages that allow you to change the contents of the tables safely outside of the Oracle Designer front-end. These packages allow you to supplement the Oracle Designer diagrammers and utilities with your own front-end programs or code. The Oracle Designer tools also use the API to insert, update, delete, and select data from the repository. Therefore, when you use the API, you are using the same method Oracle Designer uses to manipulate the repository. Figure 28-1 shows how the API works with front-end tools to access and manipulate the repository data. Note that API packages provide the only method for writing to the repository, and all front-end tools use them, whether they are Oracle Designer tools or your own.

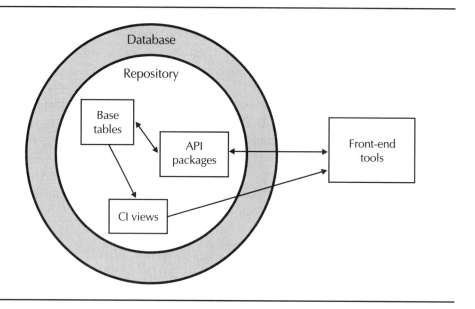

FIGURE 28-1. *API access to the repository*

NOTE
To be most effective when using the API, you need to be relatively fluent with the SQL and PL/SQL languages. If you are using only the view component of the API, the SQL language SELECT statement will serve you well. If you intend to modify or store repository data with the API packages, you will also need a good understanding of PL/SQL control structures, packages, and record variables.

Getting Started with the API

In addition to an understanding of the SQL and PL/SQL languages, you need a good understanding of the elements and properties that you want to modify or manipulate. The steps you take when using the API are typically the following:

1. Identify the views and packages you need.

2. Obtain detailed information on those views and packages.

3. Create the API code.

After you get some experience with the API, the first two steps may take no effort at all if you know the details of the views and packages. With or without experience, the first step should be straightforward. If you have suitably analyzed your needs, you should already know what elements are involved in the activity you wish to perform, or you should at least be able to look in RON to find their names.

Detailed Information on Views and Packages

Once you know the names of the element or association types, you can consult the documentation for more information. The main documentation for the API is in the online help system and in diagrams of the meta-model views that are shipped with the product.

API in the Help System

Repository Application Programmatic Interface Help, shown in Figure 28-2, is available from the Programs group of the Windows Start menu by selecting **Designer 2.1→Designer API**.

From this topic, you can load other topics that explain the meta-model in general and provide reference information as well as a sample program. The reference information contains topics on the API views (View/Element Type Definitions) and packages (API Call Information). Once you know the elements you are using, you can use these two topics to obtain detailed information on the calling syntax, view columns, and related views.

You will also find interesting and useful information in the Repository API System Release Bulletin (SRB) that you can get to by clicking **Designer 2.1 Bulletins→Repository API SRB**. For example, items 2 and 3 in the SRB will inform you that even though the style and general manner in which you use the API have not changed from version 1.3 of Oracle Designer, some of the packages have changed because of additional and removed elements.

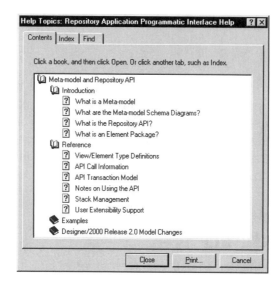

FIGURE 28-2. *API Help contents*

API in the Meta-Model Diagrams

Oracle Designer ships with a set of diagrams, in a set of hard-copy documentation called "Repository Model Documentation Set," that shows the API views and their relationships. These are standard Server Model Diagrams, with foreign key relationships between views and a notation of the view name and primary key. The views are grouped into the following subsets, with each subset taking up one page:

- Business Planning Model

- Business Requirement Model

- Database Administrator Model

- Database Schema Model

- Index Storage and Partitioning Model

- Detailed Module Design Model (General)

- Detailed Module Design Model (PL/SQL)

- Module Design Model

- Server Model

- Object Database Designer Model

Which model you need to look at depends on the type of element you are manipulating. If you want to examine Design phase elements such as tables and columns, the Database Schema Model is appropriate. If you want to view the relationships between meta-model views for the application modules, you consult the Module Design Model.

API Code

Once you have identified the views and packages you need and know the details of each, you can create the SQL or PL/SQL script to do the work. If you are just querying the views, a SQL SELECT script will work, although you can alternatively use the API packages. If you are performing an insert, update, or delete operation on a repository view, you need to write a PL/SQL script to do this. The PL/SQL block can be stored as a procedure or package in the database or run as an anonymous block from any SQL front-end tool such as SQL*Plus. The SQL SELECT syntax is no different from the code you use to perform normal queries. However, special considerations and routines apply to the PL/SQL syntax, as described in the sections "API Packages" and "API Transaction Model," later in this chapter.

API Views

The repository base tables have names with prefixes such as SDD_ and CDI_—for example, SDD_ELEMENTS, SDD_STRUCTURE_ELEMENTS, and CDI_TEXT. These tables are highly normalized, and a handful of tables serves as the basis for many different element types. For example, table definitions are stored in the SDD_ELEMENTS table with a value of "TAB" for the EL_TYPE_OF column and a value of "TABLE" for the EL_OCCUR_TYPE column. You can always look at the view definitions (in the ALL_VIEWS data dictionary view) to see how the definitions for a particular element are stored in the SDD_ELEMENTS table, but all you really need to know is the name of the view.

Most API views have names starting with CI_ and ending with the plural name of the element. For example, the view that shows entity definitions is called CI_ENTITIES, and the view that shows table definitions is called CI_TABLE_DEFINITIONS. Once you have determined the names of the views by looking in the help system topics as mentioned before, you can access the names of the columns in those views in the same help area. The column information consists of the datatype, size, and in most cases a brief description of the column and its valid values.

TIP
There are columns in all repository views called CREATED_BY and CHANGED_BY. You can use these to determine when the definition of a particular element was inserted or updated. You can, for example, issue a query that lists all table definitions that have been created or changed in the last week.

View Columns and Sample Script

View columns correspond roughly on a one-to-one basis with the properties of the element that the view represents. Each view has an ID column containing a number that identifies the element uniquely within the repository. Most element views also have a NAME column that holds the name you see in RON. In addition, there are other columns that correspond with the properties of the element. For example, the CI_ATTRIBUTES view has such columns as FORMAT (for the datatype), OPTIONAL_FLAG (which indicates whether the attribute is nullable), MAXIMUM_LENGTH, and DEFAULT_VALUE. If you know the properties of an attribute, you will be able to interpret what these view columns contain. In addition, the help system description of the columns can assist.

The CI_ATTRIBUTES view also contains a column called ENTITY_REFERENCE that contains a number acting as a foreign key that references the ID column of the CI_ENTITIES view. With this information, you can construct the following query to show details on all attributes in the EMPLOYEE entity:

L 28-1
```
SELECT a.name, a.format, a.maximum_length, a.optional_flag
   FROM ci_entities e, ci_attributes a
  WHERE e.id = a.entity_reference
    AND e.name = 'EMPLOYEE' ;
```

If you have an EMPLOYEE entity in more than one application system, you will need to work the CI_APPLICATION_SYSTEMS view into the query. This view displays information on the properties of the application systems. The unique identifier is ID, as usual, but the foreign key column in CI_ENTITIES that refers to the application system is APPLICATION_ SYSTEM_OWNED_BY. Therefore, the query to find attributes of an EMPLOYEE entity owned by an application system called CTA, version 1, would become

L 28-2
```
SELECT a.name, a.format, a.maximum_length, a.optional_flag
   FROM ci_entities e,
        ci_attributes a,
        ci_application_systems s
 WHERE e.id = a.entity_reference
   AND s.id = e.application_system_owned_by
   AND s.name = 'CTA'
   AND s.version = 1
   AND e.name = 'EMPLOYEE' ;
```

If you do not know the version number and want to ensure that you are accessing the current application system, remove the s.version = 1 and replace it with s.latest_version_flag = 'Y'.

You can use this same method—finding the element names and properties in the help system, checking for foreign key relationships, and constructing the SELECT statement with standard SQL syntax—for most API queries.

Getting API Information from the Oracle Designer Navigators

When performing queries on the API views, it is sometimes useful to know the ID of a particular element definition. You cannot see the ID number for element definitions in any of the Oracle Designer tools. To find an element definition's ID, select the element node in the hierarchy, click a property in the property palette, and press F5. A Property Details dialog will appear that contains the ID of the element along with the object type, base table name, and details of the property.

A sample Property Details dialog is shown in Figure 28-3. This dialog is based on the *Latest Version ?* property found in the Property Palette of an application system.

The Property Details dialog is divided into two sections. The top section (labeled Object Details) provides base table and view (that is, element)

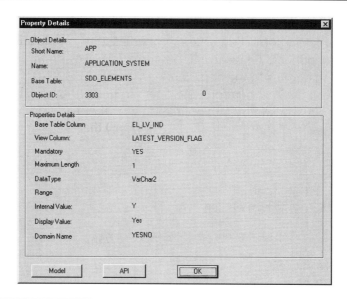

FIGURE 28-3. *A Property Details window*

information while the bottom section (labeled Properties Details) shows detailed information about what is stored in the base table (that is, property information). If you review Figure 28-3, you will find the following:

- *Short Name* A short name for the type of element. It is taken from CI_APPLICATION_SYSTEMS.ELEMENT_TYPE_NAME.

- *Name* The name of the view that is used to retrieve the property data. In this example the name is APPLICATION_SYSTEM. Since repository view names have the prefix CI_ and are plural, the name of the view is CI_APPLICATION_SYSTEMS.

- *Base Table* The name of the actual table from which the view specified in Name gets its data. The view CI_APPLICATION_ SYSTEMS is based on the table SDD_ELEMENTS.

■ *Object ID*   Almost every CI view has an ID column that uniquely identifies an element instance. In the example, this value is drawn from CI_APPLICATION_SYSTEMS.ID.

■ *Base Table Column*   The name of the column in the base table that contains the *Latest Version* ? (SDD_ELEMENTS.EL_LV_IND).

■ *View Column*   The name of the column (LATEST_VERSION_FLAG) in the view (CI_APPLICATION_SYSTEMS) that represents the *Latest Version* ? property.

■ *Mandatory*   States whether this property is mandatory or optional.

■ *Maximum Length*   States the maximum length of the property's Internal Value (described shortly).

■ *DataType*   The datatype of the Internal Value.

■ *Range*   For a property that stores a numeric value there may be a low and high numeric domain. *Latest Version ?* does not contain a numeric value so there is no range. If you look at the property's Details window for the *Version* property you will see that the range is from 1 through 999.

■ *Internal Value*   This is what actually is stored in the SDD_ELEMENTS table. Maximum Length and DataType both refer to the storage of the value in the base table.

■ *Display Value*   Represents how the Internal Value is represented in the Property Palette. The value for *Latest Version ?* is stored as "Y," but is displayed as "Yes."

■ *Domain Name*   An internal domain Oracle Designer uses as a valid values list for the property. This list is maintained in the REF_VALUES table. So, if you want to find all the possible values for this domain you could issue the query:

L 28-3
```
SELECT *
  FROM ref_values
 WHERE ref_domain = 'YESNO' ;
```

In addition to the values shown, the Property Details window includes these buttons:

- Model   Opens an HTML page displaying the Property Detail information for each of the properties on the current Property Palette.

- API   Opens an HTML page displaying information about the API package that is used to access the information in the current Property Palette. You can also retrieve a list of each API package specification in the speclist.html file in the ORACLE_HOME/CDOC70/api/specs directory.

API Packages

More than 400 PL/SQL packages make up the API. These are organized like the views, so there is one package (prefixed with CIO) for each of the repository element types—for example, CIOCOLUMN, CIOTABLE_DEFINITION, CIO_VIEW_DEFINITION, CIOAPPLICATION_SYSTEM. You can think of the views as base tables that have a one-to-one relationship with the object types in RON, and the packages as the code you use to perform DML on those tables. Each package contains procedures with the following names:

INS for insert operations
UPD for update operations
DEL for delete operations
SEL for select operations

NOTE
Some API packages and views support user-extended properties and elements as well as text types. These allow you to define and publish new extended properties and elements. Other packages contain procedures to update some user extensions and to delete user-extended elements that have not been published. More information on these packages and views is available in Chapter 27 and in the API help system under the topic "Reference – User Extensibility Support."

For example, the CIOCOLUMN.INS procedure creates a new record in the repository tables as displayed through the CI_COLUMNS view. These API procedures perform validation checking, so if a value you are updating relates to or affects another object, the repository state will not be corrupted. For example, if you try to remove a primary key column that is referenced by a foreign key constraint, the API will stop you because the constraint would then be invalid. Although you can select directly from the view, the package allows you to select from it as well (using the SEL procedure).

As mentioned, the help system for the API contains calling information for these packages.

Package Contents and Sample Code

The procedures in the API package use as parameters the ID number of the element you want to work on (for UPD, DEL, and SEL) and a record variable that contains the data (for INS, UPD, and SEL). Each package has a record variable called "data" (actually a record of records) that you can use to type a variable in your PL/SQL block. For example, if you design capture a table, its *Display Title* property will be null. If you want to fill the *Display Title* property of all the design captured tables with a value similar to what the Database Design Transformer creates, you can declare a variable, in a PL/SQL block of your own, as follows:

L 28-4
```
DECLARE
    r_tab  ciotable_definition.data;
```

You then load a member of this record variable with the value you want to use to update the property of the element:

L 28-5
```
r_tab.v.display_title := 'Employees';
```

The "v" member indicates that this is a value. The "i" member acts as an indicator to the API that you have changed this property:

L 28-6
```
r_tab.i.display_title := TRUE;
```

The last step is to issue the update statement, passing as parameters the ID number of the column definition and the PL/SQL record that contains the updated data and indicators.

L 28-7
```
ciotable_definition.upd(v_tabid, r_tab);
```

Other API package calls are needed to create a transaction and close it correctly, but the essence of the operation is in loading the record variable and passing it to the API procedure. The next section discusses the transaction model gives an example of the code you need to write to implement it. For another complete example, click the "PL/SQL Program" topic link on the main contents page of the API help system.

API Transaction Model

In addition to the API calls already mentioned, there are API calls that implement a transaction model that handles the logical beginning and end of a unit of work. This is somewhat like the standard SQL transaction model that uses COMMIT and ROLLBACK statements to mark and reverse transactions. However, the API transaction model uses a few more steps and methods to handle errors.

The intention of the transaction model is to provide a way to validate statements as a set rather than as individuals. During an API transaction, or activity, Oracle Designer constraints and rules defined for elements can be temporarily violated without aborting the operation. For example, when you enter the definition for a relationship between two entities, you have to make an entry for both ends of the relationship. However, if there is no concept of an activity and you enter the first relationship end without the second, an error state will occur, and the action will be rejected. The transaction model temporarily disables rule and validation checking until you state that the transaction is complete. This allows you to establish complex associations and dependencies as the transaction is taking place, but it still enforces the rules and validations at the end of the transaction.

The transaction model is handled mostly by the CDAPI package and consists of the steps listed in Table 28-1.

TIP
You can call cdapi.close_activity (as described in Table 28-1) without first calling cdapi.validate_activity. This will provide an increase in performance while maintaining data integrity checking, but will not display any warnings.

Step	Sample Call	Notes
Initialize	`cdapi.initialize ('CTA', 1);`	Declares which application system and version you are using. You need to perform this step only once each session for each application system.
Open	`cdapi.open_activity;`	Starts the activity (transaction).
Load record variable values	`r_tab.v.display_title := 'Employees'`	Populates a value in the record variable, representing a potential change to repository property.
Load record variable indictors	`r_tab.i.display_title := TRUE`	Signifies that a particular property value is changing.
Perform the "DML"	`ciotable_definition.upd (3712, r_tab)`	Updates the repository definition.
Validate	`cdapi.validate_activity (v_status, v_warning)`	Checks whether the action succeeded (a v_status of 'Y' is returned if the transaction succeeded).
Report Errors	`cdapi.instantiate_ message`	Returns an error message and takes as parameters values from the CI_VIOLATIONS view that is loaded automatically when an error occurs.
Close	`cdapi.close_activity (v_status)`	Validates the data and state at the end of the transaction.
Abort upon failure	`cdapi.abort_activity;`	Rolls back the transaction if an error occurs in the close process.

TABLE 28-1. *Steps in an API Transaction*

The following sample uses some of the calls shown in Table 28-1 to update the *Display Title* property of a table.

NOTE
The user running the code must have update privileges to the application system as granted in RON. See Chapter 26 for details.

L 28-8

```
DECLARE
    r_tab    ciotable_definition.data;
    v_tabid  ci_table_definitions.id%TYPE;
    v_status cdapi.activity_status%TYPE;
BEGIN
    /*
    || Get information for Repository transaction
    */
    -- Find the ID of the table to be affected
    SELECT t.id
      INTO v_tabid
      FROM ci_table_definitions t,
           ci_application_systems s
     WHERE s.id = t.application_system_owned_by
       AND s.name = 'CTA'
       AND s.version = 1
       AND t.name = 'EMPLOYEES' ;
    /*
    || Begin repository transaction
    */
    cdapi.initialize('CTA',1);
    cdapi.open_activity;
    -- Load record variable values
    r_tab.v.display_title := 'Employees';
    -- Load record variable indicator
    r_tab.i.display_title := TRUE;
    -- Perform the "DML"
    ciotable_definition.upd(v_tabid, r_tab);
    /*
    || End repository transaction
    */
```

```
   cdapi.close_activity(v_status);
     IF v_status != 'Y'
     THEN
         -- Abort upon failure
         cdapi.abort_activity;
     END IF;
END;
```

The two steps that load record variables may consist of multiple statements if you are inserting an element definition or updating more than one property at a time. In addition, you can choose to validate (close) the activity whenever you want. For example, you can loop through a number of records and update each before closing the activity. The validation will be deferred until the close, so if any of the records violate the constraints, the entire set will be rolled back. This behavior is similar to that of the SQL transaction model and should be familiar territory.

Having seen this simple example of an API script, you will find it easy to add the loop that would fulfill the post-design capture needs described earlier. Here's an example:

L 28-9

```
DECLARE
        r_tab      ciotable_definition.data;
        v_tabid    ci_table_definitions.id%TYPE;
        v_status cdapi.activity_status%TYPE;
CURSOR c_display_title
    IS
        SELECT t.id, t.name
          FROM ci_table_definitions t,
               ci_application_systems s
         WHERE s.id = t.application_system_owned_by
           AND s.name = 'CTA'
           AND s.version = 1
           AND t.display_title IS NULL ;
BEGIN
    /*
    || Begin repository transaction
    */
    cdapi.initialize('CTA',1);
```

```
cdapi.open_activity;
FOR r_display_title IN c_display_title
LOOP
   -- Load record variable values
   r_tab.v.display_title :=
        initcap(replace(r_display_title.name,'_',' '));
   -- Load record variable indicator
   r_tab.i.display_title := TRUE;
   -- Perform the "DML"
   ciotable_definition.upd(r_display_title.id, r_tab);
END LOOP;
/*
|| End repository transaction
*/
cdapi.close_activity(v_status);
IF v_status != 'Y'
THEN
   -- Abort upon failure
   cdapi.abort_activity;
END IF;
END;
```

Manipulating Multiline Text

Despite the flexibility and support for all major element and association types in the repository, the API has some limitations. One of these is that you cannot manipulate text types such as Notes, Descriptions, Derivation Expressions, Select Text, PL/SQL Blocks, and WHERE clauses. This text is stored in a table called CDI_TEXT, but application of SQL statements to this table, other than queries, is completely unsupported. The CDI_TEXT table has the following structure:

L 28-10

Name	Null?	Type
TXT_REF	NOT NULL	NUMBER(38)
TXT_SEQ	NOT NULL	NUMBER(6)
TXT_TYPE	NOT NULL	VARCHAR2(10)
TXT_NOTM		NUMBER(38)
TXT_TEXT		VARCHAR2(2000)

The TXT_REF column is the ID number of the element that this text is used by. The TXT_TYPE is a code that designates the type of text. For example, a value of CDINOT means that this text type contains notes for the element. CDIPLS is the text for the PL/SQL block. A block of text can consist of more than one record, and the TXT_SEQ column is the line number for this record. TXT_TEXT is the actual text. TXT_NOTM is an, as yet, unused column that is intended to store the number of times that this record was modified. Using this information, you can construct a SQL statement to query the CDI_TEXT table and extract any text type for any element. For example, to extract the user help text for the STUDENTS table in the CTA version 1 application system, you would issue the following SQL statement:

L 28-11
```
SELECT txt_text
    FROM cdi_text
  WHERE txt_type = 'CDHELP'
    AND txt_ref =
        (SELECT t.id
           FROM ci_table_definitions t,
                ci_application_systems a
          WHERE t.application_system_owned_by = a.id
            AND a.name = 'CTA'
            AND a.version = 1
            AND t.name = 'STUDENTS')
  ORDER by txt_ref, txt_seq;
```

TIP
You can view a list of the text types and descriptions of those types by querying the RM_TEXT_TYPES view.

A Sample Multiline Text API Script

After performing a design capture on tables, the *User/Help Text and Description* table properties remain unpopulated. Using the API, you can write a routine to put information into these properties for all of an application system's tables based on the information in the *Comment* property. This is a bit trickier than the *Display Title* example earlier because *User/Help Text* and *Description* are multiline text types and are designed to store more than one row in the repository for each table instance.

TIP
When you work in the TextPad to edit multiline text, such as Description, you can include a carriage return in the text to indicate a new line. The carriage return "character" is saved in the CDI_TEXT table, so if you use a SELECT statement similar to the one shown earlier to retrieve the multiline text data directly from the CDI_TEXT table, you will see the Description *stored as multiple lines, with a carriage return at the end of each. When you use the API to load text, remember that you can use the carriage return (CHR(10)) to create a new line.*

To write this into the multiline text property, you may use the undocumented package RMOTEXT. Through the use of RMOTEXT. READALL and RMOTEXT.WRITEALL, you can issue transactions against the repository with streams (long text strings) rather than with multiple records of scalar types. Below is an example using RMOTEXT to populate *User/Help Text* from *Comment* after design capturing tables in a schema. You could also populate the *Description*, if needed. As mentioned, this is undocumented, and, although it uses a standard API-like interface, you should be careful to back up your repository before using this (or any other) utility that you create outside the Oracle Designer front-end interface.

L 28-12
```
DECLARE
     r_tab              ciotable_definition.data;
     v_tabid            ci_table_definitions.id%TYPE;
     v_status           cdapi.activity_status%TYPE;
     v_bufwrt           integer;
     v_stream_handle rm.stream;
     -- Declare a cursor for User/Help Text.
     -- The result set of this cursor will contain
     --    the ID and COMMENT from a repository
     --    table definition for which the User/Help Text
     --    does not exist. If the Comment property is
     --    null the User/Help Text will not be populated.
```

```
    CURSOR c_uht -- uht = user_help_text
    IS
        SELECT t.id, t.remark, t.name
          FROM ci_table_definitions t,
               ci_application_systems s
         WHERE NOT EXISTS
               (SELECT NULL
                  FROM cdi_text
                 WHERE txt_type = 'CDHELP'
                   AND txt_ref = t.id
               )
           AND s.id = t.application_system_owned_by
           AND s.name = 'CTA'
           AND s.version = 1
           AND t.remark IS NOT NULL;
BEGIN
    /*
    || Begin repository transaction
    */
    cdapi.initialize('CTA',1);
    cdapi.open_activity;
    -- Update User/Help Text
    FOR r_uht IN c_uht
    LOOP
        -- Load stream value
        rmotext.open(r_uht.id,'CDHELP','w',v_stream_handle);
        rmotext.writeall(r_uht.id,'CDHELP',r_uht.remark,
            length(r_uht.remark),v_bufwrt);
        rmotext.close(r_uht.id,v_stream_handle);
    END LOOP;
    /*
    || End repository transaction
    */
    cdapi.close_activity(v_status);
    IF v_status != 'Y'
    THEN
        -- Abort upon failure
        cdapi.abort_activity;
    END IF;
END;
```

Sample Uses for the API

While you can perform a large number of tasks with the Oracle Designer front-end tools, some things are not easy or possible with those tools. Also, even if a task is easy or possible, it may be repetitive or tedious if a large number of repository objects are affected. In addition, you may need to support access to and manipulation of a user-extended property or element. The API is the perfect facility to use in all these cases.

The following sections describe some possible uses for the API. Additional ideas are presented in the sections "Supplementing the Repository Reports" and "Developing an Oracle Forms Front-End Program for the API," later in this chapter.

Loading Legacy Report Definitions

The activities in the Analysis phase include creating module definitions for legacy reports and entering a value to a user-extended property to denote the status of the report. You can accomplish these tasks with the API by writing your own front-end in Forms or another tool that allows you to enter the definitions and mark the status more easily than you could using RON. An alternative is to create a non-Oracle Designer table or file with the information on the reports and read this into an API routine that creates the module definitions.

Creating Domains from Column Definitions

In the Analysis phase, you create domain definitions that are to be used in creating the attribute definitions for entities. If you want to create an attribute for which there is no suitable domain, you would have to leave the domain name empty. An API routine can query for all attributes with null domain properties, create a domain definition for each, and attach the new domain definition to the attribute.

Making Global Changes to Column Names

In the Pre-Design phase, when the DDT creates columns from attributes, it uses the attribute name, substitutes underscore characters for spaces, and truncates the name to 30 characters. If you prefer to make your column names abbreviated versions of the attribute names, you can do this by storing the full name and abbreviation in an external table and writing an API routine to read the table, find columns with the full name, and update the definition using the abbreviated name.

Mapping Requirements to Modules

In the Pre-Design phase, you need to assign requirements to modules so you can ensure that all system requirements are being fulfilled, and track which modules or tables fulfill a specific requirement. This is a manual process of associating a requirement with a module, and you can use the Matrix Diagrammer for this purpose. The API can assist in this task, too. For this task, you need to copy the requirements mapping to the modules with an API routine that loops through all functions, finds the modules with which the functions are associated, finds the requirements that are mapped to those functions, and creates a requirements-to-modules association for that function. This can be a time-consuming task if performed manually or with the Matrix Diagrammer, but using the API will save time.

Tracking Problems

In the Test phase, and while performing unit tests in the Build phase, you need to track the problems for each module. You can write a front-end program in Forms or another tool using the API so you can easily insert, update, and delete problems and the association of problems to modules. In fact, you could open this interface up to trusted users who could log their own comments and problems into the repository (or an intermediary database table) as they are testing the forms.

Changing Free-Format View Definitions into Declarations

A limitation of the Capture Design of Server Model Database utility is that it loads view and snapshot definitions as free-format text. If you want the definition to be based on tables and columns already in your application system, you can write an API routine that reads the table names from the Select Text, finds the IDs for those table definitions in the repository, and adds a base table association for each table. The API routine can also find the IDs of the columns and attach them to the *Base Column* property of the column definition. You also need to change the *Free Format Select Text ?* property to "No," but you cannot remove the FROM clause from the view text using the API. To do that, you go into RON and edit the *Where/Validation Condition* property for the view.

Reporting on Table Usages

One of the cross-check reports you may want to run in the Application Design phase is one that shows the tables and how they are used in the modules. This report would give you a list of modules with the module component usages and the base tables under the module components. This matrix-type diagram is not available in the Matrix Diagrammer, but it can help you determine if you have provided a way to insert, update, delete, and query each table somewhere in your application. You could write an additional query that lists all tables that have no module components (in a module) with each of the operations (insert, update, delete, and query).

Reporting on Role Access to Tables

One of the security reports you need to run in the Design phase is a mapping of users or roles to tables. You need to ensure that the proper user roles are accessing the tables they need to access. The report would give a quick view into this association of users and roles to tables. You could include other database objects such as views, sequences, and packages, as well.

Loading Definitions from a File or Table

You can create a table or file that serves as a source for the definitions of any type you wish to insert or modify. An API routine you write can read the file or query the table and, based on the information in those sources, modify or insert definitions into the repository. This approach can be more convenient or faster than manual RON work when you have a large number of objects. It would be especially time-saving in a reengineering or data migration effort, where descriptions of the legacy data, typically available in COBOL copybooks or similar files, could be loaded into the repository.

Supplementing User Documentation

You can use RMOTEXT.READALL to show all help text for a definition. This offers a quick way to extract the text you wrote into the *User/Help Text* property of various elements. You can use this text to supplement and provide a basis for the user documentation. Alternatively, you could write queries against the CDI_TEXT table with a TXT_TYPE of 'CDHELP.' While this is not strictly an API view, it is accessible to repository users and offers a quick way to see any text recorded for an element.

NOTE
Working with the API is straightforward once you understand the principles. However, no matter what your level of understanding is, the API routines will take time to write, which you should weigh against the potential time savings that the API offers. Keep in mind also, though, that if the routine you are writing has a general-purpose use, you will be able to reuse it in future projects, so any extra time required creating it might be worthwhile in the long run.

Supplementing the Repository Reports

Before writing any reports on the repository elements, be sure that the Repository Reports utility does not already contain a report that can handle the job. If you cannot find a predefined repository report, you can use the API views as described earlier in this chapter to query the database. Since repository access essentially involves standard SQL, you simply need to understand the contents of the views and their relationships and write a SELECT statement to return the desired results. The Oracle Designer software set includes SQL*Plus which you can use to write these queries. You can also employ any other SQL reporting tool that connects to an Oracle database.

Using the Meta-Model Application System

Oracle Designer ships with an application system that contains the definitions of all meta-model views with their columns and relationships. You can load this application system into the repository from a .DAT load file or a .DMP archive file. The files are called Model_20.dat and Model_20.dmp, respectively, and are located in the ORACLE_HOME/ des2_70/model directory. You load the .DAT file into an empty application system using **Utilities→Load** in RON. Alternatively, you can import the .DMP file using **Application→Restore** in RON to create the application system. Either method will load the view definitions into the repository.

Once you have the view definitions loaded in an application system, you can create report modules based on them and use the Report Generator to generate Oracle Reports code for the module. One benefit of creating the reports this way is that, if you are using Oracle Designer to generate code, you already know how to generate report modules and do not have to be concerned with the details of the Reports tool. In addition, the repository reports you write will have a standard appearance, and you can generate all supported report types, including matrix and drill-down reports.

Developing an Oracle Forms Front-End Program for the API

You may have a need to access the repository that is not filled in the Oracle Designer front-end. You could develop a front-end program that interactively accesses the repository in the same way the Oracle Designer tools do. The API allows you to use a development tool you are comfortable with, such as Oracle Forms, to manipulate repository data. The following paragraphs outline the issues you need to consider when creating a Forms front-end program to access the repository. While this discussion is specific to Oracle Forms, you can translate the techniques into any other development tool that can connect to an Oracle database.

Sample Form Requirement

When you write code to perform work using the repository, it is important that you limit the scope. Completely generic programming can be extremely time-consuming, and if you never use the generalized part, it can be a wasted effort. Suppose you run the Reconcile Report to cross-reference the repository to the Oracle data dictionary, and the resulting report shows a number of differences in the Not Null properties of the database and repository definitions for some views. The database view definition may be based on tables that have the wrong Not Null constraint. What you really want is a utility that lets you see the data dictionary Not Null values side by side with the repository Not Null values. This utility can be a form you develop to show these properties side by side which will help you determine which values are wrong. At that point, you can click an item and change the value in the repository by issuing API calls to update the column definition.

The API Form

The API is as easy to call from a Developer form as it is in SQL*Plus. Forms version 5 (Oracle Developer version 2) provides PL/SQL version 2.3, which can handle direct access to the Oracle Designer API. You can develop a form that queries the data dictionary and the repository views to show the null indicator for a particular view definition. There are a few ways to do this. One way is to have a list of values from which the user can select a view definition name. Figure 28-4 shows the main work screen of such a utility.

You can then perform a query on a block based on the API view CI_COLUMNS using the selected view name. Naturally, you will need to have the user specify which application system this form is acting on. The columns block has a POST-QUERY trigger that looks up and displays the corresponding data dictionary property value in another nonbase table item. You can have a mechanism (for example, double-clicking the null indicator) that indicates that the repository value is to be changed. If the user employs this mechanism, a value is written to a nondisplayed flag item that indicates a change.

If the repository and data dictionary are in separate databases or in different user accounts, you will also need to set up database links and synonyms for those other databases.

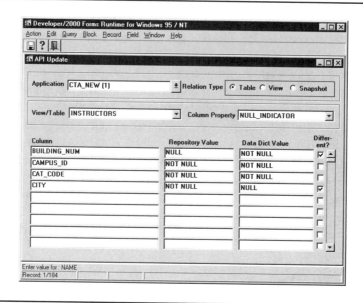

FIGURE 28-4. *The API form*

When you click the Commit button, a package procedure checks the flag item of each record to determine if the record changed. If a record was changed, the procedure calls the API routines to make the change in the repository. The form code follows the same model as code you would execute from another tool like SQL*Plus.

CHAPTER
29

Information Flow

As a thing the way is
Shadowy, indistinct.
Indistinct and shadowy,
Yet within it is an image;
Shadowy and indistinct,
Yet within it is a substance.
Dim and dark,
Yet within it is an essence.
This essence is quite genuine
And within it is something that can be tested.

—Lao Tzu

The way that information flows from one area to another in Oracle Designer may seem quite mysterious at times. Properties you set in one place are able to greatly affect your work in another place. The converse is also true: properties that you expect to have great effect later on do absolutely nothing. Knowing about this flow of information from one part of Oracle Designer to another is a key factor to successful use of the product. If you understand information flow, you can decide which properties are most important and how complete you need to be when filling out repository definitions. You are also better able to prevent errors due to missing information. Such errors can be costly when they appear later in the life cycle.

In short, there is nothing more important when working with Oracle Designer than knowing what will happen to the information in element definitions that you create in the repository. The problem is that this information is less well documented than other aspects of the product and the main way to master it is to use Oracle Designer for a couple of years. Whether you take time up front to learn the flow, or pick it up as you go, there is an inherent learning process that can be costly and, if not done completely, can actually slow down your work on a project. The result is a perception that Oracle Designer cannot easily handle many types of system development environments and methodologies. The reality is that Oracle Designer can do it but you have to be in tune with the way the product handles information.

This chapter does not attempt to explain all details about all properties in the repository. It does, however, provide you with a guide to supplement the discussion of properties in previous chapters; this chapter discusses how this information can help you be more effective in supporting a full System Development Life Cycle using the tools that Oracle Designer provides for information flow. It starts with a review of how Oracle Designer stores and transfers information in general and some methods used in the research for obtaining this information. It finishes with some detailed examples of how property values in one repository definition affect property values in other repository definitions and the program or DDL code generated from those definitions.

NOTE
Repository definitions can be manipulated by writing API scripts, and many people have done just that to extend the native utilities. There are also third-party (and even Oracle) utilities for Oracle Designer that extend the capabilities of the repository tools and the range of information flow.

Repository Review

You store information about a project as *definitions* (structured sets of details) in the Oracle Designer repository. Definitions are made up of *properties* (the details), so the process of filling in a definition requires you to supply values to properties. Figure 29-1 shows a sample properties window in the Repository Object Navigator (RON) for a Business Function definition.

Even though this element definition is valid, some property values are missing. This is typical of information in the repository. Properties like *Label* and *Short Definition* (labeled in red) are required, but other properties are not. The problem is that some nonrequired properties are important to your work later in the life cycle, and the values that you fill in for the Analysis phase of the system development can radically affect the way Oracle Designer handles design objects and code generation.

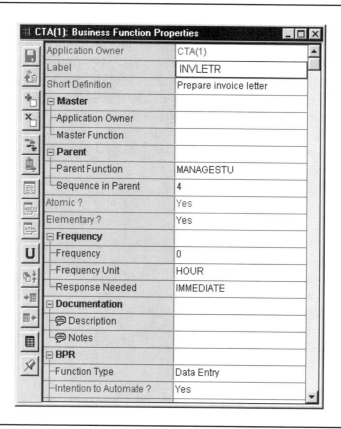

FIGURE 29-1. *Business Function definition properties window*

How Information Flows in the Repository

Information in the Oracle Designer repository definitions flows into other definitions in the repository via a set of front-end tools and utilities. Typically, each of these tools takes element definitions relevant to a specific phase of the life cycle and copies the element properties into definitions applicable to another phase of the life cycle. Further, each tool generally operates either on data-related definitions, such as entities and tables, or process-related definitions, such as functions and modules.

Figure 29-2 shows the main flows and the development phases to which they contribute. Table 29-1 lists the development phases between which flows occur and the tools or utilities that cause these flows to occur.

Oracle Designer information flow works in two directions. It operates in a traditional system development life cycle, where development proceeds from Analysis through Design and Building (Generation). It also works in design capture (reverse engineering), where information embedded in objects or applications generally produced at a later phase of the life cycle can be captured and copied to the corresponding object or definition in a previous phase. Further, although the robustness of the tools in this regard

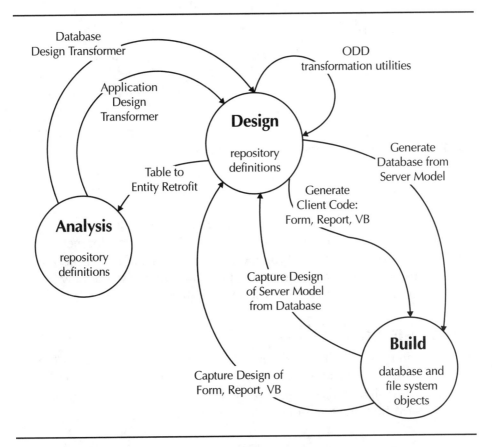

FIGURE 29-2. *Major information flows between development phases*

Flow Category	Tool or Utility
Analysis to Design	Database Design Transformer and Application Design Transformer
Design to Generation	Generate Database from Server Model and client code generators
Database Objects to Design	Capture Design of Server Model from Database
Application Modules to Design	Capture Design of Form, Report, Visual Basic; Object Database Designer: Rescan C++ Files
Design to Analysis	Table to Entity Retrofit utility
Design to Design	Object Database Designer utilities Generate Database from Type Model, Create Oracle Object Type utility, Create Object View utility

TABLE 29-1. *Oracle Designer Information Flow*

varies, the information flow is also evident in an iterative development approach such as rapid prototyping or rapid application development (RAD). For example, you could run the Database Design Transformer multiple times for the same entity, each time carrying revised or new entity-level information to the corresponding table.

Analysis to Design

Analysis definitions (Entities and Functions) in the repository serve as the logical model of the business. When you run the Database Design and Application Design Transformers, Oracle Designer copies property values into the corresponding types of design objects.

On the data side, the Database Design Transformer (DDT) creates table and column definitions, usually in a 1-to-1 mapping, from entity and attribute definitions. DDT creates a foreign key column and constraint on the many side of a 1-to-many relationship and creates a primary key constraint from the entity's unique identifier. If the entity does not have a unique identifier defined, DDT also creates a new surrogate key and makes this column the primary key for the table. DDT also resolves many-to-many relationships and subtype/supertype relationships.

DDT copies certain property values of the entities and attributes to the corresponding tables and columns. Each table and column element DDT creates has a link or association to the analysis element that was its source. For example, table definitions reference the entities they were created from. These references or associations are called Table Entity Usages and are used for documentation and design capture purposes.

Another data side utility, the Create Type Model from Entities utility in ODD, will copy entity definitions to the Type Model definitions. This creates Design elements that you can use to generate database objects or to create other database definitions such as object tables.

On the process or application side, the Application Design Transformer (ADT) creates module definitions from function definitions. It produces candidate modules—modules not yet ready for generation—which you can later accept as application modules using RON or Design Editor. After accepting a module, you can generate working code from it with any of the Oracle Designer generators. ADT creates module components with a table usage from each entity usage in the function the module is based on. These module component table usages form the basis for how the generators produce blocks for forms or groups for reports. ADT combines ownership information from the Function to Business Unit associations with the function definitions and creates a first-cut menu or module network structure.

NOTE
An example of something that the ADT copies is the Other ? property of the attribute usage. This property is copied to the Context Flag property on the bound item for the module that is created from the function.

Design to Generation

This category covers all generator options that produce finished code from repository definitions. Generate Database from Server Model produces scripts from repository definitions to create tables, views, snapshots, sequences, and other database objects. The Form, Library Report, WebServer, Visual Basic, and MS Help generators produce application code based on module definitions in the repository. In this progression from Design to Generation, the generators use properties stored in the repository's design objects to produce database objects (or the code to create them) and application program files.

Database Objects to Design

In this category, information flows from the online data dictionary or from DDL CREATE scripts that reside on the file system into definitions in the Oracle Designer repository. The Capture Design of Server Model from Database utility for database objects creates design-level definitions from extant database objects. For example, Oracle Designer can load the properties of an existing table into the repository, thereby providing a definition you can work on. As you might expect, the properties extracted from various database objects differ based on the type of object you are capturing. For example, table link properties are recorded for a foreign key constraint, but these make no sense for a primary key constraint.

One caveat is in order: when you design-capture a table, foreign keys will only be defined in the repository if the referenced table is captured at the same time, or if it is already defined in the repository. Consequently, when design capturing a database for the first time, it is useful to choose all of the tables. You can then review the results and alter or delete the unwanted definitions.

Application Modules to Design

The design capture utilities load application code for Oracle Forms, Oracle Reports, and Visual Basic source files into the repository. The utilities read the source code from the files and create module and module component table usage definitions in the repository.

The Object Database Designer provides a menu option for **Generate→Generate C++→Rescan Files**. This option examines the locations of class code in a C++ file and updates the repository with the location information. This would be useful if you had manually changed your C++ class code files and moved class information from one file to another. The utility checks for duplicates as well and updates the repository with the new class location.

Design to Analysis

The Table to Entity Retrofit utility copies table definitions to entity definitions. If you combine this with the Capture Design of Server Model from Database utility you can create analysis definitions from database objects. When you run the Table to Entity Retrofit utility, you choose which tables to retrofit from a list of candidate tables. Only tables that do not already have a Table Entity Usage (that is, tables that are not already associated with an entity, either through a previous run of this utility or by using the Database Design Transformer) are valid candidate tables. Therefore, you cannot use this utility to reconcile differences between existing table and entity definitions.

This "reverse" information flow in the repository copies properties from a later phase of development to an earlier phase. This might be required if you are adding to a legacy system; are starting to work with Oracle Designer after table design was already underway; or are adding tables to a database without first creating entity definitions for them.

Design to Design

A number of utilities in the Object Database Designer (ODD) can copy properties between Design-level definitions. If you choose **Generate→ Generate Database from Type Model** from the menu, you will be able to select Repository held Server Model. This option copies Type Model elements into element definitions in the Server Model area. You can specify that you want to generate definitions for Object Types and Tables, Relational Tables, or Relational Tables with Object Views. The property details that are copied are pretty much on a one-to-one basis, as all you are doing, in essence, is creating Oracle database elements in the Server Model area from those in the Type Model area. Note that you will not be able to perform this action again unless you unlink the Server Model from the Type model using the **Utilities→Remove Generated Server Model** or **Utilities→ Remove Server Model Mapping** menu choices.

ODD includes another utility you can use to copy elements in the repository between the Type Model and the Server Model. If you choose **Utilities→Create Oracle Object Type** from the menu, you can specify relational table definitions that you want to use as Oracle Object Types. This will create Oracle Object Type definitions, including attributes based on the columns in the table. The name of the object type will be the same as the table with a _T suffix. The properties that map from one definition to another are also fairly understandable.

You can also run the **Utilities→Create Object View** menu option of ODD to create object views from Oracle Object Types. This essentially copies the Oracle Object Type definition to an object view definition with the attributes being copied to Select text columns in the object view. The object view name will be the name of the type with a _V suffix. The *Free Format Select Text ?* property will be "Yes" and the *Select Text* will have the column names list corresponding to the attributes of the type.

These utilities allow you to create definitions that will assist in creating Oracle object elements in the repository, but they also help you reach the stage where you can generate object CREATE scripts using the Generate Database from Server Model utility.

There is another type of flow that uses design-level definitions to change other design-level definitions: you could call it Database Design to Application Design. This flow is from table, view, and snapshot definitions to Module Component Table Usages. When you create a Module Component Table Usage, Oracle Designer copies property values from the table and column definitions to the module component's table usage and bound item properties.

Yet another type of Design to Design flow appears when you generate a module. The generator makes changes to definitions if there are inconsistencies or missing values. For example, if you forget to fill in a layout placement for a particular module component, the generator will issue a message to the Messages Window, fill in the value with a default, and generate the module without stopping. After the module generates, the Generation Complete dialog will appear and you will be able to accept the changes that the generator made, browse these changes before accepting them, or cancel the changes. Therefore, the generator tries as much as possible to generate the module even if the property values are missing or inconsistent. If there is a set of values that the generator cannot resolve with defaults, it will abort and issue messages in the Messages Window.

Methods for Discovering Information Flows

The first place to look for information on the properties is the help system. If you click the Context-Sensitive Help button in the Design Editor toolbar and drop it on a property in the Property Palette, a small help window will display information about that property. It is likely that there is more information than that available and you can reach it through hypertext links in that pop-up help. This help is also available in the property dialogs by clicking the Context-Sensitive Help button in the top-right corner of the dialog and dropping the mouse cursor on the property in the dialog. In most cases, this help window shows which generators use that property and offers a link to a fuller description for that particular generator.

The help system contains some information flow tables such as the ones in this book. Navigate to the Find window in the help system and type "properties". You will get a large list that includes topics like "Repository *[element]* properties used by Form Generator" (where *[element]* is the type of repository element, like action items), which contain a wealth of information on the individual properties that the Forms Generator uses. The same types of tables exist under similar headings for the Report Generator. This is an excellent resource for the Design to Generation category of information flow.

The nature of the help system is such that regardless of how well it is organized, it will not be organized to give you everything you need in one place, and you have to hunt and peck for details. This drawback might lead you to a bit of "undercover" research to determine the way the Database Design Transformer maps properties to other properties. This research can use several techniques.

Choosing **Options→Diagnostics** (available on the menu of most tools) provides access to a feature that allows tracing in the tool session. Once Diagnostics is enabled, you will see the *** *Diagnostics ON* *** message appear in the title bar of all newly started Oracle Designer screens. You will also see this message listed in the task name in NT's Task Manager (If you are running on NT). There is no help for this option, since it is designed to be used in cooperation with Oracle Support. It should be used judiciously, since it can create a good deal of trace information, slow down the system.

The Diagnostics option provides a good insight into how Designer interacts with the database. Unfortunately, it is less useful than needed for this kind of research, since the informative details on API calls that it could provide are obscured by the tool's use of bind variables. There is no way to tell the source of the bind variable value, so one end of the information flow remains a mystery.

Another approach is to try a database trace with TKPROF (an Oracle database utility) to extract the SQL. This technique yields the same results as the diagnostics session and the same problem with bind variables.

You may also find it useful to press F5 after selecting a property value in the Property Palette of RON or the Design Editor. This will show the base table and column used to store the property in the repository.

The technique that yields the best results is to create a sample element with all properties filled in, run the transformers, and examine the properties and values that are filled in side-by-side with the original elements. Unfortunately, this is also the most tedious of the techniques.

TIP

The spreadtable view, as mentioned in Chapter 6, may be used to make the side-by-side comparison much clearer. For this example, assume that you are using RON and would like to look at the property overlap between an Entity and its corresponding Table created by DDT. You could do the following:

1. *Select the Entity and Table definition (point and click while holding the CTRL key).*

2. *Click on the SpreadTable view button in the Property Palette.*

3. *Review the two definitions in the spreadtable view.*

You will find some properties populated in the entity that are not populated in the table (or vice versa). The spreadtable view's matrix-like appearance does not reveal if that effect is due to the property not being assigned a value or because the property doesn't apply to that element. You can switch back to the default view for answers if you have this kind of question.

Examples of Analysis to Design

The Oracle Designer utilities responsible for transforming analysis objects to design objects are the Database Design Transformer and Application Design Transformer. It is useful to look at some examples of how these transformers copy (or ignore) property values. By examining the effects of the utilities, you can make better decisions about what data to enter and how complete you need to be when filling in an analysis definition. Two common analysis objects—Entities and Attributes—are examined next to show how the property values are transformed.

Entities to Tables

Table 29-2 shows entity properties and the table properties DDT loads from them. Properties that do not map from Entity to Table are not listed. This table also shows the DDT settings (in the Settings dialog) that affect the properties in the table. Some of the DDT settings pertain to properties that describe how the table will be physically stored in a particular database schema. These DDT settings actually show up as properties in the table implementation for a particular database and user rather than in the table definition itself.

CAUTION
DDT loads the table definitions when it is invoked. Therefore, if you make a change to the repository after the DDT session has been started, that change may not be reflected in the output.

Figure 29-3 shows the Other Settings tab pages of the DDT Settings dialog referenced in Table 29-2 and explained further in Chapter 12.

Attributes to Columns

DDT maps attributes directly to columns when it creates or modifies tables, as shown in Table 29-3. The columns have similar properties to the attributes.

Entity Property	DDT Setting Dialog Setting	Table or Table Implementation Property	Notes
Description		Description	
Description		User/Help Text	Used as the text supplied to the MS Help Generator, Forms help system, and WebServer Generator.
Maximum		End Rows	Default is 0.
Notes		Notes	
Plural	Table Prefix	Name	If the Table Prefix option in DDT is filled in, the table *Name* is the Table Prefix in DDT plus the *Plural* property of the Entity. Otherwise, the table *Name* is just the plural. DDT substitutes an underscore character for spaces in the entity name. If the name is not unique, DDT adds a number suffix.
Plural		Display Title	The *Plural* property in mixed case with initial characters capitalized.
Short Name		Alias	Truncated to 30 characters and suffixed with a number if the alias is not unique.

TABLE 29-2. *Entity Properties Mapped to Table Properties*

Entity Property	DDT Setting Dialog Setting	Table or Table Implementation Property	Notes
Volumes: Initial		Start Rows	Default is 0. Entity Average and Annual Growth Rate (%) are not used in the table.
(No corresponding entity property)	Columns check box in Other Settings	Col. Prefix	First four characters of Short Name.
	Database and Database User	(Database and user association)	Specifying the user and database in the DDT settings creates a table implementation under the specified database and user (schema).
	Tablespace	Tablespace	Table implementation. Choices come from the Tablespaces repository element.
	Storage Definition	Storage Definition	Table implementation. Choices come from the Storage Definitions repository element.
	Column Component Priority	(Not a property)	This orders the columns in a way you specify through this setting.

TABLE 29-2. *Entity Properties Mapped to Table Properties* (continued)

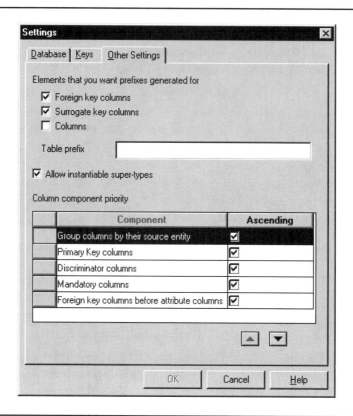

FIGURE 29-3. *Database Design Transformer Settings dialog*

Attribute Property	Column Property	Notes
Average Length	Average Length	
Comment	Hint	
Comment	Comment	
Decimal Places	Decimal Places	
Default	Default Value	

TABLE 29-3. *Attribute Properties Mapped to Column Properties*

Attribute Property	Column Property	Notes
Derivation		Does *not* map to Derivation Expression on the column.
Description	Description	
Description	User/Help Text	
Domain	Domain	
Format	Datatype	Maps nonrelational concepts like VIDEO to relational datatypes like LONG RAW.
Format	Display Type	Display Types can be set to the GUI display types, such as text items, check boxes, and radio groups. A NUMBER format yields a Text display type because a text item type of user interface object will be displayed even though the datatype for the column is NUMBER.
Maximum Length	Maximum Length	
Maximum Length	Display Length	
Name	Name	DDT substitutes an underscore character for spaces. The Columns prefix setting in DDT specifies whether the column names will be prefixed with the first four characters of the Entity short name.
Name	Prompt	In mixed case with initial capitals.

TABLE 29-3.   *Attribute Properties Mapped to Column Properties* (continued)

Attribute Property	Column Property	Notes
Name	Source Attribute	This represents the link back to the source attribute.
Notes	Notes	
Optional ?	Optional ?	
Sequence in Entity	Sequence in Table	The numbers may not be the same, but the order is the same unless you change the column order by using the DDT settings.
Sequence in Entity	Display Sequence	
Volumes: Percent Used – Initial	Initial Volume and Average Volume	Copied directly from the attribute to the column properties.
(No corresponding attribute property)	Upper Case ?	Default is No.
	Sequence	Default is null unless the column was created as a surrogate key. In that case, an Oracle sequence is also created, named EntityShortName_SEQ, and the sequence name filled in.
	Display	Default is Yes.
	Complete ?	Default is Yes.

TABLE 29-3. *Attribute Properties Mapped to Column Properties* (continued)

NOTE
You can create attributes in the ER Diagrammer or in RON. If you do this in the diagrammer and use a domain for the attribute, the comment on the domain definition copies into the comment on the attribute definition. If you change the comment and reapply the domain, your comment will be preserved. This effect does not occur in RON so the attribute definition is left comment-less even though its domain has a comment. Since the attribute's Comment property becomes the Hint property of the column, this effect is worth noting. The same effect occurs in the Design Editor when entering column definitions—domain comments are not copied.

CAUTION
When assigning a primary unique ID to an entity, that ID may be composed fully or in part of relationships. It is important to make sure that the "many" side of the relationship is mandatory. If it is not, then when the Database Design Transformer runs, it will not add the components (columns) to the primary or foreign key constraints of any of the tables. Making the from (or many) side of the relationship mandatory may seem like the obvious thing to do, but attributes and their optionality work somewhat differently. If you make an attribute optional but you do add it to a primary unique identifier, DDT will change it to mandatory.

Entity Relationships to Foreign Key Constraints

As explained in Chapter 12, DDT creates a foreign key constraint for all logical-level relationships. Other than the actual nature of the relationship (optionality and cardinality) and the columns or other relationships that participate, no properties are preserved in the transformation. The incarnation of the foreign key has almost as much to do with the options chosen in the DDT Settings dialog as it has to do with the relationship definition itself. DDT creates columns on the physical side to support a relational database implementation of the logical relationships. Table 29-4 shows how relationships are transformed to foreign key constraints and the DDT settings that affect the transformation.

Transforming Subtype/Supertype Relationships

Mapping Entities to Tables in DDT is fairly straightforward when mapping simple relationships such as 1-to-many and even many-to-many. As mentioned in Chapter 12, the mapping of subtype/supertype relationships requires some additional choices to be made. The key to creating any one of these implementations is based on what choices are made for the *In Set* check box of the Table Mappings tab of DDT.

There are four approaches to mapping these relationships.

- Supertype (single table)

- Explicit subtype (separate table)

- Implicit subtype

- Arc

SUPERTYPE (SINGLE TABLE) APPROACH   All of the supertype attributes and all of the subtype attributes are placed into one table. A new discriminator column is added to that table and it is given a name derived from the Table Short Name plus "_TYPE." An Allowable Values list is populated and contains the Short Names of the subtypes. To implement this approach, check the *In Set* check box only for the supertype entity.

Under the Other Settings tab of the DDT Settings dialog is a check box labeled "Allow instantiable super-types" (as shown in Figure 29-3). If this is

Foreign Key Property/Concept	Derived From
Constraint Name	FromTableShortName_ToTableShortName_FK.
Enforcement type	DDT option on the Keys tab of the Settings dialog for Delete rule and Update rule. The choices are Cascades, Defaults, Nullifies, and Restricted.
Foreign key column and column name	A column is created in the "to" table for every column in the primary key of the "from" table. The DDT option on the Other Settings tab of the Settings dialog to generate prefixes for foreign key columns prefixes the column name with the "from" table's *Short Name* property.
Index and Index Name	Every foreign key constraint has an index created on the "from" table to support the constraint. The index name is the constraint name with an _I suffix: FromTableShortName _ToTableShortName_FK_I
Partitioning of Foreign Key Logic	DDT option on the Keys tab of the Settings dialog for Implementation level for constraints. The choices are Server, Client, or Both. A value of "Server" means the foreign key constraints will be added to the table. A value of "Client" instructs the generators to create client-side code to maintain the referential integrity. A value of "Both" means the foreign key constraints will be enforced by creating a foreign key on the table and by creating client-side code.

TABLE 29-4.   *DDT Effects on Relationship to Foreign Key Transformation*

checked, an additional value of the supertype's Short Name will be added to the Allowable Values list of the Discriminator column.

EXPLICIT SUBTYPE (SEPARATE TABLE) APPROACH   The explicit subtype approach produces separate tables for each of the subtypes. Each of those tables contains all of the attributes (including the primary key) of the supertype in addition to their own unique attributes. The supertype entity is not created as a table. To implement this approach, specify only the subtype entities in the *In Set* check box of the Table Mappings tab of DDT.

IMPLICIT SUBTYPE APPROACH   Like the explicit subtype approach, the implicit subtype approach creates one table for each subtype. In addition, the implicit subtype approach also creates a table for the supertype. DDT will take this approach if both the supertype and its subtypes are checked in the *In Set* check box under the Table Mappings tab. The supertype, of course, will only contain columns for attributes defined in the supertype entity. It will not include columns for attributes in the subtype entities.

ARC APPROACH   The arc approach creates the supertype and all or some of its subtypes in an arc configuration. That is, the supertype table is created with foreign keys and their columns referencing the subtype tables. The subtype tables contain only the columns for attributes defined in their associated entities. The foreign key constraints between the supertype table and its subtype tables show with an arc across them.

There are two steps in using the arc approach. More accurately, you make two runs of DDT. In the first, you check In Set for the supertype and its subtypes that you want to include in the arc. In this run, you uncheck Columns and Keys under the DDT Run Options tab. This run will create the tables without any constraints or columns. In the second run, you check Columns and Keys and check Arc under the Mappings tab for the subtypes that you want to include in the arc relationship.

It may be confusing when you first look at the Server Model Diagram created for the arc approach. You will see the foreign key columns in the supertype table. You can use those columns to enforce the exclusive "OR" characteristic inherent in subtype/supertype relationships. What is a bit tricky is that you will see the many relationships on the supertype table. This is so because arcs can only be put on the "many" side of the relationships in the diagrammer and since the arc represents the word "OR", these relationships have to be on the parent side.

NOTE
No matter what approach you select, the logic to enforce the exclusive OR characteristic inherent to the subtype/supertype relationship is not generated by the Generate Database from Server Model utility. If you want to enforce the exclusive OR, you will either need to write the triggers on the tables yourself or use the Table API that can be generated from **Generate→Generate Table API** *menu option found in the Design Editor.*

Examples of Flow from Design Definitions to Generated Code

One of the main features of Oracle Designer is that it can create fully functional and robust database and application code. If this is your objective, you need to know what properties are key to making the generators perform the way you want them to. The following section examines properties in the design area of the repository and how these properties affect the output of the Oracle Designer generators, particularly the client-code generators. Property definitions are only part of the story for code generation, however, so be sure to supplement this information with knowledge of how information flows out of the templates, object libraries, and preferences to create the module source code.

The secret to successful generation of any kind of application code is in knowing the product for which you are generating that code. For example, if you do not understand the structure of an Oracle Developer Forms application or the layout elements in an Oracle Developer Reports module, you will get useful code but you will not be able to make the smart decisions needed to create production-level applications from the generators. This is not to say that you cannot approach 100 percent generation but is merely a warning that you need to understand the product and its objects and properties so you can fill out the correct Oracle Designer elements and properties.

The discussions and tables that follow use Oracle Forms as an example for client-code generator unless otherwise indicated.

Server Code

The Generate Database from Server Model utility produces the CREATE script code you would expect it to from properties in repository object definitions. For example, to generate code for a table, you enter a repository definition for a table and its columns. The properties in the definitions have an almost one-to-one correspondence with the aspects of the table and columns you need. If you know the syntax of the create statement, you will be able to find the correct properties in the repository. This is relatively straightforward, but you may wish to consult the Oracle Designer help system for explanations on the various database elements and how their properties affect the Generate Database from Server Model utility.

Client Code

The following sections explain the effects of table, column, module component table usage, and module component column (bound item) usage definitions on generated application code. The module definition itself also feeds the generators. An excellent help system topic, "Repository module properties used by Form Generator," documents this. Use the Find tab of the help system to locate this topic.

When you create a module component data usage, Oracle Designer copies some properties from the table and column definitions to the table usage and bound items. No code is created until you run the generators, but property information copies from one definition to another in this way. This affects the final code, of course, because the module data usages form the main foundation for the generated code.

Table Definitions to Generated Code

The generators use some properties directly from the table and column definitions. Other properties are used indirectly; that is, when you create a module component table usage, the initial value of certain properties is copied from the table. However, you can then change the module or module component properties if desired.

Properties from table definitions used by the application generators are summarized in Table 29-5.

Table Property	Generator Effects
Alias	Copied to the table usage's *Usage Alias* property of the module component. Becomes the block name for the form.
Display Title	Copied to the *Display Title* of the module component. Used as the block title of the generated form or the heading for the generated Web page.
End Rows	The Form Generator uses this to determine how many rows to retrieve from the first base table block in a form. (Look in the Form generator help system under the topic MAXQRY for further details). WebServer Generator uses this to determine whether to present a long list LOV. If this value is more than the number in the preference MAXQRY, the Web page will produce a prompt asking the user for more restriction on the LOV. This is useful if the list will be long.
Journal	This property determines whether the Generate Database from Server Model utility produces DDL for a Journal table to hold changes performed on the base table. In addition, this property specifies where the code to populate the journal table will be executed— server or client. If in the client, a Form trigger is generated to insert records into the Journal table. If in the server, code is generated in the Table API.
User/Help Text	Used for help system generation (MS Help or table-based). Also used by the WebServer Generator to provide help text in the Startup Web page.

TABLE 29-5. *Table Properties Used by the Generators*

Column Definitions to Generated Code

A column definition property may affect the generated code in one of two ways:

- The code generator can use its properties directly.

- Design Editor (DE) or RON can use its properties to provide a default value to the bound item. The code generator then uses the bound item and ignores the corresponding properties on the source column definition.

Table 29-6 summarizes how the generator uses column properties. The codes listed here reflect the possible types of property usages:

CD   The property on the column definition property is directly used.

MC   The property module component bound item property is used. The property received a default value from the corresponding column definition property.

Column Property	Usage	Generator Effects
AutoGen Type	CD	The generators create code for audit columns (date and user created or modified) and Sequence within Parent for blocks such as Invoice Item that needs a line item number for each row. If this is set to a value other than null, the item will not be enterable.
Column Name	MC	Copies to bound item properties *Column* and *Name*. There is a distinction in Oracle Developer version 2 between these two, which means you can create an item named differently from the column on which it is based.

TABLE 29-6. *Column Properties Used by the Generators*

Column Property	Usage	Generator Effects
Descriptor Seq	CD	The order this column is in for the descriptor list. A descriptor is used as a default column in an LOV generated from this table and also to copy the context of one canvas to another.
Display Sequence	MC	Designates the order in which this column is shown on the form (or other generated module file). The *Usage Sequence* property on the bound item stores the corresponding number.
Display Type	CD	Specifies which GUI control or datatype is used to show the column value. For example, you can specify an item as a combo box, check box, button, radio group, VBX control, OLE container, and so on. The default of null will produce a text item.
Maximum Length	MC	Oracle Designer calculates the maximum display width regardless of the column width and sets the module component bound item *Width* property to that value.
Oracle Sequence	CD	The sequence definition that will be used to provide an application-generated value for this column. The Generator produces the Forms code to accomplish this. Alternatively, the Table API can provide a server generated value.
Uppercase	CD	The generator creates code or a property in the form module to convert the input to uppercase if this property is True or Yes.

TABLE 29-6. *Column Properties Used by the Generators* (continued)

Column Property	Usage	Generator Effects
User/Help Text	Both	Used for help system generation (MS Help or table-based). The column help text is used for the *Hint* property of the bound item.
Datatype Description Hint Notes Template/Library Object	MC	These property values are not copied although they appear in both column and bound item definitions. The generator consults only the module component definitions.
Alignment Default Value Display Height (height) Display Length (width) Display Type Display ? Format Mask Formatting Highlighting Optional ? Order Seq Prompt Sort Order	MC	These all perform a function that you would expect in the generated code. For example, *Display ?* indicates whether the column should be displayed on the application module.

TABLE 29-6. *Column Properties Used by the Generators* (continued)

Module Definitions to Generated Code

Table 29-7 shows how module properties file affect the generated application file (such as the form report).

Module Property	Generator Effects
Command Line	Used for the menu module or action item call to this module. WebServer Generator uses this as a hypertext link to another URL, although it can also correctly create these links in most cases using the module name.
Implementation Name	The name of the file created from the generator. Defaults to the module short name in lowercase. Client generators (Form, Library Report, and VB) use this for the file name. The WebServer Generator uses this for the name of the package that represents the module, so this name will appear in the URL that calls the module.
Language	Which generator is used.
Layout Format	The type of default layout used, such as Master-Detail or Tabular. Applicable to Form and Report generators.
Module Type	Choices are Default, Menu, or Library. Default depends on which language is chosen when generating the module.
Name	The form name (name on the Form property sheet of Oracle Developer) if there is no Top Title or Short Title defined.
Runtime Path	The location of the form (such as C:\PROD\FORMS). This can be used for menu or action item command line calls to other forms but is not recommended because it is not portable.
Short Name	Becomes the file name of the generated code file.
Short Title	Becomes the menu item label if this is a menu item.

TABLE 29-7. *Module Properties and Their Effects on Generation*

Module Property	Generator Effects
Top/Bottom Title	Form Generator can use these to place a word or phrase as boilerplate. For Report Generator, these become top and bottom margin titles. For WebServer, the top title becomes a link to a detail page from a master page.
User/Help Text	Module help used for the Help Generator or help table text. Also used by Web generator for module title text.

TABLE 29-7. *Module Properties and Their Effects on Generation* (continued)

Module Components to Generated Code

Module components contain table usages and related objects such as item groups and unbound items. Many module component properties have great effect on the generated code, as Table 29-8 shows.

Table Usages to Generated Code

The Table Usages node of a module component stores details about the tables that comprise the module component. The table usage forms a link in the chain from the module to the bound items that make up the table usage. Table 29-9 shows some of the important properties of the table usage and how the generator interprets them.

Module Table Links to Generated Code

The table link in the module data definition is created from the table's foreign key. If you want only the table link and not the database foreign key, you can define the foreign key with the *Validate in* property to "Client." No properties are copied from the table foreign key to the module table link as such, but all client code in the generated application module will reflect that logical link.

Property	Generator Effects
Autoquery ?	Determines if code will be generated to automatically query the table when the form starts.
Canvas Width/Height	Fixes the width and height of the content canvas this block is on, but the template can override these settings. These properties override the width preferences PAGCWD (Content canvas width) and POPCWD (Stacked canvas width) and the corresponding height preferences.
Datasource Type	The type of database object that supplies the data for this table usage. The choices are Table, View, Query, PL/SQL Procedure, or None.
Datatarget Type	The type of database object that receives data from this table usage. The choices are Table, PL/SQL Procedure, Transactional Triggers, or None.
Layout Style	Specifies how the table usage will be displayed in the generated form or report. Also used by the WebServer Generator to specify how the different forms in the module will be grouped into pages.
Operations	Specify which DML operation (Insert, Delete, Update) is performed on the base table in this module component. These set block properties in the form. For WebServer Generator, they determine whether insert, delete, and update pages will be generated.
Overflow	Overrides preference and specifies what happens if a row is too wide for the canvas.
Placement	Specifies the canvas or window type that this table will be generated into.
Rows Displayed	Block property for *Number of Records Displayed*. For Web pages, the number of records displayed on the list form.

TABLE 29-8. *Module Component Properties Used by the Generators*

Property	Generator Effects
Show Maximum Rows	If this is set, the Form generator clears the *Rows Displayed* property and creates the maximum number of records displayed in the block based on the canvas size. This appears in the Display tab of the property dialog but not the Property Palette.
Title	Used for the label of the block (boilerplate text on the canvas). Copied from the table definition *Display Title* when the module component is created.
User/Help Text	Used for help system generation (MS Help or table-based).
Window/View— Width and Height	Size of the canvas or window for this block in the MDI window. The window properties are in the Window definition.
Window/View— X and Y	Location of the canvas or window for this block in the MDI window. The location coordinates of the window appear in the Window definition.

TABLE 29-8. *Module Component Properties Used by the Generators (continued)*

Items to Generated Code

The bound and unbound item properties generally affect the properties of the corresponding item in the generated form, as Table 29-10 shows. For the WebServer Generator, these properties affect which items occur on which Web page—the Query Form, Record List, View Form, Insert Form, or Delete Form. Unless otherwise indicated, these properties pertain to bound items.

The help system documents item properties that have not been included in the previous table. Navigate to the Find window in the help system and type "properties" and look for the topic "Repository *[element]* properties used by Form Generator," where *[element]* is a repository element.

Property	Generator Effects
LOV Title	Title for the LOV that displays if the table has a lookup usage type.
Table/View/Snapshot	Used as the name of block if there is no block title for a table with a Base usage type.
Usage Alias	Used by Forms as the block name for a Base table usage and the table alias in the LOV SELECT statement for a Lookup usage. Used by the Report Generator as table alias in the Query. Used by the WebServer Generator to form the name of PL/SQL procedures containing DML in the generated module.
WHERE Clause of Query	Block property *WHERE clause*. For a lookup usage, this becomes a WHERE clause in the LOV SELECT text.

TABLE 29-9.   *Selected Table Usages Properties Used by the Generators*

Examples of Database and Application Design Capture

The design capture utilities create repository definitions for existing database objects and applications. Database objects are queryable in the online data dictionary through views like ALL_TABLES and ALL_TAB_COLUMNS. The Capture Design of Server Model from Database utility basically queries these views and inserts element definitions into the repository. It can also create definitions based on code in a Data Definition Language (Create) script. On the client-code side, the Capture Design of Form (or Report) utilities read Oracle Developer source files—.FMB for Forms and .RDF for Reports—and insert module definitions into the repository.

   Figure 29-4 shows the dialog for selecting database objects for design capture.

Item Property	Generator Effects
Alignment	*Justification* item property.
Context ?	If set to "Yes" and the block spreads across multiple canvases, this value will appear in a separate item at the top of the next canvas. For the WebServer Generator, items with Context flags will appear at the top of all but the first Web page for the module component.
Default Value	*Initial Value* item property.
Derivation Text	The expression used to create a calculated "unbound" or nonbase table item. Available only for unbound items.
Display ?	*Visible* item property.
Display Type	The type of GUI control that will be generated. If no special type (list item, check box, or radio group) is selected, a text item will be generated.
Display in LOV	Means that this column will appear as a column in an LOV. This applies to tables in lookup usages. An LOV will be attached to an item if the column for the item is a foreign key or has allowed values or an associated domain with allowed values.
Format Mask	*Format Mask* item property.
Hint	*Hint* text item property.
Insert ?	Item property for *Insert Allowed*. Indicates whether the item will appear on the WebServer Insert form.
Item Group	Name of the item group, which this item is part of. The item group contributes a label, decoration, and layout to the form's appearance.
Optional ?	Specifies if this item is optional or required.

TABLE 29-10. *Module Component Item Usage Properties Used by the Generators*

Item Property	Generator Effects
Order by Sequence	Designates if this column is to appear in the *ORDER BY clause* block property and what sequence it is in for the list of Order By columns.
Prompt	*Prompt* property of the item.
Range Search	Used by the Visual Basic and WebServer Generators to specify if a To and From item will appear for queries on this column. Used to limit the query results.
Sort Order	Indicates whether columns in the Order by Sequence are in ASC (ascending) or DESC (descending) order. Default is ASC.
Template/Library Object	Can be the name of an object library object or template object that this column item will be based on.
Update ?	Item property for *Update Allowed*. Indicates whether the item will appear on the WebServer update form or be modifiable in the Form module.
User/Help Text	Used for help system generation (MS Help or table-based) and to provide text on Startup pages produced by the WebServer Generator.
Width/Height	Item *Width* and *Height* (in character cell units). Will translate into points, inches, or centimeters depending on the template's coordinate system.

TABLE 29-10. *Module Component Item Usage Properties Used by the Generators* (continued)

Tables 29-1 and 29-12 list information on what properties are populated in the repository for tables and table implementations and for columns. These results reflect a test case that included capturing the design of two tables that had a foreign key relationship but were not clustered. In these tables, '%' indicates that any of the Oracle data dictionary views—USER_, ALL_, or DBA_—could be used as the source for the property. For example,

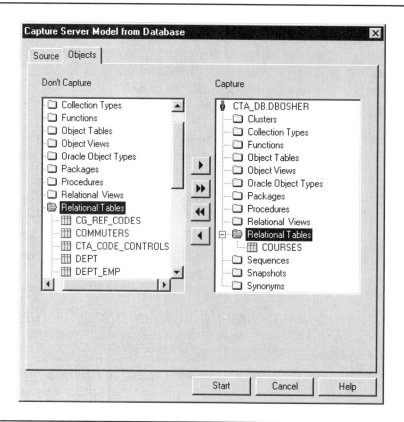

FIGURE 29-4. *Objects tab of the Capture Server Model from Database dialog*

%_TAB_COMMENTS serves as a substitute for USER_TAB_COMMENTS, DBA_TAB_COMMENTS, and ALL_TAB_COMMENTS.

Table and Table Implementation Properties

The Capture Design of Server Model from Database utility creates both table and table implementation definitions after querying the database definitions of the database objects, as Table 29-11 shows. The table implementation

Property	Source or Default Value
Cached	Taken from %_TABLES.CACHE. Set to NOT CACHED even if the table has the cache option set to Y.
Complete ?	"Yes", for both the table and table implementation.
Database	Takes the database name provided in the Capture Objects Into field of the Capture Server Model from Database dialog, not the source database name. The table implementation appears under this database node.
Database User	Takes the user name provided in the Capture Objects Into field of the Capture Server Model from Database dialog, not the name of the current user or the user who owns the objects. The table implementation appears under this database node. The table implementation appears under the specified database and user combination.
Datawarehouse Type	Set to null even if the application system that this table is captured into has a *Datawarehouse?* property of "Yes." The Datawarehouse Type property allows you to specify that this table represents a Fact or Dimension table in a datawarehouse application. You can also assign this property to an entity.
Documentation – Comment	Taken from %_TAB_COMMENTS.COMMENTS.
Global Synonym Name	Taken from %_TABLES.TABLE_NAME.
Index-organized	Yes if %_INDEXES.PCT_THRESHOLD is not null.
Init Trans	Taken from %_TABLES.INI_TRANS.
Journal	None.
Max Trans	Taken from %_TABLES.MAX_TRANS.

TABLE 29-11.   *Capture Design of Server Model from Database for Table and Table Implementation Properties*

Property	Source or Default Value
Name	Taken from %_TABLES.TABLE_NAME.
Parallel – Degree	Taken from %_TABLES.DEGREE.
Parallel – Instances	Taken from %_TABLES.INSTANCES.
Parallel – Parallel ?	Set to "Yes" if Degree and/or Instances is greater than 1 for the table definition in the database.
Pct Free	Taken from %_TABLES.PCT_FREE.
Pct Used	Taken from %_TABLES.PCT_USED.
Snapshot Log ?	"Yes" if a snapshot log is created on the table.
Storage Definition	Design capture attempts to match parameters in the source object with an existing storage definition. Otherwise, it creates a new one with the name STOREn, where n is a unique number.
Tablespace	Will be set as defined in the database if the tablespace is also design captured or is already in the application system.

TABLE 29-11. *Capture Design of Server Model from Database for Table and Table Implementation Properties* (continued)

definitions store user- and database-specific information like storage and tablespace assignments. These are needed to control the location of tables and other objects as well as how these are assigned to specific users or schemas.

Column Properties

If the table definition already exists in the repository, the Capture Design of Server Model from Database utility will add definitions for columns that are in the database table but not in the repository. However, it will not modify existing definitions or delete column definitions if the column is no longer in the database table.

If a name is specified for a not-null constraint, the constraint is design captured with the *Optional* property as "No" and with a check constraint defined at the table level in the repository. When generating DDL, two not-null constraints are placed on the table. Therefore, the developer or data administrator will have to remove one of them from the repository. If the column in question is part of a primary key constraint (where it's not possible to change *Optional* to "No"), then it will not be possible to properly name the no-null constraint. Table 29-12 shows value population of column properties after a Capture Design of Server Model from Database run.

Index Properties

Indexes appear as a subnode to specific table definitions (the Relational Tables node in the Server Model tab of DE). The index can also appear in the DB Admin tab of DE under the *User Object Index Storages* node. This node, like the table implementation, records storage parameters for the index as part of a user schema definition. Table 29-13 shows both index properties and User Object Index Storage properties for indexes that have been design captured from the database to the repository.

Primary and Foreign Key Constraint Properties

Primary and foreign key constraints are described by the view %_CONSTRAINTS of the online database catalog. As Table 29-14 shows, many properties apply to both foreign and primary key constraints, although some may apply to only one type of constraint.

Packages, Procedures, and Function Properties

Design capturing PL/SQL code creates PL/SQL definitions. One definition is created for each package, procedure, and function regardless of whether they are within the package or not. The procedures and functions within a package are linked to the package definition with the calling/called properties shown in the Design Editor (and properties accessible in RON). Implementations are also created for the captured modules. The

Column Property	Source or Default Value
Comment	Taken from %_COL_COMMENTS.COMMENTS.
Complete ?	Yes.
Datatype	Taken from %_TAB_COLUMNS.DATA_TYPE.
Decimal Places	Taken from %_TAB_COLUMNS.DATA_SCALE.
Display Length	NULL.
Display Sequence	NULL.
Display Type	Taken from %_TAB_COLUMNS.DATA_TYPE (Char if Varchar2, NULL if Raw or Long Raw). NULL.
Display ?	Yes.
Dynamic List ?	No.
Final Volume	100 if column is NOT NULL; otherwise, left blank.
Initial Volume	100 if column is NOT NULL; otherwise, left blank.
Name	Taken from %_TAB_COLUMNS.COLUMN_NAME.
Optional ?	Yes if NULLable; No if NOT NULL.
Prompt	Taken from %_TAB_COLUMNS.COLUMN_NAME.
Sequence	Taken from %_TAB_COLUMNS.COLUMN_ID.
Server Defaulted ?	No.
Server Derived ?	No.
Suggestion List ?	No.
Uppercase ?	No.

TABLE 29-12. *Capture Design of Server Model from Database for Column Properties*

Maximum Length Property (Breakdown by Datatype)	Datatype	%_tab_columns Column
	CHAR/VARCHAR2	%_TAB_COLUMNS. DATA_LENGTH
	DATE	NULL
	LONGs and LOBs	NULL
	MLSLABEL	Cannot capture
	NUMBER	%_TAB_COLUMNS. DATA_PRECISION
	RAW	%_TAB_COLUMNS. DATA_LENGTH

TABLE 29-12.   *Capture Design of Server Model from Database for Column Properties* (continued)

implementation appears under the node for the database and the user specified when the Capture Design of Server Model from Database utility is run.

Table 29-15 shows the effects of capturing PL/SQL code. PL\SQL definition properties may be populated differently, depending on whether the source was a package or a procedure or function.

Capture Design of Form Utility
The Capture Design of Form utility loads the repository with properties derived partially from the form (FMB) file itself and partially from the repository. The Tables 29-21, 29-17, and 29-18 detail these properties. The

Property (S for User Object Index Storage properties)	Source or Default Value
Complete ?	Yes.
Index Type	Unique or Not Unique; taken from %_INDEXES.UNIQUENESS, which has a value of UNIQUE or NONUNIQUE. If the index is defined as a bitmap index in the %_INDEXES view, the value of the *Index Type* property is Not Unique.
Init Trans (S)	Taken from %_INDEXES.INI_TRANS.
Max Trans (S)	Taken from %_INDEXES.MAX_TRANS.
Name	Taken from %_INDEXES.INDEX_NAME.
Percent Free (S)	Taken from %_INDEXES.PCT_FREE.
Tablespace (S)	Taken from %_INDEXES.TABLESPACE_NAME. Captured if the tablespace is also design captured or is already in the application system.

TABLE 29-13.   *Capture Design of Server Model from Database for Index Properties*

utility can successfully capture not only table usages, column usages, and table links, but also application code. It cannot capture or write changes to preference settings, the template form, or the object library. These limitations are expected.

Key Constraint Property	Constraint Type	Source or Default Value
Complete ?	Both	Yes.
Delete Rule	Foreign	Restricted, Cascades, or blank as taken from %_CONSTRAINTS. DELETE_RULE.
Enable ?	Both	Taken from %_CONSTRAINTS. STATUS (ENABLED = Yes, DISABLED = No).
Join Table	Foreign	%_CONSTRAINTS.
Mandatory ?	Foreign	True if at least one of the columns in the constraint is a Not Null column. (Primary key constraints are, by definition, mandatory.)
Name	Both	Taken from %_CONSTRAINTS. CONSTRAINT_NAME.
Table	Both	Associated table name.
Transferable ?	Both	Yes.
Update Rule	Foreign	Restricted.
Validate in	Both	Server.

TABLE 29-14. *Capture Design of Server Model from Database for Foreign and Primary and Foreign Key Properties*

Figure 29-5 shows the Capture Form Design dialog that you will see when choosing **Generate→Capture Design of→Form** from the Design Editor menu.

Property	Package Value	Procedure/Function Value
Free Format Declaration ?	No	Yes
Implementation Name	Package name	Procedure or function name as recorded in the USER_SOURCE.TEXT column by the CREATE or REPLACE statement. This could appear in mixed case if the original statement used mixed case.
Name	Package name	Procedure or function name
PL/SQL Block	Null	PL/SQL text (begin...end)
Return Type (Scalar)		Null for procedures; a datatype for functions
Scope	Private	Private if the procedure or function appears only in the package body; Public if the procedure or function is specified in both the package specification and body, or if the function or procedure is stand-alone
Short Name	Package Name	Procedure or function name
SubProgram Units	All procedures and functions including private and public	
Type	Package	Procedure (or Function)

TABLE 29-15. *Capture Design of Server Model from Database for PL/SQL Code*

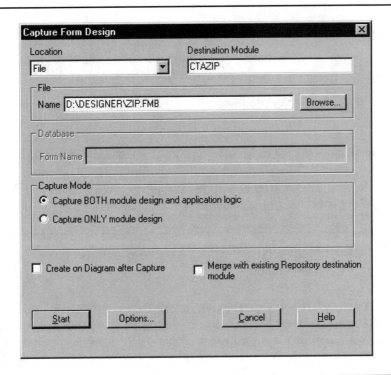

FIGURE 29-5. *Capture Form Design dialog*

Module Property	Value
Description	From Form property *Comments.*
Language	"Developer/2000 Forms."
Name	File name.
Notes	A note on when the utility created this definition. You can specify in the Capture Design of Form utility that you do not want notes by unchecking the Add Notes option.

TABLE 29-16. *Module Properties for Capture Design of Form Utility*

Module Property	Value
Purpose	*Title* property on the window properties list.
Short Name	File name.
Status	"Not Started."
Titles: Top	*Title* property on the window properties list.
Top Level	Set to "Yes." The Capture Design of Form utility does not look for modules calling modules, so all modules it creates will be at the top level of the module-calling network.

TABLE 29-16. *Module Properties for Capture Design of Form Utility* (continued)

Form to Module Component and Properties

Table 29-16 shows how form details are captured into module properties by the Capture Design of Form Utility.

Form to Module Component and Table Usage

Table 29-17 shows how form details are captured into module component and table usage properties.

Associations are created for master-detail and LOV lookup usages. These appear under the table name in the Key Based Links node. Other properties captured by the utility are detailed in the help system under the index topics "design capture – Form Builder applications – Repository *[element]* properties set during design capture." There are specific topics for different *[element]* values.

Property (M is for module component)	Value
Description (M)	*Comments* property on the block
Display:Title (M)	From the table definition *Display Title* property in the repository, not from the form.
(M) Operations and Query	*Insert Allowed, Delete Allowed, Update Allowed,* and *Query Allowed* properties set for blocks in the form.
Notes (both)	A note that the module design was captured by the utility.
Rows Displayed (M)	From *Number of Records Displayed* block property in the form.
Usage Type	"Base" from Relation property of master block or "Lookup" for lookup tables usages.
WHERE clause of Query	From the *WHERE Clause* block property in the form.
Window: Title	From the *Title* property of the main (form) window.

TABLE 29-17.   *Module Component and Table Usage Properties Supplied by Capture Design of Form Utility*

Form to Bound Item

Table 29-18 shows how form details are captured into module component bound item properties.

The utility cannot capture allowable values from poplists or check boxes. It can create definitions for summary and formula items if they are defined with the formula and summary item properties in Oracle Developer Form Builder. Again, it is best to use the help system for supplementary properties that the Design Capture utility loads into the repository. The help system also contains notes about what the utility cannot read from the form file.

Property	Value
Alignment	The item *Justification* property is used.
Datatype	From the *Data Type* item property in the form.
Display ?	From the *Visible* item property in the form.
(display sequence)	Sequence in Forms Designer Object Navigator.
Display Type	From the *Item Type* of the form item.
Format Mask	From the *Format Mask* item property in the form.
Height	From the *Height* item property in the form.
Hint	From the *Hint* item property in the form.
Notes	A note that the module design was captured by the utility.
Operations and Query	*Insert Allowed, Update Allowed,* and *Query Allowed* properties as set for items in the form.
Order By Sequence and Sort Order	From the *ORDER BY Clause* block property in the form.
Prompt	From the *Prompt* item property in the form.
Width	From the *Width* item property in the form.

TABLE 29-18. *Bound Item Properties Supplied by Capture Design of Form Utility*

Search in the help system index for the topic "design capture – Form Generator applications – What Form Generator does not capture."

Index

User-Defined Set (UDS),
917-918
Users, 36
definition, 554
repository, 930-931
Utilities (functional
category in Oracle
Designer), 42, 67-73
interface, 98-100

V

Valid values, *See*
Allowable values
Value types definition,
573
Version testing, 684
Versioning, 29, 669-670,
683-684
application systems,
232-234, 839,
920-922
specifications, 810
View Objects (in RAU),
931

Views
object, 572
changing free format
text 993
definition, 485,
543-546, 593-594
in the API, 975-977
See also Repository
views
repository, 38-39
See also API views
Visual Basic, 64, 400,
625, 638, 643, 783-790
Capture Design of
Files, 67
required components,
784-786
preferences, 785
template project, 785
Visual Basic Generator,
64, 783-790
output, 786
required components,
784-785
running, 787-788

W

Waterfall method, xxxix, 6
Web based groupware,
194
Web Forms, 704, 741
Web Server, 547, 608,
625, 643, 1025
WebServer Generator, 63,
760-778
preferences, 762,
768-775
properties, 768-775
required components,
761-763
running, 764-767
templates, 762,
776-777
Window properties, 710
Workplan, 191
example, 201
high-level, 13
Strategy, 13, 133-134
World Wide Web, 401

Get Your **FREE** Subscription to Oracle Magazine

Stay informed and increase your productivity with every issue of *Oracle Magazine*. Inside each FREE, bimonthly issue you'll get:

- Up-to-date information on Oracle Data Server, Oracle Applications, Network Computing Architecture, and tools
- Third-party news and announcements
- Technical articles on Oracle products and operating environments
- Software tuning tips
- Oracle customer application stories

Three easy ways to subscribe:

1 MAIL Cut out this page, complete the questionnaire on the back, and mail it to: *Oracle Magazine,* P.O. Box 1263, Skokie, IL 60076-8263.

2 FAX Cut out this page, complete the questionnaire on the back, and fax it to **+ 847.647.9735.**

3 WEB Visit our Web site at **www.oramag.com.** You'll find a subscription form there, plus much more!

If there are other Oracle users at your location who would like to receive their own subscription to *Oracle Magazine,* please photocopy the form and pass it along.

☐ YES! Please send me a FREE subscription to Oracle Magazine. ☐ NO, I am not interested at this time.

If you wish to receive your free bimonthly subscription to *Oracle Magazine,* you must fill out the entire form, sign it, and date it (incomplete forms cannot be processed or acknowledged). You can also subscribe at our Web site at **www.oramag.com/html/subform.html** or fax your application to *Oracle Magazine* at **+847.647.9735.**

SIGNATURE (REQUIRED) ✓	DATE

NAME _____ TITLE _____

COMPANY _____ E-MAIL ADDRESS _____

STREET/P.O. BOX _____

CITY/STATE/ZIP _____

COUNTRY _____ TELEPHONE _____

You must answer all eight questions below.

1 What is the primary business activity of your firm at this location?
(circle only one)
- 01 Agriculture, Mining, Natural Resources
- 02 Architecture, Construction
- 03 Communications
- 04 Consulting, Training
- 05 Consumer Packaged Goods
- 06 Data Processing
- 07 Education
- 08 Engineering
- 09 Financial Services
- 10 Government—Federal, Local, State, Other
- 11 Government—Military
- 12 Health Care
- 13 Manufacturing—Aerospace, Defense
- 14 Manufacturing—Computer Hardware
- 15 Manufacturing—Noncomputer Products
- 16 Real Estate, Insurance
- 17 Research & Development
- 18 Human Resources
- 19 Retailing, Wholesaling, Distribution
- 20 Software Development
- 21 Systems Integration, VAR, VAD, OEM
- 22 Transportation
- 23 Utilities (Electric, Gas, Sanitation)
- 24 Other Business and Services _____

2 Which of the following best describes your job function? *(circle only one)*
CORPORATE MANAGEMENT/STAFF
- 01 Executive Management (President, Chair, CEO, CFO, Owner, Partner, Principal)
- 02 Finance/Administrative Management (VP/Director/Manager/Controller, Purchasing, Administration)
- 03 Sales/Marketing Management (VP/Director/Manager)
- 04 Computer Systems/Operations Management (CIO/VP/Director/Manager MIS, Operations)
- 05 Other Finance/Administration Staff
- 06 Other Sales/Marketing Staff

IS/IT Staff
- 07 Systems Development/Programming Management
- 08 Systems Development/Programming Staff
- 09 Consulting
- 10 DBA/Systems Administrator
- 11 Education/Training
- 12 Engineering/R&D/Science Management
- 13 Engineering/R&D/Science Staff
- 14 Technical Support Director/Manager
- 15 Webmaster/Internet Specialist
- 16 Other Technical Management/Staff

3 What is your current primary operating platform? *(circle all that apply)*
- 01 DEC UNIX
- 02 DEC VAX VMS
- 03 Java
- 04 HP UNIX
- 05 IBM AIX
- 06 IBM UNIX
- 07 Macintosh
- 08 MPE-ix
- 09 MS-DOS
- 10 MVS
- 11 NetWare
- 12 Network Computing
- 13 OpenVMS
- 14 SCO UNIX
- 15 Sun Solaris/SunOS
- 16 SVR4
- 17 Ultrix
- 18 UnixWare
- 19 VM
- 20 Windows
- 21 Windows NT
- 22 Other _____
- 23 Other UNIX _____

4 Do you evaluate, specify, recommend, or authorize the purchase of any of the following? *(circle all that apply)*
- 01 Hardware
- 02 Software
- 03 Application Development Tools
- 04 Database Products
- 05 Internet or Intranet Products

5 In your job, do you use or plan to purchase any of the following products or services?
(check all that apply)

SOFTWARE

	Use	Plan to buy
01 Business Graphics	☐	☐
02 CAD/CAE/CAM	☐	☐
03 CASE	☐	☐
04 CIM	☐	☐
05 Communications	☐	☐
06 Database Management	☐	☐
07 File Management	☐	☐
08 Finance	☐	☐
09 Java	☐	☐
10 Materials Resource Planning	☐	☐
11 Multimedia Authoring	☐	☐
12 Networking	☐	☐
13 Office Automation	☐	☐
14 Order Entry/Inventory Control	☐	☐
15 Programming	☐	☐
16 Project Management	☐	☐
17 Scientific and Engineering	☐	☐
18 Spreadsheets	☐	☐
19 Systems Management	☐	☐
20 Workflow	☐	☐

HARDWARE

	Use	Plan to buy
21 Macintosh	☐	☐
22 Mainframe	☐	☐
23 Massively Parallel Processing	☐	☐
24 Minicomputer	☐	☐
25 PC	☐	☐
26 Network Computer	☐	☐
27 Supercomputer	☐	☐
28 Symmetric Multiprocessing	☐	☐
29 Workstation	☐	☐

PERIPHERALS

	Use	Plan to buy
30 Bridges/Routers/Hubs/Gateways	☐	☐
31 CD-ROM Drives	☐	☐
32 Disk Drives/Subsystems	☐	☐
33 Modems	☐	☐
34 Tape Drives/Subsystems	☐	☐
35 Video Boards/Multimedia	☐	☐

SERVICES

	Use	Plan to buy
36 Computer-Based Training	☐	☐
37 Consulting	☐	☐
38 Education/Training	☐	☐
39 Maintenance	☐	☐
40 Online Database Services	☐	☐
41 Support	☐	☐
42 **None of the above**	☐	☐

6 What Oracle products are in use at your site? *(circle all that apply)*
SERVER/SOFTWARE
- 01 Oracle8
- 02 Oracle7
- 03 Oracle Application Server
- 04 Oracle Data Mart Suites
- 05 Oracle Internet Commerce Server
- 06 Oracle InterOffice
- 07 Oracle Lite
- 08 Oracle Payment Server
- 09 Oracle Rdb
- 10 Oracle Security Server
- 11 Oracle Video Server
- 12 Oracle Workgroup Server

TOOLS
- 13 Designer/2000
- 14 Developer/2000 (Forms, Reports, Graphics)
- 15 Oracle OLAP Tools
- 16 Oracle Power Object

ORACLE APPLICATIONS
- 17 Oracle Automotive
- 18 Oracle Energy
- 19 Oracle Consumer Packaged Goods
- 20 Oracle Financials
- 21 Oracle Human Resources
- 22 Oracle Manufacturing
- 23 Oracle Projects
- 24 Oracle Sales Force Automation
- 25 Oracle Supply Chain Management
- 26 Other _____
- 27 **None of the above**

7 What other database products are in use at your site? *(circle all that apply)*
- 01 Access
- 02 BAAN
- 03 dbase
- 04 Gupta
- 05 IBM DB2
- 06 Informix
- 07 Ingres
- 08 Microsoft Access
- 09 Microsoft SQL Server
- 10 Peoplesoft
- 11 Progress
- 12 SAP
- 13 Sybase
- 14 VSAM
- 15 **None of the above**

8 During the next 12 months, how much do you anticipate your organization will spend on computer hardware, software, peripherals, and services for your location? *(circle only one)*
- 01 Less than $10,000
- 02 $10,000 to $49,999
- 03 $50,000 to $99,999
- 04 $100,000 to $499,999
- 05 $500,000 to $999,999
- 06 $1,000,000 and over

OMG